Social interaction

Social interaction

Thomas M. Kando, Ph.D.

Associate Professor of Sociology,
California State University at Sacramento,
Sacramento, California

with 30 illustrations

The C. V. Mosby Company

Saint Louis   1977

Library of Congress Cataloging in Publication Data

Kando, Thomas M   1941-
   Social interaction.

   Bibliography: p.
   Includes index.
   1. Social psychology.   2. Sociology.
I. Title.
HM251.K29   301.1   76-26614
ISBN 0-8016-2614-5

TS/M/M   9   8   7   6   5   4   3   2   1

To
DANIELLE

Foreword

Here we have a humanistic social psychology of direct relevance to the personal problems of our time. Not since the earlier effort by Hans Gerth and C. Wright Mills, *Character and Social Structure*—never as influential as many of us wish it were—has there been a serious attempt to bring the European tradition of Geisteswissenschaft (the science of the "spirit" or "soul"—ideals germane to the human condition) together with the distinctively American tradition of pragmatism in a textbook for those who read English. We see the same tendencies toward the mutual enrichment of the perspectives in Germany, for example, in the work of Hans Joas in Berlin, Helle in Munich, and Auwärter, Kirsch, and Schröter in Frankfurt. The same tendencies can be found in England in the recent efforts of Arthur Brittan and, to a lesser degree of completeness, David Field. Even in Japan, there is the same thrust. I can cite the untranslated recent (1975) accomplishment of Momoru Funatsu, *Discourse on Mutual Symbolic Process.* In short, an international intellectual movement can be discerned. It is also interdisciplinary, evidenced by a few publications in humanistic psychology and above all by Victor Turner, in anthropology, whose inquiries draw heavily upon the informing perspective of Florian Znaniecki's "humanistic coefficient." Quite obviously a social psychology text is needed to bring this movement to the attention of teachers and students in the United States, and this is what Professor Kando's book attempts to accomplish.

The book draws heavily on the contributions of Weber and Marx, pointing out the shortcomings of the Marx*ists* (the uncritical believers) and the unbelieving critical sociologists of the New Left, to set the stage for the contextual analysis of social order. It then follows the direction recommended by the Meadian perspective for the focused analysis of the self and social interaction.

Freud, whose work is briefly reviewed in an early chapter of the book, widened the limits of significant symbolism, while, at the same time, narrowing the circumference of universes of discourse or mind. Mead, on the other hand, anchored the meaning of symbolism in any and all social circles—the community, economy, government, school, family, friendships, and even in the internalized conversation he called the self.

Mead found the self *in* society in both its euphonious and cacophonous concerts. Freud set the individual over and against the society, and this is the way in which the problem is experienced by many today. This book recasts the issue as a practical paradox of freedom versus social order. Nor is the antithesis new to Western thought. It has certainly persisted since prebiblical times, and the fact that it is painfully experienced today, especially by youth, lends it a significance that is best described as epochal in scale. In a little book, *Conscience and Society,* Ranyard West drew the analogy between Freud's conception of the opposition between the individual and society and that of Thomas Hobbes. Certainly the problem goes back at least to the contract theorists in the thought of "modern times." For Hobbes the order ought to be imposed to harness the bestial nature of a posited presocial man. So was the monarchy justified. For John Locke the order emerged at the convenience and design of posited reasonable creatures. Democracy was thus the desirable way to order human affairs, and monarchy or oligarchy must surrender to the design of reason. Conceptions of freedom, itself, were developed grossly at odds with one another: one conceived freedom as basically destructive, grounded in feral impulse; the other, as basically constructive and founded on reason thought to characterize the human species. Different versions of the social order have also emerged. Pertinent are the conceptions of Weber and Marx. In one sense, Weber conceived the social order as stultifying. He despaired the routinization of charisma necessitated by its ritualized and bureaucratized transmission beyond the generation of the leader endowed with the "gift of grace." Marx was morally indignant at the alienation of man provoked by the economic rationalization of society by the bourgeoisie metaphorically unleashed by the rationalism of Locke.

As it developed in the United States from social pragmatism, symbolic interaction never conceptualized the dialectic in this way, although we find the distinction in the emphasis given by Cooley to the sentiments, as opposed to the emphasis given by Mead to cognitive communication. Nevertheless, the contributions of Mead loom larger, as this book so clearly demonstrates, for Mead carefully attends to the emergents of the dialectic. In the conversation between the "I" and the "me" we find the self; in the conjoint action of selves, the society. Yet the self can emerge only in interaction, where it contributes to the permanence and change of the larger social order.

A further theoretical concern of Professor Kando's book is the way in which it explicitly attends to what we have come to call the "sociology of knowledge." Social psychology has waited too long for this connection to be made in a textbook. At this writing, pop textbooks select a list of current social problems and review disconnected social science treatments of such problems in diverse disjointed aspects. They try to titillate students with accounts of bizarre and absurd difficulties found in the everyday life of the present. Pop pedagogy seems, at times, to be merely another manifestation of American kitsch, or as Eric Sevareid recently described sociology, as "slow motion journalism." We might add "journalism for those who somehow can't find the time to read the papers." This book turns the carousel around. It establishes how social problems give rise to social science perspectives and underscores the necessity for seizing those perspectives in their appropriate sociohistorical contexts, the better to implement them in the proper critical study of mankind.

But the bulk of *Social Interaction* is devoted to a review of empirical research bearing on these and other theoretical issues. As a textbook for undergraduate and graduate courses in social psychology, the primary relevance and utility of Dr. Kando's book should lie in the fact that it provides an extensive review and discussion of the research, findings, and studies done by sociologists and psychologists on such topics as love, conflict, deviance, mental illness, leadership, conformity, authority, social comparison, cognitive dissonance, helping, riots, and many other group processes.

Gregory P. Stone

Professor of Sociology and American Studies,
University of Minnesota;
President, Society for the Study
of Symbolic Interaction

Preface

The purpose of this book is twofold. In the first place, it aims to provide a basic text in social psychology, with an emphasis on *social*, thereby bridging the gap between sociology and psychology and filling a void that is particularly obvious to sociologists. Indeed, while the number of social psychology textbooks is probably second only to that of introductory texts, nearly all of them are psychological. Yet social psychology is also one of sociology's core areas. It is important that the subdiscipline be well balanced, recognizing, for example, Mead as much as McDougall, Goffman as much as Festinger, Garfinkel as much as Osgood, Cooley as much as Newcomb.

The need for such a book is now widely recognized, yet there does not seem to be much more on the market to fill that need at this time than Lindesmith and Strauss' fine example of a truly sociological social psychology text. The present text hopes to pick up where that book leaves off. While written by a sociologist, this book attempts to be of equal relevance to sociologists and to psychologists. Therefore, at this time this may be one of the few comprehensive textbooks fulfilling an interdisciplinary function.

The book's second objective is also its most distinguishing feature. In contrast to a majority of existing textbooks in social psychology, the present work reflects the current revival of humanism, qualitative methodology, nondeterminism, and existential value orientation in sociology. C. P. Snow has coined the now classical concept of the two cultures—one scientific and one humanistic. Bruyn, Zetterberg, and others have discussed the place of social psychology within that framework, Bruyn, for example, arguing that our discipline now straddles and eventually will reintegrate the two cultures, whose artificial and unhealthy separation goes back only to the beginnings of the industrial revolution.

One thing is certain: the days of sociology's total domination by the abstract empiricists are over; witness the growing popularity of qualitative methodology, phenomenological social psychology, ethnomethodology, ethnography, participant observation, documentary interpretation à la Goffman and Garfinkel, symbolic interactionism, the sociology of meaning, and critical sociology, to name but a few of the outcroppings of the new sociology. Yet few, it any, efforts have yet been made to pull together the multiple strands of this new sociology. Lyman and Scott's highly successful *A Sociology of the Absurd* proves the potential relevance of the new approach to the moral and psychological issues of the 1970s. However, that book is an unsystematic anthology of those two authors' previously published articles, not a textbook. My objective, then, has been to provide a textbook in the new sociology, or more precisely in the new social psychology.

The book tries to perform two functions: (1) it attempts to make a theoretical contribution; (2) since it is a basic textbook, it surveys much of the existing research findings in social psychology. The first two parts of the book are therefore theoretical—one reviewing the orientations which I do not adopt, the next section reviewing those, like symbolic interactionism, which are indeed mine. The remainder of the book is substantive. Chapter 7 is about language, Chapter 8 about the self, Chapter 9 about socialization, Chapter 10 about self-concept, identity, and personality, Chapter

11 about interaction, and Chapter 12 about deviance, conflict, and change. I must point out that the classification of subject matter is based on the current state of the empirical literature: the headings just listed simply represent the major categories of research in sociological social psychology at this time. Theoretically, other categories might be more defensible.

The effort involved in completing this book was considerable. An enormous amount of material had to be covered, since both the novel, "phenomenological" type of work and the more traditional research of social psychologists had to be presented to the students. The book attempts to integrate some of the informa-tion I have been dealing with in my various courses in social psychology, ethnomethodology, and humanistic social theory over the past eight years.

In view of the above, my acknowledgments must begin with the many lively people who over the years, while officially designated as my students, have just as often been my teachers. In addition, graduate assistant Ed Lavelle, reviewers Dr. Norman K. Denzin, University of Illinois at Urbana, Dr. Kenneth Feldman, State University of New York at Stony Brook, and Dr. Stanford Gregory, Kent State University, and secretaries Lois Hill and Caroline Schaefer also deserve my gratitude, all having positively contributed to this project. Finally, my special thanks to my wife, Anita, who makes it all possible.

Thomas M. Kando

Contents

12 Deviance, conflict, and change, 286

Social interaction

Introduction

The best way to approach this book is to first say what it is not. It does not deal with the statistical quantification of behavior. It is not about laboratory experiments on operant or respondent behavior. It does not conceptualize man as a mere biological organism that responds predictably to environmental cues on the basis of past conditioning. Neither does it view society as a mechanistic system in which individuals are propelled, attracted, repelled, and directed along predetermined paths.

Many beginning students of human behavior expect a simple, consistent, and more or less exhaustive formula for the understanding and solution of immediate problems. To try to seduce the reader at the outset with such a promise would be fraudulent. This book does not offer simple formulas, master keys, or even a coherent paradigm with ready applicability in such realms as social control, mental illness, deviance, therapy, and corrections. Furthermore, it also withholds the easy sop of the current revolutionary antiscience. The nihilistic anti-intellectualism and sloppy hedonism spreading over college campuses at this time are what is passed off for dialectical liberation from the technocratic power structure among much of the misguided new generation. The social psychology in this book is neither technocratic nor liberated in that perverted yet voguish sense. This book worships no more at the altar of the new left, pop sociology, or sexual liberation than at the shrine of Auguste Comte or B. F. Skinner, to drop but the first few names in this incipient game.

"Truth," as Durkheim (1964:409) knew, "is a living thing that changes ceaselessly. . . . Not so long ago, it was believed that science brings us the truth, whole and definitive. But today we know that this is not so." And "today's truth is tomorrow's error." How, then, could we attempt to offer more than tentative theories about human behavior *as we see it* at this time? Many questions will be raised but no definitive answers will be given. These must come from the reader. What we do hope to accomplish is a contribution to the never-ending process of understanding man. Perhaps the perspective offered here will open some readers' eyes to a new and meaningful reality. In that case, the game will have been worth it.

PARADIGMS

The important assumption underlying the book, its conception of social psychology, and certain convictions as to the proper socioexistential stance at this juncture in the development of American civilization lead us to believe that we need to develop and apply a new theoretical stance toward human behavior, a stance that is both coherent and yet free, both intellectual and activist, both liberated and orderly, in sum a position that synthesizes rather than separates and one that transcends paradoxes rather than reinforces parochialism. The gist of this seemingly heavy rhetoric is this: early in the book a considerable amount of emphasis will be placed on theory, because we believe that without a proper theoretical stance action remains nonsensical and the world remains absurd, particularly the world of social psychology. Furthermore, much will be said about good theory—the integrative kind—and bad theory—theory concerned with trivia.

What this statement wishes to convey is, in a nutshell, the necessity of good paradigms. Paradigm has been used in sociology, notably by Merton (1957), in the sense of "a compact outline of the major concepts, assumptions, procedures, propositions, and problems of a substantive area or a theoretical approach in sociological analysis" (Theodorson and Theodorson, 1969:290). Kuhn's classic work on the structure of scientific revolutions (1962) goes further, defining paradigm as an achievement that attracts enduring groups of individuals who subscribe to it, and is also sufficiently open-ended to leave room for further problem solving. Kuhn's definition permits the following interpretation. A paradigm is an outlook on reality that is orderly, coherent, and to a certain extent socially consensual, yet sufficiently tentative and open-ended to permit and in fact demand further inquiry and creative effort. A paradigm combines freedom with coherence. It guides action, action that by definition is constructive, since it contributes to a sociocultural system under construction. At the same time it cannot impose excessive control on the membership, for once it does it becomes dogma, a closed system requiring no further elaboration and precluding further growth. A paradigm has utility only insofar as it is becoming. A paradigm is a process of fulfillment, and the completion of that process requires, paradoxically, that the paradigm be discarded. A paradigm cannot be static.

Examples of scientific paradigms are Ptolemaic astronomy, Newtonian physics, sociological functionalism, and stimulus-response psychology. It is in this restricted sense that Kuhn uses the concept. However, the scientific paradigm has much in common with ideology, philosophy, and religion, to name but a few related words. Without lapsing into a philosophy-of-science conceptual discussion of these terms, what matters here is that ideology, philosophy, and religion (and in fact also Berger and Luckmann's symbolic universe [1966], the anthropologist's worldview, and the Germans' Weltanschauung) all share with the paradigm the fact that they provide their adherents with a coherent system of implicit or explicit meanings for the interpretation of experienced phenomena and guidelines for action.

The first major point is that in human life—that of the scientist or that of the college freshman—paradigms are the sine qua non for work and other forms of meaningful behavior. Normal behavior, like Kuhn's normal science (1962:35-42), is guided by paradigm. The alternatives to paradigm are either random, meaningless behavior or crisis and conflict. The so-called Baconian method of scientific inquiry, the random collection of data, is an example of unguided activity, and the various forms of personality disorganization termed mental illness are also examples of meaningless behavior. We grant that the other alternative to paradigm—crisis—is also of the essence. However, like Kuhn's scientific revolution, all crisis ultimately results in the institution of a new order, a new paradigm. Insofar as revolutionary activity may be termed meaningful, its meaning is derived from negation, not affirmation. To contend, as does some of the contemporary radical rhetoric, that liberation from an existing system is the ultimate meaning and justification of revolution is to put the cart before the horse.

The second major point is in diametric contrast to what has just been said: just as one must insist on paradigm to guide activity, so one must also, paradoxically, be ready to reject it once it lapses into scholasticism. Man's inherent need for order and meaning is no deeper than his need for freedom and quest. The value of paradigm, like that of life itself, is in its process. Once fully explicated, its remaining value lies, at best, in the ways in which it may influence subsequent thought. The history of ideas may be marked by the same kind of continuity as the evolution of organic life itself, but the analogy does not stop there: birth, growth, decay, death, and even willful senicide are also of the essence of both realms.[1] To explain further: the

---

[1] The best example of such an organismic interpretation of sociocultural history is Arnold Toynbee's work (1947; 1957).

more complete a paradigm becomes, the closer it is to its necessary demise. A truth stated by Marx, a truth more inescapable than ever today, applies to the socioeconomic system and to the thought system— the paradigm—in equal measure: both contain the seeds of their own destruction. As with the organism, society, and the culture, the paradigm's youthful challenge to creativity is eventually followed by sterility, stagnation, and decay. As accumulated verities increase its mass and anchor it ever deeper into an existing status quo, it is increasingly left behind by events, the changing world, life itself. Furthermore, the paradigm embodies a commitment to an established accomplishment, and this makes the exploration of unchartered territory and the creation of radically novel meanings increasingly problematic. As innovation becomes increasingly threatening, tolerance declines and deviation is either forced back into the fold or cast out into alienation. The former is accomplished through a variety of social control mechanisms ranging from crude forms of physical coercion to modern therapeutic techniques (cf. Berger and Luckman, 1966). The latter results in the creation of deviant and eventually revolutionary fringes. Thus the system becomes totalitarian, thereby setting in motion the dialectic of revolutionary change and evoking through repression the very opposition to which it will eventually succumb.

At the peak of its creative potential, the paradigm asks questions of the most fundamental importance, and it permits men to freely express their greatest creativity in their quest for truth, beauty, answers, and happiness. Later, however, it is capable only of retreading familiar ground, adding a detail here, a nuance there, exploring areas of only secondary importance. As rococo follows baroque and the silver age follows the golden era, so in the evolution of paradigms the period of greatest growth must give way to decadence and eventual demise. Life, however, goes on. And because that which is anchored in the

past cannot free itself to grasp a changing reality, only an uncommitted position provides the necessary freedom for the fresh resumption of problem-solving activity. Furthermore, the relationship between the old paradigm and the new activity is, as explained already, at least somewhat antagonistic and possibly revolutionary. The old paradigm commands a psychological commitment and represents vested interests that cannot tolerate innovation, while the emerging culture rejects, often foolishly, much of the experience of the past as irrelevant. Continuity and disjunction are both inherent in the life of the sociocultural cycle.

This book stresses the importance of a guiding paradigm, and it stresses the importance of creativity. The previous pages have described the nature of paradigm and its functions in human action. Note that the concept is used generically, applicable to scientific as well as lay conduct. Note also the claim that different paradigms may have different utility. As will be argued throughout this book, that paradigm having the greatest utility asks the most important questions and permits the most freedom for creative action. Conversely, paradigms that force us into narrowly specialized focuses and impose on us rigid controls thereby merely manifest their incipient decline.

Thus three possibilities have been established at the outset: action unguided by paradigm, action guided by an obsolescent paradigm, and action guided by and contributing to a relevant paradigm. This book may be viewed as a plea for the third possibility. It suggests a social psychology that aims to be relevant and innovative, yet does more than reject technocratic knowledge. It attempts to pass between the Scylla of traditional scientism and Charybdis of revolutionary antiscience.

The first two parts of the book are heavily theoretical, reviewing first waning paradigms, then emerging paradigms, and finally proposing a new social psychology along existential humanistic lines. However, the remainder of the book is substantive, covering the concrete body of knowledge—the "findings"—of the new social psychology under such headings as self, socialization, interaction, and finally deviance, conflict, and change. Theory and practice, thought and action. It is the inseparable unity of the two and the equal importance of both that the textbook hopes to reflect.

As a whole, this book advocates not only a particular theoretical stance—a paradigm—but also a philosophy and ultimately, let's face it, a particular morality as well. That morality follows from what has been said about paradigms in the previous pages: it follows from the aforementioned arguments that man's highest good has always been in exploration and creative accomplishment, particularly in the artistic, intellectual, scientific, and social realms. It follows that mechanical effort, routine dictated by external constraint, authority, or need, is contrary to human values. Today, modern technology makes it possible, for the first time in history perhaps, to conceive of man free from such constraints. A society could emerge where all Indians are chiefs, where all men are artists, scientists, and explorers, with computers doing the rest. Indeed, let us hope that students will someday cease training themselves to become technicians and learn to become artists, scientists, and explorers.

WANING PARADIGMS

Twentieth century social science has a vast number of competing paradigms, theories, and theory groups (cf. Mullins, 1973), forming together a mosaic not unlike the spectrum of political parties. Some are venerable and powerful, some in decline, some merely static, some still vigorously gaining adherents, some practically viewed as lunatic fringe movements, some long gone and dead, some young

and aggressively carving out their territory, some short-lived, and some representing the heritage of thoughts that reigned millenia ago.

In sociology, the grand old paradigm (G.O.P.) is undoubtedly classical positivism, or what may also be called positivistic functionalism. This paradigm was, for a long time, synonymous with sociology itself. It was launched by the Frenchman Auguste Comte in 1830, but it is American sociology that eventually, after World War II, fell heir to the tradition, most of all in the person of Talcott Parsons. Fundamental to this paradigm are the assumptions that (1) social behavior constitutes first and foremost interrelated and integrated systems[2] and that (2) it is to be studied with the same stance (objective) and the same methods (quantitative) as other phenomena. Indeed, positivism is the position which holds that all disciplines, including the study of man, must be modelled after the physical sciences and the empirical methods used by those sciences. According to this view, then, sociology is a science and its aim is to predict and control human behavior.

In psychology, the dominant theoretical position has been less unified than in sociology. However, there can be no doubt as to what the single most salient aspect of the psychological enterprise is: psychiatry. Behaviorism is psychology's most positivistic strand; it goes back to the work of Ivan Pavlov in Russia at the turn of the century and of J. B. Watson (1919) in the United States. Its best known representative today is B. F. Skinner. Psychoanalysis is the brainchild of the Austrian Sigmund Freud (1856-1939). Today, the most important cornerstone of psychology as a practical enterprise is psychiatry, which may be positivistic in its methods and assumptions, as in the case of physiological behavior modification, or not, as in the case of neo-Freudian forms of therapy. All psychiatry

---

[2]See Martindale (1960:446-447) for a concise argument as to how functionalism really differs from other possible approaches in social science.

shares the fundamental assumption that it is possible to distinguish scientifically between healthy and pathological behavior. According to this view, psychiatry is a medical science that cures mental illness. This applies to the newer forms of group therapy as well, for anything termed "therapy" is based on the assumptions that the behavior of individuals is not merely subject to moral judgment but can also be measured against certain objective standards of health, and that there are professionals in society whose judgments are based on knowledge of such objective standards, not on values.

A third paradigm we shall want to bracket in this book is the Marxian one. From Karl Marx's 1848 *Communist Manifesto* to the contemporary writings of men like Herbert Marcuse (1968) in the United States and Jurgen Habermas (1970) in Germany, all radical-critical works share the assumptions that conflict and opposition are the fundamental facts of history and that all social relations and cultural phenomena are caused by the dominant economic system, currently capitalism. All sociological analysis must be dialectical.

The new left departs from the old left in that it rejects all theory, even the revolutionary dogma of Marxism itself. It therefore has no intellectual leaders of historical stature, only followers; it is a headless mass movement, not an intellectual stance. It is experience in behavior. As will become clear in the discussion of Meadian social psychology (Chapter 6), the counterculture—for that is what we are talking about—could often be viewed as a case of the "me" in action and an absence of reflexive consciousness—the knowing "I." Yet although the counterculture is therefore not truly paradigm-based, it does have implicit values. These include pleasure, liberation, individualism, and spontaneity, and they are reflected in their adherents' sexual and consumptive life-style. The viability of this ephemeral movement—less than a decade old, yet here classified as a waning paradigm—is comparable to that of a body without a head.

Central to this book is the contention that the four preceding social orientations or paradigms are bankrupt or, less bluntly, of little relevance to the new social psychology that shall be proposed. Positivistic functionalism arbitrarily disregards the humanistic coefficient in human behavior and the innovative role man himself plays in creating his environment. Psychiatry's fallacy can best be summed up in a quote by Theodore Sarbin: "The labelling of unwanted behavior is a moral enterprise, not a scientific one." The Marxian scheme claims that its explanatory principle can account for all facts, including all forms of consciousness and all social relationships. This can only be a metaphysical assertion, a statement of faith. The counterculture rejects analysis altogether and thus drops out before the game is even underway. Finally, racial and instinctivist social psychology has been sufficiently refuted not to be taken too seriously.

HUMANISTIC PARADIGMS

Now that we have preliminarily indicated what will not be important in this book, we shall introduce those paradigms that are, either partially or closely, relevant to the new social psychology.

In sociology, there is a tradition nearly as old and just as rich as positivistic functionalism: social behaviorism. Here, the major name is Max Weber of Germany (1864-1920), according to many the greatest of all sociologists. Social behaviorism must not be confused with the psychological behaviorism discussed a short while ago; the two are on opposite sides of the fence. The paradigm of which we now speak recognizes that sociology is in the business of studying concrete human behavior and not abstract "systems" and that human culture, behavior, and experience differ fundamentally from other phenomena in that they have *meaning* for those engaged in them, not only to those observing them. This is the *humanistic coefficient*, a term coined by Florian Znaniecki in 1934. Thus the method of sociology cannot be identical to that of the physical sciences: the sociologist must transcend mere objectivity and attempt to empathetically understand—in Weber's word, *verstehen*—what a particular experience means to the actor himself.

Closely related to Weber's sociology is symbolic interactionism. The American philosopher George Herbert Mead (1863-1931) is generally considered to be the father of this school of thought. In sharp contrast with psychological behaviorism, symbolic interactionism argues that social behavior is a dialectical process in which man not only passively responds to stimuli but is also at all times influencing his environment. Thus it is the interaction process that is looked at, not the stimulus or the response. This is symbolic interactionism's first essential feature. Its second characteristic is that it recognizes the symbolic, or *meaningful*, nature of human experience. Thus symbolic interactionism differs little from Weberian sociology. The main difference between the two is that symbolic interactionism has focused on the micro whereas other forms of social behaviorism (for example, Weber's work) are more macrosociological. Since this is a textbook in social psychology, symbolic interactionism will be of exceptional importance to us, particularly the work on face-to-face interaction of contemporary American symbolic interactionists like Erving Goffman.

A third strand of the new social psychology will be ethnography. Unlike causal sociology, ethnography does not test hypotheses to explain phenomena but instead *describes* and thus tries to understand them. Whereas standard sociology and social psychology seek causal explanations, ethnography seeks description. In the past, the ethnographic tradition has been strongest in anthropology, but there is now a resurgence of descriptive sociol-ogy—sociography some call it—as well. Ethnography's foremost methodology is participant observation. That is, the sociologist is required to not only observe and study his subject matter—play the *scientist role*—but also to participate in his subject's life—play the *native role*. As Blumer (1969), Bruyn (1966), and an increasing number of sociologists argue, this dual-role combination required by the method of participant observation is a sine qua non for a better understanding of human behavior.

Phenomenology is a philosophical stance and a methodology closely related to the paradigms being discussed here. Like ethnography, phenomenology describes rather than explains. Like the participant observer, the phenomenologist believes that empirical, "objective" observation is insufficient for an adequate understanding of human phenomena. He is often said to operate "intuitively." The more exact formulation is to say that whereas the positivist pays attention only to that which appears to the *senses*, the phenomenologist observes (also) that which appears to *consciousness* (Bruyn, 1966:277). The founder of phenomenological psychology was the Austrian-German philosopher, Edmund Husserl (1859-1938). Phenomenological sociology has been primarily the accomplishment of the Austrian-American, Alfred Schutz (1899-1959).

Ethnomethodology is that branch of contemporary American sociology which claims to carry forth the phenomenological heritage. For the purposes of this preliminary introduction, it is perhaps best to define this paradigm etymologically. Garfinkel (1967), the founder of ethnomethodology, explains the meaning and origin of that word as follows. In anthropology, we have had such areas as ethnomusicology, ethnobotany, etc. These are simply the study of primitive music, the study of primitive botanical classifications, etc. Similarly, Garfinkel then coined the term enthnomethodology for the study of native methodology, only the natives are now not just primitive non-Westerners, but all of us. Thus ethnomethodology studies the cognitive methods we employ in everyday living to construct coherent and meaningful patterns of interaction. Two important corollaries follow. First, we—the natives—are generally unaware of the rules, internal structure, logic, and cognitive systems that result in what sociologists in the past have called "culture"; we are just as unaware of these things as, say, a primitive medicine man is unaware of the logical principles he unwittingly uses when classifying various herbs. Second, ethnomethodology studies the *process* of classifying, ordering, and making meaningful—nothing more and nothing less. It thus shares with symbolic interactionism and social behaviorism a processual conception of sociology's subject matter.

A sixth perspective that will be important in this book is the sociology of knowledge. This subdiscipline studies the relationship between knowledge and its social-structural bases. In other words, it seeks to explain why particular groups and individuals subscribe to particular scientific, religious, philosophical, and political theories. It assumes that they do so because of the particular social and economic positions that they occupy, and out of this follows the assumption that all knowledge is relative. Thus the sociology of knowledge calls into question—debunks—all theories, values, and perspectives, including psychiatric definitions of mental health and positivistic science's conception of truth.

The sociology of meaning builds upon the sociology of knowledge, saying that truth is what a particular group or individual chooses to believe. Stanford Lyman and Marvin Scott published the best recent book along these lines and they called it *A Sociology of the Absurd* (1970). They did this to indicate a fundamental point of the new social psychology: whereas earlier paradigms were based on the assumption that certain truths inherent in the objective world existed and could be discovered, the new social psychology recognizes that the world is inherently absurd, deriving its

meaning from the only possible source of meaning—man himself.

Finally, there is existentialism. This philosophy, complex and ramified, is an eighth important ingredient in our paradigm insofar as it too recognizes the inherent absurdity of the world. The existentialism of the Frenchman Albert Camus (1913-1960) has particular relevance for the new social psychology. It suggests that the meaning of being is in existence itself, that the value and meaning of activity is in its *subjective experience*. Some psychologists, for example Viktor Frankl (1959), have proposed a form of "therapy" that returns the whole burden of choice and responsibility to the subject. What existentialism and such humanistic psychology have in common is the fact that both hold man responsible for his actions and for their interpretation and evaluation.

Eight perspectives, or paradigms, have just been introduced, and each of these has been said to make a significant contribution to the new social psychology, unlike the four paradigms introduced in the previous section. It is Sir Charles P. Snow (1959) who coined the now classical concept of the two cultures—one humanistic and one scientific—and that, essentially, is the distinction underlying this discussion. In the final analysis, it is on the matter of validity that the two groups of paradigms differ: whereas the first claims that validity is fundamentally objective, the "humanistic" paradigms maintain that it is subjective, or intersubjective. Thus positivistic functionalism, psychiatry, psychological behaviorism, and Marxism all claim that objective truth exists and that it can be ascertained. This is *the* distinguishing feature of science—and of religion, too. On the other hand, social behaviorism and symbolic interactionism recognize the subjective nature of meaning, ethnomethodology emphasizes its emergent quality, the sociology of knowledge focuses on its relativity, and the sociology of meaning and existentialism both stress that man is its only source. Ethnography, which uses participant observation, and phenomenology, which uses "intuition," indicate the methods whereby valid knowledge is to be acquired. The aim of this book will be to reintroduce humanism into social psychology and thus redress a balance that is still all too heavily in favor of positivism, Mills' abstract empiricism. Hopefully, some day a third culture will emerge, a culture transcending the artificial and unhealthy separation of science and humanity, integrating the best of both worlds for a unified understanding of man.

THE SELF

The title of Mead's *Mind, Self and Society* (1934) has provided the headings for the organization of material in innumerable readers and textbooks in social psychology, and this book will be no exception. Mead's own analysis, while positing the prior existence of society to the individual, proceeds from individual psychology to social structure. Following that arbitrary format,[3] we shall first deal with the self and then with society.

The self may be defined as a conscious organic entity. Man is and has a self, and only man does. The choice of word is important. For example, if man is referred to as an organism, even a psychological organism, his uniqueness will be overlooked. Man's uniqueness lies in his capability for consciousness, and consciousness can only emerge from social interaction. The word "self" means all of this, and every time we refer to man as a self we will know that we mean all of these things. Thus we shall not confuse man with animals, as many psychologists do, or with numbers, as many sociologists do.

---

[3]Berger and Luckmann's *The Social Construction of Reality* is just one example of a treatise that deals with similar problems but first handles the macro and then the micro.

A self is both a process and an entity. It is a process consisting of behavior and consciousness (reflection upon behavior), and it is an entity in that it is also a physical organism. Now one good way to see how such a self is indeed conscious, and is so only because it is social, is to split it up into an "I" and a "me." These terms were initially coined by the American psychologist William James (1842-1910) and used by him and by Mead in the following sense: the I is the self as knowing subject, while the me is the self as known object. In other words, the I is in action when I think about myself. The me is the sum total of all that is mine, including my body, my personality, my social roles, and even my possessions. The I is aware of the me. The two constantly interact, the I steering, judging, readjusting, liking, or disliking those aspects of the me that come to its awareness. It is this dialogue between the I and the me that goes on in each of us all the time and that we call the mind. While common parlance has it that we have a mind, it is much better to say that we *think*, for the self is a process, an activity, a stream of consciousness, no more and no less. To say that I have a mind is just as misleading as to call the activity of alternately putting one foot ahead of the other "a walker." Just as we call that activity walking, we shall call the dialogue between I and me thinking.

It is through the process of socialization that the self comes about. Socialization is the basic social process whereby society and individual become integrated. What happens during childhood in this respect is therefore of crucial importance, although the process of socialization continues throughout everyone's life.

While the self is a process of constant change, we do nevertheless develop a feeling of permanence and identity—what philosophers call essence. Indeed, one of the outcomes of socialization is the development, within the individual, of certain *tendencies* toward given behaviors. We call such tendencies habits, and habits are, indeed, no more than tendencies. Putting together an individual's most characteristic behavioral tendencies—including of course his mental behavior—we may speak of his personality.

Identity refers to who, what, and where—socially speaking—a person is. Since identity is a social concept, it is essentially the product of how *others* view, define, and label us: personal identity is the outcome of social identification. Think of the I.D. card: it is like a name tag given to us and validating us.

Finally, self-concept is the way we see ourselves. This may, perhaps should, and generally in the long run does coincide with how others see us, but it does not inevitably have to. The most obvious and pervasive case of discrepancy between self-concept and identification is when the former is positive in some respect and the latter negative. This is a fancy way of saying that there is a problem whenever we note that someone does not like us.

SOCIETY

Although the self was introduced first, we could just as well have begun with society, for the two are inseparable, of equal importance, and neither comes first. They are merely two sides of the same coin, both emerging from social interaction.

We take our approach to society through the concept of role. This concept, for which the German sociologist Georg Simmel (1858-1918) bears particular responsibility (see Martindale, 1960:239), is the most important term in sociology and social psychology. Role refers to a pattern of behavior that is linked to a particular social position. The incumbent of that position plays out the role, just as an actor acts out the part for which he has been hired.

Of equal importance here is the concept of reference group, invented by Herbert Hyman in 1942. It refers to a group or category of people whose ideas and values serve to guide an individual's behavior, a group to which that individual may or may not belong.

We may think of roles and reference groups as being *outside* of the individual. We first focused on processes internal to the individual but now, through the concepts of role and reference group, we move out to the larger social world of which he is a part—society. Reference groups indicate where many of his ideas, values, and behavior come from; roles show us the ready-made social-structural slots and parts that society has in store for him. Thus the developing self is merely the gradual internalization of such external elements: without a society no self can develop.

Moving on to an even higher level of abstraction, we arrive at the concept of institution: this is simply an interrelated system of roles, organized for some specific purpose(s). For example, the family is an institution; it evolved to take care of a variety of functions, including the regulation of procreation and socialization. The university is another institution; its purpose is education. The government is that institution whose primary function is to rule over a nation. In every instance, the institution may be seen as an organization of roles for the satisfaction of some social need(s), with rules specifying that organization. A society's social system consists of its institutions. As we move up from the individual through the role to the institution, we gain something and lose something: institutions provide order, stability, and up to a certain point the more efficient satisfaction of common needs. However, they also curtail individual freedom and innovation.

We then arrive at society's social structure. This can be defined as the stable and lasting system of roles, statuses, and relationships that make up the society. The difference between institution and social structure is this: social structure is a *characteristic* of institutions, societies, and other social systems. More than any other concept, social structure connotes stability. This is why it is introduced at this point, for we have gradually moved out of the concrete and dynamic self through roles and institutions to finally the social structure. We are now operating at the level of society, an abstraction denoting a reality that is external to the individual, objective in Berger and Luckmann's (1966) sense, a constraining bag that envelopes the individual, in Durkheim's metaphor.

There is, finally, another concept that is as static, abstract, external, and objective—in sum, as much a property of society—as the social structure; this is culture: Culture has been defined as "the way of life of a social group" and "a group's total man-made environment" (cf. Theodorson and Theodorson, 1969:95). However, the more important point here is that culture is a property of society, enveloping and molding the individual. Culture, like social structure, stands for highly stable and repetitive patterns that far transcend the individual. Together the culture and the social structure make up the society. While social structure is an abstraction that denotes the society's most prevalent patterns of interaction, culture is an abstraction for society's most permanent and consensual beliefs, values, thoughts, etc. It is possible to anthropomorphize society for a second and realize that the culture stands to the social structure as the I stands to the me, for both culture and the I are cognitive concepts, whereas the social structure and the me have behavioral referents. But the main point to remember is that by discussing roles, institutions, social structure, and culture, we end up right in the middle of macrosociology—society.

THE CONSTRUCTION OF REALITY

An important question, one that the reader should already have asked as we meandered from the concrete self to the abstract society, is this: what, precisely, is the concrete stuff of which roles, institutions, structure, and culture are made? To juggle with those abstractions is very well, but isn't that just playing with big words?

How real are the things we have been talking about so far? This section will try to explain precisely how real roles, institutions, organizations, structure, and culture are.

One idea must now once and for all be dispelled, and that is the belief that the only reality in which we live is that of our immediate actions and those of other concrete people. There is much more to our lives, our problems, and our achievements than merely what we did yesterday and today, even more than the deeds of an allegedly evil President or those of the capitalist conspirators. We shall fail to understand the world in which we live, and fail to improve it, as long as our view is thus myopic, as long as we see only the trees instead of the forest. To say "Nixon (or whoever) did it" and count on, say, Watergate to solve our problems is easy, misleading, and futile. To recognize the structural nature of our problems is more difficult, because it is more difficult to see a social structure. That requires a different set of glasses, and it is such a perspective that this book will provide.

Throughout this book, two things will have to be kept in mind: social reality far transcends the everyday interactions in which we are engaged, but at the same time the sum total of social reality is ultimately entirely our own creation. The culture and the social structure indeed exist, and they are certainly more powerful than any one of us, but they only exist in the sense that *we enact them.* If it weren't for you and me, there would be no American culture and American society. What we mean by the social construction of reality[4] is this: the social world in which man lives is of his own making, and *it consists of nothing more than his collective enactment of it.* If it is true that man's social world ceases to be from the moment that he ceases to (behaviorally) enact it, then why, you will ask, distinguish at all between men as a plurality of concrete behaving organisms and the

---

[4]The expression is borrowed from Berger and Luckmann's (1966) seminal book by that title.

external social reality in which they live? Aren't they one and the same? The answer to this is as follows. Man's uniqueness is in his dual nature. Because man—a self, remember—has the unique capability to objectify, that is, to transcend his subjectivity through consciousness, he creates a reality that simultaneously becomes objective yet remains subjective. While bees construct hives and ants build hills, only man creates *mental constructions*, and these are of the same lasting resilience as physical structures like the Egyptian pyramids. Thus we must recognize the existence of culture, even though we must be careful not to reify it, that is, give it a life of its own.

The basis of man's complex collective mental constructions—his culture—is his ability to *symbolize,* to handle in his mind ideas that he arbitrarily chooses to attach to things, and to communicate to his fellow men through such symbols and through complex systems of symbols, languages.

Thus man's forte, above everything else, is his ability to arbitrarily *choose* from a variety of alternative ways of perceiving, naming, labelling, explaining, and evaluating whatever it is that he perceives. Indeed, a rose by any other name is not a rose, no matter what Shakespeare said, for whereas to us the word "rose" means a beautiful, pleasant-smelling, and originally pink flower of essentially esthetic value, another culture could conceivably view the rose as a food and name it, accordingly, a "sweet." We do not know and shall never know what a rose *really* is. Similarly, we shall never know what it is that men truly see. But what we can do is listen to what they *say* they see. We shall find that what they tell us depends, to use another analogy, on the glasses they wear—sunglasses keeping out some parts of the spectrum, magnifying glasses that distort reality in one way, bifocal glasses that distort it in another way, etc.

Thus the relevant question for us is not what man perceives (although philosophers must continue to ponder that), but what he *says* he perceives and how he goes about perceiving. To say this is to recognize that man defines objects and situations and that the task of sociology and social psychology is to study and understand this process of definition—nothing more and nothing less. Because of man's inherent need to make the absurd meaningful, to explain, the definition of the situation also entails the construction of explanations for his behavior. This is what we shall discuss under the heading of accounts, motives, and motivation. Rather than asking ourselves what needs, drives, predispositions, cultural factors, delinquent backgrounds, or other a priori causes can be identified as the true motivation behind given conduct, we shall examine the *explanations* that people give, often *after the facts,* for behavior, their own as well as that of others. Motive to us shall mean explanation, be it a true one or a false one.

WHOSE REALITY?

What has just been said may have left the reader with a feeling of dissatisfaction: after all, is not the goal of social psychology, as that of all science, the *valid* explanation of phenomena, that is, the discovery of their true causes and the dismissal of erroneous theories? For example we now agree, thanks to social psychology, that an important cause of behavior is the way in which an individual has been reared, while the color of his skin, the shape of his skull, and the constellation of stars at his birth, which were formerly all held to be of great significance, are now known to have relatively little impact on his subsequent behavior. Isn't this kind of knowledge the task at hand? By studying subjective motives, ex post facto explanations, and arbitrary definitions of situations and by giving equal weight to all, are we not lapsing into sophistry and relativism, that is, abdicating our scientific responsibility, which is to distinguish truth from falsehood?

According to the perspective of this book, the answer to these questions is no.

While causal explanation is an important objective of science—certainly of physical science—there is, in the study of man, an even more important goal, and that is the discovery not of what things mean "transcendentally" but of *what things mean to man himself.* In fact, the whole gist of the argument thus far has been that the discovery of objective or absolute meanings is in the realm of philosophy and religion and not of the kind of social psychology we propose. Thus we turn the table on the scientists, claiming in a way to be more scientific than they are and unmasking their enterprise for what it is, namely a metaphysical endeavor.

The new social psychology studies the meanings men attach to conduct and other phenomena. Is this not a valid objective? And can we not hope to make a great deal of headway toward that objective, assuming that we use the right methods? In fact, is that not a much more realistic goal than that pursued by the so-called behavioral scientists—we shall sometimes call them the absolutists—in the past, namely trying to discover ultimate laws that should govern social interaction? Surely we can hope to establish with some validity what conduct means to the actor, but the same cannot be said of what the absolutists are attempting to do!

Having said all this, we may now be ready to introduce the concept of game. If we agree that the new social psychology only studies the meanings and definitions arbitrarily created by various groups and individuals, we might as well face the fact that each group, individual, subculture, and even society is merely engaged in its own *game.* A game, after all, is "a body of rules associated with a lore regarding good strategies" (Goffman, 1961:35), and in a very general sense that description fits just about any conceivable interaction pattern, from the dating game enacted by two lovers to the international confrontation game played by two superpowers.

While we all play games, some games are "better" than other games in the sense that they are more acceptable to a majority. Those of us who play games that are totally idiosyncratic (for example, the schizophrenic), that go against the interests of others (the criminal), or that are unpopular for some less tangible reason (like the hippie or the homosexual) may be called deviants. We say *may be,* because it is important to understand the dual origin of deviance: a deviant act need not, in and of itself, produce a deviant role. As Professor Lemert (1951) first showed, the deviant role results only once such primary deviation is followed by secondary deviation, the processes of labelling, stigmatization, etc., processes for which, incidentally, mental and correctional institutions are primarily responsible.

Thus we are back where we started from, at the definition of the situation. As Thomas Szasz said in a recent lecture, in the animal kingdom there are only two possibilities—one eats or one is food; similarly in human society you either define or are defined. There is no alternative. Sociologically, a majority may be thought of as that subgroup which is in a position to define and to impose its definitions upon other subgroups, and in that process it either commands conformity or, in the case of incorrigibles, isolates them through deviant labels, clearly there for all to be recognized and not to be associated with lest they contaminate us.

This brings us to the final issue that must be introduced here—power. Weber (1947:152) defines power as "the probability that an actor within a social relationship will be in a position to carry out his own will despite resistance." In this book, we shall have much to say about power, because that, ultimately, is what determines how situations are defined, which groups are the defining majority, and which individuals are labelled deviant. Thus the last part of this book is headed by a question: whose reality? and the most basic answer to that question is given by Berger and Luckmann (1966:109) as follows: "He who has the bigger stick has the better chance of imposing his definitions of reality."

SUMMARY AND CONCLUSION

The purpose of this book is to contribute to a new social psychology whose strands are already widely recognized in many progressive quarters and which therefore shows all the signs of an emergent paradigm. The new social psychology departs from other perspectives theoretically, methodologically, and philosophically. It is important to emphasize, nevertheless, that the new departure is epistemological rather than ontological; that is, we shall argue for a somewhat novel approach to knowledge but shall, in accordance with phenomenology and the pragmatism that underlies symbolic interactionism, bracket any preoccupation with the nature of ultimate reality itself. We shall suspend judgment about the validity of positivism, questioning only its *relevance*, particularly in social science.

Theoretically, the new social psychology proposes a new paradigm that is holistic, dialectical, processual, and humanistic in its postulates. Methodologically, it advocates a qualitative and phenomenological approach, because its subject matter consists of the (inter)subjective meanings that man constructs. Philosophically, finally, certain value affirmations follow from the above, at least two of which will be mentioned here.

1. Theory and practice are as inseparable as their two corresponding phases of the self—the I and the me. Thus activism—political, business, revolutionary, or any other kind—and intellectual theorizing must go hand in hand, and we aim to point out certain inadequacies in the life-style of Americans in this respect, on both sides of the thirty-year demarcation line.

2. Freedom and order, too, are one, as inseparably united as the individual and society. Man's reflexive consciousness makes him inherently paradoxical, and history is nothing but the human paradox infinitely working itself out. The terms of that paradox are, of course, I and me, subject and object, individual and society. As man will continue to create a meaning without which he cannot exist, in time proselytizing and imposing it on others, he will also unceasingly reject that which is dehumanizing and oppressive, in one word: meaningless. Of that we may be sure.

REFERENCES

Berger, Peter and Thomas Luckmann
1966 The Social Construction of Reality. Garden City, N.Y.: Doubleday & Co., Inc.
Blumer, Herbert
1969 Symbolic Interactionism. Englewood Cliffs, N.J.: Prentice-Hall, Inc.
Bruyn, Severyn
1966 The Human Perspective in Sociology. Englewood Cliffs, N.J.: Prentice-Hall, Inc.
Cardwell, J. D.
1971 Social Psychology: A Symbolic Interactionist Perspective. Philadelphia: F. A. Davis Co.
Comte, Auguste
1853 The Positive Philosophy of Auguste Comte. Translated by Harriet Martineau. London: J. Chapman.
Durkheim, Emile et al.
1964 Essays on Sociology and Philosophy. Kurt H. Wolff (ed.). New York: Harper & Row, Publishers.
Frankl, Viktor
1959 Man's Search for Meaning. New York: Washington Square Press.
Freud, Sigmund
1943 General Introduction to Psychoanalysis. Translated by Joan Riviere. Garden City, N.Y.: Garden City Publishing Co.
Garfinkel, Harold
1967 Studies in Ethnomethodology. Englewood Cliffs, N.J.: Prentice-Hall, Inc.
Goffman, Erving
1961 Encounters: Two Studies in the Sociology of Interaction. New York: Bobbs-Merrill Co., Inc.
Habermas, Jurgen
1970 Toward a Rational Society; Student Protest, Science, and Politics. Translated by Jeremy J. Shapiro. Boston: Beacon Press.
Hyman, Herbert H.
1942 "The psychology of status." Archives of Psychology 269.
Kuhn, Thomas S.
1962 The Structure of Scientific Revolutions. Chicago: The University of Chicago Press.

Lemert, Edwin
  1951 Social Pathology. New York: McGraw-Hill
        Book Co.
Lindesmith, Alfred R. and Anselm L. Strauss
  1956 Social Psychology. New York: Dryden Press.
Lyman, Stanford and Marvin B. Scott
  1970 A Sociology of the Absurd. New York:
        Meredith Corp.
Marcuse, Herbert
  1968 One-Dimensional Man: Studies in the Ideol-
        ogy of Advanced Industrial Society. Boston:
        Beacon Press.
Martindale, Don
  1960 The Nature and Types of Sociological
        Theory. Boston: Houghton Mifflin Co.
Mead, George Herbert
  1934 Mind, Self and Society. Charles W. Morris
        (ed.). Chicago: University of Chicago Press.
  1956 On Social Psychology. Anselm Strauss (ed.).
        Chicago: University of Chicago Press.
Merton, Robert K.
  1957 Social Theory and Social Structure. Glencoe,
        Ill.: Free Press.
Mullins, Nicholas C.
  1973 Theories and Theory Groups in Contem-
        porary American Sociology. New York:
        Harper & Row, Publishers.
Pavlov, I. P.
  1927 Conditioned Reflexes. New York: Oxford
        University Press.

Schutz, Alfred
  1970 On Phenomenology and Social Relations.
        Helmut R. Wagner (ed.). Chicago: Univer-
        sity of Chicago Press.
Shibutani, Tamotsu
  1961 Society and Personality: An Interactionist
        Approach to Social Psychology. Englewood
        Cliffs, N.J.: Prentice-Hall, Inc.
Snow, Charles P.
  1959 The Two Cultures and The Scientific Revo-
        lution. Cambridge: Cambridge University
        Press.
Theodorson, George A. and Achilles G. Theodorson
  1969 A Modern Dictionary of Sociology. New
        York: Thomas Y. Crowell Co., Inc.
Toynbee, Arnold J.
  1947- A Study of History. Two-volume abridg-
  1957   ment by D. C. Somervell. New York: Oxford
         University Press.
Watson, J. B.
  1919 Psychology From the Standpoint of a Behav-
        iorist. Philadelphia: J. B. Lippincott Co.
Weber, Max
  1947 The Theory of Social and Economic Organi-
        zation. Talcott Parsons (ed.). Translated by
        A. M. Henderson and Talcott Parsons. Glen-
        coe, Ill.: Free Press.
Zetterberg, Hans L.
  1965 On Theory and Verification in Sociology.
        Totowa, N.J.: The Bedminster Press.
Znaniecki, Florian
  1934 The Method of Sociology. New York: Farrar
        and Rinehart.

part one

Waning paradigms

chapter 1
Scientific sociology

In sociology, the grand old paradigm is what Mullins (1973) calls standard American sociology but what should in fact be called standard international sociology. This paradigm was launched by the Frenchman Auguste Comte in 1830, an event often equated with the birth of sociology itself, because Comte at that time invented the word "sociology." After Comte, it was another Frenchman, Emile Durkheim, who more than anyone else carried the banner and the tradition of the paradigm toward the beginning of the twentieth century. Later, from about World War II on, it was American sociology which, in the form of structural-functionalism, fell heir to the grand old paradigm. The prime figures at that point became Robert Merton, George Homans, and, above all, Talcott Parsons. While the central flow of this paradigm has moved from nineteenth century French sociology to twentieth century American—and particularly Ivy League—sociology, other expressions of it were German organismic sociology (Ferdinand Tonnies), British anthropology (A. R. Radcliffe-Brown and Bronislaw Malinowski), and British sociology (Herbert Spencer).

Today, the condition and fate of the grand old paradigm (G.O.P. for short)—functionalism, it has permanently been labelled—are unclear. On the one hand, criticism of functionalism has, since the 1960s, become so much part and parcel of each new sociologist's training program that in a majority of quarters the issue is now considered a dead horse. On the other hand, the beast may very well once again be in the process of reincarnating into a form that is seemingly novel, and therefore socially acceptable, yet in substance similar to what it was in the past: the new anthropological and kinship structuralism so

voguish in Europe at this time (for example, Levi-Strauss) and the mathematical and linguistic structuralism of a growing group of young American sociologists (cf. Mullins, 1973:250-269) may be the latest extension of the systems theory earlier called functionalism. The new causal theory (Mullins, 1973:213-249) is, of course, the furthest extension to date of the positivistic program initially proposed by Comte and Durkheim.

Finally, there are two brands of microfunctionalism: one based on Kurt Lewin's pioneering work and now called group dynamics or, simply, small groups research; the other, exchange theory, based primarily on Homans' conversion to Skinnerian behaviorism. While microfunctionalism straddles the sociological and psychological G.O.P.'s, it does deserve a place under contemporary American functionalism.

With this, some of the grand old paradigm's essential features have already been touched upon. Let us identify the main contributions made to the paradigm, first by its French founders, Comte and Durkheim; second by the American functionalists, both macro and micro; and finally by the structuralists and the new causal theorists.

COMTE AND DURKHEIM

Comte (1798-1857), of course, conceived sociology. This new science, according to the Frenchman, was to be "patterned after the natural sciences, not only in its empirical methods. . .but also in the functions it would serve for mankind" (Coser, 1971:4). Sociology's methods were to be the same as those used in the natural sciences, namely, observation, experimentation and comparison (op. cit.:5). There are three stages in the evolution of human civilization—the stages of theology, metaphysics, and science. Science, then, is the culmination of social progress, and sociology was to be the queen of all sciences. Comte also called sociology *positive philosophy*, positive in the sense of scientific and empirical. Finally, society is a structured and functioning organic whole whose organs are institutions and whose elements are the individual and the family (Martindale, 1960:63). Thus Comte's work immediately reveals the two central features of the sociological G.O.P.: a positivistic methodology and an organismic or systemic conception of sociology's subject matter.

Durkheim (1858-1917) is being singled out here because he insisted, more relentlessly than anyone else, on the sui generis nature of social phenomena. In other words, it was Durkheim who argued most vigorously that in order for us to understand society, we must view it in its totality and not break it down into individuals. When it comes to the relationship between society and the individual, there are two possibilities: one can argue that institutions and culture are the *product* of individual actions, attitudes, beliefs, and values, or one can, quite to the contrary, argue that individual behavior and attitudes are the product of the culture and social institutions that envelope the individual. The former view is generally termed *reductionism*, because it essentially implies that social phenomena (institutions like the state or the family, cultures like American or German culture) can ultimately be reduced to their individual psychological component parts. The latter perspective implies *emergentism*, the assumption that at the complex social level whole new properties emerge that cannot be deduced from individual psychology. It is this perspective with which Durkheim's work remains forever associated. It is well illustrated by the analogy of the chemical compound: the properties of the compound (density,

smell, color, etc.) cannot be reduced to and deduced from those of its elements.

Thus it is of the essence of Durkheimian sociology—and of the sociological G.O.P.—to proceed from the whole to the parts, from society to the individual. Not only is the whole *more* than the sum of its parts (emergentism) but it also *determines* the behavior of the parts: society and culture are the *cause* of, and determine, individual behavior. Durkheim's metaphor of society, then, is that of a bag that constrains and surrounds the individual (cf. Stone and Farberman, 1970). A good application of the general perspective is the Frenchman's theory of suicide: here is a highly individual form of behavior, yet as suicide statistics show, the rates vary according to such factors as nationality, religion, and economic conditions. This indicates, according to Durkheim, that the true causes of suicide are social rather than psychological. In fact, there are three types of suicide: *altruistic*, where social integration is excessive (society pressures the individual to sacrifice himself for the group, as in the case of the war hero), *egoistic*, where structural integration fails (the individual is thrown upon his own devices, separated from the group), and *anomic*, where normative integration fails (the individual suffers from normlessness).

Durkheim's sociology contains many additional elements that have become cornerstones of contemporary standard international sociology. The distinction between egoistic and anomic suicide points to one such element—the distinction between structural and normative integration. According to Durkheim, there are two kinds of social integration, one mechanical and one organic. Mechanical solidarity is based primarily on normative integration and is found mostly in primitive societies; organic solidarity is based on the structural integration typical of advanced societies with a complex division of labor and a high degree of functional interdependence. For us, the crucial point is that all societies, and particularly advanced ones, are viewed as integrated organisms or systems. Durkheim's work is clearly an extension of the paradigm established by Comte, particularly since both men advocate a similarly rigorous positivistic methodology (cf. Durkheim, 1938).

CONTEMPORARY AMERICAN SOCIOLOGY

Postwar American functionalism has been subdivided into macro- and microfunctionalism (cf. Martindale, 1960). The former deals with large social units (societies, institutions, large-scale organizations) and is therefore properly sociological, whereas the latter deals with small groups, face-to-face interaction, and laboratory experiments and is therefore more social-psychological. Microfunctionalism is also called group dynamics, and as we shall see, it straddles the sociological and the psychological G.O.P.

Macrofunctionalism

The Durkheimian heritage was picked up after World War II by American sociologists, mostly at Harvard and Columbia. The social organism now became the social system (a concession to the vocabulary of our technocratic century), and society was to be analyzed in terms of its structure and functions. The paradigm remained holistic and abstract, as with Durkheim. The meaning of the emergentism-reductionism polarity was explained before, and it was pointed out that the G.O.P. is clearly on the side of emergentism. A parallel set of philosophical concepts is the nominalism-realism polarity: *nominalism* may be defined as the belief that only the parts of a phenomenon are concretely real, and *realism* is the opposite doctrine, namely that complex composite concepts (such as "society," "culture," "mind") refer to real, existing entities in the phenomenal world and are *not* mere abstractions, *not* mere heuristic devices, that is, devices invented merely to facilitate our understanding. Thus nominalism goes with reductionism, whereas realism goes with emergentism. Modern functionalism, like Durkheim's sociology, is clearly on the side of realism as well as emergentism, for it posits that "society,"

"institution," "culture," "mores," and "folkways" are real, all existing *objectively* and not merely in the conceptions of sociologists. The three major American functionalists have been Talcott Parsons, Robert Merton, and George C. Homans.

Talcott Parsons was born in 1902 and his institutional affiliation has been Harvard. He has been the most influential American sociologist. In *The Social System* (1951), he presents his theory about society and its functional prerequisites. A social system cannot function properly unless the minimum needs of (1) the individual (such as physical survival), (2) the society (for example, social order), and (3) the culture (like the availability of a common language) are met (summarized in Martindale, 1960:486). Furthermore, there are four major functional problems that all social systems must solve if they are to survive, namely adaptation, goal attainment, integration, and latency (Parsons, 1953). This has become Parsons' famous AGIL system. What he means is that all societies are subject to at least these four kinds of functional imperatives and that societies develop institutions to meet these requirements. Thus our economic institutions have important adaptive functions. Goal attainment functions are served by an institution like the government (p. 114). Integration is served by a variety of political and legislative processes. Finally latency, by which Parsons means the transmission of culture, is served by education, the family, etc. (cf. p. 113). The most serious problem with Parsonian sociology is its tendency to reify social constructs. Reification means "making a thing" out of a concept, attributing to a concept the properties of a real and independently existing object. Thus Parsonian sociology reified the idea of social system to the point where it became endowed with systemic needs that seem to have priority over those of people, needs demanding certain responses *for the sole sake of system maintenance.*

Robert Merton was born in 1910 and he has been employed mostly by Columbia. His major contributions to the functionalist paradigm include (1) the final definition of function as understood by sociologists, (2) the codification and elaboration of functionalism's prevailing postulates, (3) the addition of the concept of dysfunction, (4) the very important distinction between manifest and latent functions, and (5) his classical example of a functional analysis in "Social Structure and Anomie" (Merton, 1957). Having reviewed five major meanings of the term "function," Merton arrives at the definition relevant to a sociological functionalism, a definition explicitly adopted from biology: "the vital . . . processes considered in the respects in which they contribute to the maintenance of the organism," that is, social system (Merton, 1957:21). This, then, is the central concept in American sociological functionalism. Second, Merton points out that functionalists have generally conceived of *all* functional institutions as being functional for the *entire* system and as being therefore *indispensable* (op. cit.:25-37). This triple assumption is ill-founded, Merton explains, since there may be alternative ways to satisfy the same function. Third, it is necessary to recognize the possibility of *dysfunctions*, that is, "consequences which lessen the adaptation or adjustment of the system" (p. 51). Fourth, institutions and activities may have *manifest* functions, consequences that are intended and recognized (loc. cit.), and *latent* functions,

which are neither intended nor immediately recognized. For example, the manifest function of military service is the protection of the nation; a latent function is to reduce unemployment.

In addition, Merton has left us with a brilliant and famous functional explanation of crime and deviant behavior. In "Social Structure and Anomie" (pp. 131-160), the author shows how different kinds of individual adaptation and the high frequency of deviant behavior in America may be the result of disjunctions between culturally shared goals on the one hand and legitimate means toward such goals on the other. There is in our society a widely shared belief in success goals, but no "equivalent emphasis upon institutional means" (p. 136). Such means—for example, upward mobility through education and hard work—are either insufficiently available or insufficiently subscribed to. Hence, at least five logical possibilities exist: *conformity*, adherence to both success goals and legitimate means; *innovation*, the pursuit of success goals through the use of illegitimate means (for example, the common criminal); *ritualism*, abiding by legitimate work routine but no longer pursuing success (like a great many lower middle class workers such as petty bureaucrats); *retreatism*, rejection of both success values and hard work (like the hippie); *rebellion*, the substitution of a new set of success values and institutional means (for example, the revolutionary). Merton's typology is summarized in Table 1.

The third major American functionalist has been George Homans, born in 1910 and employed during most of his career by

TABLE 1. Merton's typology of modes of individual adaptation

Modes of adaptation	Cultural goals	Institutionalized means
I. Conformity	+	+
II. Innovation	+	−
III. Ritualism	−	+
IV. Retreatism	−	−
V. Rebellion	±	±

Harvard. In *The Human Group* (1950), Homans provides a systematic functionalistic theory. His major contribution is an attempt at distinguishing between an internal and an external system. Having established that the proper unit of sociological analysis is the human group and that this is a system, Homans proceeds to differentiate the two components of this system: the external system, which represents the group and its relationships to its environment, and the internal system, which represents the group's internally elaborated behavior. "We call the system 'internal' because it is not directly conditioned by the environment and we speak of it as an 'elaboration' because it includes forms of behavior not included under the heading of the external system" (Homans, 1950:109). Furthermore, the elements of the total system are activity, interaction, sentiment, and norms. As Martindale (1960:483) has shown, the distinction between the two subsystems may be artificial, for in the real world it may never be clear whether a given sentiment or activity belongs to the external or the internal system. In fact, the two cannot be separated, not even by calling the internal system the *social* system, as Homans does. Surely the author does not mean to restrict the external system to nonsocial variables. However, Homans remains a central figure in functionalism because his analysis—like Parsons'—is an example of modern abstract systems theory. His unit of analysis, the system, refers to *any* human group, from a subgroup in a modern factory to an entire civilization. Furthermore, large systems such as large-scale organizations and societies are made up of smaller subsystems, and it is assumed that the same sociological laws apply to all systems. We should also note at this point that Homans' focus on sentiments and activities, among other things, reveals an early behavioristic and psychological tendency. Indeed, later in his career Homans moved radically toward Skinnerian exchange theory, becoming a total psychological reductionist. This will be discussed further in the next section.

Microfunctionalism

The subject matter to be discussed under this heading does not have the same unity as macrofunctionalism. Furthermore, it overlaps with the psychological G.O.P. and will therefore be discussed in greater detail in the next chapter. Here, we shall discuss the two strands of microfunctionalism deemed properly sociological—group dynamics and exchange theory.

Group dynamics. This area is also called *small groups research.*[1] "The word 'dynamics' implies forces which are complex and interdependent in a common field or setting" (Luft, 1970:1). This subdiscipline comes out of *Gestalt psychology* and *field theory.*

It has been said that classical Gestalt psychology—to be defined shortly—has focused primarily on problems of cognition and perception, field theory turned its attention to motivation, and group dynamics is mostly concerned with interaction (cf. Deutsch and Krauss, 1965:37; Luft, 1970:1). Nevertheless, the entire area is sometimes referred to as *cognitive (social) psychology.*

Chronologically, the German Max Wertheimer's experiments in 1912 laid the first foundations of Gestalt psychology. Analyzing the visual experience that makes motion pictures possible, Wertheimer concluded that the perception of smoothly flowing *motion* cannot be reduced to the simple static stimuli (pictures) that give rise to it. The scientist called this the phi-phenomenon (Martindale, 1960:452) and it represents the prime example of a Gestalt. Gestalt is the German word for *whole,* or *configuration;* it is a phenomenon that cannot be reduced or analyzed in terms of component parts but must be

---

[1]For surveys of the field, see Deutsch and Krauss, 1965; Luft, 1970; Martindale, 1960. For a recent and representative reader, see Ofshe, 1973.

comprehended and apprehended in its totality.

Wolfgang Kohler, a colleague of Wertheimer's, was stranded in South America during World War I, at which time he carried out a number of experiments with apes, demonstrating the Gestalt experience. Caged animals were presented with a number of stimuli situations. For example, bananas were placed just out of the reach of chimps, and some sticks were lying inside the cage, potentially usable to paw in the bananas. Kohler's important discovery was that the chimps did not learn to reach the bananas through trial and error but rather perceived the solution all at once. Suddenly, the animal would "realize" what needed to be done and would grab one of the sticks and thus reach the otherwise inaccessible fruit. In fact, the chimp even chewed the end of one stick, fit it into the other one, and thus reached a banana too removed for either one stick! This so-called "aha Erlebnis," then, demonstrates that perception emerges out of consciousness as an organized whole, that is, as a Gestalt.

Kurt Koffka was also a colleague and a disciple of Wertheimer's, and he emphasized in his writings the notion of *Pragnanz:* this means that there is a tendency to achieve in any given psychological situation (for example, the perception of images, or ideas, or beliefs) the simplest, most orderly, and *best* possible organization, or Gestalt.

Another early and highly influential Gestalt psychologist was Fritz Heider, also a German. As early as 1927, Heider formulated a psychological theory that would lead to Gestalt psychology, attribution theory, and phenomenological cognitive theory, thereby making a contribution to both kinds of paradigms discussed in this book, that is, to theories which we believe are highly relevant today and to outdated paradigms as well. The German psychologist's primary focus was on *cognitive bal-ance:* a fundamental feature of naive psychology is a constant striving for maximum cognitive balance. In other words, "when the cognitive structure is in a state of imbalance, forces will arise to produce a tendency toward locomotion so as to change the psychological environment . . ." (Deutsch and Krauss, 1965:33). For example, if I am radically prejudiced against blacks but have a fine black neighbor, I will either minimize my interactions with him so as not to experience cognitive imbalance, or change my attitudes toward blacks in general, or mentally segregate my neighbor from other blacks ("he is an exception"). Heider's concept of a striving for cognitive balance is, of course, identical to Koffka's notion of *Pragnanz.* Both authors belong to the Gestalt school because they emphasize man's tendency to perceive and to know things in an organized fashion rather than disparately and man's tendency to strive for perceptual and cognitive simplicity and orderliness. It is clear that the theoretical perspective of Gestalt psychology has been functionalistic, that is, relational and holistic rather than atomistic.

When we move to *field theory,* we see a great deal of continuity with Gestalt psychology, the only significant difference being perhaps a shift in substantive emphasis, namely toward problems of *motivation* rather than perception (cf. Deutsch and Krauss, 1965:37).

The German Kurt Lewin (1890-1947) is unanimously considered the father of field theory. He began his work in Berlin but moved to the United States in 1933, working at M.I.T. and at the University of Iowa. He founded the Research Center for Group Dynamics, indicating once again the unity of Gestalt, field theory, and group dynamics. Adopting Einstein's definition of field as "a totality of coexisting facts which are conceived of as mutually interdependent" (Lewin, 1972:200), Lewin postulates that "psychology has to view the life space, including the person and his environment, as one field" (loc. cit.). Within such a field, *psychological forces* determine individual and group behavior. The two major psychological forces are *positive* and *negative* valence. A positive valence occurs when forces point toward a given region of a field. This is Lewin's conceptualization of, for example, a goal that attracts an actor. A negative valence is the opposite, namely when psychological forces point away from a region (such as a threat). "Whenever a resultant force (valence) exists, there is either a locomotion in the direction of that force or a change in the cognitive structure equivalent to this locomotion" (Lewin, 1972:205). These are some of Lewin's concepts in approaching the problem of motivation.

Lewin also focused on cognition. In addition to the dynamic psychological *forces,* the field—or life space—is also characterized by a cognitive *structure.* Lewin developed a geometric model representing such a structure, calling it *hodological space.* In sum, field theory is a paradigm that models social-psychological processes and phenomena after physical reality. It will be covered in more detail in Chapter 2.

From the standpoint of sociology, Lewin's major contributions include his study of Jewish marginality (1935) and his experimental comparison of autocratic and democratic group structures among young boys (Lewin and Lippitt, 1938). Much of his work in sociology has been highly "en-gaged," that is, relevant to the dominant political issues of the day. His preoccupation with Jews, marginality, authoritarianism, and democracy is understandable in light of the fact that he was an emigrant from Nazi Germany. His work includes comparisons of American and German national character, pointing out, for example, that the former tends to be more open than the latter at the surface but not so deep down (the stereotype of the superficially friendly American). His comparative experiments with boys showed the superiority of the democratic group (no scapegoating, less tension, more cooperation, etc.).

Lewin's work in group dynamics was carried on in the United States by Leon Festinger and his associates. Festinger, who was born in 1919 and who has worked at Minnesota and Stanford among other universities, is best known for his theories of cognitive dissonance and social comparison. Since these are more psychological than sociological, they will be reviewed in the next chapter. Here, we discuss Festinger's major contribution to sociology, *When Prophecy Fails* (Festinger et al., 1956). In this study, the authors examine a small Midwestern chiliastic sect and the group's

TABLE 2. Bales' categories for the analysis of interaction*

		Percent
Positive reactions	Shows solidarity	3.4
	Shows tension release	6.0
	Shows agreement	16.5
Problem-solving attempts	Gives suggestion	8.0
	Gives opinion	30.1
	Gives information	17.9
Questions	Asks for information	3.5
	Asks for opinion	2.4
	Asks for suggestions	1.1
Negative reactions	Shows disagreement	7.8
	Shows tension	2.7
	Shows antagonism	0.7

*From Bales, Robert F. 1950. "A set of categories for the analysis of small group analysis." American Sociological Review 15:257-263.

reaction to the failure of the prophesized messianic arrival to materialize. Through participant observation (some covert and ethically questionable), the investigators discovered the nature, strength, and persistence of these people's beliefs. Their major finding is that the reaction to disappointed expectation (the predicted destruction of the city and the coming of the messiah) is often a *strengthening* of the belief, not its abandonment. What this shows is the human tendency to avoid *cognitive dissonance*, to avoid the disharmony resulting from inconsistent cognitive elements coexisting in a person's awareness. This, in turn, is clearly in the tradition of Gestalt and field theory, which emphasizes man's tendency to perceive and to know things in harmonious configurations.

While Lewin and Festinger have been psychologists, the primary sociologist associated with small groups research has been Robert F. Bales, a colleague of Parsons at Harvard. In collaboration with Parsons, Bales has made contributions to macrofunctionalism (Parsons et al., 1953). However, his most lasting work has been the development of twelve behavioral categories for the analysis of social interaction in controlled conference type settings. Table 2 produces Bales' twelve categories, as first formulated in the *American Sociological Review* (1950) and his first book (1950).

The percentages in Table 2 are averages obtained from ninety-six group sessions conducted experimentally by Bales and his researchers. According to these findings, fifty-six percent of all acts fall into the problem-solving category (Bales, 1955:5).

Twenty years later, Bales' work was reviewed by Strodtbeck (1973). The most interesting development has been a shift from the original research on laboratory groups to therapy groups. By the late 1960s and early 1970s, Bales' work had converged with the applied therapeutic focus of the encounter movement. This will be picked up in the next chapter.

Two other important group dynamicists are Cartwright and Zander (1953). Both, like Festinger, were disciples of Lewin, carrying on the German scholar's work in this country. These researchers' focus has been on group cohesiveness, group pressures and standards, and leadership. Cartwright (1972) believes that group dynamics provide an understanding of the forces that change groups *and* individuals, and he enumerates laws accounting for such change. As we shall see in the next chapter, the study of such phenomena—leadership, group conformity, and cohesiveness—has become the hallmark of psychological social psychology today, and it is therefore to that side of the fence that men like Cartwright and Zander must primarily by assigned.

There is, then, a general field that may be termed *small group research* or *group dynamics* and that straddles sociology and psychology in terms of the academic background of its adherents. Some, like Bales, have come to the field from macrosociology, influenced by Parsons. Most, like Festinger and Cartwright, have been psychologists, influenced mostly by Lewin, who in turn was carrying forward the work of the German Gestaltists. Today, the field finds unity in its choice of topics (leadership, conformity, cohesiveness, etc.) and most of all in its strongly experimental methodology. As Vinacke (1964) views it, the laboratory situation is the miniature social situation. That, however, is precisely what begs the question. As we shall see, the major weakness of this entire field is the questionable validity of its findings, resulting from the contrived setting in which they are arrived at.

Exchange theory. George Homans, who was originally a macrofunctionalist, subsequently formulated a rationalistic and psychologistic perspective called exchange theory (see Homans, 1961; 1972). This perspective views all human interaction as exchange, that is, as the exchange of goods, services, favors, approval, disapproval, love, or the expression of any other sentiment or activity. Exchange theory views all human interaction as *transaction*. It uses concepts like "cost," "reward," and "investment" and assumes that humans calculate such things whenever interacting with one another. On that basis, it formulates laws that allegedly can predict the course of social interaction. For example, a person will cease interacting with another person whenever the cost of interaction exceeds the rewards. Since cost can be defined as the sum of the forgone alternatives, the cost of any activity can be determined by examining what alternatives the actor forgoes. Rewards include all the possible (social) psychological gratifications that can be exchanged in social interaction, for example, esteem, friendship, ego support, respect.

Exchange theory may be seen as the product of three distinct strands. In the first place, Homans' own theories are an explicit extension of Skinnerian reinforcement theory. Social exchange among humans is essentially viewed as the exchange of reinforcement. Like the Skinnerians, Homans spends a considerable amount of time showing us the similarities between humans and other animals, for example, pigeons. Both species are seen as essentially being the product of conditioning, either positively through rewards or negatively through punishments.

Distinct from this is the contribution made to exchange theory by the sociologist Alvin Gouldner (1960). In the norm of reciprocity, Gouldner is a clear functionalist in the Parsonian tradition. According to the author, we all tacitly subscribe to a norm which says that gratification, help, benefits, etc., should be reciprocated. This norm is a cultural universal—it exists in all societies—and it is one of the major mechanisms maintaining the stability of social systems. Gouldners's norm, the generalized expectation of some sort of "repayment," is an important simultaneous contribution to Parsonian functionalism and exchange theory.

Third, there is the game theoretical brand of exchange theory proposed by Thibaut and Kelley (1959). These two psychological social psychologists have been strongly influenced by Lewin and Festinger. They approach social interaction as a trading game, that is, as a series of exchanging moves through which the parties arrive at some sort of joint objective. In this conceptualization, Thibaut and Kelley make use of outcome matrices explicitly resembling the payoff matrices used in game theory (1959:24). For example, a wife likes to go dancing in the evening but the husband prefers the movies. This relationship requires trading if both parties are to obtain what they want. The outcomes are illustrated in Fig. 1-1.

In sum, contributors to exchange theory have come from at least three distinct directions: Homans' variant is the application of Skinnerian behaviorism, Gouldner's is that of Parsonian functionalism, and that of Thibaut and Kelley is game theoretical.

FIG. 1-1
Thibaut and Kelley's illustration of a relationship requiring trading.

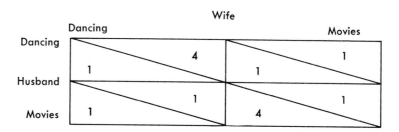

From Thibaut, John W. and Harold H. Kelley. 1959. The Social Psychology of Groups. New York: John Wiley & Sons, Inc., p. 127.

In a recent evaluation of exchange theory, Robert Schafer (1974) argued that this orientation can be successfully synthesized with symbolic interactionism, that is, with the more humanistic and phenomenological social psychology advocated in this book. According to Schafer, exchange theory's forte is that it offers a theory of motivation, that is, it addresses itself to the "why" of human behavior, something lacking in symbolic interactionism. This may be (although we do not agree that symbolic interactionism overlooks the question of motivation, as will be apparent in Chapter 11). What *is* evident, however, is exchange theory's deplorably simplistic assumptions about human nature and its inherent rationalistic reductionism. Thus, although Homans denies that he assumes rationality in human nature, that assumption is there. It may plausibly be argued that exchange theory can account for sacrifice, self-denial, suicide, self-destruction, heroism, unprovoked aggression, altruism, and other forms of human irrationality by allowing the actor to attach *subjective meaning* to his actions and to those of others. According to Schafer, this is precisely what Blau has done, thereby successfully integrating exchange theory and symbolic interactionism. However, it is our view that even so, exchange theory remains an impoverished and mechanistic metaphor that provides a mere caricature of man and that does not do justice to the full complexity of his behavior, behavior for which, as we shall see, we do *not* necessarily need to discover all-encompassing causal principles.

Structuralism: a new fad?

This new brand of social theory has become one of the most popular bandwagons since the mid-1960s, particularly in Europe. The high priest is the French anthropologist Claude Levi-Strauss (1967; 1969). Structuralism combines a variety of features, which accounts for its current popularity. It is theoretically sophisticated, leads to the development and use of mathematical models, and uses poetic intuition such as Levi-Strauss' own brilliant speculations. By offering something to everybody, structuralism has been able to attract a wide variety of young sociologists, from armchair social philosophers to computer addicts, from radical humanists to technocratic scientists. Although there can be little doubt about the genius of Levi-Strauss, structuralism has some of the earmarks of a fad and it is, as such, likely to be of ephemeral popularity. Perhaps, as with Durkheim and the Durkheimians in the beginning of the century (cf. Kando, 1976), the faddish and the lasting components of this school of thought will in time sort themselves out.

Levi-Strauss' structuralism is a theory concerned with the *cognitive* structure of the social system. It holds that underlying the accidental cultural variations of human behavior are invariant universal mental structures that may be discovered. The relationship between those preconscious structures and the concrete manifestations consists of transformation rules that can be discovered scientifically. The fundamental assumption is that all preconscious structures follow *binary* logic (like the computer).

Evidently, the study of language is what structuralism is generally about. Noam Chomsky's work (1965), postulating a linguistic deep structure, is very relevant here. Also, Levi-Strauss has devoted himself to the study of myths, the content of which he sees as coming in binary pairs of opposite themes.

The difference between European and American structuralism is, predictably, the usual difference between the grand speculative approach always more typical of European social thought and the more empiricomathematical approach of the Americans. The best-known contemporary American structuralist is Harrison White (1963). Here, as for Mullins (1973:250-269), structuralism means often the use of transformational mathematical models for the understanding of how "one structure is transformed into another" (Mullins, 1973:259).

Whatever the methodological emphasis, structuralism may be defined as a theory of knowledge, that is, a theory of "how understanding is possible" (Deetz, 1973:163). Its method consists of taking logical permutations from the binary oppositions observed or inferred, which constitutes the underlying structural unity, and finding empirical instances of those possibilities (Deetz, loc. cit.).

Structuralism is a sophisticated new look at language and cognition as the foundations of society. It shares a number of concerns with some of the paradigms to be discussed in the second part of this book, but it does that also with the static and holistic sociological G.O.P., structural-functionalism. In his 1974 presidential address to the American Sociological Association, Professor Blau pegged structuralism quite nicely, pointing out an essential difference between Levi-Strauss' concept of social structure and the classical functionalist conception, which goes back to the British anthropologist A. R. Radcliffe-Brown (1940): whereas classical functionalism views the social structure as a system referring to empirical conditions, structuralism views it as a system of logic, a cognitive *model* referring to theories, not reality. However, beyond that, both theories are profoundly holistic and abstractionistic. As Deetz (1973) explains, structuralism, too, sees the meaning of isolated events only in their relationships to the larger system of which they are a part, and that system is always more than the sum of its components.

While structuralism shares a concern for language with symbolic interactionism, and whereas it is a cognitive theory, like ethnomethodology, it nevertheless differs from those orientations in important respects: unlike symbolic interactionism, it does not focus on the essential *experiential, processual,* and *behavioral* character of human action. It is simply not truly social psychological. Furthermore, unlike ethnomethodology and phenomenological sociology, it deals in abstractions that are extremely far removed from the actor's own experience. Truth, to the structuralist, is an underlying structure to be discovered by the anthropologist, the sociologist, and the mathematician, and this is totally different from the native's knowledge. The distinction between the conscious model held by the native and the unconscious model discovered by the scientist is, of course, in sharp contrast with the ethnographic empiricism and the emic approach advocated in this book.

Computerized sociology

The furthest extension of the inherent positivism of the sociological G.O.P. is now found in what Mullins (1973:213-249) calls new causal theory but what may more appropriately be termed causal statistical methodology. During the 1950s, standard sociology was essentially functionalist sociology. As Mullins describes the situation, there was at that time a division of labor in the field, with theorists on the one hand (Parsons, Merton) and methodologists on the other (Lazarsfeld, Stouffer). The theorists were, of course, functionalists. Gradually, the theoretical component of standard American sociology began to crumble, attacked as it was by increasing numbers of dissidents and opponents. Meanwhile, standard American methodology was for the most part left in peace, questioned only by a few humanists (Berger, 1963), radicals (Mills, 1959), and interactionists (Blumer, 1969; Bruyn, 1966). Representative of the 1960s was Zetterberg's (1965) small but highly influential book on theory and methodology. Its main point was that sociological theory building—axiomatic, in the author's term—must essentially be an inductive and positivistic process.

The subsequent development of standard American methodology established the use of increasingly sophisticated statistical techniques—factor analysis, path analysis, multiple correlation, and regression techniques. Hubert Blalock (1964) wrote the authoritative works for all those now engaged in standard statistical causal analysis. The entire trend of the 1960s may be summed up as the massive elaboration of the grand old paradigm's methodological arm, while simultaneously letting its theory lapse into oblivion. New causal theory, then, is not theory at all, it is theoryless methodology.

Blalock's work indicates the close connection between causal analysis and functionalism. Both are in essence *systems analysis*, functionalism at the theoretical level, Blalock's work formulating multiple causal relationships. Fig. 1-2 provides an example out of that author's work.

Like the structuralists, the causal methodologists make extensive use of mathematical models. And like the functionalists, they study systems of interrelated and quantifiable variables. As Catton (1964: 919) observed, ". . . if all functions that actually tend to maintain the system are manifest functions (i.e. recognized by the participants) there ceases to be any real difference between functional and causal analysis."

Today, the causal statisticians dominate sociology as the functionalists did in the 1950s. According to Mullins (1973:241) the two are not likely to remain distinct for long. We can therefore envision two possible developments, both equally unsatisfactory: either causal sociology returns to an explicit functionalist perspective, or it continues on the road of abstract empiricism. In the final analysis, this brand of sociology is the eminently technocratic type of social science that this book rejects. Far from providing an alternative to the sociological G.O.P., it has merely improved and elaborated positivistic methodology. It contrasts sharply with ethnomethodology, which rejects standard sociology's positivism and instead takes a phenomenological approach.

SUMMARY AND CONCLUSION

This chapter has surveyed a number of sociologies that share characteristics and that may be said to belong to an overall "paradigm," or perspective. That perspective has been termed scientific sociology, or the grand old sociological paradigm. It is to this perspective, among other ones, that this book wishes to offer an alternative.

It was seen that the foundation of scientific sociology goes back to nineteenth century European thinkers, particularly two Frenchmen—Comte and Durkheim. In the twentieth century, American functionalism became heir to the tradition. As we saw, functionalism has been applied both at the macro and the micro level. Because our topic is social psychology, the discussion covered not only the major macrofunctionalists (Parsons, Merton, and Homans) but also two schools of microfunctionalists: the experimental study of small groups, also called group dynamics, launched by the German immigrant Kurt Lewin, and exchange theory, an approach

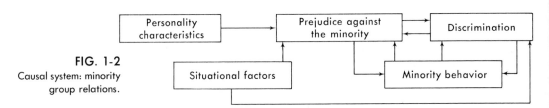

FIG. 1-2
Causal system: minority group relations.

(From Blalock, Hubert. 1970. "The formalization of sociological theory." In Theoretical Sociology. J. C. McKinney and E. A. Tiryakian [eds.]. New York: Appleton-Century-Crofts, p. 276.)

based on elements derived from Skinnerian behaviorism (Homans), macrofunctionalism (Gouldner), and game theory (Thibaut and Kelley).

Our review of structuralism began with its French founder, Levi-Strauss. This new perspective, highly popular on both sides of the Atlantic at this time, is a theory of knowledge, analyzing the social system in terms of preconscious linguistic deep structures. European structuralists tend to be more speculative, and Americans (for example, White) make extensive use of mathematical models.

Finally, new causal theory was examined ("computerized sociology"), and it was indicated that a better name would be causal *analysis,* for this group, dominant in America today, is essentially a group that applies rigorously positivistic methodology to data, with no theory in any meaningful sense of that word. Indeed, it develops complex mathematical models, specifying causal paths and multivariate relationships, but abstains from any theoretical speculation and imagery that might be inspirational rather than directly testable.

The shortcomings of the sociological G.O.P. are rooted in its theoretical and methodological assumptions. They have been pointed out many times, and frequently the paradigm under indictment has simply been functionalism. Whether or not all theories discussed in this chapter can be linked to functionalism, it is clear that they all view social behavior as a system of interrelated parts that affect one another. The system may be likened to an organism, as was done by the early Europeans, or a more abstract mechanism, as did the American functionalists. The parts of the system may be identified as individuals, actions, roles, institutions, or even concepts. The system as a whole possesses a discernible *structure,* and its parts perform specifiable *functions* for the whole.

Scott (1970) once again reviews functionalism's inability to deal with change and conflict, its inherent conservatism, and other standard criticisms. His remarks are well taken and must be supplemented with additional points, some applying narrowly to classical functionalism, some to the entire scientific paradigm.

A fundamental bias of systems analysis is its *holism,* or what philosophers term "realism." As was explained in the section on macrofunctionalism, the nominalism-realism controversy has been central in sociology. *Nominalism,* it may be recalled, is the position which holds that the ultimate reality of phenomena resides in their constitutive *parts* and that complex concepts are mere abstractions without empirical referents. *Realism* is the opposite philosophical tendency, the position holding that composite phenomena are more than just the sum of their parts, that they are real in their own right, and that complex concepts therefore refer to real objects. For sociology, the fundamental case in point is *society:* according to the realists, society exists, it is a reality sui generis. To the nominalists, it is a mere abstraction, a shorthand term underneath which reality in fact consists of actions, behavior, etc. The first section of this chapter has made clear that realism, related to emergentism, is the hallmark of classical functionalism, particularly as enunciated by Durkheim.

Functionalism, then, attributes to society an independent reality and existence. It *reifies* society, makes it into a thing, although it should be remembered that it is merely a concept. When society is thus reified, it begins to look like a giant Alcatraz (Berger, 1963), constraining us all from without. Furthermore, as Wrong (1961) pointed out, it produces an over-socialized conception of man and an erroneous conception of what socialization is all about. Man is viewed as all me, all internalized roles, no I, no id. Such total social determinism leaves no room for deviance, interpretation, freedom of choice. It views man as a total conformist, an automated and programmed sociopath.

The G.O.P.'s methodological assumptions are shared by all theories discussed in this chapter and, as we shall see, also by scientific psychology, which otherwise differs from functionalism in that it is nominalistic and reductionistic. The fundamental tenet of all scientific sociology and scientific psychology is that the study of human behavior must be *positivistic,* and the purpose of studying man is to predict and thus control his behavior. Positivistic methodology means quantitative and objective techniques. That is, man and his behavior are viewed as objective phenomena deteached from the observing sociologist, and statements about those phenomena are to take the form of quantitative propositions and laws. Positivism, then, contains the fallacy of objectivism, and as Scott (1970) explains, this leads to two problems: the (social) scientist is oblivious to the essentially *interpretive* and *meaningful* nature of his subject matter, which is human experience, and he imputes, in the form of models and theories, his own meanings to the actors. All theories discussed in this chapter are clearly guilty of this, from functionalism to structuralism, from exchange theory to causal theory.

Finally, scientific sociology's determinism gives it an air of value-neutrality, but this is highly fraudulent, for in the end it merely substitutes a pseudoscientific set of absolutes for an old-fashioned ethical vocabulary. It claims that man has no more freedom of choice than do other natural objects, and this claim, far from making scientific sociology amoral, is the grandest possible assertion of absolutes, since it states that the scientific laws governing human behavior may not be questioned.

REFERENCES

Bales, Robert F.
1950a "A set of categories for the analysis of small group analysis." American Sociological Review 15:257-263.
1950b Interaction Process Analysis. Reading, Mass.: Addison-Wesley Publishing Co., Inc.
1955 "How people interact in conferences." Scientific American (March): 3-7.

Berger, Peter L.
1963 Invitation to Sociology: A Humanistic Perspective. New York: Doubleday & Co., Inc.
Blalock, Hubert
1964 Causal Inferences in Non-Experimental Research. Chapel Hill: University of North Carolina Press.
1970 "The formalization of sociological theory." In Theoretical Sociology. J. C. McKinney and E. A. Tiryakian (eds.). New York: Appleton-Century-Crofts, pp. 272-300.
Blumer, Herbert
1969 Symbolic Interactionism. Englewood Cliffs, N.J.: Prentice-Hall, Inc.
Bruyn, Severyn
1966 The Human Perspective in Sociology. Englewood Cliffs, N.J.: Prentice-Hall, Inc.
Cartwright, Dorwin
1972 "Achieving change in people: some applications of group dynamics theory." In Classic Contributions to Social Psychology. Edwin P. Hollander and Raymond G. Hunt (eds.). New York: Oxford University Press, pp. 352-361.
Cartwright, Dorwin and Alvin Zander (eds.)
1953 Group Dynamics. Evanston, Ill.: Row, Peterson.
Catton, William R., Jr.
1964 "The development of sociological thought." In Handbook of Modern Sociology. R. E. L. Faris (ed.). Chicago: Rand-McNally, pp. 912-950.
Chomsky, Noam
1965 Aspects of the Theory of Syntax. Cambridge, Mass.: M.I.T. Press.
Coser, Lewis A. (ed.)
1971 Masters of Sociological Thought; Ideas In Historical and Social Context. New York: Harcourt, Brace, Jovanovich, Inc.
Deetz, Stanley
1973 "Structuralism: a summary of its assumptive and conceptual bases." Review of Social Theory (April):138-163.
Deutsch, Morton and Robert M. Krauss
1965 Theories in Social Psychology. New York: Basic Books, Inc.
Durkheim, Emile
1938 The Rules of Sociological Method. Chicago: University of Chicago Press.
Festinger, Leon et al.
1956 When Prophecy Fails. Minneapolis: University of Minnesota Press.
Gouldner, Alvin
1960 "The norm of reciprocity: a preliminary statement." American Sociological Review 25:161-179.
Heider, Fritz
1927 Ding und Medium. Symposium 1:109-158.
Homans, George C.
1950 The Human Group. New York: Harcourt, Brace.

1961 Social Behavior: Its Elementary Forms. New York: Harcourt, Brace.

1972 Social behavior as exchange." In Classic Contributions to Social Psychology. Edwin P. Hollander and Raymond G. Hunt (ed.). New York: Oxford University Press, pp. 150-160.

Kando, Thomas M.
1976 "L'annee sociologique: from Durkheim to today." Pacific Sociological Review (April):147-174.

Levi-Strauss, Claude
1967 Structural Anthropology. Translated by Claire Jocobson and Brook G. Schoeph. New York: Doubleday & Co., Inc.

1969 The Elementary Forms of Kinship. Translated by James H. Bell et al. Boston: Beacon Press.

Lewin, Kurt
1935 "Psycho-sociological problems of a minority group." Character and Personality 3:175-187.

1972 "Need, force, and valence in psychological fields." In Classic Contributions to Social Psychology. Edwin P. Hollander and Raymond G. Hunt (eds.). New York: Oxford University Press.

Lewin Kurt and Ronald Lippitt
1938 "An experimental approach to the study of autocracy and democracy: a preliminary note." Sociometry (January-April):292.

Luft, Joseph
1970 Group Processes: An Introduction to Group Dynamics. Palo Alto, Calif.: National Press Publications.

Martindale, Don
1960 The Nature and Types of Sociological Theory. Boston: Houghton Mifflin Co.

Mennell, Stephen
1974 Sociological Theory: Uses and Units. New York: Praeger Publishers, Inc.

Merton, Robert K.
1957 Social Theory and Social Structure. New York: The Free Press.

Mills, C. Wright
1959 The Sociological Imagination. London: Oxford University Press.

Mullins, Nicholas C.
1973 Theories and Theory Groups in Contemporary American Sociology. New York: Harper & Row, Publishers.

Ofshe, Richard J. (ed.)
1973 Interpersonal Behavior in Small Groups. Englewood Cliffs, N.J.: Prentice-Hall, Inc.

Parsons, Talcott
1951 The Social System. Glencoe, Ill.: The Free Press.

1953 "A revised analytical approach to the theory of social stratification." In Class, Status and Power. Reinhard Bendix and Seymour Lipset (eds.). Glencoe, Ill.: The Free Press, pp. 92-128.

Parsons, Talcott et al.
1953 Working Papers in the Theory of Action. Glencoe, Ill.: The Free Press.

Radcliffe-Brown, A. R.
1940 "On social structure." Journal of the Royal Anthropological Institute 70:1-12.

Schafer, Robert B.
1974 "Exchange and symbolic interaction: a further analysis of convergence." Pacific Sociological Review (October):417-434.

Scott, Marvin B.
1970 "Functional analysis: a statement of problems." In Social Psychology Through Symbolic Interaction. Gregory P. Stone and Harvey A. Farberman (eds.). Waltham, Mass.: Ginn-Blaisdell, pp. 21-28.

Stone, Gregory P. and Harvey A. Farberman
1970 Social Psychology Through Symbolic Interaction. Waltham, Mass.: Ginn-Blaisdell.

Strodtbeck, Fred L.
1973 "Bales 20 years later: a review essay." American Journal of Sociology (September):459-465.

Thibaut, John W. and Harold H. Kelley
1959 The Social Psychology of Groups. New York: John Wiley & Sons, Inc.

Vinacke, W. Edgar
1964 Dimensions of Social Psychology. Chicago: Scott, Foresman and Co.

White, Harrison C.
1963 An Anatomy of Kinship: Mathematical Models for Structures of Cumulated Roles. Englewood Cliffs: N.J.: Prentice-Hall, Inc.

Wrong, Dennis H.
1961 "The oversocialized conception of man in modern sociology." American Sociological Review (April):183-193.

Zetterberg, Hans L.
1965 On Theory and Verification in Sociology. Totowa, N.J.: Bedminster Press.

chapter 2
Scientific psychology

The psychological G.O.P. is even less unified than that of sociology. It might be questionable to speak of *a* paradigm in this field. Nevertheless, this chapter intends to review a number of theories and to show that they share some very general assumptions that distinguish them all from the phenomenological social psychology advocated in the subsequent portions of the book.

First, we shall examine behaviorism, founded by the Russian physiologist Ivan Pavlov (1849-1939) and by a number of American psychologists, featuring most prominently J. B. Watson (1878-1958). As we shall see, this school developed into neobehaviorism, which is the dominant approach in American psychology today. This approach may also be termed reinforcement theory, stimulus-response psychology, or learning theory. Key figures in the development of neobehaviorism have been B. F. Skinner and Clark Hull.

Second, we shall deal with the psychoanalytic school, which may also be divided into classical psychoanalysis and its neoanalytic heir. Towering above the entire field is, of course, the Austrian Sigmund Freud (1856-1939), who overshadows all others to such an extent that psychoanalytic psychology is also called Freudian psychology. There are, however, other important early psychoanalysts, for example Alfred Adler, Carl Jung, and Wilhelm Reich, all from the Germanic areas of Europe. Neo-Freudians are found among American psychologists (Erickson, Fromm), anthropologists (DuBois, Horney, Kardiner), and social philosophers (Brown, Marcuse). We shall also discuss the culture and personality school in anthropology, which is Freudian, and Dollard and Miller's synthesis of behaviorism and psychoanalytic psychology.

The third strand of the psychological paradigm to be examined will be psychological social psychology. By that, we mean the approach already partially discussed under microfunctionalism. Here, we shall give a more systematic presentation of the school, again distinguishing its classical origin, German Gestalt psychology, from its contemporary form in the United States. Key figures here include Solomon Asch, Leon Festinger, Theodore Newcomb, and the Sherifs. As we shall see, this group has most frequently studied such phenomena as leadership, group cohesiveness, influence, conformity, and group standards. Psychological social psychology has also focused on attitudes, for example, in Adorno's work on authoritarianism. Finally, it includes Moreno's technique of sociometry.

As a fourth area, the encounter movement will be examined, again from its origin to its current state. Among founders of this movement, we shall examine Fritz Perls, Viktor Frankl, both originally from Germany, and Abraham Maslow, Carl Rogers, Eric Shostrom, and other American humanistic psychiatrists who now advocate various forms of nondirective group therapy. As we shall see, Esalen and transactional analysis (the latter under Berne and Harris) are among the most solidly institutionalized enterprises in this field, and the most lucrative. It will be seen that countless additional businesses of this type have snowballed since the 1960s and that their services provide varying degrees of satisfaction to their customers, despite the questionable validity of the basic assumptions underlying the entire group experience movement.

Finally, we shall examine psychiatry as a general phenomenon, arguing that it constitutes the unifying feature in psychology. Indeed, psychoanalytic psychology, encounters, behavior modification, and even psychological social psychology all have one fundamental trait in common: as applied disciplines, they are in the business of altering behavior that is somehow deemed undesirable. Thus the entire mental health movement is based on the premise that a scientific and objective distinction can be made between desirable and undesirable conduct. Psychiatry is a moral enterprise, of course, and not a scientific one. We shall argue, along with Thomas Szasz and Erving Goffman, that this confusion has been the major fallacy of the psychological G.O.P., for psychiatry is nothing less than the applied arm of the entire psychological profession.

TYPICAL AMERICAN PSYCHOLOGY[1]

The roots of behaviorism can be traced to the philosophies of *associationism, hedonism,* and *utilitarianism.* As a reaction against the medieval idea of predestination, seventeenth and eighteenth century Anglo-Saxon philosophers developed what may properly be viewed as the oldest theory in social psychology. The English philosopher John Locke (1632-1704), the Scottish moral philosophers David Hume (1711-1776) and Adam Smith (1723-1790), and the American statesman Thomas Jefferson (1743-1826) proposed a social psychology called associationism. The English philosopher Jeremy Bentham (1748-1832) formulated the philosophy of hedonistic utilitarianism. The basic assumptions underlying these ideas are that (1) human behavior is governed by the pleasure-pain principle (hedonism), (2) man is rational in the pursuit of his goals (utilitarianism), and (3) he associates experiences with one another (associationism). Furthermore, man is presumed to be born a tabula rasa, which means that his behavior, habits, and personality are entirely the result of environment (the environment writing on this blank slate) and not of heredity. Theories like this have been called *monistic* or *simple and sovereign* (Henry George), because they presume to explain

everything on the basis of one simple set of principles.

While each experience is unique to every man, the rules of association are universal laws that can be discovered and systematically studied. Experience does not come in discrete units but as a continuous flow. It follows the law of place association (which states that two events occurring in the same place will be associated with one another by the subject), the law of time association, the law of logical association, and so on.

We may sum up this earliest form of social psychology as being hedonistic, utilitarian, environmental, and rationalistic (although recognizing that rationality may be *subjective,* that is, that a behavior may make sense to the actor while appearing irrational to others). It should be clear that this model of man is a direct anticipation of homo economicus, exchange theory, and all forms of behaviorism.

Behaviorism

Properly speaking, the foregoing ideas belong in the realm of philosophy, not psychology. While they provide the philosophical postulates underlying behaviorism, it is only at the turn of the twentieth century that a behavioristic psychology began to develop, based not only on theory but also on (experimental) empirical work.

Around 1900, the Russian Ivan Pavlov (1927) conducted his famous experiments on conditioned salivary responses in dogs. The basic format of the experiment is as follows. A dog is harnessed in a laboratory under such conditions that its salivation can be measured. A light (the *conditioned stimulus*) is turned on. The dog does not salivate. After a few seconds meat powder (the *unconditioned stimulus*) is delivered. The dog is hungry and eats and salivates extensively. This process is repeated several times: the light is followed by the meat, the meat by salivation. This is what is

---

[1] The following discussion owes much to classes and seminars taken with the late Arnold Rose at the University of Minnesota.

called *reinforcement*. Eventually, salivation follows the light even without meat: the *conditioned response* has been established. The process identified by Pavlov is the foundation for the entire school of behaviorism. It can be graphically represented through the concept of the *reflex arc*. This is done in Fig. 2-1.

According to classical behaviorism, the process discovered by Pavlov and described in Fig. 2-1 is *the* model for all learning. Therefore, learning is the same thing as conditioning, and conditioned habits, like the dog's salivation, develop through stimulus associations. The direct link between associationism and behaviorism should now be clear, and so should the fact that behaviorism, learning theory, stimulus-response psychology, and reinforcement theory are more or less synonymous.

Meanwhile, behaviorists had also been at work in the United States. For example, in 1898 Thorndike postulated his famous law, "pleasure stamps in, pain stamps out" (Deutsch and Krauss, 1965:79), thus adopting hedonism's pleasure-pain principle.

It was John B. Watson (1919) who was most of all responsible for establishing behaviorism as the dominant doctrine in American psychology. At the beginning of the century, the discourse about human nature ranged from an emphasis on heredity, as found among the instinctivists, to a preoccupation with subjectivity and consciousness, as typical of the introspectionists, and finally to the rationalism and enviromentalism of the associationist tradition. Watson rejected the first two of these traditions and embraced the third. Unlike the instinctivists, he argued that human behavior is initiated by environmental stimuli, in other words outside the nervous system. To be sure, he recognized the existence of reflexes, some of them inherited, but since reflexes are common to the entire species, they may be bracketed. Individual differences have nothing to do with heredity, Watson argued, but with differential conditioning (as well as possible differences in the chemical composition of the nerve connections). Extreme environmentalism, then, was the first characteristic of Watsonian behaviorism. Indeed, the American psychologist claimed that he could condition any baby to any behavior of which it is potentially physically capable.

Furthermore, Watson believed that psychology should not be concerned with consciousness, the mind and meaning. Science must be entirely *objective*. Thinking is simply subvocal speech to oneself, another form of physical behavior. Whether or not consciousness or mind exists, Watson believed that this was *epiphenomenal*, that is, irrelevant to science. It could be compared

Fig. 2-1

The reflex arc and the establishment of Pavlov's conditioned response. S_u, Unconditioned stimulus; S_c, conditioned stimulus; R_u, unconditioned response; R_c, conditioned response. *Impulse:* a physiologic stimulus conveyed by the nervous system. *Reflex:* an involuntary response consisting of simple muscular or glandular activity. This may be learned, as in the case of the conditioned response. *Conditioned response:* same thing as a *habit*, the prototype of any learned behavior.

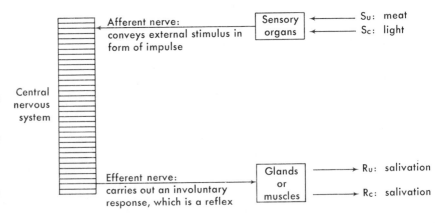

to steam escaping from an engine. Philosophers might wish to speculate about it, but not empirical scientists. Mental factors do not affect human behavior.

Third, Watsonian psychology of course concerned itself primarily with physiology, with empirically observable physical behavior. It assumed that people and "*other*" animals did not differ significantly and psychologists could therefore find out about humans by studying animals.

Finally, behaviorism has been totally *nominalistic*, conceiving of human behavior at even the most complex social level as merely the added sum of individual reflexes and habits. The school's entire contribution can be summed up as the elaboration of the reflex arc concept outlined previously. Complex behavior can be accounted for by chains of such reflex arcs, the establishment of which follows two— and only two—basic principles: (1) any conditioned stimulus is, however remotely, associated with something positive, and (2) a response can itself become a conditioned stimulus. This is how chains are established; for humans the relationship between a conditioned stimulus and the original unconditioned stimulus can be extremely remote. Beyond these principles, all else in behaviorism has been variation on the basic theme. For example, if two opposing conditioned stimuli are applied simultaneously (one associated with pain), the result may be nervous breakdown.

It was in the United States, not in Russia, that behaviorists began to experiment with people and thus developed a truly social psychology. The first real experiment in social psychology was conducted at Harvard by Floyd H. Allport (1920). He asked students to perform the same tasks (for example, painting checkerboards) individually and then together in small groups. Controlling the possible effect of learning by asking a number of students to paint checkerboards individually both before and after, Allport found that a group accomplished more than all its individual members added together. He concluded that the presence of others energizes and speeds the individual up, and he termed this *social facilitation*. However, it also cuts down on the quality of the individual's thinking. Allport's study was important because it demonstrated that stimuli can be social as well as physical. It moved behaviorism from psychology into the field of sociology.

In 1928, Peterson and Thurstone (1932) were the first behaviorists to study attitudes. By developing quantitative attitude scales, these psychologists were the first to apply the principles of psychophysical measurement to the area of attitudes. The government wanted to know how propaganda works, particularly in determining attitudes toward various nationalities. This was important in view of the fact that America was becoming increasingly involved in the Asian turmoil. Thurstone and his colleagues were hired. They selected a large number of high school students, first testing their attitudes toward the Chinese. Then the students were shown a film giving a favorable portrayal of Chinese people. When tested again the next day for their attitudes, the students were now significantly more sympathetic to the Chinese. Beyond that, some students took the test again five months later and others nineteen months later and the results showed that sixty-two percent of the students retained an improved attitude for as long as a year and a half. Interestingly, a control group of students not exposed to the film also showed signficant attitude change (albeit not as marked). This was the result of interaction between the two groups. Such work, then, represented a significant step forward in that it began the study of response to propaganda, mass media, and other *social* stimuli.

Neobehaviorism

The transition to modern-day behaviorism can be said to have begun with Clark L. Hull (1886-1952). Departing from Watson's strict environmentalism, Hull (1943) reintroduced the notion of an *internal* source of motivation, namely through the concept of *drive*. There are two kind of drives, primary, or unlearned, and secondary, or learned. Both are motives internal to the organism. The neobehaviorist's analysis, unlike that of the behaviorist, starts out with this internal drive, not with the external stimulus. The drive (for example, hunger) selects the appropriate environmental drive-reducing stimulus (food). This recognition of the organism's active and selective participation in its interaction with the environment is a great step forward.

Furthermore, Hull introduced the concept of *cue*. For example, when experimenting with rats attempting to reach food via a maze, the food, its smell, and the distance may be conceived of as cues rather than simple stimuli because they are mere signs aiding the animals rather than clear stimuli eliciting specific responses. With each new trial the rat takes less time to reach the food (the decline is curvilinear, leveling off at a minimum). This shows that cues are "remembered." How? Through positive and negative reinforcement: each time a cue is missed (for example, a wrong turn) this produces fatigue, frustration, and deprivation. Whenever a cue is observed, this brings the reward closer.

A further major step forward was the distinction between *classical* conditioning and *operant* or *instrumental* conditioning. Classical conditioning is the type of procedure involved in Pavlov's experiment, where a conditioned stimulus (the light) is used to *elicit* a conditioned response (salivation). In instrumental or operant conditioning, the response must occur *first*, accidentally, and it is then rewarded. For example, a hungry rat is in a box. When it accidentally presses a bar, this delivers some food. Soon the animal learns to press the bar to obtain the reward (food). Its be-

havior is termed an instrumental response (Deutsch and Krauss, 1965:80). This latter procedure, first proposed by E. L. Thorndike, became central in the work of Hull and his disciples at Yale—Carl Hovland, Neal Miller, and John Dollard, among others.

Additional concepts that have become central to neobehaviorism include: (1) *extinction*, meaning the decrease in the strength of a response as a result of nonreinforcement; (2) *discrimination*, which occurs when a subject distinguishes between situations in which a response will be rewarded and those in which it will not; (3) *generalization*, which is the opposite of discrimination, occurring when a response given to one stimulus is also given to other (similar) stimuli; (4) *spontaneous recovery*, the sudden return of a conditioned response after its temporary extinction; (5) *anticipatory response*, which refers to the tendency of responses "to occur before their original time in the response series" (Dollard and Miller, 1950:57); and (6) *higher-order conditioning*, meaning that if a cue elicits a certain response (such as fear), then it is possible for other cues consistently preceding that original cue to elicit the same response.

One of the major contributions made by the Yale group was the frustration-aggression hypothesis, for twenty years one of the most debated, tested, and amended propositions. The initial formulation (Dollard et al., 1939) was that frustration always leads to some form of agression and that aggression never occurs without prior frustration. A typical experiment of the Yale group would entail a rat in a maze, with food perceptible but inaccessible, for example blocked off. When such a block occurs, the frustrated animal becomes aggressive and may attack the block. If that behavior is punished (say the block is electric), aggression is turned toward some other object. We see in this simple experiment the paradigm not only for frustration and aggression, but also target substitution, or scapegoating.

Of interest to sociologists is an ex post

facto test of the frustration-aggression hypothesis in real society by Hovland and Sears (1940). A correlation of the price of cotton (a valid indicator of Southern prosperity) with the number of black lynchings in the South between 1880 and 1930 turned out significantly negative (-0.67). Months during which the price of cotton was low were followed, with a three-month lag, by months with a high frequency of lynchings. The frustration of economic depressions and recessions led to subsequent aggression and scapegoating.

Miller and Bugelski (1948) led a group of young men to believe that they were going to go out on a nice excursion. The boys were made to answer a questionnaire about Japanese and Mexican Americans. They were then told that the trip was cancelled and were instead made to take the ethnic attitude test again. The retest showed a significant increase in prejudice against Japanese and Mexicans. Again, this test shows that frustration produces not only aggression but also scapegoating. Expressing hostility toward the experimenters would have been dangerous, and it was therefore *transferred* onto the minorities.

From Thurstone to the Yale group, behaviorism has made a tremendous contribution to our understanding of ethnic prejudice. It has shown the crucial role that propaganda, mass media, and frustration can play in this area, and both Thurstone and Hovland showed that prejudice, once developed, can last very long.

In general, however, the frustration-aggression hypothesis has not been supported by all subsequent research and theory. Some theoretical possibilities overlooked in the initial formulation and stressed in subsequent research, particularly by Freudian psychologists, include the following. Frustration, far from always leading to overt aggression, can be inverted (and produce neurosis, ulcers, etc.) or sublimated into constructive channels. The latter possibility is of course the rationale for the frustrations and denials (for example, sexual) imposed on athletes be-

fore a game, soldiers before combat, and others in similar situations. Furthermore, the most crucial question is whether frustration necessarily leads to *any* of these reactions: because man *interprets* his experiences, he may choose resignation, apathy, or turning the other cheek. Here, again, our humanistic orientation compels us to observe that man's reaction to frustration is ultimately determined by his interpretation of the experience and that this invalidates the inherently deterministic frustration-aggression hypothesis.

Other important contributions to neobehaviorism were made by Bandura and Walters (1963) and Dollard and Miller (1950). A common problem area explored by these authors has been imitation and the role it plays in learning. Dollard and Miller had focused on imitation as an *operant* process, that is, as requiring that the imitated response already be, latently, in the subject's behavioral repertoire. Bandura and Walters have shown that this is not the case and that imitation actually proceeds through *observation*. For example, a young child does not necessarily learn a certain speech item by first accidentally hitting upon it and being rewarded for it (operant conditioning) but rather because the child imitates a respected significant other, such as the father.

Dollard and Miller's contribution to psychotherapy has been highly valuable. Stressing the importance of language as a cue-producing and drive-reducing mechanism, these authors propose a psychotherapy that focuses on the development of *verbal* weapons with which to tackle emotional problems. Their *Personality and Psychotherapy* (1950) is a successful integration of behaviorism, psychoanalysis, and labelling theory.

The high priest of neobehaviorism is B. F. Skinner. Born in 1904, the Harvard psychologist has been both more influential and more controversial than any other contemporary psychologist. Skinner's contribution to psychology is both substantive and methodological. Methodologically, his controlled experiments with animals (pigeons, mostly) have become the model for nearly all subsequent work in animal psychology. His "Skinnerbox" is, in essence, a laboratory environment in which nearly all variables—dependent behavioral variables (the response) and independent environmental variables (the stimulus)—are controlled by the experimenter. The methodology, then, is highly rigorous.

Building on the principles of classical behaviorism, Skinner was one of the first to make the distinction between classical and operant conditioning. Throughout his work, he has been concerned with the control of human behavior. This, plus his willingness to apply rigorous behaviorism and the results of animal experiments to human verbal and social behavior, is what makes his work so intriguing and controversial.

In *Walden Two* (1948), the author proposed a behavioristic brave new world. Then, in *Verbal Behavior* (1957), he presented his analysis of language acquisition through reinforcement. Basically, the process is one of operant conditioning, whereby the listeners (the child's verbal community) reinforce the emission of certain vocalizations. One type of verbal behavior is the *mand*, a response reinforced by a specific consequence—for example, demands, questions, commands, etc. Another type is the *tact,* which is related to generalized reinforcement—for example, naming objects correctly or any other "disinterested" behavior, behavior for which the speaker gets nothing in particular.

Osgood (1963) and Chomsky (1972) are among those who have criticized Skinner's *Verbal Behavior.* Osgood, for example, points out that semantic generalization (important in the Skinnerian scheme) is a matter of symbolic association, not phonetic association. For example, one may respond positively to the word "red," but

not because of an association with the similar sounding "bed" but because one has heard it with reference to a nice big juicy apple; then again, a description of red hot human blood may make one cringe.

Skinner's latest bestseller, *Beyond Freedom and Dignity* (1971), has led to an unprecedented flurry of arguments across disciplinary boundaries. This is where the psychologist makes his final case for the full-fledged application of social technology and scientific control to human behavior. His target is "autonomous man," that burdensome myth handed down to us by our humanistic forefathers and now standing in the way of "progress through science and technology." According to Skinner, we must recognize that freedom of choice and dignity are myths. The sooner we recognize this, the better. The ultimate victory of science and behavior control is inevitable. The question is merely: who shall control? Who shall design and implement the culture and the values? If this is recognized, then the problem boils down to ensuring that the good guys, and not a Hitler, be placed in charge.

Chomsky (1971) was again among the first to indict this latest vision. The linguist's argument was substantive rather than moral. It is not that Skinner's brave new world is repugnant but that man is simply *not* the kind of animal it describes and therefore not subject to Skinner's laws. In view of this, Skinner's enormous and growing impact on American sociology is surprising. His book has received lengthy and emotional reviews in the major journals (cf. Berger, 1972; Boguslaw, 1972; Homans, 1972; Marwell, 1972; Swanson, 1972), and sociologists continue to apply Skinnerian behaviorism in their research (cf. Conger and Killeen, 1974) and to see him as the savior of our ailing discipline (Tarter, 1973). The reviewers range from critical humanists (Berger, 1972; Boguslaw, 1972) to men like Marwell (1972) and Homans (1972) who predictably venerate Skinner. A growing number of sociologists believe that the development of positivistic social technology toward the total control of man and society is, as suggested by Skinner, the only way to go. As Friedrichs (1974) shows, American sociology may be in the process of becoming Skinnerian, and this may be in response to the realization that in order for the profession to be "replenished and expanded by public monies, (it) must be focused directly upon the resolution of what the public, through its representatives, deems its most oppressive societal problems" (Friedrichs, 1974:5). According to that author, it is no coincidence that Skinnerians like Homans and Coleman are now located at the apex of our profession's power structure. These men embody and advocate a paradigm centering around ameliorative social research and the solution of social problems through (Skinnerian) methods of behavior control. Sociology has, of course, much to gain from a federal research establishment (Health, Education and Welfare, National Institute of Mental Health) whose funding of applied research commissioned at colleges and universities has nearly tripled over the previous decade (Friedrichs, 1974:7).

Evaluation

As can be gathered from the preceding paragraphs, neobehaviorism is today the dominant social scientific force in a predominantly technocratic society. As we saw, the basic assumptions of this paradigm are (1) a strong environmentalism, (2) the continuity between man and animals, and (3) a strict nonmentalism.

As far as the environmental assumption is concerned, it should be remembered that it was Watson's early behaviorism that took the most extreme position on this issue, adopting the early associationists' tabula rasa clause. Later, in the 1930s, neobehaviorists like Hull and Skinner reintroduced a certain degree of instinctivism through the concept of drive.

Because behaviorism minimizes the differences between men and animals, the study of animals has always been of major interest to this school. While the Skinnerians have liked rats and pigeons, other social psychologists see more value in studying primates (cf. Washburn and Hamburg, 1969) and insect societies (cf. Lindesmith, Strauss, and Denzin, 1975:67-71). From the standpoint of social psychology, these are indeed the more interesting species, since they exhibit group life, communication, and, in the case of some apes, even rudimentary culture. However, it must be remembered that the study of lower animals has only evolutionary relevance to social psychology, for the absence of verbal language among *all* subhuman species indicates that human behavior has emergent properites that cannot be reduced to animal behavior, as claimed by the Skinnerians.

Finally, behaviorism is unconcerned with consciousness and meaning, and it rejects introspection as a source of data. While neobehaviorists no longer make the absurd claim that all thinking is muscular behavior, they still consider it epiphenomenal to a truly behavioristic science. As Natanson (1970:37) explains, all consciousness is translated into behavior. The problem with this perspective is that, for example, when a man extends his hand, that *is* the greeting; the raised fist *is* the anger; the smile *is* the pleasure. It is no longer necessary to separate the speaker from the speech, since the latter merely takes place *through* the former (op. cit.:38).

The paradigm's therapy is, of course, *behavior modification,* the extinction or alteration of unwanted behavior through negative reinforcement, aversion and shock therapy, and various other forms of conditioning. And since it is behaviorism that denies the mind's emergent qualities, we may add here therapy through drugs and brain surgery, those other two grimly physiological approaches to behavioral problems.

There is some indication that behavior modification works significantly better than any other form of psychotherapy (cf. Eysenck, 1961; Gyman, 1973), and this may partially explain behaviorism's ascendency in the twentieth century. From the standpoint of a truly sociological social psychology, *the* crucial question is, indeed, why behaviorism is such a dominant paradigm in American psychology today. Surely its appeal cannot be theoretical, esthetic, intellectual, or inspirational. As Arthur Koestler correctly pointed out, the paradigm is a "monstrous triviality" reminiscent in its imbecile simplicity of some medieval doctrine. More than likely, it is precisely this seductive simplicity, promising the easy mechanical solution of a frighteningly complex social reality, that attracts laymen and scientists alike, particularly those scientists who have reduced their work to visionless ritual.

Before the turn of the century, John Dewey already mounted the first attack upon this emerging paradigm, pointing out that it ignores subjective selectivity and thus reduces human interaction to a mechanical process that does not accurately represent reality. Although Dewey's point was rather obvious, and despite the fact that it has been reiterated incessantly since that time, our society has apparently not been ready for that point of view. Today, the typical college textbook is still essentially behavioristic (see, for example, the still popular Hilgard, 1957).

It is therefore the sociology of knowledge that must provide an explanation of behaviorism's popularity, and not its inherent merit or lack thereof. Indeed, why was associationism the social psychology of the Anglo-Saxon world, why has behaviorism been the psychology of the Soviet Union and the United States, while Gestalt dominated Germany and elsewhere in Europe other orientations prevailed? Clearly, associationism's tabula rasa assumption and behaviorism's environmentalism were well suited to a liberal and egalitarian society like the United States, providing the rationale for laissez-faire capitalism and equal opportunities through mass education. Behaviorism's emphasis on the scientific control and manipulation of man became popular in societies which, like the Soviet Union and the United States, are committed to social engineering and improving the human condition through science and technology. Finally, behaviorism's totalitarian potential is now clearly visible, and the question is how welcome this may become in the United States. In conclusion, let us remember that a social scientific theory is no more than a model of man and that social scientists see in man precisely the kind of creature they desire to see. As Bertrand Russell quipped "rats studied by German psychologists have been observed to sit down and think and evolve the answer out of their inner consciousness while rats studied by American psychologists have been noted to rush about with great bustle and pep, finally achieving the desired results by chance" (Martindale, 1960:452).

FREUDIAN PSYCHOLOGY

The philosophical foundations of Freudian psychology go back to the *conflict* theory of the English philosopher Thomas Hobbes (1588-1679) and the *voluntarism* and *irrationalism* of the German philosophers Arthur Schopenhauer (1788-1860) and Friedrich Nietzsche (1844-1900). Hobbes is best known for a pessimistic world view that postulates limitless human greed and hunger for power. The natural state is one of war of each against all. The German voluntarists developed a philosophy based on the concept of *will:* everything in nature and society is ultimately moved by the will to power. According to these two traditions, then, man as a natural individual is a beast, and social order and rationality are thin veneers only superficially and generally unsuccessfully concealing that fact. The fundamental problem in human existence is seen as the conflict between the beast and the socialized. It is this focus that was inherited by Freud and the Freudians.

Freud (1856-1939) must unquestionably rank—along with Marx, Einstein, and Darwin—as one of the four most influential figures in the history of the modern world. In vulgarized terms, the Austrian is now most often associated with two things: *sex* (its importance as a motive behind human behavior) and *the unconscious* (the discovery that we are frequently unaware of our motives). Related to these, we often think of Freud as the man who explained *repression*, for example sexual repression, and how this produces misery and neurosis, and the *irrational*, the instinctual and beastly in all of us. Let us discuss Freud's major contributions under the following five headings: the instinctivist foundation of his psychology, his theory of psychosexual development, his theory of personality, his psychotherapy, and his theory of society.

At the outset, Freud postulates that the organism operates on psychic energy and that there are essentially two types of energies—the life instincts, or *eros*, and the death instincts, or *thanatos*. The life instincts, also called *libido*, operate through *cathexis*, the investing of love, emotion, or psychic energy into a desired object. The opposite process, negative and often destructive, is called *anticathexis*, and it is illustrated by aggression, repression, and inhibition. It produces deprivation and frustration. This conception, by no means consistently abided by throughout Freud's writings, helps us to understand the central idea in the author's entire psychology—the unconscious. It is when the *net* cathexis (positive cathexis minus anticathexis) is negative that an idea becomes unconscious. Since both the amount of positive and negative energy operating at cross-purposes in such a manner can be enormous, that which is suppressed into unconsciousness at such cost can be very troublesome, causing great psychic tension.

It is through the various stages of psychosexual development that man gradual-

ly alters the form that libidinal energy takes. The first stage is *oral*, lasting from birth to about eighteen months. The mouth is the main erogenous zone at this point and nourishment is the prime source of gratification. The next stage is *anal*, and it lasts up to about four years. The anus becomes the major erogenous zone and excretion becomes an important source of gratification. It is during this period that sphincter control is learned. The third stage is called *phallic* or *genital* and it lasts up to six or seven years. The sex organs now provide erotic pleasure. The period encompasses the Oedipal crisis, which must be overcome if one is to develop into a healthy and mature individual. Following this, the child enters the *latency* stage, lasting until approximately twelve years. The boy has had to temporarily repress sex since he learned that his mother was not available to him. The fifth stage is *puberty*, at which time (hetero)sexual activity resumes, leading, Freud hoped, to the final developmental stage of *heterosexual maturity*. Thus all six stages are psychosexual, the first three *autoerotic*, the last three *alloerotic*.

The human personality has three components—id, ego, and superego—and these develop in line with the foregoing stages. At the outset, there is only *id*, the instinctual. It is totally unconscious, consists of energy or primary drives that seek discharge, and is ruled by the pleasure principle. Gradually, the id's interaction with the environment produces the *ego*, the experiential self, or that element of personality which helps the individual to effectively interact with the environment. It is partly unconscious, follows the secondary process of thinking, and is ruled by the reality principle. Finally, out of the ego emerges the *superego*, which represents both the conscience and the ego ideal. The superego is mostly unconscious, it consists of the internalized expectations of society (transmitted through significant others such as the mother), and it punishes the ego through guilt or rewards it through pride.

According to Freud, pathology can develop at any stage. At the oral stage, excessive or insufficient stimulation can produce fixation. For example, one hears that this may be the root of the evil of cigarette smoking. Again, improper handling of the anal stage can produce fixation at that level. Thus excessively harsh toilet training has been said to produce anally retentive individuals, for example, people who are compulsively neat and hoard money. Freudians have often been teased for some of their more humorous hypotheses. For example, the miser, in whose subconscious money is symbolic feces, is said to suffer from a "constipated" personality. Conversely, insufficient toilet training has been said to produce a sloppy, spendthrift, "diarrheatic" personality.

The problems that may develop during the genital stage are more serious. For one thing, the little girl begins to suffer from *penis envy*, and this ultimately accounts for her desire for babies. Furthermore, it is during this stage that the child falls in love with the parent of the opposite sex. The girl must overcome her *Electra complex*, the boy his *Oedipus complex*. The experience of competing with one's father for the mother's love can be traumatic. It produces *castration anxiety*, because that is the feared form of paternal punishment. Therefore, in order to avoid castration, the young boy begins to *repress* his libidinal impulses, and this is how the superego originates.

Again, Freud and the Freudians have been made fun of for some of their bizarre hypotheses. The concept of penis envy, for example, can mean that all babies are in essence substitute penises, and Freudians have also been accused of attributing a jealous and resentful personality to all women, as a result of penis envy. At least since Betty Friedan (1963), Freud has become the whipping boy of women's liberation and of every college freshman capable of spelling his name. We should note that that fad reflects radical know-nothingism rather than advances in social-psychological knowledge.

The next stage is that of *latency*. During this period, sexuality becomes latent, and members of the opposite sex are rejected. The young boy may be latently homosexual, ambivalent, or bisexual. Unless the youngster overcomes his ill-fated love affair with his mother and successfully *transfers* his love to another woman, there will be problems. It is during puberty that heterosexual activity resumes, but Freudian psychologists warn that the young teenager's first girlfriends are likely to be mother substitutes.

To all these potential pitfalls of growing up psychoanalytic psychology adds the possibility of an excessively harsh superego, that is, a sadistic and irrational superego punishing the ego with undue severity and repressing the individual's desire for growth and fulfillment. Furthermore, there are the various *defense mechanisms* of the ego against anxiety, and these, too, may be pathological. Indeed, Freud conceives of three basic emotional states: love, anger, and fear or anxiety. In order to cope with the last, particularly *neurotic* anxiety, the ego can repress, regress, engage in reaction formation, project, sublimate, or rationalize.

Freud's various diagnostic and therapeutic methods are, of course, among his most widely adopted contributions (cf. Freud, 1924). Since fixation at an earlier stage and repression are at the root of most maladjustment, psychotherapy must be a sneaky process of uncovering that which is repressed. This requires the use of *indirect* methods, ways of uncovering the camouflages imposed by the ego and superego, while avoiding awakening their resistance of defenses. This is where dream interpretation acquires its importance, as well as the interpretation of so-called Freudian slips of the tongue (which escape while the superego is unaware) and the entire array of projective techniques (Rorschach, Thematic Apperception Test, Minnesota Multiphasic Personality Inventory, etc.) so widely adopted by clinical psychology today. Also, since Oedipal fixation is the failure to transfer love from one's mother to another woman, psychoanalysis may entail the double transference process of the patient falling in and then out of love with his therapist.

Finally, Freud's perspective on contemporary society is a clear derivation from the foregoing ideas. He attributed much of modern man's misery and neurosis to libidinal repression, that is, to the puritan straightjacket into which middle-class Western society forces its members. Civilization, then, breeds discontents (1946). The road to human happiness is a less rigid socialization process, with more emphasis on love and less on the disciplinary values embodied by the concept of the superego.

Other early psychoanalytic psychologists include the Austrians Alfred Adler (1870-1937), Otto Rank (1884-1939), and Wilhelm Reich (1897-1957) and the Swiss Carl Jung (1875-1961). Adler is best known for having discovered the *inferiority complex*. The contribution is important because it views neurosis as the combination of a physical condition and a subjective interpretation thereof. *Organ inferiority* is the real condition of anyone who is abnormally short or ugly. It becomes an inferiority complex when it is interpreted as a defect. This, in turn, may lead to sublimation or compensation, as in the case of Napoleon and other short men whose quest for power was nothing but overcompensation for their perceived shortcomings.

Otto Rank emphasized the birth trauma and the role of insecurity in neurosis. Carl Jung is perhaps best known for his concepts of *animus* and *anima*, the masculine and feminine principles variously present in each of us, and for his *introvert-extrovert* typology, referring to the inwardly with-

drawn and the outgoing other-directed individual, respectively. Interestingly, Jung has been used by the American sexual liberation movements (women in their quest for sexual equality, homosexuals arguing that all men have some latent homosexual tendencies), but he was also welcomed by Nazi Germany's sexual ideology of *Kinder, Kuche und Kirche*. Indeed, a major problem in modern society, Jung felt, is that we have a higher evaluation of men than of women, and this leads women to reject their roles. However, they should recognize their inherent femininity (anima) and accept domestic roles.

Reich (1961) was one of the tragic figures in the history of science. After a highly successful career with Freud's Psychoanalytic Polyclinic in Vienna, the Nazification of Europe forced him to the United States. He discovered *orgonomy*, or the *science of the life energy*, but in 1954, the federal Food and Drug Administration sued him for his experiments, and in 1957 he was imprisoned, dying a few months later in the federal penitentiary at Lewisburg, Pennsylvania. Since the decree stipulated that "the defendants refrain from . . . disseminating information pertaining to the construction . . . of orgone . . . devices . . ." (1960:548), one cannot ascertain the value of this part of Reich's work. One should, as a matter of principle, condemn the governmental censorship of scientific work.

Current state

The number of modern-day scholars influenced by Freud cannot be estimated, and even those properly considered neo-Freudians are innumerable.

One of the classical neo-Freudian studies of childhood socialization was Rene Spitz's famous *hospitalism* (1945), which showed that children who were institutionalized and separated from their mother fared very poorly. Eric Erikson (1950), too, is best known for his work on childhood, although focusing more on the development of adolescents and identity problems. Karen Horney (1950) was among the neoanalysts concerned with developing a theory of neurosis *not* strictly based on libido theory, that is, less biological and sexual than Freud's original formulation. Erich Fromm's thrust was in the same direction, in both his sociological (1941) and his psychological (1957) work. He epitomizes the many postwar psychologists who developed a *humanistic* and ideological psychology based on Freudian principles, with prescriptions ranging from how to love to international relations. Abraham Maslow (1962) and Eric Berne (1947) belong in precisely the same category, both combining Freudianism and humanism. Berne's work has been both conventional clinical (1955) and, best known to the public, game theoretical (1964), therby moving in the antipsychiatric direction best represented by Thomas Szasz (1961). It is obvious that the *parent-adult-child* conception of personality so popularized in recent years by Berne and other transactional analysts is a simple translation of Freud's superego, ego, and id, in that order. In general, psychoanalytic developmental psychology is now called *ego psychology* (cf. Blanck and Blanck, 1974; Deutsch and Krauss, 1965:136), and it is the school of thought that proposes a psychotherapy rooted in Freud's writings.

Separate mention must be made of the *culture and personality school* in anthropology. During the 1920s, eminent anthropologists like Margaret Mead and Bronislaw Malinowski were engaged in work simultaneously influenced by and critical of Freud. For example, they demonstrated that the Oedipus complex was by no means a cross-cultural universal, as implied by Freud. Shortly before and after World War II, a number of Columbia anthropologists launched research aimed at exploring the relationship between childhood socialization, the ensuing basic personality,

and the resulting social and cultural "superstructure." Abram Kardiner was the group's mentor, and Cora Dubois did much of the field work among the Alorese Islanders (in Indonesia) to produce the analytic data. Basically, the thesis of the culture and personality school is that the childrearing patterns that prevail in a given culture tend to produce a modal personality and that institutions, in turn, reflect that modal personality.

The importance of the culture and personality thesis is that it traces the roots of various social systems (oppressive, liberal, totalitarian, or free) back to the way children are reared. For example, the Alorese islanders treat their children with neglect and inconsistency. As a result, that people's personality is frustrated and distrustful, and this in turn is reflected in the grimly punitive theology and mythology to which they subscribe. A more detailed discussion of culture and personality is provided in Chapter 9.

An entirely different group of people whose ideas also go back to Freud are radical culture critics such as Norman Brown (1959), Herbert Marcuse (1962), and Allen Wheelis (1958; 1974). These men are social commentators rather than empirical scholars. They share an extremely critical view of the contemporary technocracy, seeing it as monstrously oppressive. They advocate individual libidinal liberation, and at least to Marcuse this may have to take the form of violent revolution. The fact that these men see freedom—and the lack of it in contemporary society—in libidinal terms clearly shows their Freudian orientation.

Among the most successful attempts at an *eclectic* theory based in part on Freudianism is the psychotherapy proposed by Dollard and Miller (1950) and already touched upon previously. Selecting the best from behaviorism, psychoanalytic psychology, and labelling theory, the two Yale psychologists have formulated one of the most sensible theories of neurosis. Their etiology is Freudian, focusing on possible early fixations. Their therapy stresses the need for labelling, that is, for bringing emotional problems under the control of the secondary process.

Another important eclectic contribution was made by Harry Stack Sullivan (1953). This psychoanalyst developed a synthesis of Freudian and symbolic interactionist social psychology which holds that while the fundamental condition man must cope with is *anxiety,* maladjustment originates and is cured at the symbolic level. Sullivan's ideas will be discussed in greater detail in the chapters on socialization, communication, and mental illness.

In concluding this brief review of neoanalytic psychology, mention must be made of the school's typical diagnostic and therapeutic techniques. It follows logically from the entire Freudian scheme that all such techniques must be *indirect,* or *projective.* Among the best known tests are the *Thematic Apperception Test* developed by Morgan and Murray in 1935, the *Rorschach Inkblot Test* devised by Rorschach in 1921 (1942), and the *Minnesota Multiphasic Personality Inventory* invented by Hathaway and McKinley in the 1940s (cf. Dahlstrom and Welsh, 1960). The TAT requires the subjective interpretation of concrete photographs, the Rorschach does likewise with abstract inkblots, and the MMPI consists of verbal statements to be responded to. What all these as well as other projective tests have in common is that they (1) require the subject to *project* himself into the test and (2) require the analyst's *interpretation* of the subject's responses. Thus psychoanalytic psychotherapy stands or falls upon the validity of the tests used and the therapist's imputations of motives to the patients. This is the rub, and we shall return to it extensively in the chapter on motivation.

Finally, reference should be made to dream interpretation (cf. Freud, 1924) and to hypnosis (see Eysenck, 1969a; 1969b), two favored techniques of Freudians. Again, if it is agreed that lasting behavioral change can only be accomplished by way of the unconscious (a fundamental Freudian assumption) and that escape of unconscious material is only possible when the guards—the ego and superego—are, quite literally, asleep, the utility of hypnosis and dream interpretation becomes obvious.

Evaluation

The foregoing discussion has already included some judgments. Here, we come back to the following: (1) Freud's contribution to social psychology, (2) the discovery of the irrational, (3) the discovery of the unconscious, (4) instinctivism, and (5) psychoanalytic therapy.

As Swanson (1972) points out in his comparative evaluation of Freud and Mead, the Austrian psychologist's contribution to socialization theory (for example, through the concept of the superego) is lasting, and so is his contribution to motivation theory (for example, through the concept of the id). In addition, many of Freud's major works are entirely sociological—his *The Future of an Illusion, Moses and Monotheism,* and *Civilization and its Discontents.* There is no doubt that, as Swanson phrases it, Freud is unlikely to ". . . soon be only a curiosity in the museums of our discipline" (loc. cit.).

One of the Freudians' seminal contributions was the discovery of the irrational. Unlike the early associationists and even the behaviorists, the Freudians knew the importance of the irrational in human motivation. For example, even the pleasure-pain principle does not exclude irrationality, as in the case of the self-destructive heroin addict.

Similarly important was the "discovery" of the unconscious. While behaviorists tend to reject that notion, arguing that man *forgets* rather than *represses,* it is undeniable that unconscious factors sometimes influence behavior. Research is being conducted in this area (cf. Machotka, 1964; Shibutani, 1966). As Harry Stack Sullivan showed, the Freudian and the symbolic interactionist positions with respect to the unconscious can be reconciled: Freud emphasized purposeful *repression;* interactionism says that man perceives *selectively;* in either case, we have a basic *defense mechanism* against the pain and anxiety produced by the excessive awareness of certain stimuli.

The instinctivism that was such a pronounced feature of Freud's own psychology has been gradually deemphasized by the neo-Freudians. The less biologistic formulations of such psychologists as Erikson and Horney have made psychoanalytic psychology increasingly relevant to social psychology.

Finally, the impact of psychoanalytic psychology on psychotherapy is immeasurable. As Barton (1974) argues, orthodox Freudianism was first improved upon by Jungian therapy and finally by Carl Rogers' client-centered or existential-phenomenological brand of therapy. What this means, then, is that Freud's contributions ultimately flow into the humanistic paradigm advocated in the subsequent parts of this book.

TYPICAL AMERICAN SOCIAL PSYCHOLOGY

At the present time, there is no doubt that the field of social psychology is dominated by what is here called psychological social psychology, that is, the orientation coming out of *Gestalt* and *field theory* and

partially discussed in the previous chapter under *group dynamics.*[2]

Origins

As indicated in the section on group dynamics (see Chapter 1), the origin of this brand of social psychology goes back to the work of a number of German psychologists at the beginning of the twentieth century. Wertheimer labelled the motion picture experience the *phi phenomenon,* arguing that this was a sui generis experience not reducible to simpler terms. Kohler showed that apes arrive at solutions through a sudden total perception and realization, not through atomized trials and errors. Koffka emphasized the concept of

---

[2] A glance at my own bookshelves shows the following recent textbooks in psychological social psychology: Aronson (1972), Baron et al. (1974), Cooper and McGaugh (1963), Doby (1966), Elms (1972), Gergen (1974), Grossack and Gardner (1970), Hollander (1971), Kaluger and Unkovic (1969), Lambert and Lambert (1964), Marlowe (1971), McDavid and Harari (1974), Sampson (1971), Schellenberg (1974), Secord and Backman (1974), Watson and Johnson (1972), and Wrightsman (1972). In addition, the following are readers in the same tradition: Aronson and Helmreich (1973), Bickman and Henchy (1972), Evans and Rozelle (1973), Franklin and Kohout (1973), Hollander and Hunt (1971; 1972), Lambert and Weisbrod (1971), Lindzey and Aronson (1968), MacDonald and Schellenberg (1971), and Vinacke et al. (1964). Most of these books were published by psychologists, and they contrast with the few sociological social psychology books in existence, mostly four readers and two textbooks following the symbolic interactionist tradition.

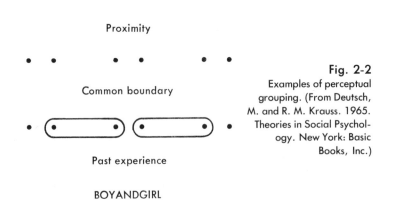

Fig. 2-2
Examples of perceptual grouping. (From Deutsch, M. and R. M. Krauss. 1965. Theories in Social Psychology. New York: Basic Books, Inc.)

pragnanz, the organism's tendency to achieve the *best* possible organization of perceptual stimuli. Heider focused on two related tendencies: *attribution* and striving for *cognitive balance,* that is, the tendencies to view the environment as coherent. Lewin, finally, launched *field theory,* a social psychology based on the notion that the individual lives and acts in a psychological field characterized by forces that propel him toward goals or repel him from threats.

The major assumptions of Gestalt and field theory may therefore be summed up as follows: (1) perception is holistic and organized, not fragmented; (2) psychological phenomena always occur in a field (in a total system) rather than as disparate stimuli; and (3) psychological processes tend toward an end state of greatest possible rest and simplicity, that is, the organization of stimuli tends to be as good as conditions permit. *Perceptual grouping,* then, is what most of us generally tend to do. This is illustrated in Fig. 2-2.

According to Gestalt psychology, the same grouping principles also apply in *social* psychology. For example, when we assign guilt by association ("all hippies are bad because Charles Manson was bad") we group by proximity, assuming that all hippies are alike because they frequent one another. When we generalize about the entire population of a nation ("all Frenchmen are amorous") we group by common boundary. Also, as Zillig (1928) showed, unpopular children are often thought to be poor performers by their classmates (cf

Deutsch and Krauss, 1965:21). This illustrates grouping by similarity.

In addition, Lewin's field theory centers around *dynamic* concepts: an individual's life space (the "field") consists of regions, some of which are in *tension,* some having *positive valence* (goal regions that attract the individual), some with *negative valence* (threats that repel him). The field, then, is characterized by a variety of *forces* operating within it and determining the *locomotion* of the individual (cf. Lewin, 1938). An example of an application of Lewin's theory is Zeigarnik's quotient (1927). According to Lewin, the tendency to recall unfinished activities should be greater than the tendency to recall completed ones, for this would leave the individual's field in psychological tension. Zeigarnik tested this hypothesis by asking a group of subjects to perform some task, then preventing half of them from completing the task, and later asking all subjects to recall the task. The results are presented in the form of the so-called Zeigarnik quotient:

$$\frac{\text{Unfinished tasks recalled (RU)}}{\text{Completed tasks recalled (RC)}}$$

And indeed, the quotient obtained was well over one (1.9), clearly supporting Lewin's theory (cf. Deutsch and Krauss, 1965:40). Of course, in some instances (for example, when recall of failure is too threatening), the quotient will be less than one.

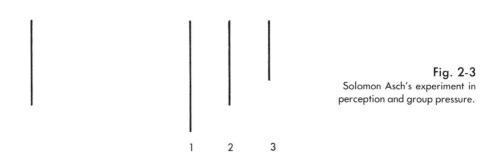

Fig. 2-3
Solomon Asch's experiment in perception and group pressure.

1   2   3

Current state

Out of the classical tradition just discussed, three major topics for social psychology have emerged: (1) Gestalt psychology opened up the study of *perception*, (2) Lewin's field theory moved into the area of *motivation*, and (3) from early German psychologists like Heider to modern American scholars such as Festinger, *cognition* has been of central concern.

One of the best known studies of perception and how it is affected by social pressures was done by Solomon Asch (1942). A group of students was shown a series of lines as in Fig. 2-3. Each student was asked to tell the researcher, in front of the group, which of the three right-hand lines was equal to the left-hand line. The rub was that prior to the experiment, all subjects had been instructed to give the wrong answer, except one student who was left naive, and who therefore alone gave the correct answer. Asch discovered that the naive subject, confronted by a majority that unanimously gives a different answer, becomes highly upset and in more than half of the cases ends up agreeing with the majority, conforming to a wrong answer. When the naive subject has an ally confronting such a majority, he is much less likely to flinch. Asch's main point is that the naive subject often comes to agree with the group not merely because of fear of rejection and the like, but because he genuinely believes that he is wrong; no longer trusts his own *perception*.

Of equal importance here is the work of the social psychologist Theodore M. Newcomb (1953; 1956), who has extended the Gestalt tradition into the areas of interpersonal communication and attraction. Newcomb has proposed and researched many hypotheses and assumptions, including the following ones:

1. Generally, when two people perceive each other positively and each is oriented toward a third person, they will develop the same attitude toward that third person.
2. In a cohesive group there will, initially at least, be an increase in communication toward deviant members (in an effort to reestablish conformity).
3. Accurate communication is generally more rewarding than punishing.
4. Interpersonal attraction varies positively with similarity.
5. It also varies positively with amount of communication.
6. It also varies with amount of interaction.

Note that many of these propositions merely translate commonsense homilies into sociologese and that they are not necessarily truer than such homilies. Is "any friend of yours indeed a friend of mine?" as 1 above suggests? Do communication and interaction indeed increase liking, as 5 and 6 state, or does familiarity, as "everyone knows," "breed contempt"?

Out of Heider's work comes the currently popular topic of *attribution*. Central to the German psychologist's work was the assumption that man tends to attribute order and causality to his environment. Far from being existentialists and from recognizing the inherent absurdity of the world, most of us not only organize our environment into orderly configurations but we also attribute to it centralized causality and often even expect it to be *ethically just!* There is much work on attribution currently going on (cf. Baron et al., 1974:341-343; Jones, 1972; Shaw and Skolnick, 1973). For example, Lerner (1965) has proposed a "just world" theory. He showed that because people must believe that the world is just, they tend to blame victims of accidents for those accidents, particularly in the case of severe occurrences. Walster (1966) speaks of "defensive attribution," which also states that a person tends to blame the victims of catastrophic occurrences for those occurrences more often than in the case of minor accidents, because otherwise he would be threatened by the possibility of the same thing happening to him. Shaw and Skolnick tested the possibility of this working in reverse; do people also attribute responsibility for *lucky* breaks? A group of subjects were told a story about a chemistry student who accidentally made a major discovery, developed a pleasant smelling compound, etc. The findings showed that while attribution did take place, it did *not* increase with the magnitude of the positive event, indicating that the "just world" theory only seems to apply to negative occurrences.

Another direct outflow of Heider's work is Festinger's famous theory of cognitive dissonance (1957), which in essence states that "the reality which impinges on a person will exert pressures in the direction of bringing the appropriate cognitive elements into correspondence with that reality" (loc. cit.). For example, after a student has decided to go to one college rather than another, the college of his choice will seem to him to become increasingly attractive compared to the other one (Deutsch and Krauss, 1965:71). This is an example of how people tend to use *dissonance-reduction* mechanisms to ensure that what happens to them, their decisions, and the consequences thereof are consistent with one another. As Festinger (1961) writes: "Rats and people come to love the things for which they have suffered." Festinger's theory of cognitive dissonance is clearly in the Gestalt and field tradition. Its propositions also resemble those of Homans' exchange theory, which predicts such things as a correspondence between the investments one makes into a social situation and the rewards one gets out of it. There have been many empirical tests of cognitive dissonance and dissonance reduction, including the famous study by Festinger and Carlsmith (1959), which showed that students receiving small rewards for deceiving someone were more likely to change their opinion than those receiving a large reward. Most of the evidence supports the theory.

Festinger's other major contribution is his theory of *social comparison* (1954). This is a series of partially obvious and commonsense propositions about how and why people tend to compare their own opinions and abilities with those of others. An important assertion, for example, is that people are more likely to compare themselves with others who are fairly similar than with people who are widely discrepant. Furthermore, there is a pressure for conformity; people preferably frequent those to whom their opinions and abilities are fairly similar, and even exert themselves to achieve similarity. For example, a golfer playing with others who shoot in the eighties will tend to play the same kind of game, even if he is otherwise capable of doing better. Festinger's point is that this happens not merely for the sake of social acceptance but so as to facilitate social comparison (see Deutsch and Krauss, 1965:63).

In general, the study of *conformity, group standards*, and *group influence* on behavior has become one of the major areas of interest to psychological social psychologists. Picking up Floyd Allport's work on *group facilitation* (see first section), social psychologists have shown that what happens is actually a *standardization of behavior*. In a wide variety of experiments, subjects have been asked to make all sorts of judgments (of the number of beans in bottles, of the lengths of lines, of a tiny spot of light in a dark room, etc.); generally the estimates of individuals in group settings tend to become alike, to cluster toward an average, a *norm*. Famous is the work of Muzafer Sherif (1935), for example, his experiments on the so-called *autokinetic effect*. This is the tendency, when one is viewing a single small light in a dark room where there is no objective basis of comparison, to see the light moving in any direction, even when the subject knows perfectly well that the light is still. Sherif asked subjects to judge the distance, position, and movements of such a light. He found that among a group of subjects a norm developed, and thereafter individual judgments converged toward that norm. Furthermore, this norm was so strong and *autonomous* (Sherif, 1935) that even a leader could not change it.

The standardization of behavior has been studied not only with reference to *perception,* as with the autokinetic effect, but also with opinions and attitudes. For example, asked whether or not they agree with a certain statement, subjects will respond significantly differently depending on the source to which the statement is attributed. Thus the statement "According to the President, nuclear energy is one of the cheapest and safest forms of energy available" will elicit significantly higher agreement scores than the same assertion not attributed to a specific source. Lambert and Lowy (1957) showed that attitudes converge toward a group average when group discussion is allowed and when the subjects know each other. Otherwise they found no convergence, and this led them to conclude that people will tend to change their attitudes only if some personal advantage follows from the change. One of the very important implications of this entire research area was already well perceived by Lewin (cf. Lambert and Lambert, 1964; 90), who noted that the best way to modify individual behavior or attitudes is to change group *norms* rather than by trying to work directly on individuals. A norm is always more acceptable, Lewin argued, whereas individual change carried the threat of becoming a deviant.

Additional topics studied extensively by psychological social psychologists include group cohesiveness (Cartwright and Zander, 1953), leadership (Bavelas, 1971; Fiedler, 1972; Hollander, 1971), sociometry (Moreno, 1960), and personality (Adorno et al., 1950; McClelland, 1961; Rokeach, 1960). Cohesiveness has been related to conformity and the establishment of group standards. Leadership, as Bavelas and Hollander point out, can be examined through trait psychology and the "great man" approach or, better, through the *situational* approach, which recognizes the situational emergence of leadership behavior. In this context, Hollander speaks of leadership *credits* that accrue to various individuals who have been helpful in group problem solving but that may be used up and lost. Also, research has clearly shown the existence of various types of leaders. For example, a group generally has a best *liked* man, as well as a most *respected* member. The former maybe the *affective* star, but the latter is the *instrumental* leader.

Sociometry is the study, developed primarily by Moreno, of group structures, relations, attraction, popularity, and leadership through such graphic devices as sociograms and sociometric stars (the group's most popular members), isolates, coalitions, subcliques, hierarchies, etc. A major social psychological journal, *Sociometry,* is dedicated to this kind of research.

Finally, personality has been studied with a concern for such traits as achievement need (McClelland, 1961) and authoritarianism (Adorno et al., 1950; Rokeach, 1960). Adorno's classical work was a timely study of fascism, measured in his F-scale. His focus on the childhood origin of the fascist personality (characterized by such things as racial prejudice and authoritarianism) makes him partially a Freudian.

Evaluation

Compared with behaviorism, Gestalt and field theories represent a great step forward insofar as our understanding of social behavior is concerned. Unlike behaviorism, Gestalt psychology recognizes that human experience is always *interpreted* experience. It is *contextual,* not disparate, as stimulus-response psychology describes it. In Becker's (1962) terms, Gestalt psychology recognizes type 3 reactivity, whereas behaviorism tends to reduce human behavior to the simple level of type 2 reactivity, the conditioned response. In line with this, we saw that the Gestaltists

```
┌─────────────────────────────────────────────┐
│            Behaviorism                        │
│   Stimulus → Organism → Response              │
│                                               │
│       Gestalt and field theory                │
│   Stimulus → Interpretive → Organism →        │
│             screen          Response          │
└─────────────────────────────────────────────┘
```

FIG. 2-4
Basic metaphors underlying
behaviorism and Gestalt
psychology.

and field theorists are far less dependent on animal experiments than the behaviorists, moving decisively into human social experimentation. Fig. 2-4 is a graphic presentation of these two competing metaphors.

Thus Gestalt recognizes the intervening variable of interpretation, a screen as it were between objective reality and its perception by the organism. This is an important step toward recognizing the subjective nature of human experience. However, as we shall see, this does not go far enough. What is ultimately required is a recognition of the *reactive* or *dialectical* relationship between man and his environment. This only an interactionist perspective provides. In turn, such a perspective raises serious doubts as to our ability to ever make valid generalizations about an objective reality at all. Instead, it implies the relativism inherent in the sociology of knowledge as well as the pragmatism of men like William James, W. I. Thomas, and George Herbert Mead and the subjective focus of the phenomenology of Alfred Schutz. These are the perspectives dealt with extensively in Part two of this book.

Two final reservations must be raised with regard to psychological social psychology, and here we focus on its methodology, which has been essentially small group experimentation: it is still not clear to what extent the findings of small group research may be generalized, because of the contrived conditions of such research. In other words, the relationship between the world of the experimenter and the real world outside has never been sufficiently explicated. Related to this is the possible *culture-boundness* of many of the findings.

As Allardt (1958) points out, the myriads of findings about need for conformity, social comparison, group cohesion, norms, and standards produced by American social psychology since the 1930s may reflect the strong conformist tendencies in United States society. Thus the group-dynamic "laws" discovered by Festinger, Newcomb, Asch, Sherif, Bales, Homans, and others may not apply, say, in India or Turkey.

THE GROUP EXPERIENCE MOVEMENT

Since the mid-1960s, millions of Americans have become caught up in the fad of group therapy, or "psychological group experience." Although the similarity between some facets of this new psychological enterprise and plain old fraudulent elixir peddling was pointed out early, the bandwagon rolls on. Somehow, millions upon millions of students, housewives, businessmen, professionals, and military people continue to turn to psychologists, facilitators, and institutions for the purchase of happiness.[3]

----

[3]Out of my own files, I select the following institutions in the business of sensitivity, group therapy, encounters, psychic liberation, personal growth, and related matters: the Alan Watts Society for Comparative Philosophy (Vallejo, Calif.), Anadysis Institute (Los Angeles), the Association for Humanistic Psychology (San Francisco), the Center for Interpersonal Development (Sacramento), Esalen (Big Sur, Calif.), EST (San Francisco), Gestalt Institute (San Francisco), Human Institute (Palo Alto), Human Relations Institute (Sacramento), Kairos (Rancho Santa Fe, Calif.), Living Love Center (Berkeley), National Training Lab (Washington, D.C.), Shambhala-Tollan Foundation (Berkeley), *Synthesis*, the new journal for those seeking self-realization (Redwood City, Calif.), Tahoe Institute (South Lake Tahoe, Calif.), and Zen Center (San Francisco). It can be seen that sensitivity training is heavily concentrated in California.

Origins

The "group experience movement"[4] is rooted in the classical theories already discussed. At least six distinct influences can be discerned, and this is what accounts for the variety of competing approaches at the present time. First, psychoanalytic psychology's impact is undeniable. Jung, Reich, and ultimately Freud himself had the most profound influence on Fritz Perls (1964), who launched the type of group experience offered at Esalen, where he in fact became one of the first gurus. The Freudian influence is also clearly noticeable in the work of Eric Berne (1964), who founded *transactional analysis*. This approach is based on a division of personality into parent, adult, and child, obviously the old Freudian trichotomy of superego, ego, and id. Perls, again, also incorporated Gestalt into his so-called *Gestalt therapy,* which stresses the importance of getting in touch with one's (subconscious) feelings and which rejects intellectualizing, words, symbols, and all verbal behavior. Third, the field of group dynamics has also had an input into the movement. Bales' IPA has, by now, veered toward group therapy (cf. Bales, 1970; Strodtbeck, 1973), and the *National Training Lab*, one of the most venerable sensitivity organizations, goes back to experimental group dynamics (cf. Luft, 1970). Fourth, Moreno (1960), who invented sociometry, also developed psychodrama, or role-playing. If anyone is to be singled out as the father of the encounter, it is Moreno. A fifth strand can be traced back to Viktor Frankl (1963) and his existential therapy and to Carl Rogers and his

nondirective therapy. Rogers, more than anyone else, popularized the concept of sensitivity training. The humanistic psychiatry of men like Frankl, Rogers, and Maslow will be singled out in subsequent chapters, since its focus on meaning makes it relevant to the phenomenological social psychology we propose. Finally, the Eastern philosophical influence from India and China must also be mentioned, although in the work of men like Carl Jung, Herman Hesse, and Wilhelm Reich this overlaps with the European psychoanalytic tradition. Indeed, both the psychoanalysts and the Eastern mysticists (Hesse, Watts, Leary) share a preoccupation with the unconscious and consciousness expansion.

Current state

It follows from the foregoing that there are now many competing types of institutionalized group experiences on the market. At least five can be distinguished, but with the many overlaps and the rapid rise and fall of new fads in this highly faddish area this classification is tentative. One brand is transactional analysis. This is an approach based on a Freudian conception of personality but aimed at the elimination of undesirable "games," by which Berne (1964) means dishonesty. It is popular and sells quite well, through slogans like "I'm okay, you're okay" (Harris, 1967). Second, the Gestalt therapy of Fritz Perls and the Esalen Institute, as stated, strives to get the person in touch with his emotions, thereby rediscovering the missing parts of his personality and becoming a whole being. Third, Glasser's reality therapy has a similar focus, and so does the existential humanistic therapy of men like Frankl (1963), Rogers (1961), and Shostrom (1968). These and other similar formulations are difficult to distinguish from one another, since they all stress such values as interpersonal closeness, honesty, feeling, self-actualization, liberation from such middle-class constraints as puritanism and materialism, and how to accomplish these objectives through unstructured group meetings. However, these approaches can

---

[4]The movement is quite flexible, coopting, as we shall see, any new behavior that promises to be lucrative, and also adroitly adjusting its rhetoric to criticism. Thus Esalen now disclaims having anything to do with therapy and rather labels itself an *educational* institution. Hence we use the term "group experience movement," which is, hopefully, sufficiently generic to cover the multiplicity of activities exemplified in footnote 3.

be distinguished from a fourth brand, the hard-hitting marathon encounter. First developed by Moreno (who also coined such well-known slogans as the "here-and-now"), the encounter may include up to thirty people and last up to seventy-two hours. It involves psychodrama and emotions of all kinds, including hostility. Encounters can be tough. Finally there is, at Esalen and in the various other sensitivity training centers, the emphasis on consciousness expansion, transcendental meditation, and other similar values derived from Eastern philosophies like Zen Buddhism. The group therapy movement has overlapped with the counterculture ever since the appearance of the first hippies, and as one moves away from multimillion dollar establishments like Esalen toward the more marginal efforts of student-like groups, group therapy and consciousness expansion begin to overlap with LSD, witchcraft, astrology, and communal marriages. In fact, even established organizations like the National Training Lab (which participates in federal foreign aid projects!) and Esalen include in their program workshops on witchcraft, telepathy, and clairvoyance.

In sum, little seems to escape the sensitivity–group therapy–encounter movement. The initial avowed focus was on psychic growth, liberation, consciousness expansion, and the development of Gestalt and awareness. Now, one can enroll in workshops on dream interpretation, voice interpretation, art appreciation, communion with nature, ecology, learning to love, sex, massage, psychedelic LSD experiences, Eastern mysticism, yoga, Zen, transcendental meditation, Taoism, use of the I-Ching, witchcraft, clairvoyance, telepathy, and the occult. A recent book, *Golf in the Kingdom* (Murphy, no date), finally shows us that golf, too, is a mystical experience.

Evaluation

The problem with the group sensitivity movement is that it mixes valuable ideas with charlatanism and criminal fraudulence. The humanism of men like Frankl (1963), Rogers (1961), and Szasz (1961) makes an important contribution. However we find, even in this group (cf. Berne, 1964; Harris, 1967; Shostrom, 1968) a deplorable tendency to offer simple slogans and facile formulas ("parent-adult-child," "I'm okay-you're okay," "man the manipulator," etc.) as panaceas for all problems of living. Such glib promises account for the popularity of the new quacks with millions of harried and naive people who hope to purchase instant happiness as one would purchase a painkiller, a holiday, or any other commodity. The inherent fraudulence of this situation lies in the fact that America's problems are more sociological, political, economic, structural, and cultural than psychological. Americans still overwhelmingly tackle their problems at the level of psychology, not sociology. In Mills' words, they do not see that their personal troubles are in fact social issues. One can argue, of course, that the various practices sold to the public by the group experience professionals work—they work the same way as superstition, opium, or a placebo works. But that is precisely the problem: as long as we take refuge in such pseudosolutions, we do not attack the fundamental social-structural roots of our collective problems. That is why this movement may entail an element of quackery.

A central feature of the group therapy–sensitivity movement is its commercialism. The Association for Humanistic Psychology circulates advertisements about conventions and workshops held in Oahu and at Squaw Valley. Esalen has branched out into the publishing and the recording business, and its staff, like that of other similar institutions, gives lucrative lectures and consultations to the campuses and businesses of America. These institutes are also in the travel business, like Kairos, which offers sensitivity tours to Japan, and the Tahoe Institute, which offers sensitivity skiing in Austria. Out of the Living Love

Center (Berkeley) comes the *Handbook to Higher Consciousness* (Ken Keyes, Jr.) and *How to Make Your Life Work or Why Aren't You Happy?* (Ken Keyes, Jr. and Tolly Burkan).

An entirely different aspect is the hostility and violence typical of some encounters. It is not uncommon for marathon sessions to feature gross verbal and physical abuse. The following account is provided not as a typical case—it represents one extremely negative experience of this nature, as against several highly positive ones—but as one that deserves exposure. Additionally, this experience is included to buttress a methodological point central to this book: good social psychology is *experiential* social psychology, that is, social psychology involving not just theory and objective observation but also subjective experience.

A few years ago at the Palo Alto Human Institute, encounter participants were ruthlessly abused and manhandled. A student was first insulted, accused of cowardice and homosexuality, then struck by screaming females and laughing males. Half a dozen group members grabbed him by his feet, hair, beard, and clothes, trying to forcibly undress him and in the process beating him unmercifully. After he somehow caused them to relent, another chap, young and timid, was provoked into fist fights with several of the heavyweight facilitators. He fought courageously but when he sued for peace, exhausted, the group leaders alternately forced him to continue. Each time the fellow fled to a corner of the room he was dragged back to the center. He was literally shaken out of his sleeping bag, and bunches of hair were pulled out of his head. He finally broke down, sobbing, which elicited unanimous ridicule but did stop the fighting. Women were similarly maltreated, forced to fight with one another while a crowd of hysterically laughing spectators encircled them. Periodically, ashtrays and other objects were hurled across the room, causing black eyes and bloody head wounds. The two dozen participants were packed together in this inferno for forty-eight hours. All doors were locked. By the second day of the marathon, the physical damage included not only head wounds but also broken ribs. Psychologically, individuals were reaching their limits, variously exhibiting hysterical, homicidal, suicidal, and catatonic symptoms. The nightmare was finally broken up at gunpoint by the Palo Alto police. The Palo Alto Institute was subsequently put out of business when a client was sufficiently distraught to return and firebomb the hanger-like structure where the meetings had been held.

Not all encounters are as sinister as the Palo Alto marathon. However, it is the custom to dish out a considerable amount of suffering under the guise of therapy. The toughness of these practices is said to benefit the clients. Synanon, the drug rehabilitation center, is often mentioned as proof that such techniques work. Esalen speaks of the *psychotic opportunity*, implying that total mental breakup may be the prelude to the rebuilding of a superior person. The rationale, then, is the same as that which underlies any brainwashing and conversion process—the brutal destruction of personality. Of course, encounters can, in a less serious vein, also be viewed as a form of leisure. But then, why pay $50 to $300 for an experience that is not necessarily more fun than a party or a fishing trip?

Back (1972:204) shows that the group experience movement "is an anti-intellectual movement in the name of science." While not all sensitivity labs opt for emotionalism and irrationalism, there is often a tendency to reject words, abstractions, and scientific and intellectual theorizing ("going to the head"), in sum to reject some basic features of middle-class Western society, because they are deemed dehumanizing. Hence stress is placed on self-actualization, uninhibitedness, honesty, and psychic liberation.

In our secularized and bureaucratized society, many of us are alienated from our feelings, turning then to sensitivity in a search for meaning and feeling. However, aside from this age-specific problem, the sensitivity movement can also be viewed in the context of the perennial dualism of reason versus emotion, the Apollonian against the Dionysian principle in man and culture. The current cultivation of "honest" emotions may, to some extent, be a retreat from reason.

PSYCHIATRY

This chapter is a critical examination of scientific psychology. Since psychiatry is nothing less than the applied branch of the entire psychological profession, we now turn to that enterprise. We shall first indicate how each of the theoretical perspectives described in this chapter led to its own brand of therapy, meshing together into general psychiatry. Next, we shall examine the case against psychiatry, discussing labelling, existential game theory, and ethics. Finally, a brief evaluation will be offered.

Behaviorism's therapeutic branch is *behavior modification,* the extinction or alteration of unwanted behavior through negative or positive reinforcement. Based on the assumption that man learns all behavior through the pleasure-pain principle, behavior modification (also called *aversion therapy*) attempts to alter behavior by associating it with rewards or punishments. For example, a homosexual who is fond of Beethoven's music is shown photographs of naked women at the sound of the *Pastorale.* In theory, he should develop a liking for the female body. Of course, the aversion toward women may be stronger than the attraction of the music, in which case the man will learn to dislike Beethoven. However, other associations can be tried (the subject's favorite food, a pleasurable scent or sensation) and somehow, in theory, he should be able to overcome his dislike for women.

Freudian therapy is, of course, psychoanalysis (cf. Alexander and Ross, 1952; Freud, 1924). Here, the assumption is that individual maladjustment is caused by (early) childhood fixation and the repression of experience into the subconscious. Therefore, therapy consists of digging up such submerged material through the lengthy process of psychoanalysis, which often requires many years. Since the individual's ego and superego repress this information, its discovery by the analyst requires indirect sneak techniques, hence the use of hypnosis, dream interpretation, and projective tests like Rorschach, TAT, and MMPI (see section on Freud and psychoanalysis). Today, ego psychology (cf. Blanck and Blanck, 1974) and transactional analysis are among the therapeutic approaches directly based on Freudian assumptions. Eric Berne (1957; 1964), as noted earlier, has simply translated Freud's superego, ego, and id into the parent-adult-child trichotomy on which transactional analysis is based.

The Gestalt and field traditions have also had their input into psychiatry. Fritz Perls' Gestalt therapy, for one, emphasizes the totality of personality, the need to recognize and to integrate one's feelings with the rest of the person. Perls was one of the co-founders of Esalen, and in one way or another all sensitivity training can be said to emphasize the effective integration of personality. Furthermore, it is this tradition that has, through group dynamics, also led to the emergence of group therapy. Here the assumption is that the small group is a microcosm of the real world and that individuals can practice and develop behavior patterns desirable for effective coping in the outside world.

The encounter then, insofar as it stresses the fight, is a therapeutic technique devised to train the subject to better fend for himself. Therapy becomes a form of psychological karate that presumably equips the patient to fight back and to avoid the recurrence of the social victimization that ended up sending him for professional help.

In addition to these distinct traditions,

there are also synthetic approaches to therapy. Dollard and Miller (1950) proposed an eclectic psychotherapy based on behaviorism and Freudianism. According to these authors, neurosis is characterized by misery and stupidity, that is, the subject's inability to deal with his personal problems at the symbolic level. Therapy consists of the development of *verbal* control over *emotional* problems. Others, like R. D. Laing (1965) and H. S. Sullivan (1953) have combined psychoanalytic and symbolic interactionist principles in their approach to mental illness and therapy. While Sullivan recognizes the centrality of anxiety in human behavior and human problems, his therapy stresses the importance of the subjective and symbolic meaning of behavior. According to these authors, conventional psychiatry fails to grasp this; therefore, rather than establishing common understanding between a subject and us, it merely imposes our norms on him.

A final brand of psychotherapy must be mentioned here—the totally physiological approach to behavior in the form of drug therapy, electric shock therapy, brain surgery, etc. While physiological psychology is mostly a branch of behaviorism, these techniques deserve separate mention because they are at the core of the controversy about psychiatry.

In his famous essay on *The Effects of Psychotherapy*, Eysenck (1961) performed a thorough comparison of the therapeutic effects of the different approaches. The gist of his findings was that (1) *neurotic patients "treated by psychotherapy recover or improved to approximately the same extent as similar neurotics receiving no psychotherapy"* and that (2) *the only procedures leading to significantly more rapid rates among patients under treatment than among patients not receiving treatment are those based on behaviorism.* In sum, as of 1961, psychiatry was accomplishing nothing, with the possible exception of behavioristic therapy. As to the group methods which have emerged since that time, they remain to be evaluated.

Antipsychiatry

Psychiatry has grown into a massive national institution as responsible for social control as the government itself and far more so than the institution it has displaced, the Church. The critical analysis of psychiatry and the identification of its true purpose has come from sociology and psychiatry itself, and it has centered around the *moral* aspects of the problem.

Sociological labelling theory is based on Edwin Lemert's (1948; 1951) distinction between primary and secondary deviation: *primary deviation* is any norm-breaking behavior that may occur but remains essentially unacknowledged, unnoticed. *Secondary deviation* occurs "when the person begins to employ his deviant behavior or a role based on it as a means of defense, attack, or adjustment to the . . . problems created by the societal reaction to it" (Lemert, 1948:28). Thus a deviant is not so much the perpetrator of a deviant act as the occasional recipient of a deviant label attached to him by society. Mental illness, according to Thomas Scheff (1966), is a form of secondary and residual deviation. It may be defined as "the stabilization of the behavior of an individual into a pattern of residual rule-breaking produced by the societal reaction called forth by the rule-breaking" (quoted in Martindale and Martindale, 1973:15). One of the major proponents of the sociological labelling approach to deviance and mental illness has been Erving Goffman (1957; 1959; 1961; 1963). Throughout his writings, Goffman focuses on society's reaction to individual behavior, stigmatization (1963), labelling, institutionalization (1961), and the ensuing identity and self-concept that develop. His main point is that mental illness is not the cause of psychiatric treatment and hospitalization, but its end result. In general, labelling theory simply turns the classical conception of deviance around: the conventional conception is that individual deviance, which is harmful to society, evokes social control; sociological labelling theory states the opposite, namely that society, by stigmatizing some individuals, creates deviants. The value position of each perspective is obvious. In one case, society is viewed as the victim, rightfully defending itself against criminals, psychotics, and other deviants. In the last case, it is the deviant who is the victim of society.[5] It is this perspective that constitutes the basis for the sociological attack on psychiatry.

The foremost renegade among psychiatrists is Thomas Szasz (1961; 1970; 1971). According to Szasz, psychiatry is a pseudoscience founded on a major conceptual error committed by such early psychiatrists as Charcot and Freud. Until the twentieth century, it was recognized that human problems could be one of two kinds— either physical or moral and behavioral. The former were the domain of medical science, the latter belonged to religion and the law. However, psychiatry introduced a third conceptual category, the *functional illness*. It did this because it noted a large number of behavioral problems with no apparent physical causes and also, on humanitarian grounds, because some harmless forms of deviance (homosexuality, hallucination) were dealt with harshly. Sin thus became illness, evil became sick, thereby absolving those deviants from responsibility for their conduct. Increasingly, certain categories of deviants were seen as driven to their actions by illness rather than by deliberate choice. The concept of guilt was replaced by incompetence, punishment by treatment.

Szasz considers the many ramifications of the psychiatric innovation and concludes that it was an error. He argues for a return to a clear distinction between the only two logical possibilities: medical problems should be treated by medical science, and moral problems should be dealt with by the law insofar as they harm society and by a new *humanistic* psychiatry insofar as they do not. As it is, the confusion is total

and individual civil liberties are trampled under: psychiatry terms itself a science, which it is not. Its most basic distinction is between neuroses and psychoses, which sometimes simply means curable versus noncurable disorders but often also refers to functional versus organic disturbances. It uses medical substances (drugs) and procedures (lobotomy) to treat mental illness, particularly those classified as psychotic or organic. All of this is nonsense, for insofar as an illness is organic, it is not mental, and conversely neuroses are not illnesses at all. What are they? According to Szasz, they represent interpersonal problems resulting from one's inability or unwillingness to play the situationally appropriate *games* or to accept the *meanings* shared by others.

For the individual, the problem boils down to an existential choice. According to Szasz, the fundamental struggle in society is about definitions, definitions of truth, reality, good, and evil. To accept the definitions of psychiatry is to acquiesce in the permanent victory of the definers over the defined. The existential choice before each of us is whether to submit to the psychiatric dogma—for psychiatry is the new church of America and psychiatrists are its priests (Szasz, 1971)—or to remain free. And as Camus (1954) knew, man is free as long as he is a rebel.

Szasz is not alone in pointing out the similarities between psychiatry and religion. According to Dr. E. Fuller Torrey's (1971) witty speech before a psychiatric convention, psychiatry has more in common with witchcraft than with science. For example, there may be "a relationship between the face paint and mask commonly adopted by therapists in other cultures and the beard and pipe used by psychiatrists in our own culture." And "dream analysis, the focal point of Freudian analysis, goes back at least 300 years to the Iroquois Indians." Also, the farther a patient goes for treatment, the greater the chance of success. "This is called the pilgrimage," said

---

[5]Howard Becker's article "Whose side are we on?" (1967) discusses this matter.

Torrey. "Thus sick people in Boston may go to the Menninger Clinic in Topeka while sick people in Topeka go to the Leahy Clinic in Boston. The resulting therapeutic effects of the trip are exactly the same as have operated at Delphi or Lourdes for centuries."

All jests aside, Szasz's position is philosophically unassailable. However, its current viability must be questioned, for psychiatry's power resides precisely in its ability to disarm all such heresies by labelling them and those who formulate them.[6]

Evaluation

Psychiatry, then, succeeds in fending off its attackers by labelling them or by coopting at least part of their arguments. As a symbolic universe (see Berger and Luckmann, 1966), it is vigorous precisely because it is capable of doing this. Its assumptions and its vocabulary provide it with the mechanisms and the conceptual tools with which to neutralize heretics such as Goffman and Szasz. Martindale and Martindale (1973) have evaluated the psychiatric and the antipsychiatric positions, assuming a somewhat moderate stance, especially vis-a-vis the issue of involuntary hospitalization. In the end, these authors nevertheless work in the hand of psychiatry, for they label the American Association for the Abolition of Involuntary Mental Hospitalization a crusade and its leaders, Szasz and Goffman, crusaders. Thus the labelling process is now underway.

The outcome of the struggle for definitions between psychiatry and such groups as the AAAIMH cannot be predicted at this time. In any event, one should pay attention to the antipsychiatric argument. It is basically a humanistic stance that sees the

prospect of total behavior control as totalitarian and repugnant. The point has been made not only in scholarly writings but also, perhaps most poignantly, in Ken Kesey's *One Flew Over the Cuckoo's Nest*. Essentially, the humanist rejects both the desirability and the feasibility of total behavior control, psychiatric programming, and an *objective* morality based on science.

SUMMARY AND CONCLUSION

This chapter has surveyed scientific psychology, focusing on the major theoretical orientations in that field today. All were found lacking. Underneath any question asked, there lies a presumed metaphor, a picture. The behavioral disciplines are based on certain images held about the nature of man, society, and communication. For example, Durkheim's sociology, which is so highly representative of the scientific sociology discussed in the previous chapter, presupposes a metaphor in which society is a container of individuals, determining and constraining those individuals' behavior (see Stone and Farberman, 1967).

The metaphors underlying the psychologies discussed in this chapter include the mechanistic metaphor, the species metaphor, and the Gestalt metaphor.[7] Behaviorism is based on the mechanistic metaphor. In Fig. 2-5, this metaphor is once again presented, along with some of its implications.

Fig. 2-5 suggests why a mechanistic metaphor has been so seductive. It fits our grammar and provides the basic format for scientific research. However, while behaviorism is the most rigorously positivistic orientation discussed in this chapter, it focuses only on what Becker (1962) calls type one and type two reactivity, the mechanical reaction of the organism to unconditioned and conditioned stimuli. We saw that neobehaviorism expands classical behaviorism's analysis by introducing such concepts

---

[6]Psychiatry is a perfect example of Berger and Luckmann's (1966) concept of the *symbolic universe*. See those authors and Berger's other treatises in the sociology of religion for brilliant discussions of the various universe maintenance mechanisms used by such systems.

[7]The next few pages go back, to a large extent, to the inspiring classes and seminars in social psychology taken from Gregory Stone at the University of Minnesota.

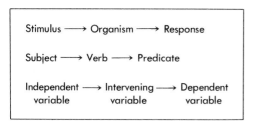

Stimulus ⟶ Organism ⟶ Response

Subject ⟶ Verb ⟶ Predicate

Independent ⟶ Intervening ⟶ Dependent
variable   variable   variable

FIG. 2-5
The mechanistic metaphor underlying behaviorism and its implications for language and research.

Unicellular organisms	Indeterminate	Mammals	Primates	Homo sapiens
(ameba)	(worm)	(dog)	(chimpanzee)	(man)

Complexity

FIG. 2-6
Species metaphor underlying Freudian psychology.

as drive and cue, recognizing thereby the internal origin of behavior. However, the overall orientation was found lacking because of its erroneous conception of the relationship between the person and his environment. Behaviorism assumes that objective environmental stimuli impinge on the person, who in turn reacts to them in a more or less passive and predictable fashion. Actually, the relationship is far more complex. The same stimulus will elicit different responses from different individuals, depending on the *meaning* each of them attaches to it, that is, depending on the subject's *definition of the situation,* which is partially the product of his personal background, partially arrived at socially with others, and always an emergent property of the situation at hand. This activity of individual interpretation is what Mead called the "I." The I makes human experience meaningful. "Stimulus," then, which is inherently meaningless, acquires an entirely new character when it comes to its experience by humans. The person is in active interaction with his environment, interpreting it and thereby altering it. This symbolic manipulation of the environment by ego is what we call *thinking*. Despite the fact that behaviorism totally overlooks these fundamental facts, Skinner and his

followers continue to have the greatest impact on scientific research, both in psychology and in sociology.

Psychoanalytic psychology, founded by Freud, took a somewhat different departure. Its major contribution was the recognition of the irrational and the subconscious element in human behavior. Reviewing Freud's stages of psychosexual development and his conception of personality—the id, ego and superego—we saw that Freud's theories have great relevance for psychiatry and for sociology.

Both the Freudians and the neo-Freudians assume that diagnosis and treatment must proceed through the uncovering of early childhood experiences, fixations, and repressions. Hence clinical psychology's widespread use of indirect techniques such as the TAT, Rorschach, and MMPI.

However, Freudian psychology, along with other forms of instinctivisms, relies on what has been termed the "species metaphor," a conception reproduced in Fig. 2-6.

The basic fallacy of this metaphor, as Becker (1962) points out, is to view the differences between the five levels of complexity in Fig. 2-6 as merely quantitative. In fact, each higher level is qualitatively different. Human conduct, for example, is distinguished by the *symbolic transformation* which takes place at that level. Thus the metaphor commits the fallacy of *anthropormorphism;* it sees human features and motives in animal conduct. One hears, for example, of dogs feeling guilt, or acting on a hypothesis. Also, Freudian psychology notoriously commits what may be called "adultomorphism," the imputation of adult motives to children.

At issue here, as throughout this book, is not so much the *validity* of the competing metaphors under review as their *relevance.* Indeed, the species metaphor provides us with some knowledge about man's metabolic requirements, and it is useful in explaining his response under extreme physical deprivation and his bizarre behavior. However, it does not answer the questions that social psychology poses. Our question is not why the organism controls man but why man controls his organism; not why man must eat but why some men eat hamburgers while others eat grasshoppers and monks fast several weeks on end. Need psychology, then, which is so typical of this orientation, is tautological and relatively useless for social psychology.

Psychological social psychology was our term for the Gestalt and field traditions. On the basis of the pioneering work of such German psychologists as Wolfgang Kohler and Kurt Lewin, American psychologists have produced a vast amount of experimental research on group dynamics. The fundamental theoretical assumption is that experience is contextual; perception, motivation, and interaction are determined by the total field of forces in which they take place. The realization that stimuli are thus *interpreted* and *make subjective sense* was a great step forward. However, the Gestalt metaphor merely adds, so to speak, an interpretive sense to man's other five senses. This does not grasp the fact that interpretation is the process of *symbolic interaction* and communication between the

subject and the environment. And since man's environment essentially consists of others, the interpretive process is a social dialogue in which all participants are both subject and object. Furthermore, as we shall see in Chapter 6 and beyond, the internal dialogue between the I and the me and our social interactions with others are closely linked to each other, for in time the me within us comes to represent others. The Gestalt perspective overlooks these complexities.

The group experience movement is our summary term for all forms of encounters, sensitivity training, group therapy, and Gestalt therapy on the market since the 1960s. The theoretical origins of this enterprise were pointed out. Furthermore, it was argued that, although some of these techniques have shown some effectiveness in satisfying their customers, the most salient characteristic of the group therapy fad has been the commercial exploitation of a gullible public.[8] In general, the public is bound to remain cheated in the bargain, for whatever it is that group experiences offer, they do not solve the basic problems plaguing society. It is a solipsist fallacy that drives millions of frustrated housewives, students, and professionals to group facilitators. In fact, today's citizen is a powerless atom in a mass society, and no amount of tinkering with the self will affect the gigantic structural and historical forces that are the true causes of individual conditions.

We finally took a separate look at psychiatry. It was shown that all major theoretical branches have had an input into the mental health profession. We examined the antipsychiatry argument of sociologists like Erving Goffman and psychiatrists such as Thomas Szasz. That argument is based on the realization that psychiatry is a moral

---

[8]A recent example is EST (Erhard Seminar Training). For $250, a person can join two hundred others in a packed hotel ballroom and spend a weekend learning how to "get it," that is, to learn a combination of vulgar Zen and plain relaxing. Since, as Festinger showed, people learn to appreciate what costs them dearly, most EST graduates profess to have become much happier (cf. *Newsweek,* 1975).

enterprise, not a scientific one, having far more in common with religion than with medicine. Thus "mental illness," as Szasz argues, is a myth, a pseudoscientific label conveniently applied to behavior deemed undesirable. As Szasz once said, in the animal kingdom there are only two possibilities, to eat or to be food; similarly, in human society one defines or one is defined. And the definitions that ultimately constitute social reality are simply, as Peter Berger noted, those imposed by the man with the biggest stick.

As Whorf (1956) concludes, "there are certain courses that psychology has elected to follow that have estranged it, perhaps permanently, from the truly mental field." According to that author, psychology is essentially behavioristic, physiological, and, in the case of Freudian psychology, only concerned with the abnormal. In the final analysis the critique of scientific psychology boils down to the same arguments as those applied against scientific sociology. The fundamental distinction underlying this book is that made for example by Douglas (1970) and Wilson (1970) in their distinction between *absolutist* or *normative paradigms* on the one hand and *phenomenological* or *interpretive approaches* on the other. The two features shared by all branches of psychology discussed in this chapter are *positivism,* a belief that the only valid data are those that are objectively and empirically observable, and *moral absolutism,* the belief that it is possible and desirable to determine a normative system for human behavior based on science and with transcendental, or objective, validity.

REFERENCES

Adorno, T. W. et al.
1950 The Authoritarian Personality. New York: Harper & Row, Publishers.
Alexander, Franz and Helen Ross
1952 "Concepts of dynamic psychiatry." Dynamic Psychiatry 12: 578.
Allardt, Erik
1958 "Sociology and small groups." Nya Argus (April):123-125.
Allport, Floyd H.
1920 Journal of Experimental Psychology 3: 159-182.
Aronson, Elliot
1972 The Social Animal. San Francisco: W. H. Freeman and Co.
Aronson, Elliot and Robert Helmreich (eds.)
1973 Social Psychology: a Transaction-Society Reader. New York: Van Nostrand Co.
Asch, Solomon E.
1942 Social Psychology. Englewood Cliffs, N.J.: Prentice-Hall, Inc., chap. 16.
Back, Kurt W.
1972 Beyond Words. Baltimore: Penguin Books.
Bales, Robert F.
1970 Personality and Interpersonal Behavior. New York: Holt, Rinehart & Winston.
Bandura, Albert and R. H. Walters
1963 Social Learning and Personality Development. New York: Holt, Rinehart and Winston.
Baron, Robert A. et al.
1974 Social Psychology: Understanding Human Interaction. Boston: Allyn and Bacon, Inc.
Barton, Anthony
1974 Three Worlds of Therapy: An Existential-Phenomenological Study of the Therapies of Freud, Jung, and Rogers. Palo Alto, Calif.: National Press Books.
Bavelas, Alex
1971 "Leadership: man and function." In Current Perspectives in Social Psychology. Edwin P. Hollander and G. Hunt (eds.). New York: Oxford University Press, pp. 495-503.
Becker, Ernest
1962 The Birth and Death of Meaning. Glencoe, Ill.: The Free Press.
Becker, Howard
1967 "Whose side are we on?" Social Problems (Winter): 239-247.
Berger, Bennett
1972 Review symposium: Beyond freedom and dignity, by B. F. Skinner. New York: Alfred A. Knopf, Inc., 1971. In American Journal of Sociology (November): 705-708.
Berger, Peter and Thomas Luckmann
1966 The Social Construction of Reality. Garden City, N.Y.: Doubleday & Co., Inc.
Berne, Eric
1947 The Mind in Action. New York: Simon and Schuster.
1957 A Layman's Guide to Psychiatry and Psychoanalysis. New York: Simon and Schuster.
1964 Games People Play—The Psychology of Human Relationships. New York: Grove Press.
Bickman, Leonard and Thomas Henchy
1972 Beyond the Laboratory: Field Research in Social Psychology. New York: McGraw-Hill Book Co.

Blanck, Gertrude and Rubin Blanck
  1974 Ego Psychology: Theory and Practice. New York: Columbia University Press.
Boguslaw, Robert
  1972 Review symposium: Beyond freedom and dignity, by B. F. Skinner. In Contemporary Sociology (January): 23-29.
Brown, Norman
  1959 Life Against Death. Middletown, Conn.: Wesleyan University Press.
Camus, Albert
  1954 The Rebel. New York: Vintage Books.
Cartwright, Dorwin and Alvin Zander (eds.)
  1953 Group Dynamics. Evanston, Ill.: Row, Peterson.
Chomsky, Noam
  1971 The case against B. F. Skinner." New York Review of Books (December): 18-24.
  1972 "On Skinner's 'verbal behavior'." In Classic Contributions to Social Psychology. Edwin P. Hollander and Raymond Hunt (eds.). New York: Oxford University Press, pp. 275-282.
Conger, Rand and Peter Killeen
  1974 "Use of concurrent operants in small group research." Pacific Sociological Review (October): 399-416.
Cooper, Joseph B. and James L. McGaugh
  1963 Integrating Principles of Social Psychology. Cambridge, Mass.: Schenkman Publishing Co., Inc.
Dahlstrom, W. Grant and George S. Welsh
  1960 An MMPI Handbook—A Guide to Use in Clinical Practice and Research. Minneapolis: University of Minnesota Press.
Deutsch, Morton and Robert M. Krauss
  1965 Theories in Social Psychology. New York: Basic Books, Inc.
Doby, John T.
  1966 Introduction to Social Psychology. New York: Appleton-Century-Crofts.
Dollard, John et al.
  1939 Frustration and Aggression. New Haven, Conn.: Yale University Press.
Dollard, John and Neal E. Miller
  1950 Personality and Psychotherapy: An Analysis in Terms of Learning, Thinking, and Culture. New York: McGraw-Hill Book Co.
Douglas, Jack D. (ed.)
  1970 Understanding Everyday Life: Toward the Reconstruction of Sociological Knowledge. Chicago: Aldine Publishing Co.
Elms, Alan C.
  1972 Social Psychology and Social Relevance. Boston: Little, Brown and Co.
Erikson, Eric H.
  1950 Childhood and Society. New York: W. W. Norton & Co.

Evans, Richard I. and Richard M. Rozelle (eds.)
  1973 Social Psychology in Life. Boston: Allyn and Bacon, Inc.
Eysenck, Hans J.
  1961 "The effects of psychotherapy." In Social Psychology Through Symbolic Interaction. Gregory P. Stone and Harvey A. Farberman (eds.). Waltham, Mass.: Ginn-Blaisdell, pp. 718-763.
  1969a "Theories of hypnosis." In Readings in Social Psychology. Alfred R. Lindesmith and Anselm L. Strauss (eds.). New York: Holt, Rinehart and Winston, pp. 192-194.
  1969b "Behavior under hypnosis." In Readings in Social Psychology. Alfred R. Lindesmith and Anselm L. Strauss (eds.). New York: Holt, Rinehart and Winston, pp. 195-202.
Festinger, Leon
  1954 "A theory of social comparison processes." Human Relations 7: 117-140.
  1957 A Theory of Cognitive Dissonance. Evanston, Ill.: Row, Peterson.
  1961 The psychological effects of insufficient reward." American Psychologist 16: 1-11.
Festinger, Leon and J. M. Carlsmith
  1959 "Cognitive consequences of forced compliance." Journal of Abnormal and Social Psychology 58: 203-210.
Fiedler, Fred E.
  1972 "Leadership and leadership effectiveness traits: a reconceptualization of the leadership trait problem." In Classic Contributions to Social Psychology. Edwin P. Hollander and Raymond G. Hunt (eds.). New York: Oxford University Press.
Frankl, Viktor
  1963 Man's Search for Meaning. New York: Beacon Press.
Franklin, Billy J. and Frank J. Kohout (eds.)
  1973 Social Psychology and Everyday Life. New York: David McKay.
Freud, Sigmund
  1924 A General Introduction to Psychoanalysis. New York: Boni and Liveright Publishing Corporation.
  1946 Civilization and Its Discontents. London: Hogarth Press.
Friedan, Betty
  1963 The Feminine Mystique. New York: Dell Publishing Co.
Friedrichs, Robert W.
  1974 "The potential impact of B. F. Skinner upon American sociology." The American Sociologist (February): 3-8.
Fromm, Erich
  1941 Escape From Freedom. New York: Farrar & Rinehart.
  1957 The Art of Loving. London: Unwin Books.
Gergen, Kenneth
  1974 Social Psychology: Explorations in Understanding. Del Mar, Calif.: CRM Books.

Goffman, Erving
1957 "Alienation from interaction." Human Relations I: 47-59.
1959 "The moral career of the mental patient." Psychiatry (May): 123-142.
1961 Asylums. Garden City, N.Y.: Doubleday & Co., Inc.
1963 Stigma: Notes on the Management of Spoiled Identity. Englewood Cliffs, N.J.: Prentice-Hall, Inc.
1967 Interaction Ritual: Essays in Face-to-Face Behavior. Chicago: Aldine Publishing Co., pp. 113-136.

Grossack, Martin and Howard Gardner
1970 Man and Men: Social Psychology as Social Science. Scranton, Pa.: International Textbook Co.

Gyman, Harry
1973 Review of Robert L. Hamblin's (et al.) The humanization processes: a social behavioral analysis of children's problems. Society (July/August): 92-93.

Harris, Thomas A.
1967 I'm OK—You're OK. New York: Avon Books.

Hilgard, Ernest R.
1957 Introduction to Psychology. New York: Harcourt, Brace and Co.

Hollander, Edwin P.
1971 Principles and Methods of Social Psychology. London: Oxford University Press.

Hollander, Edwin P. and Raymond G. Hunt (eds.)
1971 Current Perspectives in Social Psychology. New York: Oxford University Press.
1972 Classic Contributions to Social Psychology. New York: Oxford University Press.

Homans, George C.
1972 "Social behavior as exchange." In Classic Contributions to Social Psychology. Edwin P. Hollander and Raymond G. Hunt (eds.). New York: Oxford University Press, pp. 150-160.

Horney, Karen
1950 Neurosis and Human Growth. New York: W. W. Norton and Co.

Hovland, C. I. and R. R. Sears
1940 "Minor studies in aggression, VI: Correlation of lynchings with economic indices." Journal of Psychology 9: 301-310.

Hull, Clark L.
1943 Principles of Behavior. New York: Appleton Century.

Jones, E. E.
1972 Attribution: Perceiving the Causes of Behavior. New York: General Learning Press.

Kaluger, George and Charles M. Unkovic
1969 Psychology and Sociology: an Integrated Approach to Understanding Human Behavior. St. Louis: The C. V. Mosby Co.

Keyes, Ken, Jr.
Handbook to Higher Consciousness. Berkeley: Living Love Center.

Keyes, Ken, Jr. and Tolly Burkan
How to Make Your Life Work or Why Aren't You Happy? Berkeley: Living Love Center.

Laing, R. D.
1965 The Divided Self. London: Pelican Books.

Lambert, William W. and Wallace E. Lambert
1964 Social Psychology. Englewood Cliffs, N.J.: Prentice-Hall, Inc.

Lambert, William W. and F. H. Lowy
1957 "Effects of the presence of others on expresses attitudes." Canadian Journal of Psychology 11: 151-156

Lambert, William W. and Rita Weisbrod
1971 Comparative Perspectives on Social Psychology. Boston: Little, Brown and Co.

Lemert, Edwin
1948 "Some aspects of a general theory of sociopathic behavior." Proceedings of the Pacific Sociological Society 16(1): 24-25.
1951 Social Pathology. New York: McGraw-Hill Book Co.

Lerner, M. J.
1965 "Evaluation of performance as a function of performer's reward and attractiveness." Journal of Personality and Social Psychology 1: 355-360.

Lewin, Kurt
1938 "The conceptual representation and measurement of psychological forces." Contributions to Psychological Theory 1(4).

Lindesmith, Alfred R., Anselm Strauss, and Norman Denzin
1975 Social Psychology, ed. 4. Hinsdale, Ill.: The Dryden Press.

Lindzey, Gardner and Elliot Aronson
1968 The Handbook of Social Psychology (5 volumes). Reading, Mass.: Addison-Wesley Publishing Co.

Luft, Joseph
1970 Group Processes: An Introduction to Group Dynamics. Palo Alto, Calif.: National Press Books.

MacDonald, Richard R. and James A. Schellenberg (eds.)
1971 Selected Readings and Projects in Social Psychology. New York: Random House, Inc.

Machotka, Otakar
1964 The Unconscious in Social Relations. New York: Philosophical Library.

Marcuse, Herbert
1962 Eros and Civilization. New York: Vintage Books.

Marlow, Leigh
1971 Social Psychology: An Interdisciplinary Approach to Human Behavior. Boston: Holbrook Press.

Martindale, Don
1960 The Nature and Types of Sociological Theory. Boston: Houghton Mifflin Co.

Martindale, Don and Edith Martindale
1973 Psychiatry and the Law: The Crusade Against Involuntary Hospitalization. St. Paul, Minn.: Windflower Publishers.

Marwell, Gerald
1972 "Skinner: pro and con." Contemporary Sociology (January): 19-23.

Maslow, Abraham H.
1962 Toward a Psychology of Being. Princeton, N.J.: Van Nostrand Co.

McClelland, David C.
1961 The Achieving Society. Princeton, N.J.: Van Nostrand Co.

McDavid, John W. and Herbert Harari
1974 Psychology and Social Behavior. New York: Harper & Row, Publishers.

Miller, N. E. and R. Bugelski
1948 "The influence of frustrations imposed by the in-group on attitude expressed toward out-groups." Journal of Psychology 25: 437-442.

Moreno, J. L. (ed.)
1960 The Sociometry Reader. Glencoe, Ill.: Free Press.

Morgan, C. D. and H. A. Murray
1935 "A method for investigating fantasies: the Thematic Apperception Test." Archives of Neurology and Psychiatry 34: 289-306.

Murphy, Michael
Golf in the Kingdom. New York: Viking Press.

Natanson, Maurice
1970 The Journeying Self: A Study in Philosophy and Social Role. Reading, Mass.: Addison-Wesley Publishing Co.

Newcomb, Theodore M.
1953 "An approach to the study of communicative acts." Psychological Review 60: 393-404.
1956 "The prediction of interpersonal attraction." American Psychologist 11: 575-586.

Newsweek
1975 "Getting it." (February 17): 46.

Osgood, C. E.
1963 "On understanding and creating sentences." American Psychologist 18: 735-751.

Pavlov, I. P.
1927 Conditioned Reflexes. New York: Oxford University Press.

Perls, Fritz
1964 Ego Hunger and Aggression. New York: Random House, Inc.

Peterson, R. C. and L. L. Thurstone
1932 The Effect of Motion Pictures on the Social Attitudes of High School Children. Ann Arbor, Mich.: Edward Bros.

Reich, Wilhem
1961 Selected Writings: An Introduction to Orgonomy. New York: The Noonday Press.

Rogers, Carl R.
1961 On Becoming a Person. Boston: Houghton Mifflin Co.

Rokeach, Milton
1960 The Open and Closed Mind. New York: Basic Books, Inc.

Rorschach, H.
1942 Psychodiagnostics. Berne: Hans Huber.

Sampson, Edward E.
1971 Social Psychology and Contemporary Society. New York: John Wiley & Sons, Inc.

Scheff, Thomas J.
1966 Being Mentally Ill. Chicago: Aldine Publishing Co.

Schellenberg, James A.
1974 An Introduction to Social Psychology. New York: Random House, Inc.

Secord, Paul F. and Carl W. Backman
1974 Social Psychology. New York: McGraw-Hill Book Co.

Shaw, Jerry I. and Paul Skolnick
1973 "Attribution of responsibility for a happy accident." In Social Psychology in Life. Richard I. Evans and Richard M. Rozelle (eds.). Boston: Allyn and Bacon, Inc., pp. 407-416.

Sherif, Muzafer
1935 "A study of some social factors in perception." Archives of Psychology 27.

Shibutani, Tamotsu
1966 Review: The unconscious in social relations by Otakar Machotka. New York: Philosophical Library. American Journal of Sociology 71 (May): 727-728.

Shostrom, Everett L.
1968 Man the Manipulator: The Inner Journey from Manipulation to Actualization. New York: Bantam Books.

Skinner, B. F.
1948 Walden Two. New York: The Macmillan Co.
1957 Verbal Behavior. New York: Appleton-Century-Crofts.
1971 Beyond Freedom and Dignity. New York: Alfred A. Knopf.

Spitz, R.
1945 "Hospitalism." In The Psychoanalytic Study of the Child. O. Fenichel et al. (eds.). New York: International Universities Press.

Stone, Gregory P. and Harvey A. Farberman
1967 "On the edge of rapproachment: was Durkheim moving toward the perspective of symbolic interaction?" Sociological Quarterly (Spring): 149-164.
1970 Social Psychology Through Symbolic Interaction. Waltham: Mass.: Ginn-Blaisdell.

Strodtbeck, Fred L.
1973 "Bales 20 years later: a review essay." American Journal of Sociology (September): 459-465.

Sullivan, Harry Stack
1953 The Interpersonal Theory of Psychiatry. New York: W. W. Norton & Co.

Swanson, Guy E.
1972 "Mead and Freud: their relevance for social psychology." In Symbolic Interaction. Jerome G. Manis and Bernard N. Meltzer (eds.). Boston: Allyn and Bacon.

Szasz, Thomas
1961 The Myth of Mental Illness: Foundations of a Theory of Personal Conduct. New York: Dell Publishing Co.
1970 The Manufacture of Madness: A Comparative Study of the Inquisition and the Mental Health Movement. New York: Harper & Row, Publishers.
1971 "In the Church of America, psychiatrists are priests." Hospital Physician (October): 2-4.

Tarter, Donald E.
1973 "Heeding Skinner's call: toward the development of a social technology." American Sociologist 8 (November): 153-158.

Torrey, E. Fuller
1971 Interview. Los Angeles Times, March 24.

Vinacke, W. Edgar et al.
1964 Dimensions of Social Psychology. Chicago: Scott, Foresman and Co.

Walster, E.
1966 "Assignment of responsibility for an accident." Journal of Personality and Social Psychology 3: 73-79.

Washburn, Sherwood L. and David A. Hamburg
1969 "The study of primate behavior." In Readings in Social Psychology. Alfred R. Lindesmith and Anselm L. Strauss (eds.). New York: Holt, Rinehart and Winston.

Watson, Goodwin and David Johnson
1972 Social Psychology: Issues and Insights. New York: J. B. Lippincott Co.

Watson, John B.
1919 Psychology from the Standpoint of a Behaviorist. Philadelphia: J. B. Lippincott Co.

Wheelis, Allen
1958 "The quest for identity." In Analyses of Contemporary Society: I. Bernard Rosenberg (ed.). New York: Thomas Y. Crowell Co.
1974 The Moralist. Baltimore: Penguin Books.

Whorf, Benjamin Lee
1956 Language, Thought and Reality. Cambridge, Mass.: M.I.T. Press.

Wilson, Thomas P.
1970 "Normative and interpretive paradigms in sociology." In Understanding Everyday Life. Jack D. Douglas (ed.). Chicago: Aldine Publishing Co., pp. 57-79.

Wrightsman, Lawrence S.
1972 Social Psychology in the Seventies. Monterey, Calif.: Brooks-Cole Publishing Co.

Zeigarnik, Bluma
1927 "Das Behalten erledigter und unerledigter Handlungen." Psychologische Forschung 9: 1-85.

Zillig, Maria
1928 "Einstellung und Aussage." Zeitschrift fur Psychologie 106: 58-106.

chapter 3
Left-wing sociology

The first two chapters of this book have covered the two dominant establishment paradigms in the human disciplines—scientific sociology and scientific psychology. Since this is a textbook in social psychology, it is especially important to give an adequate coverage of the prevailing psychological theories. However, not everyone subscribes to one of those perspectives. A growing minority subscribes to a variety of radical notions derived from Marx or from a gut level, atheoretical stance, and this group has a growing impact on sociology, social policy, and ultimately our lives. We therefore devote a brief chapter to these tendencies.

Any discussion of leftism must begin with Karl Marx, the prophet, high priest, and evangelist of the left-wing sociological gospel. We shall also examine the varieties of neo-Marxisms, including contemporary American radicalism and critical sociology, the latter most popular in Europe but lately gaining adherents in the United States as well. In addition we shall, under a separate heading, look at the new left and the counterculture, noting that the radical youth movement of the late 1960s and 1970s contains both a rebellious and a retreatist wing. Finally, a brief evaluation will be offered. It will be suggested that Marx and the radicals have made valuable contributions to the sociology of knowledge perspective and to an understanding of our socioeconomic system, but that contemporary radicalism is neither the most enlightening theoretical perspective nor a promise of a better life for man.

MARX

Even the most superficial review of Marx's ideas must distinguish between Karl Marx (1818-1883) and Marxism. Like Freud, the German social philosopher towers over all others in his own realm, identified by history as single-handedly re-sponsible for a greater impact on mankind than perhaps anyone since Christ. However, Marxism is a loose label, referring variously to dialectical materialism, scientific socialism, communism, and a variety of radicalisms partially discussed in the subsequent parts of this chapter. In this book, we are interested in some of Marx's specific contributions because they are the foundation of the contemporary left-wing paradigm and we also, of course, examine that left-wing paradigm. *Communism*, which is the social system established in the Soviet Union and other countries in the twentieth century—also called Marxism-Leninism (cf. Sabine, 1963)—will not be dealt with. In addition to scientific socialism and dialectical materialism, we shall briefly deal with Marx's economic determinism, class conflict, and the inevitability of (violent) revolution.

It is Marx and the Marxists themselves who view their doctrine as the only form of "*scientific* socialism." Whereas the socialism of men like Henri de Saint-Simon and Pierre Proudhon was *utopian,* Marxism is allegedly scientific in that it is claimed to represent the discovery of true historical and sociological laws and to point, like any other science, to the inevitable shape of things to come. These things include revolution and the emergence of a classless society. However, ambiguity already becomes apparent when Marxism-Leninism, departing from orthodox Marxism, establishes (in Russia) the dictatorship of the proletariat and Lenin's democratic central-ism, a situation initially meant to be temporary but now of course the permanent hallmark of soviet communism, precluding forever the predicted emergence of the classless society. The emergence of the "new class" (cf. Djilas, 1957) is, of course, merely one of the innumerable problems with Marxism's scientific claims.

Of much greater inherent interest is

Marxism as a theory. As such, it is called *dialectical materialism,* indicating the two fundamental elements of Marxism—the dialectic and materialism.

Marx adopted the dialectical mode of reasoning from Georg Friedrich Hegel (1770-1831). According to that German philosopher, history is the dialectical unfolding of the absolute *idea.* It may be interpreted as follows: a proposition *(thesis)* necessarily provokes an opposite assertion *(antithesis),* and this contradiction is reconciled at a higher level of truth in the form of a third proposition (the *synthesis*). This, in turn, becomes a new thesis in the next dialectical equation, and so on ad infinitum. For example, the dominant thesis in Western society has been, since seventeenth century rationalism, a belief in reason, science, and progress through technology. The antithesis to this began to emerge in the form of nineteenth century Romanticism (of which Hegel himself was a part). Today, Western society is increasingly split between these two antagonistic ideas, one associated with the technocracy, the other with humanistic, irrational, and revolutionary opposition to it. A conceivable future synthesis might take a form not unlike that of some Asiatic conceptions of knowledge (although of course far more advanced)—reconciling science with feeling, spirit with matter.

Marxism, then, adopted from Hegel the fundamental *processual* orientation that the dialectic entails. As Engels (1941:44), Marx's life-long alter ego, wrote, "the great basic thought that the world is not to be comprehended as a complex of ready-made *things,* but as a complex of *processes*... in which, in spite of all seeming accidents and of all temporary retrogression, a progressive development asserts itself in the end—this great fundamental thought has, especially since the time of Hegel, so thoroughly permeated ordinary consciousness that in this generality it is scarcely ever contradicted."

However, Marx's important innovation was to transfer Hegel's dialectic from the realm of ideas to that of matter, hence the label dialectical materialism. A good summary of Marx's materialistic conception of history is provided by Marvin Harris (1968:4). As that author notes, "the principle (of historical materialism) holds that similar technologies applied to similar environments tend to produce similar arrangements of labour in production and distribution, and that these in turn call forth similar kinds of social groupings, which justify and co-ordinate their activities by means of similar systems of values and beliefs."

According to Marx and Engels, then, history is a dialectical process, but the moving forces in this process are not ideas, as Hegel maintained, but economic conditions. The deepest causes underlying social change are the *forces of production* (technology). These are reflected in the *relations of production* (the economic system), which in turn lead to the development of a cultural superstructure consisting essentially of ideological justifications for the existing economic relations. Religion is a case in point, since it merely functions as an opiate for the masses. The essence of Marxian materialism is that it views the economic infrastructure as cause, the cultural superstructure as effect. Marx is an economic determinist and a materialist simply because of the causal direction of his analysis, an analysis that therefore contrasts diametrically with all forms of philosophical idealism, including Hegel's and, as we shall see, Max Weber's.

If history is a dialectical process, then conflict is obviously of the essence—violent revolutionary conflict to the Marxists. As a new system of production evolves, it comes in increasing conflict with the persisting ideology appropriate to an older system (a phenomenon later called "cultural lag" by Ogburn) and with the older social classes committed to the older system. Eventually revolution is the result, after which the new productive system gradually develops itself and its ideologies. For example, the development of bourgeois capitalism made the great bourgeois revolutions of the eighteenth century (in 1776 in America, in 1789 in France, later elsewhere throughout industrializing Europe) inevitable, for the old nobility was unalterably opposed to capitalism. However, since then a new situation has gradually developed. Capitalism has created an industrial proletariat. Socialism is the indicated new economic system, but this is blocked by the increasingly obsolescent ideology of laissez-faire capitalism, which will be removed only through revolutionary class struggle between the proletariat and the capitalists.

Marxism, in sum, is based on a number of assumptions, including the following three: (1) materialism, (2) history as a dialectical process, and (3) the inevitability of conflict. These assumptions are unverified, unverifiable, and all equally questionable. (1) That true social change can only emanate from the material infrastructure is simply not so; witness the massive impact of the current cultural revolution in Western society. (2) Equally arbitrary is the assertion that there is, to every truth, an equally plausible antithesis. (3) Neither is it so, finally, that history is a succession of inevitable clashes (between classes, economic systems, or ideologies). Reform and evolution are, of course, viable alternatives to violent breaks with the past. To ignore continuity, as contemporary Marx-inspired radicalism does, is as arbitrary as to negate conflict, which was the bias of the earlier functionalists. Nevertheless, Marxism assumes for increasing numbers of radicals in the West and of course in the secular theocracies of Russia and China the exact character of a religion. Marxist texts are sacred documents (cf. Mullins, 1973:272), their interpretation is a meticulous ritual left to a handful of experts, and the power of this new religion is unrelated to its empirical validity, which is precisely the qualifying criterion for any religion. In sum, Marxism is a pow-

erful twentieth century paradigm, providing mystery, awe, meaning, and inspiration to millions of men because it combines powerful explanatory principles modelled after science with a concern with the social problem unanimously defined as the most important one by our sensate civilization—economic inequality. One might plausibly argue that mankind's crisis is a moral one, but not in today's world. Marxism is a materialistic philosophy for our overwhelmingly materialistic era.

CRITICAL SOCIOLOGY

Contemporary left-wing sociology can be divided into two strands: the populist American radicalism best exemplified by C. Wright Mills (1916-1963) and the neo-Marxian critical school, which is more theoretical and more European in its constituency.

Although Mills also oriented himself toward the Marxists (1962), his position, for example in *The Power Elite* (1956), is more accurately described as a mixture of radical populism and Weberianism. His work has often been in the symbolic interactionist (1970) and humanistic (1959) tradition. Mills' major contribution to radical sociology was his description of the American power structure as an "interlocking directorate" of the three power sectors in our society—the economy, the government, and the military. He, in effect, was responsible for the concept of the *military-industrial complex*.[1] When contemporary radicalism indicts *both* government and business, *both* the Washington bureaucracies and the corporations, it essentially follows in Mills' populist footsteps. According to this perspective, little relief can be expected from Washington, whether from one party or the other, whether from the executive, the legislative, or the judiciary, and whether from a lavish federal budget or a skimpy one, because the government and the corporations are in collusion against the work-

---

[1]It was President Eisenhower who used the concept in his Farewell Address. Thereafter, it became part of everyman's political lexicon (see Rose, 1967:36).

ingman. Thus it is a fallacy to expect taxation—viewed by the liberal as the fundamental equalizer in any society—to alleviate social injustice. Under the Millsian conception of the American power structure, governmental taxation in any form (Social Security, income tax, sales tax, tariffs) can be viewed as just another ripoff aimed at the subsidizing of ailing monopolies, the financing of political careers, and the erection of expensive bureaucracies at the expense of the working class. While this represents our own extrapolation of Mills, we feel strongly that twenty years later his vision is more accurate, and indeed more prophetic, than ever.

Current neocriticism is theoretically more esoteric. Unlike Mills' straightforward indictment of existing political conditions, the critical school engages in sophisticated forms of intellectual gamesmanship reminiscent of medieval scholastics. Indeed, the criticists recognize holy (Marxian) scriptures, canons of interpretation (such as the dialectic), and a rhetoric often clear only to the initiates. Such is the work of the so-called Frankfurt school, led by Jurgen Habermas, as well as that of French neo-Marxists and dialecticians behind the Iron Curtain (cf. East Germany's Robert Haveman's *Dialektik ohne Dogma?* [1964]).

Thus the critical school is mostly theoretical and European. One of its foremost propagators in America has been the German emigre Herbert Marcuse (1962; 1964). Well-known American criticists include Alvin Gouldner (1970), best known as the impetuous convert from functionalism who suddenly unmasked all "Western sociology"; Trent Schroyer, a critical sociologist concerned with neocapitalism; and Angela Davis, the colorful Marcuse disciple best known for her activism and her unfortunate brush with the law. Part of the American neocriticist's training often consists of the pilgrimage to Europe, as when Angela Davis spends her "stage" at Frankfurt or Alvin Gouldner his at Amsterdam. Evidence of the neocriticists' growing hold of sociology is the fact that

Tom Bottomore, best known as a neo-Marxist and life-long interpreter of Marx, became president of the International Sociological Association in 1974.

The critical school's position may be summed up in two generalizations. In the first place, it emphasizes, as did Marx, the ideological nature of all knowledge including positivistic science (cf. Schroyer, 1970). One of its major activities is therefore the study and interpretation of history, and its most valuable contribution is to the field of the sociology of knowledge. Second, its major target is technocratic capitalism, which is viewed as the source of economic injustice, as by Marx and old-line Marxists; as repressive of humanistic values and true freedom (including in some formulations sexual freedom; cf. Marcuse, 1962; 1964); and, most importantly, as the eliminator of the necessary dialectic of oppositions that makes true social change possible. Marcuse's argument (1964) is that our one-dimensional social system coopts and disarms all potential source of change, including intellectual dissent, sex, and love. The tragedy, then, is that the dialectic itself seems to come to an end.

THE NEW LEFT

We previously examined the scholarly and theoretical writings inspiring current left-wing radicalism in Western society. Those writings are essentially based on Marx. While we have labelled these authors neo-Marxists and criticists, it is not clear that all belong to the new left. Rather, they have provided the inspiration for the new left. Indeed, the major distinguishing feature of the new left has been its rejection of what it considers excessive theory and its emphasis on *activism*. Furthermore, it has tended to depart from old-line Marxism, which stresses discipline and organization, and to move toward anarchy. Whereas the old left is collectivistic, the new left is individualistic; while the old left emphasizes economic *equality,* the new left focuses on cultural and psychosexual *freedom.* Based on these criteria, Angela Davis, although a communist, may nevertheless be considered a member of the new left (her contribution has been to action more than theory), while Michael Harrington, one of America's eminent socialists, belongs to the old left. A radical student organization such as the Students for a Democratic Society belongs to the new left, but the American Communist Party belongs to the old left. Fig. 3-1 attempts to clarify these distinctions.

As Theodore Roszak (1969) noted, it is in the counterculture that Marx and Freud finally confront one another, and this is nowhere clearer than in the works of Marcuse, who therefore, despite his theoretical and Marxian orientation, straddles the old left–new left distinction. Indeed, Marcuse's work is a synthesis of Marxism and Freudianism. To the essential question "is liberation to be social or sexual, is it to be collective class struggle against the capitalists, or is it to be the psychic and cultural liberation of the individual?" Marcuse answers: both. While the philosopher recognizes that postindustrial society's central problems, unlike those of the industrial society to which Marx addressed himself, are psychological alienation and sexual repression, he nevertheless believes that technocratic capitalism is at the roots of these problems. Most exciting is Marcuse's concept of *repressive desublimation.* According to this concept, our society permits, and indeed encourages, through mass media, culture, and advertising, increasing sexual permissiveness precisely to rob sexuality of its truly subversive potential. By desexualizing sex itself, capitalism forces man to repress his true emotional needs and meanwhile reaps the benefits of an apathetic consumerism.

While Marcuse recognizes the importance of both politics and sex, other authors have become increasingly psychologistic in their radicalism. As Roszak (1969) shows, Norman Brown (1959) and others look almost exclusively at psychic liberation. Ultimately, then, radicalism reaches an entirely apolitical and retreatist position, a position best exemplified by the hippies.[2]

In sum, the counterculture of the 1960s and 1970s can best be analyzed in terms of Merton's (1957) famous typology of deviant adaptations to anomie (see Chapter 1). It contains both *rebellious* elements and a *retreatist* wing. Rebellion is the political activism and the revolutionary activity—sometimes violent, as in the case of the Symbionese Liberation Army—of the new left. Retreatism is the dropping out and the cultural revolution of the hippie, a sub-

---

[2]For an analysis of the counterculture and the various brands of youth culture and youth rebellion since World War II, see Kando (1975). This reference, along with Davis (1971), provides an extensive bibliography on the pertinent literature.

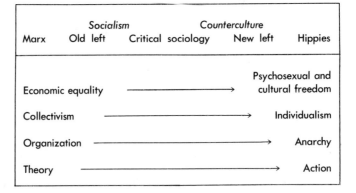

FIG. 3-1
The left.

| | Socialism | | Counterculture | |
Marx	Old left	Critical sociology	New left	Hippies
Economic equality	$\longrightarrow$			Psychosexual and cultural freedom
Collectivism	$\longrightarrow$			Individualism
Organization	$\longrightarrow$			Anarchy
Theory	$\longrightarrow$			Action

culture centering around mysticism, spiritual values, drugs, and sexual and affective bonds, among other things.

SUMMARY AND CONCLUSION

Some evaluative hints of the left-wing paradigm have already been made. It was suggested earlier that Marx and radical-critical sociology have made important theoretical contributions, but that contemporary radical activism must be viewed with skepticism, since it has demonstrated great negative power but has yet to show a far-sighted *constructive* capability.

Marx's own doctrine, as we saw, is based on a number of questionable assumptions about the nature of the world, including the dialectic and material primacy. Nevertheless, Marx launched the sophisticated analysis of culture that subsequently became known as the sociology of knowledge. When Peter Berger (1963) describes contemporary sociology as essentially a *debunking* enterprise, this in many ways restates Marx's program, a program based on the assumption that the knowledge, culture, values, attitudes, norms, and law that people frequently take for granted are actually determined by their position in society. Contemporary critcal sociology continues to make valuable contributions to the field of the sociology of knowledge, as when for example Trent Schroyer (1970) explains technocratic science as a *legitimation* of the neocapitalist economic structure. In the end, however, the sociology of knowledge must be turned on the Marxists themselves, since their own perspective needs to be related to their social-structural position. An obvious yet untested hypothesis is that Marxism, critical sociology, and conflict theories of all kinds are popular among intellectuals in proportion to and because of their alienation, powerlessness, and failure at upward mobility. This was lucidly stated by the late Joseph Schumpeter (1947), among others. A good case in point is none other than Marx himself, who became radicalized *after* early career failures.

The contemporary new left and the counterculture have failed to deliver the promises that may have been perceived in the idealistic youth movement of the 1960s. It was explained earlier that two strands can be distinguished in this sector—an actively *rebellious* new left and a *retreatist* wing commonly associated with the hippies. While the new left is political, it is generally atheoretical and anarchistic, thereby differing from the old left. Through cooptation, diffusion, and other processes, the new left is partially responsible for the end of the Vietnam war, Watergate, sexual liberation, the cultural revolution, the reconstitution of education, ecology, the crisis of confidence in authority, and, paradoxically, the increasing role of government generally associated with socialism. The retreatist wing of the counterculture is a partially hedonistic, partially spiritual movement. Important elements of this subculture include drugs and sexual liberation as well as intuition, faith, the irrational, the occult, consciousness—in sum, *alternative* forms of knowledge.

At best, the new left and the counterculture have attempted to construct alternative political structures, life-styles, values, and theories, emphasizing equality and freedom, both of which are perceived to be lacking in conventional society—hence the name *counter*culture. However, the results have often been deplorable, since alternative politics have often come to mean anarchy, alternative values nihilism, alternative life-styles sensate hedonism, and alternative theories know-nothing antiintellectualism. In the realm of values, socialization, and education, the rejection of the old has not led to its replacement by the new but often to ignorance, chaos, moral vacuum, selfishness, and failure. Radicalism has meant the courageous peace movement and freedom marches of the 1960s. However, it has also often come to mean flight into heavy drugs, anomie, retreatism, and common crime.

REFERENCES

Berger, Peter
  1963 Invitation To Sociology. Garden City, N.Y.: Doubleday & Co., Inc.

Brown, Norman
  1959 Life Against Death. Middletown, Conn.: Wesleyan University Press.

Davis, Fred
  1971 On Youth Subcultures: The Hippie Variant. New York: General Learning Corporation.

Djilas, Milovan
  1957 The New Class. New York: Frederick A. Praeger.

Engels, Friedrich
  1941 Ludwig Feuerbach and the Outcome of German Classical Philosophy. New York: International Publishers.

Gouldner, Alvin W.
  1970 The Coming Crisis of Western Sociology. New York: Basic Books, Inc.

Harris, Marvin
  1968 The Rise of Anthropology. London: Routledge and Kegan Paul.

Haveman, Robert
  1964 Dialektik ohne Dogma? Reinbek bei Hamburg: Rowohlt.

Kando, Thomas M.
  1975 Leisure and Popular Culture in Transition. St. Louis: The C. V. Mosby Co.

Marcuse, Herbert
  1962 Eros and Civilization. New York: Vintage Books.
  1964 One-Dimensional Man; Studies in the Ideology of Advanced Industrial Society. Boston: Beacon Press.

Merton, Robert K.
  1957 Social Theory and Social Structure. New York: Free Press.

Mills, C. Wright
  1956 The Power Elite. New York: Oxford University Press.
  1959 The Sociological Imagination. New York: Oxford University Press.
  1962 The Marxists. New York: Oxford University Press.
  1970 "Situated actions and vocabularies of motive." In Gregory P. Stone and Harvey A. Farberman (eds.). Social Psychology Through Symbolic Interaction. Waltham, Mass.: Ginn-Blaisdell, pp. 472-479.

Mullins, Nicholas C.
  1973 Theories and Theory Groups in Contemporary American Sociology. New York: Harper & Row, Publishers.

Rose, Arnold M.
  1967 The Power Structure; Political Process in America. New York: Oxford University Press.

Roszak, Theodore
  1969 The Making of a Counterculture. Garden City, N.Y.: Doubleday & Co., Inc.

Sabine, George H.
  1963 A History of Political Theory. London: George G. Harrap & Co. Ltd.

Schroyer, Trent
  1970 "Toward a critical theory for advanced industrial society." In Recent Sociology, No. 2. Hans Peter Dreitzel (ed.). London: The Macmillan Co.

Schumpeter, Joseph
  1947 Capitalism, Socialism and Democracy. New York: Harper & Row, Publishers.

chapter 4
Right-wing psychology*

A case can perhaps be made for viewing sociology as an *inherently* left-wing discipline and psychology as *inherently* right-wing. This is plausible if one somehow associates the political left with collectivism and the right with individualism, the left with equality and the right with both freedom and elitism. In any event, it is clear that sociology today is increasingly dominated by a series of left-wing thrusts, including feminism, third-world liberation, affirmative action, and other *collectivist* and levelling social movements.

On the other hand, psychology, as we saw, is in the throes of the group-induced psychic liberation movement—an eminently do-your-own-thing individualism. In addition, there is an older and at times more sinister form of individualism in psychology, the tradition associated with Anglo-Saxon instinctivism and ultimately the ideologies of racism and social Darwinism. Furthermore, right-wing psychology also includes French crowd psychology and German folk psychology, the latter highly collectivistic but also racist. In sum, there is a brand of psychology that rejects the environmentalist tabula rasa assumption of behaviorism and instead maximizes the importance of inborn biological differences between individuals, between races, and between social classes. In the old nature-nurture controversy, right-wing psychology opts for nature, arguing that differences in aptitude, intelligence, skill, and capabilities of all sorts are inborn, inevitable, and not the result of learning. According to this position, all men are definitely *not* created equal. While French

crowd psychology avoids the biologism of the other schools under review in this chapter, it, too, is equally elitist, certainly in the case of Gustave Le Bon. It is therefore included in the present discussion.

This chapter, then, examines right-wing psychology, pointing among other things at its recent resurgence in a number of semipopular works emphasizing aggression (Lorenz, 1966), territoriality (Ardrey, 1966), pair-bonding (Morris, 1967), and other presumably innate characteristics. The nature-nurture argument will be examined, with specific reference to six salient issues, and both sides will be evaluated. It will be shown that the "nature" position has, in some cases, validity, but that its ideological implications are in many ways dangerous.

GERMAN FOLK PYSCHOLOGY

By the middle of the nineteenth century, a reaction against the early associationists had begun to set in. One began to realize that man is by no means always rational, as the seventeenth and eighteenth century rationalists assumed—not even subjectively rational. Understandably, this realization was most marked in the national and cultural milieu least affected by the rationalist tradition, Germany. Indeed, among the various areas of the West, the reaction against rationalism (also known as romanticism) must unquestionably by associated with Germany more than with any other cultural area. Just as French culture, for example, remains predominantly anchored in the rationalist tradition, so history shows that the Germanic contributions to Western civilization became overwhelming during the Romantic era. With all due overlap granted, the most cursory examination of art, music, philosophy, and social thought shows that nineteenth century ro-

*While this entire book owes much to the teachings of my former mentors at the University of Minnesota, especially Don Martindale, the late Arnold Rose, and Gregory Stone, the influence of Arnold Rose's course in social psychology—Sociology 120—on this chapter needs special acknowledgment.

manticism must be associated first and foremost with Germanic Europe.

Thus it was in Germany that the discourse about human behavior and human psychology shifted most markedly away from environment and toward *heredity*. Man's behavior was now increasingly perceived as the product of not only his own experience but also that of his ancestors— his *folk*. To act "naturally," as opposed to rationally, came to mean acting in accordance with the folk experience. And since each folk has a different historical experience, differences in national character are due precisely to differences in ancestral experience, *not* to culture.

Men like Wilhelm Wundt (1832-1920) represent this school of thought. It includes the belief in racial memory and in Lamarckian biology, the notion (now discarded) that acquired characteristics may be transmitted genetically.

Folk psychologists, then, unlike behaviorists, were not interested in studying the individual, only the *Volksgeist*. Favorite topics of inquiry of men like Muller included mythology and language. For example, by comparing Greco-Roman, German, and Hindu mythologies, one discovers the essential features of the different *Volksgeists*. The themes found in Homer's *Iliad* and *Odyssey* and in Wagner's operas are far more meaningful and revealing than history books. Similarly, the analysis of linguistic grammar and structure provides the cue to an understanding of national character, since language is a formalization of the folk experience.

Wundt was the first man to introduce university laboratory experiments with humans. People of different nationalities were tested and compared for their reactions to a variety of stimuli. It was found that the Germans—and Nordics in general—performed best. Latins and Mediterraneans were found inferior in such experiments. The explanation was that the ancient Latin civilizations were based on corrupt and decadent cities and on the racially mongrelized population of the former Roman empire. Meanwhile, the Teutons had preserved their racial and natural purity. Living for many centuries in the Northern European forests, natural selection had preserved a more vigorous race.

The sociology of knowledge explains nicely why folk psychology has been so important to the Germans and relatively unpopular in France and the Anglo-Saxon world. For Germany, the nineteenth century was the century of national unification. Whereas countries like France and Great Britain had been nations for centuries, Germany's political unification was only now getting under way and all sectors of German arts and sciences were mobilized for the ideological legitimation of that movement. Above all, what needed to be demonstrated was that the disparate Germanic and German-speaking peoples of Europe shared a *Volksgeist* that entitled them to national unification. Thus by the time unification finally occurred in 1871, Germany had already been a *psychological* entity for some time. German folk psychology was, along with the romantic music of composers like Wagner and the philosophies of men like Nietzsche, a major ideological building block for German nationalism.

Any evaluation of German folk psychology must recognize at least three major lasting contributions. First, as indicated, Wundt was responsible for the introduction of the first laboratory experiments in psychology. Second, this school paved the way for linguistics, the study of language by psychologists, sociologists, and anthropologists. Contemporary social science accepts folk psychology's view that language determines thought (cf. Sapir, 1949; Whorf, 1956). Finally, the study of national character (cf. Martindale, 1967) can also be said to have been launched by this school, although, to be sure, differences in national character are now attributed to culture and not genetic ancestry.

On the negative side of the balance, folk

psychology is of course partially to be blamed for the nationalism and racism that eventually engulfed much of the world and led to World War II. While the German folk psychologists demonstrated experimentally that Germans perform better than other people, their colleagues across the Rhine were "proving" exactly the opposite, showing the superiority of Frenchmen. And if one accepts folk psychology's premises, all people should be superior to the Americans, since that nation is racially and culturally far more heterogenous and mixed than any other. All this of course indicates the great deal of nonsense generated by this school. Finally, as stated earlier, it was this brand of psychology that became the official doctrine of the increasingly nationalistic, militaristic, and racist social system culminating in Nazi Germany.

FRENCH CROWD PSYCHOLOGY

At about the same time, French sociologists and psychologists were also becoming aware of the irrational features of human behavior. In France, the reaction against the rationalist bias of associationism took a somewhat different form. Gustave Le Bon (1841-1931) was an aristocrat who noted with dismay the destructive violence of French revolutionaries and concluded that although man is indeed born a tabula rasa, his subsequent experience with groups and collectivities often results in a deterioration of behavior. Le Bon's main thesis was that *when individuals act in groups they descend to their lowest common denominator.* In a crowd, man becomes a beast, losing his rationality. Although Le Bon agreed that man learns from experience, he felt that social experience is by no means always good.

Le Bon looked at certain forms of collective behavior—revolutions, mobs, panics—and generalized by stating that all group experience leads to irrational behavior. He then drew the logical implications of this position for social policy: in education, a private, preferably tutorial, and always elitist system is far better than

mass public education, since the latter merely reduces the level of education to the mediocrity of the masses. In government, likewise, aristocracy is better than democracy. Society must be ruled by an elite, a select few who, unlike the masses, are rational.

It is important to keep in mind the similarities and differences between Le Bon's crowd psychology and the other schools we have discussed: like the associationists and the behaviorists, Le Bon is essentially an environmentalist. His elite, unlike that of the German folk psychologists, is *not* hereditary. He is, however, an elitist, rejecting, for example, the mass education advocated by liberal associationists like Thomas Jefferson.

Another Frenchman who was interested in collective behavior was Gabriel Tarde (1843-1904). As a judge in a Southern French town, Tarde had an opportunity to observe criminals. He was the first sociologist to note that criminal behavior was *social,* learned from others (through imitation and suggestion), representing a subculture, so to speak. This was a very important discovery, for the prevailing theories at the time held that criminality was an inborn characteristic, most prominent in individuals with certain facial and bone features (cf. Lombroso's theories in Haskell and Yablonsky, 1974). In fact, the argument about the biological determination of criminality is still raging, since we have some current research attempting to trace crime to chromosomal makeup. Thus myths die hard. Tarde showed us over a century ago that crime is a sociological phenomenon, and this fact was incorporated into the body of knowledge in the works of, for example, Sutherland (see his theory of differential association in Sutherland and Cressey, 1970). Yet there is a persistent need in our society, apparently, for ignoring facts and lapsing into the facile and fallacious notion that society can rid itself of crime and social ills if only it identifies and apprehends a class of born losers.

Tarde, then, noted that the vast majority of criminals had learned their trade from other criminals and had acted together (in gangs). *Imitation* was the central concept in his explanatory scheme. As a crowd psychologist, he shared the tabula rasa assumption of both Le Bon and the associationists. However, the main difference between the two Frenchmen was that whereas Le Bon believed that collective behavior is always bad, Tarde did not share this pessimism and elitism. Whereas Le Bon thought that aristocracy was the best form of government, Tarde was more liberal, accepting the advent of mass democracy. If man imitates whatever he perceives, then he can learn both good and bad behavior, depending on the model.

Again, the sociology of knowledge can show the historical and local conditions that produced crowd psychology: while Germany's central problems had to do with national unification, those of France (as well as Italy, where there was a similar concern with crime and violence) centered around the frequent revolutions there. Indeed, France underwent major revolutions in 1789, 1830, 1848, and 1871, and there were numerous lesser instances of national disruption. Le Bon's and Tarde's concern was understandable. Le Bon developed a "scientific" justification for conservatives, arguing that society must be ruled by a social elite. Tarde, on the other hand, believed that democracy was a possibility despite the growing pains it was experiencing at the time.

Crowd psychology has made a lasting contribution to social psychology. The modern subdiscipline of *collective behavior* (cf. Lang and Lang, 1961; Turner and Killian, 1957) is largely founded on the classical contributions of men like Tarde and Le Bon. This discipline studies mobs, riots, panics, disasters, fads, fashions, and a variety of other forms of mass behavior

characterized by short duration and lack of structure. As America undergoes the pains of the current transitional crisis, French crowd psychology seems to become increasingly relevant. On the negative side, we must note Le Bon's elitism, which avoids the pitfalls of German racism and biological determinism but nevertheless wishes to maintain inequality and offers a biased and negative conception of human nature.

ANGLO-SAXON INSTINCTIVISM

In the English-speaking world, the reaction against rationalism primarily took the form of instinctivism. Like the German folk psychologists, instinctivists began to reject the tabula rasa assumption of the associationists, noting that human behavior is frequently irrational and attributing this to nature rather than to nurture. However, unlike folk psychology, instinctivism was an individualistic psychology, not a collectivistic one. Thus irrational or "natural" human behavior was attributed to *instincts*, which came to mean *inborn tendencies for certain behavior patterns.* Alone among the schools presently under review, instinctivism assumed that man is essentially similar to other animals, a continuity later picked up by behaviorism. According to instinctivism, we have innate instincts for aggression, territoriality, dominance, etc. just like other species. Yet this school does qualify as a form of *social* psychology, for it posits that man has social instincts as well, for example, gregariousness and love. In America, William McDougall (1871-1938) stands out as the most famous instinctivist. He stressed the fact that "conative" processes (or what is today called motivation) are frequently determined by some hereditary equipment, that is, instinct (McDougall, 1918).

The rise of instinctivism in England and America is easy to comprehend in the light of the sociology of knowledge: Darwin's *Origin of the Species,* first published in 1859, signaled the spectacular rise of the biological sciences, probably the most successful scientific enterprise of the nineteenth century, and certainly developed most actively in the Anglo-Saxon countries. Biology demonstrated the importance of instinct and genetic transmission in animal behavior. Furthermore, England and the United States have had a liberal and individualistic tradition linked to these countries' laissez-faire capitalist economies. Thus when a biologistic psychology developed emphasizing inheritance over acquisition, it had to be *individual* inheritance, not collective and racial as in Germany. Certainly racism as a national ideology would have been ludicrous in a heterogeneous and mixed society such as the United States. Furthermore, Britain had an empire to justify, and America had its manifest destiny. This involved war and the subjugation of non-Western populations. Whereas France's central problem was political instability, necessitating a focus on the sources thereof and theories aimed at buttressing stability, England and America had stable governments. There the issues were of a different kind. Capitalist competition and imperialist wars needed legitimation. The ideology justifying ruthless individual competition became known as *social Darwinism,* the misapplication of Darwinian principles to the realm of human society. It became fashionable to argue that among men, as among animals, only the fittest survive and that this is an inevitable and salubrious process of natural selection. Instinctivism, then, was a logical justification of laissez-faire capitalism. Similarly, instinctivism and social Darwinism "proved" that wars—in this case the colonial wars against non-Western peoples—were natural, inevitable, and therefore moral.

The first wave of revulsion against war and its legitimating theories occurred after the needless carnage of World War I. Also, anthropology did a great deal to undermine instinctivism, since its research showed that the almost infinite variation in human behavior found around the world can only be attributed to *culture,* and not to instincts—to nurture and not to nature. Tribes were found which had never experienced war (in Polynesia), some did not know the incest taboo, some practiced institutionalized homosexuality, most practiced polygamy. It became evident that the Western ways were not necessarily the natural ways, but merely arbitrary cultural choices.

The downfall of instinctivism was furthered by the constant internal quarrels within this school about the number of human instincts. Some authors believed that there were basically two, sex and hunger. Others expanded the list to include territoriality, aggression, fear, and fear of the unknown. The critics of instinctivism pointed out that many forms of behavior attributed to instincts were in fact learned. John B. Watson, for example, showed experimentally that newborn infants only exhibit three uniform patterns of response: fear (for example, when dropped in a net), anger, and pleasure (e.g., when tickled). Apart perhaps from sucking, no behavior could be attributed to instincts in the sense of being unlearned. To accommodate such criticism, instinctivists replied that instincts are sometimes dormant, showing up later in life upon maturation. Birds, for example, only build nests (an instinct) at the appropriate stage in the life cycle. McDougall made sure to define instincts as mere *tendencies* toward certain behavior, allowing therefore for the frequent deviation from the pattern, especially when forced by circumstances.

Although there is today no unified school of instinctivism in social psychology, there are several strands that may be subsumed under the heading of neoinstinctivism: some psychologists, for example Raymond Cattell, do cross-cultural studies of human behavior and try, through factor analysis, to identify universal patterns that would presumably represent instinctive behavior. Then there are some Freudians who place emphasis on the instinctual in human behavior. Freud himself believed that man was born with life (eros) and death (thanatos) instincts, and this idea persists in some quarters, although by no means among all neo-Freudians. Finally there are ethologists like Konrad Lorenz (*On Aggression*, 1966) and anthropologists such as Robert Ardrey (*The Territorial Imperative*, 1966) and Desmond Morris (*The Naked Ape*, 1967) who have popularized the notion that man must recognize his instincts and that modern civilization owes many of its problems to the fact that it ignores man's instincts. This, too, is a Freudian notion.

An evaluation of instinctivism must start out with the recognition that it has, for better or worse, left a strong impact on several schools of contemporary psychology. In addition to psychoanalytic psychology, which, as just indicated, goes back to Freud's own instinctivism, it is in particular neobehaviorism that tends so often to degenerate into pure physiology and animal psychology, and hence carries a strong dose of instinctivism. It is now agreed that *instinct*, in contradistinction to other physiological concepts like *reflex* and *impulse*, refers not to a simple muscular or glandular response but to *a complex pattern of unlearned behavior that is common to all members of a biological stock.* Thus birds instinctively build nests, and newly born turtles instinctively walk toward the ocean from eggs that hatch inland. There is no question about the genetic anchorage of such patterns in animals. In the case of turtles, for example, the mother is not present when the eggs hatch, yet the young instinctively find their way to the water. Some years ago it was shown that the atomic tests in the Bikini atolls had effectively destroyed this instinct in the newborn turtles: they now crawled inland to die and dry up in the sand.

However, for social psychology instinctivism is of little value. As Alland (1972) recently argued, the writings of neoinstinctivists like Lorenz, Ardrey, and Morris do not address themselves to the central issues in human behavior. Aggression, territoriality, and pair-bonding may exist, but these are variables rather than constants. The main point is not that man fights, eats, and reproduces but that he does so in a multiplicity of ways depending on his culture, training, and judgment and that he in fact often chooses *not* to do so at all. To posit the existence of instincts—or inborn drives, or needs—as explanatory principles is to explain nothing at all, for instinctivism is, as all need psychology, fundamentally tautological. Unless one accepts the unfounded premise that behavior patterns are rooted in one's genes, thereby reducing social psychology to biology, such expansions merely rephrase the questions, for one must then explain why the need arose in the first place. The task of social psychology is not to redundantly show what biology has known for a long time—that man shares certain features with other animals—but precisely the opposite, namely to explain man's uniqueness. The reduction of human behavior to instincts, as Suttles (1972) showed, has the sinister ideological implication that human intervention for the alleviation of social ills, conflict, and injustice is futile and misguided since nature ought to be left alone. Most important, this assumption is metaphysical rather than scientific, for the evidence suggests not the presence but the absence of instincts behind a majority of behaviors. Thus instinctivism is an ideology. To be sure, if sufficient consensus about the existence of certain instincts (such as territoriality, greed, lust) develops, it is quite possible that we shall have a self-fulfilling prophecy whereby people conform in their behavior to the prevailing theories about human behavior. Nevertheless, we shall have to remember that the jail in which we have placed ourselves is of our own making, for existentialism and humanism teach us that we are free as long as we choose to be.

SUMMARY AND CONCLUSION

Although instinctivism has been an individualistic psychology, in a broader sense it ties in with the issue of race and the nature-nurture argument. Since the nineteenth century there have been repeated attempts to hold inborn hereditary characteristics accountable for differential behavior by individuals, groups, nationalities, and races. This is "nature." The effort has been to scientifically prove the innate superiority of some people (for example, Westerners, Caucasians, Germans, "Aryans") and the inherent inferiority of others (such as non-Western natives, Negroes, Jews, gypsies, Slavs, Latins). Thus "nature" can lead directly to racism. "Nurture," on the other hand, simply means that human behavior and psychology are shaped by what the individual is "fed," by what he experiences and learns from birth on. Nurture, then, is the position that holds the environment rather than heredity responsible for man's behavior. It is tantamount to the tabula rasa assumption and has been the dominant position in the behavioral sciences throughout this century, the dominant position of an essentially liberal scientific establishment in our liberal society. However, the environmentalists' victory is by no means final. As stated earlier, the question of biological imperatives has recently been raised again by men like Lorenz, Ardrey, and Morris. In addition, such authors as Jensen (1970) and Shockley (1970) have made it once again fashionable to hypothesize a relationship between intelligence and genes. This, as well as additional efforts at relating crime and a variety of other forms of social behavior to heredity, shows that the nature-nurture controversy is by no means settled. Let us briefly examine six issues over which the two camps have struggled.

One argument used to buttress the nature argument has been to point to the political, economic, and military supremacy of the Western world. Since the white nations of the world have produced a technologically more advanced civilization than the nations of Africa and Asia, so the argument goes, this must prove their innate racial superiority. This type of argument is advanced with particular reference to Northern Europeans, Anglo-Saxons, etc.

The refutation of this specific brand of racism is easy: for one thing, it can be shown that the ascendency of European man over other people began only approximately four centuries ago. At that time, non-Western civilizations such as the Incas, the Aztecs, the Ashanti, and the Chinese were in many ways ahead of the Europeans. History is cyclical; no group remains dominant forever. Today, indications abound to suggest that the future lies not in the West but elsewhere— perhaps in the East. Furthermore—and this is our second counterargument—what is this flaunted Western superiority anyway? From the first colonial conquests of Africa, America, and Asia, there was essentially only one area in which non-Westerners could not match the Europeans— technology, specifically military technology such as gunpowder. However, in terms of the level of intellectual, artistic, philosophical, and moral development, as well as in terms of social organization and even in terms of the level of material progress (for example, in the areas of housing and transportation), Western civilization was more rudimentary than some of the cultures it subjugated.

A second argument used in favor of the alleged racial superiority of the white man is brain size. The average brain size of modern man is approximately 1,500 cc, ranging from 1,000 to 2,000 cc. Men of Anglo-Saxon descent have been found to average 1,530 cc, Afro-Americans 1,462 cc. This, then, has led some people to argue that whites are perhaps innately more intelligent than blacks (and similarly that men have a higher IQ than women because their average brain size is 1,500 cc versus 1,450 cc for women). Klineberg (1935) showed that there is a slight but consistent correlation between brain size and intelligence. However, this argument also backfires, for certain races have a higher average brain size than modern whites. Eskimos are such a people, as well as the extinct Neanderthal man. These, along with African Zulus and the people of Java, should therefore be expected to be our intellectual superiors. The truth of the matter is that, as Hoebel (1966:149) notes, "within the normal range brain size has no functional significance."

Third, there is a hypothesis formulated by Professor Carleton Coon in 1963 that is also a potential argument in the racist's arsenal. According to Coon, "the subspecies who crossed the evolutionary threshold into the category of *homo sapiens* have evolved the most, and . . . the obvious correlation between the length of time a subspecies has been in the *sapiens* state and the levels of civilization attained by some of its populations may be related phenomena" (quoted in Hoebel, 1966:222). Coon then suggests that of the major world races, the European (Caucasoids) made it across the line first—by several hundred thousand years—which would account for his evolutionary superiority today. He would simply be on a higher rung of the evolutionary ladder.

Two counterarguments can be made here for the nurture side. First, *if* it is granted that *Homo sapiens* has been around longer in Europe than in Africa and that the contemporary inhabitants of those continents are the descendents of earlier races located there, it can be argued that the European's brain structure has evolved further toward specialization and uses that are sometimes dysfunctional in terms of changing conditions. Thus African man may have greater potential adaptability in the future. Second, there is no convincing evidence that European man crossed the threshold significantly earlier than did the other races. With Leakey's spectacular discoveries (see Hoebel, 1966:156-159; *Newsweek*, 1974:72-77) in East Africa, the origins of man are being pushed back all the time, now to four million years. Although it is not claimed that Leakey's very old findings represent specimens of *Homo sapiens*, there is no proof that *Homo sapiens* could not have evolved out of those very early *Homo* species. For now, all we know is that the family of man goes back further in Africa than anywhere else at this time.

The IQ controversy is a fourth argument in the nature-nurture debate: In the 1920s the Binet test revealed that Europeans had a higher IQ than blacks, American Indians, and Orientals. The average intelligence scores were 100, 99, 75.3, and 99 for these racial groups respectively (Hoebel, 1966:227). Racists have been able to use these findings as a scientific justification for discrimination against minorities. They provided another argument for "nature" over nurture. In addition, the 1960s and 1970s have witnessed a renaissance in the attempt to relate intelligence to race and biology. Berkeley psychologist Arthur Jensen has conducted elaborate research in this matter and his conclusion is that "the evidence for the major role of heredity factors in determining individual differences in mental ability is now so consistent and conclusive that it should require little further explication. . . . In recent years there has grown up an inordinate emphasis on the belief that environmental factors are the main cause of individual and group differences in traits relevant to educational potential. This exaggerated emphasis . . . is belied by the preponderance of evidence" (1970:122-124).

William Shockley, the Stanford physicist who won the Nobel prize for the transistor radio, has taken the same stand as Jensen (1970). This has generated a great deal of controversy, Shockley's opponents arguing that his expertise is in the area of physics, not genetics, and that he therefore does not know what he is talking about. Whether done irresponsibly, as by Shockley, or in the form of solid research, as in Jensen's case, there is a growing sentiment that the liberal environmentalism underlying our policy toward social problems must now be questioned, because those who fail to "make it" in our society (the poor, the black, etc.) lack the innate equipment for success, intelligence. These proponents of "nature" include Edward Banfield (1968), who advocates benign neglect toward the central city poor rather than expensive remedial programs, and R. J. Herrnstein (1973), who carries forward Jensen's research and thesis on the genetic fixedness of intelligence.

The counterargument to all this is a fundamental one. No IQ test is culture-free. What is being measured is learned skill, *not* innate intelligence. The early tests (Standford-Binet, etc.) were so grossly biased toward those who developed them (middle-class urban males of European origin) that they produced consistently lower scores for women than for men, for rural people than for urbanites, for members of the lower class than those of the middle class. But even the revised tests that attempt to eliminate such biases remain culture-bound, and the fact remains that psychological intelligence tests measure one thing and one thing only: the individual's ability to pass those tests.

The extremely low IQ scores of many American Indians provide a good illustration of how culture totally invalidates any claim that such tests might measure any kind of native aptitude. As anthropologists have shown (cf. Kluckhohn and Leighton, 1962), Southwestern Indians such as the Navaho are highly cooperative, not competitive and individualistic like Anglo-Americans. In their culture it is shameful to excel. Thus when tested for intelligence and aptitude, each Navaho child deliberately slowed himself down so as not to finish the test ahead of his peers.

The same point was made with a punch by Adrian Dove, a Watts social worker. The "Dove Counterbalance IQ Test" devised by that man is a witty collection of black-oriented items like:

1. "Bird" or "Yardbird" was the jacket that jazz lovers from coast to coast hung on
   a. Lester Young
   b. Peggy Lee
   c. Benny Goodman
   d. Charlie Parker
   e. "Birdman of Alcatraz"
2. Cheap chittlings (not the kind you purchase at a frozen food counter) will taste rubbery unless they are cooked long enough. How soon can you quit cooking them to eat and enjoy them?
   a. 15 minutes
   b. 2 hours
   c. 24 hours
   d. 1 week (on a low flame)
   e. 1 hour
3. If you throw the dice and seven is showing on the top, what is facing down?
   a. Seven
   b. "Snake eyes"
   c. "Boxcars"
   d. "Little Joes"
   e. Eleven

According to this test, which I took, I have an IQ of 67.

Thus intelligence tests measure cultural knowledge, not innate intelligence. Nevertheless, the labelling and classification of children according to their performance on such tests goes on, and as Rosenthal and Jacobson (1968) have shown, this frequently leads to a self-fulfilling prophecy whereby the students initially classified as slow learners indeed end up as such. Thus the measurement of intelligence, by fixing an individual's performance and labelling him accordingly, has victimized millions of youngsters who were culturally deprived but could have been educated to succeed in society if they had not been identified as unable to do so and tracked by psychologists, teachers, and agencies into second-class citizenship.

Fifth, we mention the selective migration hypothesis, another famous issue in the nature-nurture controversy. Early IQ tests produced not only higher scores for whites than for blacks, but also higher IQs for Northern blacks than for Southern blacks. Now this latter finding could mean two things: (1) either Northern blacks were more intelligent than their Southern brothers because the Northern environment (urban, industrial, etc.) was more conducive to the development of higher intelligence, or (2) it was the *innately* more intelligent Southern black who decided to migrate northward. Nurture or nature? In the 1920s, the more popular notion was the second, *selective migration.*

In the 1930s, Otto Klineberg (1935) set out to test and refute the selective migration hypothesis. He collected the school records of Southern black children (in Charleston, Nashville, and Birmingham) who were known to have moved North, and he found that they were on the average identical to the Negro school population in those cities. Thus the selective migration hypothesis was refuted. Furthermore, Klineberg measured the performance of blacks who had left the South and settled in the North. He found that those who had been in the North the shortest amount of time were closest to the level of the Southern Blacks and that the longer a Black had lived in the North, the higher his IQ tended to be, eventually to equal that of the Northern Blacks. Thus Klineberg conclusively showed that environment, not race, is the prime determinant of intelligence.

Finally, there is the more general issue of biological imperatives. Lorenz (1966), Ardrey (1966), Morris (1967), and several other authors have made it once again fashionable to base human behavior on instinct or, somehow, on biology. The works of these neoinstinctivists are quite popular. They emphasize not man's uniqueness but his similarity to other animals; not his cultures and symbols but his physiology; not his infinite variety but his species commonality; not nurture but nature. The ideological implication of neoinstinctivism is that human society is ruled by the same immutable laws of nature as the animal kingdom and that aggression, war, and inequality are inevitable, indeed wholesome, natural selection and population control mechanisms.

The counterargument to this trend of thought has been provided by Alland (1972). The entire instinctivist-racial argument can be formulated in terms of two fundamental concepts of genetics—the

genotype and the phenotype. *Genotype refers to the genetic consitution of an organism. Phenotype can be defined as the observable characteristics of an organism or a group, resulting from the interaction of that organism's genotype with the environment.* Now the argument of instinctivists and racists is always that the genotype is primarily responsible for determining the phenotype. For example, genetic constitution is said to determine intelligence, aptitude, artistry, etc. What Alland points out is that some species can tolerate far wider environmental variation than others. Man is such a species. Thus *Homo sapiens* is not subject to the same narrow genotypic determinism as most other animals. Cultural variation and individual differences are therefore the crucial points for understanding human adaptation to the environment, and adaptation involving learning, choice, decision, and subjective interpretation far more than biological limitations. This is what Alland terms the *human imperative.*

• • •

In summary, this chapter has examined the three major reactions in social psychology against the rationalistic theories of associationism and behaviorism. They all share a focus on man's irrationality, and the sociology of knowledge can shed light on the time and place of their emergence.

Associationism was the liberal, environmentalistic, and rationalistic psychology of the eighteenth century Anglo-Saxon world. During the nineteenth century, Germany's national needs led to the development of a collectivistic social psychology emphasizing racial heredity—folk psychology. France, at the same time, experienced the social instability that led some of its concerned scholars to develop crowd psychology, one brand of which (Le Bon's) was highly critical of collective behavior and another (Tarde's) less so. In the early twentieth century, England and America developed ideological theories both to account for violence and to justify existing policies—instinctivism. This brand of social psychology could degenerate into social Darwinism and thus legitimize colonialism, war, and capitalist competition.

The appeal to biology inherent in instinctivism is by no means defunct. A review of the nature-nurture controversy showed that even today there is the tendency in many quarters to reduce human conduct to the same principles as those governing animal behavior and to view racial and individual performance as genetically fixed.

On the whole, social psychology has become increasingly environmentalistic over the years. This is because it has become more and more empirical, and the brunt of the evidence is on the side of nurture, not nature. However, there is always the possibility that theories positing biological determinism and ignoring human choice will triumph. As Rene Dubos states, "getting tired of being human is a very human habit." Insofar as we put ourselves in that straitjacket, we must keep in mind that this will be our own decision. Truth, as Durkheim knew, is a function of a larger consensus. Indeed, while facts may have something to do with truth, from the standpoint of a humanistic social psychology the more pertinent observation is that truth is a human production, the product of social interaction, power, ideological indoctrination, conflict, and negotiation. This, in essence, is what the remainder of the book attempts to demonstrate.

REFERENCES

Alland, Alexander, Jr.
1972 The Human Imperative. New York: Columbia University Press.
Ardrey, Robert
1966 The Territorial Imperative. New York: Dell Publishing Co.
Banfield, Edward C.
1968 The Unheavenly City. Boston: Little, Brown and Co.
Haskell, Martin R. and Lewis Yablonsky
1974 Juvenile Delinquency. Chicago: Rand McNally.
Herrnstein, R. J.
1973 I.Q. in the Meritocracy. Boston: Little, Brown and Co.
Hoebel, E. Adamson
1966 Anthropology: The Study of Man. New York: McGraw-Hill Book Co.

Jensen, Arthur R.
1970 "Learning ability, intelligence, and educability." In Psychological Factors in Poverty. Vernon L. Allen (ed.). Chicago: Markham Publishing Co., pp. 106-132.
Klineberg, Otto H.
1935 Race Differences. New York: Harper & Row, Publishers.
Kluckhohn, Clyde and Dorothea Leighton
1962 The Navaho. New York: The Natural History Library.
Lang, Kurt and Gladys Engel Lang
1961 Collective Dynamics. New York: Thomas Y. Crowell Co.
Lorenz, Konrad
1966 On Agression. New York: Harcourt Brace.
Martindale, Don (ed.)
1967 "National character in the perspective of the social sciences." Annals of The American Academy of Political and Social Science (March).
McDougall, William
1918 Social Psychology. Boston: John W. Luce.
Morris, Desmond
1967 The Naked Ape. New York: McGraw-Hill Book Co.
Newsweek
1974 "The Leakeys' telltale skulls." Newsweek (July 15):72-77.
Rosenthal, R. and L. Jacobson
1968 Pygmalion in the Classroom: Teacher Expectation and Pupils' Intellectual Development. New York: Holt, Rinehart and Winston.
Sapir, E.
1949 "The status of linguistics as a science." In Selected Writings in Language, Culture and Personality. D. G. Mandelbaum (ed.). Berkeley: University of California Press.
Shockley, William
1970 "A 'try simplest cases' approach to the heredity-poverty-crime problem." In Psychological Factors in Poverty. Vernon L. Allen (ed.). Chicago: Markham Publishing Co., pp. 141-146.
Sutherland, Edwin H. and Donald R. Cressey
1970 Criminology. Philadelphia: J. B. Lippincott Co.
Suttles, Gerald D.
1972 The Social Construction of Communities. Chicago: The University of Chicago Press.
Turner, Ralph H. and Lewis M. Killian
1957 Collective Behavior. Englewood Cliffs, N.J.: Prentice-Hall, Inc.
Whorf, Benjamin L.
1956 Language, Thought and Reality. Cambridge, Mass.: Harvard University Press.

part two

Humanistic paradigms

chapter 5
Cultural sociology

By its very nature, social psychology straddles so many fences that its failure to develop a unified paradigm is understandable. These "fences" are ideological, substantive, and epistemological.

One of the organizing principles used to classify paradigms in the first four chapters of this book has been to examine the ideologies underlying those paradigms. From this standpoint, the classification can be summed up as in Table 3.

As Table 3 indicates, a major problem with most existing approaches in sociology and social psychology is their ideological anchorage. Our first challenge, then, will be to delineate an alternative orientation. Since this book subscribes to the fundamental sociological tenet that no sociological perspective can be objective, it is immediately admitted that the proposed alternative, too, is based on a particular philosophy. However, the new bias proposed is perhaps less blatantly political and ideological and more philosophical. In any event, it does depart from all positions summarized in Table 3. It is, at least, a new start.

Second, social psychology is, by its very nature, the meeting ground of a number of behavioral disciplines. In addition to straddling the fence between sociology and psychology, it also deals with political, economic, and anthropological phenomena. Think, for example, of studies of public opinion and voting behavior, market and motivation research, and studies of culture and personality. Thus a second difficulty in arriving at a unified social-psychological paradigm has been to agree on a specific domain of substantive inquiry, a domain distinct, for example, from both sociology and psychology.

Finally, there has been no agreement about the basic *ontological* assumptions regarding the discipline's subject matter. Here, two distinct problems have plagued social psychology from its very inception: the society-individual controversy and the science-humanity argument. Table 4 sums up the four possible positions generated by these controversies.

The challenge, then, is to develop a unified perspective that will opt neither for society nor for the individual, neither for scientific determinism nor for total freedom and unpredictability. When such a perspective is developed, it will be seen that we have also solved our second problem—the matter of substantive domain. Social psychology will, ideally, distinguish itself as a

TABLE 3. Classification of sociological and social-psychological paradigms by their underlying ideologies

Levels of analysis	Left-wing paradigms	Establishment paradigms	Right-wing paradigms
Macro	Marxism	Sociological G.O.P.	Folk psychology and racism
Micro	Psychosexual liberation (hippies; encounters)	Psychological G.O.P.	Instinctivism

perspective rather than as dealing with specific subject matter.

Much headway has been made toward the solution of the three problems just outlined. Although nineteenth century and early twentieth century social psychology was mostly speculative and ideological, it has, since the 1930s, become increasingly empirical and applied. Public opinion research from the 1930s on, studies of troop morale during World War II and thereafter, and studies of worker productivity are among the accomplishments that have gained the discipline increasing recognition. This growing empiricism has made social psychology more and more environmentalistic and less and less instinctivistic, for a recognition of facts forced it to abandon that largely unfounded and ideological orientation. Whereas at an earlier time biology had had the greatest impact on social psychology, it was now sociology, anthropology, and psychology that greatly influenced it. Sociology's basic environmentalism was gradually adopted. Anthropology demonstrated that cultural socialization accounts for most of the variation in human behavior, not biology. And psychology has always been rigorously empirical, often experimental, in its approach to facts. Thus social psychology has gradually freed itself of its earlier speculative and ideological character.

The newer social psychology presented in the remainder of this book has also received the kind of political labels applied to older brands in Table 3. Mullins (1973), for example, refers to symbolic interactionism—a cornerstone of the new social psychology—as "the loyal opposition" within sociology. Max Weber, another major contributor to the new paradigm, has been termed a liberal and a humanist (Gerth and Mills, 1958:73). Be this as it may, our contention is that the new social psychology represents the most promising avenue at this time because it is synthesizing rather than partial, broad rather than narrow, and because it focuses not on mechanical processes that human behavior may or may not share with other natural objects but on precisely those features of man that are unique to him, prime among them the capacity for *meaning*. Thus the new social psychology offers an essential antidote to the dominant technocratic culture of the day. It must be vigorously developed if man himself is not to be lost sight of.

The other two major problems just outlined are also of central concern to the new social psychology. As stated earlier, it is the emergence of a new perspective that now promises to make headway in two age-old controversies—the individual-society problem and the science-humanity argument—and to establish the discipline in terms of its theory and methods rather than as a specific domain of inquiry.

Both the sociologist E. A. Ross and the psychologist William McDougall published their social psychology texts in 1908. Thus social psychology has suffered, from its very beginning, from the dual origin and the dual allegiance that have made it so difficult to agree on a definition and, more importantly, on the relationship of society and the individual. Sociologists and psychologists may agree that social psychology

TABLE 4. Classification of sociological and social-psychological paradigms by their underlying philosophical assumptions

	Primary unit of analysis	
Approach	Society	Individual
Scientific	Sociological G.O.P.	Psychological G.O.P.
Humanistic	Humanistic sociology	Humanistic ("existential") psychology

tries to understand how people affect one another; they may, among the myriad of ways in which the discipline has been defined, both accept Allport's definition that it is "concerned with the study of actual, imagined, or anticipated person-to-person relationships in a social context as they affect the individuals involved" (quoted in Deutsch and Krauss, 1965:3). However, this or any other definition cannot hide the fact that the dual origin of social psychology has burdened it with a fundamental problem that none of the paradigms discussed previously has successfully solved. This is the individual-society problem. Predictably, psychological social psychology has focused on the individual and on interpersonal interaction as the product of individual acts. Sociology, on the other hand, assumes the independent existence of social structure and culture, and insofar as it delves into the social-psychological, it tends to view individual and interpersonal behavior as determined by those larger realities or contexts. There is, to be sure, convergence. As one example, both disciplines approach the study of leadership increasingly in situational terms rather than in personality terms. However, because of the independent development of social psychology in sociology and psychology departments, there are still two distinct approaches to human behavior divided by fundamentally different assumptions. One posits the ultimate primacy of the concrete individual and would probably agree that, in a philosophical sense, individual behavior is ultimately the starting point, building block, and independent variable for the behavioral disciplines. The other—sociological—perspective rejects such reductionism and posits the primacy of society, the independent and a priori existence of culture and social structure. As Durkheim, who epitomized this sociological perspective, ceaselessly reiterated, society is a sui generis reality.

The problem cannot be dismissed by suggesting that social psychology henceforth focus both on the individual and on the social. As with the chicken and the egg, it does not suffice to say that both are primary. What this chapter and the remainder of the book do is to show that there is a third way, a radical departure that cuts this age-old Gordian knot by reformulating the issue in such a manner that no position needs to be taken vis-a-vis the individual-society controversy. If psychological reductionism is based on a *nominalistic* philosophy (see Chapter 1) and sociological reification is based on the philosophical position of *realism*, it is a third philosophy, namely *pragmatism*, that underlies the solution we shall discuss. The pragmatic social psychology advocated in this book refuses to take sides in the individual-society controversy, because it realizes that that controversy is metaphysical, insoluble, and futile. Instead of reifying either society or the individual, the new social psychology orients itself toward *process*, not entity. By taking social process as its point of departure, it is able to view both social structures and individual selves (which admittedly possess some permanence) as emergent products within that process. Above all, by viewing human behavior as an ongoing flow, it escapes the deterministic fallacy committed by the more static conceptions of human behavior. The new social psychology is thus pragmatic in the sense that it provides the conceptual apparatus to deal with a reality that is far too complex for the older paradigms. It is, then, more realistic and therefore more useful. All this will become much clearer in subsequent chapters. Here, we now move on to a discussion of a truly *unified* social psychology that is neither psychological nor sociological but pragmatic. The founders of this new social psychology, which is, like the philosophy of pragmatism upon which it is based, primarily American, include William James (1842-1910), Charles Horton Cooley (1864-1929), and above all George Herbert Mead (1863-1931). In addition, parallel paradigmic developments occurred in the works of other scholars on both sides of the Atlantic, for example the German Max Weber (1864-1920) and the Austrian-American Alfred Schutz (1899-1959).

Finally, the development of a unified social-psychological paradigm has faced that other major obstacle, the science-humanity controversy. As Coser and Rosenberg (1969:243) have noted, the behavioral disciplines have been perennially criticized on the grounds that human behavior is free and unpredictable and that they can therefore never attain the dignity of a science. Thus social psychology was resisted both by the natural sciences, which thought that it was not a true science, and by the humanities, which argued that man cannot be explained scientifically. The behavioral disciplines, and most of all social psychology, have been the central arena for the struggle between what C. P. Snow coined "the two cultures"—one scientific and the other humanistic. The most fundamental assertion of this book is that the new social psychology must find a way to transcend this cultural schizophrenia, and the contributions discussed from here on clearly point to an emerging paradigm that will do just that.

The previous chapters have, among other things, discussed the contributions of those men who had no doubt that the study of human behavior is a science. They range from Durkheim's sociological determinism to Watson's and Skinner's psychological determinism. Here, we begin to examine an alternative body of knowledge, the contributions of all those scholars who took their basic point of departure in the recognition that *sociology and social psychology must not only deal with objectively observable physical behavior but, perhaps more primarily, with the (inter)subjective meanings and motivations of the actors.* The basic realization shared by all these authors is that human conduct is interpretive and interpreted.

Sociology, as these people see it, is not merely a behavioral science but far more a cultural and symbolic discipline.

This chapter reviews the following contributions: (1) Max Weber's "verstehende" sociology, (2) W. I. Thomas' definition of the situation and Florian Znaniecki's "humanistic coefficient," and (3) some more recent contributions to the paradigm, including those of Robert MacIver, C. Wright Mills, and Peter Berger. This leaves several relevant authors for later discussion, prime among them G. H. Mead and A. Schutz. Since Mead is the father of symbolic interactionism and Schutz the founder of sociological phenomenology, these authors' ideas will be discussed separately in subsequent chapters.

MAX WEBER [1]

Weber's relevance for the new social psychology resides primarily in his theory and his methodology. Indeed, it is Weber's conception of the nature of social life and the consequent methodology he advocates for sociology that constitute his crucial contribution to the new paradigm. There is, of course, always a relationship between methodological and epistemological assumptions on the one hand and the substantive areas of inquiry to which these lead on the other. Thus the substantive problems that preoccupied Weber in most of his work are directly related to his basic conception of sociology. These include his types of social action and the relationship between ideas and interests. However, the bulk of Weber's work is macrosociological, dealing with large-scale sociocultural and structural phenomena rather than social-psychological ones. In the following pages, we first deal with Weber's methodology, then briefly with some of the substantive problems with which he dealt, and finally with his philosophical and ideological position.

---

[1]The following review of Weber's major ideas is based, among other sources, on Coser, 1971; Gerth and Mills, 1958; Martindale, 1960; Mennell, 1974; Weber, 1947; 1958, 1968.

Weber defines sociology as "a science which attempts the interpretive understanding of social action in order thereby to arrive at a causal explanation of its course and effects" (Weber, 1947:88). This definition immediately reveals several of the central distinguishing features of Weber's sociology: the discipline is viewed as *a science* which attempts the *interpretive understanding* of *social action* in order to arrive at *causal explanations*. Already we see Weber's basic ambiguity, or better, his synthesizing tendency: he wishes to create a sociology that is both scientific and humanistic, that explains (causally) as well as interprets (intuitively). This synthesizing tendency (cf. Martindale, 1960:376-380) is indeed one of the major reasons for Weber's unsurpassed greatness. By reconciling in his sociology C. P. Snow's two antagonistic traditions, Weber promises a way out of the impasse in which so much of contemporary sociology finds itself. While advocating quantitative methods (Gerth and Mills, 1958:59) as do the positivists, Weber at the same time agreed with Dilthey (Gerth and Mills, 1958:56; Martindale, 1960:377-378) on the need to recognize man's uniqueness—to make sociology a "moral" or "cultural" science. Weber's sociology, then, is interpretive sociology.

Since so much of sociology consists of the interpretation of meaning (Weber's *sinn*) rather than the mere observation of behavior (Weber's *verhalten*), it is important to distinguish between such mere behavior and action that is subjectively meaningful. This—Weber's *handeln*—is what is meant by *action*. Next to Weber's definition of sociology, his definition of (social) action is the most important concept underlying his entire sociology. By action, Weber means "all human behavior when and insofar as the acting individual attaches a subjective meaning to it. . . . Action is social insofar as, by virtue of the subjective meaning attached to it by the acting individual (or individuals), it takes into account the behavior of others and is thereby

oriented in its course" (Weber, 1968:248). Thus Weber establishes at the very outset that sociology studies social action—subjectively meaningful action—and that such action constitutes the primitive term and basic building block of sociology's subject matter.

As Zetterberg (1965:44-46) argues, the taxonomy Weber builds upon the concept of social action is as yet unsurpassed in sociology: the next step is the *social relation*, which is defined as "the existence of a probability that there will be a course of social action" (Weber, 1947:118). A *social order*, in turn, "consists of social relations guided by a set of prescriptions" (Zetterberg, 1965:45). "An *organization* is defined as a rather closed social order and a *state* is a compulsive organization that imposes its order on anyone living in a given territory . . ." (Zetterberg, 1965:45-46). The point, here, is that Weber's taxonomy reveals his conception of sociology's subject matter: while he ends up, throughout his work, analyzing vast sociohistorical systems, he is nevertheless a *nominalist* (cf. Martindale, 1960; Chapter 1) and a reductionist. As Gerth and Mills (1958:55-56) argue, his was, at least partially, the "Robinson-Crusoe approach," the individual person being his ultimate unit of analysis. To be sure, his interpretative sociology contains a certain dose of holism, since action is viewed as the manifestation of a cultural context (Gerth and Mills, 1958:56). Nevertheless, and this is what makes Weber so eminently relevant to social psychology, the focus is on the subjective meaning of social action, on man's mind and culture, not on abstract social structures, as for example in the work of Durkheim. Even when dealing with large-scale institutions, bureaucracies, and social classes, Weber avoids the pitfall of reification, aware at all times of the fact that these are no more than behavior patterns and that they represent complexes of subjective meanings rather than objective and external realities.

Weber's comprehensive conception of sociology—a cultural science—leads him to the methodological recognition that there are two fundamental criteria for the adequacy of sociological interpretations: (1) adequacy on the level of meaning *(sinnhafte Adaquanz)* and (2) causal adequacy (Weber, 1947:88-100). The first type of adequacy occurs when the component parts of a course of conduct are recognized to constitute a "typical" complex of meaning. An example is the correct solution of an arithmetic problem (loc. cit.). Causal adequacy, on the other hand, occurs when there is a probability that the explained event will always occur in the same way. Sociological interpretations must be adequate in both of these terms.

As Weber points out, some statistics are merely statistical probabilities, devoid of meaning and hence not truly comprehensible (for example, death rates and the production rate of machines). Truly *sociological* are only those statistics that are meaningful (for example, crime rates and occupational distributions). To Weber, then, many data that have no subjective meaning (for example, hereditary uniformities) are outside the scope of sociology, and he terms such data *nonunderstandable* (Weber, 1947:88-100). However, there are facts devoid of meaning yet well within the scope of sociology—for one thing, the large amount of human behavior that is merely reactive, habitual, and traditional (loc. cit.), also such psychophysical phenomena as fatigue, habituation, and memory. Such data are devoid of meaning for they cannot be related to action in the role of the intended means and ends (loc. cit.). Thus one major task of sociology is to interpret *(deuten)* and understand at the level of meaning *(verstehen)*.

All interpretation of meaning, or comprehension (Weber's *Evidenz*), is based either on reason (logical or mathematical) or on intuition (emotional empathy or artistic appreciation). Furthermore, understanding may consist of direct observation, or it may be explanatory, that is, it may consist of understanding the *motive* of the actor. A motive is defined as "a complex of subjective meaning which seems to the actor himself or to the observer an adequate ground for the conduct in question" (loc. cit.). Weber generalizes the concept of *intended* meaning to all subjective meaning of action, whether conscious or not, whether affectual or rational. The sociological interpretation of meanings alone can only produce plausible hypotheses, not causally valid explanations.

Causal explanation was, however, Weber's ultimate goal, since he considered sociology to be a science. It is to this end that he introduced his major methodological device—the *ideal type*. While sociology differs in essence from the physical sciences in that it deals with unique historical situations, only the situations—the constellations of factors—are unique. They can nevertheless be analyzed systematically in terms of their constitutive factors. Different constellations can be compared (Gerth and Mills, 1958:59-60). Thus, to arrive at a scientific sociology with causal explanations, Weber uses the comparative method, and his prime tool is the "pure" or ideal type. An ideal type is a theoretical construct, a logically pure model. For example, democracy is defined as "the minimization of power" (Gerth and Mills, 1958:60).

The ideal type is a methodological device comparable to the physicist's perfect vacuums and frictionless surfaces not found in reality but designed as an aid to understanding reality. It is through the ideal type that Weber hoped not only to interpret the subjective meaning of social action but also, at last, discover the lawful regularities that govern society and thus make sociology a causal science in addition to being an interpretive discipline (cf. Gerth and Mills, 1958:60). An example of the use of the ideal type (which Weber merely formalized, for classical sociologists such as Comte, Maine, Tonnies, Durkheim, and many others had all made implicit use of the methodology) is the construction of a type—for example, a model of rational conduct—and then the examination of specific actions and of their deviations from the model and from one another in terms of the factors specified by the model (cf. Weber, 1947). Thus hypotheses are generated about the various factors (for example, cultural and psychological) influencing the concrete behavior.

The content of his work

It is a fundamental assumption of this book that the substantive areas of inquiry into which social psychologists move are determined by the paradigms to which they either consciously or latently subscribe. The research and tentative answers produced by social psychologists are a function of the questions they ask. As Goode and Hatt (1952:9) wrote, "theory helps to define which kinds of facts are relevant." This is the main justification for this book's emphasis on paradigms. The new social psychology is the most promising, we argue, not because it solves old problems but because it raises new questions.

Weber's dual theoretical-methodological point of departure is a case in point: he is fundamentally concerned with subjective meaning and his ideal type makes him one of the first model builders in sociology. Much of his work consists of the construction of social-psychological and cultural models of social action.

His best-known typology is that of the four types of social action in terms of rationality:

1. *Traditional* behavior is behavior that follows the habituation of long practice.
2. *Affectual behavior* is behavior determined by the feeling of the actor.
3. *Action rational in terms of values (wertrational)* is behavior that rationally selects the proper means toward an absolute value, for example a religious, ethical, esthetic, or political belief.
4. Finally, *rationally purposeful* action (*zweckrational*) occurs when both the

means and the ends are rationally taken into account and weighed (Weber, 1947).

Weber clearly intends these types of action to be merely heuristic. As he states, "it would be very unusual to find concrete cases of action . . . which were oriented *only* in one or another of these ways . . . (they are) pure . . . sociological types . . . which constitute the elements to make up (actual action). The usefulness of the classification . . . can only be judged in terms of its results" (loc. cit.). Here, then, is a prime example of Weber's modus operandi: the construction of ideal types as heuristic and methodological devices.

It should be noted that the four types of action constitute a continuum of ascending rationality and that rationality, to Weber, is close to *meaningfulness*. Traditional and affectual behavior are the least rational, that is, least meaningfully oriented, in the sense described previously. As such they are actually on the borderline of sociology, which, it may be recalled, deals with meaningful, or understandable, social action.

Weber's distinction between wertrational and zweckrational action has been one of sociology's most fertile conceptions. Zweckrational has variously been translated as expedient (Parsons et al., 1961:175), pragmatic, or rationally purposeful, while wertrational is generally translated as rational in terms of an absolute value. Thus the action of a kamikaze pilot or a Christian martyr is wertrational, rational in light of the unquestioned ultimate value for which he is willing to die (country; God). However, only when means, ends, and consequences are weighed does action become zweckrational. Such would be the case if our war pilot considered the human, military, personal, strategic, and other costs as well as benefits of his action before deciding whether or not to nosedive onto the enemy ship.

Weber assumed the inherent superiority

of rational over nonrational action. His discussion of bureaucracy, for example, although recognizing the dehumanizing potential of that institution, nevertheless assumes that it is the most efficient form of human organization because the most rational (cf. Blau and Scott, 1962; Gouldner, 1959). However, an interesting moral issue raised by the wertrational-zweckrational distinction is the expediency-versus-ethics controversy: does not rationally purposeful action—that eminently modern form so much part of our pragmatic society—represent a loss in terms of values, convictions, commitment, and ideals?

Beyond this, Weber moves into sociology proper, linking his types of social action to corresponding social structures. Relying on Tonnies' pioneering *Gemeinschaft-Gesellschaft* typology, Weber calls affectual and traditional structures *communities* (Weber, 1958:9) and rational structures *associations* or *societies* (cf. Gerth and Mills, 1958:57). His famous three types of authority—traditional, charismatic, and legal—also clearly correspond to his basic types of social action: traditional authority structures are characterized by traditional behavior; charismatic authority (ephemeral as it is) is based on affect; legal authority is, of course, the hallmark of the rational, bureaucratized society. Again, Weber's typology is at least implicitly evolutionary, with legal-rational authority representing the apex of progress toward efficiency, democracy, universalism, achievement (as opposed to ascription), and meritocracy. Although Weber recognized that the trend toward rationalization and bureaucratization also poses a threat to human values, he did share the naivete of earlier sociologists insofar as he too tended to equate bureaucracy and rationality. Today, we know, thanks both to sociologists (cf. Gouldner, 1959; Parsons, 1956; Reiss, 1972) and to the counterculturalists (cf. Roszak, 1969; 1973) that bureaucracy can turn into the very opposite

of such features as rationality, efficiency, responsiveness, and meritocracy, often impeding rather than advancing the objectives for which it was created and the interest of clients, constituency, and the public at large.

Another major topic in Weber's work is the sociology of ideas and interests (cf. Gerth and Mills, 1958). Here, his lasting contribution was to rectify Marxism's excessive emphasis on the materialistic determination of ideas. In *The Protestant Ethic and the Spirit of Capitalism,* Weber essentially complements (not refutes) Marx's thesis about the relationship between ideas and (economic) structure. Calvinism, it is shown, has been a major factor in the development of capitalism. Thus religion—and ideas and culture in general—are not mere epiphenomena, as a strict materialistic conception of history would have it. Weber did, of course, recognize that for an idea to survive, historically, it must eventually mesh with some group's interests (cf. Gerth and Mills, 1958:62-64). However, this takes place through *elective affinity:* "during the process of routinization . . . the followers 'elect' those features of the idea with which they have an 'affinity'" (op. cit.:63). Thus Weber recognizes the personal and charismatic origin of ideas and the great importance of culture. His sociology remains humanistic and cultural. It contrasts with both Marxian determinism and scientific positivism.

His humanism

Although, as noted before, Weber's concepts of rationality and bureaucracy suffered from a certain bias, this by no means indicates an endorsement of modern society's drift toward technification and bureaucratization. While a rationalist, Weber was also a humanist. Freedom, he believed, "consists not in realizing alleged historical necessities (as the Marxists claim) but in making deliberate choices between open alternatives" (Gerth and Mills, 1958:70). Choice, then, is the central feature in human existence, not determinism. Central to Weber was the concept of *charisma,* and this performed somewhat the same function in his work as the "I" in George Herbert Mead's (op. cit.:73). Both concepts serve to underscore the elements of freedom and creativity in human conduct; to remind us that man is not merely a social product, not merely the sum of his roles, his "me"; to retain in sociology the humanistic coefficient.

Weber was a humanist and a liberal. His was a cultural and ideological liberalism rather than an economic liberalism. His concern was with freedom, democracy, and the cultivation of the spirit. However, as early as 1906 (cf. Gerth and Mills, 1958:70-71), he expressed pessimism about the survival chances of both freedom and the cultivated man, even in the United States. The cultivated man, he feared, was being phased out in favor of the technical expert who, from the human point of view, is crippled. "Man," he wrote, "will again move into the house of servitude" (op. cit.:71). Thus we see Weber's concern for the two central values advanced in this book—freedom and culture. His concern for these threatened commodities make Weber's sociology cultural, humanistic, and therefore eminently relevant to the new social psychology.

THOMAS AND ZNANIECKI

W. I. Thomas (1863-1947) was an American symbolic interactionist. Florian Znaniecki (1882-1958) was a Polish sociologist who moved to the United States in 1939 and whose sociology was cultural and humanistic, quite similar in orientation to that of Max Weber. Thomas and Znaniecki met in Poland in 1913 and began to work together. Jointly they wrote *The Polish Peasant in Europe and America* (1918-1920), a five volume work which became both men's magnum opus. These two authors are discussed together because of their collaboration and because of their shared humanistic perspective. Proceeding chronologically, we first briefly touch upon *The Polish Peasant,* then Thomas' definition of the situation, and finally Znaniecki's humanistic coefficient.

The Polish Peasant

This classic study of the assimilation of Polish immigrants to the United States stands as one of the greatest contributions to symbolic interactionism (cf. Martindale, 1960:350) and humanistic social psychology. While the work was Thomas' inception and plan, Znaniecki's contribution was primarily in the area of methodology (Bierstedt, 1969:11).

The central thesis of *The Polish Peasant* is the transformation both in personality and in social structure of the Polish peasant community as it moves from Poland to America. The transition involves personality disorganization and then reorganization. This is where Thomas and Znaniecki coined their famous three personality types, three modes of adaptation to social disorganization: (1) the *philistine,* who rigidly adheres to a narrow class of traditional norms and influences, (2) the *bohemian,* who, quite to the contrary, remains flexible and open to any and all new influences, and (3) the *creative individual,* who creatively selects both traditional and innovative courses of action to achieve the best results.

It is also in this work that Thomas and Znaniecki coined their famous four wishes: (1) the desire for new experience, (2) the desire for recognition, (3) the desire for mastery (or response), and (4) the desire for security (Znaniecki, 1969:112-113). These (and other) wishes enter into the three personality types in varying degrees and combinations.

Thus *The Polish Peasant* is an eminently social-psychological work. Its central concepts include *value, attitude,* and *the social situation* and its definition. "When a natural thing assumes a meaning, it becomes thereby a social value. And naturally a social value may have many meanings, for it may refer to many different kinds of activity" (Znaniecki, 1969:70). Thus value is clearly defined in social-relational terms, just as meaning is, by George Herbert

Mead. Similarly, attitude is socially and relationally defined ("an attitude is a psychological process treated as primarily manifested in its reference to the social world and taken first of all in connection with some social value" [Znaniecki, 1969:71]) and distinguished from purely psychological processes ("the psychological process is a state *of somebody;* the attitude is an attitude *toward something*" [loc. cit.]). These distinctions lead Znaniecki to define social psychology as "the science of attitudes," namely "attitudes which are more or less generally found among the members of a social group . . . and manifest themselves in social activities of these individuals" (op. cit.:75-77). Thus *social psychology is the science of the subjective side of social culture* (op. cit.:78). Thomas, in turn, emphasizes the *situation* and its *definition,* by which he means the group's conception of the values and attitudes with which it must deal.

Finally, it is in terms of its methodology that *The Polish Peasant* makes a genuine contribution to the new humanistic-descriptive social psychology: for the first time, the case study approach and the use of personal documents are made into the central methodology of a major research project. One entire volume, for example, consists of the autobiography of a young Polish immigrant, Wladek. Thus *The Polish Peasant* is a major contribution to the new social psychology that is in part based on that tradition.

The definition of the situation

While W. I. Thomas' contributions to the new social psychology will crop up repeatedly throughout the remainder of this book, his concept of the definition of the situation must be introduced at this point. Although the concept, as we saw, was already present in *The Polish Peasant,* it was in Thomas' *The Unadjusted Girl,* first published in 1923, that it was fully developed, becoming the central object of sociology.

"Preliminary to any self-determined act of behavior there is always a stage of examination and deliberation which we may call *the definition of the situation*" (Thomas, 1931:41). The definition of the situation is, of course, a social process. Examples provided by Thomas himself include mob action, gossip, the deliberations of a jury at a trial, and the seemingly highly chaotic deliberations of the Russian *mir,* the primitive rural community gathering in that country, which nevertheless in the end produces a highly cohesive and unanimous definition of the situation. Another example would be the gradual definition of the situation arrived at by an increasing number of contemporary women. At the outset, there is an indeterminate situation of malaise, calling for *some* course of action. Gradually, it is determined that the problem is inequality and the goal liberation. The situation has thus been defined, and if a sufficient segment of the community rallies to the new definition, it is *then* considered true. However, the main point to remember is that the definition of the situation is a process of social dialogue and negotiation and emphatically *not* the discovery of a transcendental truth!

Directly related to the definition of the situation is what has become known as the "Thomas theorem": *"If men define situations as real, they are real in their consequences"* (Thomas and Thomas, 1928:571-573). "To take an extreme example," the Thomases write, "the warden of Dannemora prison recently refused to honor the order of the court to send an inmate outside the prison walls for some specific purpose. He excused himself on the ground that the man was too dangerous. He had killed several persons who had the unfortunate habit of talking to themselves on the street. From the movement of their lips he imagined that they were calling him vile names, and he behaved as if this were true" (loc. cit.). Or, to pursue the previous example of the contemporary women's movement, it is obvious that once having defined the situation as essentially a problem of sexual inequality, that situation and definition are quite real: not only do they produce such very tangible consequences as affirmative action in hiring, but they are also increasingly *perceived* as correct. Thus the Thomas theorem—probably the single most important tenet of the new social psychology—clearly reveals the *pragmatic* nature of our new paradigm. Indeed, pragmatism, the philosophy on which the new social psychology is based, is premised on the fundamental separation of *real* and *true*. Unlike earlier paradigms, it is not concerned with truth, merely with reality. Thus a pragmatic sociology does not, for example, pass judgment as to whether the claims and assertions of the contemporary women's movement are true; it does, however, consider them very real and worthy of close scrutiny.

Thomas' concept of the definition of the situation is among the most monumental contributions to the new paradigm, indeed to sociology and social psychology. The pragmatic conception of reality in terms of consequences rather than prior causes and the separation of reality from (transcendental) truth constitute the foundation of symbolic interactionism and cultural-humanistic social psychology. This reconceptualization is no longer seriously questioned by too many sociologists, and that is why it has become known as the Thomas theorem, as suggested by Merton. The concept of the definition of the situation is central to the new humanistic social psychology because it helps us refocus on the uniquely interpretive, deliberative, and conscious nature of human behavior, as distinct from that of animals. Men "have the power of refusing to obey a stimulation they followed at an earlier time" (Thomas, 1931:41). Human conduct is, at least partially, the expression of choice, or "free will." Even though definitions of the situation that are embraced by large collectivities for long periods of time become the components of what is simply known as *culture*, sometimes achieving the external facticity so much emphasized by Durkheim and his followers, Thomas reminds us,

correctly, that all culture is ultimately deliberate human construction.

The humanistic coefficient

In *The Method of Sociology* (1934), *Social Actions* (1936), and *The Social Role of the Man of Knowledge* (1940), Znaniecki consistently stressed the need to study social systems from the standpoint of the actors themselves and thus the importance of an irreducible humanistic coefficient in sociology. "The primary empirical evidence about any cultural human action is the experience of the agent himself, supplemented by the experience of those who react to his action, reproduce it, or participate in it. . . . The scientist who wants to study these actions inductively must take them as they are in the human experience of those agents and reagents; they are his empirical data inasmuch and because they are theirs" (Znaniecki, 1936:11-17). "In a word, the data of the cultural student are always 'somebody's', never 'nobody's' data. This essential character of cultural data we call the *humanistic coefficient,* because such data, as objects of the student's theoretic reflection, already belong to somebody else's active experience and are such as this active experience makes them" (Znaniecki, 1934:37). "The humanistic coefficient distinguishes cultural data from natural data, which the student assumes to be independent of the experience of human agents" (Znaniecki, 1936:11-17).

To Znaniecki as to Weber, then, sociology is a cultural discipline dealing in meanings. Sociology studies social action, which is always cultural, that is, subjectively meaningful action. It is because "the investigator must always try to discover how anything he observes . . . is experienced and evaluated by" his subjects (Znaniecki-Lopata, 1970:158) that we label the approach called for *humanistic*. Therefore, sociological methodology will always have to be *qualitative* as well as quantitative. In addition to enumerative induction, there will always be need for *analytical induction* (1934), the case study approach. Throughout, Znaniecki advocates the in-depth study of single cases, as done by ethnographers, rather than the statistical handling of many cases.

In addition, Znaniecki is critical of behavioristic psychology because it, too, ignores the subjective meaning experience has for the agent. The crucial question about (social) objects is not what they are, as behaviorists believe, but what they *mean*. Human beings are conscious, experiencing agents. The psychological reality studied by behaviorists is not the irreducible foundation of cultural life but, to the contrary, the product of cultural activity (Znaniecki, 1936:11-17).

A final contribution of relevance here is Znaniecki's study of the man of knowledge (1940). As Martindale (1960:421) sums it up, this has historically been the role of the "cultural technologist," well exemplified by Machiavelli's *The Prince*. Since Znaniecki's life-long emphasis was on the need to recognize the centrality of culture in human conduct—and therefore on sociology's essentially humanistic character—we can appreciate his elaborate treatment of the man of knowledge through the ages, a role of essential importance in the cultural process.

FURTHER CONTRIBUTIONS TO CULTURAL SOCIOLOGY

Many others have contributed to the new social-psychological paradigm. This paradigm includes not only the "cultural-humanistic" tradition discussed in this chapter but also such schools as symbolic interactionism, phenomenology, ethnomethodology, and existential-humanistic sociology, each of which is the subject of a subsequent chapter. We therefore postpone treatment of a much larger number of sociologists until those pertinent chapters, selecting for the present discussion, admittedly somewhat arbitrarily, contribu-

tions by Robert MacIver, C. Wright Mills, and Peter Berger.

Robert MacIver

In his *Social Causation* (1942), MacIver (1882-) coined a concept quite similar to Thomas' definition of the situation: the *dynamic assessment* of the situation. As MacIver explains: "A preliminary to conscious activity is a decision between alternatives—to do this or to do that, to do or not to do. In the process of decision-making the individual assesses a situation in the light of these alternatives. A choice between values congenial to the larger value-system of the individual is somehow reached" (MacIver, 1942:291-299). MacIver gives the example of a businessman who has just concluded an important deal and who now ponders whether or not to take a vacation, for how long, where, etc. As this man weighs the pros and cons of each alternative possible course of action he is dynamically assessing the situation. Although such a subjective assessment can never cover all contingencies and therefore cannot predict the outcome of any decision with absolute certainty, it is the best process available to man. It is the capacity for such rational and reflexive evaluation of means and ends, the anticipatory imagination of possible consequences, and the review of past events that distinguish man from animals. To be sure, values differ from one individual to the next, and so do the factors considered relevant in the dynamic assessment. Thus human conduct is based on the subjective interpretation of facts.

We see, then, that MacIver has much in common with Thomas, Znaniecki, Weber, and other humanistic sociologists. He insists, as do those authors, that social causation is essentially different from natural causation. It is different because it is "teleological," that is, human conduct is motivated, intentional, goal-directed. "We as human beings are immersed in the strivings, purposes, and goals that constitute the peculiar dynamics of this area of reality. The chain of social causation needs mind for its existence . . ." (paraphrased in Martindale, 1960:408). Thus the social sciences differ from the natural sciences both in subject matter and in methods. The essentially cultural, meaningful nature of sociology's subject matter make positivism inappropriate for that discipline.

C. Wright Mills

Although the work of Mills (1916-1963) remains primarily identified with the radical-critical analysis of American institutions (cf. Mills, 1951; 1956; Chapter 3), he has also made important theoretical contributions to the new paradigm. Early in *The Sociological Imagination* he states that "it is my aim in this book to define the meaning of the social sciences for the cultural tasks of our time" (1959:18). Significantly, Mills does not care much for the expression "social science," preferring "social studies" or "human disciplines" (loc. cit.). This is because his conception of sociology is a humanistic one, reconciling C. P. Snow's two antagonistic cultures (op. cit.:16-18). Mills' view is that sociology "deals with problems of biography, of history, and of their intersections within social structures" (op. cit.:143). Throughout his work, he insists, in quite Weberian fashion, on the importance of history and on the cultural context of all social action. As a humanist, Mills insists on the value of freedom and on the danger of men becoming cheerful robots, of willingly rejecting freedom. "The values involved in the cultural problem of individuality are conveniently embodied in all that is suggested by the ideal of the Renaissance Man. The threat to that ideal is the ascendancy among us of the Cheerful Robot." Furthermore, Mills believes that a major danger in contemporary society is history-by-default, "men . . . abdicating (history's) wilful making, and so merely drifting" (op. cit.:176). The thrust of Mills' argument is clearly humanistic and cultural: man is free and must assume responsibility for his destiny, and human conduct can only be understood in a historical-cultural context.

On the cultural context of human conduct, Mills had earlier written an article, "Situated Actions and Vocabularies of Motive" (1940), which has become a classic because it, practically single-handedly, provides sociology with its own theory of motivation as distinct from the conventional psychological theory of motivation. The Millsian concept of motive is eminently pragmatic, interactionist, and therefore central to the new social psychology. It is *the* sociological conception of motive.

A vocabulary of motive is a typical mode of explaining conduct. That is, it is the type of explanation an individual may be expected to provide when asked to account for his behavior. Thus motive is essentially *an explanation given after the fact* rather than a cause occurring before it. This conception of motive contrasts sharply with the conventional psychological definition, particularly the Freudian one, which views motive as the (true) prior cause of behavior, a cause to be located within the acting individual. According to Mills, the quest for "real motives" is futile, particularly in complex and multicausal processes. At the social level, motives are linguistic terms (explanations) given, negotiated, constructed in interaction. It is not the sociologist's task to speculate about what goes on inside individual organisms. What they can and must do, however, is to study both the competing vocabularies that prevail in given historical-cultural contexts and those given by actors and/or observers to account for occurring conduct.

For example, "individualistic, sexual, hedonistic, and pecuniary vocabularies of motives are apparently now dominant in many sectors of twentieth-century urban America. Under such an ethos . . . (when) a medieval monk writes that he gave food to a poor but pretty woman because it was 'for the glory of god and the eternal salvation of the soul,' why do we tend to question him and impute sexual motives? Because sex is an influential and widespread motive in our society and time" (Mills, 1940).

Thus Mills provides us with a revolutionary new concept of motive, one that is central to the new social psychology. Unlike the classical psychological conception of motive, this sociological concept is pragmatic and directly based on Weber's work and on the Thomas theorem. "Sociologically, as Max Weber put it, a motive is a term in a vocabulary which appears to the actor himself and/or to the observer to be an adequate reason for his conduct. This conception grasps the intrinsically social character of motivation" (Gerth and Mills, 1953). And as with Thomas' definition of the situation, the Millsian theory of motivation is pragmatic in that it is not so much concerned with the validity of motives as with their relevance, not with their truth but with their reality, namely a reality defined in terms of consequences rather than prior causes.

Peter Berger

In the concluding pages of his masterful little introductory textbook (1963), Peter Berger (1929-) provides one of the best justifications of sociology as a humanistic discipline. Using the metaphor of a puppet theater, Berger compares people with the puppets dancing on the miniature stage. "We learn to understand the logic of this theater and we find ourselves in its motion. We locate ourselves in society and thus recognize our own position as we hang from its subtle strings. For a moment we see ourselves as puppets indeed. But then we grasp a decisive difference between the puppet theater and our own drama. Unlike the puppets, we have the possibility of stopping in our movements, looking up and perceiving the machinery by which we have been moved" (Berger, 1963:176).

Berger's metaphor helps us conceive of sociology as both a science and a humanity, as in the case of the previous authors discussed in this chapter. There are lawful regularities governing human behavior but, on the other hand, human conduct is also reflexive, self-conscious, in one word: *free.*

Elsewhere, Berger gives (with Thomas Luckmann) a brilliant analysis of human culture-creating capacity. *The Social Construction of Reality* (1966) is unsurpassed as a treatise in cultural sociology, that is, as an analysis of the processes leading to the construction of meaning. Tracing the role and development of language, habitualization, institutionalization, sedimentation, legitimation, symbolic universes, and social structures, the authors remind us throughout their work that all meaning is man-made and that the meaning of human behavior can only be derived from the cultures and symbolic universes constructed by man himself. Much of Berger's work in his contributions to the sociology of religion and in his recent critical analysis of political ideologies (1974) is an unmasking and debunking enterprise; it shows how men construct meanings, belief systems, and cultural complexes, and how these structures become, in time, the prisons in which men throughout history seem to have deliberately placed themselves. We shall examine Berger's work in greater detail later, for example, when discussing the sociology of knowledge. As that subdiscipline shows (along with phenomenology and ethnomethodology, among other orientations), the human tendency to gradually take arbitrary conventions for granted, to cease questioning and doubting, and to reify meanings which are in fact always of man's own creation—a tendency no doubt ultimately to be understood in terms of man's desire for closure and security—makes freedom an always precarious and endangered possibility. However, a central theme in this book as in the works of humanists like Peter Berger is that freedom, while historically more often eschewed than pursued because of its anxiety-producing effect, is nevertheless of the essence of human existence. Without it, man is not truly human; with it, he is unique.

This chapter has surveyed one strand of the new social-psychological paradigm, cultural-humanistic sociology. The rallying theme of the new social psychology is that sociology and social psychology must not merely study empirically observable (physical) behavior but, more importantly, the meanings behavior has for the actors themselves. Quantitative methodology and objectivity, the defining characteristics of positivistic science, are therefore insufficient if not outright misleading. Instead, the new social psychology emphasizes the need for qualitative methodology and (inter)subjective understanding. Sociology, as Nisbet (1962) has reminded us, is also an art form.

Here, only a handful of men were discussed—those who emphasized the essential *cultural* nature of sociology and social psychology. Prime among them was Max Weber, who, while considering sociology a science, at the same time realized that the subject matter of this science is essentially different from that of the physical sciences. For our purposes, Weber's most relevant contributions were theoretical and methodological rather than substantive: he argued forcefully that sociology, in addition to providing causal explanations, must above all provide *understanding* (verstehen).

In addition to Weber, contributions were discussed by W. I. Thomas, Florian Znaniecki, Robert MacIver, C. Wright Mills, and Peter Berger. Thomas' great contribution was his concept of the definition of the situation and the "Thomas theorem": "If men define situations as real, they are real in their consequences." Znaniecki wrote about the humanistic coefficient in sociology, emphasizing the very same theoretical and methodological points as Weber. MacIver's dynamic assessment was, as we saw, somewhat similar to Thomas' definition of the situation. Mills developed a sociological concept of motive, according to which motive is not a prior and internal cause of conduct but an *explanation* given and negotiated in social inter-action. Finally, Berger has contributed to cultural-humanistic sociology both as a sociologist of knowledge who anlyzes the manmade meaning complexes called "cultures" and as a humanist who reminds us that human behavior is reflexive rather than determined.

A recent book by Abner Cohen (1974) helps us pull together the common denominator underlying this chapter. Cohen's book is a plea for the recognition of man's two dimensionality, the fact that man does not live by power and tangible interests alone but by ideas, ideals, and symbolism as well. Thus the framework of the book consists of the culture-structure dichotomy, or symbolism and power, in Cohen's terms. The dichotomy is fundamental to sociology, and for over a century our discipline has tackled many if not most of its problems in terms of that duality, or dialectic. Culture and symbolism refer, of course, to the realm of ideas. Structure refers to the realm of the material, the empirical—from power, politics, econmics to any other form of actual *behavior*. Contemporary sociology, like Marx's "scientific socialism," and contemporary psychology, behavioristic and physiological as it is, are fundamentally *materialistic*. In Cohen's dichotomy, modern social science overwhelmingly opts for the primacy of structure over culture, behavior over ideas, the empirical over the spiritual, power over symbolism. In this context, Weber and the other cultural sociologists discussed in this chapter can be termed philosophical *idealists*. They represent an important countervailing force and a tradition that must be kept alive if social science is not to degenerate into total materialism, into a paradigm that views man as a mindless and soulless stimulus-response organism. This is the importance and rallying point of cultural sociology. It explains, also, why cultural sociology is inherently humanistic.

REFERENCES

Berger, Peter L.
1963 Invitation to Sociology. Garden City, N.Y.: Doubleday and Co., Inc.
1974 Pyramids of Sacrifice: Political Ethics and Social Change. New York: Basic Books, Inc.

Berger, Peter L. and Thomas Luckmann
1966 The Social Construction of Reality. Garden City, N.Y.: Doubleday and Co., Inc.

Bierstedt, Robert
1969 Introduction. In Florian Znaniecki: On Humanistic Sociology. Chicago: University of Chicago Press.

Blau, Peter M. and W. Richard Scott
1962 Formal Organizations: A Comparative Approach. San Francisco: Chandler Publishing Co.

Cohen, Abner
1974 Two-Dimensional Man: An Essay on the Anthropology of Power and Symbolism in Complex Society. Berkeley: University of California Press.

Coser, Lewis A.
1971 Masters of Sociological Thought. New York: Harcourt Brace Jovanovich, Inc.

Coser, Lewis A. and Bernard Rosenberg
1969 Sociological Theory: A Book of Readings. London: The Macmillan Co.

Deutsch, Morton and Robert M. Krauss
1965 Theories in Social Psychology. New York: Basic Books, Inc.

Gerth, H. and C. Wright Mills
1953 Character and Social Structure. New York: Harcourt, Brace.
1958 From Max Weber: Essays in Sociology. New York: Oxford University Press.

Goode, William J. and Paul K. Hatt
1952 Methods in Social Research. New York: McGraw-Hill Book Co.

Gouldner, Alvin W.
1959 "Organizational analysis." In Sociology Today: Problems and Prospects. Robert K. Merton et al. (eds.). New York: Harper & Row, Publishers.

MacIver, Rober M.
1942 Social Causation. Boston: Ginn and Co.

Martindale, Don
1960 The Nature and Types of Sociological Theory. Boston: Houghton Mifflin Co.

McDougall, William
1908 Social Psychology. Boston: John W. Luce.

Mennell, Stephen
1974 Sociological Theory: Uses and Unities. New York: Praeger Publishers.

Mills, C. Wright
1940 "Situated actions and vocabularies of motive." American Sociological Review (October):904-913.
1951 White Collar: The American Middle Classes. New York: Oxford University Press.
1956 The Power Elite. New York: Oxford University Press.
1959 The Sociological Imagination. New York: Oxford University Press.

Mullins, Nicholas C.
1973 Theories and Theory Groups in Contemporary American Sociology. New York: Harper & Row, Publishers.

Nisbet, Robert
1962 "Sociology as an art form." Pacific Sociological Review (Fall):67-74.

Parsons, Talcott
1956 "Suggestions for a sociological theory of organization." Administrative Scientific Quarterly 1:63-85, 225-39.

Parsons, Talcott et al.
1961 Theories of Society. New York: The Free Press.

Reiss, Albert J.
1972 "Servers and served in service." In The City in the Seventies. Robert K. Yin (ed.). Itasca, Ill.: Peacock Publishers, Inc.

Ross, E. A.
   1908   Social Psychology. New York: The Mac-
          millan Co.
Roszak, Theodore
   1969   The Making of a Counterculture. Garden
          City, N.Y.: Doubleday & Co., Inc.
   1973   Where the Wasteland Ends. Garden City,
          N.Y.: Doubleday and Co., Inc.
Thomas, W. I.
   1923; The Unadjusted Girl. Boston: Little, Brown
   1931   & Co.
Thomas, W. I. and D. S. Thomas
   1928   The Child in America. New York: Alfred A.
          Knopf, Inc.
Thomas, W. I. and Florian Znaniecki
   1918- The Polish Peasant in Europe and America
   1920   (5 vols.). Chicago: University of Chicago
          Press.
Weber, Max
   1947   The Theory of Social and Economic Orga-
          nization. A. M. Henderson and Talcott Par-
          sons (trans.) and Talcott Parsons (ed.). Glen-
          coe, Ill.: Free Press.
   1958   The Protestant Ethic and the Spirit of Capi-
          talism. New York: Charles Scribner's Sons.
   1968   On Charisma and Institution Building. Chi-
          cago: The University of Chicago Press.
Zetterberg, Hans
   1965   On Theory and Verification in Sociology.
          Totowa, N.J.: The Bedminster Press.
Znaniecki, Florian
   1934   The Method of Sociology. New York: Far-
          rar and Rinehart.
   1936   Social Actions. New York: Farrar and Rine-
          hart.
   1940   The Social Role of the Man of Knowledge.
          New York: Columbia University Press.
   1969   On Humanistic Sociology. Chicago: The
          University of Chicago Press.
Znaniecki-Lopata, Helena
   1970   "On the humanistic coefficient." In Social
          Psychology Through Symbolic Interaction.
          Gregory P. Stone and Harvey A. Farberman
          (eds.). Waltham, Mass.: Ginn-Blaisdell, pp.
          156-157.

chapter 6
Symbolic interactionism

The second strand of the new social psychology to be discussed in this book is *symbolic interactionism*. This is a social-psychological perspective that finds most of its adherents among sociologists, not psychologists. It is an alternative to and, we argue, an improvement over the various psychological perspectives discussed in Chapter 2, for example, behaviorism, psychoanalytic psychology, and Gestalt and field theory. Although it will take the reader at least this entire chapter to fully grasp the meaning of symbolic interactionism, it may be defined, preliminarily, as *the type of social psychology that focuses on social interaction (rather than the individual or the social system) and on the predominantly symbolic nature of human interaction (thus clearly distinguishing it from animal behavior).*

The paradigms discussed in the first part of this book each face certain problems that symbolic interactionism successfully transcends: unlike the sociological G.O.P., symbolic interactionism does not reify social systems and structures; instead,

it emphasizes at all times that all social facts are ultimately concrete *behavioral processes*. Unlike the psychological G.O.P., symbolic interactionism is careful to avoid the fallacy of psychological reductionism, since it opts neither for the static social system nor for the atomized individual as its basic unit of analysis, but for *social process* and *social relations*. Finally, symbolic interactionism, unlike behaviorism and many other (social) psychologies, is also careful not to confuse man with animals. Central to the perspective is the concept of self, which is used to indicate that man, and man only, is simultaneously subject and object to himself, that human conduct, unlike animal behavior, is *reflexive*. Thus symbolic interactionism is, unlike the conventional sociological and psychological paradigms treated in the first part of this book, a humanistic paradigm. It is the only truly *social* psychology and the only approach that addresses itself to the central issues of human existence and experience. All this will become clearer as we proceed with the

---

[1]Textbooks in sociological theory generally recognize symbolic interactionism as one of the five or six major schools in contemporary sociology (cf. Martindale, 1960; Mullins, 1973). There are several textbooks and readers in specifically symbolic interactionist social psychology—for example, Blumer (1969), Cardwell (1971), Kinch (1973), Lindesmith and Strauss (1956), Lindesmith, Strauss, and Denzin (1975), Shibutani (1961), Warriner (1970) (textbooks); Cardwell (1973), Lindesmith and Strauss (1969), Manis and Meltzer (1972), Rose (1962), Stone and Farberman (1970) (readers).

Symbolic interactionism is one of the American Sociological Association's major classificatory categories, used to designate members' area of expertise, intellectual orientation, etc. In 1975, Gregory Stone, Harvey Farberman, and several others founded the Society for the Study of Symbolic Interaction, with its own professional journal. Many major sociology departments have long been identified as primarily symbolic interactionist. These are found mostly among

the big Midwestern universities, in what might be called "the interactionist belt." For example, during the 1930s and 1940s, the University of Chicago was the school's major center. Subsequently, disciples spread to and established strong symbolic interactionist departments at such places as Minnesota, Iowa, Missouri, Illinois, and Wisconsin.

Symbolic interactionism has, of course, its "father" and founder—George Herbert Mead—and a number of first-generation disciples responsible for disseminating the gospel. These include (alphabetically) Howard Becker, Herbert Blumer, Robert Dubin, Erving Goffman, Everett Hughes, Manford Kuhn, Alfred Lindesmith, Don Martindale, Arnold Rose, Tamotsu Shibutani, Gregory Stone, Anselm Strauss, Sheldon Stryker, Ralph Turner, to mention but a few of the vast number of sociologists responsible for the vigorous expansion of this school after World War II. Not coincidentally, most of the first-generation disciples listed above received their Ph.D. at the University of Chicago, where Mead taught.

discussion of major symbolic interactionist contributions.

Since we have designated the conventional sociological and psychological paradigms as the G.O.P., we may accept Mullins' (1973) view that symbolic interactionism is "the loyal opposition" within American sociology and social psychology. Compared, for example, to the cultural sociologists discussed in the previous chapter, symbolic interactionists definitely constitute a unified faction.[1] The school rallies, of course, around the scriptures of George Herbert Mead, whose *Mind, Self and Society* (1934) is the posthumous publication of lecture notes taken by his students at the University of Chicago. Mead can be considered the founder of the symbolic interactionist paradigm, like Marx that of communism and Freud that of psychiatry. In addition, the school also claims among its pioneers some authors already touched upon in the previous chapter, for example W. I. Thomas, Florian Znaniecki, and C. Wright Mills (cf. Martindale, 1960).

The philosophical foundation of symbolic interactionism is *pragmatism*. This philosophy can be defined as a "theory of meaning, truth and value, in which the empirically ascertainable consequences implied by an idea or statement are held to constitute the meaning of the statement. ... The pragmatic theory of value presents utility as the chief criterion of value. Exponents of pragmatism include Charles C. Pierce, William James, and John Dewey" (Theodorson and Theodorson, 1969:310).

William James (1842-1910) was one of the founders of pragmatism as well as of symbolic interactionism. He was both a philosopher and a psychologist at Harvard. Pragmatism's revolutionary contribution to the advancement of thought lies in the bold way in which that philosophy cut through a number of age-old Gordian knots and thereby helped Western thought out of a thousand-year-old impasse. Fundamental to Western thought until the nineteenth century were a number of dualisms, including the mind-matter and subject-object dichotomies. By

the nineteenth century it was apparent that these dualities were more cumbersome than enlightening. They had merely produced, throughout the centuries, unalterably opposed factions of thinkers—the idealists against the materialists, the scientists versus the humanists, the nominalists versus the realists, etc.—without any possibility of reconciliation and progress.

Pragmatism finally provided the synthesis and the fresh new departure long awaited, especially in the social sciences. James proposed that the subject-object relation is *not* fundamental. In other words, he questioned the age-old philosophical assumption that in the occurrence of "knowing" there is a subject aware of an object or thing that is known (cf. Martindale, 1960:300). That assumption—the assumption that the knower is an entity (variously called "mind," "consciousness," or whatever else)—is merely a leftover of the concept of soul, a concept that belongs in theology and metaphysics, not in empirical science. Pragmatism, then, does not postulate (nor, for that matter, does it deny) the existence of mind (or soul) as a thing within the organism. As a scientific epistemology, it is only concerned with the real world, and it defines real in terms of experience. Pragmatism therefore formulates a much more realistic postulate, namely that *the primary stuff of which everything is composed is experience.* Indeed, what could be more real than experience? Once this is established, it can be readily seen that known and knower (the mind), object and subject, are merely the two sides of experience. Experience is a process, it is activity, it is life itself. It is fundamental. At the human level, it becomes *conscious*, conscious of external phenomena as well as of itself. It turns onto itself, becomes reflexive. That is why it can be said that man (and man alone) is simultaneously subject and object to himself.

Thus James demonstrates convincingly that what has misleadingly been called "mind" and erroneously held to be an entity is actually a behavioral process, an activity. In his famous article "Does Consciousness Exist?" (1904) and in his *Principles of Psychology* (1892), James points out that an idea which makes its appearance in consciousness "is as mythological an entity as the Jack of Spades" (1892:152). Pragmatism, then, argues that (social) psychology cannot take its point of departure in the assumption that man possesses a thing or faculty called mind, because such an assumption is metaphysical.

This is, however, merely the first step, for having said this, we must immediately recognize the fact that we think. Certainly we all experience the activity called "consciousness." Therefore, James suggests, let us reconceptualize this activity as a *stream of consciousness*, a process rather than a substance. This metaphor, then, indicates the true subject matter of (social) psychology: the study of human behavior, which is first and foremost an on-going process of consciousness.

In order to facilitate the (social) psychological conception of human behavior, James proposes that we describe man, acting, thinking, and self-aware, as a *self* and that we distinguish the "I" and the "me" as the two phases of the self. The me refers to the self as known (the empirical ego) and the I refers to the self as knower (the "pure" ego). The me is all that I call mine. This can include my body, my virtues, my vices, my family, my possessions, and the social me, which is the recognition I get from my mates (James, 1892:190). I have as many me's as there are groups or individuals who recognize me. These different social me's are, of course, what we now call *roles*. Thus James' introduction of the concept of me leads to the vast work subsequently done by social psychologists on roles, role-conflict, reference groups, self-concept, and the myriad of other topics central to role theory and, indeed, to social psychology. Here, the main point to re-

member is that the me refers to myself as object, insofar as I and others are aware of it, and that it is complex and multiple, the product of all my interactions with different groups and individuals

The I, then, is the self as subject. This is the thinker, says James (op. cit.), consciousness itself. Insofar as I reflect back upon who I am, what I have done, or what I shall do, *I* am in action. The deliberative, tentative, and interpretive processes subsequently so much emphasized by symbolic interactionists are, of course, I activities. Not that any given activity (except perhaps totally habitual, instinctive, or emotional behavior) is to be classified as belonging either to the I or to the me: the I and the me are two perspectives, two *phases* of the act: the I acts in the present, and that action, when passed into memory, becomes part of the me. The I, then, represents the principle of activity in the self. The I defines the situation (cf. W. I. Thomas, Chapter 5), assesses it dynamically (cf. Robert MacIver, Chapter 5), decides, creates, chooses, imagines, reviews, judges.

Traditionally, it is the I that has been called the soul, the spirit, the mind, or the "transcendental" ego. However, James refutes that notion, pointing out that it is merely a passing state, an activity. If we do have a feeling of permanence, continuity, and identity, a feeling of being the same person today as yesterday (and it is because of this feeling that we tend to view the I as a permanent agent, a little homunculus somewhere within us), it is only because change is slow, continuous, and gradual, because we develop habits, and because we therefore behave today in some ways (but by no means all) the same way as yesterday.

James' reconceptualization of consciousness has revolutionized social psychology. From the study of objects (nervous systems, minds, people), the discipline has moved to the study of processes (activity, experience). Furthermore, the distinction between the I and the me prevents social psychology from lapsing into either a psychologistic or a sociologistic determinism.

In addition to role behavior (the me), which is socially determined, there is always the unpredictable I, which interprets, decides, defines the situation, chooses, rejects, accepts, in other words embodies *free will*. Finally, the new conception is eminently *pragmatic,* since it abandons old metaphysical and absolutist theoretical positions, posits only the primacy of *experience,* and argues for this novel theory of mind not because it can "prove" that it is the only true theory but because it is far more useful in that it provides a fresh and promising new start in social psychology, a start which finally recognizes that the most fundamental and inescapable fact about social psychology is that it studies *life,* which for man is *experience.*

The philosopher John Dewey (1859-1952) also contributed heavily to pragmatism and to a pragmatic social psychology. Like William James, he helped transcend certain age-old and insoluble philosophical issues by drastically reconceiving mind and mental activity (cf. Dewey, 1922). The problem with which philosophers like Immanuel Kant and David Hume had struggled was how to reconcile empirical and rational knowledge. Empirical knowledge is based on sensory *perception.* For example, I know that this apple fell from the tree because I just saw it fall. Rational knowledge is a matter of *conception*—theory. For example, I know that in the absence of a counterforce, any loose apple *will* fall toward the earth. The only way classical philosophers knew how to reconcile these two types of knowledge (Kant's a posteriori and a priori knowledge, respectively) was to posit the existence of things that could not be demonstrated to exist—for example, a mind, a sort of "synthesizer" that assembles perceptions into cognitions.

Dewey, however, knew from biology that life, including mental life, can best be conceived of as activity and that life furthermore is essentially *adaptive* activity, not merely a passive reaction to environmental stimuli. Classical philosophy had conceived of human psychology as mental images (ideas) elicited in a passive organism by environmental stimuli. And how environmental occurrences could produce such images remained a mystery, unless of course one was willing to posit an image-maker, a mind. Dewey abandoned such a philosophy. To him, human psychology became, as all life, adaptive behavior, *experience.* As with William James, experience and the adaptive processes called living and thinking, not static ideas or physical objects, became the fundamental point of departure in Dewey's analysis.

Dewey developed the implications of pragmatism for scientific methodology, education, and a variety of social-psychological topics, for example motivation. His theories are in total convergence with those of other pragmatists already discussed. For example, all thought and inquiry begins, according to Dewey, when a disturbance in equilibrium calls for an *analysis of the indeterminate situation.* This is, of course, quite similar to MacIver's dynamic assessment (see Chapter 5). Dewey's conception of *motive* is identical to Weber's and Mills': "A motive does not exist prior to an act and produce it. It is an act *plus* a judgment upon some element of it, the judgment being made in the light of the consequences of the act" (Dewey, 1922:120). Finally, since mental activity (intelligence) is essentially a process of and an instrument of adaptation, it follows that education and learning must be precisely that—adaptation and adjustment (cf. Martindale, 1960:302). Dewey's philosophy is called instrumentalism, which is essentially synonymous with pragmatism. The reality studied by social psychology—human activity—must be examined and appraised in light of its adaptive functions and of its instrumentality. This is where the meaning of human experience lies.

Having traced the philosophical background of symbolic interactionism through the works of two major pragmatists, this chapter will now provide a more elaborate discussion of the work of George Herbert

Mead, the founder of symbolic interactionism; some other early symbolic interactionists, including Charles H. Cooley; the major first-generation Meadians, including Herbert Blumer; a number of other interactionists, including Goffman; and other theoretical and empirical contributions to modern symbolic interactionism.

GEORGE HERBERT MEAD

Mead (1863-1931) was a philosopher and social psychologist at the University of Chicago. Today, symbolic interactionism is also termed Meadian social psychology, which indicates Mead's preponderant role in founding that school. The following discussion first traces some of the influences on Mead's thought, then touches on Mead's major concepts and theories, examines the substantive problem for which Mead's social psychology has had the greatest relevance—socialization, or the relationship of society and the individual—and finally sums up some of the subsequent evaluations of his work.

His significant others

Mead was a pragmatist, and the single greatest influence on his work came from William James (see, for example, Martindale, 1960:353-359; Mead, 1956:118; Stone and Farberman, 1970; Strauss, 1956). In addition, his work contains many references to Watson, Wundt, and Cooley, among others. There is no basic disagreement whatsoever between the perspectives of James and Mead. Both are pragmatists, both conceive of (social) psychology's subject matter as processes rather than entities, both focus on the human self with its two phases, the I and the me. The main difference is merely the fact that whereas James' theory of consciousness was primarily psychological, Mead's concern was far more *social*-psychological and sociological. James, it may be recalled, had taken experience as the fundamental process and starting point of his analysis and then

treated subject and object as distinctions arising out of it. Mead followed the same format, taking the social process of interaction as his fundamental datum and then treating both individual minds and social structures as arising out of that process. Thus just as James proposed a bold new way to do away with the cumbersome subject-object separation, so Mead showed us how to transcend the society-individual split. These contributions are essential, for they permit the development of a new social psychology that is neither totally positivistic nor totally subjective and that is the only truly *social* psychology, opting neither for the primacy of the individual nor for that of society.

Mead characterized John B. Watson's mindless behaviorism as the attitude of the Queen in *Alice in Wonderland*—"Off with their heads!" (Mead, 1956:117). While in agreement with Watson that (social) psychology must study behavior, he criticized him for totally neglecting mental phenomena. Wilhelm Wundt on the other hand, was viewed as guilty of psychophysical parallelism (op. cit.:132), of positing the separate and parallel existence of mind and body, whereby the prior existence of mind is posited to account for mental phenomena. For example, pain is said to occur at two levels, in the body and in the mind. While Mead totally rejected this, he did find value in Wundt's work on language and gestures, and he adopted much of that work. Charles H. Cooley, finally, was another early symbolic interactionist whose ideas Mead generally approved of, although with criticism for Cooley's individualistic bias (cf. Mead, 1956:244). Mead opposed what he viewed as the excessive subjectivism, introspectionism, and, indeed, solipsism (loc. cit.) of phenomenological social psychology, and he seems to have attributed these features to Cooley (see also Mead, 1929-1930:693-706).

It follows from Mead's social focus that "no very sharp line can be drawn between social psychology and individual psychology. Social psychology is especially interested in the effect which the social group has in the determination of the experience and conduct of the individual member" (Mead, 1956:115). "Psychology is not something that deals with consciousness; psychology deals with the experience of the individual in relation to the conditions under which the experience goes on. It is social psychology when the conditions are social ones. It is behavioristic when the approach to experience is made through conduct" (op. cit.:153). Thus although Mead called himself a social behaviorist (symbolic interactionism was coined by Herbert Blumer much later; cf. Blumer, 1969:1), his social psychology has virtually nothing in common with the Watsonian and Skinnerian type of psychology known today as behaviorism.

His major ideas

Since Mead meant to provide a paradigm that would enable us to understand human social conduct, the first and very important phase of his work is aimed at developing a theory and taxonomy for the understanding of communication at the specifically human level, through *language*. First, then, we have *attitudes:* attitudes are the starting point of Mead's analysis because they represent both inner states, or tendencies, of the organism and incipient acts. As Mead phrases it, "part of the act lies within the organism and only comes to expression later" (Mead, 1956:120).[2] Attitudes, then, are the internal organization

and preparation for the developing act (cf. Desmonde, 1970:57).

The next phase is the *gesture*. Wundt, according to Mead, "isolated a very valuable conception of the gesture as that which becomes later a symbol, but which is to be found in its early stages as part of a social act. It is that part of the social act which serves as a stimulus to other forms involved in the same social act" (Mead, 1956:154). Mead gives the illustration of a dog baring its teeth and another dog responding to this as a sign that the attack is about to begin. Gestures, then, are *natural signs*. They are the means of communication and interaction among nonhumans. And in terms of the logic of Mead's analysis, they go one step further than attitudes in that they are the already objectively observable, yet still early, stages in an ongoing act (cf. Desmonde, 1970:57).

Humans, however, go beyond gestures. Unlike dogs, we use not only natural signs (gestures) but also *conventional signs*, or what Mead calls *significant gestures, or symbols:* "gestures become significant symbols when they implicitly arouse, in an individual making them the same responses which the explicitly arouse, or are supposed to arouse, in other individuals, the individuals to whom they are addressed" (Mead, 1956:158-159).

---

[2]There is, perhaps as a result of the exigencies of that epoch, a strange tendency in Mead's writings to cater to biology in an attempt at grounding attitudes. For example:

> "What one must insist upon is that objectively observable behavior finds expression within the individual, not in the sense of being in another world, a subjective world, but in the sense of being within his organism. Something of this behavior is what we may term 'attitudes', the beginnings of acts. Now if we come back to such attitudes we find them giving rise to all sorts of responses. The telescope in the hands of a novice is not a telescope in the sense that it is to those on top of Mount Wilson. If we want to trace the responses of the astronomer, we have to go back into his central nervous system, back to a whole series of neurons; and we find something there that answers to the exact way in which the as-

tronomer approaches the instrument under certain conditions. That is the beginning of the act. . . . If a person did not have that particular nervous system, the instrument would be of no value. It would not be a telescope." (Mead, 1956:119)

Elsewhere Mead equates attitudes with "inner organic conduct," and he argues that it is the "innervation of certain groups of cells in the central nervous system" that initiates "in advance the later stages of the act" (op. cit.:125). Further evidence of this tendency can be found on pp. 178-179, 184 (footnote), 189, 190 et passim. It is interesting, then, that when Mead states that we can state behavioristically what we mean by an "idea," he means actually *biologically*. This explains his rejection of introspection and phenomenological social psychology. In his otherwise brilliant social psychology, Mead seems to have needlessly pinned down attitudes in the central nervous system.

Language, then, consists of such significant symbols, symbols which Mead calls *universals* (op. cit.:211) or *universes of discourse,* because their meaning is shared, that is, because they call out the same response in another that they call out in the speaker. Thus Mead's theory of the social act is based on a brilliant taxonomy that begins with the attitude and ends with language, the various components of the social act. "Language in its significant sense is that vocal gesture which tends to arouse in the individual the attitude which it arouses in others, and it is this perfecting of the self by the gesture which mediates the social activities that give rise to the process of taking the role of the other" (op. cit.:224-225).

The pragmatic reconceptualization of *meaning* that follows out of Mead's theory of the social act is more central to the new social psychology than any other concept. In essence, it states that *meaning is not inherent in an object or idea, as has been traditionally believed, but derives from the response to that object (or idea).* This follows from Mead's earlier discussion of gestures and significant symbols: since a gesture or symbol is a stimulus that elicits a specific response from another organism involved in the same social act, its meaning lies in that response. "The meaning of a gesture on the part of one organism is the adjustive response of another organism to it . . . the adjustive response of the second organism being itself directed toward . . . the com-

pletion of the act" (op. cit.:168). The logical structure of meaning is depicted in Fig. 6-1.

It should be noted that Mead's conception of meaning and "meaningful" is identical with Max Weber's. As we saw (see Chapter 5), the German sociologist explained that only rational, conscious, in sum, symbolic action is meaningful, that is, understandable. Now Mead points out, similarly, that only one type of gesture, namely the significant symbol, can be considered meaningful. This is because only the significant symbol is conscious and intended to arouse in the other some same phase of the act (response) as in oneself, and vice versa. This only the symbol does, not, for example a natural sign such as a dog's bark. Thus only human behavior can be meaningful, because only man possesses reflective intelligence, the ability to *indicate to oneself* the characters that call out the response (op. cit.:169-171).

The Meadian conception of meaning—fundamental to the new social psychology—can therefore be summed up in the theorem: *the meaning is in the response.* In a vulgar fashion one could view this as similar to the old philosophical position that "a tree falling in a remote forest makes a crashing sound only insofar as it is heard by someone." However, we saw that Mead's theory of meaning is far more sophisticated than that. The philosopher's real contribution has been to elaborate in rich detail the enormously complex social matrix of meaning, a matrix "present if the social act before . . . awareness of meaning occurs" (op. cit.:165). By relocating mean-

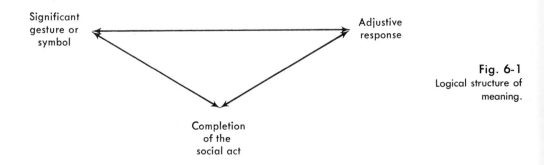

Significant gesture or symbol

Adjustive response

Completion of the social act

Fig. 6-1
Logical structure of meaning.

ing at the very center of social interaction, Mead transcends the mindless positivism of behavioristic psychology. By defining meaning pragmatically, he avoids the pitfall of absolutism, the notion that meanings are a priori inherent in phenomena regardless of their perception and interpretation by human consciousness.

Now that we understand what significant gestures or significant symbols are, we can apprehend Mead's conception of the human mind. Just as for James, the mind is not substance but process, activity. What kind of activity? It is *an internalized conversation of the individual with himself by means of (significant) gestures* (op. cit.:159). And, Mead continues, "the internalization in our experience of the external conversations of gestures which we carry on with other individuals in the social process is the essence of thinking; and the gestures thus internalized are significant symbols because they have the same meanings for all individual members of the given society or social group, that is, they respectively arouse the same attitudes in the individuals making them that they arouse in the individuals responding to them" (loc. cit.).

Thinking, then, is a reflective activity; it consists of making indications to oneself. The ability to do so distinguishes man from animals and is called *intelligence*. "Intelligence is essentially the ability to solve the problems of present behavior in terms of its future consequences as implicated on the basis of past experience. . . . It involves both memory and foresight" (op. cit.:178). Intelligent human conduct is reflective conduct; it refers "to the presence of the future in terms of ideas" (op. cit.:181). As we shall see in a moment, *social* intelligence is the ability to take the role of, or "put oneself in the place of," other individuals with whom one interacts. This is quite in line with what has just been said about intelligence, for all intelligence essentially involves the ability to think, to indicate to oneself the meanings and attitudes of others and to carry on the internal conversation in those terms (op. cit.:205-206).

Having said that the mind and thinking

essentially consist of the ability to indicate meanings to others and to oneself, we can now understand that this process is what relates the organism to the environment (op. cit.:187, 194). As Mead states it, "the organism is in a sense responsible for its environment" (op. cit.:192), for mind and thought are selective, interpretive, and organizing processes. Whereas classical psychology views the relations between the organism and the environment as one in which the former is more or less shaped by and passively responds to environmental stimuli, Mead shows that having mind means precisely the opposite: it means that the organism *endows* the environment with its meaning. The environment is as much determined by the organism as vice versa. The meaning of an environmental stimulus is in the organism's response to it.

Mentality, then, is an internal conversation of the individual with himself by means of significant gestures; it consists of self-indications, including future consequences and past experiences; it is a process of selectively and interpretively indicating to oneself environmental elements, and thus, most important of all, it is man's unique instrument to control, shape, and adapt his conduct.

Now that we understand what thought is, the question is: what kind of thing is it that can *have* thought? Mead's answer is: a *self*. A self can simply be defined "as that which can be object to itself" (op. cit.:204), that "which is reflexive, i.e. which can be both subject and object" (op. cit.:201). Indeed, the self is that unique object that can turn back upon itself, direct itself, take those experiences that belong to its own organism and identify with them (op. cit.:42); this is precisely the process called *thinking!* The self, then, represents *reflexive experience,* simultaneous organic and mental activity. Only man is capable of such, only man is a self. Lower animals have no selves. They have feelings such as pleasure and pain, but these belong to the organism, not to the self, for the feelings have no symbolic meaning (loc. cit.). The human self is "essentially a cognitive rather than an emotional phenomenon" (op. cit.:228), for even though, as Cooley (1902) showed, the self includes self-*feelings* (for example, mortification, pride, or inferiority), such feelings do not become part of the self until I am aware of them, that is, until I label them.

Following William James, Mead finds it convenient to express the dual and reflexive nature of the self through the concepts of the I and the me. "The self is essentially a social process going on with these two distinguishable phases" (Mead, 1956:233). "The 'I' is the response of the organism to the attitudes of the others; the 'me' is the organized set of attitudes of others which one himself assumes. The attitudes of the others constitute the organized 'me,' and then one reacts toward that as an 'I' " (op. cit.:230). Or, put simply, the I is the subjective and active phase of the self, the me the objective and passive phase. The me stands for the roles that have, over time, been internalized by the individual. These roles, as we shall see, are of course learned from others, and this is why Mead, in his definition, equates the me with "attitudes of others." This should not confuse us to think that the me does not represent our own attitudes. It definitely does, but they are others' because they are learned and internalized from others. The I, on the other hand, does not refer to the socialized phase of the self but to the self acting in the present. As with James, the main point to remember is that, while the I and the me mutually determine one another, neither represents the total self. What Mead wished to express, throughout his work, was the self's two-dimensionality: I am partially the product of the roles I have learned, I am partially socialized, I am partially predictable, and I am partially aware of myself. This is me. However, I am also more than that, for *in the present*, I always examine, evaluate, and interpret my environment, including my own past behavior, and how I behave at this time is never a mere reflection of my environment plus my past experience, but always something more. The I, then, indicates the *emergent* nature of the self and Mead's voluntaristic and humanistic conception of man (op. cit.:173-174).

His theory of socialization

How does the self develop? How does man become genuinely human? Central to Mead's philosophy is the argument that the self is the product of social evolution (op. cit.:40). Indeed, ever since Darwin, there has been an increasing tendency to reverse the classical notion that structures are responsible for processes (functions) and to hold, instead, that structure is the product of fuction. In this sense, Mead is a "functionalist," and so is the whole interactionist social psychology he helped create.[3]

Through what mechanism does the social process produce selves? As we just saw, a self is that which has the ability to be object to itself, that is, to make indications to itself, to symbolically converse with itself. Once symbolic thought, or *language,* has been mastered, there is a self. Now we saw that language, which consists of significant gestures or symbols, is an inherently social phenomenon, since a gesture is only significant if it evokes the same response in oneself as it is supposed to elicit in another—if it is based on *role-taking* or *taking the role of the other.* By taking the role of the other, Mead means putting oneself in the place of another individual in such a manner that one arouses the same response in both. Thus language is always social. Furthermore, *only* such significant symbolic interaction is truly social, for it alone requires role-taking. The "social" organization of ants and bees, for example, while quite complex and sophisticated (cf. Lindesmith,

---

[3]Keep in mind, however, that symbolic interactionism is precisely the antithesis of sociological functionalism, the sociological G.O.P. discussed in Chapter 1.

Strauss, and Denzin, 1975:67-71), is based on instinct, not role-taking.

Now how does linguistic role-taking develop? Obviously, only through social interaction, interaction with other selves. Early childhood socialization is characterized primarily by interaction with one's *significant others*, such figures as father and mother. Mead discusses various empathic processes involved in this interaction, including role-taking, as just defined, and playing at roles, which is a more imaginary process (for example, playing at being mother, policeman, fireman). Later, socialization requires taking the role of the *generalized other*. This refers to "the organized community or social group which gives to the individual his unity of self" (Mead, 1956:218). The difference between these two phases of socialization is similar to that between *play* and *game*, and Mead's illustrative metaphor for the latter is the baseball game. Play consists merely of taking various different roles. In contrast, the organized game requires that the child take the role of everyone else in the game and, above all, understand the rules. He must, for example, understand the position of shortstop even if he never plays at that position. The generalized other, then, refers to the entire social system in which one must be socialized if one is to develop into a mature and competent participant in that sytem. Society itself is the ultimate generalized other.

In sum, Mead's analysis gradually leads us to a discussion of society, social organization, and man's rational and democratic participation in social institutions. While Mead remains thoroughly social-psychological in his approach, never reifying his concepts ("an institution, for example, is nothing but an organization of attitudes which we all carry in us" [op. cit.:239]), it becomes increasingly clear as we follow his argument that in its logic, society precedes the individual (op. cit.:121), that the mind, self, and social institutions are ultimately all social in origin. Thus the order in which Mead and the present discussion have treated the act, mind, self, and society ac-

tually reflects a traditional and ill-founded nominalistic procedure, rather than Mead's true conception of the subject matter. To do justice to that conception, it would be appropriate to redo the entire analysis by beginning with society and gradually descending to the act. We must, however, leave that effort to someone else.[4]

Some critical appraisals

As with all major scientific inventions, Mead's work has been appraised, criticized, lauded, analyzed, and elaborated by countless subsequent scholars. Herbert Blumer has made it his life-long work to develop the implications of Mead's theories. His *Symbolic Interactionism* (1969) assembles his most important articles. Desmonde (1970), Deutsch and Krauss (1965), and Martindale (1960) summarize Mead's major theories. Meltzer (1964) does likewise and, in addition, identifies some weaknesses. Rose (1962) formalizes Mead's theories in the form of an axiomatic structure. Troyer (1946) focuses on Mead's theory of the mind, pointing out the social and biological origins of the mind. Morris (1934), Stone and Farberman (1970), and Strauss (1956) provide extensive summaries of Mead's work as introductions to their collections of Mead's and Meadian writings. These, plus others such as Becker (1962), Cardwell (1971), Lindesmith, Strauss, and Denzin (1975), and Shibutani (1961) are merely a sample of the symbolic interactionists who have been responsible for the generally *supportive* dissemination of Mead's thoughts.

Kolb (1944), Meltzer and Petras (1972), Swanson (1961), Blumer (1969), Huber (1973), and others have also identified some of the weaknesses in Mead's work. Kolb believes that Mead's I and me are em-

---

[4]See Meltzer and Petras (1972:4-22), who do precisely that, and for the very reason mentioned, as well as Troyer (1946:321).

pirically indistinguishable, that the I is a mysterious residual category that could best be eliminated and replaced by more testable concepts. Meltzer and Petras (1972) support this contention. However, Becker (1962) and others, including myself, believe that it is only thanks to the I concept that we can salvage social psychology from total sociological determinism. The I reminds us that we are more than the sum of our roles, our socialization.

Meltzer (1964), in addition, criticizes Mead for the ambiguity of many of his concepts. It has been said in defense of Mead, however (for example by Gregory Stone), that in the absence of a language oriented toward *process,* Mead had to make up his own vocabulary to deal with his subject matter, with some of the observed clumsiness as a logical outcome. Meltzer and Petras also remind us, as does Blumer (1969), that Mead's schema is purely analytical and contentless. Furthermore, they point out that Mead (unlike Cooley, in that respect) overlooks the importance of sentiment in the self.

Swanson (1961) compares Mead and Freud, their differences and complementarity, calling Mead (as does Troyer, 1946) a "functionalist." Swanson's appraisal of Mead is generally positive, but he does suggest that Mead's major premise—"that self-awareness and reflective thought are products of social interaction mediated by language signs and products of it alone"— is untestable (Swanson, 1961). The general complaint that "Mead is untestable" has indeed been a widespread one. Huber (1973), whose main criticism is that Meadian social psychology's atheoretical stance leads it to reflect the bias of whoever its subjects happen to be (we shall get back to this indictment in the conclusion), ties that to the theory's untestability. In rebuttal of the untestability argument, we conclude this section with a small sample (footnote 5) of the vast amount of excellent empirical work done by Meadians during the past two decades, most of this work explicitly testing Meadian hypotheses, and all of it doing so at least implicitly.[5]

OTHER EARLY SYMBOLIC INTERACTIONISTS

In America, the classical school of symbolic interactionism consists primarily of Mead, James, Thomas, and Cooley. Early European symbolic interactionists include Cassirer and Piaget. In addition, other early Americans who have contributed to interactionist social psychology include James Mark Baldwin, Franklin Giddings, E. A. Ross, Louis Wirth, and Ernest Burgess (cf. Blumer, 1969; Martindale, 1960; Mullins, 1973). Since Thomas was discussed in Chapter 5 in combination with Znaniecki, with whom he co-authored *The Polish Peasant,* and since we have just completed the discussion of both Mead and James, the following discussion will be primarily about Cooley, followed by a brief postscript on European symbolic interactionists.

Charles Horton Cooley (1864-1929)

As a sociologist at the University of Michigan, Cooley developed a pragmatic social psychology which followed that of James and paralleled that of his contemporary, Mead. Cooley's major contributions are (1) the concept of the looking-

---

[5]See Davis, 1956; 1961; Davis, 1947; Dubin, 1956; Glaser and Strauss, 1967; Goffman, 1959a; 1959b; 1961a; 1961b; 1963a; 1963b; 1971; Kando, 1972b; 1973; 1974; Kuhn, 1964; Kuhn and McPartland, 1954; Lindesmith, 1947; Miyamoto and Dornbusch, 1956; Quarantelli and Cooper, 1966; Ray, 1953; Stone, 1962; Stryker, 1962; Thielbar, 1970; Warshay, 1962; and Zborowski, 1952. This leaves out additional work by the very prolific interactionist Erving Goffman, the many other Iowa studies using, as do Kuhn and McPartland, the Twenty Statement Test (cf. Spitzer, Couch, and Stratton, 1971, for a review of a vast amount of Iowa TST work), and the enormously rich literature on deviance, crime, and mental illness which, insofar as it follows labelling theory (cf. Becker, 1964; Douglas, 1972; Filstead, 1972; Lemert, 1951; Matza, 1959; Rubington and Weinberg, 1973; Scheff, 1966; Schur, 1971; Spitzer and Denzin, 1968) is essentially a derivation from Meadian theory.

glass self, (2) the concept of the primary group, (3) his innovative treatment of sentiment and human nature, and (4) his use and advocacy of a humanistic methodology.

The famous concept of the looking-glass self was coined by Cooley in his *Human Nature and the Social Order* (1902). "A self-idea of this sort seems to have three principal elements: the imagination of our appearance to the other person, the imagination of his judgment of that appearance, and some sort of self-feeling, such as pride or mortification" (op. cit.:152). With the looking-glass metaphor, Cooley has exactly the same thing in mind as James' social and empirical self (op. cit.:136), the main point being that *imagination,* namely the imagination of what we appear to be and of how others respond to that, is a crucial component of the self. In fact, Cooley's basic tenet about society is that it consists of "the imaginations people have of one another," society's unity thus being fundamentally a *psychological* unity.

While Cooley is thereby in total agreement with Mead that the separation of individual and society is therefore a false one (op. cit.:35-38), he differs from the Chicago philosopher in two important ways: his theory of self is, in the first place, more psychological than Mead's and does not assert as dogmatically that *all* understanding is predicated on the internalization of language. As we saw, Mead criticized him on this ground.

A second difference is Cooley's heavier emphasis on the *feeling* aspect of the self. The self is characterized by a feeling that may be called the "my-feeling or sense of appropriation. . . . The emotional or feeling self may be regarded as instinctive" (loc. cit.).

Cooley documents his theory of self with observations of his own children. "The view that 'self' and the pronouns of the first person are names which the race has learned to apply to an instinctive attitude of mind, and which each child in turn learns to apply in a similar way, was impressed upon me by observing my child M

. . . When she was two years and two weeks old. . . she had a clear notion of the first and second persons when used possessively. When asked 'where is your nose?' she would put her hand upon it and say 'my'. She also understood that when someone said 'my' and touched an object, it meant something opposite. . ." (op. cit.).

Cooley explains how a little child learns the use of pronouns. By observing their use by others in conjunction with the appropriation of objects, the child empathizes with those appropriative feelings in others and learns to associate the pronouns with those feelings. Thus role-taking and empathy play the same role in Cooley's analysis as they do in Mead's.

Sentiment, then, is an important part of Cooley's conception of the self, even of his looking-glass self (op. cit.:152). A major part of the author's work deals with the development of sentiments (cf. Cooley, 1902; 1909; Shibutani, 1961:396-400). The thesis here is that what we generally call *human nature* consists of "those sentiments and impulses that belong to mankind at large and not to any particular race or time . . ." (Cooley, 1909:28) and that these universal sentiments, far from being inborn, are the result of the same basic *primary group* participation experienced by men the world over. "Primary groups are primary in the sense that they give the individual his earliest and completest experience of social unity, and also in the sense that they do not change in the same degree as more elaborate relations" (op. cit.:26-27). Thus because cliques, families, neighborhood groups, and juvenile gangs can be found in all societies, there exist certain universal sentiments, sentiments that are learned, to be sure, but that are shared cross-culturally. These sentiments include, particularly, "sympathy and the innumerable sentiments in which sympathy enters" (op. cit.:28). This explains how role-taking becomes possible even across cultural boundaries (cf. Shibutani, 1961:395).

In sum, Cooley's conception of society and sociology is totally social-psychological and humanistic. Social organization is ultimately only "the larger mind," since the unity of society is a mental one. As far as *understanding* social phenomena, Cooley's epistemology is as humanistic as Weber's: "Reliable social knowledge is that which captures life in its full wholeness, as it was lived" (cf. Gutman, 1958). Thus any qualitative method may be appropriate, including introspection, participant observation, the use of autobiographies, poems, and essays. Human knowledge is both behavioristic and sympathetic (Cooley, 1926). It is not merely empirical but also imaginative (loc. cit.).

Europeans

The German Ernst Cassirer (1874-1945) and the Swiss Jean Piaget (1896-) are the two major European symbolic interactionists. Cassirer's social psychology (1944) is similar to that of Mead, focusing on man's symbolic nature. Examining primitive cultures, Cassirer shows, as did Mead, that symbolic interaction produces both the self and the community with its structure and collective culture.

Piaget, too, developed an interactionist conception of self independently from Mead and other Americans (cf. Martindale, 1960). For example, in his famous *The Moral Judgment of the Child* (1932), the Swiss psychologist traces the development of reason and morality through children's games, somewhat like Mead. While Mead's metaphor was baseball, Piaget discussed marbles. This is significant, because Mead's selection of a highly organized team game indicates his greater concern with the higher forms of socialization. However, both Piaget and Mead were essentially concerned with the *rules of the game*, and as Piaget sees it, the final stage of mature morality, that of *autonomy*, is reached when the child moves from moral realism to moral democracy—in Meadian

terms, from the play to the game and to taking the role of the generalized other.

MODERN SYMBOLIC INTERACTIONISM

Since Mead, James, Cooley, Thomas, and the other early interactionists, the school has blossomed into a vast branch of modern sociology, with perhaps more adherents than any competing orientation, certainly within the subdiscipline of social psychology.[6]

Kuhn's (1964) classification of major trends in modern symbolic interactionism is based on the distinction between *determinacy* and *indeterminacy*. According to that author, there is in Mead's writings an ambiguity as to whether or not the proposed paradigm is deterministic and ambiguity centering around the nebulous meaning of the I. Although in this book we have chosen to interpret the Meadian paradigm humanistically, or nondeterministically, we agree with Kuhn that the legacy has gone both ways. Therefore, the following cursory survey of modern symbolic interactionism follows Kuhn's distinction, covering first "deterministic" or positivistic work and then nondeterministic contributions. The concluding section lists work that could not be thus classified. The present section is merely a preliminary listing of major current research by symbolic interactionists. The detailed discussion of many of these studies is presented in Chapters 7 through 12, under appropriate substantive headings.

The Iowa school

The first major category of research under this heading is Kuhn's own so-called Iowa school (see Meltzer and Petras, 1972, who subdivide symbolic interactionism precisely as we do, identifying a "scientific" Iowa school with Kuhn and a "humanistic" Chicago school primarily with Blumer).

---

[6]Today, two groups are making inroads into sociological social psychology: the new Skinnerians, led by Homans (cf. Friedrich, 1974; Lynch, 1975), and the ethnomethodologists. However, it can be safely said that the subdiscipline is still overwhelmingly interactionist.

Using primarily the Twenty Statement Test, Kuhn and his disciples have conducted a vast amout of fairly rigorous empirical research on self and self-concept.[7] Interestingly, the TST, which consists of a simple question "Who am I?" to be answered twenty times, has been both defended by its proponents and criticized by the positivists for its "sensitizing" nature, that is, for its looseness (cf. Backman, 1973). Thus from the perspective of psychological, experimental, and scientific social psychology, even the Iowa school is deemed too "journalistic," even though it is the most scientific wing of modern symbolic interactionism. Related to this work (cf. Kuhn, 1960) is other research on self-concept by symbolic interactionists, including Kinch (1963; 1973), Miyamoto and Dornbusch (1956), and Quarantelli and Cooper (1966).

Role theory, while often equated with symbolic interactionism, can perhaps better be viewed as a more deterministic brand of social psychology partially overlapping with it, but finding adherents more frequently among psychologists.[8] Merton's *self-fulfilling prophecy* is a restatement of Thomas' definition of the situation, which qualifies Merton as an interactionist (cf. Martindale, 1960:425-427). More pertinently, Merton extended Hyman's (1942) *reference group* concept. Reference group theory, then, is a subset of role theory, another important area of modern symbolic interactionism.[9]

Role theory has also produced good family sociology.[10] Related to but somewhat distinct from this is the development of the developmental family sociology of Reuben Hill (cf. Hill and Hansen, 1960).

Still under role theory should be mentioned the work on role-taking by Kando (1973) and Stryker (1957; 1962), on breadth of perspective by Warshay (1962), and on socialization by Sewell (1952).

Finally, there is the work of men like Dubin (1956) in industrial sociology (his concept of *central life interest* has led to much subsequent research), Kornhauser (1959) and Rose (with Myrdal, 1944; 1967) in political sociology and race relations, Gross (1958), Dalton (1959), and Thielbar (1970) in social organization, and Lang and Lang (1961; 1962) and Turner and Killian (1957) in collective behavior. Most if not all of this work tends to be on the deterministic side of our classification, since it tends to use quantitative survey techniques and the language of hypothesis-testing variable analysis (cf. Blumer, 1956).

The Chicago school

From our standpoint, the richer and more intriguing body of knowledge produced by Meadian theory is found on the humanistic side of the fence. Here we find the vast amount of theoretical and empirical work that constitutes the meat of the new social psychology presented in this book. For the present purposes, this body of knowledge may be classified as follows. First we have the theoretical and methodological work of men like Blumer, advocating participant observation and other qualitative techniques and leading to ethnographic and phenomenological field work. Goffman's dramaturgical school comprises the second subgroup. Third, there is the labelling theory of deviance. This branch may be subdivided into criminological labelling theory and the labelling theory of mental illness. While labelling theory deals with all sorts of deviance, the point here is to distinguish between the body of knowledge generally covered in delinquency and criminology courses on

[7]See for example Couch, 1962; Kuhn, 1960; Kuhn and McPartland, 1954; and Spitzer, Couch, and Stratton, 1971.
[8]See for example Newcomb (1943) and Sarbin (1954). In addition, the sociologist Robert Merton (1950; 1957) has been associated with role theory (cf. Deutsch and Krauss, 1965).
[9]See, in addition to Hyman and Merton, for example, Shibutani (1955; 1961) and Rose (1962).
[10]See for example Farber (1962) and the many excellent studies in Heiss' reader (1968).

the one hand and the mental illness literature on the other. The latter is more properly social-psychological and links up with the medicopsychiatric work of men like Thomas Szasz and Harry Stack Sullivan. We have, finally, a variety of humanistic, existential, and cultural contributions inspired by symbolic interactionism as well as by other humanistic perspectives. Some of the more salient contributions to these four areas will be enumerated here, while Blumer and Goffman will be covered in somewhat greater detail.

Herbert Blumer (1900-) Blumer's lifelong endeavor has been to explicate and interpret Mead's theories. This has led him to a predominantly nondeterministic interpretation (cf. Meltzer and Petras, 1972), one that this book embraces. It was Blumer who coined the term symbolic interactionism. His major contribution has been the theoretical and methodological critique of the established sociological G.O.P. and its dominant reliance on quantitative survey techniques and the advocacy of qualitative methods (primarily participant observation) so as to deal with the *meaning* of human conduct.

In his famous critique of variable anlysis (1956), Blumer points out the following shortcomings of that methodology. Today, sociologists tend to designate anything as a "variable," from simple demographic characteristics to something as vague and complex as social cohesion or anomie. There is no assurance of validity here, no assurance that sociologists are indeed measuring what they claim to measure. Furthermore, sociology has no *generic* variables, measurements of fundamental and general phenomena. For example, we have thousands of localized studies of attitudes but still do not know about the abstract nature of attitudes. Finally, variable anlysis fails to grasp the "here and now" meaning of what it purports to explain. The thrust of Blumer's argument is that variable analysis, while suited for certain types of research,

cannot do full justice to human group life, because it cannot grasp the interpretive process at the core of all social interaction. Generally, sociologists, like psychological behaviorists, merely recognize independent and dependent variables, the former presumably *causing* the behavior that the latter represents. In this process, man is viewed as a passive organism responding mechanistically to an independent variable, the stimulus. Blumer points out, however, that the crucial process occurs *between* the input and the outcome. It is the interpretive process between these two that must be our concern. As long as we ignore this process and treat man as a mysterious black box, his behavior will continue to be a mystery. Furthermore, interpretation and meaning cannot be reduced to variables (for example, "intervening" variables), for they are processses, not things. As Blumer points out, additional structural categories are constantly being devised and refined in an effort at greater precision, but this procedure is no more promising, since it is based on a scheme that refuses to recognize human beings as they are (1962:191-192). The proper approach, then, is to study human "group activity through the eyes and experience of the people who have developed the activity" (1956). In sum, Blumer concludes elsewhere, "respect the nature of the empirical world and organize a methodological stance to reflect that respect" (1969:60).

Beyond Blumer. In addition to Blumer, other authors whose contributions to symbolic interactionism have been primarily theoretical include C. Wright Mills, Hans Gerth, Nelson Foote, and Dennis Wrong. Mills, as we saw, formulated symbolic interactionism's theory of motivation. In addition, he also wrote a book on social psychology and pragmatism (1964) and, together with Hans Gerth (1953), a social-psychological analysis of social structure in which an effort is made to integrate Mead and Freud. Foote's famous article on motivation (1951) complements Mills' earlier statement, arguing that *identity* gives content to that theory, that is, that identity is the basis for motivated conduct. Wrong's (1961) equally well-known article on the oversocialized conception of man shows how conventional sociology has tended to reduce man to a role-player, to the me without the I.

The methodological works inspired by or related to Blumer's thesis include Bruyn (1966), Cicourel (1964), Denzin (1970a; 1970b), and Glaser and Strauss (1967). Beyond that, we have efforts to link up symbolic interactionism with ethnomethodology (Denzin, 1969), phenomenology with ethnomethodology (Psathas, 1969), and all of phenomenology and ethnomethodology proper (cf. Abel, 1948; Cicourel, 1970; 1974; Douglas, 1970; Garfinkel, 1967; Schultz, 1970; Truzzi, 1974; Warriner, 1969; Wax, 1967; etc.), plus some authors who themselves straddle these distinctions (such as McHugh, 1968a; 1968b).

Erving Goffman (1922-). The very prolific Goffman has, practically single-handedly, created a school called *dramaturgical sociology*. According to this perspective, life is comparable to a theater, social interaction being likened to the staged performance of the parts played by the actors. In itself, the analogy is by no means novel, going back at least to Shakespeare. In a way, it underlies *all* sociology to the extent that the *role* concept is our discipline's most important primitive term. Goffman's work is probably the most consistent extension of role theory. The analysis of all facets of social life—from international spying to surgery, from rural life in the Shetland Islands to mental wards, from blackmail to love-making, card games, and restaurants—in terms of role performance, drama, self-presentation, impression management, and interaction strategies makes for what is probably the most exiciting sociology written in America since World War II. Here, we touch briefly on the major themes found in Goffman's work. Subsequent chapters (for example, Chapters 10 and 11) pick up various parts of his work in greater detail.

Goffman always writes about face-to-face interaction, whether in public places (1963a; 1971), games (1961b), mental hospitals (1961a), or elsewhere. His style is journalistic; his methodology consists of the documentary illustration of points through the use of any available source, be it fiction, science, journalism, or everyday experience. His conception of life as drama leads him to coin such concepts as *performance* ("all the activity of a given participant on a given occasion which serves to influence in any way other participants," [1959b:15]), *performance team, audience, routine* (a "preestablished pattern of action which is unfolded during a performance and which may be presented or played through on other occasions" [op. cit.:16]), *decorum, appearance,* and *manner.* The performance takes place in *regions* (a social concept, not a geographical one!) and these have a *front*, where the performance is given (op. cit.:107), and a *back*, where the impression conveyed in the front can be contradicted (op. cit.:112). There are additional concepts to deal with the props, equipment, and setting, all conveying the theater metaphor. Furthermore, performances can be carried out in a variety of ways. Goffman describes, for example, *dramatization, idealization* (1959b) and, elsewhere, *role distance* (1961b).

One pervasive theme in many of the author's books is self-presentation (1959b), face work (1967), impression management (1959b), in sum the mechanisms involved in carrying our social masks and carrying out our scripts and performances *on the surface.* Another, related theme is the strategic or calculating and manipulative way in which people play their social *games*, particularly one very important game to Goffman, the *information game.* Thus he describes gaming encounters (1961b), strategic information games (1969), and information management by those suffering from concealable stigma (1963b), among others.

A third major theme, cutting across the

previous two, is deviance. Goffman's preoccupation with stigma (1963b), mental institutions (1961a; 1968), mental illness (1959a), and other forms of deviance (1952) led him to formulate what may be the definitive statement on labelling theory (1959a). Since it is Goffman's firm belief that mental illness is the product of labelling and of the ensuing self-identification process, he has, together with Thomas Szasz (1961; 1970) founded the American Association for the Abolition of Involuntary Mental Hospitalization (cf. Martindale and Martindale, 1973), and the two men have carried a crusade against all forms of mental hospitalization, particularly the involuntary kind.

Throughout his writings, Goffman's main unit of analysis seems to be the *social situation*. This explains his use of such terms as *setting* (1959b), *interaction membrane* (1961b), and other types of *boundaries* (1963a). Even the *total institution* (1961a; 1968)—the asylum—is a situation, not a structure. Thus Goffman is eminently an interactionist. Furthermore, one of his major contributions has been the discovery and documentation of innumerable latent norms governing various situations. These two points merge under Goffman's important concept of *situational propriety* (1961b; 1963a), and it is this contribution that makes Goffman the main forerunner if not the father of ethnomethodology (cf. Garfinkel, 1967).

Goffman's sociology has been attacked for the image of man and society it presents, an image, according to some, not congruent with reality. It is argued by some that man is not a cold, Machiavellian manipulator, as implied by Goffman (cf. Deutsch and Krauss, 1965:211), and others believe that what Goffman describes is not a natural person but a mental patient (cf. Messinger et al., 1962). Then, too, there has been criticism of Goffman's loose methodology (Deutsch and Krauss, 1965). However, in defense of Goffman, it has been pointed out that the dramaturgical model is not a theory but a methodological device, similar in purpose to Weber's ideal type—as an aid to understanding (cf. Truzzi, 1968:7).

Related contributions. Space allows only the enumeration of some related work at this point. This includes Kenneth Burke (1954), who actually predates and inspired Goffman; Messinger et al. (1962), who subscribe to the dramaturgical approach; Nelson Foote (1954); and Gregory Stone, whose work on identity (1962), urban sociology (1954), sports (1955; 1972), theory (1967), and childhood (1965) is always social-psychological and frequently Goffmanesque.

There is, in addition, the work of men like Everett Hughes (1951), Strauss (1959), and Glaser and Strauss (1965). These authors deal, in highly imaginative fashion, with the "careers," the successive social-psychological stages through which adult biography may take us, for example, in the realm of occupation (Hughes) or even terminal disease (Glaser and Strauss). Hence their focus is on such things as career trajectories, status passages, and identity alterations.

Labelling theory. In the sociology of deviance, interactionism has gradually produced a conception that is now more or less unanimous: the sociological conception of deviance says, in essence, that it is the product of interaction (namely between the acting individual and the reacting society). Thus, whereas psychology places the responsibility for deviance squarely on the individual, sociology practically reverses this, arguing that when an individual becomes a deviant, it is as much as a result of societal *labelling* as it is that of his own actions. As stated earlier, labelling theory has been applied in the fields of criminology-delinquency and mental illness, among other areas of deviance. The following paragraphs list some important work in this tradition. Many of these studies will be discussed in Chapter 12.

While Sutherland's *differential association* theory cannot properly be said to anticipate labelling theory, the criminology of Cressey, co-author of the Sutherland-Cressey (1970) text, and the delinquency of Cavan (1962) are already within the interactionist tradition. It was, however, Edwin Lemert's important distinction between primary and secondary deviation (1948; 1951) and his brilliant application of that idea to such problems as paranoia (1962) that has established the labelling perspective. Since then, there has been considerable theoretical elaboration of the interactionist-labelling approach, including Erikson (1962), Kitsuse (1968), Lofland (1969), Matza (1969), and Schur (1971). Matza's distinction between *affinity, affiliation,* and *signification* is particularly helpful in summarizing the labelling perspective (signification) and in distinguishing it from the two dominant conventional approaches (affinity and affiliation). Well-known applications of the perspective— some in fact anticipating it—include Becker's (1953) study of marijuana users, Lindesmith's classic on opiate addiction

(1947), Davis' article on the physically handicapped (1961), Reckless' (1956; 1967) work on delinquency and self-concept, as well as the dozens of studies reproduced in the Becker (1964), Filstead (1972), and Rubington and Weinberg (1973) readers.

In addition, there is the *research* on deviance that follows the labelling perspective but with a primary concern for methodological questions, that is, the need for participant observation and other qualitative methods. Douglas (1972) and Filstead (1970) make this methodological argument, and studies by Cavan on bars (1966), Humphreys on homosexuals (1970), Kando (1972a; 1973) on transsexuals, Spradley on skidrow (1970), as well as those printed in the Douglas reader (1972) provide good examples of ethnographic studies of deviance.

As applied to mental illness, sociological labelling theory received its best-known

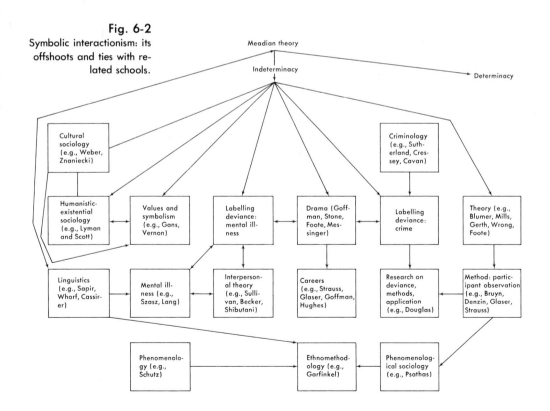

Fig. 6-2
Symbolic interactionism: its offshoots and ties with related schools.

formulation from Scheff (1966), whose concept of *residual deviance* is essentially similar to Lemert's secondary deviation; it refers to the stabilization of an individual's behavior into a deviant pattern produced by societal labelling. It is also found, for example, in the studies collected in the Spitzer and Denzin reader (1968).

At this point, sociological labelling theory merges with the work of psychiatrists such as Eysenck (1960), Laing (1959), and above all, Szasz (1961; 1970) who, renegades to their profession, turn against the very concept of mental illness. Furthermore, there is a group of scholars whose orientation is simultaneously psychoanalytic and interactionist. The psychoanalyst Sullivan's *interpersonal theory* (1953) underlies this group's orientation, and it includes such men as Becker (1962) and Shibutani (1961), both of whom, like Sullivan, incorporate Freudian concepts in an otherwise sociological approach to behavior and personality. Since labelling theory stresses the essential part that *naming*—language—plays in shaping *subsequent* behavior, this emphasis finally relates back to the linguistic work of men like Sapir (1949), Whorf (1956), and Cassirer (1944).

Humanistic-existential and cultural sociology. A final offshoot of symbolic interactionism is existential sociology, best exemplified by Lyman and Scott's *Sociology of the Absurd* (1970) and the cultural and "normative" sociology found, for example, in Gans' urban sociology (1962a; 1962b), Moskos' military sociology (1969), Kando's leisure sociology (1975), and the articles assembled in the Stein and Vidich reader (1963). Needless to say, much of this is influenced not only by symbolic interactionism but also by the cultural sociology discussed in Chapter 5.

We have attempted to summarize the enormously complex body of interrelated literature discussed in the previous pages in Fig. 6-2.

SUMMARY AND CONCLUSION

This chapter has attempted to cover symbolic interactionist social psychology, one of the major elements of the new humanistic paradigm. First the relationship between this perspective and the philosophy of *pragmatism* upon which it is based was traced, discussing the thought of two major pragmatists, William James and John Dewey. We saw that both men take their point of departure in *experience*, viewing *function*, or *process*, as primary and structure as the product thereof. This revolutionizes all previous thought on the subject.

Mead was shown to have followed the same mode of analysis, borrowing from James both the centrality of process and the dialectic conception of self, the self being viewed as the internal conversation between the I and the me. However, Mead's focus was more social than that of James. While our discussion of Mead progressed, as his own writings, from the act to the mind and the self and finally to society, it must be remembered that in Mead's scheme society—or better, social interaction—is prior to the individual. Mead was, of course, also a pragmatist. His social psychology is nondeterministic. Some critical appraisals of Mead were also discussed.

The next section covered some other early symbolic interactionists, prime among them Charles H. Cooley. Cooley's major contributions included the looking-glass self, human nature, the primary group, and sentiment. Piaget and Cassirer were mentioned as the two major European symbolic interactionists.

The final section has dealt with modern symbolic interactionism, attempting to touch on some of the vast literature produced by this school since World War II. Following Kuhn (1964), a distinction was made between a deterministic and a nondeterministic branch, what Meltzer and Petras (1972) term the Iowa and the Chicago schools, respectively. Typical of the former is work using the Twenty Statement Test and much of role theory. The second orientation's major spokesman has been Herbert Blumer, who advocates a qualitative methodology that will do justice to the interpretive nature of human inter-action. It is also in this humanistic tradition that one finds Goffman, a sociologist who has written many qualitative books and ar-ticles on face-to-face interaction in an infi-nite variety of everyday settings, ranging from primitive tribes to large-scale mod-ern organizations and from mental wards to international diplomacy. As we saw, off-shoots of this branch of symbolic interac-tionism also include labelling theory (as applied to crime, mental illness, and other forms of deviance) and existential-humanistic sociology.

Although a great deal of research was thus (admittedly cursorily) covered, this by no means exhausts the rich literature of symbolic interactionism. Additional con-tributions could have been discussed, from the theoretically important work of Cot-trell (1950), Stone and Farberman (1967), and Weinstein and Deutschberger (1963) to simple summaries of Mead (cf. Des-monde, 1970; Morris, 1934; Strauss, 1956) and of symbolic interactionism (cf. Mar-tindale, 1960; Mullins, 1973), from critical appraisals of Mead (Kolb, 1944; Meltzer and Petras, 1964; Swanson, 1961; Troyer, 1946) to symbolic interactionist textbooks (Cardwell, 1971; Lindesmith, Strauss, and Denzin, 1975; Warriner, 1970) and readers (Cardwell, 1973; Lindesmith and Strauss, 1969; Manis and Meltzer, 1972; Rose, 1962; Stone and Farberman, 1970).

Furthermore, there continue to be inter-esting and heated exchanges about the proper interpretation of Mead and the value of symbolic interactionists and those hostile to that perspective. An example of the former is found in the January, 1967, issue of the *American Journal of Sociology*, where Blumer is criticized by and in turn takes on several of his own disciples. One of them (Joseph Woelfel) suggests that the interpretation of Mead's thought be deter-mined by such expedient criteria as one's research needs, and Blumer correctly dis-misses this as nonsensical. Stone and Far-berman, in turn, disagree with Blumer

both about the character of Mead's signifi-cant symbol and about the I and the me. The protagonists differ as to the explana-tory role Mead meant to assign to struc-ture, which Stone and Farberman equate with the me but Blumer does not.

An example of the other type of de-bate—between interactionists and some-one clearly hostile to that perspective—is found in the June, 1974, *American Socio-logical Review*, where half a dozen authors react to Huber's (1973) earlier attack upon symbolic interactionism. Huber believes that in the absence of a logicodeductive component, "emergent theory" (symbolic interactionism) will reflect the bias pro-duced by the particular power distribution characteristic of whatever situation the interactionist researcher happens to be in-vestigating. In the debate that follows, the differences of opinion seem to be irrecon-cilable. Huber, a logical positivist and ra-tionalist, simply has no use for the total de-mocracy of ideas inherent in pragmatism. Schmitt's rebuttal is essentially a defense of interactionist methodology on the familiar grounds that it permits greater freedom to recognize serendipitous findings. In addi-tion, Stone et al. question whether the "logicodeductive component" so dear to someone like Huber guarantees fairness and objectivity in the research enterprise. For the rest, the two sides accuse each other of poor scholarship, bad crafts-manship, and misrepresentations.

For our purposes, the main point here is to appreciate the value of the interactionist perspective against the background of de-ductive or abstract empiricism. In the light of the enormous amount of fascinating research done on all sorts of groups, life-styles, social situations, and deviant subcul-tures (including the research by Goffman and the labelling theorists discussed in this chapter as well as work in the area of col-lective behavior), one can no longer seriously listen to those who still character-ize Meadian theory as an interesting but sterile (or nonresearchable) philosophy. As far as interactionism's alleged bias (due, according to Huber, to the absence of the logicodeductive component, and a bias that generally ends up favoring the underdog [cf. Becker, 1967]), the more accurate characterization of this inherently relativistic perspective is that it represents the final democratization of truth. To suggest that we abandon the interpretive paradigm, as Huber does, is merely an attempt to return to an outdated absolutistic conception of human conduct, what Wilson (1970) terms the "normative paradigm." In the final analysis, the central argument of this book —following Blumer, Schmitt, Stone et al.— is that interactionism is currently more promising and more meaningful than the classical mechanistic hypothesis-testing procedure because it is more inductive, more dynamic, more sensitizing, in sum more *empirical*. Unlike alternative forms of social psychology, it does justice to the reality it purports to describe, namely ongoing human *life*.

REFERENCES

Abel, Theodore
  1948 "The operation called verstehen." American Journal of Sociology 54:211-218.
Backman, Carl W.
  1973 Review of the Assessment of Self, by Stephen Spitzer et al. Contemporary Sociology (September):503-504.
Becker, Ernest
  1962 The Birth and Death of Meaning. Glencoe, Ill.: The Free Press.
Becker, Howard S.
  1953 "Becoming a marihuana user." American Journal of Sociology (November):235-242.
  1964 (ed.) The Other Side: Perspectives on Deviance. London: Collier-Macmillan Ltd.
  1967 "Whose side are we on?" Social Problems (Winter):239-247.
Blumer, Herbert
  1956 "Sociological analysis and the variable." American Sociological Review (December):683-690.
  1962 "Society as symbolic interaction." In Human Behavior and Social Processes. Arnold M. Rose (ed.). Boston: Houghton Mifflin Co., pp. 179-192.

  1967 "Reply to Woelfel, Stone and Farberman." American Journal of Sociology (January):411-412.
  1969 Symbolic Interactionism. Englewood Cliffs, N.J.: Prentice-Hall, Inc.
Bruyn, Severyn
  1966 The Human Perspective in Sociology. Englewood Cliffs, N.J.: Prentice-Hall, Inc.
Burke, Kenneth
  1954 Permanence and Change. Los Altos, Calif.: Hermes Publications.
Cardwell, J. D.
  1971 Social Psychology: A Symbolic Interactionist Perspective. Philadelphia: F. A. Davis Co.
  1973 Readings in Social Psychology: A Symbolic Interaction Perspective. Philadelphia: F. A. Davis Co.
Cassirer, Ernst
  1944 An Essay on Man: An Introduction to a Philosophy of Human Culture. New Haven, Conn.: Yale University Press.
Cavan, Ruth Shonle
  1962 Juvenile Delinquency. Philadelphia: J. B. Lippincott Co.
Cavan, Sherri
  1966 Liquor License: An Ethnography of Bar Behavior. Chicago: Aldine Publishing Co.
Cicourel, Aaron V.
  1964 Method and Measurement in Sociology. New York: The Free Press.
  1970 "The acquisition of social structure: toward a developmental sociology of language and meaning." In Understanding Everyday Life. Jack Douglas (ed.). Chicago: Aldine Publishing Co.
  1974 Cognitive Sociology: Language and Meaning in Social Interaction. New York: The Free Press.
Cooley, Charles Horton
  1902 Human Nature and the Social Order. New York: Scribner's Sons.
  1909 Social Organization. New York: Scribner's Sons.
  1926 "The roots of social knowledge." American Journal of Sociology (July):59-79.
Cottrell, Leonard S.
  1950 "Some neglected problems in social psychology." American Sociological Review (December):705-712.
Couch, Carl J.
  1962 "Family role specialization and self-attitudes in children." Sociological Quarterly (April):115-121.
Dalton, Melville
  1959 Men Who Manage: Fusions of Feeling and Theory in Administration. New York: John Wiley & Sons, Inc.
Davis, Fred
  1956 "Definitions of time and recovery in paralytic polio convalescence." American Journal of Sociology 61:582-587.

1961 "Deviance disavowal: the management of strained interaction by visibly handicapped." Social Problems (Fall):120-132.

Davis, Kingsley
1947 "Final note on a case of extreme isolation." The Bobbs-Merrill Reprint Series in the Social Sciences. American Journal of Sociology (March):432-437.

Denzin, Norman K.
1969 "Symbolic interactionism and ethnomethodology." American Sociological Review (December):922-934.
1970a "The methodologies of symbolic interaction: a critical review of research techniques." In Social Psychology Through Symbolic Interaction. Gregory P. Stone and Harvey A. Farberman (eds.). Waltham, Mass.: Ginn-Blaisdell, pp. 447-466.
1970b The Research Act: A Theoretical Introduction to Sociological Methods. Chicago: Aldine Publishing Co.

Desmonde, William H.
1970 "The position of George Herbert Mead." In Social Psychology Through Symbolic Interaction. Gregory P. Stone and Harvey A. Farbermen (eds.). Waltham, Mass.: Ginn-Blaisdell, pp. 55-62.

Deutsch, Morton and Robert M. Krauss
1965 Theories in Social Psychology. New York: Basic Books, Inc.

Dewey, John
1922 Human Nature and Conduct. New York: Holt, Rinehart and Winston.

Douglas, Jack D. (ed.)
1970 Understanding Everyday Life: Toward the Reconstruction of Sociological Knowledge. Chicago: Aldine Publishing Co.
1972 Research on Deviance. New York: Random House, Inc.

Dubin, Robert
1956 "Industrial workers' worlds: a study of the central life interests of industrial workers." Social Problems (January):131-142.

Erikson, Kai T.
1962 "Notes on the sociology of deviance." Social Problems (Spring):307-314.

Eysenck, Hans J.
1960 "The effects of psychotherapy." In Handbook of Abnormal Psychology. Hans J. Eysenck (ed.). New York: Pitman Medical Publishing Co.

Farber, Bernard
1962 "Types of family organization: child-oriented, home-oriented, and parent-oriented." In Human Behavior and Social Processes. Arnold M. Rose (ed.). Boston: Houghton Mifflin Co.

Filstead, William J.
1970 Qualitative Methodology: Firsthand Involvement with the Social World. Chicago: Markham Publishing Co.

1972 (ed.) An Introduction to Deviance: Readings in the Process of Making Deviants. Chicago: Markham Publishing Co.

Foote, Nelson N.
1951 "Identification as the basis for a theory of motivation." American Sociological Review (February):14-21.
1954 "Sex as play." Social Problems (April):159-163.

Friedrichs, Robert W.
1974 "The potential impact of B. F. Skinner upon American sociology." American Sociologist (February):3-8.

Gans, Herbert
1962a The Urban Villagers. New York: The Free Press.
1962b "Urbanism and suburbanism as ways of life: a re-evaluation of definitions." in Human Behavior and Social Processes. Arnold M. Rose (ed.). Boston: Houghton Mifflin Co., pp. 625-648.

Garfinkel, Harold
1967 Studies in Ethnomethodology. Englewood Cliffs, N.J.: Prentice-Hall, Inc.

Gerth, Hans and C. Wright Mills
1953 Character and Social Structure. New York: Harcourt, Brace, Jovanovich, Inc.

Glaser, Barney G. and Anselm L. Strauss
1965 Awareness of Dying. Chicago: Aldine Publishing Co.
1967 The Discovery of Grounded Theory: Strategies for Qualitative Research. Chicago: Aldine Publishing Co.

Goffman, Erving
1952 "On cooling the mark out: some aspects of adaptation to failure." Psychiatry: Journal for the Study of Interpersonal Relations (November):451-463.
1959a "The moral career of the mental patient." Psychiatry (May):123-142.
1959b The Presentation of Self in Everyday Life. Garden City, N.Y.: Doubleday & Co., Inc.
1961a Asylums. Garden City, N.Y.: Doubleday & Co., Inc.
1961b Encounters: Two Studies in the Sociology of Interaction. New York: Bobbs-Merrill Co., Inc.
1963a Behavior in Public Places. Glencoe, Ill.: The Free Press.
1963b Stigma: Notes on the Management of Spoiled Identity. Englewood Cliffs, N.J.: Prentice-Hall, Inc.
1967 Interaction Ritual: Essays on Face-to-Face Behavior. Chicago: Aldine Publishing Co.
1968 "Characteristics of total institutions." In The Mental Patient: Studies in the Sociology of

Deviance. Stephan P. Spitzer and Norman K. Denzin (eds.). New York: McGraw-Hill Book Co., pp. 294-297, 310-316.

1969 Strategic Interaction. Philadelphia: University of Pennsylvania Press.

1971 Relations in Public, New York: Harper & Row, Publishers.

Gross, Edward
1958 Work and Society. New York: The Thomas Y. Crowell Co.

Gutman, Robert
1958 "Cooley: a perspective." American Sociological Review (June):251-256.

Heiss, Jerold (ed.)
1968 Family Roles and Interaction: An Anthology. Chicago: Rand McNally.

Hill, Reuben and Donald A. Hansen
1960 "The identification of conceptual frameworks utilized in family study." Marriage and Family Living 22:299-311.

Huber, Joan
1973 "Symbolic interaction as a pragmatic perspective: the bias of emergent theory." American Sociological Review (April):274-284.

Hughes, Everett C.
1951 "Work and Self." In Social Psychology at the Crossroads. John H. Rohrer and Muzafer Sherif (eds.). New York: Harper & Row, Publishers, pp. 313-323.

Humphreys, Laud
1970 Tearoom Trade. Chicago: Aldine Publishing Co.

Hyman, Herbert H.
1942 "The psychology of status." Archives of Psychology 269.

James, William
1892 Principles of Psychology. New York: Henry Holt.
1904 "Does consciousness exist?" Journal of Philosophy, Psychology and Scientific Methods (September):477-491.

Kando, Thomas
1972a "Passing and stigma management: the case of the transsexual." The Sociological Quarterly (Fall):475-483.
1972b "Role strain: a comparison of males, females and transsexuals." Journal of Marriage and the Family (August):459-464.
1973 Sex Change: The Achievement of Gender Identity Among Feminized Transsexuals. Springfield, Ill.: Charles C Thomas, Publisher.
1974 "Males, females and transsexuals." Journal of Homosexuality (Fall):45-64.
1975 Leisure and Popular Culture in Transition. St. Louis: The C. V. Mosby Co.

Kinch, John W.
1963 "A formalized theory of the self-concept." American Journal of Sociology (January):481-486.
1973 Social Psychology. New York: McGraw-Hill Book Co.

Kitsuse, John I.
1968 "Societal reaction to deviant behavior: problems of theory and method." In The Mental Patient: Studies in the Sociology of Deviance. Stephan P. Spitzer and Norman K. Denzin (eds.). New York: McGraw-Hill Book Co., pp. 40-51.

Kolb, William L.
1944 "A critical evaluation of Mead's I and Me concepts." Social Forces (March):291-296.

Kornhauser, William
1959 The Politics of Mass Society. Glencoe, Ill.: The Free Press.

Kuhn, Manford H.
1960 "Self-attitudes by age, sex, and professional training." Sociological Quarterly (January):39-55.
1964 "Major trends in symbolic interaction theory in the past twenty-five years." Sociological Quarterly (Winter):61-84.

Kuhn, Manford H. and Thomas McPartland
1954 "An empirical investigation of self-attitudes." American Sociological Review 19:68-76.

Lang, R. D.
1959 The Divided Self. London: Tavistock Publications.

Lang, Kurt and Gladys Engel Lang
1961 Collective Dynamics. New York: Thomas Y. Crowell Co.
1962 "Collective dynamics: process and form." In Human Behavior and Social Processes. Arnold M. Rose (ed.). Boston: Houghton Mifflin Co., pp. 340-359.

Lemert, Edwin
1948 "Some aspects of a general theory of sociopathic behavior." Proceedings of the Pacific Sociological Society 1:24-25.
1951 Social Pathology. New York: McGraw-Hill Book Co.
1962 "Paranoia and the dynamics of exclusion." Sociometry (March):2-20.

Lindesmith, Alfred R.
1947 Opiate Addiction. Bloomington, Ind.: Principia Press.

Lindesmith, Alfred R. and Anselm L. Strauss
1956 Social Psychology. New York: Dryden Press.
1969 Readings in Social Psychology. New York: Holt, Rinehart & Winston.

Lindesmith, Alfred R., Anselm L. Strauss, and Norman K. Denzin
1975 Social Psychology (ed. 4). Hinsdale, Ill.: The Dryden Press.

Lofland, John with the assistance of Lyn H. Lofland

1969 Deviance and Identity. Englewood Cliffs, N.J.: Prentice-Hall, Inc.

Lyman, Stanford M. and Marvin B. Scott
1970 A Sociology of the Absurd. New York: Meredith Corp.

Lynch, Frederick R.
1975 "Is there a behaviorist bandwagon?" American Sociologist (May):84-91.

Manis, Jerome G. and Bernard N. Meltzer
1972 Symbolic Interaction: A Reader in Social Psychology. Boston: Allyn and Bacon, Inc.

Martindale, Don
1960 The Nature and Types of Sociological Theory. Boston: Houghton Mifflin Co.

Martindale, Don and Edith Martindale
1973 Psychiatry and the Law: The Crusade Against Involuntary Hospitalization. St. Paul, Minn.: Windflower Publishing Co.

Matza, David
1969 Becoming Deviant. Englewood Cliffs, N.J.: Prentice-Hall, Inc.

McHugh, Peter
1968a "Social disintegration as a requisite of resocialization." Social Forces (March):355-363.
1968b "Defining the situation: the organization of meaning in social interaction." New York: The Bobbs-Merrill Co.

Mead, George Herbert
1929- "Cooley's contribution to American social
1930 thought." American Journal of Sociology 35:693-706.
1934 Mind, Self and Society. Charles W. Morris (ed.). Chicago: University of Chicago Press.
1956 On Social Psychology. Anselm Strauss (ed.). Chicago: University of Chicago Press.

Meltzer, B.
1964 The Social Psychology of George Herbert Mead. Kalamazoo: Western Michigan University, Center for Sociological Research.

Meltzer, B. and John W. Petras
1972 "The Chicago and Iowa schools of symbolic interactionism." In Symbolic Interaction. Jerome G. Manis and Bernard N. Meltzer (eds.). Boston: Allyn and Bacon, Inc., pp. 43-56.

Merton, Robert K.
1957 Social Theory and Social Structure. Glencoe, Ill.: The Free Press.

Merton, Robert K. and Alice C. Kitt
1950 "Contributions to the theory of reference group behavior." In Continuities in Social Research. R. K. Merton and P. F. Lazarsfelt (eds.). Glencoe, Ill.: The Free Press, pp. 40-105.

Messinger, Sheldon L. with Harold Sampson and Robert D. Towne
1962 "Life as theater: some notes on the dramaturgic approach to social reality." Sociometry (September):98-110.

Mills, Charles Wright
1964 Sociology and Pragmatism: The Higher Learning in America. New York: Paine-Whitman.

Miyamoto, S. Frank and Sanford M. Dornbusch
1956 "A test of interactionist hypotheses of self-conception." American Journal of Sociology (March):399-403.

Morris, Charles W.
1934 Introduction. In George H. Mead. Mind, Self and Society. Chicago: University of Chicago Press, pp. 9-35.

Moskos, Charles C.
1969 "Why men fight: American combat soldiers in Vietnam." Transaction (November).

Mullins, Nicholas C.
1973 Theories and Theory Groups in Contemporary American Sociology. New York: Harper & Row, Publishers.

Myrdal, Gunnar with the assistance of Richard Sterner and Arnold Rose
1944 An American Dilemma. New York: Harper & Row, Publishers.

Newcomb, T. M.
1943 Personality and Social Change: Attitude Formation in a Student Community. New York: Dryden Press.

Piaget, Jean
1932 The Moral Judgment of the Child. New York: Harcourt Brace.

Psathas, George
1969 "Ethnomethodology and phenomenology." Social Research (April):500-520.

Quarantelli, E. L. and Joseph Cooper
1966 "Self-conceptions and others: a further test of Meadian hypotheses." Sociological Quarterly (Summer):281-297.

Ray, Verne F.
1953 "Human color perception and behavioral response." Transactions of the New York Academy of Science 16:98.

Reckless, Walter C.
1967 "Pioneering with self-concept as a vulnerability factor in delinquency." Journal of Criminal Law, Criminology and Police Science 58:515-523.

Reckless, Walter C. and Ellen Murray
1956 "Self-concept as an insulator against delinquency." American Sociological Review 21:744-746.

Rose, Arnold M. (ed.)
1962 Human Behavior and Social Processes: An Interactionist Approach. Boston: Houghton Mifflin Co.
1967 The Power Structure; Political Process in America. New York: Oxford University Press.

Rubington, Earl and Martin S. Weinberg
1973 Deviance: The Interactionist Perspective. New York: The Macmillan Co.

Sapir, E.
1949 "The status of linguistics as a science." In Selected Writings in Language, Culture and Personality. D. G. Mandelbaum (ed.). Berkeley: University of California Press.

Sarbin, Theodore R.
1954 "Role theory." In Handbook of Social Psychology. Gardner Lindzey (ed.). Cambridge, Mass.: Addison-Wesley Publishing Co., Inc.

Scheff, Thomas J.
1966 Being Mentally Ill. Chicago: Aldine Publishing Co.

Schmitt, Raymond L.
1974 "SI and emergent theory: a re-examination." American Sociological Review (June):453-456.

Schutz, Alfred
1970 On Phenomenology and Social Relations. Helmut R. Wagner (ed.). Chicago: The University of Chicago Press.

Schur, Edwin M.
1971 Labelling Deviant Behavior: Its Sociological Implications. New York: Harper & Row, Publishers.

Sewell, William H.
1952 "Infant training and the personality of the child." American Journal of Sociology 58 (July-May):150-159.

Shibutani, Tamotsu
1955 "Reference groups as perspectives." American Journal of Sociology 60:562-569.
1961 Society and Personality: An Interactionist Approach to Social Psychology. Englewood Cliffs, N.J.: Prentice-Hall, Inc.

Spitzer, Stephan P. and Norman K. Denzin (eds.)
1968 The Mental Patient: Studies in the Sociology of Deviance. New York: McGraw-Hill Book Co.

Spitzer, Stephen P., Carl Couch and John Stratton
1971 The Assessment of the Self. Iowa City: Escort, Sernoll, Inc.

Spradley, James P.
1970 You Owe Yourself a Drunk: An Ethnography of Urban Nomads. Boston: Little, Brown and Co.

Stein, Maurice and Arthur Vidich (eds.)
1963 Sociology on Trial. Englewood Cliffs, N.J.: Prentice-Hall, Inc.

Stone, Gregory P.
1954 "City shoppers and urban identification: observations on the social psychology of city life." American Journal of Sociology (July):36-45.
1955 "American sports: play and display." Chicago Review (Fall):83-100.
1962 "Appearance and the self." In Human Behavior and Social Processes. Arnold M. Rose (ed.). Boston: Houghton Mifflin Co., pp. 86-118.
1965 "The play of little children." Quest (April):23-31.
1972 (ed.) Games, Sport and Power. New Brunswick, N.J.: Transaction Books.

Stone, Gregory P. and Harvey A. Farberman
1967 "On the edge of rapproachment: was Durkheim moving toward the perspective of symbolic interaction?" Sociological Quarterly (Spring):149-164.
1970 Social Psychology Through Symbolic Interaction. Waltham, Mass.: Ginn-Blaisdell.

Stone, Gregory P. et al.
1974 "On methodology and craftsmanship in the criticism of sociological perspectives." American Sociological Review (June):456-463.

Strauss, Anselm
1956 Introduction to George Herbert Mead on Social Psychology. Chicago: University of Chicago Press.
1959 Mirrors and Masks. Glencoe, Ill.: The Free Press.

Stryker, Sheldon
1957 "Role-taking accuracy and adjustment." Sociometry (December):286-296.
1962 "Conditions of accurate role-taking: a test of Mead's theory." Human Behavior and Social Processes. Arnold M. Rose (ed.). Boston: Houghton Mifflin Co., pp. 41-62.

Sullivan, H. S.
1953 The Interpersonal Theory of Psychiatry. New York: W. W. Norton & Co.

Sutherland, Edwin H. and Donald R. Cressey
1970 Criminology. Philadelphia: J. B. Lippincott Co.

Swanson, Guy E.
1961 "Mead and Freud: their relevance for social psychology." Sociometry (December):319-339.

Szasz, Thomas
1961 The Myth of Mental Illness: Foundations of a Theory of Personal Conduct. New York: Dell Publishing Co.
1970 The Manufacture of Madness: A Comparative Study of the Inquisition and the Mental Health Movement. New York: Harper & Row, Publishers.

Theodorson, George and Achilles G. Theodorson
1969 A Modern Dictionary of Sociology. New York: Thomas Y. Crowell Co.

Thielbar, Gerald
1970 "On locals and cosmopolitans." In Social Psychology Through Symbolic Interaction. Gregory P. Stone and Harvey A. Farberman (eds.). Waltham, Mass.: Ginn-Blaisdell, pp. 259-276.

Troyer, William Lewis
1946 "Mead's social and functional theory of mind." American Sociological Review (April):198-202.

Truzzi, Marcello (ed.)
1968 Sociology and Everyday Life. Englewood Cliffs, N.J.: Prentice-Hall, Inc.
1974 Verstehen: Subjective Understanding in the Social Sciences. Reading, Mass.: Addison-Wesley Publishing Co., Inc.
Turner, Ralph H. and Lewis M. Killian
1957 Collective Behavior. Englewood Cliffs, N.J.: Prentice-Hall, Inc.
Warriner, C. K.
1969 "Social action, behavior and verstehen." Sociological Quarterly 10:501-511.
1970 The Emergence of Society. Homewood, Ill.: Dorsey Press.
Warshay, Leon H.
1962 "Breadth of perspective." In Human Behavior and Social Processes. Arnold M. Rose (ed.). Boston: Houghton Mifflin Co., pp. 148-176.
Wax, Murray L.
1967 "On misunderstanding verstehen: a reply to Abel." Sociology and Social Research (April):323-333.
Weinstein, Eugene A. and Paul Deutschberger
1963 "Some dimensions of altercasting." Sociometry (December):454-466.

Whorf, Benjamin L.
1956 Language, Thought and Reality. Cambridge, Mass.: Harvard University Press.
Wilson, Thomas P.
1970 "Normative and interpretive paradigms in sociology." In Understanding Everyday Life. Jack D. Douglas (ed.). Chicago: Aldine Publishing Co., pp. 57-59.
Woelfel, Joseph
1967 "Comment on the Blumer-Bales dialogue concerning the implication of the thought of George Herbert Mead." American Journal of Sociology (January):409.
Wrong, Dennis H.
1961 "The oversocialized conception of man in modern sociology." American Sociological Review (April):183-193.
Zborowski, Mark
1952 "Cultural components in responses to pain." Journal of Social Issues 4:16-30.

part three

The emergence of the self

chapter 7
Language

The first two parts of this book have been theoretical. Two things have been done thus far: we have disposed of the paradigms that are more or less outside the approach taken in this book, and we have introduced those theoretical approaches that are relevant to our purposes. From here on the material becomes *substantive*. While the discipline of social psychology is still in its infancy and therefore suffers from a high theory-knowledge ratio, we do already have some knowledge about human interaction. To be sure, much of this knowledge comes from humanistic contributions—from those of Shakespeare to those of Ken Kesey. But it is this more or less empirical understanding of human interaction that will be documented from here on. The reader should bear in mind that the presentation of information reflects the categories found in the existing literature rather than theoretical categories of our own construction. Such is the rationale for having a section on the self and its emergence, one on social interaction and social structure (in which we treat first elements of interaction and then their forms), and finally one titled problems, conflict, and change.

We begin, then, with the self and its emergence. The self is the minimum social concept. It encompasses "mind" and thinking, which will be discussed under the same heading. We must begin with an understanding of the emergence of the self, that is, an understanding of how a tiny bundle of nerves and muscles—the newborn baby—eventually becomes a social person. Nothing plays a more important role in this development than language, and that is why we begin our analysis with a discussion of language.

Language is a form of communication, namely verbal *symbolic* communication.

The many ways in which organisms may communicate can be classified into two broad categories: symbolic and subsymbolic. As we shall see, it is the capacity for symbolic behavior that sets humans apart from all other species.

In the first part of this chapter, we shall indicate some of the complex taxonomies that have been constructed by linguists and other students of communication. We shall point out that the most important distinction is between natural *signs* (the messages directly connected with their referents) and conventional or significant *symbols* (the units used in that specifically human form of communication called language). We shall also briefly discuss nonverbal communication, among both animals and humans.

The following section will deal with symbolic interaction, or language proper. It will indicate the subject matter of those disciplines concerned with language: psycholinguistics, sociolinguistics, and ethnomethodology, among others.

Next, we shall discuss the acquisition of language by children and the importance of what Skinner terms the "verbal community" (1957).

Finally, the functions of language will be dealt with. We will see that language, as Sapir (1949) and Whorf (1956) have shown, determines perception and that it therefore not only determines an individual's as well as a group's ideas about the world but that it is, as Mead (1956) argued, the precondition for thought, that is, mind itself. Thus it will be shown that without language, an individual cannot develop a self, an identity. Finally, the function of language in the establishment of what Mead called universes of discourse, culture, social structure, control, and order will also be treated. We shall conclude that language is a prerequisite for both selves and social structures.

NONVERBAL COMMUNICATION

Psychologists note that behavior is elicited by *cues*. Some cues are learned; these are called *signs* (cf. Lindesmith, Strauss, and Denzin 1975:117). They signify something, stand for something else. For example, smoke is a sign of fire, or a dog's growl is a sign of anger, indicating that it may bite you. Signs, in turn, can be natural, as in the case of smells or many gestures (the smell of something burning, or the dog's growl), or they may be *conventional*, as in the case of words. Conventional signs are *symbols*, or what Mead called significant symbols. Unlike natural signs, the form of symbols is arbitrary—this is what is meant by "conventional," based on conventions. For example, it would not make sense to argue that water is a sign of fire. Smoke is. We have no choice in the matter. As a symbol signifying fire, however, people of different cultures have arbitrarily used entirely different sounds: we happen to use the sound "fire." The French say "feu," the Dutch "vuur," and so on. Culture, then, arbitrarily determines the shape and form of a symbol, but not those of a sign.

Another major difference between sign and symbol is that while both stand for something else—what is called a *referent*—the relationship between a sign and its referent is direct and immediate, whereas the relationship between a symbol and its referent can be remote both in time and in space. For example, you only have smoke at the moment and place where fire occurs; the dog only growls when it is angry, it does not growl to remind you that it fought with another dog yesterday. The word "anger," however, is a symbol: it may refer to your own current state, or to your or anyone else's previous or future state, or it may even be used in the abstract. We may sum up this difference by saying that signs are concrete whereas symbols are more abstract.

Whether a message is a sign or a symbol, Fig. 7-1 shows that the process of understanding always involves three things: the message (that is, the sign or symbol), the actual object (the referent), and the subject, the interpreter.

Actually, messages are not merely of two varieties—natural signs and symbols. They range over a continuum from most concrete to most abstract. While we shall not get into this in depth, we may mention at least two refinements: as Szasz (1961:115-116), following Reichenbach (1947), notes, the most concrete signs—for example,

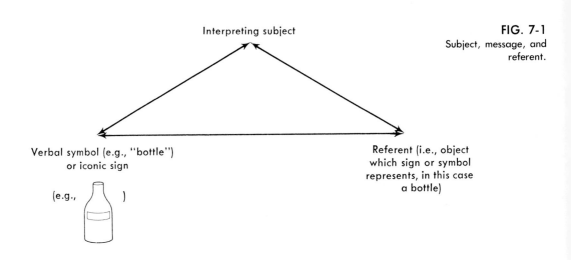

Interpreting subject

FIG. 7-1
Subject, message, and referent.

Verbal symbol (e.g., "bottle")
or iconic sign

(e.g.,   )

Referent (i.e., object
which sign or symbol
represents, in this case
a bottle)

smoke as a sign of fire—are causally related to their referents. These are called *indexical signs.* Somewhat less concrete are the so-called *iconic signs,* which merely depict their referents—for example, a picture of a man. The least concrete signs are verbal symbols. Language is not restricted to this third type. In fact, Marshall McLuhan (1964; 1969) and others have shown that writing has evolved from ideographic to phonetic, that is, the letters making up the alphabet used to be iconic signs whereas they subsequently became conventional symbols. For example, writing systems such as the Egyptian hieroglyphs and ancient Chinese consist of characters that in a way depict the objects to which they refer (cf. Tung-Sun, 1970). Kipling gave an amusing albeit fictional example of the idea: even our own letter S, he wrote, has an iconic origin, since it represents that sissing animal, the snake.

Iconic signs, then, may be considered low-level symbols. Their advantage is that, unlike verbal symbols, they are not culture-bound. This is why multilingual areas prefer to use them; witness the uniform traffic signs used in all European countries. As Fig. 7-2 shows, a given object can be represented by an infinite number of verbal symbols, but only by one concrete iconic sign.

A further classificatory refinement is the distinction between protolanguage, object language, and meta language. Protolanguage is the simplest, most concrete form of communication. It consists of iconic signs. As we shall see, one example of this is the use of hysteria and other forms of "body language" used by mental patients unable to verbalize their needs (cf. Szasz, 1961). Object language consists of words, but simple terms referring to concrete objects—for example "table," "dog." Meta language, finally, consists of more abstract terms, words that refer to other words—for example, "sentence," "norm," etc.

Among animals

Insofar as animals communicate, they are limited to the use of natural signs, not symbols. To be sure, a dog may respond to his master's order to "sit!" but the relationship between that message and the response is direct and immediate. As Kohler noted (cf. Lindesmith, Stauss, and Denzin, 1975:75), animals are limited to the here and now. The dog cannot be admonished ahead of time to remain seated the following afternoon during his master's absence. "Sit," then, is a natural sign, not a symbol.

Two main categories of animals have relevance to social psychology, both having developed (1) complex forms of social organization and (2) relatively sophisticated levels of communication. They are the insects—for example, ants and bees—and the higher primates—the great apes.

Ants, for example, may live in communities of thousands of members, with a high degree of division of labor. Some members specialize in breeding, nursing, childrearing, communal rations, feeding others, warfare, cultivating food, bequeathing "real estate" to the young, engineering, and training other insects to be slaves (Lindesmith, Strauss, and Denzin, 1975:67).

Obviously such sophisticated arrangements could not occur without communication. While ants have good com-

Object:	Iconic sign:	Verbal symbols:
A bottle		1. "Bottle" (English) 2. "Bouteille" (French) 3. "Flasche" (German) 4. Etc., etc.

FIG. 7-2
Object, iconic sign, and conventional symbols.

munication devices, it is bees that have developed astounding ways to transmit messages. As Karl Von Frisch (1950; 1955) showed, bees indicate to each other where and how far a food source is through a complicated eight-shaped dance in the air. The position of the sun and the sounds emitted during the dance are among the cues indicating estimated flying time, direction, etc. (cf. Lindesmith, Strauss, and Denzin, 1975:70-71). However, for our purposes the crux of the matter is that all insect communication is *biosocial,* that is, *instinctual* or, insofar as learned, nontransferable to a younger generation. There is no culture whatsoever among insects, no symbols, merely natural signs. This is proved by the fact that a newly hatched and totally inexperienced bee automatically "understands" the signals of other bees of its kind (Lindesmith, Strauss, and Denzin, 1975:71).

The study of primate behavior (cf. Washburn and Hamburg, 1965) has also produced important information about animal communication. Of greatest relevance here is the work done with chimpanzees, notably by Kohler (see Kohler, 1926; Lindesmith, Strauss, and Denzin, 1975; Chapter 2 of this book). Kohler found that chimps are highly social and cooperative and that they enjoy adorning themselves and playing and communicating with humans. And as we saw in Chapter 2, these great apes are even capable of perceptual "Gestalt," for example, capable of fitting together a number of boxes or sticks into a structure high or long enough to reach a fruit. However, chimpanzees are no more capable of culture and language than insects. Their "genetically determined neural substrate is not sufficient to support speech behavior" (Washburn and Hamburg, 1965).

Language consists of symbols, and symbols differ from natural signs in that they are not tied to their referents in time and space. Thus only through symbols can ex-

perience and learning be transmitted. Since animals do not use symbols, they cannot transmit their experiences to one another and therefore they cannot accumulate culture. To the social psychologist, the study of subhuman behavior is useful because it helps to understand the evolutionary origin of human behavior (cf. Lindesmith and Strauss, 1969:38). However, the superficial similarities between animal and human behavior should not obscure the fact that man is quite unique in his capacity for symbolic language. In order to apprehend this uniqueness, social psychology must of necessity be a somewhat humanistic enterprise.

Among humans

Before dealing with language, we must recognize that man, too, often engages in nonverbal communication.

The study of nonverbal communication has become increasingly popular in recent decades, leading to the emergence of a number of new disciplines. First, there is *semiotic,* the science of signs (cf. Morris, 1946; Szasz, 1961). The study of nonverbal communication is sometimes called *paralinguistics.* Insofar as such communication takes place through body movements, its study is called *kinesics* (see, for example, Davis, 1974:95; Lindesmith, Strauss, and Denzin, 1975:128), the study of "body language." This discipline can be said to have been founded by Ray Birdswhistle. Other contributors to the field include psychologists Albert Mehrabian (1974) and Albert Scheflen (1974), sociologists Erving Goffman (1959; 1974) and Gregory Stone (1962; 1970), and such authors as Flora Davis (1974) and Kenneth Johnson (1974).

Mehrabian, probably overstating the case for nonverbal communication, suggests that the total emotional impact of a message in face-to-face interaction is seven percent verbal plus thirty-eight percent vocal plus fifty-five percent facial. This finding is based on experiments conducted by that psychologist, who stresses the importance of such nonverbal components of messages as timing, distance, and posture. Mehrabian also suggests some interesting propositions. For example, "a speaker relaxes either very little or a great deal when he dislikes the person he is talking to, and to a moderate degree when he likes his companion" (Mehrabian, 1974:90-91). And: "The more you like a person, the more time you are likely to spend looking into his eyes as you talk to him" (op. cit.:91).

Goffman and Stone stress the importance of gestures and appearances in interaction. Their work and the whole dramaturgical school of sociology to which they belong are discussed elsewhere in this book. Davis and Johnson have documented different varieties of body language. Johnson, for example (1974), describes some features of black kinesics, arguing that they may be traceable to the African heritage. A case in point would be "rolling the eyes" in conflict situations. This is the practice of quickly moving the eyes from one side of the eye socket to the other. It is most common among black females.

In addition to the above and to a variety of gestures, body language also includes the use of *iconic signs* such as grooming, hair styles, etc. (cf. Lindesmith, Strauss, and Denzin, 1975:127). Thus the wearing of a tie or the smoking of a pipe by a professor is part of his body language; through such messages, he may be attempting to project a professional or an intellectual image. Furthermore, psychiatrists like Thomas Szasz (1961) are interested in a very special kind of iconic sign behavior, namely pathological body language such as hysteria, which is used as a substitute for verbal communication. According to Szasz, hysteria and some other forms of "mental illness" are merely the iconic signs of a *protolanguage* to which some people regress when unable to communicate verbally.

An entirely separate subdiscipline is *proxemics,* the study of personal space. As Edward Hall (1959) first demonstrated, space, distance, and other such physical factors are important cultural variables in communication. It is well known, for example, that South Americans and Southern Europeans stand closer to one another when talking than Anglo-Saxons. In the United States, according to Margaret Mead, "nobody has been willing to smell another human being, if they could help it, for the last fifty years" (quoted in Davis, 1974:100).

There are many other forms of nonverbal communication. For example, Shor (1972) did an interesting study of the communication systems operating between automobile drivers. These, like other systems of communication, are culture-bound. In congested cities, for example, the unwritten driving norms dictate that drivers act competitively, taking every advantage for themselves and squeezing themselves into every available space. In spacious and rural areas, on the other hand, the mutually understood driving patterns insist on mutual courtesy. The point is, in each case the proper communication of one's intentions is based on shared normative systems of interaction, a shared "language."

While humans communicate nonver-

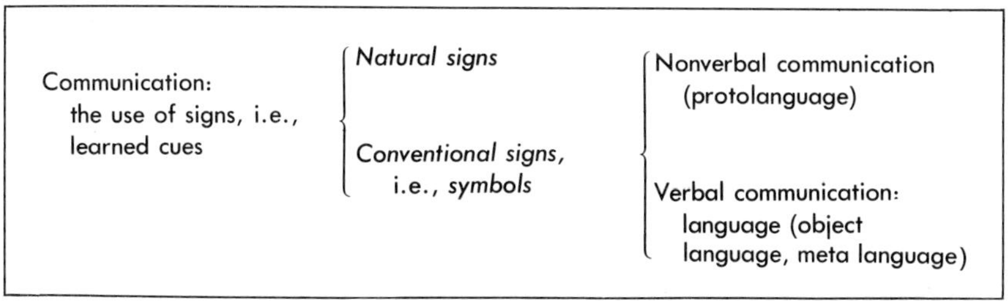

Communication: the use of signs, i.e., learned cues — Natural signs; Conventional signs, i.e., symbols — Nonverbal communication (protolanguage); Verbal communication: language (object language, meta language)

FIG. 7-3
Levels of human communication.

bally, we must remember that this is merely one of several levels of communication, as shown in Fig. 7-3. We now turn to that very important and uniquely human form, language.

LANGUAGE

The central distinction made in this chapter is between (natural) signs and symbols. The qualitative difference between man and other species boils down to the fact that only man can be stimulated by symbols (cf. Mead, 1956:36). This realization is the foundation of the linguistic sciences and of a properly humanistic social psychology, and it goes back essentially to four men: Cassirer, Mead, Sapir, and Whorf.

Ernst Cassirer (1944; Chapter 6) was a German philosopher who stressed the symbolic nature of human existence and the importance of language in the creation of man's reality. He introduced the sign-symbol dichotomy. George Herbert Mead (1956; Chapter 6) was the founder of symbolic interactionism and one of the most important contributors to the paradigm presented in this book. Edward Sapir (1949) and Benjamin Lee Whorf (1956) were authors who laid one of the most important building blocks of the modern linguistic sciences: they were among the first to realize that language determines perception, thought, and therefore human reality itself to a large extent. This seminal idea—alternatively referred to as the Sapir-Whorf hypothesis (cf. Hoebel, 1966) or the Whorfian hypothesis (cf. Hollander and Hunt, 1971)—will be discussed in detail later. Here, we note that the hypothesis is particularly important since it is relevant not only to psycholinguistics but also to the sociolinguist's interest in the cultural and symbolic origin of social reality.

Miller (1951) points out that men can make and distinguish probably no more than one hundred different monosyllabic speech sounds, or phonemes. However, the ability to put together patterns of two or more such sounds into an infinite number of combinations makes complex languages possible. This latter capability is uniquely human, made possible by man's complex nervous system, while the former skill is also related to advantageous biological equipment (a sophisticated vocal apparatus).

The development of speech during the evolution of species has been called the "human revolution" (Hockett and Ascher, 1964), and it had been completed by one million B.C. It would be improper to say that man developed speech because of his advantageous biological equipment. Biology does play an important role in the human revolution but it is, as speech itself, an outcome rather than a prior cause of that revolution. As Hockett and Ascher (1964) show, man's sophisticated vocal equipment and his complex nervous system, including an exceptionally large brain, only acquired survival value once speech had become a distinct need and possibility. At that point, natural selection produced the species now known as *Homo sapiens*. Function, as so often, preceded form. The crucial point in the human revolution was the substitution of the *open call system* for the former *closed call system:* once the protohominoids, descending from the apes, moved out of the trees to become erect bipeds, they developed a call system transmitted largely by tradition rather than by genetics (see Hockett and Ascher, 1964). For the first time, the form of messages became a matter of *convention.* The conventional symbol was born.

Another revolution in communication occurred with the invention of writing. As Goody and Watt (1962-1963) indicate, the shift from primitive oral communication to written forms of cultural transmission has drastically changed people's perceptions, notably their perception of time and space. Furthermore, the *type* of writing used in a society determines to an extent that society's way of thinking and its institutions. It is Marshall McLuhan (1964; 1969) who, more than anyone else, popularized this notion in his dictum "the medium is the message." A case in point is the already mentioned contrast between ideographic scripts (such as Chinese) and our own phonetic alphabet, which derives from ancient Greek. Goody and Watt point out that the phonetic alphabet introduced by the Greeks is directly responsible for the scientific-analytic mode of thought (including syllogistic logic) and hence, we may infer, for such core features of Western civilization as technology and rational bureaucratic institutions. The analytic nature of Western thought contrasts with the holistic primitive mind (Levi-Strauss, 1962). Whether the gradual substitution of the phonetic alphabet by television and other electronic media will reinstate Gestalt and retribalize us, as McLuhan argues, remains to be seen.

Of what does language consist?

Psychologists have been among the most active students of language. The German psychologist Wilhelm Wundt (1832-1920) can, perhaps more than anyone else, be considered the founder of psycholinguistics (cf. Blumenthal, 1970). The tradition of this subdiscipline has been to focus on the acquisition of language, including how to read (cf. Blumenthal, 1970); the structural form of language (cf. Blankenship, 1974; Hollander and Hunt, 1971; Markel, 1971); and the semantic and structural meaning of language (cf. Blankenship, 1974; Hayakawa, 1951; 1971; Osgood, Suci, and Tannenbaum, 1957). This

leaves, by default, the sociocultural context of language and meaning to the sociologists, a context which, as we shall see, cannot be overlooked for a proper understanding of meaning.

Leaving the discussion of language acquisition to the next section of this chapter, we zero in on Hollander and Hunt's (1971: 186-187) distinction between the form or structure of language and its meaning. The first of these two aspects is the business of descriptive linguistics (cf. Markel, 1971). That subdiscipline covers such topics as *phonology*, the study of the sound system of a language; *morphology*, the study of the various forms in which the sounds occur; and *paralanguage*, which deals with such things as voice quality, pitch, tempo, etc.

The problem of meaning in language has been focused upon by Blankenship (1974), Goodenough (1956), Hayakawa (1951; 1971), and Osgood, Suci, and Tannenbaum (1957), among others. Blankenship notes that meaning may be a function of three things: semantics, structure, and sound. Under semantic meaning, that author reminds us of Osgood's important distinction between *denotation* and *connotation:* "denotation is the objective reference of a word" (Blankenship, 1974:59). For example, the denotative meaning of "pencil" is that which writes. Connotation, however, is the subjectively tinted meaning at-

"The Government"

	Extremely	Very	Slightly	Neutral	Slightly	Very	Extremely	
Good								Bad
Beautiful								Ugly
Strong								Weak
Pleasant								Unpleasant
Honest								Dishonest
Peace								War
White								Black
etc. . .								etc. . .

FIG. 7-4
Semantic differential by Osgood, Suci, and Tannenbaum.

Modified from Blankenship, Jane. 1974. The resources of language. In Messages: A Reader in Human Communication. Jean M. Civikly (ed.). New York: Random House, Inc.

tached to a word by an individual. In addition to denotative meaning, most words also have connotative meaning. This is so in the case of nouns, which refer to things ("spider" not only refers to an organism of the arachnid variety but also may evoke fear or disgust, depending on the individual), and certainly so in the case of adjectives, for example "beautiful," "strong," "shallow."

Structural meaning derives from set (grammatical) rules. The English sentence "he threw the ball" is understood—by English-speaking people—to mean that a man threw a ball and not, for example, that a ball threw a man.

Sound, too, determines meaning, through such factors as loudness, pitch, duration, etc. An interesting case of the sound-meaning relationship is the *onomatopoeia* (Blankenship, 1974:73), that linguistic form in which the word imitates what it refers to. For example, we say that a cat "meows." The existence of onomatopoeia had led earlier linguists to theorize that language originated through the imitation of natural sounds, but this theory has been convincingly refuted.

Osgood, Suci, and Tannenbaum (1957), who are responsible for the distinction between denotation and connotation, devised a scale to measure connotative meaning. Their *semantic differential* consists of any concept (for example a noun) followed by a set of scales consisting of polar adjectives (good-bad, beautiful-ugly, etc.) separated by seven spaces (Fig. 7-4).

This device, according to Osgood and subsequent researchers, permits us to measure and compare such things as attitudes and the amount of consensus or disagreement about the meaning of words.

General semanticists are another group interested in meaning, particularly breakdowns of meaning (cf. Hollander and Hunt, 1971:187-188). Hayakawa, one of the leading figures in that movement, is also concerned with language as a form of control (Hayakawa, 1971), a topic to which we shall return in the final section of this chapter.

There are many other aspects to the problem of meaning in language. For example, anthropologists like Goodenough (1956) apply *componential analysis* to the study of the meaning of kinship terms. In addition, verbal behavior may be merely *expressive,* as in the case of ritualistic exchanges about the weather or in swearing. Here, the meaning of the messages sent out has little to do with the semantic meaning of the words. There is also pseudocommunication, the exchange of words that have different meanings to the different interlocutors (cf. Lindesmith, Strauss, and Denzin, 1975:125). Most important of all, however, is the sociocultural context of language, the group base of meaning. This is the aspect with which sociologists are most concerned and to which we now turn.

How does society use language?

The three major characteristics of language are that it consists of symbols that constitute systems, are not bound to the objects to which they refer, and are inherently *social,* that is, evoke the same response in their producer as in their receiver (Lindesmith, Strauss, and Denzin, 1975). A language, then, is a *shared* symbolic system. It reflects the history and interests of a group, as can be readily seen from such examples as Eskimo dialects, with their elaborate terminology for many different kinds of snow.

Having a particular language means that every group views the external world through the particular glasses—the perspective—provided by its language. The common language determines the meaning of the environment. It *is part* of the environment. Man's environment, therefore, is symbolic as well as physical.

To use language is tantamount to establishing categories. As Dewey explained, "A category. . .constitutes a point of view, a schedule, a program, a heading or caption, an orientation" (1938:237), and languages consist of categorical symbols. The general attitude implicit in the use of language has been called the "categorical attitude." As Lindesmith, Strauss, and Denzin (1975:100) describe this attitude, it consists of the "realization that (1) things can be named and talked about, (2) events and objects may be grouped or classified, and (3) by naming and classifying the features of our environment new modes of behavior, as well as new possibilities of manipulating that environment are brought into existence."

With the exception of proper nouns, all nouns, verbs, and adjectives in a language represent categories—that is, they are concepts. For example, the concept "cow" refers to all animals falling in that category. The concept "dark" refers to a variety of shades categorized in contradistinction to "light." Concepts vary in degrees of abstraction and scholars have developed hierarchical systems of classification. For example, biologists and physical anthropologists today use the system developed by the Swedish botanist Linnaeus (1707-1778). That system is given here, classifying man as an example.

	Level of classification	Man
	Kingdom	Animal
Ascending	Phylum	Chordate
	Class	Mammal
abstractness	Group	Placental
	Order	Primate
	Family	Hominid
	Genus	Homo
	Species	*Homo sapiens*
	Variety	Caucasian
	Individual	Joe Blow

Modified from Hoebel, E. Adamson. 1966. Anthropology: The Study of Man. New York: McGraw-Hill Book Co.

While everyday language is by no means as rigorous in its classifications as Linnaeus' taxonomy, the main point here is that *to use words is to categorize.* Every concept is a generalization. Some concepts refer to real things, but some merely to *fictions*, for example, Santa Claus. However, whether a concept refers to a fiction or not, it does form the basis for social action and is, in that sense, quite real. As we empha-

size throughout this book, the most meaningful definition of "real" is a pragmatic one, one best expressed in W. I. Thomas' dictum: "If men define situations as real, they are real in their consequences."

One important fiction that is quite real in its consequences is (racial) prejudice and stereotyping. As Walter Lippman (1922) and Lindesmith, Strauss, and Denzin, (1975:97-100) explain, stereotypes are oversimplified, fixed, and fallacious conceptions about some people. They are resistant to change, even in the face of contrary empirical evidence, because they constitute part of a coherent belief system, or cognitive structure. To abandon them would create cognitive dissonance. Racial stereotyping, which is one form of fictitious classification, still leads a majority of Americans to rank the following groups in an order of decreasing acceptability: (1) Americans, Canadians, and English, (2) French, Norwegians, Germans, Swedes, and other Northern Europeans, (3) Southern European peoples, (4) Jews, and (5) blacks, Turks, Chinese, and Hindus.

As we said, to use language is to categorize. Some forms of classification may be fictitious and even harmful. Other ones may be more "scientific." However—and this is the main point—all our ideas about other people, about the world, and about ourselves are determined by the categories we use. Language, as the Sapir-Whorf hypothesis states, orders the world for us and determines how we perceive it. Thus no knowledge can be totally objective, not even scientific knowledge.

It is the symbolic construction of reality and the sociocultural relativity of all language and thought that sociolinguists study. Since their work thus deals with the functional relationships between language and society, we defer discussion of typical recent work in sociolinguistics (e.g., Labov, 1972b; Moscovici, 1972) to the last section of this chapter, where we deal with the functions of language. We shall then also examine the most up-to-date effort made in the study of the relationship between language and society, that of ethnomethodologists like Cicourel (1970; 1974), Drietzel (1970), Mueller (1970), and Turner (1970). As we shall argue, ethnomethodology's current activities in the forefront of sociolinguistics are among the most exciting developments in the study of language. This radical departure from conventional sociolinguistic theories makes it at least possible to think of society, and how it operates, in an entirely new way.

LEARNING LANGUAGE

Men have been fascinated by and speculated on the origin of language for thousands of years. The Greek historian Herodotus tells us about the attempt by the ancient Egyptian king Psammeticus (663-609 B.C.) to isolate children and thereby discover the first human language. Since the ninteenth century, many more scientific efforts have been made to explain man's ability to use language. In recent decades, the number of competing theories has declined, but consensus has not yet been achieved.

Among psycholinguists, we find the behavioristic nominalism of the followers of Floyd Allport (1924) and Clark Hull (1919), who see language acquisition as the accumulation, through practice, of verbal responses that are rewarded (cf. Blumenthal, 1970:129-142). There is, too, the highly influential theory of Chomsky (1965), which posits an innate biological linguistic ability, as if the human brain were programmed with innate ideas and principles (cf. Lindesmith, Strauss, and Denzin, 1975:344-346). One of the things that led Chomsky to seek the origin of language in biology is the existence of some cross-cultural similarities in language, for example in baby talk (cf. Ferguson, 1975). However, the position taken in this book is that a sociological theory of language acquisition is far better, both because the

brunt of existing evidence points that way and because of the metaphysical character of Chomsky's theory. To simply attribute language to human nature merely relegates one more problem to that residual bag in which we throw all aspects of human behavior that we do not really understand, and if specific inheritable mental programs are posited, their existence cannot be tested, certainly not at this time.

In this section, we therefore explain language acquisition *sociologically,* as do Sullivan (1953), Lindesmith, Strauss, and Denzin (1975), and sociolinguists in general. To be sure, this focus does not deny the importance of some of the factors emphasized by other scholars. We must concur with the behaviorists that verbal responses must be socially rewarded to establish themselves, that language acquisition takes place within such a verbal reinforcement system—what Skinner (1957) terms the verbal community. Similarly, the uniquely complex nature of the human brain and nervous system must be recognized as a necessary condition in the acquisition of language. However, it is not true that certain universal onomatopoeic expressions "naturally" come to young infants the world over, with universal meaning (implying support for Chomsky's biological theory of language acquisition; cf. Blankenship, 1974; Ferguson, 1975). Studies of children who have grown up in isolation (cf. Davis. 1940; 1947; Malson, 1972) have demolished all notions of a human instinct for language. The real task of sociolinguistics is to describe the phases and differences in language learning, not to restate an unprovable and tautological single and sovereign causal principle that functions merely as a deus ex machina.

Childhood language acquisition

During most of the first year of life, the infant merely babbles and imitates itself. However, by nine or twelve months, a sort of symbolic interaction between the child and the parents begins to emerge. At first, the conversations are still in the form of gestures, not words. The child's language is still a body language. As part of such a language, a child may have a complex crying vocabulary with maybe seven different cries denoting such states as pain, anger, hunger, discomfort, etc. (Lindesmith, Strauss, and Denzin, 1975:337). Gradually, verbal utterances begin to accompany gestures, they become abbreviated gestures, and once they replace gestures, the child is in effect using symbols. As Lindesmith and co-workers (1975:336-337) stress, the infant's use of gestures and early vocalizations is *instrumental,* aimed at reaching things, getting mom's attention, and so forth. Yet such speech is still autistic, that is, private (Sullivan, 1953).

The question is, of course, how does the infant develop the use of first specific gestures and then specific words? This can occur only through interaction. In the early infant-parent interaction, it is not so much the child who imitates the parents as the parents who imitate those accidental vocalizations of the child that are linguistically meaningful, thereby rewarding their usage. For example, the infant may, at first accidentally, utter such sounds as "dadada" or "mama." The parents, by repeating such selected sounds to the infant and by other rewarding responses, encourage their usage, ignoring other sounds. This is how certain vocalizations acquire social meaning (Sullivan, 1953).

Another way in which parents may reward certain vocalizations is by selecting for the child those objects whose names are closest to the sounds (accidentally) emitted. For example, a baby may utter something like "poonie" and be given a spoon by its mother to play or attempt to eat with. Thus one important way in which the child may learn to name things is, in essence, a form of operant conditioning.

Initially, the child's use of words is inaccurate; it does not correspond to conventional adult usage. As the French linguist Guillaume (1927) has shown, children first use autonomous word-sentences (cf. Blumenthal, 1970:116), single words meaning entire sentences. The word-sentence of a child means many more things than the same word used conventionally by adults. For example, Dani, who is fourteen months old, says "dada(da)" when seeing her father, or riding back to the house, or seeing the family car as well as when she playfully approaches the dog. On the other hand, she utters "mama" and "nana" (interchangeably) when hungry, or wet, or tired. Such sounds as "(s)poon(ie)" seem to be used in connection with food, eating, and the like.

The foregoing indicates that the infant is in fact already categorizing, albeit differently than adults. The Swiss psychologist Piaget has shown that children follow logic, a logic quite different from that of adults. Earlier, the major error had been to assume that children's logic, thought, and speech are modelled—at first imperfectly—after adult categories and the written word. Guillaume (1927) has pointed out that the fact that infants initially use word-sentences negates the possibility of their categorizing words into conventional grammatical categories (cf. Blumenthal, 1970:116). What happens eventually is that the child is pressured by the parents into adopting conventional categories, something that occurs as the child learns that conventional usage is more efficient (Lindesmith and Strauss, 1956:175-176). For example, "dada" is eventually separated from the car, or from rides, or from dogs, because those (erroneous) usages are ignored by the parents (as well as by the dog).[1]

Parental pressure consists of commands, prohibitions, rewards, punishment, and indifference. Through symbolic cues (words), parents are able to control the child's behavior. Studies have shown (cf. Hull, 1933; Lindesmith and Strauss, 1956:178) that suggestibility increases greatly from age four to eight and that

---

[1]Foote (1955), always keeping humor in sociology, reminds us that the dog, too, is an important significant other within the family.

after eight the child becomes increasingly autonomous, no longer accepting his parents' word as the final law.

The gradual substitution of syntactic speech for autonomous word-sentences has been studied by Guillaume (1927), Piaget (1955), and Sullivan (1954), among others. Guillaume notes that the first two things to emerge out of word-sentences are names of people and expressions of wishes. For example, at sixteen months Dani begins to say such things as "daddy cala," in which cala probably refers to a car (ride). This is already a sentence. Sullivan (1954) distinguishes between three stages of linguistic development: prototaxis, parataxis, and syntaxis. The first of these refers to the earliest gestural form of communication just discussed. The second stage is what Piaget (1955) terms egocentric speech. This is where Dani is, at a year and a half, beginning to use sentences. Syntaxis, finally, is what Piaget calls socialized speech, the gradual adoption by the child of conventional meanings and grammar.

Communities are based on language

We have just traced language acquisition developmentally. Now, one thing must be stressed with the utmost emphasis: language acquisition is a direct function of the group in which it takes place. A person's verbal development cannot take place outside a social group, and it reflects the specific group and culture in which it occurs. Skinner (1957) terms that group the *verbal community*. This is what Mead called the generalized other, the society in which one grows up and with which one shares a common culture, notably a common language. While Skinner's treatment of language acquisition is of limited value in that it takes an (operant) conditioning approach, the concept of verbal community is useful. Following this idea, Roger Brown (1971) points out that parents (and other significant others) may be viewed as "tutors" who transmit to the child the names used in the verbal community to label objects.

Sullivan (1953) has made two important propositions with regard to this linguistic primary group—most often the parental family: (1) "the more complex the linguistic community of the primary group, the more elaborate and complex will be the speech patterns of the young child," and (2) "the greater the complexity of the community, the more rapid will be the child's acquistion of speech" (quoted in Lindesmith, Strauss, and Denzin, 1975:346).

One thing, above all, seems established: language is not instinctive, and there are no universal cross-cultural forms of speech that automatically come to children everywhere. Ferguson's (1975) comparative study of baby talk in six languages demonstrates this, demolishing both the instinctive and the onomatopoeic theories of language (cf. Blankenship, 1974). True, certain cross-cultural similarities are curious and unexplainable on the basis of cultural diffusion. For example, Comanche and Hungarian babies both call their father "api." By the same token, however, the familiar "mam(a)" and "papa" mean just as often "food" (for example in Arabic and in Spanish) as "mother" and "father." As Lindesmith and associates (1975:346) correctly explain in their criticism of Chomsky's biological reductionism, whatever cross-cultural similarities may exist should be attributed to the universality of the primary group (cf. Cooley, 1909) rather than to biology.

The study of linguistic differences in various groups, subcultures, and social classes is the major task of sociolinguistics—the discipline that studies the relationship between language and society. Good examples of such work include Ward (1971), a comparison of language learning among children in a black rural Louisiana community and a middle-class community; Labov (1972a), an examination of language and social class; and Shuy (1973), where various papers on language attitudes appear (see Grimshaw, 1973;

1974, for a two-part review symposium of these and additional books in sociolinguistics).

THE FUNCTIONS OF LANGUAGE

In this final section, we focus primarily on the relationship between language and society. Following Sapir and Whorf, we first note that language in large part determines—or better, structures—thought. Therefore, just as language shapes the individual mind, it also shapes the collective culture. Furthermore, it determines an individual's self-concept, identity, and personality. At the social level, language is our primary vehicle for communication; as many scholars since Dewey (1922) have emphasized, society itself is a vast communication process. Thus social structure, too, should be viewed as being, at least in part, a linguistic construction. While there is no longer much that is new about this last assertion, it is only recently, as we shall see, that a notable group of researchers often calling themselves (or grouped by others as) ethnomethodologists has begun with the nitty-gritty of empirically dissecting the linguistic fabric of social structure.

Consciousness

The basic thesis underlying this final discussion is, again, the Sapir-Whorf hypothesis. The essential point made by Sapir (for example, 1949) and Whorf (for example, 1956) is that language plays an important role as an independent variable. And although Whorf did anthropological field work demonstrating some of the relationships between language on the one hand and cognitive and behavioral concomitants on the other, the problem with the thesis has been a lack of specification of those concomitants, of the variables presumably affected by language. Fishman (1960) has provided a useful systematization of the Whorfian hypothesis, specifying four levels of variables affected by language. He argues that the lexical and grammatical characteristics of language can each be expected to have cultural as well as behavioral consequences. Table 5 schematizes these four logical possibilities.

An example of a level 1 relationship in Table 5 is the Eskimo's many words for different kinds of snow. Eskimo culture reflects their vocabulary. At level 2, studies have shown that the linguistic codification of colors determines how people respond to colors. For example, in a society that has a single word for a color, people will recall that color more rapidly than in a culture that requires a phrase to describe the same color. Thus behavior reflects vocabulary. A level 3 example is the relationship noted between the Navaho's language structure and their passive fatalism. Culture reflects grammar. Finally, at level 4, an experiment found Navahos classifying objects in accordance with some grammatical characteristics of their language. Behavior reflects grammar. (All examples cited in Fishman, 1960.)

Elements of the general Whorfian hypothesis are found in a large amount of literature. Since the literature on this subject does not follow Fishman's neat systematization, our discussion must also deviate from it. One emphasis, found in Whorf's own writings, is the relationship between language and perception. From this, it follows that language also determines behavior. Lindesmith, Strauss and Denzin (1975:348-352) discuss two cases of the relationship between language, consciousness, and subsequent behavior: one is the learning, by American children, of racial concepts and classifications. As the Clarks

TABLE 5.   Four ways in which language may determine thought and society*

	Things affected	
Language characteristics	*Culture*	*Behavior*
Lexicon	Level 1	Level 2
Grammar	Level 3	Level 4

*Modified from Fishman, Joshua A. 1960. "A systematization of the Whorfian hypothesis." Behavioral Science 5:323-339.

(1952) show, children learn racial identifications (or self-identifications), classification criteria, and evaluations linguistically, as they grow older. They then acquire and begin to act out their roles accordingly. Another case is the acquistion of conceptions of money, studied by Strauss (1952). Here, too, the learned concepts result in specific attitudes, values, and behaviors.

The relationship of language and thought has been of concern to many other scholars. From a Marxian point of departure, Soviet scholars (e.g., Luria, 1966a; 1966b; Vygotsky, 1962) have reached conclusions converging with those derived from Meadian social psychology. Also, there has been an interest in *aphasia* (cf. Goldstein, 1940; Head, 1926), the impairment or loss of speech, and other speech pathologies as a cause of behavioral incompetence.

Luria (1966a; 1966b) and Vygotsky (1962) emphasize the inseparability of thought and language. This confirms, according to Luria, the Marxian premise that human mental activity is sociohistorical in origin. Vygotsky criticizes Piaget for committing the dualistic fallacy of regarding thought and language as independent from one another. Scholars who have dealt with aphasia (Goldstein, 1940; Head, 1926) stress that the pathology—whether due to amnesia, organic causes, or other factors—results in an inability to conceptualize abstractly, which is an essential tool in successful living. This ties in with the important psychotherapeutic notion that mental patients, in order to deal with their emotional problems, must somehow learn to label them so as to acquire verbal control over them and learn to channel, structure, manipulate, and control their conduct toward a more desirable adjustment (cf. Bois, 1974; Dollard and Miller, 1950).

Although language and thought are inseparable, Lindesmith, Strauss and Denzin (1975:144-155) remind us that they

are not identical. Not only do animals also think, but so do human, often nonverbally. The so-called nondiscursive thought of artists is a case in point, and so are fantasizing (daydreaming) as well as dreaming.

In this section, then, we have dealt with language and one of its dependent variables—thought, or consciousness. It is discussed in many additional sources, including, for example, Chomsky (1968) and Liebendorfer (1960). Whether the posited relationship is between language and thought, or language and consciousness, or language and mind makes no difference, for we must remember that mind is thought, no more and no less. This is the central point of Meadian social psychology. Now let us examine some of language's other dependent variables.

Culture

In Fishman's (1960) systematization of the Whorfian hypothesis (see Fig. 7-4), levels 1 and 3 refer to the fact that the culture of a society, the knowledge of any group, is a reflection of their language. An article by Tung-Sun (1970) makes this point well. It shows that Western knowledge and Chinese knowledge differ because they are based on radically different languages, that is, different ways of categorizing and hence perceiving the world. Aristotelian logic is largely a formalization of Greek grammar, and it is primarily analytical and characterized by the assumption that substance always underlies appearance, thing always precedes activity. The typical sentence in the typical Indo-European language is: "The man (subject) carries (verb) the book (object)," or: "the rose (substance) is yellow (appearance)." This, then, accounts for a world view that assumes that activity emanates from thing, that ultimate reality resides in things, and that the world consists of things that can be separated (analyzed) in order to be understood. Quite different is Chinese logic, which emphasized the relational significance of phenomena, their mutual implication or inherence (Tung-Sun, 1970). For example, positive and negative, or male and female, or large and small, all these are not separate features of separate objects, but, quite to the contrary, they mutually imply each other and are therefore ultimately one.

In the final analysis, the Whorfian hypothesis' main point, at the cultural level, is that all knowledge is a function of the linguistic categories employed, and this puts a sharp dent in the possibility of objective scientific knowledge. Of course, this does not warrant total defeatism. Hockett, quoted in Fishman (1960), points out that languages differ in the degree to which they transcend their limitations. In other words, man's task is to devise *better* languages so as to improve the conception and communication of ideas.

The self

As we saw, even though language and thought are not identical, the higher mental processes—the ability to think abstractly—does fully depend on language. Furthermore, by determining how and what a person thinks, language also greatly determines personality development; that is, it determines what a person becomes. This means that language is at least partially responsible for a person's self-concept, identity, personality, attitudes, social and emotional adjustment, in sum his *self*.

How do the absence of language, or restrictions in linguistic proficiency, affect the human self? Lindesmith, Strauss, and Denzin (1975:237-259) discuss a number of such situations, including feral children and individuals who are blind-deaf, aphasic, mentally retarded, and schizophrenic. Their point throughout may be summed up as follows: the development of a mature, healthy, and competent self requires adequate mastery of the language used by

one's significant group. Failure to adequately master a language is the major aspect of inadequate socialization. Fig. 7-5 sums up the relationship between language, the self, and the group to which one belongs.

Feral children are those few children who, once in a while in history, have been found to have grown up in absolute isolation from other human beings. Feral is derived from the Latin word *fera,* meaning wild beast. These children are also called wolf children (cf. Malson, 1972). Well-known cases include Anna and Isabelle, described by Davis (1940; 1947), the wolf boy of Agra, described by Ogburn (1959), and the wild boy of Aveyron, discovered in Southern France in the nineteenth century. The relevance of such cases is twofold: in the absence of language, these children, some as old as seven or eight when discovered, were not truly human in terms of an ability to communicate symbolically, take roles, and play roles; they had no selves. However, once brought into human society, even a seven-year-old child has a good chance to "catch up," and this is primarily a verbal development.

Probably the most famous blind-deaf person was Helen Keller (1917), who, despite her condition, eventually learned to speak, read, and write proficiently. As Lindesmith, Strauss, and Denzin (1975: 239-242) note, Keller's learning of language enabled her to conceptualize sounds and colors, thereby proving that such conceptualization does not depend on specific sensory data. In her case, logical analogies were sufficient.

Aphasia, as we saw, is the loss or impair-

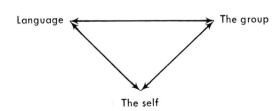

FIG. 7-5
Language, the group,
and the self.

ment of speech. Students of aphasic individuals (such as Goldstein, 1940; Head, 1926) have shown that the main problem resulting from (partial) aphasia is the inability to think abstractly, a regression to a more concrete categorical attitude. In this respect, then, aphasics are similar to the mentally retarded, who also have difficulty with symbolism and whose perceptions are concrete and personal rather than abstract (cf. Lindesmith, Strauss, and Denzin, 1975:242-244).

Aphasics also share with schizophrenics an inability to take the role of others, to empathize. Their frame of mind, as that of young children, is egocentric. The schizophrenic's language is idiosyncratic, depriving him of a common ground with his social environment. A beautiful fictional illustration of such a situation is given in Green (1964).

In general, internal thought and social dialogue are two sides of the same coin, both predicated upon language. What young children, aphasics, the mentally retarded, and schizophrenics have in common is (1) their inadequate mastery of language, (2) their inability to take the role of others (their egocentricity), (3) their consequently asocial existence, and (4) their asocial nature. By living (partially) outside society, they are not social and have no developed selves.

Finally, it must be remembered that language affects the self in a variety of other "normal" ways as well. As Strauss (1959) shows, personal identity greatly depends on the names, titles, and labels applied to a person. This is, of course, also the realization underlying the labelling theory of deviance, a theory that states that the linguistic labels society attaches to individuals affect their self-concept, identity, and behavior. Through a self-fulfilling prophecy, negative labels may produce negative behavior.[2]

[2]See Chapter 6 for a discussion and bibliography of labelling theory.

Also, a good illustration of how language affects the self is the profound personality change immigrants may undergo after switching from their earlier mother tongue to, say, English.

Communication

Much of the literature on communication deals with the verbal and nonverbal ways in which people succeed in conveying messages to one another, for example requests (Satir, 1974). There is often a focus on problems in communication, or on how to improve communication (such as Cathcart and Samovar, 1970; Civikly, 1974), and on communicative compentence (see Gumperz and Hymes, 1972). We have already touched on this subject when dealing with various linguistic impairments such as aphasia.

A fascinating approach to the problem of communication is found in the phenomenological literature. Schutz (1970), for example, approaches the phenomenon with the fundamental question: what is the structure of interhuman understanding? Similarly, Spiegelberg (1973) asks: on what grounds do we assume the "right" to say "we"? The phenomenologist is concerned with the basic structure of *intersubjectivity:* how is understanding possible, for example the profound form of communication sometimes called *communion*? (cf. Schmalenbach, 1965).

Phenomenologists recognize that a very important part of the answer will be provided by linguistic analysis, especially the examination of linguistic *deep structure* (cf. Chomsky, 1965; Cicourel, 1974), that is, the basic rules of linguistic interpretation. According to the philosopher Natanson (1970:35-40), communication involves dialogue, analogy, behavior, and interpretation as its four basic methods. Schutz (1970, chapter 9) goes into a very special kind of communication, namely the musical communication between a composer and a performer. Two such men may be separated by centuries of time, yet the *duree,* the inner time through which the music is experienced, is a bridge between them. Communication, Schutz notes, also requires "tuning in."

Important knowledge about the structure of communication will now probably be provided by the ethnomethodologists, a group important enough to deserve separate treatment in the next section of this chapter. Indeed, we discuss ethnomethodology under the final heading—social structure—because that is what an examination of language must ultimately lead to. As Blumer (1962), Dewey (1922), Ross (1973), and others have explained, society can ultimately be viewed as a vast communicative structure, a structure that exists in the sense that it is ongoingly being acted out by its members. What ethnomethodology attempts to discover are the linguistic and cognitive practices and methods used by members to sustain the social structure.

Social structure

The final relationship to be examined in this chapter—that between language and social structure—is a functional one. It is a two-way process. On the one hand there has been a focus on the social-structural determination of, or constraints on, language. Much current work in sociolinguistics deals with this. On the other hand there is the ethnomethodologists' attempt to discover the underlying linguistic and cognitive procedures used by members of society to arrive at a sense of social structure.

A good sample of the first of these orientations is reviewed by Grimshaw in *Contemporary Sociology* (1973; 1974). Much of this body of literature is concerned with the relationship between social class, socialization, and language (for example, Bernstein, 1971; 1973; Cook-Gumperz, 1973, Labov, 1972b; Moscovici, 1972) and the relationship between ethnicity and language (Labov, 1972a; Ward, 1971). One example (from Labov, 1972a) shows the stratification of language: there is, among upwardly mobile lower-middle-class speakers, a phenomenon of linguistic

hypercorrection, they correct *more* in careful speech than do upper middle-class speakers. The focus on external constraints on language is also found in the work of Mueller (1970), who, like Bernstein (see above), converges toward the critical sociology of Habermas and Marcuse. Such work shows that class positions and power relations restrict and distort language and communication. Thus one's position in the social structure determines one's access to language and therefore one's level of consciousness. One of the consequences of the sociopolitical structure is the inability of groups and individuals to verbalize an awareness of social reality and to communicate with one another. In sum, social structure not only means economic inequality but also cognitive handicap for groups and individuals.

A different matter is the linguistic construction of social structure, something stressed ever since Mead (1934) and subsequent Meadians (for example Duncan, 1962). It has been pointed out that *to speak is to do, accomplish, perform.* Hayakawa (1971), the semanticist, shows that language is directive, it controls, it makes things happen. However, it is the ethnomethodologists who, more than anyone, have studied language as *the enactment of society.* Turner (1970) picks up Austin's concept of *performative* to show that to speak is to do. While Austin merely applied this notion to expressions such as "I apologize" or "I hereby pronounce you husband and wife" (expressions representing actions as they are spoken), Turner argues that all speech is performance.

Finally, ethnomethodology delves into the nitty-gritty of how people go about making sense out of utterances and thereby sustain a sense of social structure. Let us go back to Schutz's phenomenological question: what is the structure of everyday understanding? Garfinkel was among the first to attempt to discover the specific properties of practical reasoning. Consider the following exchange (from Garfinkel, 1967:38-39).

HUSBAND: Dana succeeded in putting a penny in a parking meter today without being picked up.

WIFE: Did you take him to the record store?

Obviously the above communication between husband and wife presupposes several tacit assumptions. Actually, the exchange implies something like this:

HUSBAND: This afternoon as I was bringing Dana, our four-year-old son, home from the nursery school, he succeeded in reaching high enough to put a penny in a parking meter when we parked in a meter parking zone, whereas before he has always had to be picked up to reach that high.

WIFE: Since he put a penny in a meter that means that you stopped while he was with you. I know that you stopped at the record store either on the way to get him or on the way back. Was it on the way back, so that he was with you or did you stop there on the way to get him and somewhere else on the way back?

What rules did both husband and wife tacitly employ to accomplish understanding with a minimum of words? Garfinkel lists several, including the facts that (1) there were many matters that the partners understood they were talking about that they did not mention, (2) many matters that the partners understood were understood on the basis not only of what was actually said but what was left unspoken, (3) many matters were understood through a process of attending to the temporal series of utterances as documentary evidences of a developing conversation rather than as a string of terms. Garfinkel lists several additional rules. It is this type of tacit procedures that ethnomethodologists have been discovering and inventorizing.

Similarly, Cicourel (1974) attempts to discover the basic interpretive rules employed by people to achieve common-sense understanding in everyday interaction. He views these interpretive rules, or proce-

dures, as somewhat similar to Chomsky's (1965) linguistic deep-structure, which, through transformational grammar, results in semantically meaningful utterances. We must, Cicourel argues, acquire a set of such interpretive rules (a deep-structure?), or else how could we speak and understand sentences that we have never heard previously?

There are many unanswered questions in Cicourel's work, particularly with respect to the exact nature of the "deep-structure." Chomsky views deep-structure (or the transformational rules?) as context-free, or cross-culturally universal. This may be what prompts him to descend into biology in his linguistic theories (see section on learning language above). Cicourel seems to reject the needless assertion of a context-free linguistic base (1974:48), but this is not all that clear, particularly when it comes to his discussion of interpretive procedures. One also wonders whether these efforts parallel those of Levi-Strauss and the structuralists at discovering basic *codes* underlying cultures. Or are these sociolinguists merely telling us that there is a *grammar* underlying language and that we all use grammatical rules, notably syntactical rules, or else we do not understand utterances? Deutscher's (1975) interpretation of Cicourel's deep-structure does not clear matters up either, since it first (Deutscher, 1975:175) states that "norms" are surface rules, but later (op. cit.:177) equates them with linguistic deep-structure! Cicourel would endorse the first statement, not the second.

The main point about Cicourel, as well as Garfinkel and the Schutzian tradition in sociology, is that it is an exciting pioneering effort that deserves our full attention at this time. Misunderstandings and confusion are to some extent inevitable at such a stage. Paradigm clarification takes place through a gradual communication process in the scientific community.

SUMMARY AND CONCLUSION

This chapter has examined the nature and functions of language, in view of the essential part it plays in the development of self and society. Preliminarily, we dealt with nonverbal communication among humans and such animals as insects (ants, bees) and the higher primates (chimpanzees). The second section distinguished between the psychological and the sociological study of language. Traditionally, psychologists have focused mostly on the structure, the semantic meaning, and the acquisition of language, while sociologists have stressed the relationship between language and society. The subsequent section dealt with the acquisition of language by children and the role of the verbal community in this process. The final section, taking its point of departure in the Sapir-Whorf hypothesis, discussed the relationships between language, primarily as an independent variable, and the following concomitants: individual consciousness, culture, the self, communication, and social structure.

REFERENCES

Allport, Floyd H.
  1924 Social Psychology. Boston: Houghton Mifflin Co.
Bernstein, Basil (ed.)
  1971 Class, Codes and Control, I: Theoretical Studies towards a Sociology of Language. London: Routledge and Kegan Paul.
  1973 Class, Codes and Control, II: Applied Studies towards a Sociology of Language. London: Routledge and Kegan Paul.
Blankenship, Jane
  1974 "The resources of language." In Messages: A Reader in Human Communication. Jean M. Civikly (ed.). New York: Random House, Inc., pp. 52-81.
Blumenthal, Arthur L. (ed.)
  1970 Language and Psychology. New York: John Wiley & Sons, Inc.
Blumer, Herbert
  1962 "Society as symbolic interaction." In Human Behavior and Social Processes. Arnold M. Rose (ed.). Boston: Houghton Mifflin Co., pp. 179-192.
Bois, J. Samuel
  1974 "The power of words." In Messages: A Reader in Human Communication. Jean M. Civikly (ed.). New York: Random House, Inc., pp. 81-87.
Brown, Roger
  1971 "How shall a thing be called." In Current Perspectives in Social Psychology. Edwin P.

Hollander and Raymond G. Hunt (eds.). New York: Oxford University Press, pp. 219-225.
Cassirer, Ernst
  1944 An Essay on Man: An Introduction to a Philosophy of Human Culture. New Haven, Conn.: Yale University Press.
Cathcart, Robert S. and Larry A. Samovar
  1970 Small Group Communication: A Reader. Dubuque, Iowa: William C. Brown Co., Publisher.
Chomsky, Noam
  1965 Aspects of the Theory of Syntax. Cambridge, Mass.: The M.I.T. Press.
  1968 Language and Mind. New York: Harcourt, Brace and World.
Cicourel, Aaron V.
  1970 "The acquisition of social structure: toward a developmental sociology of language and meaning." In Understanding Everyday Life. Jack D. Douglas (ed.). Chicago: Aldine Publishing Co., pp. 136-168.
  1974 Cognitive Sociology: Language and Meaning in Social Interaction. New York: The Free Press.
Civikly, Jean M.
  1974 Messages: A Reader in Human Communication. New York: Random House, Inc.
Clark, K. and M. Clark
  1952 "Racial identification and preference in Negro children." In Readings in Social Psychology. G. E. Swanson, T. M. Newcomb, and E. L. Hartley (eds.). New York: Holt, Rinehart and Winston, Inc.
Cook-Gumperz, Jenny
  1973 Social Control and Socialization: A Study of Class Differences in the Language of Maternal Control. London: Routledge and Kegan Paul.
Cooley, Charles Horton
  1909 Social Organization. New York: Scribner's Sons.
Davis, Flora
  1974 "How to read body language." In Messages: A Reader in Human Communication. Jean M. Civikly (ed.). New York: Random House, Inc.
Davis, Kingsley
  1940 "Extreme social isolation of a child." American Journal of Sociology (January):554-565.
  1947 "Final note on a case of extreme isolation." American Journal of Sociology (March):432-437.
Deutscher, Irwin
  1975 "Review essay on cognitive sociology by Cicourel." American Journal of Sociology (July):174-179.

Dewey, John
  1922 Human Nature and Conduct. New York:
        Holt, Rinehart and Winston, Inc.
  1938 The Theory of Inquiry. New York: Holt,
        Rinehart and Winston, Inc.
Dollard, John and Neal E. Miller
  1950 Personality and Psychotherapy: An Analysis
        in Terms of Learning, Thinking, and Cul-
        ture. New York: McGraw-Hill Book Co.
Dreitzel, Hans Peter
  1970 Recent Sociology. London: Collier-Mac-
        millan Ltd.
Duncan, Hugh Dalziel
  1962 Communication and Social Order. Totowa,
        N.J.: The Bedminster Press.
Ferguson, Charles A.
  1975 "Baby talk in six languages." In Readings in
        Social Psychology. Alfred R. Lindesmith et
        al. (eds.). Hinsdale, Ill.: Dryden Press, pp.
        210-221.
Fishman, Joshua A.
  1960 "A systematization of the whorfian hypothe-
        sis." Behavioral Science 5:323-339.
Foote, Nelson N.
  1955 "A neglected member of the family." Mar-
        riage and Family Living 18:213-218.
Garfinkel, Harold
  1967 Studies in Ethnomethodology. Englewood
        Cliffs, N.J.: Prentice-Hall, Inc.
Goffman, Erving
  1959 The Presentation of Self in Everyday Life.
        Garden City, N.Y.: Doubleday & Co., Inc.
  1974 "Communication boundaries." In Messages:
        A Reader in Human Communication. Jean
        M. Civikly (ed.). New York: Random House,
        Inc.
Goldstein, Kurt
  1940 Human Nature in the Light of Psychopatho-
        logy. Cambridge, Mass.: Harvard University
        Press.
Goodenough, Ward H.
  1956 "Componential analysis and the study of
        meaning." Language (January-March):195-
        216.
Goody, J. and I. Watt
  1962- "The consequences of literacy." Compara-
  1963 tive Studies in Society and History (V.) Cam-
        bridge: Cambridge University Press.
Green, Hannah
  1964 I Never Promised You a Rose Garden. New
        York: The New American Library.
Grimshaw, Allen D.
  1973 "Survey essay: on language in society: Part
        I." Contemporary Sociology (November):
        575-585.
  1974 "Survey essay: on language in society: Part
        II." Contemporary Sociology (January):3-
        11.

Guillaume, Paul
  1927 "Les debuts de la phrase dans le language de
        l'enfant." Journal de Psychologie 24:1-25.
Gumperz, John J. and Dell Hymes (eds.)
  1972 Directions in Sociolinguistics: The Eth-
        nography of Communication. New York:
        Holt, Rinehart and Winston.
Hall, Edward T.
  1959 The Silent Language. New York: Doubleday
        & Co., Inc.
Hayakawa, S. I.
  1951 Language in Thought and Action. New
        York: Harcourt Brace.
  1971 "The language of social control." In Current
        Perspectives in Social Psychology. Edwin P.
        Hollander and Raymond G. Hunt (eds.).
        New York: Oxford University Press, pp.
        211-219.
Head, Henry
  1926 Aphasia and Kindred Disorders of Speech,
        Vol. I. New York: The Macmillan Co.
Hockett, Charles F. and Robert Ascher
  1964 "The human revolution." Current Anthro-
        pology V-3:135-147, 166-168.
Hoebel, E. Adamson
  1966 Anthropology: The Study of Man. New
        York: McGraw-Hill Book Co.
Hollander, Edwin P. and Raymond G. Hunt (eds.)
  1971 Current Perspectives in Social Psychology.
        New York: Oxford University Press.
Hull, Clark L.
  1933 Hypnosis and Suggestibility. New York: Ap-
        pleton-Century.
Hull, Clark and Bertha Hull
  1919 "Parallel learning curves of an infant in vo-
        cabulary and in voluntary control of the
        bladder." Pedagogical Seminary 26:272-283.
Johnson, Kenneth R.
  1974 "Black kinesics—some non-verbal com-
        munication patterns in the black culture." In
        Messages: A Reader in Human Com-
        munication. Jean M. Civikly (ed.). New
        York: Random House Inc., pp. 103-115.
Keller, Helen
  1917 The Story of My Life. Garden City, N.Y.:
        Doubleday & Co., Inc.
Kohler, Wolfgang
  1926 The Mentality of Apes. New York: Harcourt
        Brace Janovanovich, Inc.
Labov, William
  1972a Language in the Inner City: Studies in the
         Black English Vernacular. Philadelphia:
         University of Pennsylvania Press.
  1972b Sociolinguistic Patterns. Philadelphia: Uni-
         versity of Pennsylvania Press.
Levi-Strauss, Claude
  1962 La Pensee Sauvage. Paris: Plon.
Liebendorfer, R.
  1960 "Mind, self and society." Today's Speech
        1:31-33.
Lindesmith, Alfred R. and Anselm L. Strauss

1956 Social Psychology: The Revised Edition. New York: Holt, Rinehart and Winston.

1969 Readings in Social Psychology. New York: Holt, Rinehart and Winston.

Lindesmith, Alfred R., Anselm L. Strauss, and Norman K. Denzin
1975 Social Psychology (ed. 4). Hinsdale, Ill.: The Dryden Press.

Lippmann, Walter
1922 Public Opinion. New York: Harcourt, Brace.

Luria, A. R.
1966a Higher Cortical Functions in Man. New York: Basic Books, Inc.

1966 Human Brain and Psychological Processes. New York: Harper & Row, Publishers.

Malson, Lucien
1972 Wolf Children and the Problem of Human Nature. New York: Monthly Review Press.

Markel, Norman N.
1971 "The basic principles of descriptive linguistic analysis." In Current Perspectives in Social Psychology. Edwin P. Hollander and Raymond G. Hunt (eds.). New York: Oxford University Press, pp. 203-211.

McLuhan, Marshall
1964 Understanding Media: The Extensions of Man. New York: McGraw-Hill Book Co.

1969 "Playboy interview: Marshall McLuhan." Playboy (March): 53-56, 59-74, 157-158.

Mead, George Herbert
1934 Mind, Self and Society. Charles W. Morris (ed.). Chicago: University of Chicago Press.

1956 On Social Psychology. Anselm Strauss (ed.). Chicago: University of Chicago Press.

Mehrabian, Albert
1974 "Communication without words." In Messages: A Reader in Human Communication. Jean M. Civikly (ed.). New York: Random House, Inc.

Miller, George A.
1951 Language and Communication. New York: McGraw-Hill Book Co.

Morris, C. W.
1946 Signs, Language and Behavior. New York: Prentice-Hall, Inc.

Moscovici, Serge (ed.)
1972 The Psychosociology of Language. Chicago: Markham.

Mueller, Claus
1970 "Notes on the repression of communicative behavior." In Recent Sociology. Hans Peter Dreitzel (ed.). London: Collier-Macmillan, Ltd.

Natanson, Maurice
1970 The "Journeying Self: A Study in Philosophy and Social Role. Menlo Park, Calif.: Addison-Wesley Publishing Co.

Ogburn, William Fielding
1959 "The wolf boy of Agra." American Journal of Sociology (March):449-467.

Osgood, C. E., G. J. Suci, and P. H. Tannenbaum

1957 The Measurement of Meaning. Urbana, Ill.: University of Illinois Press.

Piaget, Jean
1955 The Language and Thought of the Child. New York: Meridan Books.

Reichenbach, H.
1947 Elements of Symbolic Logic. New York: The Macmillan Co.

Ross, Ralph
1973 "Communication, symbols, and society." In Readings in Social Psychology—A Symbolic Interaction Perspective. J. D. Cardwell (ed.). Philadelphia: F. A. Davis Co., pp. 3-18.

Sapir, E.
1949 "The status of linguistics as a science." In Selected Writings in Language, Culture and Personality. D. G. Mandelbaum (ed.). Berkeley: University of California Press.

Satir, Virginia
1974 "Communication: a verbal and nonverbal process of making requests of the receiver." In Messages: A Reader in Human Communication. Jean M. Civikly (ed.). New York: Random House, Inc.

Scheflen, Albert E.
1974 How Behavior Means. Garden City, N.Y.: Doubleday & Co., Inc.

Schmalenbach, Herman
1965 "The sociological category of communion." In Theories of Society. Talcott Parsons et al. (eds.). Glencoe, Ill.: The Free Press.

Schutz, Alfred
1970 On Phenomenology and Social Relations. Helmut R. Wagner (ed.). Chicago: The University of Chicago Press.

Shor, Ronald E.
1972 "Shared patterns of nonverbal normative expectations in automobile driving." In Beyond the Laboratory: Field Research in Social Psychology. Leonard Bickman and Thomas Henchy (eds.). New York: McGraw-Hill Book Co., pp. 319-324.

Shuy, Rodger W. (ed.)
1973 Sociolinguistics: Current Trends and Prospects. 23rd Annual Roundtable, Monograph Series on Languages and Linguistics, Number 25. Washington, D.C.: Georgetown University Press.

Skinner, B. F.
1957 Verbal Behavior. New York: Appleton-Century-Crofts.

Spiegelberg, Herbert
1973 "On the right to say 'We': a linguistic and phenomenological analysis." In Phenomenological Sociology: Issues and Applications. George Psathas (ed.). New York: John Wiley & Sons, Inc., pp. 129-158.

Stone, Gregory P.
  1962 "Appearance and the self." In Human Behavior and Social Processes. Arnold M. Rose (ed.). Boston: Houghton Mifflin Co., pp. 86-118.
Stone, Gregory P. and Harvey A. Farberman
  1970 Social Psychology Through Symbolic Interaction. Waltham, Mass.: Ginn-Blaisdell.
Strauss, Anselm L.
  1952 "The development and transformation of monetary meanings in the child." American Sociological Review 17:275-286.
  1959 Mirrors and Masks. Glencoe, Ill.: The Free Press.
Sullivan, Harry Stack
  1953 The Interpersonal Theory of Psychiatry. New York: W. W. Norton & Co., Inc.
  1954 The Psychiatric Interview. New York: W. W. Norton & Co., Inc.
Szasz, Thomas
  1961 The Myth of Mental Illness: Foundations of a Theory of Personal Conduct. New York: Dell Publishing Co.
Tung-Sun, Chang
  1970 "A Chinese philosopher's theory of knowledge." In Social Psychology Through Symbolic Interaction. Gregory P. Stone and Harvey A. Farberman (eds.). Waltham, Mass.: Ginn-Blaisdell, pp. 121-139.
Turner, Roy
  1970 "Words, utterances, and activities." In Understanding Everyday Life. Jack D. Douglas (ed.). Chicago: Aldine Publishing Co., pp. 169-187.
Von Frisch, Karl
  1950 Bees: Their Vision, Chemical Sense, and Language. Ithaca, N.Y.: Cornell University Press.
  1955 The Dancing Bees. New York: Harcourt, Brace, Jovanovich, Inc.
Vygotsky, Lev
  1962 Thought and Language. Cambridge, Mass.: The M.I.T. Press.
Ward, Martha C.
  1971 Them Children: A Study in Language Learning. New York: Holt, Rinehart & Winston.
Washburn, Sherwood L. and David A. Hamburg
  1965 "The study of primate behavior." In Primate Behavior: Field Studies of Monkeys and Apes. Ivan DeVore (ed.). New York: Holt, Rinehart and Winston, Inc., pp. 1-6.
Whorf, Benjamin L.
  1956 Language, Thought and Reality. Cambridge, Mass.: Harvard University Press.

chapter 8
The self

Having discussed the nature and role of language in human life, we now proceed to a discussion of the central concept in social psychology—the self. First, we shall describe the human mind, which is the subjective component of the self. Next, the self will be described, as viewed from at least three different perspectives, namely those of personality psychology, sociological social psychology, and phenomenology. As throughout this book, the stance taken will be sociological and phenomenological. The next section will deal with self-concept and the psychiatric focus on the place of anxiety and defense in self-concept. Subsequently, the relationship of self to others will be treated, including the fundamental role played by others as sources of self and such aspects of social interaction as self-presentation. The final section will cover the relation of self and social structure. Traditional structural sources as well as other societal sources of self and self-control will be discussed.

THE MIND

At the outset, we must reiterate that the mind *is* mental behavior, the activity called thinking. It is no more, no less. It is not an entity. Thought and mind are therefore synonymous.

We saw in the previous chapter that although not all thought is verbal (linguistic), language nevertheless plays a preponderant role in thinking. In addition, we saw that language can only be learned socially. Thus the human mind can only develop through interaction. A major argument presented in this section, therefore, is that the human mind owes its vast superiority over that of animals to its capacity for symbolism but that this potential is only realized because men live in societies. It is also argued that social psychol-

ogy cannot understand man without dealing with his mind and that the proper conception of the human mind is one that recognizes the primary relevance of *consciousness*, rather than that, for example, of overt physical behavior as done by the behaviorists, or that of subconscious drives as done by the Freudians.

The mind is symbolic

An outstanding discussion of this subject is provided by Ernest Becker (1962), who reminds us, with the anthropologist Leslie White (1960), that "mind" is originally the activity of minding, that is, in a way reacting to the environment. In this sense, even the ameba minds. However, this is merely what Becker and White call *type 1 reactivity:* the organism reacts automatically to environmental stimuli, with no choice in the matter whatsoever.

As the species evolves, however, higher levels of sensitivity emerge. A great step toward liberation from the total environmental enslavement of type 1 reactivity is accomplished when an organism can be conditioned to respond to a stimulus substituted for an original stimulus. This, termed *type 2 reactivity,* is what happens with Pavlov's dog (see Chapter 2). The dog has learned to respond (salivate) to *signs* (a bell, a light). The crucial point here is that the response is no longer determined by the intrinsic properties of the stimulus.

Even more evolved is *type 3 reactivity,* which is exemplified by Kohler's chimpanzees (see Chapter 2). These animals are capable not only of responding to signs but also of mentally combining in their mind several separate stimuli into more complex structures, which requires imagination. For example, the chimps realize mentally that fitting together several boxes will enable them to reach a suspended banana.

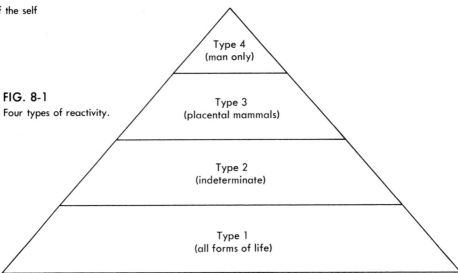

FIG. 8-1
Four types of reactivity.

Finally, *type 4 reactivity* is that form of mental activity of which only man is capable, namely the ability to respond to symbols, not just signs, and to interpret these. Fig. 8-1 sums up Becker's four reactivity types.

The evolution of mind is therefore a progressive liberation from enslavement to the inherent properties of the environment. Each of the four steps represents a qualitative jump, not merely one that is quantitative. Finally, at level 4, the response involves choice (choosing whether or not and how to respond) and interpretation (assigning properties to the environment in the form of meanings). Because man's environment, unlike that of animals, is largely symbolic, it can be said that it is of his own making. Becker gives a good example: "Nature provided all of life with H_2O, but only man could create a world in which 'holy' water generates a special stimulus" (Becker, 1962:20).

What is unique about the human mind is its ability to symbolize, and to symbolize "extrinsically" (Becker, 1962:22), that is, to respond to symbols and to share symbols with one another, socially. The "symbolic transformation" (cf. Langer, 1948) that constitutes type 4 reactivity, then, is a social act. Symbolic social behavior is what we call

language. Without language, the human mind would remain as primitive as that of lower animals. Thus the mind is both linguistic and social behavior. As both linguists (cf. Chomsky, 1968) and symbolic interactionists (cf. Liebendorfer, 1960), including of course, Mead (1934) himself, always remind us, linguistic interaction is the basis of mind, self, and society.

The mind is social

Becker (1962) also stresses the distinction between extrinsic and intrinsic symbolism: dogs, for example, may symbolize intrinsically. They dream, which indicates that they conjure and remember mental imagery. However, only man can transmit and share symbols. The first recorded examples we have of this process are the paleolithic cave drawings. For the first time, some forty thousand years ago, one animal was able to share symbolic experience with others.

As we saw, social scientists everywhere have now come to agree that thought is indeed inherently social in origin and that speech plays a preponderant part in its development. In America, this realization goes back to Mead (1934), Cooley (1902), and the other founders of symbolic interactionism. In Europe, scholars like Cassirer (1944) and Piaget (1932) have come to the same conclusions, and so have Soviet psychologists, for example Luria (1966) and Vygotsky (1962). Luria, for example, stresses the sociohistorical genesis of all thought, thereby indicating the convergence, in this respect, of the Marxian and the symbolic interactionist traditions. He also emphasizes the *mediate structure* of human thought, by which he means the fact that humans are able to mentally connect ideas and objects that are not intrinsically related. For example, I may tie a knot in my handkerchief to remind myself of a task, a task having obviously nothing to do with a handkerchief.

It is understandable that studies of children and childhood socialization loom large in the literature on the social genesis of human thought (cf. Cooley, 1902; Piaget, 1932; Davis, 1940; 1947; Lindesmith, Strauss, and Denzen, 1975). We shall return to these in a subsequent chapter. Here, the main point is perhaps best summed up by Becker when he states that "the popular 'two heads are better than one' might better be changed to 'two heads are needed for one' " (Becker, 1962:22).

The mind as social psychology sees it

This book argues that in order to understand man and in order to best research human behavior, it is important to recognize consciousness (cf. Quill, 1972). This contrasts with what the behaviorists have to say about mind. To them, words like "mind" and "consciousness" are needless baggage, referring to phenomena that either cannot be measured (and are therefore outside the scope of science and psychology) or that can best be handled through behavioral concepts and indicators. However, there is more to consciousness than observable behavior, and in order for psychology to deal adequately with the human mind (which is, we believe, the proper definition of the discipline), its approach cannot be entirely objective and positivistic. It must be at least partially phenomenological.

The Freudian idea of mind differs from ours primarily in its focus, not so much in its conception. There, a very important part of the human mind is *subconscious* and *emotional* (cf. Freud, 1924:26). At first, this may seem to differ markedly from our view, but the two conceptions are actually remarkably parallel. When the Freudians refer to the primitive, subconscious, creative, biological, and emotional aspects of the mind, they use the term "id" (or some translation of it, like transactional analysis' concept of "child"). The Meadians' I concept refers to many of the same things. Nevertheless, we believe that the Freudians are biased. To them, that side of the mind is irrational, powerful, repressed, biological, and sexual. Sociological social psychology handles it better. The I does represent freedom, creativity, and the like, but it is not necessarily irrational, sexual, biological, or in conflict with the socialized self.

A good case in point is the difference between the Freudian and the interactionist view of dreaming. The latter view, which we share, rejects the Freudian claim that dreaming is an indication of subconscious mental activity, a subconscious that is primeval, independent from, and antithetical to the other parts of the self. As Fellows (1968) shows, dreaming should be viewed within the same *symbolic* framework as other mental activities. And insofar as the mind and the self also embody *sentiment*, we shall see that it, too, can be handled sociologically (cf. Cooley, 1902; 1909) rather than biologistically.

Ever since Darwin, the human sciences have had to reorient themselves toward *process*. The mind is a process. Dewey and James stressed that it is experience, Cooley showed that it is a social and reflective mechanism, Mead demonstrated that it is a development. This is the social-psychological conception of the mind. It recognizes that mind is an inner dialogue between the I and the me, that is, a process whereby I, the subject, talk to myself, an imaginary audience. If man is simultaneously subject and object, he cannot be studied as a mere object, as would behaviorists and other "scientific" psychologists and sociologists. Since the primary task of psychology is, by definition, the understanding of the human mind, pure objectivism will not suffice. The (social) psychologist must recognize that to study the human mind is, at least in part, to study oneself. The human disciplines must therefore be at least partially phenomenological in methodology and in orientation. In addition to sense data, introspection and consciousness remain important sources of knowledge (cf. Bruyn, 1966).

THE SELF

From the mind, which is inner mental activity, we now move to the self, which is the total acting person as a subject and viewed as an object by himself and by others.

The concept of self is nebulous and its interpretations are as varied as the large literature on the subject. Nevertheless, the many different approaches can be bunched into a few distinct tendencies. This is done, for example, by Gordon and Gergen (1968), whose reader on the self includes articles written in three distinct traditions. There is, first, the conventional conception that views the self as a somewhat static *thing,* a personality. Psychologists (such as Carl Rogers, Abraham Maslow, Karen Horney) have often conceived of the self in such a fashion. Then there is the conception of self emphasized in this book, an interactionist conception that views the self as ongoing process, change, and development. According to this view, the social situation, including its subjective definition by the self, is of greater importance for an understanding of the self and its behavior than background and personality characteristics. This is the way sociologists and sociological social psychologists (for example, James Baldwin, Harold Garfinkel,

Erving Goffman, William James) approach the self. The first of these approaches treats the self as an (experimental) object. The second approach does not do this to the same extent, recognizing that the self consists of both I and me. However, it, too, has difficulty dealing with the self as subject. For example, a major instrument used by sociological social psychologists to measure the self—the Twenty Statement Test—only deals with the me—roles and self-concept—not with the I.

The more serious effort to deal with the self as subject is that of a third group, the phenomenologists. Schutz (1970), more than anyone else, has brought to sociology (and in the process refined) the phenomenological insights of philosophers like Sartre and Husserl. Our study of the self must follow the sociological and the phenomenological leads, recognizing that the self is inherently social, dynamic, and subjective.

The self is always changing

According to Deutsch and Krauss (1965:181), sociological social psychologists "have developed and employed the concept of the self as a cognitive structure which emerges from the interaction of the human organism and its social environment." This definition is typical of the many other ones found in the literature. In the majority of instances, the self soon becomes self-concept, that is, mere object. Cardwell (1971:77), for example, prefers to speak of self-definition rather than self. Similarly, the many authors who have used the Twenty Statement Test (see Kuhn and McPartland, 1954, and Spitzer, Couch, and Stratton, 1971, who have collected in one volume the bulk of the Iowa school's research with the TST) have measured such things as self-concept, self-attitudes, self-esteem, but not self. It is difficult to distinguish such work from work which, like that of Kinch (1963), deals avowedly with self-concept.

The classical founders of symbolic interactionism were more cognizant of the self's *dual* character. William James, as we saw, distinguished between the two phases of the self, which he called the I—the self as knower (subject)—and the me—the self as known (object) (see James, 1890; Chapter 6). Mead (1934), whose major contribution was the thorough analysis of the social nature and origin of the self, conceived of the self in a similar fashion.

Having duly noted the two phases of the self, James then focused on the objective phase, the me. He distinguished between the material me (my body), the spiritual me (my mind, my thoughts), and the social me (my roles). Ever since then, sociologists have primarily zeroed in on this last component, the social self, studying the multiplicity of social selves ("me's" from my own standpoint, roles from the standpoint of society) within each of us. We have, as James and Mead first pointed out, as many social selves as there are groups of other persons about whose opinions we care, groups from which we learn our roles.

This latter aspect—the interaction between individual and others that leads to the emergence of the social self—was discussed most famously by Cooley (1902), who used the metaphor of the looking-glass self. That imagery indicates that the self consists of (1) the imagination of our appearance to the other person, (2) the imagination of his judgment of that appearance, and (3) some sort of self-feeling, such as pride or mortification. Thus Cooley stresses the role played by others, and by our imagination of others, in our self-concept. A major contribution, also, is his recognition of *sentiment* (for example, pride or mortification) as an integral part of the self.

Francis Merrill (1961) has shown that the French novelist Stendhal already knew, a century and a half ago, that the social self is essentially an emergent process reflecting primarily one's (significant) others and the social situations, definitions, and interactions experienced. This is the sociological conception of the self. Stendhal's hero in *Le Rouge et le Noir*, Julien Sorel, is a very self-conscious fellow (not unlike Stendhal himself). His self develops as a reflection of direct others, intermediate others, and the ideological other. The direct others are, as always, significant others such as parents. Intermediate others are reference groups—professional groups or any other groups important to the individual. The ideological other refers here to the generalized societal *Zeitgeist*, in this case the spirit of Napoleonic France anno 1810. This led Sorel to develop a lofty ego-ideal that he could not accomplish or reconcile with his self-concept, leading him to ultimate destruction.

The sociological conception of the self emphasizes change from one situation to another. However, psychologists, particularly "personality" psychologists, have stressed precisely the opposite tendency, the strong *continuity* of behavior observed from one situation to another. Indeed, it must be granted that we are not all adaptable, all that free today from what we did yesterday. Why? Surely what we did yesterday is gone forever. We must not assume that what makes us repeat our errors, or succeed again and again at a difficult task, or feel the same dislike for a person or an object is caused by a little persona inside us. What it is, really, is *habit*, that is, the acquisition of conditioned reflexes. As Becker (1962) illustrates, we may react involuntarily and reverently toward "holy water" long after we have been converted to another religion. Habits are difficult to shake, and this is a good thing anyway, as James (1890:143) points out, for if it were not for habits, what would hold society together, what would prevent both individual and social chaos, why would people perform their necessary but often unpleasant tasks?

Change is difficult also because the elements making up the self (habits, beliefs, reflexes, thoughts) represent a coherent organization, a Gestalt. It is this problem that cognitive psychologists and field theorists (cf. Festinger, 1954; Heider,

1946; Deutsch and Krauss, 1965, chapters 2 and 3) have so thoroughly documented. Since the self is a *consistent* cognitive structure, any partial change may create dissonance, disturbance, pain, anxiety.

It is habit—which is merely the repetition of more or less the same behavior—that creates the *illusion* (cf. Sullivan, 1964) of self and mind as substances. The continuity in our behavior makes us feel that we have a self and a mind inside us, a little person as it were. At the same time, the beauty of our capacity for symbolic interaction is the freedom that thereby becomes possible: to respond to a symbol is to respond to an arbitrary meaning. We collectively define the symbolic stimuli to which we respond; we determine their meaning. Symbols need not have the immediacy of concrete objects. Their meaning can be subjectively controlled. With the power to control the meaning of stimuli comes freedom.

Symbolic interactionism has shown us that the self is social. This is extremely important. However, after James had indicated that the self is both subjective (the I) and objective (the me), subsequent research on the self became increasingly limited to the objective self, the me, the self-concept, self-definitions.[1] In order to find an adequate recognition of the self as subject, we must now turn to the phenomenologists.

The self is an experience

The self as subject. Phenomenologists are not so much interested in tracing the origin of the self and of consciousness as in describing the nature of those experiences. While they recognize with Mead that society is chronologically prior to the individual self (all humans are born into some society and without a society's socializing effect they would not develop selves), they argue that phenomenologically, in terms of one's subjective experience, individual consciousness must be the starting point of one's analysis (cf. Natanson, 1970:5-6).

The tradition of taking consciousness as one's point of departure includes the Frenchman Rene Descartes and his well-known axiom "I think, therefore I am." Similarly, William James regards the belief that "people feel themselves thinking . . . as the most fundamental of all postulates in psychology. . . . That we have cogitations of some sort is the 'inconcessum' . . ." (quoted in Schutz, 1970:57). Edmund Husserl, the founder of phenomenology, is primarily concerned with establishing an "a priori psychological discipline" (loc. cit.), that is, determining the nature of thinking as a phenomenon. Schutz extends Husserl's work toward the social, and his point of departure is also subjective consciousness (cf. Schutz, 1970:53-71). Like rationalists and existentialists, phenomenologists start out with the subjective. Therefore, an important assumption follows: the self, the notion that I exist and that I am distinct from the environment and from other persons, is basic. Although that assumption has been questioned by anthropologists (cf. Gergen, 1971:8), it is not questioned by phenomenologists. To them, the self is the experience of individual existence and identity, and it is not something that is only experienced in certain individualistic cultures but not in others. The distinction between self and environment is basic.

An excellent phenomenological study of self as subjective experience is that carried out by Manning and Fabrega (1973) among the Chiapas Indians of Mexico. The research focuses on the relation between body and self, in health and in illness. To medicine, the body is just that—a biological organism with a set of specific properties. However, the authors rightly point out that sociology errs in adopting that exclusively biologistic conception of the body (p. 255). For sociology, the rele-

---

[1] Granted, the so-called Chicago school of symbolic interactionism led by Herbert Blumer is not as guilty of neglecting the subjective self as Manford Kuhn's Iowa school (see Meltzer and Petras, 1970).

vant fact is that like other objects, one's body is subjectively experienced in certain ways, imbued with certain meanings. The body is a socially and subjectively meaningful object, and the authors list some of the body's sociological characteristics (pp. 256-257). For example "(a) the body moves through time and space, thereby altering the physical location from which the social world is viewed . . . (b) body appearances alter social choices (among the more obvious—marriage, courtship and dating, career and occupational success)."

From this theoretical vantage point, they compare three medical care systems, three contrasting settings for the interpretation of the relationship between body and self. The Mayan system is based on a belief in sin and moral responsibility as the causes of illness. The self and the body are continuous, cure is through magic and shamanism. The Mestizo system posits moral and social causes for illness. Finally, Western scientific medicine attributes illness to impersonal physiological factors (p. 261). The authors show that as one moves from system 1 to system 3, the conception of the body changes from a *sacred* one to a *machine-like instrument*. A neat linguistic study of the Apache by Basso (1967) is quoted to show that the tribe uses the body as the model, the conceptual base, and the linguistic root for extensions to other objects. Table 6 gives some examples.

Western civilization has come to turn this kind of metaphor around, increasingly using the machine as a model for man.

The behavioral disciplines are particularly guilty of this dehumanizing tendency. A typical social-psychological description of a man might read as follows: he is inner-directed, properly integrated into his primary social system, releasing tension through motor exercise, and operating at a high level of output and efficiency as a result of a strong drive, the input received in early socialization, and the use of corrective feedback mechanisms to monitor and readjust his behavior to changing external conditions. Similarly, the concept of mental illness (cf. Szasz, 1961) is a pseudo-scientific attempt at reducing consciousness and social interaction to manipulable machine-like mechanisms. In a technocratic civilization, there is thus a growing estrangement between body and self, between my body as an object and the I as a thinking and feeling subject.

A phenomenologically fascinating topic raised in the Manning-Febrega study is (physical) pain. Here is a concept whose referent cannot possibly be relegated in its totality either to the objectively physical or to the subjectively spiritual realm. There are some studies dealing with pain as a sociological phenomenon (see Zborowski, 1952; Wolff and Langley, 1968). Zborowski shows nicely how pain is interpreted, defined, in sum experienced differently, for example, by Jewish, Italian, and Anglo-Saxon Americans.

TABLE 6. Western Apache anatomical terms with extended meanings*

Apache anatomical terms	Anatomical terms (re: man)	Extended meanings (re: auto)
WOS	shoulder	front fender(s)
Čị	nose	hood
ǰisolɛ	lung	radiator
Zɛ	mouth	opening of pipe leading to gas tank

*From Basso, Keith H. 1967. "Semantic aspects of linguistic acculturation." American Anthropologist 69:472. Reproduced by permission of the American Anthropological Association. Cited in Manning, Peter K. and Horacio Fabrega, Jr. 1973. The experience of self and body: health and illness in the Chiapas Highlands. In Phenomenological Sociology: Issues and Applications. George Psathas (ed.). New York: John Wiley and Sons.

Pain does not enter the self as a neuro-physiological occurrence. Pain, one's body, or any other object or occurrence enters the self as subjective experiences. To separate subjective experience from that which is experienced, as does objectivist science, is to miss the point. Phenomenological research such as the Manning-Fabrega study reminds us of the essential reflexivity of the self, of the oneness, in man's case, of subject and object and of the impossibility of dealing with experience and that which is experienced separately.

The self and intersubjectivity. The self, then, can simply be defined as that which can be an object to itself.

Under the sociological conception of the self, we saw that the individual self originates in and reflects social interaction. Under the phenomenological approach to the self, we have seen that the self is subjective. We shall now show that these two approaches complement one another and provide a unified conception of the self as inherently social and uniquely human.

The self is that inner interaction that both originates in and reflects the outer interaction between the individual and others. Cooley's (1902) description of his own children's socialization, Mead's (1934) work, and much subsequent research demonstrates this process of *internalization*. The I-me interaction within and the I-other interaction outside are therefore two sides of the same coin. This means that just as with the inner I-me dialogue, whenever I interact with another human being, I interact with more than just an object in my environment; I interact with a very special kind of object, namely one that is (just like me) *another subject!*

The self's ability to interact with others meaningfully has been described in terms of empathy, role-taking, imagination, sympathy, putting oneself in the other's shoes, identification, and other processes by many authors, including Cooley, Mead, Sarbin, and Scheler. However, phenome-nologists rightly point out that until the problem of *intersubjectivity* is explained, interhuman communication (and therefore ultimately society itself) remain mysteries. Intersubjectivity generally means "what is cognitively common to various individuals" (Schutz, 1970:319). The problem of intersubjectivity refers to the question: how is the other self constituted in my mind as a self of basically the same essential characteristics as my own self, and how is the experience of my understanding the other and his understanding me constituted (and possible) (loc. cit.)?

Schutz (1970:163) truly comes to grips with the problem. Under a *theory of the alter ego* that differs somewhat from Sartre's (see Schutz, 1948), the author explains that the basis for all interhuman communication lies in the mutual recognition of structural, temporal, and ontological parallelism between my own consciousness and that of the other. This does not imply empathy or projection, merely the basic assumption that the other is, literally, *an alter ego*—another self, like me. This is the rock-bottom foundation of phenomenological sociology. It is the only logical justification for the "we phenomenon" (cf. Spiegelberg, 1973) and the only explanation for intersubjectivity.

Any relationship between two selves is, to use Wagner's (1970:32) fine analogy, elliptical: it has two subjective foci. Then, too, there are different categories of social situations. For example, Schutz (1970:175-178) distinguishes between the situation in which I merely observe and attempt to understand the other, and the situation in which the other also tries to communicate to me. At this point, we move from psychology to sociology, from the insights of James and Husserl to those of Mead and Schutz, from the self to society. This transition will be our point of departure in Part 4 of the book.

SELF-CONCEPT

Although Chapter 10 is largely devoted to the self-concept, we must briefly discuss this topic here as well. This is because of the widespread confusion between self and self-concept and the tendency to equate the two. Cooley's looking-glass self already did that, describing the self as our imagination of our appearance to others, their judgment of us, and our consequent feelings. More recently, Gergen (1971:22-23) defined the self as "that process by which the person conceptualizes . . . his behavior . . . (and) the system of concepts available to the person in attempting to define himself." Similarly, Kuhn's definition is, among other ones, "the individual as viewed (defined) by the individual, a social object among social objects" (Kuhn, 1964:629).

Such definitions, then, refer essentially to *self-concept.* They may include such things as self-attitudes and self-esteem, but they refer to the self as object, the me. Nevertheless, this is variously referred to as self-conception (Gergen, 1971; Kuhn, 1964), self-concept (Gergen, 1971; Kinch, 1963), self-definition (Cardwell, 1971), self-awareness (Lindesmith, Strauss, and Denzin, 1975), self-attitudes (Kuhn and McPartland, 1954), or simply self (Gergen, 1971; Kuhn, 1964; Spitzer, Couch, and Stratton, 1971). It is particularly the Iowa school of symbolic interactionism (cf. Kuhn, 1964; Kuhn and McPartland, 1954; Spitzer, Couch, and Stratton, 1971) that has tended to equate self and self-concept. On the other hand, Goffman in his work on self-presentation (1959), Blumer (1969), and the Chicago branch of symbolic interactionism in general have dealt more with the self as subject. So have the phenomenologists, as we saw. This section deals with the self as object to oneself.

The self is how I view myself

Lindesmith, Strauss, and Denzin (1975:302-307) point out that the infant at first has no self-awareness, that is, no awareness of the boundaries of his own body and of the boundary between himself and the environment. This undifferentiated perception was called "dissociation" by Piaget. This initial confusion between self and nonself has been nicely docu-

mented in studies by Cooley (1930) and Bain (1936), who showed that young children have particular difficulty with the acquisition of personal pronouns, confusing, for example, first, second, and third persons. A three-year-old may say to himself: "You be careful, William get hurt. NO! I won't get hurt" (Lindesmith, Strauss, and Denzin, 1975:305).

It is through the process of role-taking that the child gradually develops self-awareness. By taking the role of significant others the child learns to view himself as he imagines that they view him. At first there is only the I, and through role-taking the child develops a me, self-awareness and a self-concept (see next section for more details).

It is the outcome of this developmental process—the self-concept—that has often been studied empirically while being called the self. Manford Kuhn and many sociologists from the University of Iowa (for example, Carl Couch, Norman Denzin, Dean Dorn, Edwin Driver, David Lee, Thomas McPartland, Harold Mulford, Stephen Spitzer) have used the Twenty Statement Test. A respondent is given a sheet of paper with twenty blank lines on it and a single question on top:

> In the space below, please give twenty different answers to the question "Who Am I?" Give these as if you were giving them to yourself, not to someone else. Write fairly rapidly, for the time is limited.

This instrument has produced many interesting results (see Chapter 10). For example Kuhn and McPartland (1954) distinguished between two kinds of responses one may make to the TST: consensual answers, or answers of fact ("I am a student," "I am twenty-one"), and subconsensual ones, or answers of opinion ("I am happy," "I am a good wife"). The authors found that most people tend to first exhaust consensual references before going to the subconsensual ones but that this varies. For example, people belonging to minority-type religions (such as Jews or small sects) tended to focus more on consensual self-definitions than people of "respectable" majority faiths. "Minority" people, then, may anchor their self-concept more exclusively in consensually recognized roles and statuses.

There are, as Tucker (1966) showed, several unsolved problems with the TST, including the matters of validity and reliability of the instrument and the assumptions it requires. However, our main point here is a different one, namely that work such as the above measures one thing and one thing only: self-concept. Nothing shows this better than the definition of self-concept given by a specialist in that area (Kinch, 1963:481): "The self-concept is that organization of qualities that the individual attributes to himself." This includes "both attributes . . . adjectives (ambitions, intelligence) and . . . roles (father, doctor, etc.)." Kinch's definition of self-concept includes precisely the two elements termed "consensual" and "subconsensual" by Kuhn and McPartland.

The self and mental health

Becker (1962:35) points to the fundamental role played by anxiety in human existence. In addition to the inescapable fact of being mortal, we are faced with the possible realization of being, even while alive, inadequate, or worse, irrelevant. This adds up to the unbearable realization that our existence may be ultimately meaningless, absurd. Such a realization would be totally incapacitating. We would, like Goncharov's Oblomov, no longer get up in the morning, eat, work, or act in the world in any other fashion. "The basic predicate for human action is a qualitative feeling of self-value" (Becker, 1962:163). To perceive our worthlessness would produce intolerable anxiety.

According to Sullivan, it is the self's fundamental function to ensure that awareness of worthlessness and the ensuing anxiety do not break through and thereby incapacitate and indeed destroy the person. The discovery of this function has been the major contribution of psychiatrists and psychoanalysts, including Freud. As Becker (1962) shows, Freud correctly perceived the significance of the Oedipal transition for personal self-esteem. Self-esteem initially depends upon maternal love; later, approval must generally be sought and found elsewhere. In any event, we can agree with Freud and Sullivan (1964) that the roots of anxiety have much to do with parental rejection and the ensuing feelings of object loss and worthlessness.

The self and anxiety are, in a way, antithetical. Psychiatrically, the former embodies mental health, the latter can mean mental illness. The self represents the state when one is comfortable about one's self-respect and the like, and it is primarily concerned with avoiding the distressing (Sullivan, 1964). How? Since the self operates symbolically, it buffers anxiety precisely in that fashion—linguistically. By naming, interpreting, and categorizing, the self erects symbolic defenses against that which would undermine the feeling of self-worth.

Sullivan (1953) and Lindesmith, Strauss, and Denzin (1975:451-456) discuss some of the self's defense mechanisms, what Sullivan terms "security operations." These include selective inattention, evasion of responsibility, rationalization, pretense, and the disowning of undesirable qualities in oneself (Lindesmith, Strauss, and Denzin, 1975:451). An example of rationalization would be the shoplifter who claims that his action does no harm and is in fact just, since he is stealing from a rich capitalist chain store. Selective inattention can be illustrated by an unattractive individual's tendency to "overlook" the fact that he has frequently been turned down by prospective dates. He may opt for permanent bachelorhood and subsequently define this as a much better life-style, providing freedom, etc.

Also, according to Sullivan, children distinguish between the "good me," the "bad me," and the "not me." The "not me" refers to the most anxiety-provoking acts and emotions and can only be faced obliquely, for example in nightmares (Lindesmith, Strauss, and Denzin, 1975:451-452). There are additional mechanisms—for example, displacement, projection, identification with one's aggressor, detachment, and humor (loc. cit.). All these and other ones serve to protect the self against anxiety. Sullivan is careful to point out that excessive preoccupation with anxiety reduction can mean a loss to the individual. Through selective inattention a person may block out painful but perhaps useful insights. He may become fixated on costly habits. Distress can be the prelude to growth, and desirable personality change may require discomfort. For example, an obese person may only decide to lose weight and thereby save both his health and his social life after he has been brutally made aware of his repulsive appearance.

SELF AND OTHERS

The self emerges from the interaction between the individual and others and in turn affects subsequent interaction. For example, from early childhood on a person may have been frequently beaten, attacked, and reprimanded by his parents. He may develop a hostile and aggressive self and in turn interact that way with others in later life. Many parents guilty of child abuse have themselves been abused as children.

However, the interaction between self and others is far more complex than the preceding example would suggest. The self is not merely the sum of the conditioned responses acquired through exposure to environmental stimuli. Two children may both be raised brutally, as in our example, yet one may turn into a criminal and the other into a saint. For one thing, the subsequent situations each of them encounters in life may be different. More importantly, every experience, every stimulus, everything that ever happens to an individual is subjectively interpreted, that is, interpreted in a unique way that leads to unique conclusions and consequences. The cliche "no two individuals are alike" means that no two individuals ever interpret a phenomenon in exactly the same way. The self does not merely respond to others: it interprets the behavior of others, and then acts; one possible course of action is to not respond at all. In this section, we briefly examine interaction from the standpoint of self and other.

What do others think of me?

The impact of others on the self is a variable, a question mark. It cannot be taken for granted. Some others may have a great impact on us, some none. Those individuals who have the greatest impact on us are called the *significant others*. The groups that have the greatest impact are called *reference groups*. The society that has the greatest impact is called the *generalized other*.

According to Mead (1934), the individual learns from all these others by *taking their role*. At first, the young child is only capable of taking the role of single, significant others, for example, the mother or father. This is, according to Mead, the play stage. The young girl learns roles through the (often imaginary) identification with others; she may, for example, play at being a mother. Later, a person learns to take the role of more generalized others, entire groups. This is the game stage. Take baseball as a metaphor, Mead suggests: in order for the boy to learn to participate in that game, he must not only take the role of a single, significant other—learn the rules pertaining to *one* position (such as pitcher or first baseman)—he must internalize the entire game, all the rules pertaining to all the positions.[2] This is what is meant by taking the role of the generalized other. The baseball team represents, of course, society.

---

[2]On the confusion about roles and other matters in Little League baseball, see Watson and Kando (1976).

Two aspects of the impact of others on the self have just been discussed: (1) the other's "significance" and (2) the self's capacity for role-taking. Cardwell (1971:84) discusses two further crucial aspects: the self, by taking the role of others, begins to take itself as an object, to see itself as others see it; and it also evaluates what it sees and develops certain feelings about it. For example, the child taking the role of an apparently disapproving and resentful mother begins to view himself as the mother views him and he develops a negative self-feeling.

These last two aspects of self-other interaction are found in Cooley's looking-glass self. As that author reminds us, the feelings we have about ourselves result from our *imagination* of how others see us. We can never know for certain how they really see us, for we are not inside their mind. The correspondence between how we see ourselves and how others see us is probably never exact. Examples of extreme discrepancies are provided by several great stars who, while at the apex of success and adulated by millions, nevertheless have such strong negative self-feelings that this drives some of them, like Marilyn Monroe, Billie Holiday, and Judy Garland, to suicide or other forms of self-destruction. The crucial element in self-other interaction is not what the other "really" thinks of us or "really" means by his words, but how we interpret those things and the motives and meanings that we impute to him. It is on this latter basis only that the other has an impact on us. In many instances, the others with the greatest social-psychological impact upon us are not even aware of our existence. Think of how often celebrities and remote reference groups function as role-models! Is there better proof that the self, far from being a passive reactor, in fact interprets and *selects* that to which it responds?

Weinstein and Deutschberger (1963) have coined the term *altercasting* to refer to the process whereby others "typecast" us, put us into specific roles and identities, and treat us on the basis of the images they have of us. In this fashion, others—some others—most definitely affect our self-concept. To some extent, we begin to see ourselves as they see us, we assume the roles and identities assigned to us.

However, the self is not a mirror, a passive reflector of the other's behavior. In the first place, the other's impact depends on many different variables. For example, studies have shown that another's impact on self-concept is particularly strong when the other is "credible" (when he is viewed as knowledgeable, respectable, of high status, and the like, as, for example, a professor) and when the interaction is personal (rather than indirect, as with television and newspapers, or impersonal, as when you are merely part of a mass audience, or when you are treated like a number) (see Gergen, 1971:43-44). Thus if a respected professor personally criticizes a college student for his stupidity, this may have a more profound impact than similar criticism from the student's working-class mother, to whom he already feels superior, or from an impersonal administrative clerk.

Most importantly, the other's impact is largely determined by how the self *interprets* his behavior. This is why it is essential to recognize that the interpretive process is part of the self, something that is insufficiently realized by most social psychologists (for example Gergen, 1971). If the self is equated with self-concept, it becomes the task of social psychology to predict the self's behavior on the basis of how others treat it or have treated it in the past. The self is viewed as mere response to others. This is the impasse in which most of the professions dealing with delinquents, criminals, the mentally ill, and deviants in general are so hopelessly bogged down. They assume that the self can be predicted and controlled through antecedent (social) stimuli. This is an illusion. In fact, the self always remains subject to reinterpretation.

The self, then, is an active participant in interaction. Stone (1962) has made the crucial distinction between identification *with* and identification *of:* before the first of these processes can take place, a person must actually identify who the other *is.* In other words, before role-taking can take place, one must first (correctly) apprehend who the other is, what his actual role is. This initial identification process is based on appearance. The apprehension of the other's identity is never fully correct, and this is why communication can be so problematic.

Stone points out that communication can range from *boredom* to *nonsense.* Boredom is the never fully realized idea of total communication; this occurs when two or more persons know exactly who the other is, understand exactly what he means; they have identified him exactly and taken his role perfectly. At the opposite pole of the continuum is nonsense. This occurs when interactors totally fail to identify one another and the meanings they attempt to convey. The question is always whether the program (the identity, the self) presented by a person is validated by others. It may, or it may not. If it is challenged, complications and conflict may result.

Appearance is one of the elements of one's identity that is presented by the self and must be validated by others in order for interaction to proceed meaningfully. In many social situations, a person's gender and often age and occupational status must be determined, at the very least, before interaction can proceed. In a dating situation, one of the first orders of business is to determine the other's marital status—an identity element of crucial importance in that situation. When the other is a policeman, his uniform certainly helps in settling the preliminary matter of his occupational identity. Even plainclothesmen must officially identify themselves before the business at hand (arrest, surveillance, search, inquiry) can proceed. An example of serious complications resulting from misidentification was reported by a trans-vestite-transsexual respondent (see Kando, 1973). A transvestite would go out on a date with a heterosexual male who, at some time during the evening, would begin to make sexual advances, having wrongly identified him as a bona fide female. Somewhere down the road the subject had to put a stop to the sexual foreplay or else, or course, be found out.

We each present a self that we deem to be the correct, true, appropriate, and real me in any given situation. Goffman has produced the best-known work on this subject. For example, he quotes Sansom's (in Goffman, 1959:4-5) description of Preedy, an Englishman making his *debut* on a summer resort beach:

> But in any case he took care to avoid catching anyone's eye. First of all, he had to make it clear to those potential companions of his holiday that they were of no concern to him whatsoever. He stared through them, round them, over them—eyes lost in space. The beach might have been empty. If by chance a ball was thrown his way, he looked surprised; then let a smile of amusement lighten his face (Kindly Preedy), looked around dazed to see that there were people on the beach, tossed it back with a smile to himself and not a smile at the people, and then resumed carelessly his nonchalant survey of space.
>
> But it was time to institute a little parade, the parade of the ideal Preedy. By devious handlings he gave any who wanted a chance to see the title of his book—a Spanish translation of Homer, classic thus, but not daring, cosmopolitan too—and then gathered together his beach-wrap and bag into a neat sand-resistant pile (Methodical and Sensible Preedy), rose slowly to stretch his huge frame (Big-Cat Preedy), and tossed aside his sandals (Carefree Preedy, after all).

We have seen that the other determines, through altercasting, who we are. Now we must recognize a complementary process: the self, through what Denzin (1969) terms *self-lodging,* determines who he is to the other: we all attempt to lodge those features that we deem crucial to our self, to our identity, into the structure of interaction. We present to others an appearance, an identity, in sum a self that we deem to be us. Foote (1951) noted this long ago when he observed that identification provides the basis for motivation. In the absence of self-validation by others, the person can be expected to depart from the scene (although this, too, is a variable and contingent on other factors, such as the availability of perceived alternatives). The ultimate departure is, of course, suicide. In general, as Denzin (1969) notes, "humans return to those interactional quarters where the most basic features of their selves have been lodged."

SELF AND SOCIAL STRUCTURE

The self does not operate in a vacuum, and neither is it enough to say that it interacts with others. The social world in which the self operates is so vast and includes so many others who sustain so many relationships with one another that it acquires the character of a *structure*. A structure is a more or less stable edifice. It may change over time, like the body, but its processes are fairly predictable. Revolutions and civil wars occasionally destroy or fundamentally alter a social structure, but between those relatively rare events, societies function for many years in stable and repetitive ways. The media may try to impress us with the shocking new developments that occur every day (*news* is their business), but if one were to list in one column all the things in society that are done today and weren't done yesterday, and in another column all the things that were done yesterday and are still done today, the second column would be much longer. Most of us still get up in the morning, wash, brush our teeth, get dressed, go to work or to school, eat our meals at regular times, sleep at night, relax on weekends, speak the same common language as last year, marry to one another (one man to one woman, in most cases), value the dollar, read books and newspapers, watch television, elect politicians of one of the same two old parties to fixed terms in office.

Why is it that behavior (note that we only

describe behavior, in the above example and everywhere else in this book), when taken at the aggregate level of millions or even hundreds of people, takes on such a sluggish character that we may then begin to call it a structure? Let us first state a law: *change (process) is generally slower at the aggregate level and for large phenomena than at the elemental level and for small phenomena.* The life-span of an elephant is millions of times longer than that of a mosquito. Societal change is immensely slower than individual change. The two cannot be measured with the same yardstick.

As the body consists of molecules, so the social structure consists of actions. Weber (1947; Chapter 5) and Berger and Luckmann (1966) are among the sociologists who have provided taxonomies that bring us up from the level of individual action to that of social structure: when individual action becomes repetitive we say that it becomes a *habit*. When it becomes a (mutual) social pattern, we call it a *relationship*. When social relationships become patterned into a stable system of interaction, we have an *institution*. The sum of institutionalized social interaction in society is the *social structure*. Thus the behavior of individuals (a dynamic process) translates into the structure of society (a static entity).

To be sure, size is not the only factor. The United States, with more than 215 million people, changes more rapidly than a South American jungle tribe of 215 individuals. Another factor, therefore, is the rate at which a society's self-consciousness can be raised. By virtue of the instant information dissemination made possible by modern technology, American society is, as a collective consciousness, not nearly as sluggish as its size would suggest.

The analysis of society at the structural level (what we have called the aggregate level) is the task of sociology, not social psychology. At that level, structural-functionalism (described in Chapter 1 as the "sociological G.O.P.") is a valid perspective. Durkheim's lasting contribution (1933; 1938; Chapter 1) has been to establish the existence of social structure as a phenomenon *qualitatively* different from the behavior of individual selves. He also discusses society as a collective consciousness, as well as the role of modern mass communication in speeding up societal change (1933).

Social psychology is only interested in the relationship between social structure and the self (cf. Gerth and Mills, 1953). Having established that society is indeed, as Durkheim described it, a massive, external, constraining social fact, or as Berger and Luckman emphasize, an *objective* reality with a facticity independent of individual consciousness, the question is: how does society affect the self?

Self-control comes from society

According to Lindesmith, Strauss, and Denzin (1975:310), "the self is an organization or integration of behavior imposed upon the individual by societal expectations and demands." At birth there is no self; there is only the I. Then the socialization process begins. As the person interacts in society, an internal differentiation process occurs, which is the emergence of the me. The me that emerges represents internalized societal elements: roles, norms, values, and self-control.

At first, an infant's behavior is uncontrolled. The I is mere (spontaneous) behavior. Insofar as there is control—when to eat, when to go to bed, not to destroy valuables, not to tear up dad's manuscript or mom's shopping list—this is externally imposed (if necessary through a spanking). As the I becomes increasingly socialized, spawning in its interaction with society the social me, control becomes internalized. Language plays a crucial part in this process. The do's and don'ts that are first voiced by mother and father gradually become *inner* directives. Miko, at three, is often heard talking to himself in this vein: "No Miko! . . . Don't jump on the table, Miko!"

There are various aspects to self-control. It may be physical (as when a sport or a craft is mastered), or it may be intellectual, as when one has learned to speed-read or to concentrate on the sequential steps necessary to solve a mathematical problem. The most frequently discussed aspect of self-control is what is called *conscience,* or what the Freudians call the *superego,* the internalized moral values of a society.

There is great variation in the consensus about values and what these values ought to be. Furthermore, socialization into societal values does not proceed through the internalization of linguistic abstractions but through the behavioral concretization given to abstract values. For example, we may assume that the word "courage" has a positive connotation to most Americans. It represents a positive value. However, only under certain concrete behavioral conditions will a person feel, in his conscience, that he has failed to live up to this moral value and hence feel ashamed or guilty. In one instance a boy may feel that courage consists of punching another fellow in the nose for a perceived insult, in another instance courage might mean precisely the opposite, being "big" enough to shrug it off and walk away from trouble.

Variation between cultures is, of course, even greater than within cultures. As the above example suggests, the important thing is not that abstract value concepts vary but that the interpretation of behavior does. Every society in the world probably recognizes equivalents of such concepts as "virtue," "good," "evil," "courage," "honesty." At the same time, the behavioral referent of such a concept may be one concrete act in one group, at one time, when committed by one individual in one type of situation, and *its exact opposite* in another case. Killing, for example, may be an act of courage, justice, compassion (think of euthanasia), love of country, pride, love of one's group, or evil.

Insofar as moral values have been internalized, the self has a conscience and the function of the conscience is to control the self internally, so that external societal control becomes unnecessary. Anthropol-

208

ogists (see Benedict, 1946; Lindesmith, Strauss, and Denzin, 1975:313-314) have tried to distinguish between various sanctions at the conscience's disposal for enforcing self-control, including guilt and shame. Such feelings are brought into action when the dictates of conscience have been transgressed—an internal punishment.

A crucial issue must be raised at this point. The necessity (and, some may argue, proliferation) of external forms of social control in society—prime among them, the police—indicates that conscience itself cannot do the job. The question is: to what extent does the very *presence* of conscience—of (internalized) values—vary? Psychologists have argued that certain categories of people (for example psychopaths, autistic children) lack internalized morality altogether. Is it possible that societies vary in terms of the strength of their members' conscience? It is said, for example, that as America rushes toward the end of the century, becoming ever more Gesellschaft-like, control is becoming increasingly *externalized:* unlike in more Gemeinschaft-like societies, the contemporary population is sometimes said to refrain from crime, dishonesty, violence, and selfishness only out of fear for the law. The crime rate is soaring and only through scientific external controls such as drug treatment and behavior modification does our society hope to force its deviants back into the fold. Internal self-control and guilt for one's wrongdoings are on the wane. As a current saying goes, "the worst crime is to get caught."

Three points can be made in response to the moral alarmists. First, those who are seen as amoral and psychopathic by the dominant groups are merely different. They have a morality of their own. Since no value can be declared transcendentally valid, the morality of any deviant is as good as that of the dominant group. Crime, killing, robbery, and violence become condonable political acts.

Second, the increasing normative disintegration of our society indeed means a growing nihilism comparable to the corrupt and immoral culture of the falling Roman Empire.

The first of these arguments is radically liberal, the second conservative. A third argument, in our view a better one, is a Durkheimian one. The current situation is one of moral pluralism and moral transition. Many people may be morally confused, and some may have lost all convictions or merely retained the value of self-survival. However, that too is a value. Crisis and rapid change may produce anomie, but the absence of self-control or its total substitution by external manipulation a la 1984 cannot be permanently applied to human society.

My self comes from society

In addition to self-control, the self also derives its roles and identity from society. We already saw this in our discussion of the self's interaction with others. We may distinguish between two types of sources of self: (1) the traditional social-structural roles that may represent the cornerstone of our identity and (2) alternative sources of meaning and identity.

Work structures are a case in point. As Hughes (1951) and others have shown, formal organizations have long provided the basis for our identity—at least to many of us. Our occupational positions, the roles we play vis-a-vis our colleagues, these are crucial features of our selves. They determine in large part who we are. To Dr. Livingston, teaching history at the State University is the most important part of his life. But that anchorage in the social structure (his membership in the State University's faculty as a professor of history) is not the only way his work determines his self. His identity and self-concept also follow from the facts that he is chairman of his department's curriculum committee, that he is on the academic senate, that he is respected by most of his colleagues (except the conservative wing, whose hostility is a compliment, really), and that he has published a major textbook in American history widely used in his own department.

The formal organizations to which we belong are important sources of self, work still being one such major source of identity. In my example, would Dr. Livingston, if forced to retire, not suffer from identity loss and self-doubt?

According to Young (1972), however, modern large-scale organizations no longer require an individual's self-involvement. In our technocracy, people must increasingly rely on alternative sources of self. Although Young's thesis must be questioned with respect to the professional class, it is true that insofar as people are alienated from their work, work is no longer a major source of self. Whether or not we are moving toward the leisure society (see Kando, 1975) is a moot point, but Young is correct in pointing to the existence of alternative sources of self. Such alternative structures might include encounter groups, communal friendship circles, or underground churches (Young's countercultural examples), or simply any recreational or informal group to which the individual belongs. Thus thirty-one-year-old, all-American looking, athletic, and jovial Jim Pozluzni works five days a week for the telephone company. He gives little thought to his job. A job is a job. This one pays well and there is security. However, Jim is also a member of an amateur car racing team. He has won several trophies on the tour in recent years. Thousands of Jim's dollars have gone into his souped-up Corvette, which has seen action up and down the coast from Monterey to Ontario. Jim is an amateur race driver and he feels that he is good and becoming better.

SUMMARY AND CONCLUSION

This chapter has discussed the self in a more or less descriptive fashion. We began with a discussion of mind, which is the inner dialogue between the I and the me—the activity of thinking. The self, of which mind is only the inner mental aspect, was discussed next. Three concep-

tions of the self were explained, two of which are central to this book. The static (psychological) conception of self that more or less equates self and personality is *not* the view we have proposed to explore. Instead, we have suggested a combination of a dynamic sociological conception that recognizes that the self *is* behavior, that it therefore changes and that the ongoing situation in large part determines the self-as-behavior, and a phenomenological approach that posits that the self is first and foremost subjective and explains the possibility of meaningful social interaction through the concept of intersubjectivity.

The following section dealt with the self as self-concept and the tendency of many sociologists to equate self and self-concept. By doing so, sociology misses one of Mead's two main points, which are that the self is *both* object and subject. As social research on the self becomes more positivistic (using, for example, the Iowa School's TST), it becomes unable to deal with the phenomenological view of self as subject.

The last two sections have dealt with the ways in which society and others act upon and interact with the self. While it is true that others have a great impact on the self, we must remember that the self does not merely react to others passively. It selects, interprets, judges, and screens environmental stimuli. It acts positively on its environment, has volition, presents itself, attempts to lodge crucial identity features into the social situation. We also saw that society may—and generally does—inject into the self both an identity based on the roles played by the self in the social structure and self-control in the form of a conscience, which enforces societal values internally. However, internal moral control may be weak—as some people claim it is becoming in our society today—in which case society must rely on external forms of control, for example, formal law enforcement.

The self is a developmental process. It emerges through such processes as socialization, internalization and interaction with significant others and reference groups. We now turn to these processes in greater detail.

REFERENCES

Bain, Read
  1936 "The self- and other words of a child." American Journal of Sociology (May): 767-775.
Basso, Keith
  1967 "Semantic aspects of linguistic acculturation." American Anthropologist 69:471-477.
Becker, Ernest
  1962 The Birth and Death of Meaning. Glencoe, Ill.: The Free Press.
Benedict, Ruth
  1946 The Chrysanthemum and The Sword. Boston: Houghton Mifflin Co.
Berger, Peter L. and Thomas Luckmann
  1966 The Social Construction of Reality. Garden City, N.Y.: Doubleday & Co., Inc.
Blumer, Herbert
  1969 Symbolic Interactionism. Englewood Cliffs, N.J.: Prentice-Hall, Inc.
Bruyn, Severyn
  1966 The Human Perspective in Sociology. Englewood Cliffs, N.J.: Prentice-Hall, Inc.
Cardwell, J. D.
  1971 Social Psychology: A Symbolic Interactionist Perspective. Philadelphia: F. A. Davis Co.
Cassirer, Ernst
  1944 An Essay on Man: An Introduction to a Philosophy of Human Culture. New Haven, Conn.: Yale University Press.
Chomsky, Noam
  1968 Language and Mind. New York: Harcourt, Brace, and World.
Cooley, Charles Horton
  1902 Human Nature and the Social Order. New York: Scribner's.
  1909 Social Organization. New York: Scribner's.
  1930 "A study of the early use of self-words by a child." In Sociological Theory and Social Research. By Charles Horton Cooley. New York: Rinehart and Winston, Inc.
Davis, Kingsley
  1940 "Extreme social isolation of a child." American Journal of Sociology (January): 554-565.
  1947 "Final note on a case of extreme isolation." American Journal of Sociology (March): 432-437.
Denzin, Norman K.
  1969 "Symbolic interactionism and ethnomethodology." American Sociological Review (December): 922-934.
Deutsch, Morton and Robert M. Krauss
  1965 Theories in Social Psychology. New York: Basic Books, Inc.
Durkheim, Emile
  1933 The Division of Labor in Society. New York: The Macmillan Co.
  1938 The Rules of Sociological Method. Chicago: University of Chicago Press.
Fellows, Jean
  1968 "Dreams and the self." Unpublished paper. Minneapolis: University of Minnesota Press.
Festinger, Leon
  1954 "A theory of social comparison processes." Human Relations 7:117-140.
Foote, Nelson N.
  1951 "Identification as the basis for a theory of motivation." American Sociological Review (February): 14-21.
Freud, Sigmund
  1924 A General Introduction to .Psychoanalysis. New York: Boni & Liveright Publishing Corporation.
Gergen, Kenneth J.
  1971 The Concept of Self. Theodore R. Sarbin (ed.). New York: Holt, Rinehart and Winston, Inc.
Gerth, Hans and C. Wright Mills
  1953 Character and Social Structure. New York: Harcourt, Brace Jovanovich, Inc.
Goffman, Erving
  1959 The Presentation of Self in Everyday Life. Garden City, N.Y.: Doubleday & Co., Inc.
Gordon, Chad and Kenneth J. Gergen
  1968 The Self in Social Interaction. New York: John Wiley & Sons, Inc.
Heider, Fritz
  1946 "Attitudes and cognitive organization." Journal of Psychology 21:107-112.
Hughes, Everett C.
  1951 "Work and self." In Social Psychology at the Crossroads. John H. Rohrer and Muzafer Sherif (eds.). New York: Harper & Row, Publishers, pp. 313-323.
James, William
  1890 Principles of Psychology. New York: Henry Holt.
Kando, Thomas
  1973 Sex Change: The Achievement of Gender Identity Among Feminized Transsexuals. Springfield, Ill.: Charles C Thomas, Publisher.
  1975 Leisure and Popular Culture in Transition. St. Louis: The C. V. Mosby Co.
Kinch, John W.
  1963 "A formalized theory of the self-concept." American Journal of Sociology (January): 481-486.
Kuhn, Manford H.
  1964 "Major trends in symbolic interaction theory in the past twenty-five years." Sociological Quarterly (Winter): 61-84.

Kuhn, Manford H. and Thomas S. McPartland
1954 "An empirical investigation of self-attitudes." American Sociological Review 19:
68-76.
Langer, Suzanne
1948 Philosophy in a New Key. New York:
Penguin Books, Inc.
Liebendorfer, R.
1960 "Mind, self and society." Today's Speech
1:31-33.
Lindesmith, Alfred R., Anselm L. Strauss, and Norman K. Denzin
1975 Social Psychology (ed. 4). Hinsdale, Ill.: The
Dryden Press.
Luria, A. R.
1966 Human Brain and Psychological Processes.
New York: Harper & Row, Publishers.
Manning, Peter K. and Horacio Fabrega, Jr.
1973 "The experience of self and body: health
and illness in the Chiapas Highlands." In
Phenomenological Sociology: Issues and Applications. George Psathas (ed.). New York:
John Wiley & Sons, Inc., pp. 251-304.
Mead, George Herbert
1934 Mind, Self and Society. Charles W. Morris
(ed.). Chicago: University of Chicago Press.
Meltzer, Bernard N. and John W. Petras
1970 "The Chicago and Iowa schools of symbolic
interactionism." In Human Nature and Collective Behavior: Papers in Honor of Herbert Blumer. Tamotsu Shibutani (ed.). Englewood Cliffs, N.J.: Prentice-Hall, Inc.
Merrill, Francis E.
1961 "Stendhal and the self: a study in the sociology of literature." American Journal of Sociology (March): 446-453.
Natanson, Maurice
1970 The Journeying Self: A Study in Philosophy
and Social Role. Menlo Park, Calif.: Addison-Wesley Publishing Co., Inc.
Piaget, Jean
1932 The Moral Judgment of the Child. New
York: Harcourt, Brace.
Quill, William G.
1972 Subjective Psychology: A Concept of Mind
for the Behavioral Sciences and Philosophy.
New York: Spartan Books.
Schutz, Alfred
1948 "Sartre's theory of the alter ego." Philosophical and Phenomenological Research 9:181-
199.
1970 On Phenomenology and Social Relations.
Helmut R. Wagner (ed.). Chicago: The University of Chicago Press.
Spiegelberg, Herbert
1973 "On the right to say "we": a linguistic and
phenomenological analysis." In Phenomenological Sociology: Issues and Applications.
George Psathas (ed.). New York: John Wiley
& Sons, Inc. pp. 129-158.
Spitzer, Stephen, Carl Couch, and John Stratton

1971 The Assessment of the Self. Iowa City: Escort, Sernoll, Inc.
Stone, Gregory P.
1962 "Appearance and the self." In Human Behavior and Social Processes. Arnold M. Rose
(ed.). Boston: Houghton Mifflin Co., pp. 86-
118.
Sullivan, Harry Stack
1953 The Interpersonal Theory of Psychiatry.
New York: W. W. Norton & Co., Inc.
1964 "The illusion of personal individuality." In
The Fusion of Psychiatry and Social Science.
Helen Swick Perry (ed.). New York: W. W.
Norton & Co., Inc.
Szasz, Thomas
1961 The Myth of Mental Illness: Foundations of
a Theory of Personal Conduct. New York:
Dell Publishing Co.
Tucker, Charles W.
1966 'Some methodological problems of Kuhn's
self theory." Sociological Quarterly (Sum-
mer):345-358.
Vygotsky, Lev
1962 Thought and Language. Cambridge, Mass.:
The M.I.T. Press.
Wagner, Helmut (ed.)
1970. Alfred Schutz on Phenomenology and So-
cial Relations. Chicago: The University of
Chicago Press.
Watson, Geoffrey G. and Thomas M. Kando
1976 "The meaning of rules and rituals in Little
League baseball." Pacific Sociological Review
(Summer).
Weber, Max
1947 The Theory of Social and Economic Organi-
zation. A. M. Henderson and Talcott Par-
sons (trans.) and Talcott Parsons (ed.). Glen-
coe, Ill.: The Free Press.
Weinstein, Eugene A. and Paul Deutschberger
1963 "Some dimensions of altercasting." Sociom-
etry (December):454-466.
White, Leslie A.
1960 "Four stages in the evolution of minding." In
The Evolution of Man: Man, Culture and
Society, vol. 2 of Evolution After Darwin. Sol
Tax (ed.). Chicago: University of Chicago
Press.
Wolff, B. B. and S. Langley
1968 "Cultural factors and the response to pain: a
review." American Anthropologist 70:494-
501.
Young, T. R.
1972 New Sources of Self. New York: Pergamon
Press.
Zborowski, Mark
1952 "Cultural Components in responses to pain."
Journal of Social Issues 4:16-30.

chapter 9
Socialization

The human self is in part the product of millions of years of evolution and in part that of the socialization process that begins at the birth of each individual. We have already discussed some of the ways in which the human self represents the culmination of the evolutionary process: Becker's (1962) four types of reactivity (see Chapter 8), of which the last is symbolic interaction; Hockett and Ascher's (1964) anthropological demonstration of how speech was first mastered by the protohominoids some one million years ago; Mead's (1934) emphasis on the neural substratum upon which symbolic thought and interaction are predicated.

However, what evolution has produced is an organism with a *potential* for human behavior only. As studies of feral children (cf. Davis, 1947) show, that potential is not realized unless a person engages in social interaction. Therefore, in order to understand how each of us acquires a self during our lifetime, biology is insufficient. We must deal with the problem of socialization, and this is a sociological question.

In America, the concept of socialization was introduced by Franklin Giddings (1897:2), who conceived of it "as the development of a social nature or character—a social state of mind—in the individuals who associate." Today, there are practically as many definitions of socialization as there are authors writing about it. For example, Elkin (1960:4) defines socialization as "the process by which someone learns the ways of a given society or social group well enough so that he can function within it." Theodorson and Theodorson (1969:396) define it as "the basic social process through which an individual becomes integrated into a social group by learning the group's culture and his role in the group."

Instead of proposing one more specific definition, like Clausen and associates (1968), we prefer to indicate what socialization is by discussing some of the questions dealt with under that heading. One question raised by socialization is: How do newcomers learn to participate effectively in social groups? By "newcomers" is meant, in the first place, babies. A somewhat different question is: How does the infant develop into a value-seeking person? Furthermore, socialization deals with adults, too, not just children. It also asks such questions as: How do people learn, change, adjust, adapt at *any* stage of the life cycle? How do they become resocialized from one self, role, or identity to another? What are the differences between the socialization of children (primary socialization) and later forms of socialization (secondary socialization)?

There is no consensus among social psychologists as to the exact mechanisms involved in socialization. There are still a number of competing schools. The (neo-) behaviorists see socialization as the *learning* of behaviors that are rewarded through positive reinforcements (see Chapter 2). They derive this conclusion mostly from research done with animals, not with humans. Psychologists who subscribe to this theory (such as Clark Hull) view socialization as the piece by piece accretion of small behavioral increments, or habits. This is the learning theory of socialization.

A much improved conception of socialization is that presented by the field theorists and the Gestalt psychologists (see Chapter 2), who have noted that each new (learning) experience not only adds an increment to the self but actually changes its total Gestalt, its entire configuration. However, this school has not studied socialization very much, focusing more on perception and cognition.

The Freudian or psychoanalytic orientation to socialization was dominant in the 1950s (see Chapter 2). These psychologists focused almost entirely on early childhood socialization, maintaining that what occurs early in life pretty much determines subsequent behavior. This determinism has, in some instances, been so excessive that some (neo-) Freudians have been called "chamberpot determinists." This epithet is only partially facetious, since some psychologists, such as the Britisher Otto Rank, have argued that the birth trauma—the process of being born, with its varied amount of pain—may be a crucial determinant of personality. In addition, the Freudians' other distinctive feature is their focus on pathological behavior, that is, on faulty socialization.

In addition to behaviorism, Gestalt psychology, and Freudian psychology, the major contribution to socialization theory comes from symbolic interactionism. Here, as elsewhere in this book, we wish to adopt the valid points made by the other schools while recognizing that it is interactionism's treatment of socialization that "puts it together" in the best possible fashion.

It is somewhat true, as behaviorism argues, that man becomes socialized into new behavior patterns through a natural selection process, a process of conditioning (Shibutani, 1961:474). It is also true that successful behavior—behavior that leads to the solution of a problem, the attainment of a goal, behavior that is therefore somehow rewarded—is likely to be repeated. Thus learning is indeed in part a trial-and-error conditioning process. However, and this is where behaviorism falls short, the behavior of the self is not merely a response to physical or other "objective" stimuli. It is far more often a response to symbolic rewards, to such things as respect, status, self-esteem, sentiment, and innumerable other subjective values that can in no way be objectified, as attempted by psychologists who develop "hierarchies of needs" (cf. Maslow, 1962).

A further error, as we saw, is to view socialization as the gradual accretion of small habits, or behavioral increments. Rather, it is the continuous reorganization and readjustment of the self to the environment (cf. Shibutani, 1961:500).

The Freudians make an important contribution to socialization theory by showing us that man develops a variety of defense mechanisms to cope with his environment, including some that may be viewed as pathological. However, this group's excessive childhood determinism is another misconception. As we shall see, it is important to recognize that socialization is a life-long process, taking place in adulthood as well as during childhood. A person does not stop changing early in life, and his behavior is not necessarily determined by his early childhood experiences.

Socialization is essentially a communicative process (cf. Shibutani, 1961: 499-500) whereby the individual gradually learns to (1) anticipate the reaction of others (role-taking), (2) conform to expectations, and (3) control his own behavior. It is important to realize that childhood socialization is merely one phase of the socialization process, what is termed *primary socialization.* It is through primary socialization that we become members of society itself. However, there is in addition *secondary socialization,* the subsequent processes that induct already socialized individuals into new sectors of society—for example, a university, the army, a profession, marriage. While the brunt of the literature on socialization is still limited to primary socialization (cf. Danziger, 1971, for a recent example), this chapter will document the rich and growing information about all phases of socialization.

CHILDHOOD

In this section we examine two things: children and the socialization of children. The distinction is meaningful, because we all too often tend to view children as mere protoadults, homunculi, "little people" who only await socialization into adulthood. As Aries (1968) showed, children are in fact a different breed of people, and this was not "discovered" until the sixteenth century, at least in a society such as France. It is therefore proper to first treat children in their own terms, in their own right.

The second part of this section, then, will deal with the vastly more familiar topic of childhood socialization, the process and mechanisms whereby children become adults. Here, the major issue to be raised is the question of childhood determinism: is it true, as the (neo-)Freudians have argued, that early emotional nurturing is crucial to healthy development, or has this been an exaggeration? We shall also examine some of the developmental schemes proposed by various social psychologists, among them those of Baldwin and Sullivan. We shall then discuss two important issues following from the various developmental discussions of childhood socialization. One is the matter of value: what constitutes a mature, well-adjusted, healthy, in sum "good" person? This issue has preoccupied many psychologists, including such neo-Freudian humanists as Fromm, Maslow, and Rogers. The other question is the more neutral examination of the role of language in the development of a competent self. This focus is found in the works of Sullivan, Mead, and symbolic interactionists generally. We shall propose a reconciliation of these two preoccupations found in the literature.

What is childhood?

As stated in the previous paragraphs, the field of socialization has overwhelmingly focused on *how children become adults,* that is, it has viewed childhood mostly as a preparatory stage in human life. It is therefore appropriate to complement that approach by also dealing briefly with children per se, that is, by viewing children as a particular category of people, a subculture in their own right.

The Frenchman Phillip Aries (1968) provided the classic demonstration that "childhood' as a concept and as a social identity is not a universal condition but the product of a sociocultural definition of the situation. In other words, the idea of childhood was invented in France in the beginning of the seventeeth century. It may also, of course, have occurred elsewhere, for example in ancient Greece.

Before the seventeenth century, there were two categories of humans: infants (who were swaddled) and adults. There was nothing in between. Children were *homunculi,* little people. They were dressed and treated in many ways as adults, in both the upper and the lower strata. Louis XIII, for example, sang and played the violin at seventeen months, danced at three, and read and wrote at four. He was not a child prodigy (Aries, 1968, paraphrased in Stone, 1965). Anyone familiar with pre-Renaissance art—paintings by Brueghel and other Flemish primitives, for example—may notice that the children of commoners look like little adults and participate in such adult settings as taverns and wine shops.

Stone (1965) develops Aries' thesis a bit further, pointing out that childhood emerged earlier in the Catholic world than in the more work-oriented Protestant societies. With the rise of Calvinism, capitalism, and industrialism, work became the central value and activity in Western civilization (cf. Kando, 1975; Stone, 1965; Weber, 1958). This meant that insofar as play survived, it was relegated to childhood. Earlier, play had *not* necessarily been associated with children. In fact, children and adults played the very same types of games (cf. Stone, 1965).

While Protestant countries such as the United States conferred the privileges of play upon children later than, for example, France, it is now a fact that in order to understand the subculture of childhood one must examine the meanings of play. Stone (1965) does this, pointing out first that his interest is not, like Mead's (1934), the developmental meaning of a play-game contrast and relationship but merely the examination of *play* as a crucial element in the subculture of childhood. Following that author, we shall now briefly discuss five themes in childhood play.

To the child, play means in the first place *drama,* the dramatization of his personal identity. Stone provides a fine proof that the building of personal identity is a prime function of child play: "Indeed, in playing house, it is difficult to recruit a child to play the role of child or baby. Such a role has no implication for the building of his own identity. A doll, therefore, is better suited to the role" (Stone, 1965).

Child play is of course to an extent socialization. However, it is only partially *anticipatory* socialization (Merton, 1957), for much of it is also what Stone terms *fantastic* socialization, for example, playing such unreal identities as cowboy, Indian, or creatures from outer space. Fantastic drama, then, may serve to keep alive some of the culture's myths and legends, as well as to anticipate the future (as in space adventure play).

A third feature of the play-centered childhood subculture is the incomplete knowledge children have of the roles they enact. Stone again gives a good example: a boy and a girl play house in a front yard. The girl busily sweeps up the play area, rearranges furniture, cares for baby dolls, and the like. The boy, however, only leaves the play area on his tricycle, disappears to the back of the (real) house, remains there for a while, reappears in the play area, and lies down, feigning sleep. "For the boy, a father was one who disappeared, reappeared, and slept, *ad infinitum!*" (op. cit.).

A fourth aspect of childhood play occurs when play functions as a means of *satisfying tabooed curiosity,* and a fifth meaning is the *testing of poise.* The best example of the fourth—most of us can probably remember this rather vividly— is playing "nurse" or "doctor," the quasispontaneous discovery and exploration of sexuality by children.

As examples of the last feature, Stone points to the many ways in which children deliberately push and trip each other, spin about to induce dizziness, disrupt play, disarrange clothing, and perform all sorts of other pranks. Amusement parks, Stone points out, are an implicit modern technol-ogy to facilitate this fifth function of play, the testing of poise.

The point of this section, then, has been to get away from the banal and incomplete notion that childhood is merely or even primarily a preparatory stage in socialization toward adulthood and instead to do justice to childhood as a subculture, to children as a specific type of people.

Two additional groups of social scientists are now studying childhood in the sense used here: some ethnomethodologists focus on the organization of children's culture (such as Speier, 1970:91). They do this by studying the conversational resources available to children (and to their interlocutors) in their routine interactions (op. cit.:192). Recognizing, as Turner (1970) does, that talking is doing, they examine the interactional basis of talk. As Speier convincingly argues, words to children are *not* in the first place categorical concepts or ideas, but *tools* in action. To a young child, the meaning of the word "box" is not the idea of a box but the fact that by uttering that sound he will probably obtain a desired object—a particular box. Thus words are actions; to speak is to accomplish.

Finally, we know from anthropologists and ethnographic sociologists that childhood does come to an end and that this necessitates some rite of passage (cf. Van Gennep, 1909). A heart-rending description of such a rite is found in Gatheru's (1964) autobiographical account of the circumcision rite which, in his African culture, changes him from child to man. The rite of passage is a test of courage, of one's ability to endure excruciating pain. If the test is passed successfully, the transition in identity is itself the reward, for being a man means the acquisition of status and power in the community.

How are children socialized?

The induction of newborn members into an ongoing society takes place through *primary socialization.* As Berger and Luckmann (1966) point out, primary socialization is the sine qua non for the successful integration of new members into society, for society's continued success as a stable and ongoing enterprise. In primary socialization, the new member—the infant—has no choice as to *what* to internalize and as to his socializing agents. He cannot choose his parents. The child does not choose the world it joins. That world is given as inevitable and absolute. Its ways are the only truths. The internalization of these ways are both cognitive and affective. That is, primary socialization not only means the acquisition of knowledge but also the internalization of a firm belief that this knowledge is right.

In their primary interactions with their socializing agents—parents mostly—children not only take on those agents' identities but also their social world. In Meadian terminology, the child not only takes the role of individual significant others but of the general other as well.

As Berger and Luckmann phrase it, primary socialization is society's "confidence trick" on the individual: society succeeds in making *accident* appear *necessity*. When a child of Jewish parents is raised in the Jewish faith and Jewish customs, this does not appear to him to be a matter of choice, one possibility among many; it is *the only right way*. Primary socialization, then, is the internalization of cultural elements that at the time have the character of absolutes. These elements include language, programs of behavior, and motives—self-evident explanations. The little boy does not doubt, for example, that he must be brave and honest, and he does not doubt the reasons given to him for this. At the level of primary socialization, there is no room for doubt. Even in periods of rapid cultural change, when for example, as today, many basic assumptions about such things as sex roles are questioned, young children must be socialized into *some* set of primary roles, values, and assumptions

with consistency. These may be liberated or traditional, but they must, from the child's primary perspective, have the character of being firmly correct. Doubt, questioning, and reinterpretation occur later, when individuals begin to opt between alternative and often contradictory institutions, subworlds, subcultures, and values, socialization into which is *secondary*. Doubt and choice are parts of the secondary socialization process, the life-long process experienced by each of us as we begin to move through schools, colleges, armed forces, occupations, family roles, and other institutional slots. This surely is the major reason why the impact of secondary socialization is not as profound and as lasting as that of primary socialization.

The foregoing discussion reflects somewhat the functionalist approach to socialization, the major approach in sociology over the past thirty years. This approach (by no means endorsed by Berger and Luckmann, whose conception of socialization is, in addition to what has just been said, also social-psychological) views socialization as a functional imperative, a systemic need. That is, in order for the social system to successfully maintain itself, it must transmit and inculcate into the new members certain qualities, skills, and values. This is the functional imperative that socialization performs. Works such as Inkeles (1968) and Clausen and associates (1968) still reflect this tradition. Clausen (1968:130-188) deals with such traditional but important aspects of socialization as its sequence and scheduling, focusing on the three major agents of socialization—the parents, the schools, and the peers. He makes the important point that whereas in the middle class the various socializing agents reinforce one another, they often work at cross purposes in the lower class. Clearly, when youngsters are exposed to competing parties, each of which is attempting to inculcate them with a culture that is antagonistic to the others, everyone suffers—youngsters, parents, teachers.

There are, however, some extremely relevant aspects of socialization that have not received as much attention in the literature thus far, and it is the responsibility of this book to focus on those issues rather than to once again sum up familiar ground. The central controversy in the field of socialization concerns the importance of early childhood socialization. To simplify matters for a moment, we may say that there are two opposing schools: those who subscribe to a fairly rigid childhood determinism (and are thus often Freudian in orientation), and those who do not. The brunt of the background research for this book brings us to believe that the latter group is correct, that there is no scientific justification for thinking of the individual as being "locked up" in his earliest socialization experiences.

Many (social) psychologists have proposed developmental schemes. Freud's stages of psychosexual development have already been discussed (see Chapter 2). They include the oral, anal, phallic, latency, and puberty stages. As we saw, the underlying theme in Freud's developmental theory is the organism's management of sexuality.

James Mark Baldwin (1861-1934), an American child psychologist, distinguished between three stages of child development. Unlike Freud, he was concerned with the emergence of consciousness. Baldwin called the first stage of child development *projective:* at this point, the child is shaped by the various suggestions of his significant others (such as his mother). The second stage is *subjective;* now the child becomes aware of himself, develops volition, is capable of effort. Finally, the *ejective* stage is reached, at which point the child becomes able to identify with others, becomes able to say, in effect, "what I feel, others must feel" (Baldwin, 1906).

George Herbert Mead's developmental metaphor of play versus game has already been disscussed (see Chapters 6 and 8). In essence, Mead uses "play" to denote the most elementary level of role-taking, while "game" occurs later, when the child learns to take on multiple roles and to internalize rules of complex interactions.

Piaget (1932) has been primarily concerned with the moral development of the child. According to this child psychologist, the earliest form of morality found in children is *heteronomous;* rules are unquestioningly accepted, as is all authority. Later, morality becomes *autonomous;* that is, rather than conforming uncritically to authority, older children gradually learn choice and judgment. As Mead uses the baseball metaphor to convey his ideas, so Piaget, a European, based his theory on observations of children playing marbles. He noted that authority—the source of unquestioned rules—is often represented not by parents but by older peers.

A particularly important developmental typology is provided by Harry Stack Sullivan (1953-1954) who, although incorporating Freudian elements, focuses on symbolic rather than psychosexual development. The child's symbolic development proceeds through three stages: (1) the prototaxic, (2) the parataxic, and (3) the syntaxic. The prototaxic stage consists of partially unconscious experiences. The syntaxic stage consists of experiences that are fully encompassed by symbolic formulations. These can now be *thought* about (discussed with oneself) and communicated (discussed with others). The child's development, then, proceeds from the uncommunicable through the partially communicable to the wholly communicable. The beauty of Sullivan's theory is that it allows for unconscious experience without the necessity to posit an unconscious mind. It reconciles Freudian and symbolic interactionist social pyschology.

Sullivan describes seven specific stages in human development. (1) *Infancy* lasts from birth up to the emergence of articulate speech. (2) *Childhood* lasts up to the emergence of the need for playmates. It is at this stage that sensible communication with others emerges. (3) *The juvenile era* lasts up to the appearance of the need for intimate relations with others of equal status. During this stage, both peers and new authority figures appear. Parents no longer appear to be perfect. Egocentrism is gradually replaced by sociability. Belonging and being accepted acquire crucial importance. The youngster's self-concept becomes a reflection of his relations with his peer groups. (4) *Preadolescence,* then, is the period when the need for intimate relations with others of the same sex appears. There may be homosexual tendencies at this point, but the intimacy in question is of course primarily a Platonic one. This is also the age of gang activity. (5) *Adolescence,* according to Sullivan, is when sexual lust and genital interest erupt. This is the last of the maturation needs. (6) *Late adolescence* is when sexual activity becomes patterned, and further development from here on, through (7) *adulthood,* consists essentially of further growth in syntaxic experience, for example through education, work, and civic participation.

Sullivan's scheme is excellent in its emphases: like the Freudians, he recognizes the possibility of mishaps at each stage. For example, lack of interactional success during the juvenile and preadolescent stages may result in negative self-concept, neurosis, or psychosis. Preadolescence and adolescence may produce persistent homosexual habits. However, the crucial and eminently *reasonable* point throughout Sullivan's analysis—based, incidentally, on extensive first-hand experience as a psychiatrist and not on armchair theory—is that each stage is a threshold providing the possibility for a fresh new start. There is no sexual determinism. The earlier and more fundamental need is not lust but intimacy. Furthermore, an individual's personality is not a replica of his primary socialization. Think, for example, of those children who are nursed and raised by servants, their earliest significant others. Surely such upper-class children do not develop the character traits of servants themselves!

The gradual vulgarization of Freudianism has led to the point where today vast numbers of laymen and professionals alike unquestioningly accept a variety of false determinisms. While this may make life easier for some, it does not benefit children and future generations. Sullivan convinces us that these simplistic determinisms are often shackles of our own making.

The issue of childhood determinism is an old one. The widespread adoption of the Freudian perspective by Americans began in the 1940s. Spitz's (1945) classic study of *hospitalism* was one of the most famous and most frequently cited sources of evidence to support the general Freudian contention that the nature of infant socialization is of the utmost importance in determining such things as mental and emotional health, intelligence, personality, and even physical health. Specifically, Spitz compared two groups of infants raised in two different institutional settings—a nursery and a foundling home. In the nursery the children were raised by their own mothers; in the foundling home, they were taken care of by overworked personnel. Spitz found that the rate of retardation, depression, and even mortality was far higher in the latter group, despite similar health and housing care in both instances. He attributed the deterioration among foundlings to the lack of mothering, a condition termed "marasmus," indicating affective-emotional starvation. In some form or another, the crucial importance of early childhood socialization in determining mental health and personality has been accepted by most neo-Freudians (such as Erickson, Fromm, Margaret Mead, Spock), and indeed by most psychologists.

Both Spitz's study and the general Freudian conclusions just alluded to have been discussed and criticized many times during the past three decades. Of particular interest is the work of Jerome Kagan (1973), who discovered a village in Guatemala which seems to undermine the conventional assumptions about child development. In Guatemala, Kagan observed hundreds of children who were isolated from their homes and their parents during the first years of their lives. The local culture prescribes a way of life whereby young infants are kept in windowless huts, without toys. By one and a half years, these children were very retarded. However, Kagan's significant discovery was that the children *recover*. The eleven-year-olds in this Guatemalan village were beautiful, alert, intelligent, and healthy. Similar findings have been reported from villages in the Eastern Netherlands (Kagan, 1973).

Sewell's (1952) earlier work has the same kind of bearing on the issue as Kagan's. In an empirical test of nine specific hypotheses, Sewell showed that whether or not an infant is breast-fed, whether or not it is fed on self-demand, whether or not weaning is abrupt, whether bowel and bladder training take place late or early, whether or not the infant sleeps with the mother, and whether or not it is punished for toilet training has *no significant impact on later personality development.*

One aspect of the controversy presently under review concerns male-female personality differences. Orthodox Freudians have argued that the feminine superego is less well developed than that of the male because of inescapable biological differences. "Castration threats, so the reasoning goes, are simply not as convincing to young girls as they are to young boys" (Stone and Farberman, 1970:512). In other words, there is no way for parents to discipline and socialize girls as adequately as boys. This is one variant, then, of the Freudian dictum "anatomy is destiny." Stone and Farberman (1970:512-513) offer a speculative but fascinating interpretation of male-female differences in the modern world, one that does not reject the Freudians' *observations*, merely their *interpretation*. In our society, the authors first point out, it may (at least until recently) have been more difficult for boys to become men than for girls to become women, but once adulthood is established men may have an easier time being men

than women do being women.[1] Now the Freudian inference of weak female superego may reflect social rather than biological reality. Since in our society social structures are built for men, men's identities revolve around rational behaviors—Stone's "value." Women, on the other hand, have had to rely on the more "emotional" bases of interpersonal interaction for their identities. This may be why many psychoanalysts have believed that men have stronger superegos than women—male personality has simply tended to reflect, more frequently than that of women, the rational and controlled work structures that are still so overwhelmingly male-dominated.

It seems clear, then, that the self is neither chained to anatomy nor to the earliest stages of development. This is the persistent argument made by symbolic interactionism, the paradigm that gives due recognition to the centrality of language in human development. If this is granted, then it is indeed difficult to see how preverbal experience—Sullivan's prototaxic stage—can be as important as conventional (Freudian) child psychology would have it.

Empirical work documenting the role of language in the development of the self has already been discussed (see Chapter 7). Such work goes back to Cooley (1902) and a good recent example is Denzin (1972). This author notes, once again, how the

[1] Today, women's liberation seems to support the latter part of this hypothesis. However, sexual inversion problems have, until recently, been more frequent among men than among women. This goes for homosexuality (cf. Humphreys, 1970) as well as for the more extreme conditions of transvestism and transsexualism (cf. Kando, 1972; 1973). The best sociological interpretation of transsexualism is that it represents an inability to carry the roles and burdens of one's own gender. Thus whether male sexual inversion (notably transsexualism) has only been more *visible* than that of females, or indeed more *frequent*, thereby reflecting the greater difficulty men have in carrying out male roles than do women in carrying out theirs, remains to be seen.

child gradually masters personal pronouns and thereby acquires a self, being, by age three, able to see himself as an object. Denzin points out that the emergence of the self is not only indicated by the increasing mastery over personal pronouns and one's own name but also by a variety of "possessive" behaviors (op. cit.:200). This was, of course, also noted by Cooley, who viewed the self as "appropriative," aggressive, militant, and possessive (Cooley, 1902).

Sociologists have also shown some of the more subtle processes involved in socialization. Stone (1962) has pointed out that it is often the parent who imitates the child, vocalizing and representing to the child sounds that are emitted randomly by the child but that acquire meaning once imitated by the parent. Rheingold (1969) shows how the infant socializes his caretaker(s) in many ways, teaching adults, for example, the power of smiling and crying and the meaning of tenderness. Thus the infant, too, is a teacher.

Out of psychiatry, which has been so heavily influenced by the Freudian perspective, have come many attempts to define mental health, maturity, and happiness—in other words, to determine what constitutes a proper "self." The current conception is a humanistic one, listing such items as freedom, autonomy, love, self-actualization, and the ability for free expression of creativity and, to some extent, emotion (compare various writings by such men as Eric Berne, Abraham Maslow, Erich Fromm, Carl Rogers, Everett Shostrom). To this, each author may add or substitute his own conceptions of health and maturity. Blitsten (1971), for example, mentions such things as the ability to relate, to give, and to sustain institutions. Thus in addition to the traditional psychiatric focus on mental illness (cf. Hilgard, 1964, for a study in social heredity, of how mothers transmit their own pathologies to their children), psychologists are increasingly interested in *values* and in formulat-

ing guidelines for proper values. Tolley's (1973) study of how children responded to the Vietnam war found, rather obviously, that the parents had much more to do with this than either the teachers or the media. Implicit was, of course, the author's condemnation of the war itself.

Out of symbolic interactionism and the writings of some psychiatrists (such as Sullivan, 1953; Szasz, 1961), on the other hand, comes a more neutral conception of "proper" personal and social adjustment. Here the focus is primarily on interpersonal and communicative competence. Thus from a pragmatic standpoint, that self develops properly which is capable of meaningful (symbolic) interaction within its community.

Without passing judgment on the values found in the writings of the humanistic psychiatrists, it seems to us that the two kinds of recommendations—let us term one idealistic and the other pragmatic—both have a function, but in the following manner. The task of empirical social psychology is to examine and evaluate the self primarily in terms of interpersonal and communicative competence. In addition, sociologists may privately advocate certain values that they would like to see implemented by the culture at large. However, we must remember that there is, in the ultimate and transcendental sense, no absolute behavioral form that can be termed healthy or, conversely, pathological. By the same token, it must be recognized that human existence without *some* value is meaningless and that all human values must to some extent be shared, for man is inherently and uniquely social.

WHERE DOES SOCIALIZATION COME FROM?

To say that the human self is inherently social is to say that its development reflects the others with whom it interacts. The individual's socialization reflects his family, his social class, the institutions and culture in which he grows up. The school, the media, and many other individuals and institutions contribute to the individual's development.

This section discusses concepts and research dealing with the role of others in the socialization process. Seminal were the contributions of Mead (1934), who was concerned with the interaction between self and significant and generalized others, and Hyman (1942), who coined the concept of *reference group*. We shall trace the history and the revisions of such concepts and document some of their recent applications, for example, in the area of deviant behavior. A central distinction, as we shall see, is between membership group and reference group. Once this is understood, it becomes clear why human behavior so often fails to reflect those groups to which the individual belongs and those others with whom he is in direct interaction.

The origins of socialization theory

As we saw, Mead (1934) discussed the development of the self under the impact of significant others and, eventually, the generalized other. The former are the individual's immediate others, his parents, his peers, those people who exert their influence during primary socialization, as well as others who exert profound and lasting influence on him. The latter is the total community or group into which the individual is eventually socialized.

As Hyman and Singer (1971:67) point out, the ancient and almost self-evident notion that men act in accordance with the groups of which they are a part is at times belied by contradictory examples: upper-class individuals with radical ideologies and revolutionary allegiances, the renegade Catholic, the nonconformist who comes from an orthodox milieu, etc. It is via the concept of reference group that such cases can be reconciled with the fundamental principles of socialization. Hyman (1942) was the first to distinguish between a *membership group* (the group to which someone actually belongs) and a *reference group* (the group which someone employs as a basis of comparison for self-appraisal). "The fact that men may shape their attitudes by reference to groups other than their own and their self-evalua-

tions by the choice of unusual points of social comparison is perhaps the most distinctive contribution of reference group theory" (Hyman and Singer, 1971:67).

Other early contributions to reference group theory by psychologists include those of Newcomb (1943), who studied attitude change among the students of Bennington College, and Sherif (1948), who recognized the importance of reference groups in his textbook. An important extension made by Newcomb was the distinction between *positive* and *negative reference groups*. For example, an upwardly mobile person coming from a poor family may use the working class as a negative reference group—he dislikes the group from which he originates and aspires to become a member of the upper class, which is his positive reference group.

Sociologists who made early contributions to reference group theory include Stouffer and associates (1949) and Merton and Kitt (1950). In *The American Soldier,* Stouffer found that a soldier's dissatisfaction did not always reflect the actual extent of his deprivation but the standards he used in evaluating his deprivation. For example, Southern blacks felt generally happier in the army than Northern blacks. Merton and Kitt explained this through the concept of *relative deprivation:* the reason why the Southern black felt less deprived than his Northern brother was that he evaluated his condition relative to that of the Southern black civilian, whereas the Northern black soldier used the better-off Northern black civilian as a standard.

The central import of reference group theory, then, is that "individuals may orient themselves to groups other than their own, not merely to their membership groups, and (this) explains why the attitudes and behavior of individuals may deviate from what would be predicted on the basis of their group membership" (Hyman and Singer, 1971:69). A reference group, then, is not necessarily a membership group; it may be an *identification group.* This is the fundamental distinction.

Other early contributions highlighting this distinction include Festinger (1954), Smith et al. (1956), Merton and Rossi (1957), and Siegel and Siegel (1973). Festinger's theory of *social comparison* parallels the earlier findings of *The American Soldier:* individuals, Festinger suggests, tend to compare themselves with others close to their own level of ability, or status. Smith and his colleagues found that the attitudes *held* by an individual tend to reflect his reference group, while the attitudes *expressed* tend to reflect the membership group. Indeed, since the membership group will sanction an individual member who *reveals* nonconformity, it can be expected that an individual will conform to his membership group overtly, even though his private thoughts may reflect a different group— his reference group.

Merton also coined the concept of *anticipatory socialization,* the process whereby an individual adopts the attitudes of a group to which he does not yet belong—a reference group—but which he hopes to join at a later point. For example, to a graduate student who anticipates becoming a professor, the student body is the membership group, but the faculty is his reference group.

A study by Siegel and Siegel (1973) deals with the crucial distinction between reference group and membership group. Two groups of college students were compared. Both had sororities as their reference groups, but after their freshman year, only one of the groups was permitted to go live in the sorority houses, at which point that group's reference group and membership group became identical. The other girls had to live elsewhere. The authors found that the students who joined their reference groups (who moved into the sororities they had pledged) retained the attitudes prevailing in those sororities, whereas the students who could not move

in gradually developed different attitudes.

Although the Siegel study shows that membership in one's reference group strengthens one's conformity to that group's attitudes, it remains to be emphasized that physical membership is merely one form of group membership. Indeed, the distinction between membership group and reference group acquires an entirely different meaning if it is realized, in accordance with symbolic interactionist principles, that group membership may be *symbolic* as well as physical. For example, in a symbolic sense, the conservative lower middle-class individual is a member of the ruling establishment. Marxists may term his consciousness "false," but the fact remains that he identifies with the ruling class, that he equates his interests with the status quo, and that he is therefore part of those.

Revisions of socialization theory

Everett Hughes (1962) was one of the first sociologists to point out, impatiently, that it is one thing to state the obvious truism that individuals react to others, but quite another to systematically examine the extent and direction of this sensitivity. Previous insights into this question had been provided by W. I. Thomas and F. Znaniecki (1918-1920) and David Riesman (1950). Thomas and Znaniecki had distinguished between three personality types— the philistine, the bohemian, and the creative man. The first of these could be characterized as excessively conforming to others' expectations, the second insufficiently so. The creative type is the kind of person who is capable of responding to others in a selective and constructive fashion. Riesman's distinction between inner-directed, other-directed, and autonomous man is similar. While the first of these types was typical of the rugged nineteenth century pioneering individualist, the twentieth century has seen the ascendency of the second type, the conformist, the role-player, the "selfless" individual who is totally group-oriented, that is, other-directed. Riesman wishes for the advent of autonomous man, a happy balance between the other two extremes.

Hughes' recommendations follow this tradition, pointing out that the self's responsiveness to others is a variable. "Many of the saints, the heretics and villains, have fanatically rejected the opinions of all 'others'—wife, children, kin, friends, class, brothers in the faith, and professional colleagues" (Hughes, 1962:121). And when it comes to the question "what other?" in today's world, the professions are often among the most "significant" others toward which conduct is directed (op. cit.:125). In fact, a new profession may, as a whole, use an already established profession as its reference group. Thus social work's "other" has been psychiatry, sociology's and psychology's other (or model, if you wish) has been physical science, for nurses it has been physicians, and so forth.

Manford Kuhn (1964) also reconsidered the concepts of the other and the reference group. He introduced an important new concept, that of the *orientational other.* Denzin (1966), who tested this concept, defined it in contradistinction to the *role-specific other.* The orientational other is the kind of person who is important to the individual transsituationally, who provides him with his basic vocabulary, self-concept, and the like. The role-specific other is only significant to the individual in a highly role-specific sense. For example, an individual's parents may be (among) his orientational others, whereas his teachers or his employers may only be role-specific others.

Additional refinements and extensions of reference group theory have been provided by Shibutani (1955; 1961), Rose (1962), Kemper (1968), and Schmitt (1972). Shibutani discussed the idea of social world, the "culture area, the boundaries of which are set neither by territory nor by formal group membership, but by the limits of effective communication" (Shibutani, 1961:130), and this led him to a redefinition of reference group as an *audience,* as "that group, real or imaginary, whose standpoint is being used as the frame of reference by the actor" (op.

cit.:257). A reference group, Shibutani (1962) also pointed out, is a *perspective.*

Kemper examined the relationship between reference groups and achievement. He suggested that three different types of reference groups act together to foster achievement: the normative group, the role model, and the audience. "The normative group defines the roles the individual is to assume, the model provides exemplification of how the role is to be performed . . . and the audience provides anticipation of rewards for outstanding performance in the role" (Kemper, 1968:31).

Rose (1962:11) argued that the concept "reference relationship" would be better than reference group, and Schmitt (1972), who surveyed the reference group literature, combined the entire discussion under the concept "reference other."

Some recent applications

Apart from such isolated instances as Foote's (1955) humorous article about the dog as one of man's developmental significant others, most empirical tests of Meadian socialization theory are relatively recent. Denzin (1966), as stated previously, tested Kuhn's distinction between the orientational other and the role-specific other in a college population. He found, for example, that female college students tend to mention family members as orientational others more frequently than do male students. As far as role-specific others are concerned, Denzin found that males tend to orient themselves more to faculty during their freshman year and less so later. Females orient themselves increasingly toward relatives and friends as they move through college.

Moore, Schmitt, and Grupp (1973) retested the very same concepts, using the same format as Denzin. Unlike that author, however, they did not find significant differences between males and females or between different college classes. They did, on the other hand, support Denzin's conclusion that individuals tend to use different others as their orientational others and as their role-specific others. Predictably, faculty and administrators were more often mentioned as role-specific others, while family and friends were more frequently mentioned as orientational others.

Webster and associates (1972) tested six alternative models of the ways in which individuals accept and organize information from others. In other words, how do various significant others influence the individual? The authors concluded that a simple "additive model" is the best, that is, people evaluate information acquired from others and use it in a simple additive fashion. This research was subsequently criticized and defended by Shelly (1974) and Webster and co-workers (1974) on methodological grounds.

Hartnagel (1974) recently studied the measurement of the significance of others, using data collected through the semantic differential. He concluded that current methodology (such as partial correlations) has not dealt adequately with the concept of "significant other," that this concept has either inadequately been researched or is itself simply inadequate.

In a larger sense, reference group theory has perhaps received its widest application in the areas of deviance, crime, and delinquency (cf. Clark, 1972). This goes back to Sutherland's (1947) differential association theory, which states that crime is a form of behavior which, like any other behavior, is learned and which will be committed by individuals who have been widely exposed to reference groups that favor law violation. Reference groups, then, account for deviant and delinquent behavior, as they account for other behavior. This involves, among other things, role models (cf. Glaser, 1973).

Drug use is a case in point. As Becker (1953; 1962) shows, one becomes a mari-

juana user when general social controls are replaced by those of a subculture, that is, when one is socialized into such a particular (normative) reference group. One learns to enjoy marijuana by adopting a definition of the situation that defines the experience as enjoyable.

Johnson and Cressey (1963) studied the rehabilitation of heroin addicts who joined Synanon. Their main finding was that joining and remaining in the antidrug community significantly reduced the probability of relapse. This supports Sutherland's theory of differential association and reference group theory in general.

Recently, Weis (1974) extended Becker's work by specifying different types (or styles) of drug use among middle-class suburban adolescents. He identified such adolescent types as "hard guys" (the "punks" who are status losers within the school and whose domain is the street), "brains" (the studious and intelligent students), "hippies," "athletes," and "city-goers" (those whose social ties and reference points are mostly in the central city). The different ways and extent to which each of these types participated in the drug scene were examined, and the importance of the *learning milieu* was stressed. This study is therefore another application of reference group theory in the area of deviance and delinquency.

In sum, the central issue in this section has been the socializing impact of others on the self. In a way, the many experimental studies by social psychologists on group influence also have relevance in this context. Chapter 2 reviewed, for example, work by Asch (1942) and Newcomb (1953; 1956) on group pressure toward conformity, Festinger (1954) on social comparison, Sherif (1935) on the autokinetic effect, and Lambert and Lowy (1957) on the convergence of group attitudes. However, the development of the self is most significantly affected by a variety of influences that cannot be studied in a laboratory setting—for example, institutional sources of influence (the individual's school and his occupation), the individual's position in the social structure (notably his social class), and other cultural influences (the individual's nation, his religion, the cultural, economic, and political system in which he grows up). The sum of an individual's attitudes and personality—his total self— reflect all these influences. This is why no two individuals are identical and why no single person can develop a comprehensive and objective perspective. We all reflect the partial influences under which we have been socialized.

WHAT DOES SOCIALIZATION DO?

In this section, we survey two further broad areas of socialization. First, the various processes that have been conceptualized by social psychologists in their studies of various aspects of socialization will be discussed. Basically, according to behaviorists, socialization is a learning process. However, there is much more to it than just that. What is meant, for example, by *internalization*? How does this process lead to self-control and morality? What is *habitualization*? How does this differ from such pathological developments as *addiction* and *fixation*? What are *acculturation* and *enculturation*? These and other related concepts will be discussed and documented, in an effort to clarify some of the major dimensions of socialization discussed in the literature.

In addition, we shall survey some of the substantive contents of socialization, for example, roles, symbols (language), morality (values), self-control, personal identity, self-esteem, and culture. These are among the things acquired through the various processes of socialization.

How does socialization work?

Sociology, psychology, and anthropology have all been interested in socialization, albeit with different emphases. All three disciplines have, at times, been guilty of a biased conception of socialization and this has led to a great deal of confusion in terminology. Social psychology may provide a balanced understanding of the process if it succeeds in disentangling a number of related concepts and thereby indicating the different possibilities within socialization.

As Dennis Wrong (1961) pointed out in his classic paper on the oversocialized conception of man, functionalist sociology has tended to equate socialization, internalization, and habitualization. This goes back to Durkheim's distinction between external and internal controls and his view that man learns to conform to the norms and morality of his culture by gradually internalizing them, a process of gradual substitution of internal conscience for external controls. According to this view, the socialized adult obeys the law not out of fear of apprehension by the police but out of his internal conscience. Parsonian sociology in America has more or less adopted the same view.

Freud, too, contributed to this view through his concept of the superego; which is the inner conscience, the morality of society internalized. Although Freud did not forget that inner tension between the forces of individualism and the internalized forces of society—between the id and the superego—remain, he too helped create the idea that a socialized person is simply one who has internalized the culture and its moral code.

Many learning theorists have been guilty of a similar kind of simplification. As Maccoby (1968) showed, socialization to them has often meant the same thing as learning and the internalization of self-control. This takes place through such processes as positive reinforcement, conditioning, negative reinforcement, extinction, stimulus generalization, and discrimination.

Even Piaget's developmental theory, while different from learning theory, views moral development as proceeding through a process of internalization that eventually leads to moral autonomy (cf. Maccoby, 1968).

In anthropology, finally, one finds many authors who practically equate socialization and enculturation (or acculturation). The three terms are sometimes used nearly interchangeably (cf. Williams, 1972; Theodorson and Theodorson, 1969). They are defined as either the transmission of culture or its acquisition, that is internalization, and the process is explained largely in terms of learning theory (cf. Williams, 1972).

The following problems emerge from the foregoing: on the basis of an implicit or explicit distinction between external and internal (moral) controls, it is generally believed that socialization produces moral behavior (such things as altruism, autonomy, conformity; cf. Maccoby, 1968) because it consists of the internalization of control and morality—self-control replaces social control. Socialization is viewed as the internalization of culture and values. This explains the confusion with respect to such terms as socialization, internalization, and habitualization, used synonymously, for example, by Berger and Luckmann (1966); socialization and en- or acculturation (cf. Williams, 1972; Theodorson and Theodorson, 1969); and socialization and learning (cf. Maccoby, 1968; Wrong, 1961).

Fortunately, several sociologists (such as Lindesmith, Strauss, and Denzin, 1975; Shibutani, 1961; Stone and Farberman, 1970; Wrong, 1961) do recognize the profound difference between socialization on the one hand and such related but narrower terms as internalization, learning, enculturation, and habitualization on the other.

Wrong (1961) shows, in the first place, that man conforms to societal expectations not only because he has internalized those expectations but also because, as Sullivan stressed, of a fundamental (but variable!) anxiety and need for acceptance. One does not necessarily conform in order to reduce one's guilt, as "internalization theory" would have it, since one often feels guilty and uneasy precisely because one has been

a (cowardly) conformist instead of following one's inner dictates. Even more crucial is Wrong's point that socialization does not necessarily mean conformity at all. Human behavior, as Stone and Farberman (1970:13-14) point out, must be approached dialectically, always recognizing *both* the mechanisms that may produce social order and integration (such processes as internalization and conformity) *and* the principles of individuality referred to by such concepts as the id and the I. Man, Wrong concludes, is social, but not necessarily socialized in the sense that he inevitably internalizes his culture and conforms to it. A totally static conception of human social behavior would, Maccoby (1968) recognizes, make intergenerational change not understandable.

To be socialized, then, is to be human. It does not necessarily mean being a perfect role-player, being as other-directed as Riesman and associates (1950) see the emerging typical American. As Goffman (1961) showed, roles may be played with role-distance, as in the case of the surgeon or medic who performs with visible detachment. It is true that all men who grow up in human society are socialized. Only feral children are not. To what extent each of us has internalized certain values and been acculturated (or enculturated) is an empirical question. The idea that socialization always means conformity may simply be a reflection of the particular era in which we live. If such a model of man is made into a fundamental postulate—"sociological man" replacing such earlier models as "economic man" or "political man"—it is not because it is any more in accordance with basic human nature than were those earlier models but because it reflects the modal behavior in bureaucratic mass society. Since human behavior is essentially reflexive, there is of course no possibility of a permanent self-fulfilling prophecy whereby "sociological man"—Mills' "cheerful robot," Marcuse's one-dimensional man—would become, indeed, natural man. Our awareness of that possibility precludes it.

A few additional terms must now be mentioned briefly. Beyond habit formation (which, as we saw, is only one minor dimension of socialization), there are also such phenomena as fixation and addiction. These terms are used to denote the more extreme and pathological forms of learned behavior. Examples of fixations may include excessive chattering, obesity, drinking, smoking, and the compulsive pursuit of pleasures. As Shibutani (1961:495) points out, fixations have a *defensive* function, they are defense mechanisms or defensive meanings held rigidly in order to avoid pain or anxiety. Maier (1949) found that rats develop two types of stable behavior patterns—habits and fixations. Habits were established through rewards. Fixations developed as defense mechanisms under frustrating conditons, when the animals were unable to reach their goal. Maier found that habits could be modified by altering the reward patterns (for example, using food as a positive reinforcement or electric shocks as a negative one) but that punishment of a fixation merely strengthens it rather than extinguishes it.

Addiction to drugs, according to Lindesmith, Strauss, and Denzin (1975:224-234), is one type of fixation. The main point about addiction to a heavy drug such as heroin is that it only occurs after the individual has realized that nonuse of the drug produces certain painful withdrawal effects and that these effects can only be avoided by using the drug. Thus while the withdrawal reaction is biological (it occurs in newborn infants whose mothers are addicts and in animals), addiction to the drug is not the same thing as the habit itself, and neither can it be explained on the grounds of the "pleasure" provided by the drug, since placebos have been found to produce the same amount of pleasure as the drug itself. In order for addiction to become established, the individual must first label his withdrawal pain and connect it with drug use. It is the withdrawal distress, recognized by the patient, that causes addiction, and not the pleasurable effect of the drug (Lindesmith, Strauss, and Denzin, 1975:

231). Since addiction only occurs after the individual has arrived at a certain definition of the situation, one cannot say that animals can be "addicted."

What does socialization provide?

While the previous section dealt with the "how" of socialization, we now turn to the "what." Danziger (1971) discusses such "outcomes" of socialization as sex typing, moral development, ego development, and cognitive functioning. These are the things we mean by "contents." What, specifically, is it that is being transmitted and acquired through socialization? It is cognitive skills (language), roles, an internalized morality (conscience), a culture, components of identity such as gender and personal idiom, ego development, and personality.

As we saw in Chapter 7, the acquisition of language is the sine qua non for the development of the self. It is primarily as a demonstration of this fundamental fact that studies of feral children, "wolf children" who were not raised by any other human beings and merely managed to survive biologically (cf. Davis, 1940; 1947; Itard, 1932; Malson, 1972; Ogburn, 1959), have relevance. The development of cognitive skills may occur quite late without causing permanent retardation. Davis' (1947) paper documents the case of a feral girl, Isabelle, who was nearly seven when she was discovered but who subsequently managed to catch up, doing as well as her age mates in school. Within a year and a half, Isabelle's IQ tripled. Kagan's (1973) study of Guatemalan Indians, who are sometimes totally neglected during their first years of childhood, also shows that these children catch up later on.

Whether cognitive-linguistic socialization occurs early or late depends on such factors as culture, biography, and accident. However, sooner or later the prototaxic stage, as Sullivan (1953) shows us, must make way for the parataxic and eventually the syntaxic stage in order for the individual to develop a competent self. One of the early aspects of this development is the mastery over personal names and pronouns (cf. Cooley, 1909; Denzin, 1972), which, more than anything else, provides a *sense of self.*

Hess and Shipman (1974) studied a topical aspect of cognitive socialization—the differential acquisition of language by children from middle-class and from culturally disadvantaged backgrounds. These researchers interviewed a sample of black mothers ranging from college-educated upper middle-class professionals to lower-class welfare recipients. They found a correlation between this variable and a linguistic dependent variable, namely the kind of language the mother tends to use as she addresses her child: (upper) middle-class mothers tended to use elaborated codes, whereas lower-class mothers used more restricted codes. That is, lower-class communication is more direct, concrete, and restricted. For example, a child is merely told to "shut up." In the middle class, communication is more elaborate. For example, a child will be told "please keep quiet for a minute; I want to talk on the phone." The linguistic socialization of lower-class children puts them at a disadvantage, for restricted codes do not enable an individual to handle abstractions and complex problems. This is why lower-class ghetto children cannot cope in school.

Socialization also means the transmission and acquisition of roles. Mead, of course, stressed the inseparability of socialization into language and socialization into roles. Flavell (1974) provides a framework to study this process, the development of role-taking and communication skills. He traces previous theoretical contributions by Mead (1934), Piaget (1926), and Vygotsky (1962) and zeroes in, as did the last author, on the crucial difference between *inner speech* and *social speech.* Inner speech is always condensed and abbrevi-

ated, and it needs to be extensively recoded before accurate social communication can take place. For example, the inner verbal expression of "I guess I'll go there tomorrow" might be "go tomorrow" or simply "tomorrow." As Vygotsky (1962:145) stated, "it is as much a law of inner speech to omit subjects as it is a law of written speech to contain both subjects and predicates." Thus inner speech is egocentric, that is, it is typical of the way children communicate. The hallmark of adult social communication is that such egocentric speech is recoded into nonegocentric forms when it is externalized. Only in this fashion does accurate role-taking occur; only thus can the gulf between speaker and listener be bridged.

Moral development is another facet of socialization. We saw in the previous section that most social scientists have conceived of this as a process of internalization. For example, Freud's concept of the superego stands for the internalized morality of society, that is, for society's morality transmitted to the individual through socializing agents such as the father and internalized by the individual. It means the same thing as conscience, and conscience is socially acquired. Piaget (1932) traces the moral development of children from an egocentric stage to an autonomous stage, a stage at which the child has "interiorized" rules, following them out of a sense of respect and cooperation (see Maccoby, 1968). Sociologists have often adopted the same view, arguing that self-control gradually replaces external control (cf. Shibutani, 1961). However, we saw in the previous section that this process of internalization should not be taken for granted. As Wrong (1961), Maccoby (1968), and others have argued, socialization does not preclude disagreement with existing rules and change from one generation to the next.

Anthropologists have dealt largely with static and homogeneous societies, and this has led many of them to equate socialization, enculturation (also called acculturation), and internalization (cf. Williams,

1972). Here the general idea is that socialization consists of internalizing the *culture* in which one grows up, including its language and its values.

Enculturation is also what occurs when a member of one culture suddenly joins another. Kroeber described the American Indian Ishi, who was discovered in California in 1911. Ishi was the latest survivor of the Yahi tribe and he had, up to his discovery by whites, succeeded in avoiding all contacts with Western culture. Once he was brought into American society, he underwent a process of drastic enculturation. This is one of the most spectacular cases on record. Ishi's enculturation was nearly as drastic as the socialization of feral children, the only difference being that the Indian's point of departure, unlike that of wolf children, was an aboriginal culture of which he was the sole surviving representative.

Anthropology has also produced the so-called culture and personality school, which uses psychoanalytic principles to explain different "modal" personalities found in different societies. Psychoanalytic psychology, as we saw, holds that an individual's personality is largely determined by the way he was weaned, nursed, swaddled, toilet trained, and generally treated during his earliest infancy. Otto Rank even stressed the birth trauma itself, arguing that it is a major source of anxiety in later life. Spitz (1945) argued that maternal deprivation leads to a pathological condition—marasmus.

Following these ideas, anthropologists like Kardiner (1939; 1945) and Cora DuBois (1944) developed and tested the proposition that different societies produce different modal or basic personality types because they rear their children differently. Cora DuBois, for example, studied the Alorese people, who live on the island of Timor in Eastern Indonesia. She described the overall treatment of children in Alor as one of neglect and inconsistency. The Alorese mother works hard in the fields and has little time for her child. The child's hunger pangs are irregularly met. Sometimes whoever happens to be around absentmindedly masturbates the child to calm him down. The breast-seeking child is often pushed away or slapped. As a consequence, DuBois and Kardiner argue, the basic personality that Alorese people develop is one of distrust, fearfulness, and deception. Adults have a weak ego and social conscience. They are selfish and unreliable. Alorese institutions also reflect this. For example, when the Alorese wage war against another tribe, it is a disorganized and vengeful enterprise. The economy is a primitive and egotistical form of capitalism. Religious art is careless and irreverent. The most common motifs in Alorese folklore are parental frustration and hatred. For example:

> In one tale, a child is told by his mother to fetch some water with a water tube which she has deliberately punctured at the bottom. While the child is vainly attempting to fill the tube the parents abandon him. Years later, at his marriage feast, the parents reappear and are presented with food tubes filled with feces. (Kardiner and Preble, 1961:218-219)

The culture and personality school refers to the whole complex of child treatment as the *primary institutions* and to the other social institutions such as religion, government, and mythology as the *secondary institutions*. The basic hypothesis states that a society's primary institutions pro-

FIG. 9-1
The culture and personality thesis.

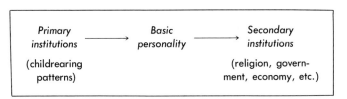

Primary institutions → Basic personality → Secondary institutions

(childrearing patterns)

(religion, government, economy, etc.)

duce the basic personality of its members and that this personality, in turn, affects the nature of that society's secondary institutions. Fig. 9-1 summarizes the hypothesis.

A similar logic has been applied to other peoples. Geoffrey Gorer (1951) has explained the Russian national character as follows: Russian babies have traditionally been swaddled very tightly during the first year of life. Occasionally, however, (for example at feeding and bathing time), they are unswaddled and enjoy complete freedom of movement for a brief period of time. This early contrast between total restraint of motion and total freedom accounts, according to Gorer, for the typical Russian character, which is highly temperamental and submissive on the one hand but frustrated, aggressive, and hostile on the other. This shows why Russians are so unpredictable, at times submissive and gentle but frequently also violent and revolutionary.

Similarly Gorer (1943) traced the character of adult Japanese back to their early childhood training. The Japanese baby is carried spread-eagled on the back of his mother during the first two years of life. Also, the Japanese house is dangerous for the baby—built of fragile material and heated with open charcoal burners. These early forms of body discipline account for the impassivity and the anxiety about proper etiquette, sitting, and bowing typical of adult Japanese.

Margaret Mead's (1942) analysis of the American national character runs along similar lines. American children feel anxiety as to whether they will successfully retain parental love. This love is conditional, given only if the child achieves certain performance standards and certain goals set for him. However, these goals are generally well within the child's reach and can be achieved with some but not too much effort. Hence, adult Americans are success-oriented, competitive, and boastful, but they are also optimistic.

Because of the worldwide impact of German National Socialism three decades ago, numerous speculations have been written about German national character and the childhood socialization practices that could account for it. The general argument has been that, historically, the parent-child relationship in Germany has been a rigidly authoritarian one, the child being totally submissive and the father all-domineering. This, presumably, explains the traditional German blind submission to authority and hierarchy, his acceptance of his "place," his insistence on rank and title. Also, the repression of the tender tie with the devoted, despised, but idealized mother explains that sentimental longing for a lost happiness and a promised land, the emotional difficulties of adolescence and the introspective and tormented self-dissection (Dicks, 1950).[2]

Culture and personality anthropology has been criticized from the very moment it appeared, particularly on the grounds of its (Freudian) assumptions and its speculative and ill-founded generalizations (cf. Lindesmith and Strauss, 1956; Orlansky, 1949; Shibutani, 1961). Indeed, explanations such as Gorer's and Mead's can degenerate into facile ad hoc generalizations that amount to little more than chauvinistic stereotypes of some outgroup. As argued earlier in this chapter, there is little evidence to support the extreme childhood determinism of the Freudian and culture and personality schools, and much evidence (cf. Kagan, 1973; Sewell, 1952) that refutes it. As Orlansky (1949) pointed out, postinfantile experiences are probably more important than prelingual ones. Nevertheless, anyone with cross-cultural experience has to be struck by the amazing similarities in character traits sometimes shared by the members of a society and clearly distin-

---

[2]For summary treatments of culture and personality anthropology, see Deutsch and Krauss (1965) and Hoebel (1966). For critical appraisals, see Lindesmith and Strauss (1956) and Shibutani (1961). For an anthology of culture and personality writings, see Kaplan (1961).

guishing them from those of another. As statisticians say, within-group variation is frequently far less than between-group variation. Thus the study of national character (cf. Martindale, 1967) must be recognized as a valid enterprise. Social scientists continue to discover many interesting cross-cultural and cross-national differences, and many of these are indeed the outcome of different socialization practices. For example, Clausen (1966) found that French children conform more to adults while American children conform more to their peers. Rosenblatt (1966), sampling twenty-one societies from the Human Relations Area Files, found a strong correlation between oral frustration (in childhood) and belief in romantic love (as a basis of marriage later on). Other interesting cross-cultural differences in socialization and personality are reported in Lambert and Weisbrod (1971).

Thus far we have seen that socialization means the transmission and acquisition of (1) language, (2) roles, (3) morality, and, generally, (4) culture, personality, and perhaps a national character—although this fourth aspect of socialization, studied primarily by anthropologists, is by no means cleared up at this time.

In addition, we must now mention identities (for example gender), individual idiom, and such things as ego development and self-esteem.

Identity will be discussed in detail in the next chapter. Here, we merely mention that it, too, is a content or "outcome" of socialization and that it consists of such components as occupational, racial, and gender identity. Gender identity is the outcome of sex typing. In every society, little boys are socialized into men and little girls into women, learning the roles that are appropriate for their sex and learning to think of themselves as men or as women. In some rare instances, as I (1972; 1973) showed, the socialization process fails and men grow up thinking that they are women and vice versa. As Richard Green and John Money (1969) have shown, the causes of this condition—transsexualism—

clearly lie in faulty socialization. The parents may, for example, have wanted a little girl and when a boy is born they begin to treat him like a little girl anyway, giving him girl's toys, girl's clothes, and the like. In some instances, the little boy simply does not know that he is a boy. By the time he begins school at age five, six, or seven, he has firmly internalized a feminine gender identity and self-concept. Doctors, teachers, and friends may try to confront him with an inescapable biological reality—after all, he has a penis—but psychology prevails over biology: the boy "knows" that he is a girl. Eventually, he may, as thousands have in the United States over the past decade, undergo sex change surgery so as to adjust his body to his mind, thereby moving in a direction opposite to that of conventional psychotherapy, which is of course essentially an effort to change the mind.

Individual idiom must also be recognized as an important outcome of socialization. As Shibutani (1961:565) explains, not all people who grow up in the same (cultural) environment turn out alike, and often people from very different backgrounds resemble one another. Thus with biological, cultural, and biographical factors all affecting personal development, it must be recognized that in the end every one of us is, to some extent, idiosyncratic.

Ultimately, social psychologists must ask what constitutes a "desirable" outcome of socialization and this raises, again, matters of value. Smith (1968) deals with "competence" and socialization, offering a conception of a competent self that incorporates such features as hope and self-respect. Many psychologists would also agree that a "healthy" and competent self is an individual with a well-developed ego and self-esteem. However, let us, again, keep in mind that these are the arbitrary contents given to socialization by twentieth century humanistic psychiatrists whose conception of mental health and proper socialization is as culture-bound as the antithesis they reject. For example, the earlier Christian ethic had argued precisely the opposite, namely that a mature and good man is a humble man (cf. Gergen, 1971). Similarly, the Eastern philosophies that reached our shores during the countercultural 1960s state that a strong ego and self-love are negative assets, not signs of mental health and proper socialization. In conclusion, if the ideas of proper socialization and interpersonal competence are to be salvaged, they must be restricted to *communicative* competence.

LATER STAGES OF SOCIALIZATION

According to Berger and Luckmann (1966), secondary socialization consists of the internalization of institutional subworlds, that is, the acquisition of role-specific knowledge, of roles rooted in the division of labor. Since the content of secondary socialization is superimposed on that of primary socialization, personal life is easiest and secondary socialization most effective when there is consistency between the two. It makes more sense for a gentle young man raised in intellectual, contemplative, and peaceful values to opt for a career in academia or the ministry than in rock and roll or the marines.

Secondary socialization need not be as affective as primary socialization: one loves one's mother but need not love one's instructors. The agents of secondary socialization are, then, not significant others. They are role-specific rather than orientational others (cf. Denzin, 1966; Kuhn, 1964). There is nothing inevitable about what they transmit to us. Majoring in psychology and becoming a social worker are merely choices made out of many alternatives. It is possible to establish *role distance* from the content of secondary socialization, but not from that of primary socialization. One can separate one's self from those specific roles. An employee of the city animal control department is more

likely to take offense if he is told that he is not a real man (through such short-hand terms as "sissy" or "faggot") than if he is accused of being a poor animal controller. We are far more emotionally involved in such primary identities as gender than in the specific roles acquired through secondary socialization.

It follows that the more secondary socialization approximates the effective character of primary socialization, the more effective it is likely to be. Institutions such as churches, the military, fraternities, rehabilitation centers, political parties, and therapy groups understand that in order to gain a recruit's lasting commitment, they must make his socialization an intense emotional experience. In this section, we examine various forms of secondary socialization, including those intensely traumatic experiences termed conversions and brainwashing.

Adolescence

Although social psychology was earlier guilty of neglecting all phases of socialization beyond childhood, this lacuna is now being filled. Elder (1972), for example, has written a book that attempts to integrate the theories of Sullivan, Piaget, and Erikson and that deals with adolescent socialization in such areas as interpersonal competence, self-esteem, identity formation, moral development, vocational development, and even physical growth. Kagan and Coles (1972) have assembled a very good reader dealing with the same areas among early adolescents, from age twelve to sixteen.

Cavan's (1970) content analysis of children's etiquette books deals with three age categories: young children (from four to eight), preadolescents (from eight to twelve), and adolescents (from thirteen to eighteen). The author shows how etiquette books gradually socialize children into an adult world view. Whereas the view presented in the books addressed to the youngest children is a utopia in which honesty and virtue always prevail, by the time adolescence is reached the youngster is taught that vice, jealousy, hostility, selfishness, and fraudulence are inevitable features of human nature and society. Dating manuals, for example, explicitly teach how to lie, manipulate, and succeed with fraudulence.

Thomas and Weigert (1971) did a cross-cultural study of adolescent conformity, comparing middle-class Catholic youngsters in New York, St. Paul, Puerto Rico, and Yucatan. They found, predictably, that those four settings rank as listed in terms of the youngsters' conformity to "authoritative others" (that is, parents) and that parental *support* is more conducive to conformity than parental *control.*

Conformity has been one persistent theme in the sociological literature on adolescence (see also Hollingshead, 1949). In America, particularly in certain lower-class delinquent subcultures (cf. Cohen, 1955), it is the peer group that above all commands conformity. In France (Clausen, 1966) and in more traditional settings generally, parents are more important in that respect. Related to conformity is that other oft-cited adolescent characteristic—insecurity (cf. Rose, 1944).

One thing is known: in American society, adolescence is a problematic stage of the life cycle, and the reasons for this are sociological. If American adolescents are insecure and as a result often blindly conform to a variety of social pressures, including pressure toward delinquency, it is because of social arrangements peculiar to our society and not universal. As Lewis (1972) and I (1975) and other students of modern youth culture have shown, the teenager or the adolescent as a social identity is just as clearly a historical creation as the earlier identity of child (cf. Aries, 1968; Stone, 1965). Only since World War II has the teenager been a prominent presence on the American scene, and this is probably the result of economic forces—the teenager represents an important category of consumers.

The teenager, then, is a postwar American creation and one that was, incidentally, exported to other parts of the world only several years later as part of the mod-rock explosion, which, although by now a near worldwide uniculture, clearly originated on Madison Avenue. At the same time, the American adolescent's social-psychological condition is not a rosy one. As Friedenberg (1963), Gottlieb (1974), and others (see the reader by Manning and Truzzi, 1972) point out, they are second-class citizens, often legally discriminated against. The crux of the problem has been stated by Bloch and Niederhoffer (1958) in the context of delinquency sociology. The trouble with our social structure, these authors suggest, is that it fails to provide puberty rites and other formal status passages which in other, non-Western societies confer social-psychological manhood on the boy. In America, adolescence is a social-psychological identity crisis, a void where the individual is no longer a child but neither yet a man, in terms of rights and responsibilities. It is this void and undignified position that gangs and delinquent behavior attempt, in a perverted way, to remedy. Goodman (1960) made a similar point in *Growing Up Absurd,* a point as valid today as ever.

Adulthood and beyond

Sewell's (1963) review of recent developments in socialization research points out again that the earlier dominance of the field by psychoanalytic psychology and its excessive preoccupation with early childhood have now been tempered by the role-theoretical study of later socialization. A good example is Brim (1968), whose paper discusses the three major areas of adult socialization—occupational, family, and community socialization. Another is Becker (1970), who discusses personal change in such adult settings as college, medical school, and prison along the change-stability axis: situations make for change, Becker argues, and commitments make for stability. The author's notion of "side bets" is interesting: the longer one remains in a situation, the more likely one is to become committed or "rooted" to that situation. For example, the more years a college professor has taught at a particular institution, the more likely he is to have bought a home, obtained tenure, developed community ties, established a family, in sum pulled roots. These "side bets" diminish an individual's potential for mobility.

With Becker's article we have already touched on one major area of adult socialization—occupational career. Ashton (1974) examines the transition from school to work, distinguishing three patterns: the careerless, the working-class career, and the middle-class career. In each pattern there is clear continuity between school and work. Layder (1974) distinguishes two different types of middle-class careers, one termed bureaucratic and one public-audience. The bureaucratic career is a closed one in terms of roles, statuses, rights, and obligations. The public-audience career is much freer. Examples of the latter would include freelance artists and professionals.

Layder's distinction is probably related to the classic sociological distinction between *localites* and *cosmopolites* (see, for example, Gouldner, 1957-1958; Merton, 1957; Thielbar, 1970). These are two contrasting types of adaptation found in communities and occupational organizations. The localite is the individual who identifies with the local organization or community, striving to achieve local success and recognition. For example, a college faculty member becomes increasingly active in local committees and community affairs and climbs up to become an administrator or local politician. The cosmopolite, on the other hand, identifies with the nationwide professional community of which he is a member. He is much more likely to be mobile. For example, a sociology professor flies around the country to professional conventions and might move to another

university or to a consultant position in Washington.

The sociological concept of career becomes interesting when it assumes a *generic* meaning. That is, the occupational career can be viewed as the model or prototype for "careers" in other spheres of life as well, for example deviance, sex, or social-psychological development. Thus Goffman (1959) traced the moral career of the mental patient. Such a career consists, just like an occupational career, of a step-by-step succession of stages, statuses, roles, and identities, each ushered by status passage, sometimes ritualized, each resembling in some way promotion, demotion, transfer, or some other occupational transition. Similarly, one can speak of the alcoholic's "career," of how becoming an alcoholic constitutes a career (cf. Spradley, 1970).

Becker and Strauss (1956) are among the most eloquent spokesmen for such a use of the career concept. As they phrase it:

> The crises and turning points of life aren't entirely institutionalized, but their occurrence and the terms which define and help to solve them are illuminated when seen in the context of career lines. In so far as some populations do not have careers in the sense that professional and business people have them, then the focus of attention ought still to be positional passage, but with domestic, age, and other escalators to the forefront. This done, it may turn out that the model sketched here must undergo revision. (Becker and Strauss, 1956:263)

These two authors provide additional insights, all stemming from the application of the career concept to both occupational and nonoccupational processes. For example, when an individual passes from one status into another, this may be preceded by ritualized leave-taking and followed by a "probationary" period during which mistakes are tolerantly attributed to a temporary lack of experience. An occupational example would be graduation from college and assumption of one's first teaching job, a transition entailing both a graduation ceremony and a probationary period in the new role. More interesting is the application of the framework to nonoccupational transitions, for example marriage. That transition is, of course, highly ritualized and it, too, may be followed by an initial "grace period" during which the young wife's charcoal a la mode and other bumbling culinary efforts are laughed off by a good-humored husband. Later on, they may be grounds for divorce.

Becker and Strauss also advance the now familiar proposition that those new to a certain status may embrace it with greater zeal than veterans. They may, as the French say, be "plus royaliste que le roi." For example, a rookie patrolman on the police force may at first carry out his law enforcement duties with zeal, enthusiasm, idealism, and rigor, imbued with an awareness of his station and importance in the social order. Later, as a veteran, he may adopt a more compromising and "realistic" attitude and be less apt to cite people for minor infractions.

There is, Becker and Strauss point out, also a mutual interdependence of careers: those who have already escalated the ladder may function as sponsors to those still on their way up, their proteges. This is seen, for example, in the professor–graduate student relationship.

Manning (1970) has written about organizational socialization in a somewhat different vein, but one that deserves mention at this point because it, too, examines the nature of the individual's participation in social organizations. As an ethnomethodologist, Manning emphasizes the importance of language in organizational socialization. That is, socialization into an organization means learning not only the lexicon of the organization but also applying the rules for the use of that lexicon. Since an organization is a constant process of change, Manning would agree that socialization is not something that occurs prior to (effective) participation in the organization but that the two are in fact identical. The socialization process *is* the functioning organization, and socialization into a role ends only when one relinquishes that role.

The ethnomethodologist's approach to socialization is still difficult to integrate into existing social psychology. More in line with what has been discussed thus far are the writings of Strauss (1959) and Glaser and Strauss (1971), whose work on such things as *status passage* and *identity transformation* is, again, an elaboration of the career concept and its application to all areas of life.

The Belgian anthropologist Arnold Van Gennep (1909) was the first to develop the concept of *rite of passage,* documenting its existence in different cultures and showing that it represents a three-phased process of separation, transition, and incorporation. Glaser and Strauss have developed the idea of status passage in great detail, with particular attention to its social-psychological concomitants. As Strauss (1959:108) writes: "the movement from status to status, as well as the frustration of having to remain unwillingly in a status, sets conditions for the change and development of identities."

Strauss also introduced such terms as coaching and scheduling. For example, the psychiatrist can be said to be the coach of his patient, scheduling his identity change and his changing adaptation to the environment.

While we all have a sense of personal identity and continuity, "the awareness of constancy in identity is in the eye of the beholder rather than 'in' the behavior itself" (Strauss, 1959:147). As Erikson said, "a sense of identity is never gained nor maintained once and for all. Like a good conscience, it is constantly lost and regained" (quoted in Strauss, 1959:109). The building of one's present identity often entails redefining past experiences, rewriting history, so to speak. For example, a young man may at one time have engaged in semidelinquent activities that even led to a brush with the law. While that may have seemed a major crisis at the time, eliciting severe condemnation from others and pointing to a career in delinquency, the same man—now a young lawyer with a wife, two children, a suburban home, and a bright career ahead—may at this time feel that he was merely "sowing his wild oats." He has redefined the situation.

Change and continuity are the two fundamental axes of human life. Among the more drastic changes that can occur in a person's life is *conversion*. The term comes initially from religion, meaning of course a sudden change in an individual's religious commitment. However, social psychologists and philosophers have secularized the idea (cf. Burke, 1954), showing that *any* sudden and drastic change in identity and allegiance may be viewed as a conversion. For example, Robert Coles (1973) is a psychologist who began as a detached "scientific" researcher but who subsequently became involved as an activist in radical causes such as the civil rights movement, and this had an effect on his work as well.

Berger (1963:51) has argued that the term *alternation* may be more appropriate than conversion to denote such secular changes in attitudes and identity as experienced by Coles. However, Travisano (1970), who compared Jews who converted to a fundamental Christian faith and Jews who converted to a more liberal faith like Unitarianism, believes that conversion is a very traumatic and basic change, while alternation is a smoother type of transition. For example, when a fiance becomes a husband or when a husband becomes a father, these are instances of alternation, not conversion. Conversion entails a change in general identity; it is very fundamental. Alternation may, as in the examples just given, only mean a cumulative identity sequence: new identities are added on top of earlier identities; the change is not as drastic or traumatic.

A related concept is that of *resocialization*. Criminologists (cf. Landis, Mercer, and Wolff, 1969), for example, have examined the resocialization of criminals into law-abiding citizens and what accounts for success and failure among probationers. Kennedy and Kerber (1973) look at three major areas of resocialization: the rehabilitation of criminals, the training of hardcore unemployed, and compensatory education. Resocialization, then, often refers to the attempt at bringing the disadvantaged and deviants back into the dominant (middle-class) social system.

According to McHugh (1970), resocialization must first be preceded by social disintegration. Here we begin to see that conversion, resocialization, and even alternation all entail, to some extent, some of the processes that are often discussed under the heading of *brainwashing*. McHugh's point is that truly profound personality change can only occur if an individual's former attitudes and social relations have been made meaningless, randomized so to speak.

Lifton (1969) and Schein (1964) are among the psychologists who have studied Chinese brainwashing. Lifton interviewed several Westerners who had been imprisoned by the Chinese communists and subjected to "thought reform." He found that the treatment involved assault upon personal identity, the creation of strong guilt feelings, and the breakdown of social ties. The prisoners eventually broke down and confessed what their captors wished to hear. They in effect underwent the psychological death and rebirth meant by the term conversion. Schein studied American prisoners of war who had been subjected to the same treatment during the Korean War. He too found that the secret to the Chinese success in thought reform was the fact that they worked at the level of the group, not the individual. By breaking down the individual's social ties, identifications, reference groups, and peer-group support, the Chinese accomplished an indoctrination that no amount of cortical intervention—through drugs, hypnosis, electrodes, or whatever else—could have effected.

In Chapter 2 we described a psychological group encounter that used the same principles. Coincidentally or not, that Palo

Alto Institute had been founded by a Chinese. Several other therapy groups in the United States operate in a similar way. Some, like Synanon and Alcoholics Anonymous, successfully "cure" heroin users and alcoholics *as long as the ex-user remains within the reinforcing therapeutic community.* Whether the drastic manipulation of man for purposes of fundamental change is viewed as ruthless and sinister indoctrination or benevolent therapy depends on whose ox is being gored. Most Americans probably believe that brainwashing a prisoner of war into communism is evil, but rehabilitating a criminal or a heroin addict is not. In any event, various sources concur that such resocialization generally involves an attack on a person's identity, the break-up of supportive social ties, the creation of guilt feelings, and the reorganization of the individual's total pattern of beliefs and attitudes.

Besides occupational careers, the other major area in adult socialization consists of the series of marital, postparental, and other role transitions that together make up the life cycle. Many of these roles are sex-specific. As Josselyn (1970) points out, while sexual identity presents the most problems during adolescence, sexual identity crises occur throughout life.

Socialization into marital roles is perhaps the major form of socialization experienced by most adults. While Sewell (1963) deplored the lack of research on this topic, a good subsequent study of precisely this process (among working-class families) was done by Komarovsky (1964). She showed that the couples' socializing agents and role models included relatives and friends of the same sex, in-laws of the same sex, mass media, and, more rarely, relatives and in-laws of the opposite sex as well as experts, such as professional counselors.

Deutscher (1962) examined socialization into the next stage—postparental life. He showed that parents are prepared for this stage through a process of anticipatory socialization. For example, children often leave home temporarily (for example, to go to college) before they leave permanently. This gives parents the opportunity to learn postparental roles ahead of time, and that is why the transition, when it finally comes, is rarely painful.

The next stage, old age, is currently becoming a major concern of American social scientists (for example, Eisdorfer and Lawton, 1973). The study of old age is called *gerontology.* This field is growing because our population pyramid is aging so rapidly. Since 1950, the number of Americans over sixty-five years of age has nearly doubled, from 12.3 million to 21.5 million. Much of the literature in gerontology (cf. Havighurst, 1960; Kaplan, 1960) emphasizes the need to provide good leisure (cf. Kando, 1975) for the retired. A central concept is *disengagement theory* (cf. Hochschild, 1975), which states that growing old involves a gradual and "inevitable mutual withdrawal or disengagement, resulting in decreased interaction between an aging person and others in the social systems he belongs to" (Cumming and Henry, 1961:14).

In America, entering old age is often a traumatic experience. As Blau (1956) found, retirement is particularly painful, more so in fact than the death of a spouse. Retirement often has a very negative effect on self-concept. As Cavan (1962) therefore suggests, the major remedy to the problems of the aged would be to provide acceptable roles and self-images. For example, grandparents can, even in America, feel good about their role if it is recognized by them and by their friends and relatives as a useful one.

There are many other areas of adult socialization. Some of us must learn to adjust to a stigmatized role. For example, Scott (1973) describes how the blind are socialized into their position. Then, too, most of us must at times learn to live with failure. Goffman (1952) shows how the "mark" (the loser, the "sucker") is socialized into accepting that fate.

Here, the final major socialization experience to be touched on is adjustment to death. For reasons that are not altogether clear, death has recently come to the fore of American thought, both in popular culture and in social science.[3] *Thanatology* is the term for the (scientific) study of death. The field has attracted psychologists (Kastenbaum and Aisenberg, 1972; Schneidman, 1973), anthropologists (Becker, 1973; Gorer, 1965), and sociologists (Fulton, 1965; Glaser and Strauss, 1965; 1968).

In sociology, Glaser and Strauss' *Awareness of Dying* (1965) is probably the best known work on death. The authors, who studied terminal patients in six hospitals, distinguish four awareness contexts: closed, suspicion, mutual pretense, and open.

A closed awareness context is one where the terminal patient is unaware of his condition, while the staff does know. At this stage, the staff frequently uses such tactics as the construction of fictitious future biographies for the patient, in effect lying to him.

The suspicion awareness context is one in which the patient is frequently on the psychological offensive, while the staff is on the defensive: he suspects and tries to find out what his true condition is. Occasionally, however, a patient will want to suppress or ignore the truth. The staff may drop hints about it.

The mutual pretense context is one where both sides know but pretend not to know. A "truth game" can be initiated by either the staff or the patient, but there are strict rules to such a game.

Open awareness, finally, develops when

mutual pretense can no longer be sustained. This can occur abruptly or gradually. The patient's self-concept has now made the full transition from a healthy self to a dying self. Now questions of timing and norms (manners) arise. Not all patients live up to proper standards as to how to die. Yet terminal patients aware of their condition are held responsible for their behavior. They are expected to die in a manly fashion, and they are not expected to bring about their own (premature) death. Except for very old patients, the staff is hostile toward suicidal patients. Staff members expect terminal patients to maintain their dignity and cheerfulness and to remain nice and cooperative. Patients are told how to die gracefully, and this is part of a trade-off, for they also receive certain privileges.

Glaser and Strauss enumerate a number of situations in which awareness is discounted: premature babies, the hopelessly comatose (what Goffman terms a nonperson), the senile patient (who is already socially dead), and patients regarded with little respect (such as a hobo). Also, there are spatial and other situational variations: if a patient's heart has stopped beating, heroic efforts will be undertaken to keep him alive. Here, any pretense that may have existed will be dropped.

There is a widespread feeling today that it may be better "to know." Glaser and Strauss quote a statistic indicating that eighty-two percent of the patients wanted to know their true condition. Also, the authors believe that the four awareness contexts often represent a sequence—patients moving from stage 1 to stage 4. Elsewhere (1968), they deal with the dying trajectory as a status passage.

Others do not agree that dying consists of a series of successive psychological stages. Schneidman (1973) finds that patients alternate back and forth between acceptance and denial of death. Becker (1973), who recently died of cancer himself (see Horowitz, 1975), wrote his last book precisely on this subject—the meaning and denial of death.

One thing above all seems clear: death,

---

[3]Schneidman (1973), himself a thanatologist, attributes today's violence, disrespect for life, and self-destructive tendencies such as drug use to the atom bomb. The resurrection of this deus ex machina out of the 1950s (when all social problems were suddenly attributed to the alleged social-psychological impact of the threat of nuclear anihilation) is both odd and implausible.

the one condition that the self cannot experience, has become highly problematic in modern Western society. Gorer's (1965) study of death, grief, and mourning in Britain indicates that in that country there is also a general repudiation of death and grief, so that the survivor is as ill-equipped to cope after the death of a spouse or relative as are hospital staff, relatives, and the patient himself before. Traditional religious and community sources of support are no longer available, but no alternatives have yet been provided.

SUMMARY AND CONCLUSION

This chapter has dealt with socialization at all points of life. Beginning with childhood socialization, the earliest stages of that process were traced. Next, the sources of socialization were examined, which led to a discussion of significant others and reference groups. Having then dealt with the major dimensions and outcomes of socialization, the final section picked up where childhood socialization was left off—adolescence. Youth problems and youth culture were examined, followed by a discussion of the major aspects of adult socialization. Here, socialization into occupational and family roles as well as the general problems of the fundamental identity changes termed "conversion" and allegedly involving brainwashing were dealt with. Finally, life's last status passage was examined—dying.

The ultimate question regarding socialization is, of course, how to imprtove the process (cf. Lippitt, 1968; Kennedy and Kerber, 1973). It is, more than anything else, the socialization process that determines the quality of a society and therefore the well-being of its members. Socialization is education in its broadest sense. The single major cause of Western man's troubles at this time may not be economic, ecological, or political. It may be the failure of the socialization process.

REFERENCES

Aries, Phillip
　1968　Centuries of Childhood. New York: Vintage Books.

Asch, Solomon E.
　1942　Social Psychology (chap. 16). Englewood Cliffs, N.J.: Prentice-Hall, Inc.
Ashton, David N.
　1974　"Careers and commitment: the movement from school to work." In Social Psychology for Sociologists. David Field (ed.). New York: John Wiley & Sons, Inc., pp. 171-186.
Baldwin, James Mark
　1906　The Mental Development in the Child and the Race. New York: The Macmillan Co.
Becker, Ernest
　1962　The Birth and Death of Meaning. Glencoe, Ill.: The Free Press.
　1973　The Denial of Death. New York: The Free Press.
Becker, Howard S.
　1953　"Becoming a marihuana user." American Journal of Sociology (November):235-242.
　1962　"Marihuana use and social control." In Human Behavior and Social Processes. Arnold M. Rose (ed.). Boston: Houghton Mifflin Co., pp. 589-607.
　1970　"Personal change in adult life." In Social Psychology Through Symbolic Interaction. Gregory P. Stone and Harvey A. Farberman (eds.). Waltham, Mass.: Ginn-Blaisdell, pp. 583-593.
Becker, Howard and Anselm L. Strauss
　1956　"Careers, personality and adult socialization." American Journal of Sociology (November):253-263.
Berger, Peter L.
　1963　Invitation to Sociology. Garden City, N.Y.: Doubleday & Co., Inc.
Berger, Peter L. and Thomas Luckmann
　1966　The Social Construction of Reality. Garden City, N.Y.: Doubleday & Co., Inc.
Blau, Zena Smith
　1956　"Changes in status and age identification." American Sociological Review (April):198-203.
Blitsten, Dorothy R.
　1971　Human Social Development: Psychobiological Roots and Social Consequences. New Haven, Conn.: College and University Press.
Bloch, Herbert and Arthur Niederhoffer
　1958　The Gang: A Study in Adolescent Behavior. New York: Philosophical Library.
Brim, Orville G., Jr.
　1968　"Adult socialization." In Socialization and Society. John A. Clausen (ed.). Boston: Little, Brown and Co., pp. 182-227.
Burke, Kenneth
　1954　Permanence and Change. Los Altos, Calif.: Hermes Publication.
Cavan, Ruth Shonle
　1962　"Self and role in adjustment during old age." In Human Behavior and Social Processes.

Arnold M. Rose (ed.). Boston: Houghton Mifflin Co., pp. 526-536.

Cavan, Sherri
1970 "The etiquette of youth." In Social Psychology Through Symbolic Interaction. Gregory P. Stone and Harvey A. Farberman (eds.). Waltham, Mass.: Ginn-Blaisdell, pp. 554-565.

Clark, Robert E.
1972 Reference Group Theory and Delinquency. New York: Behavioral Publications.

Clausen, John A.
1966 "Research on socialization and personality development in the United States and France: remarks on the paper by P. H. Chombart de Lauwe." American Sociological Review (April):248-258.

Clausen, John A. et al.
1968 Socialization and Society. John A. Clausen (ed.). Boston: Little, Brown and Co.

Cohen, A. K.
1955 Delinquent Boys. New York: The Macmillan Co.

Coles, Robert
1973 "A psychiatrist joins the movement." In Social Psychology: A Transaction-Society Reader. Elliot Aronson and Robert Helmreich (eds.). New York: D. Van Nostrand, pp. 61-66.

Cooley, Charles Horton
1902 Human Nature and the Social Order. New York: Scribner's.
1909 Social Organization. New York: Scribner's.

Cumming, Elaine and William Henry
1961 Growing Old. New York: Basic Books, Inc.

Danziger, Kurt
1971 Socialization. Middlesex, England: Penguin Books, Ltd.

Davis, Kingsley
1940 "Extreme social isolation of a child." American Journal of Sociology (January):554-565.
1947 "Final note on a case of extreme isolation." American Journal of Sociology (March):432-437.

Denzin, Norman K.
1966 "The significant others of a college population." Sociological Quarterly (Summer):298-310.
1972 "The genesis of self in early childhood." Sociological Quarterly (Summer):291-314.

Deutsch, Morton and Robert M. Krauss
1965 Theories in Social Psychology. New York: Basic Books, Inc.

Deutscher, Irwin
1962 "Socialization for postparental life." In Human Behavior and Social Processes. Arnold M. Rose (ed.) Boston: Houghton Mifflin Co., pp. 506-525.

Dicks, H. V.
1950 "Personality traits and national socialist ideology." Human Relations 3:11-154.

DuBois, Cora
1944 The People of Alor. Minneapolis: University of Minnesota Press.

Eisdorfer, Carl and M. Powell Lawton (eds.)
1973 The Psychology of Adult Development and Aging. Washington, D.C.: American Psychological Association.

Elder, Glen H.
1972 Adolescent Socialization and Personality Development. Chicago: Rand McNally and Co.

Elkin, F.
1960 The Child and Society: The Process of Socialization. New York: Random House, Inc.

Festinger, Leon
1954 A Theory of Social Comparison Processes. Human Relations 7:117-140.

Flavell, John
1974 "The development of role-taking and communication skills in children." In Social Psychology for Sociologists. David Field (ed.). New York: John Wiley & Sons, Inc., pp. 47-61.

Foote, Nelson N.
1955 "A neglected member of the family." Marriage and Family Living 18:213-218.

Friedenberg, Edgar Z.
1963 "The image of the adolescent minority." Dissent Magazine (Spring):149-158.

Fulton, Robert (ed.)
1965 Death and Identity. New York: John Wiley & Sons, Inc.

Gatheru, R. Mugo
1964 Child of Two Worlds. London: Routledge and Kegan Paul.

Gergen, Kenneth J.
1971 The Concept of Self. New York: Holt, Rinehart and Winston.

Giddings, F. P.
1897 The Theory of Socialization. New York: The Macmillan Co.

Glaser, Barney G. and Anselm L. Strauss
1965 Awareness of Dying. Chicago: Aldine Publishing Co.
1968 Time for Dying. Chicago: Aldine Publishing Co.
1971 Status Passage: A Formal Theory. Chicago: Aldine Publishing Co.

Glaser, Daniel
1973 "Role models and differential association." In Deviance: The Interactionist Perspective. Earl Rubington and Martin S. Weinberg (eds.). New York: The Macmillan Co.

Goffman, Erving
1952 "On cooling the mark out: some aspects of adaptation to failure." Psychiatry: Journal for the Study of Interpersonal Relations (November):451-463.
1959 "The moral career of the mental patient." Psychiatry (May):123-142.

1961 "Encounters: Two Studies in the Sociology of Interaction." Indianapolis: Bobbs-Merrills Co.

Goodman, Paul
1961 Growing Up Absurd. New York: Random House, Inc.

Gorer, Geoffrey
1943 "Themes in Japanese culture." Transactions of the New York Academy of Science (Ser. II, 5):106-124.
1951 "Swaddling and the Russians." New Leader (May 21):19-20.
1965 Death, Grief and Mourning. Garden City, N.Y.: Doubleday & Co., Inc.

Gottlieb, David
1973 Childrens Liberation. Englewood Cliffs, N.J.: Prentice-Hall, Inc.

Gouldner, Alvin W.
1957-1958 "Cosmopolitans and locals: toward an analysis of latent social roles." Administrative Science Quarterly 2:281-306, 444-448.

Green, Richard and John Money
1969 Transsexualism and Sex Reassignment. Baltimore: Johns Hopkins Press.

Hartnagel, Timothy F.
1974 "Measuring the significance of others: a methodological note." American Journal of Sociology (September):397-401.

Havighurst, Robert J.
1960 "Life beyond family and work." In Aging in Western Societies. E. W. Burgess (ed.). Chicago: University of Chicago Press, pp. 299-353.

Hess, Robert D. and Virginia C. Shipman
1974 "Early experience and the socialization of cognitive modes in children." In Social Psychology for Sociologists. David Field (ed.). New York: John Wiley & Sons, Inc., pp. 103-115.

Hilgard, Josephine R.
1964 "Sibling rivalry and social heredity." In Dimensions of Social Psychology. E. W. Vinacke, W. R. Wilson, and G. M. Meredith (eds.). Chicago: Scott, Foresman, pp. 94-100.

Hochschild, Arlie Russell
1975 "Disengagement theory: a critique and proposal." American Sociological Review (October):553-569.

Hockett, Charles F. and Robert Ascher
1964 "The human revolution." Current Anthropology V-3:135-147, 166-168.

Hoebel, E. Adamson
1966 Anthropology: The Study of Man. New York: McGraw-Hill Book Co.

Hollingshead, August B.
1949 Elmstown's Youth. New York: John Wiley & Sons, Inc.

Horowitz, Irving Louis
1975 "Ernest Becker: an appreciation of a life that began September 27, 1924 and ended March 6, 1974." American Sociologist (February):25-28.

Hughes, Everett C.
1962 "What other?" In Human Behavior and Social Processes. Arnold M. Rose (ed.). Boston: Houghton Mifflin Co., pp. 119-127.

Humphreys, Laud
1970 Tearoom Trade: Impersonal Sex in Public Places. Chicago: Aldine Publishing Co.

Hyman, Herbert H.
1942 "The psychology of status." Archives of Psychology 269.

Hyman, Herbert H. and Eleanor Singer
1971 "An introduction to reference group theory and research." In Current Perspectives in Social Psychology. Edwin P. Hollander and Raymond G. Hunt (eds.). New York: Oxford University Press, pp. 67-77.

Inkeles, Alex
1968 "Society, social structure, and child socialization." In Socialization and Society. John A. Clausen (ed.). Boston: Little, Brown and Co., pp. 73-130.

Itard, J. M. G.
1932 The Wild Boy of Aveyron. New York: Appleton-Century-Crofts.

Johnson, Rita Volkman and Donald R. Cressey
1963 "Differential association and the rehabilitation of drug addicts." American Journal of Sociology (September):129-142.

Josselyn, Irene M.
1970 "Sexual identity crises in the life cycle." In Sex Roles in Changing Society. Georgene H. Seward and Robert C. Williamson (eds.). New York: Random House, Inc., pp. 67-93.

Kagan, Jerome
1973 "A conversation with Jerome Kagan." Saturday Review (March 10).

Kagan, Jerome and Robert Coles (eds.)
1972 Twelve to Sixteen: Early Adolescence. New York: W. W. Norton.

Kando, Thomas
1972 "Role strain: a comparison of males, females and transsexuals." Journal of Marriage and the Family (August):459-464.
1973 Sex Change: The Achievement of Gender Identity Among Feminized Transsexuals. Springfield, Ill.: Charles C Thomas, Publisher.
1975 Leisure and Popular Culture in Transition. St. Louis: The C. V. Mosby Co.

Kaplan, Bert (ed.)
1961 Studying Personality Cross-Culturally. New York: Harper & Row, Publishers.

Kaplan, Max
1960 "The uses of leisure." In Handbook of Social Gerontology: Societal Aspects of Aging. C. Tibbits (ed.). Chicago: University of Chicago Press, pp. 407-443.

Kardiner, Abram
  1939 The Individual and his Society. New York: Columbia University Press.
  1945 The Psychological Frontiers of Society. New York: Columbia University Press.
Kardiner, Abram and E. Preble
  1961 They Studied Man. New York: World Publishing Co.
Kastenbaum, Robert and Ruth Aisenberg
  1972 The Psychology of Death. New York: Springer.
Kemper, Theodore D.
  1968 "Reference groups, socialization and achievement." American Sociological Review (February):31-46.
Kennedy, Daniel B. and August Kerber
  1973 Resocialization: An American Experiment. New York: Behavioral Publications.
Komarovsky, Mirra
  1964 Blue-Collar Marriage. New York: Random House, Inc.
Kuhn, Manford H.
  1964 "The reference group reconsidered." The Sociological Quarterly (Winter):6-21.
Lambert, Wallace E. and F. H. Lowy
  1957 "Effects of the presence of others on expressed attitudes." Canadian Journal of Psychology 11:151-156.
Lambert, William W. and Rita Weisbrod
  1971 Comparative Perspectives on Social Psychology. Boston: Little, Brown and Co.
Landis, Judson R., James D. Mercer, and Carole E. Wolff
  1969 "Success and failure of adult probationers in California." Journal of Research in Crime and Delinquency (January):34-40.
Layder, Derek R.
  1974 "Notes on variations in middle class careers." In Social Psychology for Sociologists. David Field (ed.). New York: John Wiley & Sons, Inc., pp. 161-170.
Lewis, George H.
  1972 Side-Saddle on the Golden Calf: Social Structure and Popular Culture in America. Pacific Palisades, Calif.: Goodyear Publishing.
Lifton, Robert
  1969 "Thought reform: psychological steps in death and rebirth." In Readings in Social Psychology. Alfred R. Lindesmith and Anselm L. Strauss (eds.). New York: Holt, Rinehart and Winston, pp. 324-340.
Lindesmith, Alfred R. and Anselm L. Strauss
  1956 Social Psychology: The Revised Edition. New York: Holt, Rinehart and Winston.
Lindesmith, Alfred R., Anselm L. Strauss, and Norman K. Denzin

  1975 Social Psychology (ed. 4). Hinsdale, Ill.: The Dryden Press.
Lippitt, Ronald
  1968 "Improving the socialization process." In Socialization and Society. John A. Clausen (ed.). Boston: Little, Brown and Co., pp. 321-375.
Maccoby, Eleanor E.
  1968 "The development of moral values and behavior in children." In Socialization and Society. John A. Clausen (ed.). Boston: Little, Brown and Co., pp. 227-270.
Maier, Norman R. F.
  1949 Frustration: The Study of Behavior Without a Goal. New York: McGraw-Hill Book Co.
Malson, Lucien
  1972 Wolf Children and the Problem of Human Nature. New York: Monthly Review Press.
Manning, Peter K.
  1970 "Talking and becoming: a view of organizational socialization." In Understanding Everyday Life. Jack D. Douglas (ed.). Chicago: Aldine Publishing Co., pp. 239-256.
Manning, Peter K. and Marcello Truzzi (eds.)
  1972 Youth and Sociology. Englewood Cliffs, N.J.: Prentice-Hall, Inc.
Martindale, Don (ed.)
  1967 National Character in the Perspective of the Social Sciences. The Annals of The American Academy of Political and Social Science (March).
Maslow, Abraham H.
  1962 Toward a Psychology of Being. Princeton, N.J.: D. Van Nostrand Co.
McHugh, Peter
  1970 "Social disintegration as a requisite of resocialization." In Social Psychology Through Symbolic Interaction. Gregory P. Stone and Harvey A. Farberman (eds.). Waltham, Mass.: Ginn-Blaisdell, pp. 699-708.
Mead, George Herbert
  1934 Mind, Self and Society. Charles W. Morris (ed.). Chicago: University of Chicago Press.
Mead, Margaret
  1942 And Keep Your Powder Dry: An Anthropologist Looks at America. New York: William Morrow and Co.
Merton, Robert K.
  1957 Social Theory and Social Structure. Glencoe, Ill.: The Free Press.
Merton, Robert K. and Alice C. Kitt
  1950 "Contributions to the theory of reference group behavior." In Continuities in Social Research. R. K. Merton and P. F. Lazarsfeld (eds.). Glencoe, Ill.: Free Press, pp. 40-105.
Merton, Robert K. and Alice K. Rossi
  1957 "Contributions to the theory of reference group behavior." In Social Theory and Social Structure. R. K. Merton (ed.). New York: The Free Press.

Moore, Harvey A., Raymond L. Schmitt, and Stanley E. Grupp
  1973 "Observations on the role-specific and orientational other." Pacific Sociological Review (October):509-518.
Newcomb, Theodore M.
  1943 Personality and Social Change: Attitude Formation in a Student Community. New York: Dryden Press.
  1953 "An approach to the study of communicative acts." Psychological Review 60:393-404.
  1956 "The prediction of interpersonal attraction." American Psychologist 11:575-586.
Ogburn, William Fielding
  1959 "The wolf boy of Agra." American Journal of Sociology (March):449-467.
Orlansky, Harold
  1949 "Infant care and personality." Psychological Bulletin 46:1-48.
Piaget, Jean
  1926 The Language and Thought of the Child. New York: Harcourt, Brace.
  1932 The Moral Judgment of the Child. New York: Harcourt, Brace.
Rheingold, Harriet L.
  1969 "The social and socializing infant." In Handbook of Socialization and Research. David A. Goslin (ed.). Chicago: Rand McNally, pp. 779-790.
Riesman, David, with Nathan Glazer and Reul Denney
  1950 The Lonely Crowd. New Haven, Conn.: Yale University Press.
Rose, Arnold A.
  1944 "Insecurity feelings in adolescent girls." Nervous Child 4:46-59.
Rose, Arnold M.
  1962 (Ed.) Human Behavior and Social Processes: An Interactionist Approach. Boston: Houghton Mifflin Co.
Rosenblatt, Paul C.
  1966 "A cross-cultural study of child rearing and romantic love." Journal of Personality and Social Psychology (3):336-338.
Schein, Edgar H.
  1964 "Reaction patterns to severe, chronic stress in American army prisoners of war of the Chinese." In Dimensions of Social Psychology. W. Edgar Vinacke and Warner W. Wilson (eds.). Chicago: Scott, Foresman and Co., pp. 224-229.
Schmitt, Raymond L.
  1972 The Reference Other Orientation: An Extention of the Reference Group Concept. Edwardsville, Ill.: Southern Illinois University Press.
Schneidman, Edwin S.
  1973 Deaths of Man. New York: Quadrangle Books.
Scott, Robert A.
  1973 "The socialization of the blind in personal interaction." In Social Psychology in Everyday Life. Billy J. Franklin and Frank J. Kohout (eds.). New York: David McKay, pp. 423-432.
Sewell, William H.
  1952 "Infant training and the personality of the child." American Journal of Sociology 58:150-159.
  1963 "Some recent developments in socialization theory and research." The Annals of the American Academy of Political and Social Science (September):163-181.
Shelly, Robert K.
  1974 "On 'accepting significant others'." American Journal of Sociology (May):1477-1480.
Sherif, Muzafer
  1935 "A study of some social factors in perception." Archives of Psychology 27.
  1948 An Outline of Social Psychology. New York: Harper & Row, Publisher.
Shibutani, Tamotsu
  1955 "Reference groups as perspectives." American Journal of Sociology 60:562-569.
  1961 Society and Personality: An Interactionist Approach to Social Psychology. Englewood Cliffs, N.J.: Prentice-Hall, Inc.
  1962 "Reference groups and social control." In Human Behavior and Social Processes. Arnold M. Rose (ed.). Boston: Houghton Mifflin Co., pp. 128-147.
Siegel, Alberta E. and Sidney Siegel
  1973 "Reference groups, membership groups, and attitude change." In Social Psychology in Life. Richard I. Evans and Richard M. Rozelle (eds.). Boston: Allyn and Bacon, pp. 332-342.
Smith, M. B. et al.
  1956 Opinions and Personality. New York: John Wiley & Sons, Inc.
Smith, M. Brewster
  1968 "Competence and socialization." In Socialization and Society. John A. Clausen (ed.). Boston: Little, Brown and Co., pp. 270-320.
Speier, Matthew
  1970 "The everyday world of the child." In Understanding Everyday Life. Jack D. Douglas (ed.). Chicago: Aldine Publishing Co., pp. 188-217.
Spitz, R.
  1945 "Hospitalism." In Psychoanalytic Study of the Child (Vol. I). O. Fenichel et al. (eds.). New York: International Universities Press.
Spradley, James P.
  1970 You Owe Yourself a Drunk: An Ethnography of Urban Nomads. Boston: Little, Brown Co.
Stone, Gregory P.
  1962 "Appearance and the self." In Human Be-

havior and Social Processes. Arnold M. Rose (ed.). Boston: Houghton Mifflin Co., pp. 86-118.

1965 "The play of little children." Quest (April): 23-31.

Stone, Gregory P. and Harvey A. Farberman
1970 Social Psychology Through Symbolic Interaction. Waltham, Mass.: Ginn-Blaisdell.

Stouffer, S. A. et al.
1949 The American Soldier (2 vols.). Princeton, N.J.: Princeton University Press.

Strauss, Anselm L.
1959 Mirrors and Masks. Glencoe, Ill.: The Free Press.

Sullivan, Harry Stack
1953 The Interpersonal Theory of Psychiatry. New York: W. W. Norton & Co.
1954 The Psychiatric Interview. New York: W. W. Norton & Co.

Sutherland, Edwin H.
1947 Principles of Criminology. New York: J. B. Lippincott Co.

Szasz, Thomas
1961 The Myth of Mental Illness: Foundations of a Theory of Personal Conduct. New York: Dell Publishing Co.

Theodorson, George A. and Achilles G. Theodorson
1969 A Modern Dictionary of Sociology. New York: Thomas Y. Crowell Co.

Thielbar, Gerald
1970 "On locals and cosmopolitans." In Social Psychology Through Symbolic Interaction. Gregory P. Stone and Harvey A. Farberman (eds.). Waltham, Mass.: Ginn-Blaisdell, pp. 259-276.

Thomas, Darwin L. and Andrew J. Weigert
1971 "Socialization and adolescent conformity to significant others: a cross-national analysis." American Sociological Review (October): 835-847.

Thomas, W. I. and F. Znaniecki
1918- The Polish Peasant in Europe and America
1920 (5 vols.). Chicago: University of Chicago Press.

Tolley, Howard, Jr.
1973 Children and War: Political Socialization to International Conflict. New York: Teachers College Press.

Travisano, Richard V.
1970 "Alternation and conversion as qualitatively different transformations." In Social Psychology Through Symbolic Interaction. Gregory P. Stone and Harvey A. Farberman (eds.). Waltham, Mass.: Ginn-Blaisdell, pp. 594-605.

Turner, Roy
1970 "Words, utterances, and activities." In Understanding Everyday Life. Jack D. Douglas (ed.). Chicago: Aldine Publishing Co., pp. 169-187.

Van Gennep, Arnold
1909 Les Rites de Passage. Paris: E. Nourry.

Vygotsky, Lev
1962 Thought and Language. Cambridge, Mass.: The M.I.T. Press.

Weber, Max
1958 The Protestant Ethic and the Spirit of Capitalism. New York: Charles Scribner's Sons.

Webster, Murray, Jr. et al.
1972 "Accepting 'significant others': six models." American Journal of Sociology (November):576-598.
1974 "Reply to Shelly." American Journal of Sociology (May):1480-1483.

Weis, Joseph G.
1974 "Styles of middle-class adolescent drug use." Pacific Sociological Review (July):251-283.

Williams, Thomas Rhys
1972 Introduction to Socialization: Human Culture Transmitted. St. Louis: The C. V. Mosby Co.

Wrong, Dennis H.
1961 "The oversocialized conception of man in modern sociology." American Sociological Review (April):183-193.

chapter 10
Self-concept, identity, and personality

Although we have already touched on such aspects of the self as personality and self-concept in the previous chapters, we must now systematically review the literature, the issues, and the research done on these nebulous concepts.

In this chapter, we devote one major section to self-concept, one to identity, and one to personality. While these three terms are often ill-defined and overlap with one another as well as with such related terms as self, self-definition, and self-attitudes, we arrive at this organization of the material on the basis of what has been found in the literature: there is, simply, a large body of literature on self-concept, identity, and personality. Much of the research on self-concept is by interactionists (that is, sociological social psychologists), while personality has been researched primarily by psychologists. Identity is seemingly dealt with by both psychologists and sociologists a great deal.

The section on self-concept will first examine work done with the Twenty Statement Test by the Iowa school, a school that has tended to equate self and self-concept. Next, it will examine other contributions to the study of self-concept, both by interactionists and by psychological social psychologists. We shall subsequently discuss the relationship between self-concept and deviance, that crucial component of self-concept—self-esteem—and finally change in the self-concept.

The section on identity will deal with such bases of personal identity as sex, race, and occupation, with identity change, and finally with an important theme in the modern world: the possible loss, or erosion, of personal identity in our atomized mass society.

The third section, personality, will first examine the concept and the instruments that have been used to measure it. Then some major correlates of personality will be examined, for example culture, class, race, and sex. The following part will deal with such aspects of personality as emotions, intelligence, attitudes, values, and beliefs. We shall examine political, racial, religious, and cultist attitudes. Finally, two attitude problems will be discussed—the problem of dissonance and the attitude-behavior problem. In the conclusion we shall argue that whether or not social psychology uses the concept of personality—a concept with obvious *static* rather than dynamic implications—it must recognize the essential role of change in human existence.

SELF-CONCEPT

As was stated earlier, it is not clear to what extent the study of the self and that of self-concept differ or overlap. Recent books devoted to the self (cf. Ziller, 1973) also deal with self-concept and books written about the self-concept (cf. Gergen, 1971) deal with the self. Since the term self-concept is also used interchangeably with such expressions as "self-definition" (Cardwell, 1971:85-86), self-attitudes, and (self-) identity (see Gergen's definition, 1971:22-23), the confusion is great.

According to Gergen (1971:1-5), interest in the self has historically taken four foci:

1. The ancient Greek philosophers and their subsequent disciples have been concerned mostly with *identity*, with knowing oneself. As Plato admonishes us: "know thyself."

2. A second tradition stresses *self-evalua-*

tion. Here, we have both the Christian emphasis on humility (negative self-evaluation) and a contemporary trend that runs counter to that, namely modern humanistic psychiatry's recommendation that one love oneself (cf. Fromm, 1957).

3. A third theme is the self versus society controversy, with many authors throughout the ages deploring society's tyrannical intrusions into the self, liberty, and individual integrity, but some, like Machiavelli, arguing the opposite, namely that the flexible adaptation of self to societal roles is desirable.

4. Finally, there is the focus taken by such authors as Herman Hesse (in his *Steppenwolf*), who stresses the limitations of the self.

Gergen (1971:15-18) grapples with the problematic relationship between the self and self-concept, as he reminds us of William James' and George Herbert Mead's basic characterization of the self as a dual or two-phased process, namely as both knower and known, both I and me, both subject and object. The author's solution to this problem is a positivistic one and therefore no solution at all. As soon as one reduces the study of the self to the study of purely empirical indicators such as questionnaire responses or overt behaviors, one ceases to study the full self and merely studies the "me," that is, objective human behavior.

However, a positivistic definition of self-concept and a positivistic strategy to study that phenomenon are defensible, for the self-concept may indeed be equated with the me, with the self as object.

Thus it must be clear that the self and self-concept are not identical. Of the more than two thousand empirical studies of the self done since World War II (Gergen, 1971:11), only a fraction deal with self-concept, namely those that deal with *the way the individual sees himself, objectifies himself.* As we shall see, this process entails role-taking, objectifying oneself from the standpoint of (significant) others.

How I view myself

Manford Kuhn and his disciples at the University of Iowa have relied primarily on the Twenty Statement Test to measure the self. This test simply consists of asking the respondent to quickly answer twenty times in a row the question "Who am I?" It therefore measures self-concept, not self.

Some of the research of the Iowa school has already been discussed in Chapter 8. Kuhn himself (see Kuhn, 1960; Kuhn and McPartland, 1954) worked several times with the TST to determine, among other things, what references different demographic groups tend to use the most to define themselves. He found (1960) that sex references increase with age, that women identify themselves by sex and kin more frequently than men but less by race, and that occupational self-identification increases with age.

Carl Couch (1962) related respondents' self-attitudes (as measured by the TST) to the degree of role specialization found in their family. A family with a high degree of role specialization is a family where, say, the father is clearly and alone responsible for earning money, where it is always the mother who shops for groceries, cooks, and the like. Respondents who come from families in which sex roles are thus clearly and traditionally defined can be expected to identify themselves first and foremost on the basis of sex. After all, they grew up in an environment where gender identity and sex roles were clearly demarcated and all-important. On the other hand, a man, say, with a more liberated background might start identifying himself on the TST as a "human being," an "Aries," or an "American" and only further down write that he is a male. To him, his gender is less salient, a less crucial part of his total identity. Couch found, interestingly, that this prediction only materialized for men, not among women.

Driver (1969) used the TST in a cross-cultural comparison of self-conceptions. This study essentially replicates in India the study by Kuhn and McPartland (1954) on the salience of religion in the self-conception of different religious denominations (see Chapter 8). Driver concludes that the TST is cross-culturally valid, non-culturebound.

Nevertheless, controversy regarding the validity and reliability of the TST continues. In 1971, Spitzer and associates published *The Assessment of the Self,* a collection of most of the studies conducted at the University of Iowa and using the TST. Carl Backman (1973), in his review of this anthology, points out that the TST has both the advantages and the disadvantages of such a subjective methodology. The TST has an open response format, of course; it is merely a sensitizing test. This renders it rather unreliable, Backman argues, and he proposes more structured approaches to the study of self(-concept), for example the semantic differential (see Chapter 7).

Backman, in his review, and Tucker (1966), earlier, both raise a point about the TST that is of the utmost importance. The question "Who am I?" asked abstractly may be meaningless if no regard is given to the specific context or situation in which it is asked. Thus it is not clear what the TST measures, since we know so little about how such factors as the testing situation and subjective interpretation affect the re-

sponses.[1] Until this difficulty is resolved, the validity of the TST remains in doubt.

What determines how I view myself?

It was Cooley who, shortly after the turn of the century, made the great discovery that the self is essentially the product of how one interprets and responds to others' perceptions of oneself. He called this the *looking-glass self.* Thanks to Cooley, then, we now know that our self-concept somehow basically originates in our interactions with others.

Cooley's theory has been articulated, operationalized, and tested by many social psychologists since then. John Kinch, for example (1963; 1973) has "formalized" Cooley's theory of the looking-glass self. The author's main conclusion is that the theory contains the following four propositions:

1. The individual's conception of him-

[1]There is, of course, a great deal of literature about such methodological problems. It generally falls under the heading of "reactivity" or "(un)obtrusive measures" (cf. Webb et al., 1966). A good recent example is Landis et al. (1973), who asked a sample of women whether they agree or disagree with a series of feminist statements (such as "women are definitely discriminated against"). These authors found that the respondents were more feminist when the interviewer was male than when she was a female. This, then, is a clear demonstration of "reactivity."

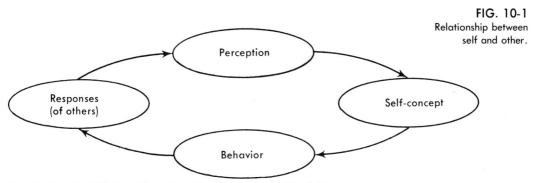

FIG. 10-1
Relationship between
self and other.

From Kinch, J. W. 1973. Social Psychology. New York: McGraw-Hill Book Co.

self is based on his perception of the way others are responding to him.

2. The individual's conception of himself functions to direct his behavior.
3. The individual's perceptions of others' responses are an accurate reflection of the actual responses that the others are directing toward the individual.
4. These actual responses are based on their (others') reaction to the individual's behavior.

These four propositions add up to a circular model, as depicted in Fig. 10-1.

To illustrate this theory, Kinch describes an experiment in which a number of graduate students took out and otherwise interacted with a (naive) coed as if she were very attractive, although in fact she was quite plain. By the end of the experiment, several weeks later, the girl had begun to be quite popular, having begun to dress up and to take care of her appearance, looking much more beautiful and indeed becoming an attractive date in great demand.

Kinch recognizes that his theory is circular, and the self-fulfilling anecdote we have just related also points up a major gap in this formulation: one should not take the correspondence between self-concept and others' responses and attitudes for granted. In fact, the amount of overlap between these two things is, just as with role-taking, a variable. Sometimes we see ourselves as others see us, but often we do not. We confidently hypothesize that most people view themselves more favorably than others see them. At the same time, people manage to hold on to unrealistically positive self-concepts by believing that others see them as they see themselves. More often than not, life is a comedy of mutual misunderstanding and self-deception.

Other researchers have faced this problem more squarely than Kinch. For example, Miyamoto and Dornbusch (1956) told a number of subjects to rate themselves along such dimensions as intelligence, attractiveness, and self-confidence. The subjects then rated their significant others' conception of them along the same dimensions, and the significant others made the same ratings on the subjects. The study confirmed the basic hypothesis that *there is greater agreement between one's own conception of self and one's perception of others' evaluation than between one's own conception and the actual attitude of others.*

Quarantelli and Cooper (1970) replicated this study, using an improved methodology. They, too, concluded that a person's conception of self is more closely linked to *how he thinks* the other feels about him than to how the other actually regards him.

Reeder and co-workers (1960) studied the sources of self-concept in military groups. They found, among other things, a high degree of correspondence between self-conception and the perceived generalized other, but not between self-conception and the actual responses of others, except for persons who rated themselves low.

Clearly, then, Kinch's formalization has done violence to Cooley, who did recognize the always problematical nature of role-taking. Although Kinch subsequently recognizes that research must determine to what extent and under which conditions his four interconnected propositions hold, he has in fact put the cart before the horse: in reality, the relationship between self-concept and others' responses is a highly problematical one. This is the matter that must be researched, along with people's amazing ability to operate on the basis of discrepant assumptions. To posit congruence between one's self-concept and how others view us (even in the long run) and to view the self as essentially the predictable product of how others respond to us are to deny the I, the subjective, the indeterminate, the complex and irreducible aspects of the human self.

There is, in American social science, a traditional tendency to subscribe to what Wrong (1961) has termed an *oversocialized conception of man.* This may reflect the fact that Americans are, indeed, an exceptionally conformist or what Riesman (1950) calls other-directed people. Veblen (1899) already noted that people's self-esteem often depends more on how much they own in comparison with others than on their absolute wealth. The *conspicuous consumption* in which the very rich engage (such as lighting your cigar with a $100 bill) is aimed at impressing others and thus enhancing one's self-esteem. In 1954, Festinger launched his theory of *social comparison,* which systematized such observations as Veblen's: people, Festinger argued, derive their self-conceptions from comparisons with others (who are generally not too different, either in a positive or a negative direction). Thus it must be recognized that social comparisons—and, more generally, *external* sources—are one important origin of self-concept.

Despite what had just been said, we must, once again, remember that there is an important subjective or "internal" side to self-concept as well. Dave Franks (1974), for example, following White (1959), stresses the fact that one extremely important source of self-esteem is so-called *competency motivation,* the inner knowledge and feeling of being consequential, of being "a cause," knowing that one's intentions accomplish something in the world. Lacking this inner source of self-esteem and having to rely entirely on external sources (the opinions of others), one becomes alienated, insecure, or worse, mentally ill. Contemporary man's malaise has frequently been diagnosed in precisely these terms. Riesman et al. (1950), Mills (1951), Whyte (1956), Wheelis (1958), and Goodman (1960) are but a few of the many authors who have documented and deplored modern man's growing other-directedness, his *selflessness.* Examples abound to indicate that the strength of an inner sense of effectiveness and meaning cannot be matched by external social rewards, when the inner conviction and belief in oneself exist. This is demonstrated by many cases throughout history, from the early Christian martyrs to Copernicus, Van Gogh, Solzhenitsyn, and all other lonely great men driven by the inner flame rather than the motive to impress others.

As a final source of self-concept, we should mention the various biases and defense mechanisms through which we sustain a positive self-image and thereby protect our ego and ourselves against excessive anxiety. Sullivan's (1953) theory of interpersonal psychiatry was primarily based on this recognition. More recently, Gergen (1971:53) has dealt with the same idea under the concept of *biased scanning,* the individual's tendency to select those cues and responses of others that are positive, or at least those that permit him to see himself as he wishes to be.

Along the same lines, Vroom (1964) showed that a person accurately perceives characteristics that are part of his self-concept only in others whom he likes and who are similar to him in those characteristics. Also, a person is likely to project a characteristic central to his self-concept to others he likes, but not to those he dislikes. For example, if I feel that one of my main personality chracteristics is a good sense of humor, I am likely to attribute a sense of humor to my good friend and colleague down the hall, but not to the administrator who voted against my promotion last year.

Becoming deviant

Walter Reckless (1960) was one of the first to apply the interactionist concept of the self—Cooley's looking-glass self—to juvenile delinquency. He found that delinquents often had a negative self-image. These boys often begin to see themselves as others see them, whereupon they begin to act accordingly, thus effecting a self-fulfilling prophecy.

Recently, psychologist Howard Kaplan (1975) has amplifed precisely the same idea, although this author seems totally unaware of Reckless' pioneering work. Kaplan suggests two basic hypotheses: (1) "individuals who have developed relatively stable negative self-attitudes are predisposed or motivated to seek out and adopt deviant patterns" and (2) "the adoption of deviant patterns by self-rejecting persons will tend to result in increased self-acceptance . . ." (Kaplan, 1975:67-68). The author then examines these two mechanisms in the areas of crime, delinquency, drug use, alcoholism, aggression, suicide, and mental illness.

Klapp (1962) has dealt with the dynamics of *self-typing,* the ways in which all of us, including deviants, categorize and label ourselves according to the typologies provided by our culture. Klapp's work shows, as does all labelling theory, that while the relationship between an individual's self-concept and his behavior is a close one, we can no longer accept the traditional conception of deviance that views deviant behavior as the cause of the stigmatization that ensues: when it comes to the cause and effect relationship between deviant behavior on the one hand and negative self-other processes on the other, the question is often of a chicken or egg variety.

Once delinquents have established deviant patterns, however, they do employ mechanisms that firm up those patterns. Sykes and Matza (1957) list several so-called *neutralization techniques* which serve that purpose. For example, the delinquent may deny responsibility for his acts, such as when he uses the liberal "sociological" rhetoric of a poor and disadvantaged socioeconomic background to justify his illegal acts. Or he may deny that he is victimizing anyone and assert that he is actually performing a Robin Hood type of justice, as was done for example by the Symbionese Liberation Army and other groups robbing banks under the guise of political activism. Then, too, the delinquent may condemn the condemners, such as when he accuses the police of brutality and the teachers of rigidity. Such techniques enable delinquents to neutralize negative self-images.

Finally, there is research that deals with the rehabilitation of deviants in relation to their self-concept. For example, Schwartz and co-workers (1966) have shown that among emotionally disturbed youngsters, those with the most positive and stable self-attitudes are in fact the most committed to the disturbed role and therefore the least favorable prognoses: they have come to accept that role.

Litman (1962) studied the physically handicapped and he found that a positive self-conception was correlated with a good response to rehabilitation. Thus a positive self-concept may signify different things, depending on what an individual's stigma is.

Liking and disliking oneself

A major aspect of the self studied by social psychologists has been self-esteem (cf. Gergen, 1971:11). As Kinch (1973:79-80) explains, self-esteem differs from self-concept in that it is unidimensional, it refers only to how highly the individual regards himself. William James (1890), in his discussion of the me, pointed out that self-esteem is a fraction of which pretensions are the denominator and success the numerator:

$$\text{Self-esteem} = \frac{\text{Success}}{\text{Pretensions}}$$

Thus to increase one's self-esteem, one can either diminish the denominator or increase the numerator. For example, Fran Tarkenton and the Minnesota Vikings may be miserably unhappy because they are only the second best football team in the world. Failing to win the Superbowl (which would be the only way to increase the numerator), they can only improve their self-esteem by lowering their ambition, that is, deciding that being one of the best is also satisfactory.

Although it is true, as this suggests, that self-esteem is situational, social psychologists have also established some of the necessary *antecedents* of self-esteem, the factors that account for an individual's more or less permanent sense of self-worth (or conversely, his feeling of inferiority). For example, Coopersmith (1967) found that for children to develop a healthy amount of self-esteem, parents must have clearly defined rules of behavior, and these must be enforced with consistency. Self-esteem, these authors found, is much more closely related to rules than to such things as physical attractiveness.

In addition, according to Shibutani (1961:553), "the development of an adequate level of self-esteem depends upon one's being the object of disinterested love."

Helmreich and Radloff (1973) relate self-esteem to stress, arguing that stress leads to lower self-esteem. Applying exchange-theoretical concepts (see Chapter 1) to the occupation of astronaut, they predict that while spaceflight may currently be a rewarding experience, it may not be so in the future. Today, the rewards of spaceflight are high by way of self-esteem, since such work makes one an overnight celebrity. In the future, when spaceflight becomes more common, this reward will decrease, but the cost—stress—is likely to remain high.

Webster and Sobieszek (1974) have published a sophisticated monograph on the sources of self-evaluation. They confirm such existing hypotheses as that self-conceptions give particular weight to the opinions of others of high status and great ability, in sum to others who are particularly significant in such terms. These authors also point out (p. 163) that self-esteem should not be conceived of as something transsituational. For example, the traditional notion that blacks have a low self-esteem is mistaken. Ghetto kids may exhibit a lack of self-confidence in certain middle-class academic settings, but this does not carry over into other situations such as the home.

Rosenberg (1972) compared adolescents in fourteen ethnic groups and arrived at the same conclusion as Webster and Sobieszek regarding this point: the self-esteem of blacks was found to be just about equal to that of whites. Apparently an individual's self-image is not necessarily based on his society's ethnic rankings. A study by Yancey and others (1972) also shows that the impact of racial status on self-esteem is negligible compared to that of occupation and marital status. Thus the traditional idea that blacks suffer from a negative self-concept may reflect white social scientists' projections rather than reality!

In general, all sources seem to concur that a reasonably high level of self-esteem is a necessary ingredient of mental health. We have not come across any study or theory arguing that self-esteem is undesirable. Yet we must remember that this new consensus in modern social psychology is as biased and culture-bound as the earlier Christian ethic, according to which humility, or low self-esteem, was the proper attitude.

Pepitone and his colleagues (1971) report a series of studies on the relationship between self-esteem on the one hand and such things as competitive and exploitative behavior on the other. American, Italian, and French students were used as subjects. The Americans generally had a higher level of self-esteem than the other two nationalities. And, more central to the study, those students into whom a high level of self-esteem was (experimentally) induced behaved more competitively than the other ones, and, as a way to compensate for inner insecurity, so did those who suffered from chronic low self-esteem (Pepitone et al., 1971:90).

A final issue pertaining to self-esteem is, again, the relative importance of internal versus external sources of self-esteem. Earlier, we already joined the ranks of such authors as Wrong (1961), White (1959), and Franks (1974) in arguing that there must be internal forces influencing the self-concept, no matter how other-directed (modern) man may have become. Stephen Crane's *The Red Badge of Courage* (1925) deals with this issue very nicely. A young Union soldier finds himself running away from combat during a Civil War engagement. Later on, he discovers that his fellow soldiers had not run away cowardly, as he had, and Crane describes the inner turmoil, recriminations, and various rationalizations the young man employs to redeem his self-esteem. A crucial point is that the other men did not notice his temporary desertion. Therefore, he feels that since "he had performed his mistakes in the dark . . . he was still a man." Of course, the matter of self-esteem is not thereby resolved. To what extent an individual's self-esteem will remain unbruised in such situations depends on the strength of his superego, the inner watchdog that may punish him even if no one else in the entire world knows of his failings.

Change in the self-concept

As we saw earlier, Kinch's (1963) formalization of the interactionist theory of the self-concept misses a major point, in that it takes congruence between self-concept and others' responses as its point of departure. However, that author answers this potential criticism in his subsequent work (1968; 1973). In one experiment, Kinch specifies four conditions under which an individual will tend to change his self-concept so as to align it with other people's responses to him: *frequency, importance, temporal proximity,* and *consistency.* For example, an individual may feel that he has only mediocre leadership qualities. He is then told that he has great leadership qualities. Now this is inconsistent with his self-concept. Kinch shows that the more *often* and the more *consistently* the individual is given this type of feedback, the more likely he is to develop the feeling that he is, indeed, a great leader. Simiarly, the more *important* the source of this (new) evaluation is, the more likely it is that the individual will bring his self-concept in line with the novel evaluation (begin to think of himself as a great leader). Finally, the *earliest* evaluations of an individual also tend to

have a greater influence on his self-concept than later evaluations.

What Kinch said can also be phrased in reverse. It is of course the same set of variables that account for both change and permanence in the self-concept, depending on their degree. Thus Backman, Second, and Pierce (1971) approach the same problem, but from the opposite direction, showing in a study that any feature of the self-concept is more resistant to change if there is consensus among (significant) others that it is indeed an important and typical characteristic of that individual. In essence, then, these authors specify one more variable that accounts for the extent to which an individual's self-concept will change or remain the same.

Finally, social psychologists have also dealt with change and resilience in deviant self-concepts. For example, an individual may retain a deviant self-image even after his behavior has changed, and this can impede rehabilitation. Ray (1973) shows how this process causes former heroin addicts to relapse.

IDENTITY

My self-concept is who I am in my own eyes. My identity is who I am in the eyes of others as well. Identity, then, is more objective than self-concept. Think of identity in the first place literally as an identity card that establishes your objective identity (name, rank, and serial number, so to speak) immediately and unequivocally in the eyes of those requesting the information. Such elements of identity have been called *consensual* (cf. Kuhn and McPartland, 1954) because there is no possible disagreement about them: you are twenty-one or you are not; it is not a matter of opinion.

On the other hand, novelists (cf. Pasternak, 1971) and social scientists (cf. Erikson, 1959) have used identity in a more *subconsensual* sense as well, in a subjective sense that comes close to that of the self-concept. Pasternak, for example, equates identity with the self-concept that emerges through interaction with others. This is identical with Cooley's looking-glass self. Erikson, who has done more than anyone else to popularize the concept of identity, proposes a modified psychoanalytic theory of *ego identity:* ego identity is formed out of the (congenial) blending of an individual's personal interests with the values of his group, with which he cooperates. According to Erikson, it is important to develop a good and healthy ego identity and not to suffer from ego diffusion.

Even though men like Erikson and Pasternak also recognize that identity must always (unlike self-concept) be consensually validated, their concept of identity is broader than the mere notion of an identification tag, because it also incorporates subconsensual elements. For example, to the leader of a delinquent gang, that role may be a cornerstone of his identity, both in his own eyes and in those of his peers. However, law enforcement could, for example, by locking him up, deprive him of this identity and replace it with that of felon, convict, delinquent, loser, or deviant.

To meaningfully distinguish identity from self-concept (as well as from such terms as personality, character, and self), we must agree that it represents a fairly objective description of the individual, a description primarily in terms of consensual elements such as name, sex, age, and race and in terms of roles (for example, occupational and family roles), rather than feelings such as that he is "strong" or "self-confident." Finally, it must be understood that no two individuals on earth have the same identity and that one individual has only one total identity. This, too, distinguishes identity from self-concept and personality.

What determines one's identity?

Identity, then, is based on one's demographic, sociological, and psychological characteristics.

One of the fundamental cornerstones of identity is sex—or, rather, gender. Sex is a biological fact, gender is a social-psychological concept. Therefore, we should only speak of gender identity, not sexual identity.

To most people, it may seem that if there is anything in personal identity that is not socially negotiable, it is this attribute—one's sex. However, students of a rare form of sexual inversion—transsexualism (cf. Garfinkel, 1967; Kando, 1972; 1973a; 1973b; 1974; Stoller, 1968)—have shown that a person's biological sex does not guarantee that he or she will have the same gender identity. There are thousands of natural-born females who have a firmly established *male* gender identity, and vice versa. Many of these people decide to undergo sex change surgery, which is a way to align the body to the mind, rather than the mind to the body, as psychiatry would attempt to do. The reason that these individuals' gender identity differs from their sex is that they have, from birth on, been treated as if they were of the opposite sex by their significant others. Thus we see once again that self-concept and identity—even gender identity—is the product of how others respond to us.

Nevertheless, it must be recognized that a vast majority of the people have the same gender identity as their biological sex at birth, not the opposite. Men, women, homosexuals, lesbians, women's liberationists, and even transvestites (cross-dressers) all know that they are either males or females, without any doubt, and this is confirmed in official documents such as drivers' licenses.

In our society, race is unfortunately also a crucial component of identity. Social scientists such as Moynihan (1965) and Rainwater (1972) have often emphasized two ways in which lower-class blacks are said to differ from the rest of us: (1) the frequent absence of a father figure from their families produces faulty socialization, particularly for the boys, who fail to develop proper discipline and male identification, and (2) the societywide prejudice and discrimination against them leads to a negative self-concept, to a low level of self-esteem. Rainwater (1972) documents the latter process within the lower-class black family. Each member constantly seems to be demeaning his brothers, sisters, children, and parents. The boys are told by their mother that their father was a no-good bum, the daughters retort that the mother could not be much better than they are if she was unable to get a hold of and hold on to a decent man, the girls prepare each other for failure by predicting unwanted pregancies, and so forth.

A classic study by the Clarks (1952) has often been quoted in support of the low black self-esteem thesis. That study showed that black children expressed preference for and identified more with white dolls than black dolls.

Since then, it has been fashionable to state that to many blacks, the Negro community functions as a negative reference group, and this presumably reflects self-hate, again, a low self-esteem. Gary Marx (1971) showed the amusing parallels between these "Negro whites" and the "white Negroes," that is, the hip wasps who reject their own white middle-class identity and try to emulate jazz musicians and other blacks, for whom they have great admiration. Norman Mailer (1957) embodies a good example of this reverse prejudice.

It is generally believed that this kind of phony escape from one's socioethnic origin is bad, whether engaged in by the black bourgeoisie or by white hipsters. There is, however, as Hall et al. (1975) describe it, a series of stages through which blacks may pass when encountering blackness in themselves, and the outcome of this cycle of identity transformation is, when completed, quite good. The stages are: (1) first seeing oneself as nonblack or antiblack, (2) realizing one's blackness, (3) being totally immersed in blackness and black pride, and finally (4) internalizing one's own

identity as black and being able to identify with a larger sense of community.

Beyond that, one has to seriously question the low black self-esteem thesis. We have already reviewed solid empirical evidence (cf. Rosenberg, 1972; Webster and Sobieszek, 1974; Yancey et al., 1972) undermining that thesis. And as Epstein et al. (1975) have shown, black children do not necessarily express a preference for white dolls over black dolls. What they do prefer are dolls that are neat and clean. Perhaps blacks have developed a new pride in themselves. More likely, the Clarks' findings have been misinterpreted.

The truth of the matter is that the meaning of color is by no means well understood at this time. Our crude transpositions from people to dolls to self may be a total misunderstanding, and so may the very concepts of "black" and "white." Actually, those Americans we call black are not black but range in complexion from fairly dark brown to the beige of many Europeans. In turn, so-called whites often have darker skins than blacks, and they are never white. Fig. 10-2 shows the objective distribution of skin color in the population.

As we see from Fig. 10-2, actual skin color has little to do with black and white. If a European-American is more likely to be classified as a white and an Afro-American as a black, it is because the two groups differ slightly, on the whole, in the average darkness of their coloring. However, people with the darkest possible skin are sometimes classified as Caucasians (whites) and people with very light skin are at times classified as blacks. For example, the federal government classifies Dravidian Indians as whites, although their skin color is often much darker than that of most American Negroes, and on the other hand men like Senator Edward Brooke and former Congressman Adam Clayton Powell probably have a lighter skin than many European Americans.

While it may be difficult (although, as we saw, not impossible) to chose one's gender identity, choice of racial identity should be

FIG. 10-2
The actual distribution
of skin color.

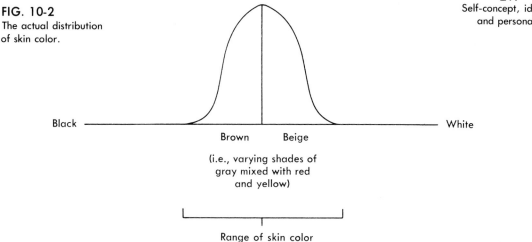

Black ——————————————— White

Brown   Beige

(i.e., varying shades of
gray mixed with red
and yellow)

Range of skin color

a cinch. We know of the many light-skinned mulattoes who have passed as whites. A more striking example is that of the Harlem jazz musician Mezz Mezzrow (cf. Mezzrow and Wolfe, 1975) who was Jewish by birth but black by choice!

Clearly, ethnic classifications are not about to disappear, for various governmental bureaucracies are enforcing them with a zeal reminiscent of the antebellum South. However, let us be clear about the fact that their basis is symbolic, not biological. It can be reasonably argued that the identities of "black" and "white" are no more rationally constructed than the designation of communists as "reds."

Another important source of personal identity is work, but the importance of this component varies by occupational stratum. As Dubin (1962) showed, work does not represent a central life interest to many blue-collar workers. However, for professionals, it often does (see Orzack, 1963; Wilensky, 1963).

Also, Carper and Becker (1970) showed in a study of college students that identification with an occupational choice is more or less difficult depending on that occupation's cultural acceptability. For example, students who decided to become mechanical engineers encountered no criticism, but those who chose physiology did, and those who decided to become philoso-

phers received the greatest amount of flack (from friends, relatives, and parents).

There are, of course, many other sources of identity. As Gregory Stone points out, one can even derive a sense of identity from one's city or community, and this is one of the functions of fandom. For example, the enthusiastic supporters of the Steelers and Pirates in the city of Pittsburgh derive a great deal of pride from their home teams' achievements. Identification with those teams and with the city they symbolize is an important source of identity, particularly in the absence of more concrete and personal alternatives.

Changes in identity

Even though a man generally has a single, coherent identity at a given time, this identity changes over time. Such change is, just as the sense of identity itself, always "in the eye of the beholder," as Erikson and Strauss point out. Whether the question "am I the same person today as yesterday?" is answered in the affirmative or not, *any* answer must inevitably be subjective.

Strauss (1962) has explicated this point nicely. Identity transformation, he points out, is a matter of a new self-evaluation taking hold, a new definition about a person being agreed upon, by himself and others. The actual behavioral changes upon which such a new definition is based may have occurred earlier, gradually, or not at all.

Often, a new identity arises at one of the *turning points* in an individual's life. As Strauss explains, change in an individual's relations with others is generally quite gradual. Then a sudden occurrence may trigger a new realization and the emergence of a new identity. An example is the immigrant who returns to the old country for the first time after many years. It then dawns on him how much he has changed, culturally and social-psychologically. His identity is now, finally, that of an American, or at least that of an immigrant to America.

Another turning point is often, in retrospect, when a person announces a position, climbing out on a limb, so to speak, and then having to live up to his new commitment. Or an individual may fill in for someone else on a certain job—say, as a counselor—and do unexpectedly well. This can be the discovery of a new "me," leading, accidentally, to a whole new occupational career and identity. These, then, are some examples of turning points in a person's development, turning points in identity and self-conception.

A transformation in identity often entails schedule and ritual. This may be done by an individual voluntarily, as when George Bernard Shaw withdrew from public life for eight years to reemerge as a converted socialist, having voluntarily submitted to a ritual moratorium. Or the process may be institutionalized in the form of such practices as the honeymoon.

The sense of personal continuity, or of identity, as well as significant change, is always a symbolic matter. Actual behavioral occurrences are less relevant than the subjective ordering of all events into a meaningful and coherent biography. One has a coherent identity to the extent that one succeeds in arranging one's experiences into a design, a scheme that makes sense in terms of the current self, the end product. In such a case, past experiences are accepted as "part of me." Even deviant events are incorporated. For example, past trouble and antisocial behavior become "learning experiences" or part of the psychological growth process. Such a unified interpretation is necessary or else the individual will suffer from a sense of personal discontinuity and existential meaninglessness. But in any event, constancy in identity is a subjective accomplishment, a psychological integration not necessarily dependent on actual events.

To what great lengths some individuals will go to achieve a sense of personal identity (and still often fail) is illustrated in Shaw's (1969) speculative account of the life of Simon Bolivar, the man who liberated much of Latin America from the Spaniards. Bolivar was constantly plagued by self-doubt. His great historical feats represented, among other things, an attempt to escape those doubts. But such externalization of his inner conflicts[2] did not satisfy him, for in the end, at the apex of power and glory, he doubted the value of his accomplishments and turned against them.

A final matter to be raised in this section is the relationship between identity and stigma. For example, MacGregor (1974) recently studied the impact of facial deformity on social relations and identity. Focusing on how the culture often deter-

---

[2]It has often been said that the real motivation underlying the earthshaking acts of many great historical figures has been some unresolved inner conflict, whether a physical inferiority complex, as allegedly in dictators of small stature such as Hitler and Napoleon, or Oedipal problems, as in the case of Christ, or some other neurosis. This has, in turn, led some authors to argue that we must be thankful for neuroses and other inner tensions, for they are often the internal forces that drive men to accomplish great deeds that they would not perform if they were normally contented. Be this as it may, we must remember that all such Freudian imputations of motives are hazardous and largely unprovable. For this reason, sociology wisely suggests that students of society and history abstain from such psychological speculation and limit themselves to the study of historical events and of their relationship to social definitions.

mines how others will interpret and respond to such stigmas, the author found, for example, that a slight facial scar was very upsetting to a woman from Puerto Rico because in her society that meant unfaithfulness.

Physical stigma is a visible stigma. It is, at least in face-to-face interaction, what Goffman (1963) calls *discredited* stigma, visible and known to others. On the other hand, stigma can also be *discreditable,* known only to oneself. Example of this type might include the covert homosexual, the undetected female impersonator, the former mental patient, and the exconvict. To conceal a stigma and present to others an identity that is not truly or completely one's own is called *passing.* It must be noted that just about any stigma can, under certain conditions, be discreditable, that is, concealed from others. All deviants (that is, bearers of stigma) can at times pass. For example, even the blind and the physically handicapped can pass, say in a telephone conversation. In turn, a stammerer can pass as long as he does not speak.

Passing has been most thoroughly documented among American blacks (cf. Myrdal, 1962). In the past, light-skinned mulattoes have often passed for Filipinos or Mediterranean Europeans in an effort to climb up a notch on the American ethnic stratification ladder. As a matter of fact, this led Myrdal to the conclusion that this process of "racial purification" is resulting in the gradual darkening of the American black population, since only the darker Negroes remain in that category!

Upwardly mobile light-skinned blacks have at times passed partially. For example, they may pass professionally but preserve a Negro circle of friends. Such partial passing may be a transitional stage toward complete and permanent passing (Myrdal, 1962:685). As Goffman (1963: 79-80) explains, this is often accompanied by a rite of passage and moving to another city or environment to then, "like a butterfly, emerging to try the brand new wings."

A few years ago, I studied an interesting group of stigmatized individuals—feminized transsexuals (cf. Kando, 1972; 1973a; 1974). These individuals had all been born natural males, but they had now all been surgically, cosmetically, and endocrinologically converted into females. *Were they women?* What was their true identity? The responses of the feminized transsexuals ranged from total acknowledgment of their background to near-total passing. There was at least one transsexual who was married to a man who did not know that she had, at one time, been a biological male. Passing, then, was a possibility of which at least some of the transsexuals made use. However, it was the feeling of just about everyone, including the subjects themselves, that the identity thus presented was not the "true" identity, that passing was a fraudulent thing.

Indeed, passing presents several hazards. Goffman (1963) discusses the anxieties and problems of those who must cope with discreditable stigma. For example, there is always the danger that one will, accidentally or of necessity, reveal discrediting information about oneself and eventually the discredited identity itself. And the effort at sustaining a normal identity may lead to misunderstandings and hurt feelings, such as when a deaf person is merely seen as gauche and snobbish.

A passer always lives a double life (Goffman, 1963:77), interacting with two distinct sets of others: those who know the whole man and those who don't. Sociologically, the passer is interesting because he is *aware* of social situations and problems that others handle automatically. For example, it can be argued (cf. Garfinkel, 1967; Kando, 1973a) that only feminized transsexuals know exactly what rules must be followed in order to be a woman. Natural born women don't know it; they merely do it.

Loss of identity

Perhaps transsexuals are only doing in the extreme what most of us also do. Indeed, according to a growing number of contemporary social commentators, one of the major problems confronting man in postindustrial mass society is the loss of permanent identity, the advent of the role-player, the selfless individual, the social chameleon. Ellul (1964), Goodman (1960), Mills (1951), Reich (1970), Riesman et al. (1950), Toffler (1970), Wheelis (1958), and Whyte (1956) are among the authors who have identified and deplored this trend.

Allen Wheelis (1958), for example, believes that the new social character in America is one that places a premium on adaptability, change, role-playing, and superficial and ephemeral interaction. This is because, as Toffler (1970) later emphasized, things are changing at an ever increasing pace in our society, technologically as well as politically and culturally. Modern mass man must therefore constantly adapt to new roles, new situations, fads, new rhetorics, and new values. For instance, loyalty and commitment to flag, country, political party, institution, colleagues, or superiors are now seen as anachronistic. Expediency replaces fixed moral principles. If we follow Wheelis' Freudian analysis, we may say that whereas earlier the major source of anxiety and neurosis was an excessively strong superego (conscience), today it is the absence of it, the selflessness of modern mass man.

Although Shakespeare noted a long time ago that life is, in a sense, a stage, it is particularly under the modern conditions outlined in the previous paragraph that the stage metaphor becomes valid. Sociology—the discipline that analyzes human behavior in terms of *roles*—is an eminently twentieth century enterprise. And it is the dramaturgical sociology of men like Goffman, Stone, Lyman, and Scott that grasps particularly well the theatricality (one might say, also the superficiality) of human interaction in modern society. Indeed, according to Lyman and Scott's *Sociology of the Absurd* (1970), modern life is a staged game in which we all act out our parts with greater or lesser competence, guided by a Machiavellian ethic, an ethic of expediency and public relations. The problem, of course, is that if life is a theater, then we must all inevitably suffer from stage fright (cf. Lyman and Scott, 1970), except the most ruthless sociopaths among us. Role-playing is not an adequate substitute for true inner identity.

PERSONALITY

Allport (see Lindesmith and Strauss, 1956:484) has classified fifty definitions of personality, pointing out that there is no single correct definition, only many different approaches—biological, elementaristic, Freudian, sociological, theological, and juridicial. For example, biological conceptions of personality go back to Ancient Greeks such as Empedocles and the founder of medicine, Hippocrates. This led to the *humoral* conception of personality, according to which the four humors in the body—blood, black bile, yellow bile, and phlegm—produce the four human personality types: sanguine, melancholic, choleric, and phlegmatic.

The elementaristic conception views personality as the sum of a person's traits, attitudes, habits, and ideas. The Freudian approach, on the other hand, is more holistic; it recognizes that there is an organizing principle to personality, an *ego*. The outcome of psychosexual development produces different personality types, for example, the oral, anal, and genital personality types.

None of the above conceptions of personality gives due recognition to its sociocultural origin and to the fact that it manifests itself in a social context. Furthermore, they all suffer from a psychologistic intrapersonal bias, since they all view personality as somehow internal to the individual. Today, many social psychologists have become critical of the traditional intrapersonal and psychologistic conception of personality (cf. Hunt, 1971; Yinger, 1971), and insofar as they use the concept, it is in an interactionist sense. In addition, many agree that personality is a behavioral concept. Yinger (1971), for example, distinguishes it from *character* as follows. Whereas character is the individual's organization of predispositions to behavior, that is, what the individual brings into the situation, *personality is the flow of behavior itself.* Such a conception of personality, then, distinguishes that term from self and identity.

Still, the best-known tests for the measurement of personality are those used by the (neo-) Freudians and clinical psychologists, and these tests are very blatant in their assumption that personality, far from being the empirically observable behavior of the moment, is a "thing" that is internal to the organism, a permanent entity, and often largely concealed from awareness. There are the so-called projective or indirect tests such as the Thematic Apperception Test (cf. Morgan and Murray, 1935) and the Rorschach Inkblot Test (see Rorschach, 1942), and personality inventories such as the Minnesota Multiphasic Personality Inventory (see Dahlstrom and Welsh, 1960) and the California Psychological Inventory (cf. Gough, 1957).

The TAT consists of twenty pictures about which the subject tells stories. For example, a picture like Fig. 10-3 might be shown.

One subject who was shown a picture similar to the one in Fig. 10-3, a veteran now in college, gave the following interpretation:

She has prepared this room for someone's arrival and is opening the door for a last general look over the room. She is probably expecting her son home. She tries to place everything as it was when he left. She seems like a very tyrannical character. She led her son's life for him and is going to take over again as soon as he gets back. This is merely the beginning of her rule, and the son is definitely cowed by this overbearing attitude of hers and will slip back into her well-ordered way of life. He will go through life plodding down the tracks she has laid down for him. All this represents her complete domination of his life until she dies (Arnold, 1949; quoted in Hilgard, 1957:482).

The Rorschach test is also a method for eliciting subjective interpretations from subjects (which presumably reveal latent personality traits and problems), but instead of pictures, abstract inkblots are shown.

Finally, personality inventories consist of a large number of questions submitted to subjects for their agreement or disagreement. For example, the MMPI consists of 495 statements such as the following ones:

I daydream very little.
I like to read newspaper editorials.
I have never done anything dangerous for the thrill of it.

A subject is asked to sort out these statements into three categories—those that he judges to be true, those that are false, and those about which he cannot say—and on

FIG. 10-3
A picture similar to
one of the TAT.

From Hilgard, Ernest R. 1957. Introduction to Psychology.
New York: Harcourt, Brace and Co., p. 481.

that basis clinical psychologists construct his profile(s).

The rationale behind personality tests is good, but their validity has long been questioned. Projective techniques such as the TAT and the Rorschach assume that the subjects' responses express inner personality characteristics or problems. Personality inventories like the MMPI assume that the items used are not culturebound. These are only a few of the problems. Nevertheless, within bounds, such tests have proved to be quite useful. For example, the MMPI has revealed consistent differences between the profiles of various categories of people, for example men, women, neurotics, psychotics, etc.

To the sociologist, personality has been a far less appealing concept. Nevertheless, some sociologists have attempted personality typologies. For example, Thomas and Znaniecki (1918-1921) argued that social disorganization could produce three types of personalities, three modes of adaptation: the philistine, who rigidly overconforms in an attempt at assuaging his inner anxieties; the bohemian, who does the opposite and is totally disorganized and carefree; and the creative man, who is both flexible and organized, thus combining the best elements of the other two types. One often sees young people among the bohemians and older people among the philistines.

If an individual's behavior sometimes displays cross-situational continuities, it is because of certain habits and roles he has acquired. Habits are merely tendencies to act in a certain way, and so is one's personality (cf. Shibutani, 1961:284). Roles are programs of action within given situations. Thus while there are continuities in human behavior, there is no need to posit a priori personality traits that are internal to the individual and exist prior to the act. A properly interactionist social psychology must avoid the reification of personality, an error recognized perhaps more elo-

quently by Tolstoy than by any sociologist:

> One of the most widespread superstitions is that every man has his own special, definite qualities; that a man is kind, cruel, wise, stupid, energetic, apathetic, etc. Men are not like that. . . . Men are like rivers: the water is the same in each, and alike in all; but every river is narrow here, is more rapid there, here slower, there broader, now clear, now cold, now dull, now warm. It is the same with men. Every man carries in himself the germ of every human quality, and sometimes one manifests itself, sometimes another, and the man often becomes unlike himself, while still remaining the same man. (Leo Tolstoy; quoted in Luft, 1970:51)

Some correlates of personality

Although personality must only be used in the limited sense of a *tendency* to behave in a certain fashion, it is a fact that these tendencies are not randomly distributed. As statisticians would say, there is often more variance among the various social and demographic groups than within them. For example, sex, race, social class, and (national) culture are among the variables significantly correlated with personality.

Freud's dictum "anatomy is destiny" is today considered an unforgivable faux pas. Simone de Beauvoir, who was liberated long before women's liberation had been heard of, states that "the passivity that is the essential characteristic of the 'feminine' woman is a trait that develops in her from the earliest years. But it is wrong to assert a biological datum is concerned; it is in fact a destiny imposed upon her by her teachers and by society" (Simone de Beauvoir; quoted in Aronson and Helmreich, 1973:19). I have elsewhere (cf. Kando, 1973b) discussed the nature-nurture controversy regarding gender characteristics and joined the nurture side. However, the current ideological climate must not make us oblivious to the fact that there are some genuine physiological bases for male-female personality differences. Bardwick (1971), for example, pays due attention to the natural hormonal differences between the sexes, differences that may account for some inescapable personality differences.

Whether masculinity-femininity is totally the product of culture and socialization or only partially so, the fact is that most women's scores on existing masculinity-femininity scales are more feminine than those of most men (cf. Kando, 1973a). Insofar as masculinity-femininity is learned, many studies have shown that this has a great deal to do with the presence or absence of gender identity figures, in sum with role-taking. For example, Barclay and Cusumano (1973) show that boys who grew up in a home with older males around them score higher on masculinity. They also quote another source that found that boys with absent fathers often had more feminine fantasies. For example, such a boy "might be less likely to dream of *making* a million dollars than of having the money simply fall into his lap. He would dream not of becoming a great industrial tycoon, but of holding a winning lottery ticket, being befriended by a wealthy benefactor, or being left a fortune by a distant relative" (Barclay and Cusumano, 1973:29).

Racial personality differences have been studied by many sociologists and psychologists. Guterman's (1972) reader contains many good studies about black personality, and Hernandez, Wagner, and Haug's (1971) does likewise for chicanos. Most racial personality studies have utilized one of the existing personality inventories, most frequently the MMPI. Many MMPI studies have found blacks to be (1) high on such things as defeatism, cynicism, and egocentricity, (2) low on affection need, idealism, and naivete, (3) high on withdrawal, alienation, and self-doubt, and (4) high on warmth, hyperactivity, and lack of inhibition (Guterman, 1972:163). However, a recent study by Baughman and Dahlstrom (1972) failed to find significant black-white differences in affection need and idealism.

As stated earlier, two pet sociological generalizations about modal black personality have been that (1) many ghetto males fail to develop adequate masculinity because they often grow up in a matriarchal home and (2) blacks suffer from a negative self-concept (Pettigrew, 1971). Today, both generalizations are increasingly questioned. For example, Hannerz (1972) shows that blacks find alternative male identity figures and role models when lacking a father.

Chicanos and American Indians have generally also been found to have "handicapped" personalities in terms of what personality inventories measure. For example, Mason (1971) used the California Psychological Inventory to demonstrate significant racial (and sexual) differences in such characteristics as security, achievement, sociability, and success orientation. White males scored highest, Indians and females scored lowest. Kamaroff et al. (1971) showed that Mexicans and blacks have more trouble readjusting to life crises such as death in the family and divorce than do whites.

Personality has also frequently been found to be correlated with social class. A classic study by Hollingshead and Redlich (1958) showed correlations between social class and various forms of mental illness. More recently, Banfield (1968; 1974), Allen (1971), and others have argued that a crucial differentiating factor between the social strata is the complex consisting of *time perspective* and *deferred gratification*. That is, the working and lower classes are said to be more present-oriented and less future-oriented, more oriented toward immediate gratification and less inclined to plan ahead and save for the future. Furthermore, the lower strata are also often said to believe that their lives are externally controlled, whereas members of the middle and upper strata believe in the efficacy of their own efforts (cf. Allen, 1971). Finally, the lower strata are often described as more spontaneous than the upper and middle strata.

The relationship between culture and personality has already been discussed (see Chapter 9). As we saw, there is a group of Freudian anthropologists (such as Kardiner, 1945) who believe that the kinds of infant disciplines used in a given culture determine that society's modal personality type and that this personality is in turn reflected by the society's secondary institutions. Although there is much that is tenuous about the culture and personality school (for an early critical evaluation, see Lindesmith and Strauss, 1956), it is undeniable that there are such things as national characters (cf. Martindale, 1967). Cultural configurations do, somehow, have their counterparts in individual personalities. For example there is definitely such a thing as a "typical American," certainly from the standpoint of a Frenchman or a Russian. Whether white, black, brown, or red, the typical American is generally slightly more spontaneous, free, friendly, casual, slovenly, boastful, optimistic, and dynamic than the typical Frenchman, Russian, German, or Dutchman. At a time when Americans are maximizing every minute internal ethnic and subcultural difference among themselves, calling themselves Afro-Americans, Italian-Americans, Mexican-Americans, Oriental, Scandinavian, Welsh, Irish, and every other conceivable name but the only true one—American—such stereotyping may be offensive. It is nevertheless valid.

Attitudes, values, and beliefs

The study of attitudes has long been a central concern of social psychology. To Floyd Allport (1924), attitudes were preparations for response, set up in the neuromuscular system. Obviously, this is an extremely behavioristic conception. Mead's (1956) definition was also surprisingly behavioristic. To the Chicago philosopher, attitudes were "the beginnings of acts . . . (found) in the central nervous system . . ." (Mead, 1956:119) or "inner organic conduct" (op. cit.: 120). "In the form of physiological attitudes (expressed in specific physiological sets) different possible completions to the given act are there in advance of its actual completion . . .; so that the purposive element in behavior has a physiological seat, a behavioristic basis, and is not fundamentally nor necessarily conscious nor psychichal" (op. cit.:178-179).

More acceptably, Thomas and Znaniecki (1918-1920) understood "by attitude . . . a process of individual consciousness which determines real or possible activity of the individual in the social world. (For example,) hunger that compels the consumption of the foodstuff; the workman's decision to use the tool. . . ."

Pioneering work in the study of attitudes was done by Newcomb (1943) in his famous study of attitude change among Bennington students and by Likert (1932),

	Strongly agree	Agree	Undecided	Disagree	Strongly disagree
Item 1					
Item 2					
Item 3					
. . . . . .					
Item N					

FIG. 10-4
Likert scale for the measurement of attitudes.

Summated agreement score (Σ):
Average agreement score $\left(\dfrac{\Sigma}{N}\right)$:

who devised what became the most widely used technique for attitude measurement. The basic format of Likert's attitude scale is presented in Fig. 10-4.

Related to the attitude concept is the concept of *value*. According to Thomas and Znaniecki (1918-1920) a value is anything with "a meaning with regard to which it . . . may be an object of activity. (For example), a foodstuff, an instrument, a scientific theory. . . ." Such a definition equates value with the thing that is valued—for example, money or freedom. However, Glenn Vernon (1973) has stressed the important distinction between value and value definition, two concepts insufficiently distinguished by sociologists. A value definition is a statement that calls attention to the human decision that (more or less arbitrarily) confers value on an object. For example, "In America, we consider money important."

"A belief differs from a value, in that while a value concerns what a person regards as good or desirable, a belief is a statement of what he regards as true or factual" (Theodorson and Theodorson, 1969:28). Although belief can be based on empirical criteria such as tradition, heresay, or faith (nonscientific belief), most sociological research on beliefs has been about the last kind. There is an enormous literature on prejudice (racial and otherwise), religious and cultist beliefs, and political beliefs and attitudes. Since American social science is overwhelmingly in the mainstream of our country's liberal tradition, it is the near-consensus of this research that extreme beliefs—whether (anti-) ethnic, religious, or political—are bad.

That American society is exceptionally racially prejudiced has been a tenet of American social science for at least forty years. The number of books and articles indicting American racial prejudice can no longer be estimated. Recent readers include Glock and Siegelman (1969), Guterman (1972), and Hernandez, Wagner, and Haug (1971). Since Gordon Allport's (1954) classic book on *The Nature of Preju-*

dice, more than five thousand social-scientific articles have appeared on this subject. Ehrlich (1973) reviewed six hundred of these, reducing this mass to twenty-two main psychological principles, such as (#22): "marginal persons manifest more favorable atitudes toward ethnic targets than do the more socially integrated," and (#12.1): "the greater the perceived similarity between an ethnic person and the actor, the lower the prejudice."

The matter of ethnic prejudice may now have been talked to death. That much, at least, has been accomplished by the innumerable writings and college courses in the sociology of intercultural relations. However, there are other forms of prejudice as well, less familiar and more interesting. For example, Goldberg (1973) showed that when women are asked to evaluate articles attributed to male authors, they give those articles a higher evaluation than when they are attributed to female authors. This clearly reveals that women tend to be biased against women.

Prejudice has also been examined in a religious context. Rokeach (1973), for example, building on Allport's classic work on prejudice, noted the frequent relationship between religious commitment (particularly of the fundamentalist kind) and racial and other forms of bigotry. It is the enduring paradox of religion everywhere that it engenders exclusionary ideas and thus develops an antihumanitarianism that is in diametrical contradiction with its original teachings. Rokeach might note that today men still kill each other far more frequently in the name of religion than anything else. Ireland, the Middle-East, Lebanon, India and Pakistan—such cases still outnumber those where political ideology or economics are the avowed bones of contention.

On the origins of religious beliefs, Lambert and associates (1964), who compared sixty-two societies in the Human Relations Area Files, found that cultures in which infants are reared punitively tend to have religions that stress the malevolence of the gods, whereas cultures where child-rearing is nurturing and affectionate have mostly benevolent deities.

Sociologists have also studied the various occult beliefs, for example gnosticism, nazism, alchemy, Irish fairies, Rosicrucians, tarot, freemasonry, witchcraft, ethnomethodology (Tiryakian, 1974), and doomsday and flying saucers cults (cf. Buckner, 1973; Festinger, Riecker, and Schachter, 1956; Lofland, 1966). Buckner found that the membership of flying saucers clubs consists primarily of older, lonely people who seek escape and find excitement, hope, and meaning in such beliefs. We might add a suggestion for longitudinal research testing the relationship between the frequency of UFO sightings and the business cycle. Certainly there seems to have been a sharp increase in such reports during the deep recession of the early 1970s.

The social scientist's interest in political beliefs has often centered on extremism and radical commitment (cf. Bell, 1964; Hoffer, 1951; Kornhauser, 1962). During and after World War II, fascism and anti-semitism were salient issues. It was in that climate that Adorno and associates (1950) carried out their classic study, *The Authoritarian Personality*, using the California Fascism Scale. Later work on the authoritarian personality includes Rokeach (1960) and Lipset (1959), who noted the prevalence of working-class authoritarianism.

The radical *right* has been the social scientist's most popular target. Studies repeatedly show the regional, religious, and sociological correlates of right-wing extremism, which is said to be concentrated in the South (Chmaj, 1969) and in Southern California (McEvoy, 1972), among religious zealots, suburbanites, and professions such as physicians (McEvoy, 1972).

However, when sociologists examine left-wing militancy, it is with an entirely different flavor. For example, militancy among blacks is said to be *unfortunately* low, as Gary Marx (1972) sees it, because of blacks' high degree of alienation and low self-esteem. Curle (1972) typologized people into four daringly evaluative categories—(1) low awareness individuals with weak belonging identity, (2) low awareness individuals with strong belonging identity, (3) high awareness individuals with strong belonging identity, and (4) high awareness individuals with weak belonging identity—and then proceeded to tell us in no uncertain terms who the good guys and the bad guys are. Category one includes loners, sometimes the criminals. Two includes the beer-drinking hard-hatters and the elitist professors. Three includes militant students. Finally, four comprises great lone figures such as Freud and Martin Luther King. Thus, according to Curle, it is easy to identify the peacemakers and, on the other hand, the opponents of justice. They are, respectively, groups three and two.

This example illustrates the bankrupt state of much of (political) sociology today. It often persists in beating dead horses such as organized religion and in "unmasking" the bigotry of the working class. The American working man has been stereotyped as an Archie Bunker, in liberal sociology as in the liberal media. If political sociology is to regain its value, it will have to abandon its blatant elitism as well as the boring dogmatism found in most current studies in this area.

In concluding this section, we now turn to the two central problems in the social-psychological study of attitudes. One of these is the attitude-behavior problem: what we say is rarely exactly the same thing as what we do. As Raab and Lipset (1971) note with respect to racial prejudice, the real problem is that many people, despite professing to be tolerant and unprejudiced, do not act that way. What respondents tell sociologists who interview them may not be a valid indicator of how they really feel and would act (cf. Deutscher, 1973). DeFleur and Westlie (1973), for example, asked respondents to state their racial attitudes and then requested them to sign an authorization to have a photograph taken of them with a member of another race and disseminated in varying degrees (for example, printed in a local paper, shown in a nationally televised advertisement for racial integration, etc.). Thus respondents would have to put their money where their mouth is, so to speak. As it turned out, in at least one third of the cases there was some discrepancy between avowed racial attitude and behavior.

Researchers have devised ingenious methods to get around the attitude-behavior problem, that is, to find out what people (would) really do. For example, Campbell and associates (1972) simply measured racial and sexual prejudice by examining the seating aggregations among students in the classroom. They measured the extent to which races and sexes tended to segregate themselves. Milgram's (1972)

lost-letter technique is another good unobtrusive method to measure real attitudes and behavior: a large number of letters are dropped throughout a city, addressed and stamped but unposted. The letters are of two kinds. One is addressed to a medical center, the other kind to the Communist Party, as shown in Fig. 10-5. The question is, what do people do when they find these letters? Do they mail them, open them, destroy them? And do they treat the letters differently depending on their destination? Milgram found that the medical research letters were turned in nearly three times as frequently as the communist letters. The significance of such work is in its methodology, which provides a more valid estimate of real attitudes than would interviewing. Milgram's technique can be used

---

Mr. Thuringer

Medical Research Associates
P.O. Box 7147
304 Columbus Avenue
New Haven 11, Connecticut

Attention: Mr. Walter Carnap

Mr. Thuringer

Friends of the Communist Party
P.O. Box 7147
304 Columbus Avenue
New Haven 11, Connecticut

Attention: Mr. Walter Carnap

FIG. 10-5
How envelopes might be addressed in the lost-letter technique.

From Milgram, Stanley. 1972. "The lost-letter technique." In Beyond the Laboratory: Field Research in Social Psychology. Leonard Bickman and Thomas Henchy (eds.). New York: McGraw-Hill Book Co., p. 246.

with different letters to measure attitudes toward other things.

The second major issue in the study of attitudes is the problem of *consistency*. As we saw in Chapter 2, Heider's concept of psychological balance led Festinger to develop his theory of cognitive dissonance (Festinger, 1957). This theory begins with the assumption that consonance, or consistency, of attitudes is the "natural" and desired psychological state. That is, individuals have a desire, insofar as possible, to hold attitudes, beliefs, and ideas that are consistent with one another and with their perceptions. For example, patriotic Americans who believe that America and the American government represent justice and liberty have difficulty in believing that we fought to suppress justice and liberty in Vietnam. This is one example of cognitive dissonance. On the other hand, that moral reevaluation is, itself, an ex post facto dissonance-reduction mechanism. Initially, most Americans did not doubt that the country was doing the right thing in Vietnam. However, once it became apparent that the war was being lost, we also had to convince ourselves that we were morally wrong. Otherwise, American public opinion would have suffered from severe cognitive dissonance.

Festinger explains that dissonance is, just like hunger, fear, and frustration, a basic human motivation toward action. Because dissonance is unpleasant, individuals will tend to attempt to reduce it. Much of Festinger's work consists of the enumeration and illustration of dissonance-reduction techniques. For example, one may simply change one's behavior. Or one may refuse to accept information contradicting one's beliefs.

In *When Prophecy Fails* (Festinger et al., 1956), the author and his colleagues studied a small Midwestern sect that followed a housewife who claimed to have received messages from the planet "Clarion" predicting the town's destruction by a flood.

The authors' major conclusion is that when the prophecy failed, the believers, far from abandoning their beliefs, could in fact have embraced them with even greater fanaticism and begun to proselytize in an effort to gain additional group support.

Nevertheless, people do learn to live with dissonance. Sometimes an individual is simply unable to establish consonance. Then, too, the capacity to tolerate dissonance varies. In fact, the so-called authoritarian personality can be conceived of precisely in these terms, as a person with a low tolerance for cognitive dissonance.

Festinger's dissonance theory has spawned an enormous amount of research. Aronson (1971) has reviewed some of it. Some researchers have explored how word retention may be facilitated by the use of cognitive dissonance and congruence principles (Havron and Cofer, 1964). Some have explored the potential of dissonance techniques to change attitudes (Smith, 1972).

One of the more interesting ramifications of the theory is found in the work of Jack Brehm and his associates. These authors have explored the various psychological aspects of the phenomenon of *choice*. For example, in an experiment (Brehm and Cohen, 1964a) children were given choices between similar toys, other ones between dissimilar ones. The researchers found, among other things, that the children who were given choices between dissimilar toys learned to like the toy(s) of their choice more (in contrast with the toys not chosen) than the other group. This is an example of how the strength of cognitive dissonance operates. In another study, Brehm and Cohen (1964b) examined the effect of choice upon how a person feels about some unpleasant situation (in which he finds himself).

Finally, Brehm (1971) formulated his theory of *psychological reactance*: when a free behavior is threatened or eliminated, "reactance" is aroused to restore it, that is, there seems to be a motive to enhance the attractiveness of the choice alternative that is threatened. For example, if Diane is dating both Johnny and Tom and her parents tell her that she may no longer go out with Tom (without further explanation), then Diane should experience reactance, that is, an increased desire to go out with Tom.

In general, whether or not people have an "inherent" need for consistency remains a moot point. In the first place, consistency may be a conceptual scheme in the mind of the social scientist, not in the subject. Something that may appear dissonant to a sociological observer may make perfect sense to the subject. Furthermore, sociology teaches us that we play different roles in different situations and that there is therefore no need to posit a tendency toward cross-situational consistency. It is quite possible for an individual, for example, to conceive of himself as a strong and authoritarian boss in one setting (say, at the office) and a meek and submissive mouse in another (at home, vis-a-vis his wife). As Gergen explains, if there is a tendency toward consistency, it may not be because of a genetic basis but because "Western culture simply does not seem prone to accepting both a proposition and its antithesis simultaneously" (Gergen,

1971:21). By the same token, if the generalizations made in the concluding paragraphs of our discussion of identity are correct, then it follows that modern Western man should exhibit an increasing tolerance for inconsistency and dissonance.

Intelligence

One of the perennial controversies regarding human personality differences has been the matter of capability or, more specifically, intelligence. Always in life, some people do better than others. Why? Are they *inherently* more capable, or have they just had the breaks, for example, by way of a better socialization?

The scientific measurement of intelligence was begun by the French psychologist Alfred Binet in 1904. He distinguished between an individual's mental age (MA) and his chronological age (CA). On the average for most people, MA equals CA. However, a bright individual's MA will exceed his CA, and a dull person's MA will be below his CA. Subsequently, the standard measure of intelligence de-

FIG. 10-6

Two examples of items used in intelligence testing.

1. Mark F if the sentence is foolish; mark S if it is sensible:

   S F Mrs. Smith has had no children, and I understand that the same was true of her mother.

2. In each row mark every card that is like the first card in the row:

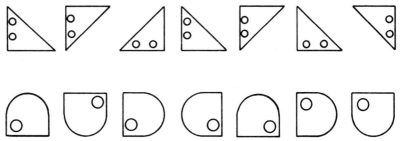

From Thurstone, L. L., and T. G. Thurstone. 1941. "Factorial studies of intelligence." Psychometry Monogram 2; reproduced in Hilgard, Ernest R. 1957. Introduction to Psychology. New York: Harcourt, Brace and Co., p. 481.

veloped in the United States became the Stanford-Binet test, according to which a person's intelligence quotient (IQ) is equal to his MA divided by his CA and multiplied by 100, as shown in the formula below:

$$IQ = 100 \; \frac{\text{Mental age (MA)}}{\text{Chronological age (CA)}}$$

Thus the average IQ is 100, and intelligence has been found to be normally distributed on both sides of this average. IQ is measured through a variety of items, verbal, pictorial, mathematical, concrete (culture-bound), and abstract. Fig. 10-6 gives two examples of items that have been used in some intelligence tests.

The question about intelligence is, of course, whether it is inborn or learned. This is the so-called nature-nurture issue. One area in which this issue has been researched and debated is sex. Are male-female differences in intelligence biogenic or sociogenic? Fitt and Rogers (1950) found a higher mean IQ among females than males but attributed this to the verbal nature of the tests. However, there is research attributing performance to sex hormones, at least among animals (cf. Douglas, Hanson, and Zucker, 1948), and a line of research currently gaining in popularity deals with cerebral hemispheres (cf. Ten Houten and Kaplan, 1973). It is postulated that one side of the brain—the side most dominant in females—is the locus of "appositional thought," while the other, the male side, is where "propositional thought" takes place. Thus women are good with tarot cards and the I Ching, but men excel in science. If this sounds absurd, it is partially intentional, for it is difficult to accept such biological simplification. However, the value of these ideas will, admittedly, have to be determined by research and not prejudice.

The nature-nurture issue has been debated more vigorously with respect to race than to sex, thus far. As we saw in Chapter 4, the evidence supporting the nurture (environmentalist) position goes back at least to Klineberg's (1935) refutation of the selective migration hypothesis, and it has been argued innumerable times that intelligence tests measure cultural knowledge, not innate intelligence (see the Dove Counterbalance Test, Chapter 4). Nevertheless, many authors have recently exhumed the nature proposition, researching the possible inborn-hereditary nature of intelligence. Jensen (1970), Shockley (1970), Eysenck (1971), and Herrnstein (1973) are among the scholars who recently did empirical research on this taboo subject and gained notoriety as a result.

Meanwhile, liberals—including most sociologists—redouble their critique of such research (cf. Hager, 1974; Leggett, 1973), sometimes labelling it racist, elitist, fascist, or social-Darwinistic, and attempting to ban it.

In sociology, which is unanimously on the nurture side of the controversy, the key expression to explain the poor performance of minorities in school and in society has been "cultural deprivation" (cf. Ausubel, 1966; Della-Dora, 1966; Himes, 1966). In other words, blacks are not only deprived socioeconomically but *verbally* as well (cf. Newton, 1966). Worst off are black males (Woronoff, 1966), who suffer the double jeopardy of racial discrimination and a matriarchal upbringing.

Some authors (cf. Pasamanick and Knobloch, 1966) have found a category of possible determinants of intelligence that falls between the nature and the nurture variables. Many minority infants are born retarded because of injury suffered in utero, for example as a result of hypertension, bleeding, premature birth, and other pregnancy problems particularly affecting the black and the poor. This, then, is an organic cause, although not a racial-genetic one. The same applies to diet, which may be significantly inferior among ghetto minorities and may thus affect school performance.

On the whole, much of the "cultural deprivation" sociology is bad ideological rhetoric rather than good research, in contrast, one must say, with the rigorous and methodical work of men like Jensen, Herrnstein, and Eysenck.

A proper conception of intelligence cannot be found in biological reductionism. Symbolic interactionists have long noted that intelligence is (1) a symbolic process, (2) a social phenomenon, and (3) often the product of a self-fulfilling definition of the situation. Intelligence is the ability to interpret and respond to signs and symbols. It is the uniquely human capacity for conceptual thought. For example, *memory,* which is such an important element in intelligence, is entirely dependent on symbolic ability. It is known that aphasia produces amnesia and that preverbal childhood memories are not, as Freud believed, repressed but merely not remembered because they are simply not recollectable! (cf. Lindesmith and Strauss, 1956:113).

Mead (1934) and Piaget (1950) both stressed the inescapable social nature of intelligence. Intelligence, to Mead, was the ability to point things out to oneself, the capacity for reflection. This, of course, requires putting oneself in the place of another, role-taking. The feral girl Isabelle described by Davis (1947) proves the point. Prior to her discovery, she was no more capable of verbal communication than an animal. Then, once brought into contact with people, her IQ trebled within a year and a half.

As Rosenthal and Jacobson's (1968) famous study shows, pupils' intelligence is not independent from the teachers' expectations. A student's poor performance may often be the result of labelling rather than its cause. This is what minorities have been complaining about. Cicourel and coworkers (1974) have recently criticized intelligence testing and the tracking of students for these reasons. This excellent study unmasks the ill-conceived assumptions underlying testing and tracking, concluding that there is little that is objective and scientific about them.

In the final analysis, a meaningful conception of intelligence must be broad, humanistic, and behavioral. It must incorporate such elements as competence in interpersonal living (cf. Foote and Cottrell, 1955), breadth of perspective (cf. Warshay, 1962), and above all the ability to suspend judgment, to hypothesize, to mentally and reflexively consider alternative possibilities in terms of their possible consequences (cf. Dewey, 1910). Man shares impulse and conditioning with other animals; he alone possesses intelligence and imagination.

SUMMARY AND CONCLUSION

This chapter has discussed self-concept, identity, and personality. These concepts, describing three fundamental aspects of the self, seem to imply something static. However, we must keep in mind that change is inevitable. While personality may be a useful concept, it is only an illusion (Sullivan, 1964). Even when we reach maturity, as Sullivan notes, this does not mean that we then have a set personality. Maturity means the ability to learn from new experiences, from failure as well as success.

As we saw, a biography can be construed as a "career." Not atypically, a man first establishes a stable sexual relationship, then his occupation absorbs him increasingly, and as he moves up the occupational status hierarchy, he gains in social power. The career concept, as we saw, can apply to many of life's transitions, not only to the occupational realm.

The transition from one status to another may be smooth or abrupt. As we saw, life inevitably contains crises, turning points, even drastic conversions. Change, in whichever form, is inescapable. No self remains the same. Attitudes, values, beliefs, and intelligence, too, change and fluctuate.

REFERENCES
Adorno, T. W. et al.
1950 The Authoritarian Personality. New York: Harper & Row, Publishers.

Allen, Vernon L. (ed.)
1971 Psychological Factors in Poverty. Chicago: Markham Publishing Co.

Allport, Floyd H.
1924 Social Psychology. Boston: Houghton Mifflin Co.

Allport, Gordon
1954 The Nature of Prejudice. Reading, Mass.: Addison-Wesley Publishing Co., Inc.

Arnold, M.
1949 "A demonstrational analysis of the TAT in a clinical setting." Journal of Abnormal Social Psychology 44:97-111.

Aronson, Elliot
1971 "Dissonance theory: progress and problems." In Current Perspectives in Social Psychology. Edwin P. Hollander and Raymond G. Hunt (eds.). New York: Oxford University Press, pp. 359-372.

Aronson, Elliot and Robert Helmreich (eds.)
1973 Social Psychology: a Transaction/Society Reader. New York: D. Van Nostrand Co.

Ausubel, David P.
1966 "The effects of cultural deprivation on learning patterns." In Understanding the Educational Problems of the Disadvantaged Learner. Staten W. Webster (ed.). San Francisco: Chandler Publishing Co., pp. 251-258.

Backman, Carl W.
1973 Review of the Assessment of Self, by Stephen Spitzer et al. Contemporary Sociology (September):503-504.

Backman, Carl W., Paul F. Second, and Jerry R. Pierce
1971 "Resistance to change in the self-concept." In Selected Readings and Projects in Social Psychology. Richard R. MacDonald and James A. Schellenberg (eds.). New York: Random House, Inc., p. 130.

Banfield, Edward C.
1968 The Unheavenly City. Boston: Little, Brown and Co.
1974 The Unheavenly City Revisited. Boston: Little, Brown and Co.

Barclay, Allan G. and D. R. Cusumano
1973 "Testing masculinity in boys without fathers." In Social Psychology: A Transaction/Society Reader. Elliot Aronson and R. Helmreich (eds.). New York: D. Van Nostrand Co., pp. 27-29.

Bardwick, Judith M.
1971 Psychology of Women: A Study of Bio-Cultural Conflicts. New York: Harper & Row, Publishers.

Baughman, E. Earl and W. Grant Dahlstrom
1972 "Racial differences on the Minnesota Multiphasic Personality Inventory." In Black Psyche: The Modal Personality Patterns of Black Americans. Stanley S. Guterman (ed.). Berkeley, Calif.: The Glendessary Press.

Bell, Daniel
1964 The Radical Right. Garden City, N.Y.: Doubleday & Co., Inc.

Brehm, Jack W.
1971 "A theory of psychological reactance." In Current Perspectives in Social Psychology. Edwin P. Hollander and Raymond G. Hunt (eds.). New York: Oxford University Press, pp. 35-43.

Brehm, Jack W. and Arther R. Cohen
1964a "Re-evaluation of choice alternatives as a function of their number and qualitative similarity." In Dimensions of Social Psychology. W. Edgar Vinacke et al. (eds.). Chicago: Scott, Foresman & Co., pp. 156-162.
1964b "Choice and chance relative deprivation as determinants of cognitive dissonance." In Dimensions of Social Psychology. W. Edgar Vinacke et al. (eds.). Chicago: Scott, Foresman & Co., pp. 162-166.

Buckner, H. Taylor
1973 "Flying saucers are for people." In Social Psychology: a Transaction/Society Reader. Elliot Aronson and Robert Helmreich (eds.). New York: D. Van Nostrand Co., pp. 56-60.

Campbell, Donald T. et al.
1972 "Seating aggregation as an index of attitude." In Beyond the Laboratory: Field Research in Social Psychology. Leonard Bickman and Thomas Henchy (eds.). New York: McGraw-Hill Book Co., pp. 146-155.

Cardwell, J. D.
1971 Social Psychology: A Symbolic Interactionist Perspective. Philadelphia; F. A. Davis Co.

Carper, James W. and Howard S. Becker
1970 "Adjustments to conflicting expectations in the development of identification with an occupation." In Social Psychology Through Symbolic Interaction. Gregory P. Stone and Harvey A. Farberman (eds.). Waltham, Mass.: Ginn-Blaisdell, pp. 606-612.

Chmaj, Betty E.
1969 "Paranoid patriotism: the radical right and the south." In Current Perspectives on Social Problems. Judson R. Landis (ed.). Belmont, Calif.: Wadsworth Publishing Co., pp. 392-406.

Cicourel, Aaron V. et al.
1974 Language Use and School Performance. New York: Academic Press, Inc.

Clark, K. and M. Clark
1952 "Racial identification and preference in Negro children." In Readings in Social Psychology. E. E. Swanson, T. M. Newcomb, and E. L. Hartley (eds.). New York: Holt, Rinehart & Winston.

Coopersmith, Stanley
1967 The Antecedents of Self-Esteem. San Francisco: W. H. Freeman and Co., Publishers.

Couch, Carl J.
1962 "Family role specialization and self-attitudes in children." Sociological Quarterly (April):115-121.

Crane, Stephen
1925 The Red Badge of Courage. New York: D. Appleton and Company.

Curle, Adam
1972 Mystics and Militants: A Study of Awareness, Identity, and Social Action. London: Tavistock Publishers.

Dahlstrom, W. Grant and George Schlager Welsh
1960 An MMPI Handbook—A Guide to Use in Clinical Practice and Research. Minneapolis: University of Minnesota Press.

Davis, Kingsley
1947 "Final note on a case of extreme isolation." American Journal of Sociology (March): 432-437.

Defleur, Melvin L. and Frank R. Westlie
1973 "Verbal attitudes and overt acts: an experiment in the salience of attitudes." In What We Say/What We Do. Irwin Deutscher (ed.). Glenview, Ill.: Scott, Foresman and Co., pp. 67-76.

Della-Dora, Delmo
1966 "The culturally disadvantaged: educational implications of certain social-cultural phenomena." In Understanding the Educational Problems of the Disadvantaged Learner. Staten W. Webster (ed.). San Francisco: Chandler Publishing Co., pp. 267-276.

Deutscher, Irwin
1973 What We Say/What We Do: Sentiments and Acts. Glenview, Ill.: Scott, Foresman and Co.

Dewey, John
1910 How We Think. Lexington Mass.: D. C. Heath & Co.

Douglas, J. W. B., D. A. Hanson, and S. Zucker
1948 "The effect of sex hormones on the performance of a learned response." Journal of Experimental Biology 25:395-405.

Driver, Edwin D.
1969 "Self-conceptions in India and the United States: a cross-cultural validation of the Twenty Statement Test." Sociological Quarterly (Summer):341-354.

Dubin, Robert
1962 "Industrial workers' worlds: a study of the 'central life interests' of industrial workers." In Human Behavior and Social Processes. Arnold M. Rose (ed.). Boston: Houghton Mifflin Co., pp. 247-266.

Ehrlich, Howard J.
1973 The Social Psychology of Prejudice: A Systematic Theoretical Review and Propositional Inventory of the American Social Psychological Study of Prejudice. New York: John Wiley & Sons, Inc.

Ellul, Jacques
1964 The Technological Society. New York: Alfred Knopf, Inc.

Epstein, Yakov M. et al.
1975 "Clean is beautiful." In Psychology is Social. Edward Krupat (ed.). Glenview, Ill.: Scott, Foresman and Co., pp. 34-43.

Erikson, Erik H.
1959 "The problem of ego identity." Psychological Issues 1:101-166.

Eysenck, Hans J.
1971 The I.Q. Argument: Race, Intelligence and Education. New York: The Library Press.

Festinger, Leon
1957 A Theory of Cognitive Dissonance. Evanston, Ill.: Row, Peterson.

Festinger, Leon, Henry W. Riecker, and Stanley Schachter
1956 When Prophecy Fails. Minneapolis: University of Minnesota Press.

Fitt, A. B. and C. A. Rogers
1950 "The sex factor in the Cattell Intelligence Tests, Scale III." Journal of British Psychology 41:186-192.

Foote, Nelson and Leonard S. Cottrell, Jr.
1955 Identity and Interpersonal Competence: A New Direction in Family Research. Chicago: University of Chicago Press.

Franks, David D.
1974 "Current conceptions of competency motivation and self-validation." In Social Psychology for Sociologists. David Field (ed.). New York: John Wiley & Sons, Inc.

Fromm, Erich
1957 The Art of Loving. London: Unwin Books.

Garfinkel, Harold
1967 Studies in Ethnomethodology. Englewood Cliffs, N.J.: Prentice-Hall, Inc.

Gergen, Kenneth J.
1971 The Concept of Self. New York: Holt, Rinehart and Winston, Inc.

Glock, Charles Y. and Ellen Siegelman
1969 Prejudice U.S.A. New York: Praeger Publishers.

Goffman, Erving
1963 Stigma: Notes on the Management of Spoiled Identity. Englewood Cliffs, N.J.: Prentice-Hall, Inc.

Goldberg, Philip
1973 "Are women prejudiced against women?" In Social Psychology in Everyday Life. Billy J. Franklin and Frank J. Kohout (eds.). New York: David McKay Co., pp. 249-254.

Goodman, Paul
1960 Growing Up Absurd. New York: Vintage Books.

Gough, H. G.
1957 California Psychological Inventory Manual. Palo Alto: Consulting Psychologists Press.

Guterman, Stanley S. (ed.)
  1972 Black Psyche: The Modal Personality Patterns of Black Americans. Berkeley, Calif.: The Glendessary Press.
Hager, Don J.
  1974 Review of I.Q. in the Meritocracy, by R. J. Herrnstein. Contemporary Sociology (March):116-118.
Hall, William S. et al.
  1975 "Stages in the development of black awareness." In Psychology is Social. Edward Krupat (ed.). Glenview, Ill.: Scott Foresman and Co., pp. 27-33.
Hannerz, Ulf
  1972 "The significance of 'soul'." In Black Psyche: the Modal Personality Patterns of Black Americans. Stanley Guterman (ed.). Berkeley, Calif.: The Glendessary Press.
Havron, M. D. and C. N. Cofer
  1964 "On the learning of material congruent and incongruent with attitudes." In Dimensions of Social Psychology. W. Edgar Vinacke et al. (eds.). Chicago, Ill.: Scott, Foresman and Co., pp. 152-156.
Helmreich, Robert and Roland Radloff
  1973 "Environmental stress and the maintenance of self-esteem." In Social Psychology: A Transaction—Society Reader. Elliot Aronson and Robert Helmreich (eds.). New York: D. Van Nostrand Co., pp. 156-161.
Hernandez, Carrol, Nathaniel N. Wagner, and Marsha J. Haug
  1976 Chicanos: Social and Psychological Perspectives. St. Louis: The C. V. Mosby Co.
Herrnstein, R. J.
  1973 I.Q. in the Meritocracy. Boston: Little, Brown and Co.
Hilgard, Ernest R.
  1957 Introduction to Psychology. New York: Harcourt, Brace and Co.
Himes, Joseph S.
  1966 "Negro teen-age culture." In Knowing the Disadvantaged. Staten W. Webster (ed.). San Francisco: Chandler Publishing Co., pp. 161-175.
Hoffer, Eric
  1951 The True Believer. New York: Harper & Row, Publishers.
Hollingshead, August B. and Frederick C. Redlick
  1958 Social Class and Mental Illness: A Community Study. New York: John Wiley & Sons, Inc.
Hunt, J. McVicker
  1971 "Traditional personality theory in the light of recent evidence." In Current Perspectives in Social Psychology. Edwin P. Hollander and Raymond G. Hunt (eds.). New York: Oxford University Press, pp. 134-144.

James, William
  1890 Principles of Psychology. New York: Henry Holt.
Jensen, Arthur R.
  1970 "Learning ability, intelligence and educability." In Psychological Factors in Poverty. Vernon L. Allen (ed.). Chicago: Markham Publishing Co., pp. 106-132.
Kamaroff, Anthony L. et al.
  1971 "The social readjustment rating scale: a comparative study of Negro, Mexican and White Americans." In Chicanos: Social and Psychological Perspectives. Carrol Hernandez, Nathaniel N. Wagner, and Marsha J. Haug (eds.). St. Louis: The C. V. Mosby Co.
Kando, Thomas
  1972 "Role strain: a comparison of males, females and transsexuals." Journal of Marriage and the Family (August):459-464.
  1973a Sex Change: The Achievement of Gender Identity Among Feminized Transsexuals. Springfield, Ill.: Charles C Thomas, Publisher.
  1973b "Sex roles and socialization: a contemporary problem." The Highlander (May 10, 17, and 24):5, 17; 4, 24; 6, 33.
  1974 "Males, females and transsexuals." Journal of Homosexuality (Fall):45-64.
Kaplan, Howard B.
  1975 Self-Attitudes and Deviant Behavior. Pacific Palisades, Calif.: Goodyear Publishing Co.
Kardiner, Abram
  1945 The Psychological Frontiers of Society. New York: Columbia University Press.
Kinch, John W.
  1963 "A formalized theory of the self-concept." American Journal of Sociology (January):481-486.
  1968 "Experiments on factors related to self-concept change." Journal of Social Psychology 74:251-258.
  1973 Social Psychology. New York: McGraw-Hill Book Co.
Klapp, Orrin E.
  1962 Heroes, Villains and Fools: The Changing American Character. Englewood Cliffs, N.J.: Prentice-Hall, Inc.
Klineberg, Otto H.
  1935 Race Differences. New York: Harper & Row, Publishers.
Kornhauser, William
  1962 "Social bases of political commitment: a study of liberals and radicals." In Human Behavior and Social Processes. Arnold M. Rose (ed.). Boston: Houghton Mifflin Co., pp. 321-339.
Kuhn, Manford H.
  1960 "Self-attitudes by age, sex, and professional training." Sociology Quarterly (January):39-55.
Kuhn, Manford H. and Thomas S. McPartland
  1954 "An empirical investigation of self-atti-

tudes." American Sociological Review 19:68-76.

Lambert, William W. et al.
1964 "Some correlates of beliefs in the malevolence and benevolence of supernatural beings: a cross-societal study." In Dimensions of Social Psychology. W. E. Vinacke et al. (eds.). Chicago: Scott, Foresman and Co., pp. 107-114.

Landis, Judson R. et al.
1973 "Feminist attitudes as related to sex of the interviewer." Pacific Sociological Review (July):305-314.

Leggett, John C.
1973 Review of Hans J. Eysenck's the I.Q. Argument: Race, Intelligence and Education. Society (July/August):79-84.

Likert, Rensis
1932 "A technique for the measurement of attitudes." Archives of Psychology 21 (4).

Lindesmith, Alfred R. and Anselm L. Strauss
1956 Social Psychology: The Revised Edition. New York: Holt, Rinehart and Winston.

Lipset, Seymour Martin
1959 Political Man: The Social Bases of Politics. Garden City, N.Y.: Doubleday & Co., Inc.

Litman, Theodor J.
1962 "Self-conception and physical rehabilitation." In Human Behavior and Social Processes. Arnold M. Rose (ed.). Boston: Houghton Mifflin Co., pp. 550-574.

Lofland, John
1966 Doomsday Cult. Englewood Cliffs, N.J.: Prentice-Hall, Inc.

Luft, Joseph
1970 Group Processes: An Introduction to Group Dynamics. Palo Alto, Calif.: National Press Books.

Lyman, Stanford M. and Marvin B. Scott
1970 A Sociology of the Absurd. New York: Meredith Corp.

MacGregor, Frances Cooke
1974 Transformation and Identity: The Face and Plastic Surgery. New York: New York Times Book Co.

Mailer, Norman
1958 "The white Negro." Voices of Dissent (Autumn):195-214.

Martindale, Don (ed.)
1967 "National character in the perspective of the social sciences." Annals of The American Academy of Political and Social Science (March).

Marx, Gary T.
1971 "The white Negro and the Negro white." In Social Psychology in Everyday Life. Billy J. Franklin and Frank J. Kohout (eds.). New York: David McKay Co., pp. 137-149.
1972 "The psychological context of militancy." In Black Psyche: The Modal Personality Patterns of Black Americans. Stanley Guterman (ed.). Berkeley, Calif.: The Glendessary Press.

Mason, Evelyn P.
1971 "Cross-validation study of personality characteristics of junior high students from American Indian, Mexican, and Caucasian ethnic backgrounds." In Chicanos: Social and Psychological Perspectives. Carrol Hernandez, Nathaniel N. Wagner, and Marsha J. Haug (eds.). St. Louis: The C. V. Mosby Co.

McEvoy, James et al.
1972 "Content analysis of a super patriot protest." In Beyond the Laboratory: Field Research in Social Psychology. Leonard Bickman and Thomas Henchy (eds.). New York: McGraw-Hill Book Co., pp. 302-309.

Mead, George Herbert
1934 Mind, Self and Society. Charles W. Morris (ed.). Chicago: University of Chicago Press.
1956 On Social Psychology. Anselm Strauss (ed.). Chicago: University of Chicago Press.

Mezzrow, Milton and Bernard Wolfe
1975 "Really the blues." In Readings in Social Psychology. Alfred R. Lindesmith et al. (eds.). Hinsdale, Ill.: The Dryden Press, pp. 77-82.

Milgram, Stanley
1972 "The lost-letter technique." In Beyond the Laboratory: Field Research in Social Psychology. Leonard Bickman and Thomas Henchy (eds.). New York: McGraw-Hill Book Co., pp. 245-251.

Mills, C. Wright
1951 White Collar: The American Middle Classes. New York: Oxford University Press.

Miyamoto, S. Frank and Sanford M. Dornbusch
1956 "A test of interactionist hypotheses of self-conception." American Journal of Sociology (March):399-403.

Morgan, C. D. and M. A. Murray
1935 "A method for investigating fantasies: The Thematic Apperception Test." Archives of Neurological Psychiatry 34:289-306.

Moynihan, Daniel Patrick
1965 The Negro Family: The Case for National Action. Washington, D.C.: U.S. Government Printing Office.

Myrdal, Gunnar
1962 An American Dilemma. New York: Harper & Row, Publishers.

Newcomb, T. M.
1943 Personality and Social Change: Attitude Formation in a Student Community. New York: Dryden Press.

Newton, Eunice S.
1966 "Verbal destitution: the pivotal barrier to learner." In Understanding the Educational Problems of the Disadvantaged Learner.

Staten W. Webster (ed.). San Francisco: Chandler Publishing Co., pp. 333-338.

Orzack, Louis
  1963 "Work as a 'central life interest' of professionals." In Work and Leisure—A Contemporary Social Problem. Erwin O. Smigel (ed.). New Haven, Conn.: College and University Press, pp. 73-84.

Pasamanick, Benjamin and Hilda Knobloch
  1966 "The contribution of some organic factors to school retardation in Negro children." In Understanding the Educational Problems of the Disadvantaged Learner. Staten W. Webster (ed.). San Francisco: Chandler Publishing Co., pp. 286-293.

Pasternak, Boris
  1971 "Identity: you in others." In Selected Readings and Projects in Social Psychology. Richard R. MacDonald and James A. Schellenberg (eds.). New York: Random House, Inc., p. 48.

Pepitone, Albert et al.
  1971 "The role of self-esteem in comparative choice behavior." In Comparative Perspectives on Social Psychology. William Wilson et al. (eds.). Boston: Little, Brown and Co., pp. 76-92.

Pettigrew, Thomas
  1971 "Negro American personality: the role and its burdens." In Current Perspectives in Social Psychology. Edwin P. Hollander and Raymond G. Hunt (eds.). New York: Oxford University Press, pp. 159-166.

Piaget, J.
  1950 "The socialization of individual intelligence." In The Psychology of Intelligence. London: Routledge and Keagan Paul, Ltd., pp. 157-166.

Quarantelli, E. L. and Joseph Cooper
  1966 "Self-conceptions and others: a further test of Meadian hypotheses." Sociological Quarterly (Summer):281-297.

Raab, Earl and Seymour Martin Lipset
  1971 "The prejudiced society." In Chicanos: Social and Psychological Perspectives. Carrol Hernandez, Nathaniel N. Wagner, and Marsha J. Haug (eds.). St. Louis: The C. V. Mosby Co., pp. 5-18.

Rainwater, Lee
  1972 "Crucible of identity: the Negro lower-class family." In Black Psyche: The Modal Personality Patterns of Black Americans. Stanley S. Guterman (ed.). Berkeley, Calif.: The Glendessary Press.

Ray, Marsh B.
  1973 "Abstinence cycles and heroin addicts." In Deviance: The Interactionist Perspective.

Earl Rubington and Martin S. Weinberg (eds.). New York: The Macmillan Co., p. 427.

Reckless, Walter C.
  1960 The Crime Problem. New York: Appleton-Century-Crofts.

Reeder, Leo G. et al.
  1960 "Conceptions of self and others." American Journal of Sociology (September):153-159.

Reich, Charles A.
  1970 The Greening of America. New York: Random House, Inc.

Riesman, David et al.
  1950 The Lonely Crowd. New Haven, Conn.: Yale University Press.

Rokeach, Milton
  1960 The Open and Closed Mind. New York: Basic Books, Inc.
  1973 "Paradoxes of religious belief." In Social Psychology: a Transaction—Society Reader. Elliot Aronson and Robert Helmreich (eds.). New York: D. Van Nostrand Co., pp. 169-172.

Rorschach, H.
  1942 Psychodiagnostics. Berne: Hans Huber.

Rosenberg, Morris
  1972 "Race, ethnicity, and self-esteem." In Black Psyche: The Modal Personality Patterns of Black Americans. Berkeley, Calif.: The Glendessary Press.

Rosenthal, Robert and L. Jacobson
  1968 Pygmalion in the Classroom: Teacher Expectation and Pupils' Intellectual Development. New York: Holt, Rinehart, and Winston.

Schwartz, Michael et al.
  1966 "A note on self-conception and the emotionally disturbed role." Sociometry (September):300-305.

Shaw, Louis C.
  1969 "Identity crisis and social change." In Readings in Social Psychology. Alfred R. Lindesmith and Anselm L. Strauss (eds.). New York: Holt, Rinehart and Winston, pp. 315-323.

Shibutani, Tamotsu
  1961 Society and Personality: An Interactionist Approach to Social Psychology. Englewood Cliffs, N.J.: Prentice-Hall, Inc.

Shockley, William
  1970 "A 'try simplest cases' approach to the heredity-poverty-crime problem." In Psychological Factors in Poverty. Vernon L. Allen (ed.). Chicago: Markham Publishing Co.

Smith, Ewart E.
  1972 "The power of dissonance techniques to change attitudes." In Beyond the Laboratory: Field Research in Social Psychology. Leonard Bickman and Thomas Henchy (eds.). New York: McGraw-Hill Book Co., pp. 237-245.

Spitzer, Stephen, Carl Couch and John Stratton
1971 The Assessment of the Self. Iowa City: Escort, Sernoll, Inc.

Stoller, Robert J.
1968 Sex and Gender: On the Development of Masculinity and Femininity. New York: Science House.

Strauss, Anselm
1962 "Transformations of identity." In Human Behavior and Social Processes. Arnold M. Rose (ed.). Boston: Houghton Mifflin Co., pp. 63-85.

Sullivan, Harry S.
1953 The Interpersonal Theory of Psychiatry. New York: W. W. Norton & Co.
1964 "The illusion of personal individuality." In The Fusion of Psychiatry and Social Science. Helen S. Perry (ed.). New York: W. W. Norton & Co.

Sykes, Gresham and David Matza
1957 "Techniques of neutralization: a theory of delinquency." American Sociological Review (December):667-670.

Ten Houten, Warren D. and Charles Kaplan
1973 Science and its Mirror Image: A Theory of Inquiry. New York: Harper & Row, Publishers.

Theodorson, George A. and Achilles G. Theodorson
1969 A Modern Dictionary of Sociology. New York: Thomas Y. Crowell Co.

Thomas, W. I. and F. Znaniecki
1918- The Polish Peasant in Europe and America
1920 (5 vols.). Chicago: University of Chicago Press.

Thurstone, L. L. and T. G. Thurstone
1941 "Factorial studies of intelligence." Psychometry Monogram 2. Chicago: University of Chicago Press.

Tiryakian, Edward A.
1974 On the Margin of the Visible: Sociology, the Esoteric and the Occult. New York: John Wiley & Sons, Inc.

Toffler, Alvin
1970 Future Shock. New York: Bantam Books, Inc.

Tucker, Charles W.
1966 "Some methodological problems of Kuhn's self theory." Sociological Quarterly (Summer):345-358.

Veblen, Thorstein
1899 The Theory of the Leisure Class. New York: The Macmillan Co.

Vernon, Glenn M.
1973 "Values, value definitions, and symbolic interaction." In Readings in Social Psychology—A Symbolic Interaction Perspective. J. D. Cardwell (ed.). Philadelphia: F A. Davis Co., pp. 37-48.

Vroom, Victor H.
1964 "Projection, negation, and the self concept." In Dimensions of Social Psychology. W.

Edgar Vinacke et al. (eds.). Chicago: Scott, Foresman, and Co., pp. 169-175.

Warshay, Leon H.
1962 "Breadth of perspective." In Human Behavior and Social Processes. Arnold M. Rose (ed.). Boston: Houghton Mifflin Co., pp. 148-176.

Webb, Eugene J. et al.
1966 Unobtrusive Measures: Nonreactive Research in the Social Sciences. Chicago: Rand McNally and Co.

Webster, Murray and Barbara Sobieszek
1974 Sources of Self-Evaluation: A Formal Theory of Significant Others and Social Influence. New York: John Wiley & Sons, Inc.

Wheelis, Allen
1958 The Quest for Identity. New York: W. W. Norton & Co.

White, Robert W.
1959 "Motivation reconsidered: the concept of competence." The Bobbs-Merrill Reprint Series in the Social Sciences. reprinted from The Psychological Review (September):297-333.

Whyte, William H., Jr.
1956 The Organization Man. Garden City, N.Y.: Doubleday & Co., Inc.

Wilensky, H. L.
1963 "The uneven distribution of leisure: the impact of economic growth on 'free time.'" In Work and Leisure—A Contemporary Social Problem. Erwin O. Smigel (ed.). New Haven, Conn.: College and University Press, pp. 107-145.

Woronoff, Israel
1966 "Negro male identification problems and the education process." In Understanding the Educational Problems of the Disadvantaged Learner. Staten W. Webster (ed.). San Francisco: Chandler Publishing Co., pp. 293-296.

Wrong, Dennis H.
1961 "The oversocialized conception of man in modern sociology." American Sociological Review (April):183-193.

Yancey, William L. et al.
1972 "Social position and self-evaluation: the relative importance of race." American Journal of Sociology (September):338-359.

Yinger, J. Milton
1971 "Personality, character, and the self." In Current Perspectives in Social Psychology. Edwin P. Hollander and Raymond G. Hunt (eds.). New York: Oxford University Press, pp. 152-159.

Ziller, Robert C.
1973 The Social Self. Elmsford, N.Y.: Pergamon Press, Inc.

part four

Interaction
and social change

chapter 11
Social interaction

Throughout this book, man's basic social nature has been emphasized. Nevertheless, Chapters 7 and 10 have actually only dealt with the individual, albeit always in a social context. Now we turn to social interaction itself. From here on, the individual is of no concern to us, not even as a unit of discussion.

The first thing to understand about sociology is that it is not interested in individuals or in the behavior of individuals. Neither is sociology primarily interested in the behavior of aggregates (many individuals), although a subbranch of it, demography, is. Sociology's fundamental unit of analysis is the *role,* and its empirical subject matter is *interaction.* A sociologist would not, for example, be interested in Richard Nixon, no matter how revealing that president's behavior has been. He would be interested in *the presidency* of the United States, which is a role. In his study of that role, he might use material provided by the particular case of Richard Nixon. Perhaps nothing proves better sociology's indifference to concrete individuals than its standard practice to use pseudonyms and anonymity, both with reference to individuals and to communities.

What has just been said about sociology also applies to social psychology. The only difference between these two disciplines is that the former moves up from roles to the study of social structures, which are often very large and abstract, whereas the latter remains more concerned with the concrete behavioral manifestations of roles in interaction.

The first section of this chapter, then, is about roles and role theory. Although role theory is considered to be a particular approach in social psychology, it should be clear from the foregoing that to the extent that sociology is, by definition, the study of roles, role theory is simply basic sociology and basic social psychology.

The second section will discuss a major aspect of role behavior—role-taking—which is the prerequisite for communication.

Finally, we shall examine a variety of forms and elements of interaction. Since this is a textbook in social psychology, we shall concentrate on face-to-face interaction, especially on its brilliant dissection by Goffman and the other followers of "dramaturgical sociology." Among the elements of interaction to be discussed will be physical space, influence, hierarchy, sentiment, perception, motivation, and self-control. Some of the types of interaction to be examined will be play, negotiation, love, sociability, problem-solving, embarrassment, and privacy.

THE CONCEPT OF ROLE

The concept of role has been defined in many different ways. A widely used introductory textbook defines role as "a set of more or less shared expectations that members of a group have about a social category" (Gouldner and Gouldner, 1963:184). Deutsch and Krauss (1965), who review role theory and several different definitions of role, suggest that it means, among other things, "the system of expectations which exist in the social world surrounding the occupant of a position—expectations regarding his behavior toward occupants of some other position. This may be termed the prescribed role" (Deutsch and Krauss, 1965:175). Stone defines role as "the expectations mobilized by an identity in a specified social situation." Thus we see that roles are invariably defined as (sets of) *expectations.* That is the crucial common term in all the above definitions.

This helps to distinguish role from such related terms as *status, position, station,* and *office.* According to Davis (1942), a position is simply a place in a social structure. Status and office are two different kinds of positions. The latter is a position in a deliberately created organization, for example, the office of president. The former, status, is "a position in the general institutional system," for example the status of husband. And as Linton (1936) showed, statuses may be ascribed, as the status of nobility or slave, or they may be achieved, as the status of professor or wife. A station, finally, is a "cluster of positions which may be combined in one individual and recognized as so combined in a great many cases" (Davis, 1942:310)—for example, the typical middle-aged, middle-class, white-collar worker who heads up a family and whose primary function is no longer upward mobility but providing for the security of his dependents, the mortgage payments, the college education of his children, etc.

Status, station, and office are all positions. They are structural units. Roles, on the other hand, are behavioral units. A role is the behavior that is expected from someone who occupies a given position. A role is what a person is expected to do to validate his occupancy of a certain status. Role expectations are generally classified into two categories: (1) rights (or privileges) and (2) duties (obligations). For example, a physician is expected to delve into a patient's personal privacy (right) and is also expected to prescribe what is deemed to be the best possible cure (duty).

We have distinguished roles from various types of positions. A role must also be distinguished from the self. As Sarbin (1954) views it, roles are what one *does*—they are acts—while the self refers to what one *is*—qualities. The extent to which the two coincide varies. The more they do, the more self-involved a person is in his roles, that is, in what he does. Thus an assemblyline worker may not be very much self-involved in his role, but a passionate lover is.

As Deutsch and Krauss (1965:175) indicate, there is no consensus about whether role refers to actual behavior or expected behavior. Here, we shall follow the majority of sociologists who believe that it is the latter. Role, then, must also be distinguished from role *performance,* or *role enactment.* We must, above all, understand

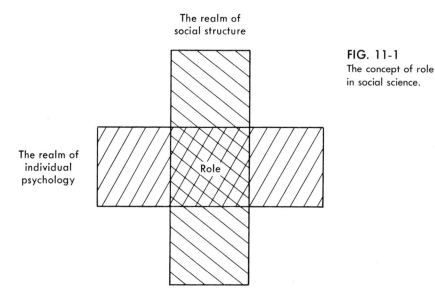

The realm of
social structure

The realm of
individual
psychology

Role

FIG. 11-1
The concept of role
in social science.

that a role is an abstraction, a concept linked to a position and not to concrete individuals. A role is a behavioral norm. Its actual enactment may coincide with it, or it may deviate from it.

Without the role concept, sociology would not exist. It is only through the role concept that we can make the conceptual jump from individual psychology to social structure. What is subjectively seen as a "me" becomes objectively a role. Fig. 11-1 indicates the conceptual position of the term role.

Classical role theory

In their discussion of role theory, Deutsch and Krauss (1965) single out three men as the major exponents of that orientation: George Herbert Mead, Robert Merton, and Erving Goffman. In addition, most sociologists would have to agree that other contributors to role theory of equal importance include Ralph Linton and Georg Simmel, among others (cf. Hooning, 1957).

Mead and the other pragmatists introduced the role concept in their analyses because they realized that, in order to account for group action without recourse to instinctivist explanations, sociology needed a concept such as role, a concept that is neither individualistic nor supraindividualistic, a concept essentially denoting, to Mead, a communicative process (Lindesmith and Strauss, 1956:373-374).

It was Merton (1957) and the structural anthropologists (for example, Ralph Linton, 1936) who linked role to status, position, and office to indicate the inseparability of individual activities from the larger organization of society. Merton then examined roles and institutions (which are complex clusters of roles) in terms of their *functions* for the larger system of which they are a part. Roles and institutions may be *functional* (beneficial and useful for the social system) or they may be *dysfunctional* (harmful). Their functions may be *manifest,* that is, intended and obvious, or they may be *latent,* unanticipated and at first unknown. For example, the

manifest function of churches is religious, but an equally important although latent function is social.

The idea that life is a drama in which we each play our parts (roles), learning the appropriate scripts, is as old as theater itself. However, it is Erving Goffman and the dramaturgical sociology he and his disciples spawned during the past fifteen years that has methodically carried out the implications of this paradigm.

Finally, there is Simmel's phenomenological discussion of the concept of *vocation* (*Beruf* in German), perhaps the most beautiful anticipation of modern role theory. "The concept of vocation refers (to the fact that) on the one hand, society within itself produces and offers to the individual a place which . . . can be filled by many individuals, and which is, for this reason, something anonymous, as it were. On the other hand, this place, in spite of its general character, is nevertheless taken by the individual on the basis of an inner calling, a qualification felt to be intimately personal" (Simmel, 1971:21).

Simmel's conception of vocation is related to "calling," as used for example by Weber in his discussion of Lutheran Protestantism. As we see, it denotes an *anonymous* position that can be filled by many individuals—precisely what modern sociology calls a role! It is, Simmel noted with brilliance, the a priori that makes society possible. And he added, significantly: "For such a thing as vocation to be possible, there must exist that harmony, whatever its origin, between the structure and development of society, and individual qualities and impulses" (loc. cit.).

Basic role processes

The central question, at this point, is *how* roles are enacted. As Lindesmith and Strauss (1956:385-386) analyze this process, it involves, first, the identification of self and the definition of the situation, and then behaving in a manner appropriate to that identification and definition. For example, the instructor enters the classroom, determines that this is his class and the appropriate time, is consciously aware that he is the instructor (self-identification), and on that basis proceeds to deliver the lecture for the day.

However, role enactment is never so totally automatic. So far, we have only discussed *role-playing,* that is, the enactment of roles. In addition—or better, as a crucial *part* of role-playing—there is *role-taking:* this means imaginatively taking the point of view of others, imagining oneself from the others' standpoint. The enactment of a role is very flexible, very much on-the-spot improvised response to what others do or are believed to do. Thus how the instructor behaves in any given class depends on whether the students are rowdy, apathetic, attentive, friendly, hostile, or something else. If on a particular day no students show up, he goes home instead of lecturing. A robot might deliver the lecture for which it has been programmed to an empty classroom. A robot cannot take role.

Thus we see that others are crucial in role enactment. Whenever people interact with each other, they typify, personify, and altercast one another. A *typification* is simply the act of placing someone into a general social category, assigning him to a role and an identity (cf. Berger and Luckmann, 1966:30-31). For example, a male professor may share a committee with a female colleague. It makes a great deal of difference in their mutual interaction whether he typifies her as a "fellow professor" or as a "woman."

Personifications, according to Shibutani (1961:351-352) are constructed through an imputation of motives." For example, "the lover imputes the finest motives to his sweetheart, always gives her the benefit of the doubt." Personifications are what people *mean* to each other (op. cit.:111), what we make of others, in our own eyes, rather than what they in fact are.

Altercasting is the "casting (of) alter into a particular identity or role type. . . . It is a basic technique of interpersonal control" (Weinstein and Deutschberger, 1963). In their effort to control one another, people create identities for each other congruent with their goals. This is termed altercasting. For example, the derelict approaches the passing businessman and says: "Sir, as a generous gentleman, can you spare a quarter?"

Roles vary, according to Goffman (1961:88-90) in the amount of *commitment* and *attachment* with which they are enacted. Commitment is a coercive thing. An individual is committed to a role to the extent that he is stuck with it. For example, the employee has invested a lifetime of seniority into his job, has tenure, and owns his home in the locality; for him, for these and other reasons, mobility and change have become inconceivable.

Attachment, on the other hand, is the voluntary and enthusiastic embracement of a role. As individual is attached to a role insofar as he likes it. Ideally, an individual should be attached to the roles to which he is committed. When this does not occur, as so often in modern mass society, there is alienation.

Roles have been classified in many different ways. One distinction is between the *prescribed role* and the *subjective role.* The former is the role as defined by the society's norms and expectations. The latter consists of the specific role expectations that one perceives as applying to oneself in a given role. For example, there is a culturally prescribed role of mother, but the subjective definition of that role by a particular mother may be such that she feels expected to be very loving or, conversely, very demanding of her children.

Sociologists have also distinguished *general roles* from *segmental roles.* For example, "male" is a general role, which can then be subdivided into such smaller segmental roles as "father" and "husband."

What makes role analysis such an enormously complex enterprise is the fact that individuals and statuses have *multiple roles* with each role related to other roles. A set of roles centering around one particular status is what Merton (1957:369) called a *role-set.* "For example, the status of university professor frequently involves the roles of teacher, research technician, adviser to students, consultant to industry and government, administrator, clerk, author, specialist in a professional discipline, and so forth (Theodorson and Theodorson, 1969:356). Each of these roles is related to some other role, and often these role relationships are complementary—for example, the teacher-student relationship or the consultant-client relationship. Without one, you cannot have the other. Some authors speak of this phenomenon in terms of roles and *counterroles,* or ego and alter. Merton's concept of role-set is illustrated in Fig. 11-2.

Although we all have multiple roles, this does not necessarily cause problems as long as we keep our different roles separate. We do this by scheduling our roles and by segregating our audiences, aided in this by the social system. For example, the vast majority of people have no trouble separating their occupational roles from their family roles. The two are scheduled for different times, and they are generally

carried out in different places—at work and at home.

However, we also often experience *role conflict.* This occurs when the various roles a person is expected to play do not mesh with one another (Gouldner and Gouldner, 1963:187), which is termed *interrole conflict,* or when an existing role contains inherent contradictions, which is called *intrarole conflict.* Interrole conflict may simply be the result of bad scheduling. For example, a wife calls her husband (a busy physician) at work to ask him to discipline the children. This produces role conflict for the husband simply because he cannot be both father and physician at the same time.

In general, it is only under exceptional circumstances that people may suddenly have to choose between roles that are otherwise nonoverlapping and not perceived to be in conflict. Killian (1952) studied the reaction of persons in four Southwestern communities to physical disasters such as explosions and tornadoes. For example, "a worker in an oil refinery, forced with the choice of aiding an injured friend or saving the plant, might be torn between the

FIG. 11-2
An example of role-set.

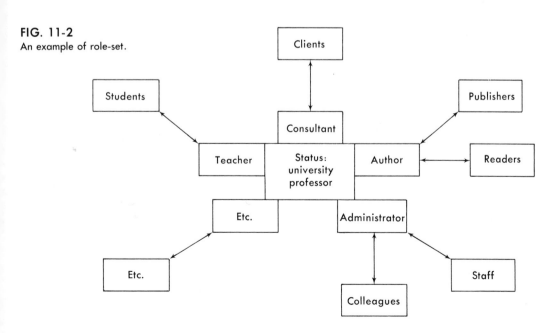

obligations of his friendship and his occupation" (Deutsch and Krauss, 1965: 179). In general, Killian found that such conflicts tended to be resolved in favor of one's family and peers, not the community as a whole.

Often interrole conflict occurs when two roles, although performed at different times, make conflicting demands on the individual—for example, the man who is a ruthless businessman during the week and a pious churchgoer on Sunday. To avoid experiencing role conflict in such cases, an individual must know how to mentally *compartmentalize* his different roles, otherwise, he may experience guilt and cognitive dissonance.

Some roles are inherently contradictory. In such cases, there is intrarole conflict. For example, the role of the army chaplain is a difficult one, since he must simultaneously profess Christian pacifist principles and condone the army's avowed function, which is to kill men. Similarly, the teaching assistant in a university has the difficult task of reconciling allegiance to the student body with identification with the faculty.

Zurcher and his co-workers (1973) studied the intrarole conflict suffered by the hashers, the college boys who work part-time in sororities setting tables, washing dishes, mopping floors, disposing of garbage, and on occasion carrying luggage for the girls. Obviously, it is difficult to reconcile these lowly activities with being "college men." Zurcher and his associates found that the hashers cope by using a variety of defense mechanisms. For example, they rationalize by saying that the job is only temporary, or they project—state that the girls are "low born." Also, they compensate by emphasizing discussions of sexual dominance, and they express verbal hostility toward the girls.

The problematic multiple-group membership illustrated in our example of the teaching assistant has been called *marginality* (cf. Park, 1928; Stonequist, 1937). The marginal man is the man who lives on the boundary between two or more (sub)cultures. This often produces role conflict, status inconsistency, and incongruence in perspectives (Shibutani, 1961:574-575).

Marginality has been studied with respect to foreign students spending a year in an American college. Brewster Smith (1956) points out that the foreign student, being on a fairly long-term but nevertheless temporary visit to the United States, is a good case for the study of marginality. He is not motivated to conform altogether, since he eventually returns to his home country, and unlike the immigrant, he does not become alienated from his home country. On the other hand, he becomes far more involved in American life than the tourist. The author found that, as expected, foreign students from culturally distant nations (in the third world) adjusted less easily than students from kin societies such as Australia and Northern Europe. In general, all students went through a four-phase cycle: from first being mere spectators, they became increasingly involved, then reached some modus vivendi, and finally spent the last few months in anticipation of their return.

Sewell and Davidsen (1956) examined the adjustment of Scandinavian foreign students. They found adjustment to be positively correlated with such factors as facility with the English language, American appearance, socioeconomic status at home, urban background, and frequency of contacts with Americans. More interesting was the authors' finding of a U-shaped type of adjustment over the year spent in the United States. At first, attitudes toward America are highly favorable, then less so, but toward the end of the year they become increasingly favorable again. Why? At first, America is viewed with all the preconceptions of the outsider, the experience is novel and exciting, and the foreign students are treated preferentially. Then disenchantment sets in, while the home country is still the reference group. Finally, there is a coming to terms with reality, while America becomes, for an increasing number of students, the new reference group. Some, particularly those who are not highly committed to the home country in the first place, become permanent United States immigrants.

Marginality offers as many opportunities as difficulties. This was at first insufficiently realized. Often, the marginal man is highly flexible, achieving an integrated personality capable of moving smoothly from status to status. In fact, we are all marginal in the sense that each of us has many different reference groups and perspectives (cf. Shibutani, 1962:138-139). As Simmel (1955) noted, each individual stands at the point where the unique combination of all his social circles intersect. In modern pluralistic society, man inevitably leads a compartmentalized life, belonging to many different groups.

Social psychologists have demonstrated that multiple-group allegiance is often handled successfully and is in fact beneficial. For example, Child (1943) studied second-generation Italian-Americans. He found three distinct modes of adaptation: some totally rejected their Italian background, some totally rejected the American ways, and some withdrew apathetically from thinking of themselves in ethnic terms, trying to avoid the issue of ethnicity and claiming that there are no significant differences between Italians and Americans. However, this was unsuccessful and merely resulted in a loss of identity.

Lambert and Gardner (1961) examined French-Americans and found the same three groups identified by Child, plus a fourth one: some subjects had successfully established a comfortable bicultural and bilingual identity. These individuals were well adjusted in both cultural settings.

Sieber (1974) has recently argued that role accumulation provides more advantages than disadvantages. While multiple roles may cause role conflict, role strain, and overload, they provide rewards like role privileges, status security, resources for status enhancement and role perform-

ance, and enrichment of the personality and ego gratification.

Many other role problems have been dealt with in the literature, not all pertaining to multiple roles. For example, sociologists have described role failure, role disruption (cf. Merton, 1957:379), and role strain. Role strain is a feeling of difficulty or stress in fulfilling the demands of one's role obligations (Goode, 1960). And as I have shown (Kando, 1972), males, females, and transsexuals differ significantly in the amounts of sex-role strain they experience: men and transsexuals suffer from relatively little role strain, but women suffer from a great deal.

Role theory today

According to Goffman (1961:93), classical role analysis is too rigid. It assumes that the social system is a neat structure of positions and roles and that individuals merely have to learn these roles and then carry them out. However, in real life, a given position is perceived and defined at least somewhat differently each time, and the performance of a given role will vary, depending on the performer and, above all, on the *situation*. Thus Goffman switches from classical sociology's concept of the social system to the *situated activity system,* or simply the situation. The role therefore becomes a situated role, a bundle of activities visibly performed and embedded in a concrete situation. While classical sociology assumes that "doing is being," so to speak—that an individual plays the role of doctor because he *is* a doctor—Goffman's refined framework makes it possible to ask the central questions about role performance: What is the relationship between the self (the person) and the role? Why does the individual deviate from the conventional role? Is an individual playing the role, or merely playing *at* it, that is, pretending?

Throughout his work, Goffman is concerned with the problem of *expression,* the individual's effort to establish a desired identity in the eyes of others. Role enactment is not, as classical sociology assumed, the mechanical enactment of a learned script. It involves explanations, apologies, humor, and other control and corrective mechanisms.

It is under the concept of *role distance* that Goffman probes in depth the relationship between the self and the role. As noted earlier, the degree of attachment to a given role can vary from one individual to another, even though both carry out the same role. When an individual is totally attached to a role, when he fully embraces it, that is when we might say that doing is being. The self and the role are one and the same. However, individuals often express role distance, which is a mechanism to express rejection of the self implied in the role. Goffman describes the five-year-old boy riding the merry-go-round: unlike the three or four-year-old, he must now demonstrate that riding a wooden horse is kid stuff. He may hold on to the post with one hand and lean back as far as possible looking up to the sky, or he may keep time to the music. The boy is saying that he is not just someone who can barely manage to stay on a wooden horse (Goffman, 1961:107).

Another example is the chief surgeon. If any role may be expected to elicit total self-involvement, it is that one—what with the television image of the surgeon as a shining hero and all. Yet here, too, we see role distance, for example, "instead of employing technical terms at all times, (the surgeon) may tease the nurses by using homey appellations: 'give me the small knife, we'll go in just below the belly button'; and he may call the electric cauterizer by the apt name of 'sizzler'. . ." (op. cit.:119). The main function of such role distance on the part of the surgeon is to serve the needs of the social situation; the surgeon must give up some of the dignity to which he is formally entitled for the benefit of the activity system, the smooth completion of the operation.

Role-distance theory has been elaborated subsequently by Coser (1966), Ford et al. (1974), and Stebbins (1967; 1969), among others. Coser has suggested that Goffman's concept of role distance subsumes at least two distinct types of behavior: (1) pretense of detachment from some status, such as when the surgeon uses humor, in the previous example, and (2) taking distance from one role in order to prepare for taking another role. This latter type of role distance occurs during socialization, as the individual moves up from one status to another.

Stebbins (1969) examined role distance among jazz musicians, and Ford and co-workers (1974) have argued that members of the lower class, unlike the middle class, are incapable of role distance, which is a serious social handicap.

Goffman was among the first to transcend some of the limitations of classical role theory, along with Herbert Blumer, who also spent a lifetime refining Mead's vague theoretical concepts (cf. Blumer, 1969). However, it is ethnomethodology that is now submitting such traditional concepts as "role," "status," and "norm" to the most critical and constructive analysis. Cicourel (1974) asks whether such terms are of any relevance to the people sociologists study and whether or not they help sociologists understand those people. As long as the terms remain abstract labels, they are fairly useless. What needs to be done is to specify the *interpretive procedures* that both the actors and the observers (the sociologists) use to construct their typifications, to negotiate roles and statuses, to reach definitions of actions as "normal" and "proper." Cicourel, basing himself on Schutz's phenomenology, proposes several such interpretive rules. One such rule is the rule of *reciprocity of perspective*. According to this rule, speaker and hearer in interaction assume that "their mutual experiences of the interaction scene are the same, even if they were to change places." Furthermore, each participant disregards "personal differences in how each assigns meaning to everyday activities." For example, when I ask a question, I have in mind a more elaborated version than what I actually ask you. I assume that you will fill in, despite receiving only a deleted surface message. The same works in reverse, when you give me your answer. Therefore, both participants presume that the other will generate recognizable and intelligible utterances as a necessary condition for meaningful interaction (Cicourel, 1974: 34-35). Thus the analysis of roles and interaction becomes, with ethnomethodology, an in-depth probe into the exact mechanisms underlying (role) behavior.

Some studies in role

The interactionist framework has generated a great deal of research on roles, particularly in family sociology (cf. Heiss, 1968; Hill and Hansen, 1960; Stryker, 1972). Then, too, the 1970s have seen the rise of "sex roles" as a new academic discipline, but this is mostly a neologism for the sociology of marriage and the family.

Farber's (1962) typology of families is an example of symbolic interactionist family sociology. The author identifies three types of families: the child-oriented, the home-oriented, and the parent-oriented family. The difference lies in the pattern of intrafamily interaction.

Another example of the application of the interactionist framework to family processes is Willard Waller's classic analysis of marital alienation (cf. Waller, 1957; Waller and Hill, 1951). The central point of this analysis is that alienation is a vicious cycle, an inexorable process once it is underway, and one in which the outside group represents a wedge between husband and wife, dividing them and further reinforcing their mutual alienation. Waller's analysis of this profoundly painful process is poignant. At each step of the process, the two partners' responses to one another merely reinforce their mutual alienation. "Even the attempts at reconciliation usually end by impoverishing the relationship, for they end in renewed disagreement" (Waller and Hill, 1951). The critical threshold is when the quarreling partners "go public," make their alienation known to their friends, begin to wash their dirty laundry in the open. This is the point of no return, for now the alienation is socially defined, fixed, and the two partners are cast in roles from which they cannot escape. "Husbands and wives who have begun to quarrel find themselves unable to stop until it is too late. Mayhap their disagreements bring heartache to both; they discuss them fully and frankly and agree to stop; no matter, the quarrels go on. . . . When alienation starts it marches inevitably, love alone cannot stop it, soon the relationship is bankrupt and those involved do not wish any longer to become reconciled" (Waller, 1957).

In recent years, a redefinition has taken place whereby we hear, in sociology, less and less about marriage and the family as a subdiscipline and more and more about sex roles. This translation is linked to the women's movement, or, more generally, to the sex revolution (cf. Sorokin, 1956) as evidenced by the fact that most of what is being written under the heading of sex roles deals with the differences between male and female roles and the disadvantages of the latter. Williamson (1970:172), for example, who reviews the sociological literature on marriage roles, concludes with the fundamental point "that the wife makes the major adjustment in marriage because of the cultural definition of sex roles" and that "especially the woman's role is not precisely defined." Much of the literature on sex roles is feminist polemic (cf. Amundsen, 1971; Andreas, 1971; Bem and Bem, 1975; Boston Women's Health Book Collective, 1973; Cade, 1970; Chafetz, 1963; Gornick and Moran, 1971; Sullerot, 1971; Tanner, 1970; Thompson, 1964) or pop sociology (cf. Delora and Delora, 1972) rather than good scholarship. However, one also finds some good studies on the bandwagon—for example, the

Goldberg (1975) study mentioned earlier, showing that women tend to be prejudiced against women, and a study by Horner (1975), which shows that women are socialized in such a manner that they are fearful of (occupational) success.

Furthermore, the latest spinoff of the sex revolution in terms of sex-role equalization is a growing body of paperback literature on the joys of fatherhood. For example, Lee Salk has written a refreshingly healthy paper on "how great it is to be a father." In it, the author highlights the many potential rewards of the father-child relationship. For example, "can there be anything that builds a man up more than knowing his overwhelming importance to his daughter?" And does the father not recapture—or improve upon—the joys of his own childhood through the enjoyment of his children's? Why, then, aren't most fathers getting more out of it? Dr. Salk goes on to suggest ways to improve this potentially fulfilling role. For example, to deal with the universal problem of coming home late and tired, why not first attend to one's basic needs, take a shower, change, tell the boy that you will play with him in an hour, and *then* go about having a relaxed good time with your son? In general, then, the father-child relationship can be most rewarding for both parties if mutual needs are frankly acknowledged and respected.

The study of roles has taken place in many other areas besides sex roles. For example, deviant roles are examined in Erikson's (1973) study of patients and Giallombardo's (1972) study of prison women, political roles are studied by Brooks (1972), and even the role of social-psychologist has been the object of study (cf. Martin, 1973). Here, we conclude with a brief examination of an entirely different approach to roles: the fascinating *phenomenology of social types* of men like Simmel and Schutz.

In his description of *the adventurer*, Sim-

mel (1971:187-198) first states that "the most general form of adventure is its dropping out of the continuity of life." Like a work of art, an adventure is a more or less autonomous experience, it is cut out from the continuous flow of routine life and stands on its own. That is why we tend to remember it as a dream. The adventurer, like the artist, is "the extreme example of the ahistorical figure, the man who lives totally in the present" (op. cit.:190). For example, Casanova, in the course of his erotic adventures, frequently intended to marry the woman with whom he was in love at the time. This was quite impossible, as Simmel shows, since Casanova's very intention to marry each of these women was a reflection of the fact that he was totally dominated by the feeling of the present.

If the adventurer shares much in common with the artist, he must be distinguished from the gambler: "the gambler has abandoned himself to the meaninglessness of chance" (op. cit.:190-191). By contrast, the beauty of the adventure lies in the fact that it synthesizes chance and necessity. "The adventurer makes a system out of his life's lack of system" (op. cit.:190).

In a sense, life as a whole is an adventure. To perceive this, "one must sense above its totality a higher unity, a super-life" (op. cit.:192). "Whoever senses through all actual life a secret, timeless existence of the soul . . . will perceive life in its given and limited wholeness as an adventure . . ." (loc cit.).

The adventure is a *form of experiencing*. The content of this experience can be manifold, but the erotic adventure epitomizes the experience best. Simmel claims that the love affair is more likely to be an adventure for men than for women: "Man plays the courting, attacking, often violently grasping role" (op. cit.:196). In old age, adventure is rare, for "only youth knows the predominance of the process of life over its substance . . ." (op. cit.:198).

In another similar essay, Simmel characterizes *the stranger* (1971:143-149) as follows. Unlike the drifter, who comes and goes, the stranger comes and stays. He brings to a situation qualities that are not indigenous to it. Because of his greater objectivity (but not nonparticipation), the stranger is sometimes relied upon as an arbiter or judge, as in the past in Italy. Since the stranger examines conditions with less prejudice, he is a freer man, practically and theoretically (op. cit.:146). Often, he becomes the scapegoat, blamed as the outside agitator responsible for turmoil within the in-group.

Schutz (1944), too, has written on the stranger. In addition, he has sketched the phenomenology of *the homecomer* (1970: 294-308). Unlike the stranger, the homecomer's strangeness upon his return is only temporary, or so he believes, for he expects to return to an environment of which he still has intimate knowledge (op. cit.:295).

To understand the homecomer, we must first understand the meaning of home. "The home is the starting point as well as terminus. It is the null-point of the system of coordinates which we ascribe to the world in order to find our bearings in it" (op. cit.:296). It is a *primary group*. Now an outstanding example of the homecomer is the returning veteran. According to a U.S. Department of Defense survey, forty percent of the discharged World War II veterans being sent back to civilian life through Eastern "separation centers" did not want their old jobs back and did not want even to return to their old communities (Schutz, 1970:305). Why? The major problem is that the war experience has added something to the perspective of the veteran, something that makes him radically different from the man being awaited back home. While he may be able to pick up where he left off because of his familiarity with the home environment, this capability is not reciprocal: those who stayed home have no way to relate to the veteran's new "personality" dimensions.

The analyses of social types and social forms undertaken by Simmel and Schutz are sociology at its best. To grasp them fully, the reader must go to the originals.

These will show that sociology can, in the hands of brilliant and perceptive minds, provide a profound understanding of human experience.

COMMUNICATION

Whether or not symbolic interactionism is correct in equating communication and interaction, the fact is that communication is a crucial part of interaction. The major form and medium of communication —symbolic language—is discussed in Chapter 7. Here, our focus will be on the *phenomenology of communication*.

Following Max Scheler (1970), we shall discuss some of the taxonomies that exist to describe different types of communication—such things as empathy, sympathy, communion, and love. The traditional conceptual distinction here has been between the affective and the cognitive levels of communication. The use and understanding of language are seen as cognitive processes, whereas empathy, sympathy, communion, and love are considered to be the affective elements in communication. However, the central point of the present textbook in humanistic social psychology is that this distinction is phony. Man is of one piece. One cannot separate his head from his heart. A humanistic conception of communication must integrate the cognitive and the affective, the scientific and the artistic, the message and the medium, content and form. Thus communication must encompass both Scheler's various types of "fellow-feeling" and symbolic language.

Because of the centrality of role-taking in the sociological analysis of communication and interaction, we begin with a discussion of that concept. Then various aspects of the phenomenology of communication will be examined. Although we shall also briefly look at some symbolic and other forms of communication, the burden of this section is on the various "empathic processes," that is, the affective level of communication, since language is discussed in Chapter 7. This will involve an excursus into love. Finally, the problem of noncommunication will be discussed.

Role-taking

To repeat, role-taking means the imaginary taking of the attitudes and point of view of another person in order to anticipate his behavior and to understand oneself from his standpoint. Simply, it means putting oneself in his shoes.

Turner (1962) has pointed out that part of this communicative process is *role-making*. By this the author means the mechanism discussed in the previous section under *typification, personification,* and *alter-casting*. Man often "makes" roles toward which he behaves, rather than behaving toward preexisting roles. In highly structured organizations such as the military, this may not be the case, but in many other settings man typically shapes his social environment into roles and then acts toward them. Thus human behavior is, to a large extent, free and subjective.

Roles, then, are the matrices that give consistency and meaning to actions. For example, spanking and kissing a child are consistent with one another: they both constitute part of the parent role. Often, therefore, there is no role conflict where a social scientist might logically expect one to be. In this light, as Turner indicates, role-taking becomes the devising and discovering of consistent behavior on the part of others. It is far more than merely conforming to others' expectations, as classical role theory would have it. It is a creative and interpretive process.

Role-taking is further complicated by the question of the *significance* of the other. As we saw in our discussion of reference groups (see Chapter 9), Hughes (1962) has shown that role-taking depends a great deal on whose role we take, how important that other person is to us, whether we choose our significant others or whether

they are imposed on us, and so forth. In other words, other-directedness is a variable, and role-taking must be an empirical question, not an assumption. As Hughes points out, some individuals creatively compromise among the various others they choose, freely and autonomously, as their significant others. Other ones are tyrannized and enslaved by one person or one group, no matter how destructive that association might be. For example, a weak man may be terribly infatuated with a beautiful woman who manipulates and humiliates him; nevertheless, he cannot free himself from this human bondage.

Although role-taking involves a certain amount of role-making, there is also an undeniable objective reality that must be grasped by an individual if he is to communicate meaningfully with others. Communication will be smooth to the extent that role-taking is accurate. For example, Kuhn (1962) has discussed the poor quality of role-taking between the social worker —who is generally middle class—and his client, who is often lower class, and between teachers and inner-city students, who are similarly different. The failure of education and of many social programs is in part caused by inadequate communication, which in turn is the result of inadequate role-taking.

Stryker (1957; 1962) has explored accuracy of role-taking between parents and their offspring. He operationalized role-taking as the ability to predict the other's attitudes about certain things. Thus two operations had to be performed: a group of respondents had to be asked to *guess* another group's attitudes, and this other group's attitudes had to be determined. For example, the grown-up offspring in a family were asked to estimate their parents' attitudes toward sexual permissiveness, and the parents' actual attitudes toward sexual permissiveness were determined. To the extent that the offspring's guesses were accurate, they could be said to take their parents' role well. Stryker found, among other things, that persons of blood relationship take each other's roles better than in-laws, persons of similar occupations take each other's roles more accurately than persons of different occupations, and persons of the same sex (for example, a mother and a daughter) take each other's roles better than persons of different sex (for example, a father and his daughter or a mother and her son).

What is communication?

Limiting himself to what he terms phenomena of *fellow-feeling*, Max Scheler (1970) discusses four such modes, four different ways in which individuals "resonate" with each other. (1) *Feeling in common* is illustrated by a mother and father coming together and sharing the anguish of burying a dead child. (2) *Feeling about something* would be the case of a close friend of the aggrieved parents commiserating with them. (3) *Mere emotional infection* occurs, for example, when a newcomer to a party or bar is swept up into the gaiety and cheerfulness of the prevailing atmosphere. (4) *Emotional identification* is exemplified by the spectator who is so absorbed by the acrobat in a circus that he reproduces, within himself, the acrobat's very movements (Scheler, 1970; Stone and Farberman, 1970:278).

Turning now to related terminologies proposed by other authors to deal with the various nonsymbolic levels of communication, we mention, first, Cooley's *sympathetic introspection*. This is the phenomenological stance advocated by humanistic social psychologists as the desirable method to understand the behavior of people. It entails relating to others on the basis of the fact that one shares with them both a basic and universal humanness and specific experiences. The modern sociological method of *participant observation* (cf. Blumer, 1969; Bruyn, 1966) is based on this.

Mead (1934), Sullivan (1970), and others have stressed the importance of *empathy*. Generally, empathy is distinguished from sympathy in that it is primarily a cognitive process, whereas sympathy is affective. For example, a policeman chasing a robber must empathize with him—that is, antici-

pate the robber's moves so as to apprehend him—but he does not sympathize with him. However, the difficulty with the concept of empathy is that it is sometimes used as an affective concept and sometimes as a synonym of role-taking, which means the mere anticipation of another's behavior. To Mead and Sullivan, empathy certainly includes an affective component. For example, it is said to account for the difficulties in feeding the baby when the mother is made apprehensive by a telegram, even though that is not communicated by her tone of voice (Sullivan, 1970:389). For this reason, some authors (such as Stryker, 1962) prefer to speak only of role-taking rather than using the ambiguous term empathy.

Goodman and Ofshe (1968), however, in a study of empathy, communication efficiency, and marital status, equated empathy and accuracy of role-taking. The technique used was similar to television's "Password" quiz show. One of the members of each couple had to guess a given word about which his or her partner could only give cues. Comparing (1) randomly paired strangers, (2) newly engaged couples, and (3) married couples, the authors found that communication, as expected, becomes more efficient from group 1 to group 3, and that there is also, generally, a correlation between empathy and communication efficiency. Goodman and Ofshe provide some interesting examples of communication in this format. For example, one of the married couples arrived at the goal word "hospital," with wife giving the cues, quite rapidly:

	Cue		Response
She:	1. Ulcer	*He:*	1. Aggravation
	2. Summer		2. Hospital

On the other hand, one dyad of strangers was quite clumsy in its attempt to communicate the word "family:"

	Cue		Response
She:	1. Nuclear	*He:*	1. Warfare
	2. Group		2. Atoms

Cue		Response	
She:	3. Primary	**He:**	3. Electrons
	4. Father		4. Einstein
	5. Primary		5. Reactor
	6. Children		6. Molecules
	7. Human		7. Matter
	8. Mother		8. Family*

Phenomenologists have often grappled with the fundamental nature of communication. Natanson (1970), Schutz (1970), and Spiegelberg (1973) are among the philosophers who have analyzed the nature and structure of interpersonal understanding. The basic problem, as phenomenologists see it, is that of *intersubjectivity*—"how is the experience of my 'understanding' the other and his 'understanding' me constituted?" (Schutz, 1970: 319). Schutz, as we saw in Chapter 7, answers this question by way of his general thesis of the alter ego, thereby criticizing empathy theory. As far as communication is concerned, Schutz discusses a variety of "vehicles of thought" (op. cit.:200), including signs, gestural expression, linguistic presentation, visual presentation, and music.

A major aspect of interpersonal interaction on which phenomenologists have focused is the "we-relationship" (cf. Schutz, 1970; Natanson, 1970). Spiegelberg (1973) offers an interesting linguistic analysis of the word "we" in everyday discourse, listing many rules and assumptions underlying usage of that word. For example, "the referents of 'we' must be personal beings who the speaking 'I' believes to be human beings. 'We' is inapplicable to nonspeaking beings, inanimate and animate, below the human level except in animal fables . . ." (Spiegelberg, 1973:133). The author concludes that the word "we" is often horribly abused and that its use must, on moral grounds, be limited.

A final concept of importance here is

---

*From Goodman, Norman, and Richard Ofshe. 1968. "Empathy, communication, efficiency, and marital status." Journal of Marriage and the Family, Nov., pp. 597-604. Copyright 1968 by National Council on Family Relations. Reprinted by permission.

communion. Schmalenbach (1965) has argued that Tonnies' *Gemeinschaft,* often translated as "community," has often mistakenly been held to cover such things as love and sentiment. Actually, community—the type of social bond found in peasant society—is as often devoid of those things as is urban life. What characterizes community is a reliance on tradition and blood ties. Thus it is *communion* that refers to the highly emotional bond found, for example, between a religious leader and his masses of followers.

Love

Classical philosophers and contemporary social scientists alike have wondered about the theoretical importance of love (cf. Goode, 1959). The Russian anarchist Kropotkin, for example, rejected the principles of hedonism, enlightened egoism, and utilitarianism underlying the theories of men like Bentham, Hobbes, and Adam Smith. Far from being inherently selfish, man's most basic instincts, he argued, are gregariousness and sympathy. If hedonism and egoism are salient features of modern society, it is because of the particular economic system (competitive capitalism) that prevails at this time. Thus the bias of classical economics and of such modern social psychological theories as exchange theory (and indeed the prevailing vocabulary of motives in twentieth century America) is to view human individualism and selfishness as immutably rooted in human nature. The collectivism of socialist thinkers and the growing interest in the phenomenon of love on the part of psychologists represent a healthy correction of this bias.

The Greeks already knew that love embodies many different kinds of attitudes. They distinguished, for example, between *eros* and *agape* (cf. Foote, 1970:321). Eros is romantic love, or what has aptly been termed cardiac-respiratory love. Agape is brotherly love. An outstanding example of the latter type of love was provided in the musical *Fiddler on the Roof.* When asked by her husband whether she loves him, Golde replies:

"Do I love you?
For twenty-five years I have lived with him,
fought with him, starved with him,
for twenty-five years my bed is his,
if that's not love, what is?

In modern Western society, romantic love (eros) is in the forefront of people's preoccupation. Freud helped to create this situation, by stressing that eros—the sexual—inevitably underlies agape (cf. Foote, loc. cit.). Sociologists and psychologists who have researched love have, therefore, often limited themselves to the study of romantic love and interpersonal physical attraction (cf. Beigel, 1951; Murstein, 1971; Rubin, 1973a; 1973b; Walster et al., 1973). Rubin, for example, has devised a love scale measuring romantic love, that is the response of an individual to a specific other, and not the general tendency to love everyone. The author distinguishes three components of romantic love: affiliative and dependent need, predisposition to help, and orientation of exclusiveness and absorption. The following items are examples of Rubin's love-scale items:

1. Affiliative and dependent need: for example, "If I could never be with ＿＿, I would feel miserable."
2. Predisposition to help: for example, "If ＿＿ were feeling badly, my first duty would be to cheer him (her) up.
3. Exclusiveness and absorption: For example, "I feel very possessive toward ＿＿."

Some of Rubin's findings are interesting. For example, the correlation between people's love scores and their liking scores turned out low. On the other hand, some are trivial. College dating couples with high love scores spend more time gazing into one another's eyes than those with low scores. In general, Harlow (1958:673) is still correct: "So far as love or affection is concerned, psychologists have failed in their mission. The little we know about love does not transcend simple observation, and the little we write about it has been written better by poets and novelists."

The excessive preoccupation with romantic love, both by laymen and by social psychologists, is a reflection of our culture.

The important sociological fact about love is that it has, throughout history, been controlled and directed into approved channels by the social structure and the kinship system so as not to disrupt society (cf. Goode, 1959). While our culture can hardly be expected to return to the agape variety exemplified in the previous quotation from *Fiddler on the Roof,* the most viable alternative to that may not be eros, romantic love. Waller and Hill (1951), for example, see the "consistent debunking of the romantic complex" as salutary. What may be needed at this time is the adoption of the humanistic conception of love found in the writings of such men as Fromm (1966), Sullivan (1947), and Foote (1970). Sullivan, for example, states that love occurs "when the satisfaction or the security of another person becomes as significant to one as is one's own satisfaction or security" (Sullivan, 1947:20). Foote, expanding on this definition, argues that "love is that relationship between one person and another which is most conducive to the optimal development of both" (Foote, 1970:322). According to this view, then, love is a dramatic presentation aimed at including another person over a long period of time without violating his or her autonomy.

Other forms of communication

As we saw in Chapter 7, *(natural) signs* and *(verbal) symbols* are the two major vehicles of communication. Mead (1934) discussed these concepts and their ramifications. For example, the *gesture* is an important concept in the Meadian taxonomy, referring to that part of the social act that serves as a stimulus to other forms involved in the same social act. Thus the meaning of a gesture is in the behavior that follows it. When they arouse the same response in oneself as in the other, gestures become significant symbols. Significant symbols, unlike natural signs, are shared meanings.

Although ethnomethodologists violently object to being likened to symbolic interactionists (cf. Denzin, 1969; the reply to Denzin by Zimmerman and Wieder, 1970), there is no fundamental conflict between the preceding paragraph and the ethnomethodologists' essential conception of meaning. Wieder (1970:108) criticizes semanticists and linguists for conceptualizing the usage of everyday language in terms of a rule-like semantics, an abstract and transsituational grammar. This does not make sense, the author argues, since, as ethnomethodologists have discovered, everyday talk consists mostly of indexical and occasional expressions, "expressions the sense of which is relative to the place in which it is spoken, what the hearer knows about the speaker, the time at which it is spoken, and an infinitely extendable collection of other contextual matters" (loc. cit.). Wieder's conclusion—that meaning is hardly determined by grammatical rules—is entirely in accord with symbolic interactionism.

Scheff (1970) has discussed another aspect of communication—*consensus.* He points out that consensus is not based on agreement but on coorientation. What this means is that, often, consensus is based on the *belief* by all parties that there is agreement, rather than an actual agreement. For example, when a public opinion poll reveals that seventy-seven percent of the people believe that the economy is recovering or that racial integration is desirable, this can mean two things: respondents have either answered what they really believe, or they have answered what they thought most people believe. In the latter case, consensus is merely a matter of coorientation.

A further form of communication discussed in the literature is humor. For example, Farina (1973) studied the extent and function of humor appreciation in social communication. In an experiment, students were shown cartoons under dif-

ferent conditions. Farina showed that when the cartoons were presented face to face by sexy female experimenters, so that the students could express themselves directly to the experimenters, the students exhibited a greater appreciation for the humor in the cartoons. Thus humor appreciation was found to be a vehicle to communicate sexual attraction.

Related to humor is sarcasm. As Ball (1970:313) defines it, sarcasm is "a common everyday linguistic form of biting communication, especially . . . an oral one." It prevails at the higher status levels, where verbal facility is greatest and where symbolic aggression replaces physical assault. The function of sarcasm is to isolate others and thus to control them. It is important to remember that whether or not a given phrase is sarcastic depends not so much on its content as on its form—how it is presented, tone, expression, etc. For example, "the meaning of the words 'nice job' remains obscure without additional information; it may be high praise or low criticism," depending on how the message is communicated and the cultural context (Ball, 1970:314).

Noncommunication

Finally, we must give due recognition to the fact that human interaction is far from always being characterized by neat mutual understanding, as perhaps implied in Meadian social psychology. Indeed, one finds in Mead's writings numerous statements such as the following: "We say something that means something to a certain group. But it not only means that to the group, it also means that to us. It has the same meaning for both" (Mead, 1956:37)

Social psychologists have often criticized Mead for this "rationalist" bias, for assuming greater mutual understanding in human communication than is actually the case. Gregory Stone has pointed out that meaning varies from what he terms *boredom* to *nonsense.* When subject A addresses subject B, his message (a word, a symbol) elicits a response both in B and in

A himself. To the extent that these responses are identical, A's message has the same meaning for both interlocutors. If such overlap in meaning is perfect, there is total communication. Stone terms this, perhaps somewhat facetiously, "boredom" because it means that the two interlocutors are in such total agreement that there is nothing left to explore, to discuss. Think, for example, of a couple married for many years and so accustomed to every communicative nuance of the other partner that mutual talk has, over the years, become practically "unnecessary."

However, the opposite extreme is also possible; a totally different response may be elicited in B by A's message than in A himself. For example, a French male out on a date with an American girl, utters the sound "doo," meaning to compliment her for her softness (doux = soft). She, however, interprets this as a demand for sexual action. Stone terms such total absence of overlap in response to a cue "nonsense." Fig. 11-3 sums up the variability of meaning as conceptualized by Stone.

Several areas of noncommunication have been dealt with in the literature. For example, Gibb (1974) discusses *defensive communication,* which is "behavior which occurs when an individual perceives threat or anticipates threat in the group." Such perception is likely to occur when the climate in the group is judgmental, authoritarian, one of control and superiority, among other things. Under such conditions, people become defensive and communication presumably suffers.

Ichheiser (1970) is a sociological theorist who has made the valuable contribution of linking up symbolic interactionism and conflict theory (cf. Schwartz, 1973a:1283). Unlike Mead, Ichheiser's central theme is the recognition that human relations are characterized by frequent misunderstandings, conflict, and imperfection. Such a recognition is important. A valid appraisal of social interaction must inevitably contain a certain dose of pessimism about the current state of human communication.

INTERACTION

The subject matter of this section is, perhaps, the most central one in this entire book. In the final analysis, social interaction is what social psychology is all about. There is such a vast amount of research dealing, somehow or other, with social interaction that the following discussion must inevitably remain selective and cursory.

The first topic to be discussed in this section will be face-to-face interaction, particularly as analyzed by Goffman and the other representatives of the dramaturgical school of sociology. This will lead us into the next topic—the matter of space in human interaction—which is also of great concern to such authors as Goffman. A third area will consist of a variety of group processes, with particular focus on the oft-studied topics of power, influence, leader-

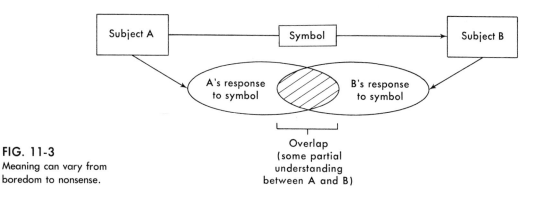

FIG. 11-3
Meaning can vary from
boredom to nonsense.

ship, and various other forms of pressures and influences. Under the next heading—motivation—we shall delineate the distinct theory of motivation offered by sociology, as well as examine such related subjects as need achievement and attribution theory. The following section will deal with play, leisure, sports, and other related activities, while the next section deals with somewhat of the opposite, namely activities that are *not* spontaneous but in fact calculative. Finally, there will be a discussion of some aspects of love, helping behavior, and (physical) attraction.

Life is a drama

While sociologists and social psychologists have long been concerned with face-to-face interaction and "visual interaction" (cf. Simmel, 1970), it is Goffman's dramaturgical school that has thoroughly pursued the analysis of a myriad of different facets of face-to-face behavior. As we saw in Chapter 6, Goffman's *The Presentation of Self in Everyday Life* (1959) depicts the individual as essentially a performer, an actor, a role-player who *stages* his appearance to others, presents a *front* in an ever-ongoing preoccupation with the management of how he impresses others. Another sociologist with a similar interest in the presentation of (physical) appearance in interaction is Stone (1962), whose article "Appearance and the Self" has already been discussed.

An interesting phenomenon studied both by Goffman (1956) and by Stone (Gross and Stone, 1970) is embarrassment. While Goffman had focused on the place and function of embarrassment in social organization, Gross and Stone relate it to role performance. Embarrassment, these authors argue, occurs when identity, poise, and confidence are lost, that is, when the requirements of basic role performance are not met. *Poise* is a crucial element in role performance. It can be defined as the appropriate presentation of the self, the allocation of approriate attention to one's various roles and identities in a given situation. Poise and self-presentation are predicated on at least five elements in a situation: space, props, equipment, clothing, and the body. For example, an instructor's self-presentation takes into account the physical and social boundaries within the classroom, and he may use such props as a cigarette and the blackboard. While interacting parties may lessen embarrassment, when it occurs, through such mechanisms as *tact*, embarrassment does have socializing functions. For example, through hazing, initiation, and deliberate insults, new members in groups are often schooled in poise maintenance.

As we saw in the first section of this chapter, one of Goffman's long-term efforts has been the systematic use of the *situation* as the unit of analysis. In *Behavior in Public Places*, he argues again for situational analysis (1963:245-246). Although this means that the analysis shifts from culture (norms, sanctions, rules) to *action*, Goffman does zero in on a central "cultural" feature of situations, namely *situational proprieties* (op. cit.:24). A fundamental situational "rule" in this sense is the rule that says that one must maintain an "interaction tonus": one must demonstrate physically, with one's body, that one is involved and participating in the situation at the level appropriate to one's role. The rule applies, in its general form, to all of us. Its specific content varies from role to role. For example, in a superior-subordiante relationship, the "interaction tonus" rule, applied to both participants, means that the former must display at least some role distance while the latter must at least feign total involvement. As so often, Goffman's work is outstanding ethnomethodology *avant la lettre*.

The concept of situational propriety (and impropriety, which is the violation of a situational propriety) leads Goffman to one of his discussions of a major theme throughout his writings—mental illness. As elsewhere, Goffman rejects the psychiatrist's distinction between the symptoms of a mental illness and the underlying disorder itself. He also sees little use for the distinction between organic and functional disorders, rejecting, as does Thomas Szasz (1961; Chapter 12) the very concept of mental illness. What psychiatrists call mental symptoms are no more than situational offenses with which the offender is unable to get away (op. cit.:240) and for which he is unable to give a convincing motive or account.

Messinger and associates (1962) have shown that Goffman's dramaturgical approach to social reality tends to view all of us more or less as mental patients. The distinguishing characteristic of the mental patient is the fact that he is "on," that he is forced to prove to others, through his behavior, that he is becoming normal again. And unlike others who are also often "on" (for example, movie actors), what the mental patient must "stage" is his total and basic self. This presents the serious problem that while he may put on a show that convinces others, he himself remains unconvinced of his own normality. The mental patient's dilemma, then, is that he is not satisfied to *appear* normal, but he also strives to *be* normal. To the extent that Goffman and other sociologists describe man as being "on," as consciously staging his behavior, and at the same time as being aware of doing so and thereby doing violence to his true self, they indeed describe him as an alienated creature, as a "mental patient."

Another pervasive theme in Goffman's work is *ritual.* His book *Interaction Ritual* (1967) contains various articles dealing with this subject. For example, in "On Face Work," the author deals with *face*—the presentation of a positive self—and the social mechanisms needed to preserve it. Face work consists of corrective, cooperative, ritualistic, and sometimes aggressive acts. For example, an individual may express modesty so as to induce praise. In *Relations in Public* (1971), Goffman deals with additional rituals. For example, when people greet one another to say farewell to each other, they are in effect engaging in *supportive rituals.* When they apologize or give accounts (explanations) for their behavior, this is *remedial ritual,* interchange aimed at shoring up and repairing the ongoing interaction.

At the present time, the study of face-to-face interaction is being extended by ethnomethodologists. Authors such as Psathas (1973), while in strong agreement with Goffman's work, wish to extend it and make it more precise and phenomenologically more rigorous. A textbook by Speier (1973) picks up many of Goffman's concepts—the remedial interchange, situational involvement, interaction ritual—and develops the ananlysis with particular focus on *talk* and *conversation.* For example, Speier indicates that a conversation must first of all be analyzed in terms of two elements: speaking (competently) and hearing (competently). To illustrate what is meant by competent hearing, Speier (op. cit.:86) gives the following example from a speech that took place at a household dinner table:

A: Did you hear what's happening with the mail strike?
B: No, what?
C: No, I'm asking you.

How do we handle our territory

For several years now, it has been fashionable to aver that the study of animal behavior with respect to habitat, which is called *ethology,* and such things as aggression (cf. Lorenz, 1966) and territoriality (Ardrey, 1966) have direct relevance to human behavior. Human territoriality is now of interest to many social scientists (cf. Martin, 1972; Van den Berghe, 1975), and there exists a tendency to reduce human behavior to spatial and biological variables and to overlook the cultural-symbolic level. Insofar as social psychologists are guilty of this, they are currently repeating the fallacy of the ecological school of urban sociology, which flourished in Chicago nearly fifty years ago (cf. Gordon, 1963).

Nevertheless, the study of spatial arrangements, boundaries, personal space, and the symbolic use of physical features of social settings is a highly valid enterprise. There is, for example, some value to *proxemics,* the study of physical proximity in human interaction. For example, Watson (1970) compared the proxemic behavior of one hundred twenty-six male foreign students at the University of Colorado. He concluded that some cultures are "contact cultures" whereas other ones are not. American students, for example, were found much less likely to touch than many of the foreign students.

The study of space becomes truly interesting when it is conceived of as social space and when regions and boundaries are approached in their symbolic complexity rather than reduced to physical simplicity. Here, again, Goffman (1959) has been the major pioneer. A crucial distinction established by that author is the distinction between *front region* and *back region.* A region, it may be recalled (Chapter 6), is a "place that is bounded to some degree by barriers to perception" (op. cit.:106). A *front region* refers "to the place where the performance is given" (op. cit.:107), whereas "a back region or back stage may be defined as a place, relative to a given performance, where the impression fostered by the performance is knowingly contradicted as a matter of course" (op. cit.:112).

Many authors have either been implicitly inspired by Goffman's work, extending his theories, or have explicitly tested some of his hypotheses. For example Mac-Cannell (1973) has studied tourist settings, showing that tourists attempt to penetrate the natives' back region because they associate it with intimacy and authenticity. However, tourists are often fooled, since the natives provide various intermediate spaces that may seem to be part of their private life space but in fact are not.

Schwartz (1973b), too, has addressed the topic of privacy in the Goffmanesque tradition. He points out that structural provisions for privacy vary by social status. In other words, high status provides privacy. For example, the chairman of the board or the higher official is protected by a series of anterooms, each occupied by a watchdog-like secretary.

Other authors who have built upon Goffman's pioneering work in social space include Bennett and Bennett (1970) and Smith (1973). Bennett and Bennett make the important point that in order to understand variation in the flow and character of a social gathering (say, a party), one must not only look at the participants but also at the combination of elements and structure that are introduced into the situation. For example, what kind of music is being played? Are drinks served formally, or are guests free to gravitate toward the kitchen refrigerator to serve themselves? Smith examines household space and family organization, pointing out that the front and the back are not always clearly separated. In certain (sub)cultures, for example in the lower class and in Mexico, one does not find as much insulation and privacy as in middle-class American families.

Goffman himself has made recent additional contributions to the study of social space. In *Relations in Public* (1971), he introduces a variety of concepts to deal with what he terms territorial "preserves," territories of the self. For example, the *stall,* based on ethological analogy, is the personal "space to which individuals can lay temporary claim" (op. cit.:32) and which they may temporarily leave while retaining their claim. When leaving one's stall, *markers* should be left to indicate one's claim.

Sommer is a psychological social psychologist who has done much work on personal space and territoriality (cf. Felipe and Sommer, 1972; Sommer, 1959; 1969; 1974; Sommer and Becker, 1972) and who has also been influenced by Goffman. For example, a series of studies by Sommer and Becker (1972) demonstrates how students (in library areas and soda fountains) defend their preserves, using markers as well as "neighbors," people sitting next to them who indicate to potential intruders, when an individual has temporarily left his stall, that the place is occupied.

Lyman and Scott (1967) provide an excellent analysis of the social and symbolic dimensions of personal space, proposing a typology of territories that ranges from public spaces to one's body. These authors also point out that interactional territories may be mobile, as in walking conversations, and that even the body may become an interactional territory, as in marriage or love.

It is, finally, in the area of urban studies that one finds the greatest preoccupation with space as a variable in human life. Simmel (1903), in his classical article on "The Metropolis and Mental Life," pointed out early that the urban dweller, because of excessive social and sensory stimulation (what is now termed the urban "overload"), is compelled to develop a protective shield. This is why the urban dweller often appears indifferent, cold, blasé. Thus Simmel attributes certain uniform psychological characteristics shared by all urbanites to ecological conditions. The study of such ecological variables as population size, density, and migration became the hallmark of the Chicago school of urban sociology (cf. Park et al., 1925).

Today, concern about the population explosion has rekindled the interest of social psychologists in urban conditions and in the effects of such things as crowding and density. It is now fashionable to devote a section of social psychology books to these problems and to relate them to animal ethology (cf. Krupat, 1975). A frequent topic, in this context, is what may be termed the "Genovese syndrome." This refers to the 1964 murder of Catherine Genovese in Queens. Coming home from a night job in the early morning, the young woman was stabbed repeatedly, over a long period of time. At least thirty-eight residents witnessed the attack, but none went to her aid, and no one called the police until she was dead. This incident presumably proved how uninvolved, anomic, and alienated the big-city dweller is, and that, in turn, has often been attributed to excessive population density. Indeed, repeated reference is made to studies (cf. Marsden, 1975) showing that mice, rats, and other animals, when reaching a certain density threshold, begin to develop various behavioral pathologies. Such studies often lead to ethological extrapolations to human society, as when Marsden (op. cit.) somehow sees parallels between the behavior of his mice and the behavior of men as described by Toffler in *Future Shock* (1970). This may be popular with students and laymen and attuned to the population-ecology fad, but it is neither necessarily valid nor relevant to our still somewhat underpopulated continent.

In the final analysis, the character and forms of social interaction that emerge in urban places have far more to do with culture than with physical space. Milgram (1972) has focused on such cultural variables as "urban atmosphere," comparing, for example, New York, London, and Paris. While these three cities are all enormous—each in excess of eight million inhabitants, and each quite densely populated—they differ sharply in character. An interesting study by Feldman (1968) indicates marked differences in behavior toward foreigners and compatriots in Paris, Athens, and Boston. For example, Parisians were significantly less apt to cheat foreigners than were the Athenians or the Bostonians (so much for the stereotype of the virtuous New Englander!), and in fact they were the only citizens who were more honest with foreigners than with compatriots in this experiment.

The importance of cultural and social-psychological dimensions—as distinct from ecological ones—has been stressed repeatedly (cf. Gans, 1962; Stone, 1954). We mention, as a final case in point, the matter of public transit (cf. Davis and Levine, 1972). While it may be true that public transit, as these authors show, is a rather problematical social situation always characterized by (minor) conflicts, it is also interesting to note the different cultural adaptations to that situation. For example, the New York subway commuter may shield himself every day behind the *New York Times* or the *Daily News.* However, the Amsterdam tram rider is generally an enormously gregarious and jovial fellow. In the Dutch capital, one cannot get work done while commuting. That time is frequently one of the day's social occasions.

Group processes

So far in this section we have covered face-to-face interaction, which has been studied primarily by sociological social psychologists (most of them influenced by Goffman), and the matter of space and territory, which has been investigated both by that group and by psychological social psychologists (such as Sommers) and by ethologists. Now we turn to a realm that has been researched almost exclusively by psychological social psychologists, often in the form of laboratory controlled, small-group experiments. This general area may be referred to as the (social) psychology of conformity and leadership (cf. Hollander, 1971; Hollander and Willis, 1971). It is under this umbrella that one finds the enormous literature dealing with such things as conformity, obedience, compliance, influence, persuasion, manipulation, power, leadership, and various other aspects of group dynamics and group structures.[1] Here, the approach is far less

---

[1]For some reason that only the sociology of knowledge might explain, conformity has been researched primarily by psychologists, while deviance has been almost exclusively studied by sociologists. As Hollander and Willis (1971) point out, psychologists have neglected to study nonconformity (except, one should add, insofar as nonconformity means leadership rather than deviance). Perhaps psychologists are conformists and sociologists are, more often, deviants. In any event, it is because of this given state of affairs in the disciplines that we discuss conformity here and devote Chapter 12 separately to the immense and predominantly sociological literature on deviance.

humanistic than the general tenor of this book. Most of the research covered in the present section is in the tradition discussed in Chapter 2: psychological (and scientific) social psychology.

As Hollander and Willis (1971) remind us, Sherif's (1935) experiments on the autokinetic effect and Asch's (1952) experiments on conformity to group norms are among the early and now classical investigations into conformity. This work was discussed in Chapter 2.

Theoretical contributions to the social psychology of conformity and nonconformity include articles by Willis (1972), who defines conformity as "behavior intended to fulfill normative group expectations as these expectations are perceived by the individual" (op. cit.:372) and nonconformity as "behavior which is intended to facilitate the attainment of some goal other than that of fulfilling perceived normative group expectations" (op. cit.:373), and by Hollander (1972). This author introduces the useful notion of *idiosyncrasy credit.* "This represents an accumulation of positively-disposed impressions residing in the perceptions of relevant others; it is defined operationally in terms of the degree to which an individual may deviate from the common expectancies of the group" (Hollander, 1972:365-366). Thus each individual has a certain "credit balance" with his group, that is, a certain degree of freedom to deviate before the group rejects him. When his credit balance reaches zero, the group will sanction or reject him. For example, a fraternity member may deviate from his peers' norms up to a certain point—he may stay away from parties, dress sloppily, drink and smoke excessively (or insufficiently), not participate in sports and games, engage in homosexuality, and do too well (or too poorly) in school. Once he has exhausted his credit with his fraternity brothers, he will be ostracized.

Perhaps the most famous recent research on conformity is that of Milgram, who has provided some spectacular and controversial tests of people's tendency to conform and to obey orders even if it means hurting others (cf. Milgram, 1964; 1965; 1974; Elms and Milgram, 1966; Meyer, 1970; Wenglinsky, 1975). In a series of studies, Milgram and his associates deal with the relationship between group pressure and conformity (Milgram (1964), seek (and fail) to identify personality correlates of obedience (Elms and Milgram, 1966), and, of central interest here, examine the conditions of obedience and disobedience to authority (Milgram, 1965; 1974). This research has been quoted innumerable times and discussed in the mass media because it presumably bears on the fundamental moral issues raised by such historical events as the postwar Nuremburg trials of Nazi war criminals and the My Lai massacre in Vietnam. The question is: are men indeed so immoral—or better, amoral—that most of them would have little trouble blindly following orders to perform monstrous acts? As Meyer puts it, "if Hitler asked you to electrocute a stranger, would you?" Milgram's experiment consists of asking people to administer electric shocks of increasing intensity to other people as part of a scientific experiment. They are left naive, that is, led to believe that they are actually hurting the experimental subjects, who are in fact confederates of the experimenter and instructed to scream, holler, and feign excruciating pain. The gist of the findings is the remarkable ease that seemingly nice and honorable people have in complying with the experimenter's orders to hurt other subjects.

According to Meyer (1970) and many others, Milgram's is a brilliant (although perhaps somewhat unethical) demonstration of the inhumanness in all of us, of the fact that we are all potential Nazis, that "it can happen here." However, Wenglinsky (1975:615) makes a far more relevant point. "All Milgram shows is that if you work hard enough you can lull people into evil by making the situation resemble a non-evil one in as many ways as possible." After all, the subjects had been told repeatedly that they were doing important scientific work, and *not* engaging in cruel and unusual punishment. The parallel with Nazi Germany is questionable. In fact, Milgram's subjects had a hunch that turned out correct: they were not hurting anyone!

Conformity and obedience are responses. Their stimulus counterpart is *influence*. Theodorson and Theodorson (1969:202) define influence as "the power to effect a voluntary change in a person's attitude or opinion through persuasive action." We should add that influence can also produce *behavioral* change and that persuasion is merely one of several forms of influence. Influence can range from coercion, in which case it is indistinct from power, to a variety of persuasive techniques. The use of threat (cf. Aronson, 1973) and brainwashing (Schein, 1973) represent coercive influence. Then, too, an individual's status (Hofling et al., 1972) and the environmental setting (Vidulich and Wilson, 1972) also affect the amount of influence he may exert.

Influence can also be exerted through a variety of techniques that do not involve the tremendous coercive pressures of brainwashing or even those exerted upon the subjects of Milgram's experiments. For example, social psychologists have documented such noncoercive techniques of influence as picketing (Lupfer et al., 1972) and petitioning (Helson et al., 1972), showing that such techniques are quite effective under certain conditions.

Also, Freedman and Fraser (1973) have demonstrated the effectiveness of the "foot-in-the-door" technique, the gradual inducement of people to large requests by first inducing them to small ones. The authors divided a sample of one hundred fifty-six Palo Alto housewives into four groups, each subjected to an increasing imposition by the interviewers. Under the guise of market research, the first group was simply contacted once by the interviewers. The second group was contacted twice and familiarized thoroughly with the alleged nature of the project. The third group underwent the same treatment as the second group, but in addition these housewives were asked whether or not they would agree to answer some questions about the types of household products they use. Then they were told that they might be contacted later to answer the questionnaire. Finally the fourth group was submitted to the same treatment as group 3, but in addition these housewives were made to answer the household product questionnaire (a short and innocuous one) on the spot.

Now all four groups of housewives were also asked whether they would be willing to submit, later on, to a long visit by six researchers who would have to be given permission to browse freely through the entire house for two hours. This, of course, was never carried out. The "foot-in-the-door" hypothesis was that the four groups would agree to comply with the large request in an ascending order. As Table 7 indicates, the hypothesis was verified.

Further techniques of influence include flattery (cf. Jones, 1973) and *one-down-manship* (Weinstein, 1973). By this, Weinstein means such ploys as *preinterpretation,*

TABLE 7.   Percentage of subjects complying with large request, by degree of imposition*

Groups	Percent
4. Performance	52.8
3. Agree-only	33.3
2. Familiarization	27.8†
1. One-contact	22.2‡

*Note: N=36 for each group. Significance levels represent differences from the performance condition. From Freedman, Jonathan L., and Scott C. Fraser, 1973. "Compliance without pressure: the foot-in-the-door technique." In Social Psychology in Everyday Life. Billy J. Franklin and Frank J. Kobout (eds.). New York: David McKay Co., p. 99.
†p < .07.
‡p < .02.

postinterpretation, and postapology. For example, an individual may preface an insult to another with an assertion that nothing detrimental is intended, as when he says, "I think you've done a great job and I don't want you to get me wrong, but. . . ." This is preinterpretation. When a speaker begins a statement with something like "I haven't had the chance to read up on this yet, but it seems to me that . . ." (Weinstein, 1973:97), we have a preapology. These, then, are techniques used to establish interpersonal influence.

The opposite of one-downmanship is discussed by Ableson and Miller (1972), who show how personal insult can stiffen people into opposition. Clearly, if we seek to influence others, the worst thing we can do is to elicit this type of "boomerang effect."

Another important form of influence is manipulation. Some social scientists see the use of manipulative techniques as rooted in what may be termed a Machiavellian personality (cf. Christie and Geis, 1971), some believe that it is a sign of inadequacy (as do humanistic psychiatrists such as Berne [1964] and Shostrom [1968], but some, reflecting perhaps our day and age, argue that a Machiavellian approach to life is desirable (Lyman and Scott, 1970). In any event, manipulation refers to a variety of calculative techniques for influencing others, generally to one's own ends.

Distinct (but not clearly so) from influence is *power,* about which there is also an enormous literature. To begin with, there is the vast taxonomic and definitional effort of social scientists attempting to define and distinguish such concepts as power, authority, influence, and persuasion. Weber's (1947:152) classic definition of power is: "the probability that one actor within a social relationship will be in a position to carry out his own will despite resistance." Authority is defined as "the probability that certain specific commands (or all commands) from a given source will be obeyed by a given group of persons" (op. cit.:324). The major difference between power and authority is that *authority is legit-*

imate power, it is voluntarily obeyed. This does not necessarily apply to all power. For example, the stick-up man has the power to abscond with his victim's wallet; he does not have the authority. More recent conceptual discussions of power can be found in French and Raven (1971), Olsen (1971), and Summers (1976), among other sources.

The study of power has taken place at a number of different levels: there is the focus on political power at the macrosociological level, as found in Mills' classic *The Power Elite* (1956), and there is the social-psychological study of interpersonal power. In addition, students of social organization are also interested in power, as are for example Blau and Scott (1962). Blau belongs to an important theoretical school in the study of power—*exchange theory* (see Chapter 1). We return to this in a later section of this chapter.

An overview of small-group research on power is provided by Jacobson (1972), and additional recent empirical work on power includes Thomas and co-workers (1972) and Berger and associates (1976). The last authors show that an individual's characteristic relevant to the task at hand determines his power in the group. Thomas and his colleagues demonstrate that role-taking can be a substitute for power when a subordinate (having no power) wishes to control a superior. For example, fathers were found to be less accurate role-takers than mothers, who in turn were less accurate than children: the more power one has, the less one needs to "bother" with role-taking!

In considerable overlap with the topics discussed so far in this section is *leadership.* Hollander (1972) and some other social psychologists approach leadership as a form of nonconformity. Leaders are viewed as those individuals who *set* group standards, rather than follow them. To earn the right to do this, one must accumulate "idiosyncrasy credits." That is, if the innovative ideas introduced by an individual are valuable to the group, he accumulates credits and becomes a leader. If

the innovations are unsuccessful, he loses the opportunity to lead and may in fact become a deviant.

A pervasive theme throughout the literature on leadership is the distinction between the *instrumental* and the *affective* leader. The former, according to Bales, is an individual with a strong desire to control others while keeping himself free of control. He is sort of cold, respected, but not loved or liked. On the other hand, there is the individual who is sensitive to the needs of others and who helps them. This is the well-liked leader. Generally, the instrumental leader, who provides the best ideas for the solution of the group's problems and who is respected, and the affective leader, who provides emotional support and is liked, are two different individuals.

Related to this is the controversial question of whether leadership (be it instrumental or affective) is primarily a function of personality or of the situation. Fiedler (1968; 1972) is one of the social psychologists who side with personality, arguing that leaders have distinct character traits such as a strong sense of perceptual discrimination. Obviously, psychological social psychologists have been more inclined toward this perspective, whereas sociological social psychologists consider the situation more important. Trait research, as Bavelas (1971) points out, means the attempt to identify leader types, who are presumably more intelligent, better adjusted, and more socially active than other people.

However, the sociological view is now gaining ground. It is increasingly being realized that an individual often exhibits leadership as a result of the situation he is in rather than because of his personality. For example, a military officer may fall apart in a democratic civilian setting. Today, leadership is increasingly viewed as an organizational function. For example, when management wishes to recruit a new man for an executive position, the question is not "which applicant is most gifted," but "who will fit in best?"

Traditionally, Bavelas points out, leadership qualities have included such things as quickness of decision, coolness under duress, intuition, and the ability to make decisions involving risks. However, modern organizations increasingly stress the ability to plan, to organize, and to use rational calculation rather than hunches. Thus the new bureaucratic culture has less use for the brilliant innovator and the rare genius than for the effective organization man. Leadership, then, is primarily situational. A good proof of this is the fact that a psychotic man may, in societies such as ours, be locked away but in tribal societies be elevated to such leadership positions as shaman or medicine man!

A topic of current interest is leadership in crisis. We know from history that changes in leadership are likely to be far more frequent during periods of crisis than during normal times. Hamblin (1964) is among the social psychologists who have tested this idea experimentally. Table 8 reproduces a portion of that author's findings.

Public and political leaders have been studied by a variety of authors (cf. Klapp, 1964), and most agree that the quality of contemporary American leadership is poor (cf. Nisbet, 1974). A long time ago,

Maslow (1942) made the following profound observation. Many who seek leadership do so to satisfy themselves (for example, their neurotic power drives) rather than to help the community. Those who would be motivated by the good of the community generally do not seek power. Why, then, do we not choose our leaders, rather than having them choose themselves? How apt Maslow's comments are, at a time (Spring, 1976) when more than a dozen political opportunists have jumped on the lucrative federally funded presidential campaign bandwagon!

Related to the matter of leadership is the question of how groups are run. For example, do groups perform better under authoritarian leadership, or does democracy work better? Is it better to have cooperation or competition? During and after World War II, social psychologists were highly interested in determining these matters empirically, because totalitarian systems such as Nazi Germany and the Soviet Union had made a claim on superior efficiency. Lewin and co-workers (1939), for example, showed in an experiment at the University of Iowa that the members of democratic groups of young boys liked their leaders more and engaged in less scapegoating than did boys in groups that were run autocratically.

French (1941) also compared two types of groups: (1) groups consisting of unacquainted undergraduates and (2) groups such as college athletic teams. Both the organized and the unorganized groups were told to perform certain tasks for which there was in fact no solution. For example, they were asked to fill in rows and columns of numbers in tables to add up to certain sums already given in the margins, which could never be done. The question was: how would the two types of groups react to such frustration? French found that the organized groups experienced more disruption, hostility, and aggression, because their motivation to succeed in the joint effort was greater.

Other early studies on the effects of variation in group structure include McCand-

TABLE 8. Replacement of leaders in crisis group and in control group*

	Leader replaced	Leader not replaced
Crisis groups	9	3
Control groups	3	9

*Chi square, one-tailed test, corrected for continuity, p < .05. From Hamblin, Robert L. 1958. "Leadership and crises." Sociometry 21:332.

less (1942), Deutsch (1949), and Leavitt (1951). This latter author compared the effect of four different communication patterns on group performance and group satisfaction. Four five-member groups were established, each group having to solve some problem. Each member of each group received certain clues to the problem, but the manner in which the subjects were permitted to transmit messages to one another varied in the different groups. Four transmission patterns were created: a circle (O), a straight line (I), a Y, and an X. This is shown in Fig. 11-4.

In the circle pattern each person was allowed to communicate with those on either side of him. In the straight line too, communication was allowed to persons on both sides, except for the two end men, who could only communicate with one other person. In the X and Y patterns, as can be seen, one individual becomes central to the communication flow. In fact, only the circle pattern is completely democratic in this respect.

Leavitt found, first, that the more democratic patterns (O and I) were less efficient in problem-solving, that is more error-prone than the two other patterns. This is shown in Table 9.

TABLE 9. Mean number of errors made in different communication network patterns over an identical number of trials*

| Patterns | Number of errors | |
	Fifteen trials	Eight trials
O	16.6	7.6
I	9.8	2.8
Y	2.6	0
X	9.8	0.6

*Adapted from Leavitt, Harold J. 1951. "Some effects of certain communication patterns on group performance." Journal of Abnormal and Social Psychology 46:38-50.

While the more centralized group patterns were found to be more efficient, Leavitt also found that they were less satisfying to their members and that they did not always correct errors as well as the more democratic patterns.

It is hazardous to apply the findings of experimental studies to real society. Often, social psychologists find whatever they are seeking, sometimes showing that democracy, cooperation, love, and equality are better, sometimes demonstrating the opposite. Neither is it clear in terms of what criteria these elements are found to be better or worse than power, competition, inequality, and subordination.

In the end, the argument remains a philosophical-ideological one. There are those who, in the tradition of Hobbes, Machiavelli, Nietzsche, and LeDantec, maintain that human nature is fundamentally selfish and predatory and that the human condition is therefore inevitably one of inequality. Goldberg (1973), for example, recently wrote a provocative book about the inevitability of patriarchy, arguing that men are destined to dominate social authority structures, since their higher level of testosterone makes them inherently more aggressive than women. However, most social scientists recognize that power, whether in a sexual context or in any other framework, is merely one of several fundamental variables in human behavior. Andre (1975), for example, has proposed a dual theory of human nature based on a power-love axis. Goode (1972), in his presidential address to the American Sociological Association, viewed force as only one of the four great social control systems in the history of mankind. Three of the four

FIG. 11-4
Leavitt's four communication patterns.

great principles recognized by Goode are presumably forces for inequality. However, the fourth one—less well understood and less researched—is love.

The position taken in this book is that the phenomena of power, domination, subordination, and inequality must, in the first place, be clearly described and understood, just like other forms of social interaction. In this light, the phenomenological analyses of men like Simmel (1971) and Schutz (1970) are perhaps more illuminating than many quantitative social-psychological experiments that attempt to establish cause and effect relationships while failing to understand the complex *nature* of the processes under examination. Simmel (1971:121), for example, opens our eyes to the fact that subordination may be at the hands of an individual (for example, a ruler, a boss, or a husband), a group (a government), or an objective force or principle (the law, or a debt, or one's conscience).

Schutz (1970:308-313) discusses equality, opportunity, and the Aristotelian principle of *distributive justice,* according to which rewards should not necessarily be absolutely equal but proportional to merit, or what exchange theorists term "investments" (cf. Homans, 1961).

Insofar as a value position is taken in the present book, it is in line with this principle, and with the admonitions of those authors (cf. Samuel, 1975:464-467) who warn against the 1984 nightmare of total equalization—an impossibility anyway. However, this is less relevant than the need to understand the essentially *symbolic* nature of such things as "force," "freedom," "equality," and "domination." Laboratory psychologists may attempt to establish the objective parameters of these phenomena and ideologues may appeal to that perennial deus ex machina—human nature. In fact, they are merely adding additional layers of meanings to concepts whose nature and meaning are determined by how

they are used and responded to by man and society. Here, we touch upon the central theme of the following section.

Motivation

It is under the heading of motivation that we must deal with the extreme relativity of all social-psychological truths. Because social psychology deals with symbolic behavior and with the uniquely reflexive and self-conscious conduct of which only man is capable, it must recognize as its fundamental characteristic the fact that it is a cultural discipline, not a natural-scientific one, a discipline that describes subjective and relative social arrangements rather than immutable laws of nature. This is what was alluded to in the concluding paragraph of the previous section.

As with the discussion of any other basic subject, it would be best to begin with a definition of motive and motivation. However, this is not possible, precisely because there is no agreement as to what motives refer to. What is possible, nevertheless, is to think of motives in the following manner. *Motives are answers to the question "why?" with respect to human conduct.* Thus, although social scientists disagree as to the empirical referents of motives—as to what the answer to the question is—they can probably all agree that this is, indeed, the fundamental question in the field of motivation.

Many competing theories of motivation have been offered. The hedonists argued that man was basically motivated by the pleasure-pain principle and that he was rational in the pursuit of pleasure and the avoidance of pain. The instinctivists proposed that man's basic motives were instincts, or drives, such as sex, hunger, and aggression, and that he was far from rational. Freud's views, which will be discussed in a moment, belong here. Plato, much earlier but already much wiser, believed that the three principles of human motivation were affection (feeling), conation (striving), and cognition (thought). There are, of course, also the various religious explanations of human behavior, and in the nineteenth century (cf. Chapter 4), some early social psychologists suggested that man's behavior reflected the crowds in which he acted out, and some believed that all human conduct could be explained through the principles of imitation and suggestion. Then, too, there is the Marxian view of motive, according to which human behavior is entirely the reflection of political and economic institutional arrangements.

Today, the fundamental cleavage is between the psychological and the sociological conception of motive, or between the classical and what may be termed the pragmatist conception. As Peters (1960) shows, the dominant way to think about motive—both among laymen and among professionals—is to view it as a *cause* of behavior. This is typical of Freudian psychology, of need psychology, in sum of psychiatry in toto.

Freud begins with the assumption that the human organism is a closed and fixed energy system activated by innate biological needs. Only two basic instincts are recognized—*eros,* or the life instinct, and *thanatos,* the death instinct. Motivation can be of three kinds: sexual (the libido), unconscious, and conscious. Freud was perhaps the first psychologist to stress sexual motivation at all levels, including childhood. Because, according to Freud, every experience is preserved, at least in the unconscious, this is another important source of motivation. For example, we all use a variety of defense mechanisms and we often do so unconsciously. Finally, there are the ego drives and the conscious needs that also represent a significant source of motivation.

Thus we see that in the Freudian scheme, all three major sources of motivation are internal to the organism, and they all follow the pleasure-pain principle. There is, in Freudian and neo-Freudian psychology, always a biological and often a sexual determinism. Consider, for example, the fact that during the first few days of January, we often continue to date our checks by the previous year. Why? General

psychologists might explain this as the persistence of motor habits. Psychoanalysts, on the other hand, might impute as a motive the fear of growing old and of losing one's vitality.

According to psychoanalytic psychology, then, *real* motives can be imputed to actors, who in turn may often not even be conscious of their motives. Thus arises the distinction between "real motives" and *rationalizations* as well as *sublimation.* A rationalization is an explanation presented by the actor for his conduct, but a false one, in other words a false motive. For example, a young man at the supermarket gallantly helps an attractive housewife carry her grocery bags to her automobile and gives as his motive for doing this the desire to fulfill his Christian duty. A psychologist might argue that this is a rationalization, imputing to the young man sexual intentions as his true motive. Similarly, sublimation refers to the subtitution of some "secondary" activity for a more basic, more primary, and generally sexual one, such as when a young man sublimates his strong sexual urges by writing poetry or lifting weights. Again, the Freudian psychologist would claim that the young man's real motive for exerting himself is not posterity or a healthy body, but sex.

Related to but somewhat different from the Freudian theory of motivation is drive theory. Drives, according to Tolman (cf. Peters, 1960:101), are states of tension that initiate directed behavior. As Peters (op. cit.:122-123) points out, "drive" is merely a mechanistic translation of the earlier concept of need, the two terms being essentially synonymous. Earlier, psychologists limited the drive concept to inborn tendencies, thus equating it with instinct. However, Hull, Miller, Dollard, and others (see Chapter 2) have extended it to incorporate acquired behaviors as well. In any event, drives have been among the psychologist's major category of motives, referring generally to some inner force aimed at the reduction of tension. Oddly, then, a drive is a force aimed at drive reduction, that is, aimed at eliminating itself. For example, hunger is said to be a drive. The hunger drive is to reduce hunger. A drive is to reduce a drive. This circularity makes the concept rather useless.

The motivation theories discussed so far all share a hedonistic assumption: both the Freudian and the drive theories view motivation essentially as drive reduction.

Neo-Freudians like Abraham Maslow (1955) have attempted to distinguish between two types of needs: *deficiency motivation* and *growth motivation.* The former refers to the traditionally recognized homeostatic needs, the needs for the reduction of tension just discussed. In addition, however, Maslow also postulates needs for love, growth, self-actualization, stimulation, etc.

Thus it appears that need psychology commits one of two possible fallacies: *teleology* or *tautology.* Maslow's articulation of the paradigm is teleological. An end state in the future (say, maturity or self-actualization) is postulated to be a cause of present conduct. The concept of growth motivation is fallacious, since cause must precede effect.

Otherwise, need psychology is inherently tautological. To the question "Why do people engage in activity X?" it answers "because they have a basic need for activity X." In other words, the observed conduct is renamed, and causality is attributed to the new name.

Otto Klineberg, in an attempt to circumvent the tautological fallacy, has formulated three criteria for the identification of what he terms "dependable motives": universality, organic basis, and phylogenetic continuity. However, this does not produce much more than such basic needs as hunger, thirst, excretion, and oxygen.

Returning to the psychoanalytic theory of motivation, its problems are equally serious. In the first place, it establishes an unwarranted hierarchy of needs. Yet we know that sexual and other biogenic needs are no more primary or "important" in any meaningful sense of the word than are sociogenic and symbolic needs. As Coutu (quoted in Lindesmith and Strauss, 1956:281) aptly pointed out: "people need whatever they think they need.,'

Psychiatrists dismiss avowed motives as rationalizations, looking instead for real motives and causes of behavior. Yet, as Shibutani (1961:184) indicates, one's stated motives are just as real, especially since they are rooted in a socially shared vocabulary of motives. What distinguishes the psychiatrist from the subject is not that the former has access to the truth whereas the latter is lying, but the fact that the two are employing different and competing vocabularies of motives. When the psychiatrist succeeds in convincing the subject of his imputations, we have what Kenneth Burke terms a *secular conversion:* the patient has been converted to the psychoanalytic rhetoric of motives.

It can be seen at this point that the sociological theory of motivation first arose out of a critique of the psychological theory. As an individual, one may turn the table on the psychiatrist and say that when he imputes a motive to a subject he is merely projecting (cf. Lindesmith and Strauss, 1956:306). Thus one can plausibly claim that when the psychiatrist "interprets" his subject's behavior as being the result of sexual repression, or, more common in the 1970s, when the encounter leader or group facilitator tells his subjects that they are uptight, emotionally starved, and need to express love and free body contact, the fact of the matter is that these are the group leader's own desires, no one else's. More to the point, as a sociologist, one must remember that role-taking is the basic mark of human behavior and that part of this is motive imputation.

The sociologist, therefore, recognizes the critical difference between *motive* and *cause.* Whereas the cause of a given action must precede it, a motive is the explanation given after the fact. Whereas causes must be public and verifiable, motives are personal and private. Motives, unlike causes, are part of the act, requiring understanding themselves (cf. Lindesmith and Strauss, 1956:300). Furthermore, motives are "linguistic designations of intentions" (Shibutani, 1961:183), generally rooted in the vocabulary that prevails in one's group or society at a given time. Thus change in group affiliation often requires that one also switch motives. And since motives, as just stated, refer to avowed intentions and to the consciously volitional aspect of human conduct, the Freudian notion of "unconscious motive" is a contradiction in terms (Lindesmith and Strauss, 1956:294).

The foundations of a sociological theory of motive were laid quite early by such men as Dewey (1922) and Weber (1947). However, it is a famous article by C. Wright Mills (1940) that is generally acknowledged as the most crucial contribution here. Mills first indicates that there are three basic types of motivations: (1) physiochemical, aimed at health restoration, (2) psychological, aimed at pleasure, and (3) social, aimed at the facilitation of interaction. There is no reason to view the third type as epiphenomenal, as the Freudians have tended to do. Sociologically, motives must be viewed as terms used in interaction and communication to explain behavior, and these terms, as stated earlier, are vocabularies that are the product of historical and cultural definitions. For example, as the consumption ethic replaces the work ethic and as the new hedonism replaces puritan values, motives change. There is even a tendency to reinterpret past events and to impute twentieth century motives such as financial greed, sexual repression, an inferiority complex, or an Oedipal fixation to historical figures such as Leonardo Da Vinci and Jesus Christ. This is clearly wrong.

Martindale (1960) raises a good point about Mills' theory of motives. If a motive is to be thought of as an ex post facto explanation, then the distinction between truth and lie disappears. If motives are only judged in terms of their acceptability, regardless of their validity, this implies that human motivation is essentially an opportunistic and deceitful strategy.

Sociologists have not stopped at the mere reporting of whatever motives subjects happen to use to explain their conduct, and this partially answers Martindale's criticism. For one thing, sociologists do concern themselves with the matter of validity. According to Stone, validity is a function of empirical evidence, logic, and the power of the negotiating parties. Furthermore, Foote (1951), Shibutani (1961:247), and Denzin (1969), among others, have identified an important antecedent basis for motivation, identity and self-concept. To understand the motivation of an individual, one must know who he is, both in his own eyes and in those of others.

The main point to remember about the sociological conception of motivation is that *motive refers to the way conduct is interpreted and explained by the subject himself and by others.* For example, organic needs such as sex and hunger can only be termed motives after they have been interpreted as such. As Lindesmith and Strauss (1956:272) note, hunger for food is learned, just like hunger for drugs. The wolf children who have survived total abandonment did not eat instinctively, but probably as a result of operant conditioning—random accident.

That human needs are always symbolic as well as biological is evidenced by the cultural nature of most of our eating habits. We all know how certain dishes—say fried ants or escargot—may be considered an exquisite delicacy in one culture and disgusting in another. Scott, on his fateful expedition to the South Pole, refused to eat his dogs despite the fact that this meant hunger and may have contributed to his death. To eat dog meat, he believed, was beneath the dignity of an English gentleman.

Modern psychologists have approached motivation in an entirely different fashion. One of their key concerns has been *achievement motivation*. McClelland (1961; 1971) has spent his career measuring this drive-like learned personality characteristic, arguing that different cultures socialize their members into different levels of achievement motivation and that this accounts for the differences in rates of development between such societies as India and the United States.

Various social and ethnic groups within American society have also been compared in terms of need achievement. Gurin and associates (1972) and Rosen (1972), for example, examine race, the former authors noting that black youths generally do not believe that internal control has a significant effect on achievement and that this may account for a low achievement motivation. Pareek (1971) examined achievement motivation among the poor, and Ellis (1968) studied achievement-oriented women, showing a high incidence of emotional maladjustment in that group.

Today, psychology has a new approach termed *attribution theory*, thereby finally converging with the sociological conception of motivation. Attribution theory is concerned with causal perception, with how people infer causes about the behavior of others. Clearly, this is related to the topic of motive imputation discussed before. Research on attribution theory includes Jones and his co-workers (1972), various selections in Krupat (1975), Lerner (1965), Shaw and Skolnick (1973), Walster (1966), and Weiner (1974). The last book is of particular interest since it attempts to relate attribution theory to achievement motivation. "Causes of behavior, Weiner points out, for example success or failure, can be attributed to (1) personal, internal forces (e.g. individual ability or effort) or (2) situational, external forces (e.g. the difficulty of the task or luck)" (paraphrased in Sullivan, 1975:425). Weiner found that

both the high achievers and the low achievers tend to perceive their successes and failures as caused by themselves, that is resulting from their own ability or lack thereof. The high achievers attribute their failures to a lack of effort. Thus high acievers reinforce themselves for further achievement in the future, while low achievers also go through such a self-fulfilling prophecy, setting themselves up for future failure.

Motivation has been approached from a variety of additional standpoints. As we saw earlier, Franks (1974), following White (1959), focused on *competence,* showing that this, too, can be an important motivational force. Here, we return to the sociological-phenomenological conception that views motives as rooted in the system of relevance used by the actor (cf. Schutz, 1970; Weigert, 1975) and in the vocabulary available to him (cf. Mills, 1940).

The sociological study of motives focuses on their social construction, ascription (cf. Blum and McHugh, 1971), and negotiation, that is, on how people *account* (cf. Blumstein et al., 1974; Scott and Lyman, 1972) for conduct. For example, the last two authors distinguish between two types of accounts: excuses and justifications. Both are answers to the question "why did you do it?" but they differ in terms of the moral commitment of the actor to his behavior.

The sociology of motivation deals with explanations of human behavior. However, unlike conventional psychology, it does not equate motive with cause. It defines motive as any explanation used to account for human conduct. For example,one may note, cynically, that the motive for the presence of white Russian soldiers in Angola is the international struggle against racism and imperialism, while the motive for the presence of white American soldiers in Vietnam was racist imperialism, at least in the system of relevance that dominates the world forum at this time. In that same system of relevance, the military invasion and occupation of Czechoslovakia in 1968 is explained as people's liberation, whereas the invasion of Cuba would be an act of imperialism.

Motives are linguistic devices, and as the preceding examples suggest, language in the modern world is often made subservient to ideological exigencies—call it rape. As Orwell unforgettably showed in *1984*, war becomes peace, more becomes less, and newspeak soon renders all words meaningless. It is precisely because of the infuriating fact that motives are no more than liguistic devices used to explain, justify, excuse, discredit, indict, or otherwise account for behavior that it is so important to discover how motives are constructed, used, evaluated, and negotiated. That is our only chance to overcome the absurd and nihilistic newspeak that characterizes modern mass society, both East and West, at this time.

Playing and helping

In this final section, we focus on some residual activities not yet discussed and which, for the most part, share with one another the fact that they are *spontaneous.*

According to Grathoff (1970:9), there are at least two fundamentally different types of social action: typified and non-typified. The former type refers essentially to role behavior, to the bulk of what sociology and social psychology study, and what has been the subject matter of this chapter. Nontypified behavior, on the other hand, is spontaneous behavior—play and, to some extent, game.

Having said this, one must immediately concur with those sociologists (cf. Mead, 1934; Goffman, 1961) who have noted that play also involves role-playing and that game, in addition to involving even more role-playing than play, is by definition rule-following behavior. Thus sociologists can be "serious about fun" (Goffman, 1961), that is, they can apply role analysis to the domain of play and game just as they have used it to study social organization.

The distinguishing feature of play and game is not that they do not involve roles and rules but the manner in which they are

enacted. For example, Goffman (op. cit.) lists such features as euphoria and spontaneous involvement among the prerequisites of fun. In addition, one must also distinguish play and game from one another (cf. Kando, 1975:28-35). To Mead (1934), play was a rather simple and fanciful activity, whereas the game was a far more complex and structured process, as illustrated by the game of baseball. Watson and I (1976) have recently studied precisely this phenomenon, showing the role and operation of rules in Little League baseball. Play and game form a continuum. Play refers to the more spontaneous and child-like activities, while game behavior refers, at times, to extreme calculation and rule-following conduct.

The study of this sector of social life is the sociology of leisure (cf. Kando, 1975), or what some call the sociology of good times (cf. Blumenstiel, 1973). Various authors have focused on different specific forms of play and leisure. Foote, for example, wrote nice articles about sex as play (1954) and family living as play (1955), Cavan (1966) studied the leisure activity of going to bars, Simmel (1949) wrote about sociability for its own sake, and Stone (1955; 1972) examined sports and a variety of other leisure activities. The common denominator in all leisure activities—all that is fun and play rather than work—is that they are done for their *intrinsic* reward rather than as a means to some ulterior end such as money. Leisure and play, then, are those activities in which one engages voluntarily. To be sure, one man's work (such as being a successful businessman or writing a book) can be another's play.

Games, as was noted earlier, are more calculative than play. They involve stricter rules. Above all, whereas play's reward is its intrinsic fun, the object of almost any game is to win. There is generally a mixture of motivations in game-playing. On the one hand, few individuals engage in gambling, pool, poker, golf, handball, football, or any other game without wishing to win. On the other hand, few of us want total prior assurance of a victory either. This is why opponents are generally expected to be fairly well matched, if necessary through handicap. Vince Lombardi was wrong: winning is not everything. It may be important, but so is fun.

Game, then, refers to a competitive relationship in which each party is attempting to win. This has led social scientists to develop mathematical game theory (cf. Rapoport, 1962; Von Neumann and Morgenstern, 1944) as well as the game theory of humanistic psychiatrists such as Berne (1964) and Shostrom (1968), who believe that most people play games with each other and that this is wrong, because it is tantamount to dishonesty and manipulation.

The game model, then, has spawned a great deal of social-psychological research on how people manipulate each other and attempt to acquire power and control over one another, often through coalition politics. The triad has long been a favored setting for the examination of such problems (Bond and Vinacke, 1964; Simmel, 1969). The focus leads to the study of coalitions (Aronson and Cope, 1973; Bond and Vinacke, 1964; Burhans, 1973; Gamson, 1961) and power relationships (Nagle, 1973; Solomon, 1964), and this is sometimes made relevant to real-life politics, for example the strategy of black power (Rustin, 1969).

While game theory is the analysis of the choices and moves made by the parties involved in a conflict or a competitive relationship, there is a somewhat related research focus called *exchange theory* (see Chapter 1). This approach deals with another area of calculative interaction, namely the exchange of social and symbolic rewards between parties involved in a relationship for the purpose of maximum reward to themselves. Thus exchange theory asserts that individuals and groups reward one another because—and only insofar as—they obtain something in return. Their model is *homo economicus,* a model eminently suited to our rationalistic-materialistic age.

Early writings on exchange include Simmel (1907), who focused specifically on economic exchange. Later exchange theorists (cf. Blau, 1964; Homans, 1961; Thibaut and Kelley, 1959) have applied the model to many other areas of human interaction, sometimes claiming, as does Homans (1961), that *all* human interaction can be understood as exchange.

Specific applications of exchange theory include Conviser (1973) and Roth (1962). Roth studied the bargaining process between hospital patients and staff; Conviser has examined the matter of trust in exchange relationships.

Since the rigid formulations of Homans, exchange theory has been made to accommodate symbolic interaction (cf. Singleman, 1972) and, most importantly, power. It is obvious that exchange is a meaningful concept only as long as all parties have the freedom to sustain or reliquish the relationship at hand. When an individual has no choice, the relationship is not one of exchange. It is not sufficient to state, as Homans does, that the absence of alternatives reduces the cost of an activity and that this restores the balance of the exchange relationship. The relationship between a slave and his owner, or a prisoner and his guard, or a ruler and his subject is one of exploitation or oppression, not exchange. Gouldner (1960) understood this, in his classic *Norm of Reciprocity.* Recently, Schwartz (1974) has shown how waiting— a cost—is distributed through the social system. His main thesis is that there is an inverse relationship between waiting and power, that is, between waiting and one's position in the social structure.

Starting out with play, the discussion led to games, game theory, and finally exchange. Here, then, we are dealing with calculative behavior par excellence, the very antithesis of spontaneity. Let us now return to a final category of spontaneous behavior studied by social psychologists: helping.

As we saw earlier in this chapter, Milgram (1965) and many other people worry about the "Genovese syndrome," the increasing tendency of people, particularly in big cities, not to care, not to help, to be indifferent even when someone is being killed on their front porch. Latané and Darley (1969; 1970; Darley and Latané, 1973) are among the social psychologists who have studied this problem experimentally, asking the basic question: why do people not help, when someone around them is in trouble? In one study, these authors (Latané and Darley, 1969) found that three mechanisms seem to be operating: (1) people either don't notice the event, or (2) they don't perceive it as being their personal responsibility, or (3) they don't define it as being an emergency. A major finding, in addition, was that there is really no safety in number: the more people around, the more diffused the responsibility for intervention becomes, and the less likely it is that any one individual will come to a victim's aid. For example, Darley and Latané (1973) conducted an experiment in which subjects were made to overhear an epileptic seizure and led to believe that they were alone, or that one or four other subjects were also present and also heard the seizure. The question was: under which conditions were the subjects most likely to report the seizure and thus provide help? The results are shown in Table 10.

Table 10 indicates that there does not seem to be safety in numbers. However, Piliavin and associates (1972) did a field experiment that failed to support these findings. In a New York subway, teams of students staged various crises, such as a person suddenly being very ill or helplessly drunk. The experimenters found that the frequency of help did not decrease with group size. Another interesting finding of this study was that the longer the emergency continued without anyone helping, the more likely it was that people would begin leaving the area.

The question can, of course, also be turned around. Rather than asking why people don't help, one may also ask why they do. This is what was done for example by London (1975), who, unlike Hughes (1964; Chapter 12) and others, was more interested in those (Christian) Germans who saved Jews in Nazi Germany than those who participated in the slaughter. He found that these individuals often tended to be adventurous and socially marginal and that they identified with a very moral parent. Thus one can bemoan, like Milgram (1965) and Meyer (1970), the

TABLE 10. Effects of group size on likelihood and speed of response*

Group size	Number	Percent responding by end of fit	Time seconds	Speed score
2 (subject and victim)	13	85	52	.87
3 (subject, victim, one other)	26	62	93	.72
6 (subject, victim, four others)	13	31	166	.51

*From Darley, John M. and Bibb Latané. 1968. "Bystander intervention in emergencies; diffusion of responsibility." Journal of Personality and Social Psychology 8(4):377-383. Copyright 1968 by the American Psychological Association. Reprinted by permission.

fact that "it could happen here," or one can focus on the fact that "it did not happen (to everyone) there."

When it comes to helping behavior, altruism, and love, one should also mention the related topic of interpersonal attraction (cf. Newcomb, 1956) and the bases for it. Social psychologists have studied the role of physical attractiveness (Walster et al., 1973; Wiggins et al., 1968), and they have shown a positive correlation, for example, between the importance placed upon such things as facial attractiveness and the need to affiliate with others (cf. Atkinson and Walker, 1964). No doubt, then, helping behavior is in large part determined by how attractive the victim is and by how attached one is to him. Thus one is more likely to come to the rescue of an attractive girl than an average fellow, and one will protect one's children and friends before one comes to the rescue of strangers.

Finally, "helping" must also be placed in the context of the helping relationship (cf. Rogers, 1974), viewed as a general, benevolent, and altruistic attitude toward others, regardless of whether or not an emergency is taking place. Helping also means what the good parent, counselor, teacher, and friend routinely do for their children, clients, students, and friends, by virtue of simply being tolerant, supportive, kind, and respectful of them as human beings, while at the same time caring enough to dare make recommendations rather than let them "do their thing," which is often synonymous with letting them stew in their own juice.

SUMMARY AND CONCLUSION

This chapter, perhaps the central one in this book, has attempted to cover a multiplicity of forms and elements of social interaction. We began with an examination of roles and basic role theory and showed how Goffman and others have extended classical role analysis toward an ever richer study of the intricacies of everyday behavior.

Next, role-taking led to an examination of communication. Various forms of communication were discussed, both at the cognitive and the affective level. It was in that context that love was also examined.

Under the heading of interaction, we dealt with face-to-face interaction viewed as drama, with the spatial aspects of social behavior, and with such group processes as conformity, leadership, power, and influence. A thorough discussion of motivation was also provided, indicating that social psychology needs to conceive of motives as the verbal components of conduct used for the explanation of that conduct, rather than as prior (or organic) causes.

Finally, playing and helping were discussed. While most of the behaviors under this last heading were shown to be somewhat spontaneous and thereby distinguishable from role behavior, our discussion of play led to an examination of precisely the opposite of spontaneity, namely the highly calculative behavior studied by game theorists and exchange theorists.

Now, the finishing touch to our imagery of man and society can be added: deviance, conflict, and change.

REFERENCES

Ableson, Robert P. and James C. Miller
1972 "Negative persuasion via personal insult." In Beyond the Laboratory: Field Research in Social Psychology. Leonard Bickman and Thomas Henchy (eds.). New York: McGraw-Hill Book Co., pp. 208-216.

Amundsen, Kirsten
1971 The Silenced Majority: Women and American Democracy. Englewood Cliffs, N.J.: Prentice-Hall, Inc.

Andre, J.
1975 "Toward a psychological theory of politics," Department of Psychology, California State University, Sacramento.

Andreas, Carol
1971 Sex and Caste in America. Englewood Cliffs, N.J.: Prentice-Hall, Inc.

Ardrey, Robert
1966 The Territorial Imperative. New York: Dell Publishing Co.

Aronson, Elliot
1973 "Threat and obedience." In Social Psychology: a Transaction Society Reader. Elliot Aronson and Robert Helmreich (eds.). New York: D. Van Nostrand Co., pp. 13-15.

Aronson, Elliot and Vernon Cope
1973 "My enemy's enemy is my friend." In Social Psychology in Everyday Life. Billy J. Franklin and Frank J. Kohout (eds.). New York: David McKay Co., pp. 307-316.

Asch, Solomon E.
1952 Social Psychology (chap. 16). Englewood Cliffs, N.J.: Prentice-Hall, Inc.

Atkinson, John W. and Edward L. Walker
1964 "The affiliation motive and perceptual sensitivity to faces." In Dimensions of Social Psychology. W. Edgar Vinacke and Warner W. Wilson (eds.). Chicago: Scott, Foresman and Co., pp. 196-200.

Ball, Donald W.
1970 "Sarcasm as sociation: the rhetoric of interaction." In Social Psychology Through Symbolic Interaction. Gregory P. Stone and Harvey A. Farberman (eds.). Waltham, Mass.: Ginn-Blaisdell, pp. 312-318.

Bavelas, Alex
1971 "Leadership: man and function." In Current Perspectives in Social Psychology. Edwin P. Hollander and G. Hunt (eds.). New York: Oxford University Press, pp. 495-503.

Beigel, Hugo G.
1951 "Romantic love." American Sociological Review (June): 326-334.

Bem, Sandra L. and Daryl J. Bem
1975 "Homogenizing the American woman: the power of an unconscious ideology." In Psychology is Social. Edward Krupat (ed.). Glenview, Ill.: Scott, Foresman and Co., pp. 60-73.

Bennett, David J. and Judith D. Bennett
1970 "Making the scene." In Social Psychology Through Symbolic Interaction. Gregory P. Stone and Harvey A. Farberman (eds.). Waltham, Mass.: Ginn-Blaisdell, pp. 190-195.

Berger, Joseph et al.
1976 "Paths of relevance and the determination of power and prestige orders." Pacific Sociological Review (January):45-62.

Berger, Peter L. and Thomas Luckmann
1966 The Social Construction of Reality. Garden City, N.Y.: Doubleday & Co., Inc.

Berne, Eric
1964 Games People Play—The Psychology of Human Relationships. New York: Grove Press.

Blau, Peter M.
1964 Exchange and Power in Social Life. New York: John Wiley & Sons, Inc.

Blau, Peter M. and W. Richard Scott
1962 Formal Organizations: A Comparative Approach. San Francisco: Chandler Publishing Co.

Blum, Alan F. and Peter McHugh
1971 "The social ascription of motives." American Sociological Review (February):98-110.

Blumenstiel, Alexander D.
1973 "The sociology of good times." In Phenomenological Sociology: Issues and Applications. George Psathas (ed.). New York: John Wiley & Sons, Inc., pp. 187-218.

Blumer, Herbert
1969 Symbolic Interactionism. Englewood Cliffs, N.J.: Prentice-Hall, Inc.

Blumstein, Philip W. et al.
1974 "The honoring of accounts." American Sociological Review (August):551-566.

Bond, John R. and W. Edgar Vinacke
1964 "Coalitions in mixed-sex triads." In Dimensions of Social Psychology. W. Edgar Vinacke and Warner W. Wilson (eds.). Chicago: Scott, Foresman and Co., pp. 397-406.

Boston Women's Health Book Collective
1973 Our Bodies, Our Selves. A Book By and For Women. New York: Simon and Schuster.

Brooks, Richard S.
1972 "The self and political role: a symbolic interactionist approach to political ideology." In Symbolic Interaction. Jerome G. Manis and Bernard M. Meltzer (eds.). Boston: Allyn and Bacon, Inc., pp. 462-471.

Bruyn, Severyn
1966 The Human Perspective in Sociology. Englewood Cliffs, N.J.: Prentice-Hall, Inc.

Burhans, David T., Jr.
1973 "Coalition game research: a reexamination." American Journal of Sociology (September):289-408.

Cade, Toni (ed.)
1970 The Black Woman: An Anthology. New York: The New American Library.

Cavan, Sherri
1966 Liquor License: An Ethnography of Bar Behavior. Chicago: Aldine Publishing Co.

Chafetz, Janet Saltzman
1963 Masculine, Feminine or Human? Itasca, Ill.: F. E. Peacock Publishers, Inc.

Child, I.
1943 Italian or American? The Second Generation in Conflict. New Haven, Conn.: Yale University Press.

Christie, Richard and Florence Geis
1971 "Some consequences of taking Machiavelli seriously." In Current Perspectives in Social Psychology. Edwin P. Hollander and Raymond G. Hunt (eds.). New York: Oxford University Press, pp. 175-185.

Cicourel, Aaron
1974 Cognitive Sociology: Language and Mean-

ing in Social Interaction. New York: The Free Press.

Conviser, Richard H.
1973 "Toward a theory of interpersonal trust." Pacific Sociological Review (July):377-399.

Coser, Rose Laub
1966 "Role distance, sociological ambivalence, and transitional status systems." American Journal of Sociology (September):173-187.

Darley, John M. and Bibb Latané
1973 "Bystander intervention in emergencies: diffusion of responsibility." In Social Psychology in Everyday Life. Billy J. Franklin and Frank J. Kohout (eds.). New York: David McKay Co., pp. 107-119.

Davis, Kingsley
1942 "A conceptual analysis of stratification." American Sociological Review (June):309-321.

Davis, Morris and Sol Levine
1972 "Toward a sociology of public transit." In Beyond the Laboratory: Field Research in Social Psychology. Leonard Bickman and Thomas Henchy (eds.). New York: McGraw-Hill Book Co., pp. 324-329.

Delora, Joann S. and Jack R. Delora (eds.)
1972 Intimate Life Styles. Marriage and its Alternatives. Pacific Palisades, Calif.: Goodyear Publishing Co.

Denzin, Norman K.
1969 "Symbolic interactionism and ethnomethodology." American Sociological Review (December):922-934.

Deutsch, Morton
1949 "A theory of cooperation and competition." Human Relations 2:129-152, 199-232.

Deutsch, Morton and Robert M. Krauss
1965 Theories in Social Psychology. New York: Basic Books, Inc.

Dewey, John
1922 Human Nature and Conduct. New York: Holt, Rinehart and Winston.

Ellis, Evelyn
1968 "Social psychological correlates of upward social mobility among unmarried career women." In The Mental Patient: Studies in the Sociology of Deviance. Stephen P. Spitzer and Norman K. Denzin (eds.). New York: McGraw-Hill Book Co., pp. 147-154.

Elms, Alan C. and Stanley Milgram
1966 "Personality characteristics associated with obedience and defiance toward authorative command." Journal of Experimental Research in Personality 1:282-289.

Erikson, Kai T.
1973 "Patient role and social uncertainty." In Deviance: The Interactionist Perspective. Earl Rubington and Martin S. Weinberg (eds.). New York: The Macmillan Co., pp. 385-391.

Farber, Bernard
1962 "Types of family organization: child-oriented, home-oriented, and parent-oriented." In Human Behavior and Social Processes. Arnold M. Rose (ed.). Boston: Houghton Mifflin Co., pp. 285-306.

Farina, Amerigo
1973 "Humor appreciation as social communication." In Social Psychology in Everyday Life. Billy J. Franklin and Frank J. Kohout (eds.). New York: David McKay Co., Inc., pp. 212-219.

Feldman, R. E.
1968 "Response to compatriot and foreigner who seek assistance." Journal of Personality and Social Psychology 10:202-214.

Felipe, Nancy Jo and Robert Sommer
1972 "Invasions of personal space." In Beyond the Laboratory: Field Research in Social Psychology. Leonard Bickman and Thomas Henchy (eds.). New York: McGraw-Hill Book Co., pp. 181-187.

Fiedler, Fred E.
1968 "Personality and situational determinants of leadership effectiveness." In Group Dynamics. Dorwin Cartwright and Alvin Zander (eds.). New York: Harper & Row, Publishers, pp. 362-373.
1972 "Leadership and leadership effectiveness traits: a reconceptualization of the leadership trait problem." In Classic Contributions to Social Psychology. Edwin P. Hollander and Raymond G. Hunt (eds.). New York: Oxford University Press, pp. 378-383.

Foote, Nelson N.
1951 "Identification as the basis for a theory of motivation." American Sociological Review (February):14-21.
1954 "Sex as play." Social Problems (April):159-163.
1955 "Family living as play." Marriage and Family Living 17:296-301.
1970 "Love." In Social Psychology Through Symbolic Interaction. Gregory P. Stone and Harvey A. Farberman (eds.). Waltham, Mass.: Ginn-Blaisdell, pp. 319-326.

Ford, Julienne et al.
1974 "Functional autonomy, role distance and social class." In Social Psychology for Sociologists. David Field (ed.). New York: John Wiley & Sons, Inc., pp. 116-125.

Franks, David D.
1974 "Current conceptions of competency motivation and selfvalidations." In Social Psychology for Sociologists. David Field (ed.). New York: John Wiley & Sons, Inc.

Freedman, Jonathan L. and Scott C. Fraser
1973 "Compliance without pressure: the foot-in-the-door technique." In Social Psychology in

Everyday Life. Billy J. Franklin and Frank J. Kohout (eds.). New York: David McKay Co., pp. 94-107.

French, John R. P.
1941 "The disruption and cohesion of groups." Journal of Abnormal Social Psychology 36:361-377.

French, John R. P. and Bertram H. Raven
1971 "The bases of power." In Current Perspectives in Social Psychology. Edwin P. Hollander and Raymond G. Hunt (eds.). New York: Oxford University Press, pp. 525-533.

Fromm, Erich
1966 The Art of Loving. London: Unwin Books.

Gamson, W.
1961 "A theory of coalition formation." American Sociological Review 26:373-382.

Gans, Herbert
1962 The Urban Villagers. New York: The Free Press.

Giallombardo, Rose
1972 "Social roles in a prison for women." In The Social Dimension of Human Sexuality. Robert R. Bell and Michael Gordon (eds.). Boston: Little, Brown and Co., pp. 189-215.

Gibb, Jack R.
1974 "Defensive communication." In Small Group Communication: A Reader. Robert S. Cathcart and Larry A. Samovar (eds.). Dubuque, Iowa: William C. Brown Co., Publishers, pp. 327-333.

Goffman, Erving
1956 "Embarrassment and social organization." American Journal of Sociology 62:264-271.
1959 The Presentation of Self in Everyday Life. Garden City, N.Y.: Doubleday & Company, Inc.
1961 Encounters: Two Studies of the Sociology of Interaction. Indianapolis: Bobbs-Merrill Co., Inc.
1963 Behavior in Public Places. Glencoe, Ill.: The Free Press.
1967 Interaction Ritual: Essays on Face-to-Face Behavior. Chicago: Aldine Publishing Co.
1971 Relations in Public. New York: Harper & Row, Publishers.

Goldberg, Philip
1973 "Are women prejudiced against women?" In Social Psychology in Everyday Life. Billy J. Franklin and Frank J. Kohout (eds.). New York: David McKay Co., Inc., pp. 249-254.

Goldberg, Steven
1973 The Inevitability of Patriarchy. New York: William Morrow and Co.

Goode, William J.
1959 "The theoretical importance of love." American Sociological Review 24:38-47.
1960 "A theory of role strain." American Journal of Sociology (August).

1972 "The place of force in human society." American Sociological Review (October): 507-520.

Goodman, Norman and Richard Ofshe
1968 "Empathy, communication efficiency, and marital status." Journal of Marriage and the Family 30:597-604.

Gordon, Milton M.
1963 Social Class in American Sociology. New York: McGraw-Hill Book Co.

Gornick, Vivian and Barbara K. Moran (eds.)
1971 Woman in Sexist Society. New York: New American Library.

Gouldner, Alvin
1960 "The norm of reciprocity: a preliminary statement." American Sociological Review 25:161-179.

Gouldner, Alvin and Helen Gouldner
1963 Modern Sociology: An Introduction to the Study of Human Interaction. New York: Harcourt, Brace and World.

Grathoff, Richard H.
1970 The Structure of Social Inconsistencies: A Contribution to a Unified Theory of Play, Game and Social Action. The Hague: Martinus Nijhoff Co.

Gross, Edward and Gregory P. Stone
1970 "Embarrassment and the analysis of role requirements." In Social Psychology Through Symbolic Interaction. Gregory P. Stone and Harvey A. Farberman (eds.). Waltham, Mass.: Ginn-Blaisdell, pp. 174-189.

Gurin, Patricia et al.
1972 "Internal-external control in the motivational dynamics of Negro youth." In Black Psyche: The Modal Personality Patterns of Black Americans. Stanley Guterman (ed.). Berkeley, California: The Glendessary Press, pp. 289-306.

Hamblin, Robert L.
1964 "Leadership and crises." In Dimensions of Social Psychology. W. Edgar Vinacke and Warner W. Wilson (eds.). Chicago: Scott, Foresman and Co., pp. 229-236.

Harlow, H. F.
1958 "The nature of love." American Psychologist 13:673-685.

Heiss, Jerold (ed.)
1968 Family Roles and Interaction: An Anthology. Chicago: Rand McNally.

Helson, Harry et al.
1972 "Petition-signing as adjustment to situational and personal factors." In Beyond the Laboratory: Field Research in Social Psychology. Leonard Bickman and Thomas Henchy (eds.). New York: McGraw-Hill Book Co., pp. 78-82.

Hill, Reuben and Donald A. Hansen
1960 "The identification of conceptual frameworks utilized in family study." Marriage and Family Living 22:299-311.
Hofling, Charles K. et al.
1972 "An experimental study in nurse-physician relationships." In Beyond the Laboratory: Field Research in Social Psychology. Leonard Bickman and Thomas Hency (eds.). New York: McGraw-Hill Book Co., pp. 60-68.
Hollander, Edwin P.
1971 "Leadership, innovation and influence: an overview." In Current Perspectives in Social Psychology. Edwin P. Hollander and Raymond G. Hunt (eds.). New York: Oxford University Press, pp. 495-503.
1972 "Conformity, status, and idiosyncrasy credit." In Classic Contributions to Social Psychology. Edwin P. Hollander and Raymond G. Hunt (eds.). New York: Oxford University Press, pp. 362-371.
Hollander, Edwin P. and Richard H. Willis
1971 "Some current issues in the psychology of conformity and nonconformity." In Current Perspectives in Social Psychology. Edwin P. Hollander and Raymond G. Hunt (eds.). New York: Oxford University Press, pp. 435-450.
Homans, George Caspar
1961 Social Behavior: Its Elementary Forms. Robert K. Merton (ed.). New York: Harcourt, Brace and World.
Hooning, T. J. S.
1957 "The concept of role in sociology." Mens Maat. 5:270-284.
Horner, Matina S.
1975 "Femininity and successful achievement: a basic inconsistency." In Psychology is Social. Edward Krupat (ed.). Glenview, Ill.: Scott, Foresman and Co., pp. 78-85.
Hughes, Everett C.
1962 "What other?" In Human Behavior and Social Processes. Arnold M. Rose (ed.). Boston: Houghton Mifflin Co., pp. 119-127.
1964 "Good people and dirty work." In The Other Side: Perspectives on Deviance. Howard S. Becker (ed.). Glencoe, Ill. The Free Press of Glencoe.
Ichheiser, Gustav
1970 Appearances and Realities. San Francisco: Jossey-Bass, Inc.
Jacobson, Wally D.
1972 Power and Interpersonal Relations. Belmont, Calif.: Wadsworth Publishing Co.
Jones, Edward E.
1973 "Flattery will get you somewhere." In Social Psychology: A Transaction-Society Reader. Elliot Aronson and Robert Helmreich (eds.). New York: D. Van Nostrand Co., pp. 91-95.
Jones, Edward E. et al.
1972 Attribution: Perceiving the Causes of Behavior. New York: General Learning Press.
Kando, Thomas
1972 "Role strain: a comparison of males, females and transsexuals." Journal of Marriage and the Family (August):459-464.
1975 Leisure and Popular Culture in Transition. St. Louis: The C. V. Mosby Co.
Killian, Lewis M.
1952 "Significance of multiple-group membership in disaster." American Journal of Sociology 57:309-314.
Klapp, Orrin E.
1964 Symbolic Leaders: Public Dramas and Public Men. Chicago: Aldine Publishing Co.
Krupat, Edward (ed.)
1975 Psychology is Social. Glenview, Ill.: Scott, Foresman and Co.
Kuhn, Manford H.
1964 "The interview and the professional relationship." In Human Behavior and Social Processes. Arnold M. Rose (ed.). Boston: Houghton Mifflin Co., pp. 193-206.
Lambert, W. E. and R. C. Gardner
1961 A Study of the Roles of Attitudes and Motivation in Second-Language Learning. Washington, D.C.: U.S. Office of Education.
Latané, Bibb and John M. Darley
1969 "Bystander 'apathy'." American Scientist 57:244-268.
1970 "Social determinants of bystander intervention in emergencies." In Altruism and Helping Behavior: Social Psychological Studies of Some Antecedents and Consequences. J. Macauley and L. Berkowitz (eds.). New York: Academic Press, Inc.
Leavitt, Harold J.
1951 "Some effects of certain communication patterns on group performance." Journal of Abnormal and Social Psychology 46:38-50.
Lerner, M. J.
1965 "Evaluation of performance as a function of performer's reward and attractiveness." Journal of Personality and Social Psychology 1:355-360.
Lewin, Kurt et al.
1939 "Patterns of aggressive behavior in experimentally created 'social climates'." Journal of Social Psychology 10:271-299.
Lindesmith, Alfred R. and Anselm L. Strauss
1956 Social Psychology: The Revised Edition. New York: Holt, Rinehart and Winston.
Linton, Ralph
1936 The Study of Man: An Introduction. New York: Appleton-Century-Crofts.
London, Perry
1975 "The rescuers: motivational hypotheses

about Christians who saved Jews from the Nazis." In Psychology is Social. Edward Krupat (ed.). Glenview, Ill.: Scott, Foresman and Co., pp. 265-271.

Lorenz, Konrad
1966 On Aggression. New York: Harcourt Brace.

Lupfer, Michael et al.
1972 "The influence of picketing on the purchase of toy guns." In Beyond the Laboratory: Field Research in Social Psychology. Leonard Bickman and Thomas Henchy (eds.). New York: McGraw-Hill Book Co., pp. 82-84.

Lyman, Stanford M. and Marvin B. Scott
1967 "Territoriality: a neglected sociological dimension." Social Problems (Fall):236-249.
1970 A Sociology of the Absurd. New York: Meredith Corp.

MacCannell, Dean
1973 "Staged authenticity: arrangements of social space in tourist settings." American Journal of Sociology (November): 589-603.

Marsden, Halsey M.
1975 "Crowding and animal behavior." In Psychology is Social. Edward Krupat (ed.). Glenview, Ill.: Scott, Foresman and Co., pp. 303-310.

Martin, J. David
1973 "Suspicion and the experimental confederate: a study of role and credibility." In Social Psychology in Everyday Life. Billy J. Franklin and Frank J. Kohout (eds.). New York: David McKay Co., pp. 533-547.

Martin, R. D.
1972 "Concepts of human teritoriality: the ethological viewpoint." Reprint from Man, Settlement and Urbanism. Peter Ucko et al. Cambridge, Mass.: Schenkman Publishing Co., pp. 1-19.

Martindale, Don
1960 The Nature and Types of Sociological Theory Boston: Houghton Mifflin Co.

Maslow, A. H.
1942 "Liberal leadership and personality." Freedom 2:27-30.
1955 "Deficiency motivation and growth motivation." Nebraska Symposium on Motivation. Quoted in The Concept of Motivation. R. S. Peters. 1956. London: Routledge and Kegan Paul.

McCandless, Boyd R.
1942 "Changing relationships between dominance and social acceptability during group democratization." American Journal of Orthopsychiatry 12:529-535.

McClelland, David C.
1961 The Achieving Society. Princeton, N.J.: Van Nostrand.
1971 "The achievement motive in economic growth." In Comparative Perspectives on Social Psychology. William Wilson Lambert and Rita Weisbrod (eds.). Boston: Little, Brown and Co., pp. 274-296.

Mead, George Herbert
1934 Mind, Self and Society. Charles W. Morris (ed.). Chicago: University of Chicago Press.
1956 On Social Psychology. Anselm Strauss (ed.). Chicago: University of Chicago Press.

Merton, Robert K.
1957 Social Theory and Social Structure. Glencoe, Ill.: Free Press.

Messinger, Sheldon et al.
1962 "Life as theater: some notes on the dramaturgic approach to social reality." Sociometry (September):98-110.

Meyer, Philip
1970 "If Hitler asked you to electrocute a stranger, would you?" Esquire 74:72, 128-132.

Milgram, Stanley
1964 "Group pressure and action against a person." Journal of Abnormal and Social Psychology 69(2):137-143.
1965 "Some conditions of obedience and disobedience to authority." Human Relations 18:57-76.
1972 "The experience of living in cities." In The City in the Seventies. Robert K. Yin (ed.). Itasca, Ill.: F. E. Peacock Publishers, pp. 250-259.
1974 Obedience to Authority: An Experimental View. New York: Harper & Row, Publishers.

Mills, C. Wright
1940 "Situated actions and vocabularies of motive." American Sociological Review (October):904-913.
1956 The Power Elite. New York: Oxford University Press.

Murstein, Bernard I.
1971 Theories of Attraction and Love. New York: Springer.

Nagle, James A.
1973 "Power, stability, and friendship in coalitions." Pacific Sociological Review (October):519-536.

Natanson, Maurice
1970 The Journeying Self: A Study in Philosophy and Social Role. Menlo Park, Calif.: Addison-Wesley Publishing Co.

Newcomb, Theodore M.
1956 "The prediction of interpersonal attraction." American Psychologist 11:575-586.

Nisbet, Robert A.
1974 "Leadership and social crisis." In Small Group Communication: A Reader. Robert S. Cathcart and Larry A. Samovar (eds.). Dubuque, Iowa: William C. Brown, Publishers, pp. 353-357.

Olsen, Marvin E.
1971 "The process of social power." In Current Perspectives in Social Psychology. Edwin P. Hollander and Raymond G. Hunt (eds.). New York: Oxford University Press, pp. 533-544.

Pareek, Udai
1971 "Poverty and motivation: figure and ground." In Psychological Factors in Poverty. Vernon L. Allen (ed.). Chicago: Markham Publishing Co., pp. 300-317.

Park, Robert E. et al.
1925 The City. Chicago: University of Chicago Press.
1928 "Human migration and the marginal man." Journal of American Society (May): 881-893.

Peters, R. S.
1960 The Concept of Motivation. R. F. Holland (ed.). London: Humanities Press.

Piliavin, Irving M. et al.
1972 "Good samaritanism: an underground phenomenon." In Beyond the Laboratory: Field Research in Social Psychology. Leonard Bickman and Thomas Henchy (eds.). New York: McGraw-Hill Book Co., pp. 34-44.

Psathas, George (ed.)
1973 Phenomenological Sociology: Issues and Applications. New York: John Wiley & Sons, Inc.

Rapoport, Anatol
1962 "The use and misuse of game theory." Scientific American (December):108-118.

Rogers, Carl R.
1974 "The characteristics of a helping relationship." In Messages. Jean M. Civikly (ed.). New York: Random House, Inc., pp. 190-205.

Rosen, Bernard C.
1972 "Race, ethnicity, and the achievement syndrome." In Black Psyche: The Modal Personality Patterns of Black Americans. Berkeley, Calif.: The Glendessary Press.

Roth, Julius A.
1962 "The treatment of tuberculosis as a bargaining process." In Human Behavior and Social Processes. Arnold M. Rose (ed.). Boston: Houghton Mifflin Co., pp. 575-588.

Rubin, Zick
1973a Liking and Loving: An Invitation to Social Psychology. New York: Holt, Rinehart and Winston.
1973b "Measurement of romantic love." In Social Psychology in Life. Richard E. Evans and Richard M. Rozelle (eds.). Boston: Allyn and Bacon, Inc., pp. 456-474.

Rustin, Bayard
1969 "Black power and coalition politics."In Current Perspectives on Social Problems (ed. 2). Judson Landis (ed.). Belmont, Calif.: Wadsworth Publishing Co., pp. 125-138.

Samuel, William
1975 Contemporary Social Psychology: An Introduction. Englewood Cliffs, N.J.: Prentice-Hall, Inc.

Sarbin, Theodore R.
1954 "Role theory." In Handbook of Social Psychology. Gardner Lindzey (ed.). Reading, Mass.: Addison-Wesley Publishing Co.

Scheff, Thomas J.
1970 "Toward a sociological model of consensus." In Social Psychology Through Symbolic Interaction. Gregory P. Stone and Harvey A. Farberman (eds.). Waltham, Mass.: Ginn-Blaisdell, pp. 348-466.

Schein, Edgar H.
1973 "Interpersonal communication, group solidarity, and social influence." In Social Psychology in Everyday Life. Billy J. Franklin and Frank J. Kohout (eds.). New York: David McKay Co., Inc., pp. 231-244.

Scheler, Max
1970 "Classification of the phenomena of fellow feeling." In Social Psychology Through Symbolic Interaction. Gregory P. Stone and Harvey A. Farberman (eds.). Waltham, Mass.: Ginn-Blaisdell, pp. 303-311.

Schmalenbach, Herman
1965 "The sociological category of communion." In Theories of Society. Talcott Parsons et al. (eds.). Glencoe, Ill.: The Free Press, pp. 331-347.

Schutz, Alfred
1944 "The stranger: an essay in social psychology." American Journal of Sociology 49(6):499-507.
1970 On Phenomonology and Social Relations. Helmut R. Wagner (ed.). Chicago: The University of Chicago Press.

Schwartz, Barry
1973a "Review of Appearances and Realities, by Gustav Ichheiser." American Journal of Sociology (March):1281-1284.
1973b "The social psychology of privacy." In Social Psychology and Everyday Life. Billy J. Franklin and Frank J. Kohout (eds.). New York: David McKay Co., pp. 3-18.
1974 "Waiting, exchange, and power: the distribution of time in social systems." American Journal of Sociology (January):841-870.

Scott, Marvin B. and Stanford M. Lyman
1972 "Accounts." In Symbolic Interaction. Jerome G. Manis and Bernard N. Meltzer (eds.). Boston: Allyn and Bacon, Inc., pp. 404-429

Sewell, William H. and Oluf M. Davidsen
1956 "The adjustment of Scandinavian students." Journal of Social Studies 13(1):10-19.

Shaw, Jerry and Paul Skolnick
1973 "Attribution of responsibility for a happy accident." In Social Psychology in Life. Richard T. Evans and Richard M. Rozelle (eds.). Boston: Allyn and Bacon, Inc., pp. 407-416.

Sherif, Muzafer
1935 "A study of some social factors in perception." Archives of Psychology 27.

Shibutani, Tamotsu
1961 Society and Personality: An Interactionist Approach to Social Psychology. Englewood Cliffs, N.J.: Prentice-Hall, Inc.
1962 "Reference groups and social control." In Human Behavior and Social Processes. Arnold M. Rose (ed.). Boston: Houghton Mifflin Co., pp. 128-147.

Shostrom, Everett L.
1968 Man, the Manipulator: The Inner Journey From Manipulation to Actualization. New York: Bantam Books.

Sieber, Sam D.
1974 "Toward a theory of role accumulation." American Sociological Review (August):567-578.

Simmel, Georg
1903 Die Grosstadte und das Geistesleben die Grosstadt. Dresden, Germany: Jansch.
1907 Philosophie des Geldes. Leipzig, Germany: Duncker and Humblot.
1949 "The sociology of sociability." American Journal of Sociology 55(3):254-261.
1955 Conflict and the Webb of Group Affiliations. Glencoe, Ill.: The Free Press.
1969 "The triad." In The Sociology of Georg Simmel. Kurt H. Wolff (ed.). New York: The Free Press, pp. 145-162.
1970 "On visual interaction." In Social Psychology Through Symbolic Interaction. Gregory P. Stone and Harvey A. Farberman (eds.). Waltham, Mass.: Ginn-Blaisdell, pp. 300-302.
1971 On Individuality and Social Forms. Donald N. Levine (ed.). Chicago: The University of Chicago Press.

Singleman, Peter
1972 "Exchange as symbolic interaction." American Journal of Sociology (August):414-424.

Smith, Dorothy E.
1973 "Household space and family organization." In Readings in Social Psychology—A Symbolic Interaction Perspective. J. D. Cardwell (ed.). Philadelphia: F. A. Davis Co., pp. 78-98.

Smith, M. Brewster
1956 "Cross-cultural education as a research area." Journal of Social Studies 12(1):3-8.

Solomon, Leonard
1964 "The influence of some types of power relationships and game strategies upon the development of interpersonal trust." In Dimensions of Social Psychology. W. Edgar Vinacke and Warner W. Wilson (eds.). Chicago: Scott, Foresman and Co., pp. 390-397.

Sommer, Robert
1959 "A study in personal space." Bobbs-Merrill Reprint Series in the Social Sciences. Reprinted from Sociometry (September):247-348.
1969 Personal Space: The Behavioral Basis of Design. Englewood Cliffs, N.J.: Prentice-Hall, Inc.
1974 "Studies of small group ecology." In Small Group Communication: A Reader. Robert S. Cathcart and Larry A. Samovar (eds.). Dubuque, Iowa: William C. Brown Publishers, pp. 283-293.

Sommer, Robert and Franklin D. Becker
1972 "Territorial defense and the good neighbor." In Beyond the Laboratory: A Field Study in Social Psychology. Leonard Bickman and Thomas Henchy (eds.). New York: McGraw-Hill Book Co., pp. 173-181.

Sorokin, Pitirim
1956 The American Sex Revolution. Boston: Porter Sargent Publisher.

Speier, Matthew
1973 How to Observe Face-to-Face Communication: A Sociological Introduction. Pacific Palisades, Calif.: Goodyear Publishing Co.

Spiegelberg, Herbert
1973 "On the right to say 'we': a linguistic and phenomenological analysis." In Phenomenological Sociology: Issues and Applications. George Psathas (ed.). New York: John Wiley & Sons, Inc., pp. 129-158.

Stebbins, R. A.
1967 "A note on the concept of role distance." American Journal of Sociology 73:247-250.
1969 "Role distance, role distance behavior, and jazz musicians." British Journal of Sociology 20:406-415.

Stone, Gregory P.
1954 "City shoppers and urban identification: observations on the social psychology of city life." American Journal of Sociology (July):36-45.
1955 "American sports: play and display." Chicago Review (Fall):83-100.
1962 "Appearance and the self." In Human Behavior and Social Processes. Arnold M. Rose (ed.). Boston: Houghton Mifflin Co., pp. 86-118.
1972 (ed.) Games, Sport and Power. New Brunswick, N.J.: Transaction Books.

Stone, Gregory P. and Harvey A. Farberman
1970 Social Psychology Through Symbolic Interaction. Waltham, Mass.: Ginn-Blaisdell.

Stonequist, Everett V.
1937 The Marginal Man. New York: Charles Scribner's Sons.
Stryker, Sheldon
1957 "Role-taking accuracy and adjustment." Sociometry (December):286-296.
1962 "Conditions of accurate role-taking: a test of Mead's theory." In Human Behavior and Social Processes. Arnold M. Rose (ed.). Boston: Houghton Mifflin Co., pp. 41-62.
1972 "Symbolic interaction as an approach to family research." In Symbolic Interaction. Jerome G. Manis and Bernard Meltzer (eds.). Boston: Allyn & Bacon, pp. 435-446.
Sullerot, Evelyne
1971 Woman, Society and Change. New York: McGraw-Hill Book Co.
Sullivan, Harry Stack
1947 Conceptions of Modern Psychiatry. Washington, D.C.: William Alanson White Psychiatric Foundation.
1970 "Self as concept and illusion." In Social Psychology Through Symbolic Interaction. Gregory P. Stone and Harvey A. Farberman (eds.). Waltham, Mass.: Ginn-Blaisdell, pp. 386-393.
Sullivan, Thomas J.
1975 "Review of Achievement Motivation and Attribution Theory, by Bernard Weiner (ed.)." Contemporary Sociology (July):425-427.
Summers, Worth C.
1976 "Power, goals and resources: notes on the generic concept of power." Pacific Sociological Association (March).
Szasz, Thomas
1961 The Myth of Mental Illness: Foundations of a Theory of Personal Conduct. New York: Dell Publishing Co.
Tanner, Leslie B. (ed.)
1970 Voices from Women's Liberation. New York: New American Library.
Theodorson, George A. and Achilles G. Theodorson
1969 A Modern Dictionary of Sociology. New York: Thomas Y. Crowell Co.
Thibaut, John W. and Harold H. Kelley
1959 The Social Psychology of Groups. New York: John Wiley & Sons, Inc.
Thomas, Darwin L. et al.
1972 "Role-taking and power in social psychology." American Sociological Review (October):605-614.
Thompson, Clara M.
1964 On Women. New York: New American Library.
Toffler, Alvin
1970 Future Shock. New York: Bantam Books, Inc.

Turner, Ralph H.
1962 "Role-taking: process versus conformity." In Human Behavior and Social Processes. Arnold M. Rose (ed.). Boston: Houghton Mifflin Co., pp. 20-40.
Van den Berghe, Pierre L.
1975 Man in Society. A Biosocial View. New York: Elsevier Publishing Co.
Vidulich, Robert N. and Donna Jean Wilson
1972 "The environmental setting as a factor in social influence." In Beyond the Laboratory: Field Research in Social Psychology. Leonard Bickman and Thomas Henchy (eds.). New York: McGraw-Hill Book Co., pp. 108-113.
Von Neumann, John and Oskar Morgenstern
1944 Theory of Games and Economic Behavior. Princeton, N.J.: Princeton University Press.
Waller, Willard
1957 The Old Love and the New. New York: Liveright.
Waller, Willard and Reuben Hill
1951 The Family: A Dynamic Interpretation. New York: Holt, Rinehart and Winston, Inc.
Walster, E.
1966 "Assignment of responsibility for an accident." Journal of Personality and Social Psychology 3:73-79.
Walster, E. et al.
1973 "Importance of physical attractiveness in dating behavior." In Social Psychology in Everyday Life. Billy J. Franklin and Frank J. Kohout (eds.). New York: David McKay Co., pp. 316-330.
Watson, Geoffrey G. and Thomas M. Kando
1976 "The meaning of rules and rituals in Little League baseball." Pacific Sociological Review (Summer):291-316.
Watson, O. Michael
1970 Proxemic Behavior: A Cultural Study. The Hague, Netherlands: Morton and Co.
Weber, Max
1947 The Theory of Social and Economic Organization. A. M. Henderson and Talcott Parsons (trans.) and Talcott Parsons (ed.). Glencoe, Ill.: The Free Press.
Weigert, Andrew J.
1975 "Alfred Schutz on a theory of motivation." Pacific Sociological Review (January):83-102.
Weiner, Bernard (ed.)
1974 Achievement Motivation and Attribution Theory. Morristown, N.J.: General Learning Press.
Weinstein, Eugene A.
1973 "The applied art on one-downmanship." In Social Psychology: a Transaction-Society Reader. Elliot Aronson and Robert Helmreich (eds.). New York: D. Van Nostrand Co., pp. 96-98.

Weinstein, Eugene A. and Paul Deutschberger
  1963 "Some dimensions of altercasting." Sociometry (December);454-466.
Wenglinsky, Martin
  1975 "Review of Obedience to Authority: An Experimental View, by Stanley Milgram." Contemporary Sociology (November): 613-617.
White, Robert W.
  1959 "Motivation reconsidered: the concept of competence." The Bobbs-Merrill Reprint Series. Reprinted from The Psychological Review (September):297-333.
Wieder, D. Lawrence
  1970 "On meaning by rule." In Understanding Everyday Life. Jack D. Douglas (ed.). Chicago: Aldine Publishing Co., pp. 107-135.
Wiggings, Jerry S. et al.
  1968 "Correlates of heterosexual somatic preference." Journal of Personality and Social Psychology 10(1):1-9.
Williamson, Robert C.
  1970 "Marriage roles, American style." In Sex Roles in Changing Society. Georgene H. Se-

ward and Robert C. Williamson (eds.). New York: Random House, Inc., pp. 150-177.
Willis, Richard H.
  1972 "The basic response modes of conformity." In Classic Contributions to Soccial Psychology. Edwin P. Hollander and Raymond G. Hunt (eds.). New York: Oxford University Press, pp. 372-377
Zimmerman, Don H. and Lawrence D. Wieder
  1970 "Ethnomethodology and the problem of order: comment on Denzin." In Understanding Everyday Life. Jack D. Douglas (ed.). Chicago: Aldine Publishing Co., pp. 287-302.
Zurcher, Louis A. et al.
  1973 "The hasher: a study of role conflict." In Social Psychology and Everyday Life. Billy J. Franklin and Frank J. Kohout (eds.). New York: David McKay Co., pp. 25-38.

chapter 12

Deviance, conflict, and change

In this final chapter we discuss, first, a variety of subjects often assigned to the realm of the sociology of deviance and of social problems. Because this is a book in social psychology, the focus is on such (inter) personal aspects of social problems as stigmatization and labelling, rather than on their larger political implications. Alternative theories of deviance are discussed, and the major categories of social problems are treated, including mental illness, drug addiction, alcoholism, suicide, physical stigmas such as illness and blindness, social stigmas such as poverty, race, and stupidity, sexual stigmas such as homosexuality, divorce, and prostitution, and problems of crime and delinquency. Throughout, the emphasis is social-psychological, and topics such as mental illness are, of course, of central concern.

The following section examines conflict and politics. The question is raised as to when deviance becomes conflict, and this leads to a discussion of the role of power.

Finally, we conclude with a discussion of social and cultural change. As a case in point, sex roles and women's liberation are discussed. Some of the costs of change are also examined. Because the argument, throughout this book, has been that social psychology is a cultural discipline, we finally return to a brief examination of culture, treating change primarily as a cultural and psychological process, as change in social consciousness. The point to remember throughout is that this dimension of social change merits our full attention. It does that not only because it is, to use Durkheim's favorite phrase, a reality sui generis, a fact totally ignored by the materialistic philosophy that prevails both East and West today, but mostly because that is,

by definition, the subject matter of sociology. We have engineering, economics, political science, biology, and geography to study the technological, economic, political, and ecological forces that contribute to social change. The task of sociology and social psychology is to focus on human consciousness as an independent variable.

THE SOCIOLOGY OF DEVIANCE

A widely used traditional definition of deviance is "behavior which violates institutionalized expectations—that is, expectations which are shared and recognized as legitimate within a social system" (Cohen, 1959:462). However, the issue is far more complex than this definition would seem to indicate, for conceptions of deviance range from that just given to far more subjective-relativistic ones, and there are in fact those who would prefer to discard the concept altogether, since they believe that it is inherently judgmental.

To throw out the term deviance is impossible, for an immense amount of sociological and social-psychological work has been done under that heading. However, it is possible—and desirable—to compare and contrast various competing conceptions of deviance. That is what this section does.

It will be seen that although there is a variety of theories dealing with deviant behavior, the fundamental cleavage is between a classical-absolutist conception of deviance and a pragmatic-relativistic one, or between what some authors have termed the normative and the interpretive-phenomenological approaches (cf. Shearing and Petrunik, 1972; Wilson, 1970).

Of equal relevance here is the sociological conception of *social problem*. A social problem may be said to exist when "some social conditions and processes are out of harmony with certain social values, and when these affect a sizable number in the population in substantially the same way" (cf. Burgess, 1962; Rose, 1962a:381). This is, indeed, the proper sociological conception of social problems. It indicates that *a social problem can only exist in the minds of people,* that it is the product of a (collective) definition of the situation. For example, analphabetism was not a social problem in medieval Europe; slavery was not a social problem in America in 1830, and much less was racial discrimination.

As will become apparent in the next few pages, the proper social-psychological conception of deviance is the "phenomenological" one, or the pragmatic-relativistic one that is in line with the definition of social problem just given. It cannot be an absolutist or normative one.

The traditional conception of deviance

The earliest explanations of deviant behavior were *biological,* as in the case of the Italian criminologist Lombroso's assertions that criminals were individuals who were born with criminal tendencies and who could be identified by such physical stigmata as a low forehead and a high tolerance for pain.

Less atavistic than Lombrosian criminology is what Matza (1969) terms *affinity.* This is the still widely followed practice of explaining deviant behavior by reference to such antecedent factors as poverty and social deprivation.

Of even more recent vintage is what Matza (op cit.) calls *affiliation,* which is the mode of explanation found for example in Sutherland's (1947) differential association theory: an individual becomes deviant through his associations with other deviants. Cloward (1959) has attempted to integrate this approach with the previous one, affinity.

As Matza (op. cit.) points out, a fourth major way in which social scientists have approached deviant behavior is by focus-

ing on the process of *signification.* This is the "new" (cf. Gibbs, 1966) approach, the phenomenological approach most frequently referred to as labelling theory. We return to this in detail in the next section.

A further theory of deviance that must be initially disposed of is the *functionalist* explanation. Going back to Durkeim (1938), Erikson (1962) has presented the now familiar idea that deviant behavior, far from always being destructive of the social system, is in fact often an important resource that makes a valuable contribution to the system's well-being. How? It helps to maintain the boundaries of permissible behavior by serving as a living example of that which is not permissible. For example, some families can perhaps "remain intact only if one of its members becomes a visible deviant to serve as a focus for the rest" (Erikson, op. cit.).

If deviant forms of behavior are often beneficial to society, Erikson asks, could it be that societies are organized in such a way as to promote this resource? It would seem that this is indeed often the case. As this chapter will demonstrate, the *production* of deviants through such mechanisms as labelling, scapegoating, ostracism, statistics, and punishments is a major activity in social systems. Groups—whether small encounter groups (cf. Daniels, 1970) or nation states such as Germany and the United States—seem to require scapegoats and deviants for the maintenance of their morale and cohesion. This is a basic social-psychological law.

Ball (1975) has recently provided empirical evidence for the functionalist view that the apprehension of deviants functions to dramatize the system's normative boundaries. He found, cross-culturally, an inverse relationship between the severity with which certain violations (such as illicit sex) are punished and the degree to which these violations may be publicly observed. In other words, in societies where certain illicit acts can and do often take place in

287
Deviance, conflict, and change

great privacy, such acts are more severely punished when they are discovered than in societies where there is less privacy in that matter.

Finally, laymen and sociologists (cf. Buckner, 1971a:245-249) have both noted an important latent function of deviance: it provides clients for social control agencies and thus jobs for social workers and other helping professionals. A major function of the consistently high crime statistics so widely publicized by correctional agencies and the media is their contribution to a full-employment economy.

A different conception of deviance

To fully understand how sociology and social psychology approach deviance today, we must discuss the theoretical tradition upon which the current approach is based. The foundation of this tradition was laid by W. I. Thomas and Florian Znaniecki (1918-1920; Thomas, 1923) with the concept of the *definition of the situation*. It may be recalled from Chapter 6 that this refers to the "stage of examination and deliberation which . . . (is) preliminary to any self-determined act of behavior" (Thomas, op. cit.), in other words, the process of interpreting a situation and determining what is going on, who the actors are, what their intentions are, what the proper course of action is, and so forth. The crucial point is to remember that, from a pragmatic standpoint, a situation is what it is defined to be. In Thomas and Thomas' (1928) famous words, "if men define situations as real, they are real in their consequences." Now this should not be extended to its absurd consequence. When two armies confront one another in the field or two boxers in the ring, it is not up to them to decide that they will have a picnic. What Thomas meant was of course the more subtle fact that within certain bounds, the participants to a social situation determine and negotiate the nature of their interaction. For example, whether an encounter between acquaintances at a party, husband and wife in bed, or teacher and students in the classroom will be pleasant, hostile, or boring depends a great deal on how the participants define the situation.

Pragmatism represents a radical departure from classical thought about social phenomena. Henceforth, men's identities, social situations, proper behavior, good and evil, and all other elements of social life are no longer viewed as being determined by absolute and external criteria but as emerging from the social process itself (cf. McHugh, 1968) and therefore as relative to time, place, culture, and situation.

The amount of subsequent work in the tradition of what is now known as the "Thomas theorem" (cf. Merton, 1948) is immeasurable. Merton's (1948) concept of the *self-fulfilling prophecy* is an important extension of that theorem. By this are meant the innumerable instances in life when things come true because our mental and verbal actions propel the social process in their direction. Think of the student who fails because he *anticipates* failure, the fight that takes place because the protagonists *expect* mutual hostility, the real enemies that all paranoids have, the deviance that *results* from being punished.

Other scholars, like Whorf (1956), have emphasized the role of language in contributing to the definition of the situation. Anthropologists have shown how even such things as response to pain (Zborowski, 1952) and crying (Fortes, 1962) are part of the definition of the situation. The concept of the definition of the situation has been applied to a myriad of settings, from the college classroom (Waller, 1961) to the stolen base in a baseball game (McCall and Simmons, 1966) and from deviant subcultures (see next section) to gynecological examinations (cf. Emerson, 1970; Henslin and Biggs, 1971).

Recent empirical research on the definition of the situation also includes McHugh's (1968) ethnomethodological research and experiments by Kohn and associates (1972) and Stebbins (1972). Stebbins, for example, carried out the following experiment: a class where the instructor was presenting the Darwinian theory of evolution was disrupted by two well-dressed men (aged twenty-two and thirty-eight) who entered and acted as if they were zealots from the community. Hired by the experimenter, these two men had been instructed to argue with the professor, accusing him of being an atheist, a subversive, and a communist. The question was: how would the students in the class define these two men and the situation? Stebbins submitted a questionnaire to each of the one hundred twenty students to determine this. Table 11 reproduces some of his results.

Now the study also established similar tabulations of how the students defined other aspects of the situation—for example, how they felt about the two disruptors. By cross-tabulating these variables, Stebbins established the existence (statistically significant) of two clusters, or two definitions of the situation. (1) "These two men are religious figures of some sort. Their beliefs are being seriously threatened by the lectures, and as a result they want them either corrected or stopped. Their activities are outrageous and highly resented. (2) These two men are only non-student

intruders. They somehow feel that the lectures are having a bad influence upon us students, and as a result want them either corrected or stopped. Their activities are mildly disgusting" (Stebbins, loc. cit.). Here, then, is a good demonstration of the empirical meaning of the definition of the situation.

A further strand in the pragmatist-relativist tradition is the *sociology of knowledge*—a sociological subdiscipline that traces our thoughts and how we define situations to the position we occupy in the world. Current colloquialisms such as "where a person is at" and "where a person is coming from" grasp the essence of the sociology of knowledge well. They indicate, as was first realized by such sociologists as Marx (Marx and Engels, 1930) and Mannheim (1936), that everything we believe and know is colored by our culture, class, social position, and environment. Thus no one is right and no one is wrong. The Chinese communists see the world one way, American capitalists define it in another way; ghetto blacks know one kind of truth, suburban taxpayers another.

To be sure, the sociology of knowledge

TABLE 11. Student identifications of two men who attacked a professor verbally for presenting the Darwinian theory of evolution*

Identifications	Number	Percent
Religious figures (clergymen, zealous laymen, theology students, etc.)	25	20.8
Nonstudent intruders or outsiders	16	13.3
Troublemakers, fanatics, cranks, etc.	10	8.3
Narrow-minded, conservative men	7	5.8
Know them by name	3	2.5
Suspect or know they are students	8	6.7
Newcomers to the course	6	5.0
Have been invited by the instructor (teaching assistants, graduate students, professors, etc.)	7	5.8
Other and unable to make identification	38	31.8
Totals	120	100.0

*Modified from Stebbins, Robert A. "Studying the definition of the situation: theory and field research strategies." In Symbolic Interaction. Jerome G. Manis and Bernard N. Meltzer (eds.). Boston, Allyn and Bacon, pp. 347.

goes beyond such platitudinous relativism. It notes that groups do develop consensual definitions, what we call cultures. It makes a true contribution when it helps us understand, as do for example Berger and Luckmann (1966) in their masterful way, *how* men construct their truths, how they define the situation, how they construct reality.

Good examples of social-psychological studies in the sociology of knowledge include Powell (1962), who critically examines the constructions of the beat generation, and Berger and Kellner (1970), who show how marriage is based on a (precarious) jointly constructed definition of reality. When two individuals enter into marriage, they develop and stabilize a new joint "culture" that is sustained through conversation and that requires the redefinition of roles and of past events.

Durkheim (Durkheim et al., 1964) already noted that two fundamentally different "paradigms" or modes of thought face one another today, the old and the new, the dogmatic and the pragmatic, the absolutist and the relativist. Many other terms have been used to refer to this dualism (cf. Wilson, 1970). What is meant, basically, is of course the contrast between the two alternative approaches in sociology and social psychology, one being the traditional notion that the study of human behavior can reveal laws and standards that are true simply because they represent objective reality, and the other being the relativistic conception that argues that social reality is essentially subjective, or at best intersubjective—always a function of human judgment and interpretation. According to the classical conception, then, knowledge reflects reality. According to the modern approach, it is the other way around: reality is determined by our knowledge of it. The definition of the situation and the sociology of knowledge are, of course, part of the modern approach.

Today, it can be safely assumed that whenever one speaks of the *sociological* approach to deviance—as distinct from the psychological approach—one means the pragmatic-relativist approach: deviance is viewed more as the product of the societal reaction to an individual's behavior than as the result of things inherent in that behavior.

Society produces deviance

While a following section will cover in detail the application of the sociological theory of deviance to specific behaviors, the present section introduces the general theoretical apparatus.

Basically, the sociological approach to deviance focuses on the *societal reaction* to deviant behavior and on how that reaction contributes to deviance, rather than on the deviant behavior itself. Today, this focus is most frequently termed *labelling theory*. The radical nature of labelling theory lies in the fact that whereas the classical approach to deviance essentially views the deviant and his behavior as the causes of the problem of deviance, labelling theory turns this around, implying that society is responsible for the production of deviance (by labelling individuals).

The contributions to this theoretical focus go back quite far. For example, it may be said to have been at least indirectly anticipated by the early work of social scientists on stereotypes (cf. Lippman, 1922) and prejudice (cf. Bogardus, 1928). These are uniform and inaccurate mental pictures and attitudes that we use to categorize all members of an outgroup, whether this be a foreign nation or a domestic minority.

It is not clear who is directly responsible for coining the term labelling, but Tannenbaum (1938) wrote quite early of the process of *tagging*, and Becker (1963; 1964) wrote specifically about "labelling outsiders."

Further seminal contributions include Lemert's (1951a) distinction between *primary and secondary deviation*, Garfinkel's (1956) article about *degradation ceremonies*, Goffman's (1959) article about the *moral career* of the mental patient, Scheff's (1966) use of the concept of *residual deviance* and his application of *typification* to the area of deviance (1973), Matza's (1969) concept of *signification,* several authors' use of such terms as *deviance amplification* and *feedback* mechanisms (cf. Buckner, 1971b: 106-110; Wender, 1968; Wilkins, 1969), and the many other books and articles that deal generally and specifically with labelling (cf. Filstead, 1972; Schur, 1971).

Lemert (1951a) was among the first to note that a deviant act need not lead to deviant status, that the latter only occurs when deviant behavior is socially recognized and leads to labelling, hence the distinction between primary and secondary deviation. Garfinkel (1956) described how, in order for an individual to become isolated as a deviant, he must be degraded in public and shown to have infringed on group norms, not merely on the interests of another member. Goffman (1959) has shown that the mental patient undergoes a career whereby he is gradually humiliated, deprived of crucial elements of identity and self-esteem, and eventually internalizes the belief that he is, indeed, mentally ill. Thus hospitalization is more a cause of mental illness than its consequence. Scheff (1966) explains mental illness as the stabilization of the behavior of an individual into a pattern of residual rule-breaking produced by societal reaction. For example, most people who act deviantly are treated as eccentrics or comics, but some are designated as insane by society.

Concepts such as signification (Matza, 1969), deviance amplification (Wender, 1968; Wilkins, 1969), and feedback (Buckner, 1971b; Wender, 1968) all refer to the notion, already discussed under Merton's self-fulfilling prophecy, that an individual may be "sucked" into a deviant career by self-reinforcing social mechanisms (for example, labelling) that are far more responsible for the creation of deviance than are whatever norm infractions that may have occurred in the first place.

Related to and in overlap with labelling

is *scapegoating.* Work on this includes Burke (1969), Daniels (1970), and Klapp (1962). Daniels, for example, describes the process of scapegoating in a sensitivity group. Sutter, an Eastern Jew, is the member who gets it. The rest of the group sees him as a villain and a fool. "As a villain he was a flouter, a troublemaker, . . . an intruder, a suspicious isolate; and as a fool he was pompous . . . a square or an eccentric misfit . . . and an eager beaver" (Daniels, 1970:245). As always with scapegoating and labelling, the typifications have little to do with the actual behavior of the victim, who is damned if he does and damned if he doesn't. Like Goffman's mental patient, once labelling has taken place, Sutter can decide to interact with the group and fight back, in which case he is an intruder or a troublemaker, or he can withdraw, in which case he is a suspicious isolate and confirms the label he has been assigned. Nevertheless, Daniels believes that the scapegoat—the labellee—does have it within his power to counterattack. He can do this by applying counterlabels to his accusers, questioning their motives, and vilifying them in the eyes of those who have not yet joined the wolfpack. For example, Sutter began to make observations as the following:

. . .There are a lot of preconceived ideas (in this encounter group) about New York people; and I think that in parenthesis this also says "Jewish.". . . The people who have given me the roughest times . . . have been a little clique made up of (three second-year residents). They are the guys who have really given me the business left and right. . . . They are utilizing the conferences as a means of showing how sophisticated they were . . . they didn't give a damn if it helped me . . . or hurt me (Daniels, 1970:247-248).

The ruthlessness of the group has been documented in a variety of other settings. The nineteenth century French social psychologist Gustave Le Bon believed, perhaps with some justification, that whenever men act in groups, they degenerate. In his novel, *Lord of the Flies,* Golding describes how a group of youngsters, stranded on a desert island during the war, gradually regress into barbarism. Although one or two among them desperately try to hold on to civilized and rational social practices, the group as a force inevitably gravitates toward brutish and destructive behavior, scapegoating, and destroying its more sensitive and intelligent members.

In traditional communities, deviance may mean the barbarous immolation of individuals who may or may not have transgressed social norms, or it may mean *ostracism*, which often is tantamount to death. Plath and Sugihara (1973), however, show how the members of a Japanese village who were ostracized ended up building their own alternative and highly viable community.

As a last point in this section, we mention such illuminating work as Cicourel (1968), Freidson (1973), and Kitsuse and Cicourel (1972), showing that deviance is, in the final analysis, also a statistical production process. That is, what our crime rates, mental illness rates, drug addiction rates, and other official statistics on various forms of deviant behavior reflect is *not* the large amount of deviant behavior in America but the methods, criteria, work habits, and motives of statisticians, record keepers, mental health officials and correctional officers.

The social psychology of deviance today

Typical of the modern sociological approach to deviance are, among other books, Becker (1963; 1964), Filstead (1972), Lofland (1969), Jacobs (1974), and Rubington and Weinberg (1973). These books all share the labelling perspective previously outlined, a preoccupation with the societal reaction to and production of deviance—as well as the features discussed next.

As a social-psychological enterprise, the sociology of deviance focuses, first, on the stigmatization resulting from deviant behavior and from society's reaction to it. Of central interest, here, is the management of stigma by deviants. Goffman (1963) has dealt with a wide variety of stigma management techniques, while others have zeroed in on specific methods or specific stigmas. For example, Davis (1961) wrote a famous article about deviance *disavowal* among the physically handicapped, Hughes (1970) has written about whites passing for blacks, and Kando (1972a; 1973) discussed transsexuals passing for natural-born women and using various rationalizations. For example, transsexuals and transvestites rationalize their life-style by claiming that they enjoy life more fully than normal persons, who have to deny half of their full personality.

Other sociologists have also enumerated some of the so-called *neutralization techniques* employed by various other categories of deviants to rationalize their behavior and thus better adjust to their social stigma. As noted earlier, Sykes and Matza (1957) list the various ways in which juvenile delinquents justify their activities and thus neutralize potential guilt. Similarly, homosexuals use such neutralization techniques as "most great men were homosexuals; think of Socrates and Plato," and "all men have latent homosexual tendencies; homosexuals are merely more honest about their true feelings."

A further central feature of the sociology of deviance is its position that deviance is whatever behavior a politically dominant majority happens to define as such and that one must therefore recognize the fact of *cultural pluralism,* the fact that there are, besides a dominant culture, various deviant subcultures and contracultures (cf. Matza, 1961; Yinger, 1960) in which so-called deviant behavior is perfectly normal.

The inherent relativism of the sociology of deviance has implications for its methodology: cultural pluralism means that no subculture, not even the politically dominant one, has the right to apply its standards to another. Therefore, the valid sociological method of inquiry is an emic one. Through participant observation and empathetic role-taking, the sociologist must live the life of his subjects (cf. Douglas, 1972), no matter how deviant they are and no matter how dangerous the moral and legal implications of this methodology are. Only in this manner can the sociologist hope to discover the true subjective meaning of the behavior at hand.

Thus a basic question about the sociology of deviance arises, one aptly phrased by Becker (1967): Whose side are we on? Labelling theory's radical departure from the classical approach to deviance has turned the table on society, on institutions of social control, and on politically dominant majorities. The deviant, who earlier was the predator, the enemy of society, now becomes the victim, the scapegoat. Value judgments are difficult to avoid, and it seems at times that sociology has lapsed into a radical antiestablishmentarian dogmatism that equals the earlier conservatism of the Parsonains.

Today, the argument rages back and forth, with some authors (such as Martindale and Martindale, 1973; Merton and Nisbet, 1971) denouncing labelling theory as a simplification and the exaggeration of a point that is otherwise well taken, other ones (such as Kitsuse, 1972) coming to the rescue of the perspective by clarifying its concepts, and some pointing out that the different approaches to deviance might coexist, since they each attempt to answer different questions. Gibbs (1966), for example, explains that it is one thing to ask questions about deviance and another to examine society's reaction to deviance. Both are valid enterprises. Then, too, the functionalist and the labelling theories of deviance can be reconciled if it is recognized that social institutions indeed produce deviants (as labelling theory asserts) and that this is, up to a point, functional for the system (the functionalist argument).

In any event, the sociological issue at this time is not why crime and deviance are so frequent, and what can be done to make people stop acting that way, but to understand why Americans perceive so much deviance around them (as reflected, for example, in the crime statistics) and how they handle their perceptions. One can hardly deny that a substantial amount of anxiety, hostility, and counterproductive symbolic interaction is currently taking place, that we live in an era of consciousness of social problems. However, it is insufficiently understood that social problems are inevitably symbolic. It is more important to determine how our collective thought processes function than to speculate about the causes of phenomena that are mere reifications anyway. If one is to be practical about, say, driving a car or skiing down a slope, one asks *how* to do it, not *why*. Similarly, an understanding of our society will not come about by labelling individuals and asking *why* they misbehave, but by asking *how* the labelling occurs. Clearly, the entire multibillion dollar correctional–mental health establishment is on the wrong track.

TYPES OF DEVIANCE

This section deals with the application of the theory just presented to specific areas of deviance. First, mental illness is examined, as well as such related problems as alienation, drug addiction, and suicide. Next, physical, socioeconomic, and criminal problems are discussed. Throughout, the focus is on such social-psychological processes as stigmatization and stigma management and on social interaction. In line with a moderate labelling perspective, we assume that it always takes at least two parties to produce deviance and social problems—society and the individual, self and other. Deviance and social problems are in the same category of terms as the concept of *conflict*: they refer to interactional processes, not to the behavior of one individual or one group.

Mental illness and related problems

The single most important business of psychology has always been mental illness. Despite the realization by a growing number of laymen and professionals that the concept of mental illness and the psychiatric enterprise are bankrupt, Szasz's (1971) allegation still holds: "In the Church of America, psychiatrists are priests."

The case against psychiatry is not so much for its abolition as for its reconceptualization. Conventional psychiatry, based on such works as Freud (1924), Dollard and Miller (1950), Maslow and Mittelman (1951), and innumerable others, posits the objective existence of mental health and mental illness and the scientific possibility (as well as necessity) of curing those who are mentally ill. In recent years, the profession has attempted to respond to the growing questioning of its scientific-medical status with various existential-humanistic-phenomenological spinoffs (cf. Barton, 1974; Frankl, 1963; Shostrom, 1968), by sending into the community the mod-liberal "community psychiatrist" (cf. Dumont, 1968), and of course with its innumerable sensitivity-encounter activities following the precepts of such gurus as Fritz Perls (1969) and Carl Rogers (1961).

Nevertheless, the issue remains. While some sociologists have kept their traditional sideline position, accepting mental illness as a social fact (cf. Clausen, 1971; Mechanic, 1969), it is primarily the sociologist (and the sociological psychologist and psychiatrist) who has mounted the attack upon scientific psychiatry. The problem, as Szasz (1961) put it in his classic discussion, is with the scientific-medical model on which psychiatry is based. The methods, criteria, and objectives of psychotherapy are no more scientific than were those of such practices as phrenology, bloodletting, and witchraft in the past. And like those earlier methods, psychotherapy frequently does more harm than good and is at best inconsequential (cf. Eysenck, 1960). In fact, mental illness is a *myth* (Szasz, 1961).

Even the jazzed-up "humanistic psychiatry" movement of today is still in the business of imposing behavioral standards upon individuals, claiming objective validity for those standards. Nothing makes this clearer than the one-sided emphasis found in all sensitivity groups on relating to others and learning to be emotionally free. It is assumed that the individual who does not wish to participate in the social game and who values privacy is maladjusted. It is not perceived that in the nineteenth (and perhaps twenty-first) century, things might be or have been the other way around—persons behaving as "expressively" as current group facilitators being locked up.

Whatever behavioral norms and values are defined as wholesome, the fundamental point is this: psychiatrists, therapists, counselors, and group facilitators are not medics but moral leaders, comparable to priests. Their business is moral leadership and social control, not cure. Once this is realized, one can still agree to the real utility of this role in a society that seems to be moving toward moral chaos and anomie.

The theoretical foundation of the position just outlined is found in symbolic interactionism and labelling theory. Sullivan (1953), it may be recalled, was a psychiatrist whose brilliant pioneering work established the fact that so-called mental illness is essentially a breakdown in interpersonal communication. Szasz (1961; 1963), also a psychiatrist, analyzes mental illness in the same terms. What psychiatrists erroneously view as symptoms of underlying mental illnesses are simply idiosyncratic forms of communication used by individuals with interpersonal problems. For example, hysteria is not a symptom of mental illness but an attempt at communication, an "iconic" language. The individual who uses such a language is not ill in the medical sense. He merely uses the wrong language, the wrong script, plays the wrong game. The success of psychotherapy should not be termed "cure" but the bringing back of the patient in the universe of discourse employed by his relevant others. For example, what is meant by *transference* is, in effect, what occurs when the therapist manages to bring the patient back into the social game deemed appropriate for him by society.

The labelling of individuals who suffer from communication problems (classifying them as "mentally ill," "neurotic," "psychotic," "schizophrenic") has been part of the problem, not the solution. The evolution of madness through history has been studied by several authors (cf. Rosen, 1969; Szasz, 1970b), and it is shown that the various forms and categories of mental illness are the product of the labels that were devised at different times to deal with deviant behavior (Szasz, 1970b). Thus a common form of "mental illness" during the sixteenth century was the St. Vitus dance, and one widespread during the eighteenth and nineteenth centuries was melancholia.

The labelling theory of mental illness is, of course, the application of the labelling perspective discussed in the previous section to a specific area of deviant behavior. Its major contributors include Denzin (1968), Goffman (1959), Scheff (1964; 1966; 1968; 1970; 1974), and Szasz (1956). A representative reader is Spitzer and Denzin (1968). The basic assertion of the labelling theory of mental illness is that the diagnostic labels used by psychiatrists do not reflect the prior mental illnesses of patients but in fact contribute more to deviant careers—that is, careers in mental illness—than any other single cause (Scheff, 1966:92-93).

Labels tell us more about those who use them than about those to whom they are applied. As Szasz (1956) shows, for example, the concept of *malingering* is not a diagnosis but an expression of social condemnation. It would be useful to conceive of malingering as the refusal by a patient to face the unfinished tasks in his life.

As Goffman (1959), Scheff (1966), and other sociologists tell us, the mentally ill are in a terrible bind, because they are told that they are deviant but at the same time they are rewarded for remaining deviant and punished when attempting to return to conventional roles (cf. Scheff, 1966:84-

87). The following excerpts from a poem from R. D. Laing's *Knots* express this quandary vividly:

> He does not think there is anything the matter with him because
>   one of the things that is
>   the matter with him
>   is that he does not think that there is anything
>   the matter with him
>   . . .
> There is something the matter with him
> because he thinks
>   there must be something the matter with us
> for trying to help him to see
> that there must be something the matter with him
> to think that there is something the matter with us
> for trying to help him to see that
>   we are helping him
>   . . .

The debate about the labelling theory of mental illness rages on. Gove (1970; 1974) believes that it is essentially incorrect, that mental illness exists prior to labelling; Martindale and Martindale (1973) think that Scheff's theory is a gross simplification; and Chauncey (1975) accuses Scheff of sociological imperialism, of wishing to explain everything sociologically. Coulter (1973) is also critical of labelling theory, but his work is a contribution to that very approach. Scheff (1975), finally, replies to his critics that he does not mean for labelling theory to replace psychiatry but to complement it.

In the final analysis, the question seems to boil down to whether an author is more sympathetic to the labellers or to the labellees. Critics of labelling theory may well share in common the view that deviants are those others who are destructive, have little in common with us, and are themselves the cause of their problems. The proponents of labelling theory may be more sensitive to the possibility that anyone may, at one time or another, be at the short end of the stick, that is, be an outsider.

Now the fact remains that sociological social psychology has had to deal with the established psychiatric taxonomy. How has it done this?

In the first place, sociology recognizes the fact of *disorganization.* In animals, for example, simultaneous feeding and punishing (the simultaneous presentation of reward and punishment) can cause disorganization. This is called experimental neurosis. While human behavior is symbolic and therefore much more complex, human disorganization—for example, neurosis—may also be viewed as the result of conflicting impulses.

Neurosis has traditionally been used to refer to a category of disorders that are somehow less serious than those classified as *psychoses.* This includes such things as conversion hysteria, obsessions, phobias, compulsions, anxiety, guilt, feelings of inadequacy, and instability. As Fig. 12-1 indicates, normality, neurosis, and psychosis may be seen as forming a continuum.

Psychiatrists have tried to establish the qualitative difference between neurosis and psychosis, sometimes equating the former with functional disorders and the latter with organic ones. However, this effort has been fraught with complications, and in the end it must be viewed as a failure. While "all mental processes are also bodily processes" (Rose, 1962b:539), the conceptual separation of mind and body is unwarranted. Neurosis, as Rose explains, must be viewed as the "inability to act reasonably effectively in society." This description also applies to psychosis, which may be distinguishable from neurosis

quantitatively; that is, it may refer to more serious behavioral disturbances, but not etiologically.

Psychosis, then, refers to the most serious forms of mental illness. Within this category, too, an attempt has been made to separate organic and functional disorders. Organic psychosis is said to be the result of brain damage, advanced syphilis (paresis), alcoholism (delirium tremens), and other permanent damage to the central nervous system (cf. Lindesmith and Strauss, 1956:640).

When a category of functional psychoses is established, it is not clear how these disorders differ from neuroses, except perhaps by being, somehow, more "severe." Well-known functional psychoses include manic-depression, paranoia, and schizophrenia. The manic-depressive is the individual who alternates rapidly between overactivity and apathy. The paranoid is the person who erroneously thinks that others are conspiring against him. Schizophrenia is a catchall label for a variety of people who have entirely withdrawn into their private mental world.

The inadequacy of the classical psychiatric etiology and conception of mental illness appears most clearly in the case of the ambiguous functional disorder—the neuroses and such functional psychoses as schizophrenia. The only clear datum about these individuals, particularly the schizophrenic, is that they no longer communicate effectively with their environment. They no longer use the same linguistic categories, words no longer have conventionally established meanings for them. As Szasz (1961) points out, these are

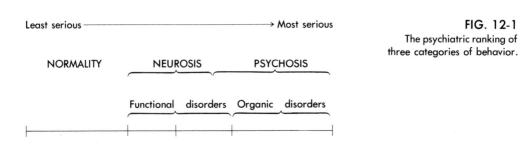

FIG. 12-1
The psychiatric ranking of
three categories of behavior.

behavioral problems, not mental illnesses. In only one instance can such problems be viewed as *symptoms* of underlying illness: when organic damage can be demonstrated. But then we have physical illness, which is in the realm of medicine, not psychiatry. The concept of functional illness must be discarded.

In the meantime, sociologists have brought their perspective to bear upon what psychiatrists classify as psychoses. Bowers (1974) and Jewell (1973) have studied psychosis, the latter author showing how a Navaho youngster who happened to be lost was mislabelled as a psychotic. Paranoia has been explained by Cameron (1943) as essentially resulting from deficiency in role-playing, Gaugh (1968) has explained psychopathy in the same fashion, and other sociologists (cf. Lemert, 1962; Lyman and Scott, 1970) have provided brilliant analyses of the self-fulfilling social process termed paranoia. As Lemert explains, the paranoid does have real enemies, and as in the case of most deviants, others contribute heavily to his predicament. Schizophrenia (cf. Laing, 1959) has been shown to result not from negative early childhood experiences but from the cumulative impact of one's inability to meet problems in adult life (cf. Rogler and Hollingsnead, 1971). In general, then, sociologists have shown that role failure, role conflict, breakdowns in communication, and the reinforcing labels used by others go a long way toward explaining mental illness, which must essentially be viewed as behavioral disorganization. To be sure, people use a variety of adjustments to such problems, including dissociation (of potentially conflicting roles), redefining the situation, role compartmentalization, and rationalization (cf. Lindesmith and Strauss, 1956:627). One should also note that a certain amount of disorganization is salutary, since it may be the stimulus to personal development.

A major area of research has been the *epidemiology of mental illness* (cf. Gruenberg, 1954; Spitzer and Denzin, 1968; Part two), that is, the study of the social, demo-graphic, ecological, and geographical distribution of mental illness. Faris and Dunham (1939) studied the ecological distribution of psychoses in Chicago (its distribution by urban areas), showing its high concentration in the central city. Hollingshead and Redlich (1958), Jackson (1962), and Kaplan and associates (1968) have discussed the relationship between social class and mental illness. They all found that psychosis is more common in the lower strata than in the upper strata, at least detected and treated psychosis (Kaplan et al., 1968). This holds not only in the United States but in the United Kingdom as well (Jackson, 1962). However, neurosis is more frequent in the upper strata (Hollingshead and Redlich, 1958). Of course, it is not clear what these statistics mean, since psychiatrists who are overwhelmingly middle class may be guilty of bias in their diagnoses of lower-class behavior, behavior that in their eyes may be psychotic but that in fact is not so within the lower-class subculture.

The relationship between sex and mental illness has gained interest under the impact of the women's movement. The acute question is: why are women so much more frequently mentally ill than men? Rejecting labelling theory, several authors (cf. Chesler, 1972; Gove and Tudor, 1973) have argued that this is a consequence of the greater role strain, role conflict, and other role problems suffered by women, in other words a result of their generally inferior status in society. One should note that this does not necessarily conflict with labelling theory.

Significant ethnic, racial (cf. Szasz, 1970a), religious (cf. Murphy, Wittkower, Fried, and Ellenberger, 1968) immigration (Roberts and Myers, 1968), and cultural (Opler, 1957; Townsend, 1975) differences in mental illness have also been found. Opler (1957), for example, found that among Irish-Americans schizophrenia is often caused by a domineering mother, whereas among Italian-Americans it is often because of a domineering father.

There is, too, the social criticism of men like Fromm and Marcuse (cf. Szasz, 1970b:320-321), who argue that some societies are, in toto, more mentally ill than other ones. It is not clear whether such usage of the concept of mental illness is metaphorical or not.

The sociological focus has also led to studies of family interaction as the arena where mental illness unfolds (cf. Sampson et al., 1973; Yarrow et al., 1973), studies of how mental patients compare with physical patients in terms of their role perceptions (Sobel and Ingalls, 1968), and the examination of the relationship between mental illness and self-concept (Dinitz et al., 1968; McPartland et al., 1967; Rosengren, 1972). Dinitz and associates (1968) found that the self-concept of mental patients did not differ significantly from how their relatives and staff perceive them. McPartland and his colleagues (1967) found that different types of self-concept (as measured by the TST) are significantly related to different types of behavioral disturbances. Rosengren (1972) found, among emotionally disturbed boys in a hospital, improvement over a one-year period in the amount of harmony between how they saw themselves and how they thought others saw them, in other words, in their self-integration.

As with the labelling theory of deviance in general, sociologists who study mental illness frequently focus on the stigmatization process (cf. Cumming and Cumming, 1968; Palmer, 1968; Whatley, 1968) and on the tremendously arbitrary ways in which some individuals become mental patients while other ones, not necessarily different, do not. Bittner (1972) focuses on police discretion in this matter, Denzin and Spitzer (1966) show the role played by such things as whether an individual is committed or a voluntary patient, and Mechanic (1968) points to the importance of the situation.

Perhaps the most massive psychiatric labelling process in existence is the routine creation of diagnostic dossiers about the millions upon millions of men passing through the armed forces. Caldwell (1944; 1949) indicates that neuropsychiatric problems constituted the largest single cause of loss of manpower during World War II. Between 1942 and 1945, of fifteen million men examined, twelve percent were rejected for neuropsychiatric reasons. And of the twelve million army personnel, one million were admitted to army mental hospitals, while fully half of all medical discharges were for neuropsychiatric disorders. Daniels (1972; 1973) examines the methods used in the construction of military psychiatric diagnoses. She points out that they resemble everyday decisions that involve value judgments. They are not scientific. Indeed, it is only since the advent of psychiatry that a combat soldier is incapacitated by, say, conversion neurosis. Prior to that, the cause was called fear.

The conclusion is therefore inescapable: psychotherapy is not a science. It is, in whatever form, not significantly more effective in curing individuals than is spontaneous recovery. Eysenck's (1960) excellent study demonstrates this, although that author for some reason pins his hopes on behavior modification. Psychiatry, sociologists point out, is essentially a subculture, a particular way of viewing the world, a specific value orientation. Kadushin (1966), Loeb (1968), and Smith and Thrasher (1968) have described various aspects of this subculture.

The argument against psychiatry finally becomes a political and moral one, and it becomes most acrimonious with respect to (involuntary) mental hospitalization. It is increasingly realized that psychiatric labels are judgments pronounced by men in power upon what Krim (1970) terms "behavioral pioneers." As psychiatrists themselves now begin to perceive (cf. Henry, 1973), the problems of society are moral, not medical. Thus the meaning of mental hospitalization becomes a drastically different one: it is a 1984-like euphemistic substitution for the cruder but more honest tradition of imprisonment. It is a new and insidious form of social control. This is the point of brilliant novels such as Ken Kesey's (1962), the sociological analyses of Goffman (1958; 1959; 1961; 1969), and mounting empirical evidence that mental hospitalization contributes to, rather than cures, mental illness.

Fortunately, there has been some progress on this front. For example, in 1970, Professors Szasz and Goffman, among others, founded the American Association for the Abolition of Involuntary Mental Hospitalization. This organization, in conjunction with other efforts, contributes to legal reform in the field of mental illness. For example, in the spring of 1976, the State of California was about to pass legislation significantly restricting the use of involuntary mental chemotherapy and electrotherapy.

Lest the reader misinterpret antipsychiatry (see Chapter 2) as just another liberal and misguided assault on the social order, it advocates a return to moral responsibility and criminal accountability. Psychiatry has provided the socially harmful and destructive individual with a justificatory rhetoric, absolving him of guilt and responsibility. This game is played with vigor and enthusiasm by both the court psychiatrists and the criminals. Antipsychiatry proposes to unmask the subterfuge, returning responsibility to the individual. Far from promoting further liberal license, antipsychiatry stresses that proper living is a serious business. This is responsible humanism.

Alienation. Of current interest is a problem that should perhaps be distinguished from mental illness, although the distinction is not clear-cut: *alienation.* While Marx used the word primarily to denote alienation from work, early psychiatrists were called *alienists,* thus indicating the close relationship between alienation and mental illness.

Goffman (1957) has described alienation from interaction, the opposite of spontaneous involvement. However, such alienation may become pathological—it is then termed self-alienation (cf. Gergen, 1971: 86)—and in the extreme it is identical with schizophrenia. In its moderate form, it is perhaps a condition from which most of us in contemporary society suffer to some extent. Blauner (1964) has distinguished four dimensions of such alienation: powerlessness, meaninglessness, isolation, and self-estrangement.

Perhaps the best way to describe alienation as a moral-psychological problem is to say that it is the condition of acting in ways inconsistent with one's principles and beliefs; of doing what one dislikes to do; of being bored and repelled by one's job and one's associations, while nevertheless sticking to these for the sake of money, power, and security; of smiling, pretending, and knowingly being dishonest with others and oneself. This is the condition deplored by existential social critics under such concepts as *sham* (cf. Henry, 1973) and *bad faith* (cf. Natanson, 1970; Sartre, 1956). It is the general human condition in advanced societies, where chameleon-like role behavior is a prerequisite for survival.

Boredom and loneliness. Related to alienation are the problems of boredom and loneliness. Now that we have atomic submarine crews and astronauts who must sometimes spend considerable amounts of time in restricted total environments, problems such as boredom, lack of social stimulation, and claustrophobia are gaining in interest. Haythorn and Altman (1973) and Heron (1957) are among the authors who have examined such problems. A recent book by Weiss (1973) assembles various studies about loneliness. This author points out the importance of distinguishing between emotional loneliness and social isolation. Following Sullivan, loneliness is defined as "an exceedingly unpleasant and driving experience connected with inadequate discharge of the need for human intimacy." Studies of widows and aged people show that less than half of these isolated people complained of loneliness. Although loneliness can be very debilitating, one must remember that it is a subjective experience produced by one's definition of the situation, not necessarily an objective condition. Riesman, Glazer, and Denney's (1950) *The Lonely Crowd* and many subsequent works have described the acute loneliness of modern urban Americans who, ironically, are physically surrounded by far more people than earlier generations.

Drugs. What about drugs? Modern American society's increasing reliance on drugs is inescapable. Oakley Ray (1972) speaks of a "biological revolution," Berg (1969) asks why Americans hide behind a chemical curtain, Farber (1970) notes that drugs are becoming America's new god. Different types of drugs affect different segments of the population (cf. Scher, 1970), but no group is immune. For example, our respectable and well-to-do physicians have an opiate addiction rate thirty times higher than the general population (Winick, 1964).

Psychologists have been concerned with how drugs affect behavior, studying, for example, the impact of opiates on rats (Nichols, 1965). LSD and other drugs have been used in psychotherapy and alcoholism treatment (Abramson, 1966), but it is questionable whether the benefits of drug treatment outweigh the costs (Barron et al., 1964).

The question of greatest interest is: what is addiction? Sociology answers this question far more promisingly than the worn-out biologistic explanations on which most drug-related policies in America are based. The sociological explanation of (opiate) addiction has been provided by, above all, Alfred Lindesmith (1947; 1968; 1969; Lindesmith, Strauss, and Denzin, 1975) on the basis of his observations of a large number of drug addicts. It is that author's basic conclusion that (opiate) addiction is

not caused by the euphoria that the drug produces but by the pain of withdrawal sickness. "It is the repetition of the experience of using drugs to alleviate withdrawal distress (when the latter is recognized and properly identified) that appears to lead rapidly to the changed orientation toward the drug and to the other behavior that constitutes addiction" (Lindesmith, Strauss, and Denzin, 1975:226).

Recently, McAuliffe and Gordon (1974) have tested and, so they claim, refuted Lindesmith's theory. These authors show that all long-term addicts interviewed experience euphoria, most of them nearly every day of the month. This leads them to conclude that Lindesmith was wrong, that opiate addiction results from the *positive reinforcement* of euphoria and not the negative reinforcement of withdrawal pain. This conclusion justifies the current use of such chemotherapies as methadone, which are aimed at blocking the euphoric effects of opiates.

In his reply to McAuliffe and Gordon, Lindesmith (1975) points out that they confuse verbalized motive and cause—an error, one should add, common to those unfamiliar with the interactionist perspective (see Chapter 11). While many addicts claim to experience euphoria from opiate use, this is an ex post facto observation and not necessarily the cause of addiction. To attribute causality here, Lindesmith argues, is like "asserting that malaria is caused by intermittent chills and fevers" (Lindesmith, 1975:148). While McAuliffe and Gordon make some valid counterarguments, the fact remains that their study does not represent a refutation of Lindesmith's work. That work demonstrates that addiction results from the combination of (1) withdrawal pain (a biological fact) and (2) the definition of the situation.

Abstinence cycles, relapse, and the rehabilitation of heroin addicts have been studied by Akers and associates (1968), Ray (1961), and Johnson and Cressey (1963), among others, and Rodriguez (1974) provides an interesting autobiographical account of a former addict. In each of these instances, we see the crucial role played by the definition of the situation. Rodriguez, for example, shows how part of successfully remaining a *former* addict is to (re)define and reinterpret the consequences of heroin use as negatively as possible.

Now this is the crucial point with regard to the meaning of drugs, and sociologists (Becker, 1953; 1962; 1969; Watts, 1971) have made the same point with respect to marijuana, LSD, and other drugs as well. In order to become a successful marijuana user, as Becker (1953; 1962) has shown, one must learn to define the experience as pleasurable. This is a socialization process requiring the support of an ingroup, or reference group, which defines the situation for the novice. Similarly, Becker (1969) has pointed out that the meaning and consequences of LSD are determined by how the experience is defined. In the 1960s, a sensationalist press and an alarmist public opinion attached such labels as "psychosis" and "psychotic break" to the LSD experience, possibly thereby *causing* many naive youngsters to expect and therefore to have "bad trips." In due time, Becker notes, LSD might be viewed with the same equanimity as marijuana, another drug that, in the 1920s, was said to cause psychosis and dementia.

The problem with drug use, as with all forms of deviance, is that two issues are being confused: drug use and society's posture toward drug use. America, which prides itself on being pragmatic, has in fact tended to adopt an Austinian approach to social control rather than a legal-realistic one. By doing so, it has often exacerbated the problems it seeks to remedy. It is my personal opinion that the widespread use of drugs—from aspirin to LSD, from coffee to heroin, and from alcohol to marijuana—is undesirable. This opinion is rooted in a humanistic-existential stance that values freedom and choice and rejects all forms of enslavement. However, our national drug policy is two-faced: it claims to help and rehabilitate drug users, while in fact it punishes, scapegoats, and weak-

ens them (cf. Szasz, 1972a). It claims that drug use causes much of the current increase in crime, when in fact there is not evidence for this (Blum, 1970). It substitutes unconstitutional infringements on individual rights and a pseudoscientific legitimation of drug use ("chemotherapy") for the alleged evils of self-administered drugs (cf. Szasz, 1972b).

The overwhelmingly valid generalization is that the drug user harms himself rather than others. The major exception to this consists of traffic accidents, but of course the vast majority of all drug-caused accidents are the result of one very specific drug: alcohol. The use of drugs is something that every individual must consider, if at all, with intelligence and deliberation (and legal restrictions on youth's access to drugs are indeed appropriate). But surely the worst of all is to have someone else make the decision for us.

Alcohol. While alcohol is, of course, a drug, we follow the de facto custom of discussing it separately. Sociologists have studied drinking and bar behavior as a form of (harmless) recreation (cf. Cavan, 1966; Gottlieb, 1957). Of course, it is alcoholism, addiction to alcohol (cf. Jellinek, 1952) that interests us here.

Again, the proper definition of this problem is one that takes the labelling process into consideration. Alcoholism, defined as "a label attached to certain persons because their patterns of heavy drinking have led to difficulties with employers, spouses, and community officials" (Spitzer and Denzin, 1968:89) has been found to be most common among those divorced or unmarried, male, Baptist, and in high-status occupations (Mulford, 1968). As Gusfield (1972) shows, alcoholism has undergone a moral passage in the history of this country—from the repentent drinker through the enemy drinker to, today, the sick drinker. The major rehabilitative institution, Alcoholics Anonymous (Cain, 1969; Lofland Lejune, 1960), of course totally endorses the medical vocabulary. For the skid row alcoholic, there are no such aids as AA. His return to society, as Wiseman (1973) indicates, is most difficult, since there are no legitimate statuses available to him on discharge from the institution.

Suicide. As a final form of deviance in this section, we touch briefly on suicide. Since Durkheim's (1897) classical work on this subject, sociologists (cf. Gibbs, 1961) and others (cf. Blum, 1972) have discussed the social dimensions of this problem. From a social-psychological standpoint, suicide must, like all other forms of behavior, be viewed in a social context (cf. Douglas, 1967), as the product of social interaction between the individual and others. Durkheim already recognized this, since his three forms of suicide—egoistic, altruistic, and anomic—were meant to reflect different kinds and degrees of social integration. Egoistic suicide, according to the French sociologist, prevails when a social system suffers from insufficient functional integration. Anomic suicide occurs primarily when normative integration is inadequate. Altruistic suicide occurs when society is excessively integrated. It represents the self-sacrifice of the individual for the sake of the group. Examples of altruistic suicide are provided by the Japanese custom of hara-kiri as well as World War II's kamikaze pilots.

The symbolic interactionist approach to suicide focuses on the behavior of both the individual and his significant others. Breed (1964), for example, found in a study of two hundred fifty suicides in New Orleans that role failure was often at the root of suicide, that the problem lay in the relationship between the individual and such others as peers and relatives.

Physical deviance

Physical illness is, of course, first of all a medical problem. However, it also has important social aspects (cf. Cooley, 1951),

and the social-psychological study of ill people has revealed interesting things about the manner in which roles, identities, and situations are defined, the labels and definitions that emerge from and influence the interaction between patients and staff, and the consequences of these social-psychological factors.

To be physically ill is to be a permanent or temporary deviant (cf. Lorber, 1967). In some cases, the "physicians" themselves are also cast in deviant roles. For example, Whitehurst (1974) studied a Mexican border-town "clinic" that catered to Americans who suffered from chronic arthritis. While the clinic used "miracle drugs" (such as cortisone) that could produce serious side effects such as bleeding ulcers, the physicians got results. The patients blindly accepted the authority of the physicians, who had complete control over the definition of the situation, and they felt cured.

As Davis (1969:148) points out, "it is an oft-repeated, although seldom analyzed truism that recovery from a disease is as much a psychological process as it is a physiochemical process." The role played by the definition of the situation is crucial. Davis (1969; 1972) shows this in several publications. For example, in the case of paralytic polio convalescents, physicians were shown to define time and recovery and patients learn to go along. Also, physicians protect themselves from the discomfort of having to tell parents that their child will be permanently impaired by stretching the period of uncertainty.

As we saw in Chapter 9, Glazer and Strauss (1965) did similar work among terminally ill patients, showing how four different awareness contexts operate, each representing a different definition of the situation.

A related condition is permanent physical handicap. This, too, has been examined by Davis (1961), who focused on the stages of interaction between this stigmatized group and normal individuals. First, there is fictional acceptance; the parties act as if there were nothing abnormal. Then a "breaking through" occurs, a facilitation of mutual role-taking, and finally, a more or less normal relationship is stabilized. This last stage is definitely reached when both parties think that the normal person has a right to joke about the handicapped individual's condition, such as when a paraplegic is told by his old friend to stop "acting like a helpless cripple."

Various other forms of physical deviance have been studied by social psychologists, including blindness (Scott, 1972), obesity (Anonymous, 1974; Nisbett and Kanouse, 1972), and stuttering (Lemert, 1951b; Johnson, 1973). As the last two authors show, stuttering is largely the product of a vicious cycle of labelling and societal reaction that exacerbates the condition. This may begin in early childhood, when parents identify a child as a stutterer and seek professional help (Johnson, 1973), and it is further reinforced whenever the stutterer provokes laughter, or embarrassment, or irritation, or awkward sympathy, such as the impulsive tendency to supply words for the stutterer, finishing sentences for him, or breaking eye contact as he speaks (Lemert, 1951b).

Socioeconomic deviance

Social psychology has also examined a variety of social and economic factors, including occupational status, immigrant status, and membership in deviant subcultures such as skid row. Here, we briefly touch upon the social psychology of poverty, race, and stupidity.

A reader edited by Allen (1970) contains some useful theoretical (Rainwater, 1970; Sarbin, 1970) and empirical (Clinard, 1970; Hess, 1970) contributions to the social psychology of poverty. The labelling-role theoretical approach provides the best understanding of the problem of poverty. As Sarbin explains, the poor primarily enact roles that have been ascribed to them by society, and when they fail to enact such ascribed roles, they experience severe degradation and negative evaluation. As Clinard's (1970) study of urban slums in India

indicates, the combination of role ascription, passivity, and degradation results in a negative self-image, the most basic problem of the poor. Thus the first step toward breaking the psychological vicious cycle of poverty is to make (role) achievement possible for the poor. This means ceasing the mere channelling of outside funds and services into an essentially passive slum population and fostering self-help.

In conjunction with this, the socialization of the poor must be drastically altered. As Hess (1970) suggests in a study of one hundred sixty black families representing four different social classes, the role of the mother is crucial in orienting the child toward authority figures, but whereas the lower-class mother socializes her child for apathy and underachievement, the middle-class woman does not. For example, mothers were asked: "Your child is going to school for the first time, what will you do, what will you tell him?" A typical lower-class mother's answer was:

. . . to obey the teacher. Do what the teacher asks her to do and that's all to do or say. Just tell her to sit quiet and listen at the teacher and do whatever the teacher tells her to do and get her lessons.

However, characteristic of a middle-class mother was the following reply:

I will tell (her) that she is beginning her education. And here she will learn to listen to the teacher and how to act properly in a control situation such as not talking out any time she wants to. . . . And I will tell her to be very cooperative and do whatever the teacher wants her to do. And try to be friendly and get along with the children.

Race is another major social-psychological variable. It is, indeed, social-psychological in the most fundamental sense, rather than biological. As Hughes (1970) demonstrates, an individual may pass for white or for black, reverse himself, and leave everyone wondering what his or her "true race" is. This is because race is, in the final analysis, defined as important, despite the fact that objective racial differences are frequently very difficult to determine, since everyone of us is of an infinitely mixed ancestry. However, as the Thomas theorem teaches us, if men define something as important, then it has important consequences. In today's world, the two single most frequent labels in the name of which men kill each other, at least on an organized warfare basis, are religion and race. This occurs, at the time of this writing, in Ireland, Lebanon, other parts of the Middle East, Southeast Asia, Angola, and other parts of Africa, among other places.

Those of us who do not kill for racial reasons do, at least, discriminate. A study by Gaertner and Bickman (1972) showed this ingeniously through the "wrong-number technique." A sample of five hundred forty blacks and five hundred sixty-nine whites received what was ostensibly a wrong-number telephone call. The caller, using an idiom and speech pattern that clearly identified him as black or white, explained that his car had broken down and that he was trying to reach his mechanic. He asked the subject to contact the mechanic for him, since he had run out of change. Table 12 shows the frequency with which the various subjects agreed to help. The striking finding is not only that whites helped other whites more often than they helped blacks, but that blacks themselves also discriminated against blacks (although statistical support for the latter finding was merely directional and not significant; chi square=2.34, p < .20).

A final social stigma to be discussed here is "stupidity" (cf. Dexter, 1964). The difficulty with this category is that it encompasses both the congenitally subnormal—that is the mentally retarded—and the slow learners who are somehow handicapped because of their subculture and their socialization. The mentally retarded range from the vegetable-like idiot, through the imbecile, to the near-normal moron (Lindesmith, Strauss, and Denzin, 1975:242).

As with other stigmas, labelling and societal reaction are among the crucial and often causal components of the problem. Mercer (1973) has shown the devastating effects that IQ classifications can have upon both the mentally retarded and those who are merely culturally handicapped. Labelling often results in a self-fulfilling prophecy. Jacobs (1974) shows that misdiagnosis is an integral part of this labelling process, and Edgerton's (1971) study of forty-eight mental retardates highlights the ways in which societal reaction both impedes and facilitates the adjustment of this minority.

TABLE 12. The frequency with which blacks and whites extended assistance to black and white victims*

	White subjects		Black subjects	
	White victim	Black victim	White victim	Black victim
Frequency help	164	125	167	145
Frequency no help	88	111	82	95
Percent help	65	53	67	60.4

*From Gaetner, Samuel and Leonard Bickman. 1972. "A nonreactive indicator of racial discrimination: the wrong-number technique." In Beyond the Laboratory: Field Research in Social Psychology. Leonard Bickman and Thomas Henchy (eds.). New York: McGraw-Hill Book Co., p. 166.

Another major area of interest to social psychologists has been sex and sexual deviance.[1]

Homosexuality is the most common form of sexual deviance, although increasingly homosexuals themselves and the liberal society at large prefer to term it an alternative life-style. For example, the American Psychiatric Association recently removed homosexuality from its list of pathologies. While homosexuality is the generic term for sexual relationships among members of the same sex, common parlance generally restricts it to refer to *male* homosexuality, using lesbianism for female homosexuality. Kinsey and his colleagues (1948) found that one out of every three men in America has engaged in some homosexuality, and one out of twenty-five is a confirmed homosexual. It is agreed that homosexuality is a learned condition, not one that is caused by chemical-glandular factors.

Homosexuals are often found concentrated in certain occupations such as fashion and ballet because this enables them to meet one another. Thus homosexuals form a subculture—or a number of subcultural communities—and this has been the major focus of sociologists who have studied them (cf. Cory, 1971; Hooker, 1965; Reiss, 1973; Warren, 1972).

Actually, there are at least two types of homosexuals, the overt and the secretive ones. Humphreys (1970) studied the latter group, showing that it consists often of respectable married men. Today, homosex-

uals seem to be coming "out of the closets" (cf. Humphreys, 1972), but labelling and discrimination are still prevalent (cf. Kitsuse, 1973; McIntosh, 1972; Miller, 1972). Homosexuals are still stigmatized deviants.

Lesbianism (cf. Gagnon and Simon, 1967) has long been a recognized phenomenon, for example in prisons for women (cf. Ward and Kassebaum, 1964). However, only recently, in connection with the emancipation of women, has it too come out in the open, sometimes even assuming ideological meaning. The more radical elements of the women's movement have argued that lesbianism is better than heterosexuality.

Transvestism is the desire, found in some men, to dress in women's clothes and thereby experience sexual stimulation and gratification (cf. Benjamin, 1954; Brown, 1961; Buckner, 1970; Hamburger et al., 1953; Bruce, 1967). Transvestites are not necessarily homosexuals. They should be distinguished from "drag queens." Buckner, for example, found that heterosexual potency can often be assured only after partial cross-dressing, for example in a female nightgown.

Transsexualism goes beyond transvestism. Here, we have individuals (both males and females) who are unalterably convinced that they belong to the opposite sex and that nature made a mistake by giving them the wrong body. Thus they are physiologically of one sex, psychologically of the other. They seek and often obtain sex-change surgery.

There may be more than one hundred thousand transsexuals in the United States, and probably over four thousand have already changed sex, beginning with Christine Jorgensen (1968), who obtained her sex change in Denmark in 1954. Today, a significant and growing proportion of transsexuals are women who seek and obtain surgery converting them into men (cf. Pauly, 1973).

Benjamin (1966) believes that transsex-

___
[1]Excluding the large literature that belongs more directly to such disciplines as sex roles, marriage and the family, and deviance, I find the following books on the *social psychology of sex behavior and sex problems* on my shelves: Bardwick (1971), Bell and Gordon (1972), Benjamin (1966), Brecher and Brecher (1966), Edwards (1972), Gagnon and Simon (1967; 1970), Heiss (1968), Henslin (1971b), Juhasz and Williamson (1970), and Stoller (1968). These books and readers contain a variety of articles and material about sex, sex problems, and specific forms of sexual deviance such as homosexuality, lesbianism, and transsexualism. Some of this is discussed in the following paragraphs.

ualism may essentially be a more severe pathology than homosexuality and transvestism, and that the three conditions form a continuum. This is shown in Fig. 12-2.

Research on transsexualism includes Driscoll (1971), Garfinkel (1967), Green and Money (1969), Kando (1972a; 1972b, 1972c; 1973; 1974), and Stoller (1968). Of particular relevance here is the work of Garfinkel, who shows the methods used by a transsexual to define reality in her own—alternative—manner, and some of my own research (Kando, 1974) also shows some of the psychological mechanisms used by these individuals as they attempt to reject stigma and define reality in the most advantageous way possible. For example, most of my subjects turned out to be sexually more conservative than either normal males or normal females, as shown in Table 13.

The sexual conservatism in Table 13 refers to attitudes toward established sex roles. For example, a person who strongly endorses statements like "men must compete, women must cooperate" and "a man does, a woman is" is sexually conservative. Table 13 reveals a common psychological mechanism. Individuals who have committed themselves to a new status, particularly such a very fundamental status as gender identity, often endorse the values that buttress that status with exceptional zeal. Examples of this abound in other areas as well: the immigrant who is more pro-American than old Americans, the former radical who becomes superconservative once he is upwardly mobile, the convert

TABLE 13. Sexual conservatism of males, females, and transsexuals*

Males	Females	Transsexuals
16	5	3.5
1	9	18
26.5	22	6
25	26.5	2
10	33.5	3.5
15	42	28
20	47	31
30	36	7
32	38	8
14	44.5	24
12	43	29
13	39	35
23	33.5	41
11	50	37
51	49	21
44.5	48	40
17	46	19

$H = 11.55$
$df = 2$
$p < .01$

*Sample ranked according to respondents' sexual conservatism (respondent 1 is the most conservative of the total sample, respondent 51 the least conservative). From Kando, Thomas M. 1974, "Males, females, and transsexuals." Journal of Homosexuality, pp. 45-64.

who embraces his new faith with extreme dogmatism.

Other sex problems and sexual deviations that have been studied by sociologists and social psychologists include frigidity (Anonymous, 1972), illegitimacy (Vincent, 1968), abortion (Ball, 1970; Henslin, 1971a; Manning, 1971), divorce (Cantor, 1969), incest (Weinberg, 1972), prostitution (Bryan, 1973; Hirschi, 1962), and rape (Greer, 1973; Chappell et al., 1971).

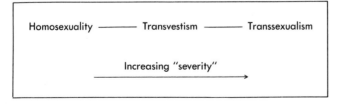

FIG. 12-2
Three forms of sexual deviance.

Again, from a social-psychological stand-point, the relevant questions about all these phenomena are: How do such individuals interact with others, including "normal" people? How are they stigmatized? How does the labelling process aggravate their condition? How do they define the situation?

For example, rape is now often said to include acts that were formerly classified as acts of seduction (cf. Greer, 1973). While rape is an admittedly heinous crime, its alleged increase during the 1970s has more to do with a changing consciousness, the greater willingness to make something of it (both on the part of the victims and the prosecutors), and a changing definition of the situation.

Crime and delinquency

As with previous social problems discussed in this chapter, the study of crime and delinquency is, itself, an entire (sub)discipline. Here, we briefly touch on the social-psychological study of these phenomena.

Chronologically as well as logically and causally in most instances, juvenile delinquency precedes crime. Social psychologists have, of course, been interested in the *socialization* processes that lead to delinquency. However, it was pointed out earlier in this chapter that the simplistic causal determinism implied in the traditional explanatory schema termed *affinity* by Matza may be a bankrupt idea, even though it still dominates the entire field of corrections.

More promising has been the line of research that follows interactionist and labelling-theoretical recommendations. For example, Reckless and his associates (cf. Reckless, 1967; Reckless and Murray, 1956; Reckless et al., 1957) have emphasized the role played by the self-concept in potential delinquency and nondelinquency. And as Deutscher (1962) points out, a youngster's self-concept is of course heavily dependent on how others view him and define him. Thus labelling and the definition of the situation (cf. Werthman, 1970) are of crucial importance in account-

ing for juvenile delinquency. Then, too, as Cicourel (1968) and others show, the amount of juvenile delinquency in society is not so much a function of how youngsters behave as of how policemen, statisticians, record keepers, the courts, and juvenile institutions behave.

A further topic of interest to social psychologists has been the juvenile gang, especially from the standpoint of the group processes taking place within it (cf. Miller, 1973; Miller et al., 1961; Short and Strodtbeck, 1965).

With respect to adult crime, sociologists have often focused on the criminal world as a subculture, while social psychologists have attempted to understand the causes and processes involved in criminal careers. As a subculture, the criminal world has its own language, mores, customs, code of ethics, and life-style. Often, criminals' goals are short-range, they spend their money right away and conspicuously, and they rarely marry (cf. Lindesmith and Strauss, 1956:672). There is one psychological feature that may distinguish the typical criminal from the rest of us—extreme suspicion, or paranoia. However, in general, psychological problems—neuroses and psychoses—are as dysfunctional in the criminal world as elsewhere (Lindesmith and Strauss, op. cit.).

A major theory in explaining criminal behavior has been Sutherland's *differential association*. Social psychologists have extended and researched this theory a great deal (cf. Burgess and Akers, 1966; Cressey, 1955; 1962; Glaser, 1962), showing for the most part that Sutherland was, indeed, correct: crime is learned, like any other behavior, and it results from exposure to an excessive amount of definitions favorable to law violation.

Other social psychological aspects of crime that have been researched include the identity of the criminal (cf. Cameron, 1973) and, above all, the negative labels (cf. Payne, 1973; Zimbardo, 1973) produced by imprisonment and, in general, the tremendous contribution prisons make to crime in society. Indeed, on one point there is nearly unanimous consensus among social psychologists: *no other institution in society contributes more heavily to crime –through recruitment, socialization, labelling, branding, the creation of a criminal self-concept, and witholding legitimate statuses from exconvicts upon release–than prisons and other correctional institutions.* Schwartz and Skolnick (1964), for example, show the very detrimental effects of a criminal record.

There is a final category of crime that has been of interest to social psychologists: so-called war crimes and other forms of organized and often legitimized evil (cf. Duster, 1971; Hughes, 1964; Sanford and Comstock, 1971). Hughes (1964) and Opton (1971) are among the authors who have shown how "good," "decent" citizens in Germany were capable of guiltless participation in mass slaughter, and how they rationalized their behavior. As we saw earlier, Milgram (1965) made the same point experimentally. The message seems to be that given the proper social context and the proper justificatory definitions, we are all potential criminals and killers.

VIOLENCE AND CONFLICT

In this section, we discuss the psychological and the sociological aspects of conflict and violence. First, we examine briefly the nature-nurture argument with respect to aggression and violence. These two terms must be understood to refer either to motives or to behaviors. Then the social process termed conflict is examined, and we deal, among other things, with collective behavior. As we shall see, conflict, like deviance, is a process requiring interaction between at least two parties. However, as Lofland (1969) explained, deviance and conflict differ in the following manner. When the enemy is small and weak, we label him and he is a mere deviant; but when the enemy is large and powerful,

there is mutual discreditation and hostility taking place. In such a case the enemy can hardly be conceived of as a deviant. For example, while we might wish that we could label the Soviet Communists deviants, in actuality their relationship with us is not one of deviance but one of conflict. In today's international community we ourselves may soon be the deviants.

Violence

Ardrey (1966), Lorenz (1966), and Morris (1967) are the inevitable triad cited to exemplify the resurgence of instinctivism as a way of explaining human aggression. Indeed, there is, once again today, a tendency to emphasize the universal, biological, and natural causes of violent behavior. In sociology, Pierre van den Berghe (1974; 1975; Fisher et al., 1975) is making a reputation for himself by "bringing the beast back in."[2] Others, like Storr (1972), combine the Lorenz-Ardrey premises with psychoanalytic explanations. According to Storr, humans are inevitably destructive because of the *paranoid projection,* a fatal character flaw resulting from infant helplessness and anxiety. Scherer and colleagues (1975) provide an excellent discussion of the biological factors in human aggression, while reminding us that these may be necessary but not sufficient conditions. Aggression, like other motives, is a label that gives meaning to behavior. It can, therefore, only occur among humans. The lion's behavior, as it attacks the antelope, cannot be termed "aggressive." It is merely an automatic response to a survival imperative.

---

[2]This is not to imply that van den Berghe's recent and controversial text is not fascinating—and in many ways valid. His analysis of society's ills, human stupidity, and his realistic appraisal of the American condition are brilliantly correct. Why he needs to appeal to biology, however, is unclear. The book is a case of correct conclusions based on wrong premises. In line with the fundamental point of this book, I suggest that it is far more plausible to trace contemporary social ills and conditions to culture, not nature. Like all other phenomena, culture can range from the healthy to the rotten. To deny this is to deny our responsibility—as humans—for our destiny.

Social psychology provides an understanding of human aggression, not biology. Aggression is learned, not instinctive (cf. Sanford and Comstock, 1971).

Psychologists like Berkowitz (1972) and Walters (1966) have studied experimentally such things as frustration, aggression, catharsis, and exposure to violence. Of central concern has been the relevance of such studies for real life. For example, does frequent exposure to media violence cause juvenile delinquency, crime, and violence, or does it, on the contrary, provide a catharsis effect? (cf. Bandura et al., 1963; Feshbach, 1961). Current evidence (cf. Scherer et al., 1975) provides very little support for the catharsis hypothesis and much support for the opposite effect. The contribution made by television and the other media to the overall level of violence in our society is becoming inescapable. This, too, might be by way of the creation of a definition of the situation, a general climate conducive to violence.

Fromm (1973) is critical of the Ardrey-Lorenz biologism, but he also rejects the learning theory of aggression. Instead, he views cruelty and human destructiveness as character traits. Personality psychology, Fromm believes, explains best such men as Stalin, Hitler, and Eichmann.

All in all, one must attempt to transcend all forms of psychologistic explanations and understand that violence is, most importantly, a reflection of sociological conditions. The novelist Arthur Miller (1969) understands this well, when he analyzes the causes of juvenile delinquency in America. The main cause, as that author sees it, is not poverty or excessive affluence but the depersonalization and spiritlessness of our times.

As to why American society is so unusually violent (an assumption shared by most observers), we must first of all remember that different cultures produce different personality types (cf. Lambert, 1971). Beyond that, there is, among sociologists and many laymen alike, an incredible mea culpa attitude (or is it, deep down, a perverted pride?) that sees America as *the* violent society (cf. Arnold, 1969; Bloomberg, 1969; Lukacs, 1969; Toby, 1972; Williams, 1972; Zinn, 1969). The self-incriminatory litany inevitably includes the observation that our culture is excessively competitive (cf. Toby, 1972; Williams, 1972) and that we have killed many Indians (cf. Zinn, 1969). One must remember, however, that the level of achievement motivation—competitive or not—may today be higher in such societies as Germany and Japan, and indeed in the Soviet orbit, where a collectivist ideology should not obfuscate the extremely vigorous work ethic and the competitiveness that manifests itself in industry, international relations, and international sports, among others. As far as American genocidal violence is concerned, it ranks well below the millions of Jews, Africans, Asians, Slavs, gypsies, and other Europeans killed by Imperial Germany, Great Britain, Belgium, France, The Netherlands, Russia, Spain, and Portugal.

And what about the other manifestations of American violence played up in recent years? Thirteen students died during the 1970 campus riots—not a very impressive statistic. Some foreign governments think little of mowing down thirty-two students in one single demonstration. Each season, a few beer cans are thrown at umpires and referees. In Latin America, soccer matches have ended in over one hundred deaths and in international war.

That social conditions breed crime and violence is a truism at this point. The Kerner report (1968) and Marmor (1969), for example, deal with racism as a cause, Coles (1969) focuses on poverty and other slum conditions, and Scherer and associates (1975), Glaser (1970), Christiansen (1970), and many others have stressed the urbanization process itself.

Conflict, riots, and mass movements

As noted in the introduction to this section, conflict is a social process in which both protagonists have some power. It is a generic concept referring to a social *form* (cf. Simmel, 1971) that may involve two individuals, as in a marital quarrel, or two billion persons, as in World War II.

At the microlevel, we have the classical experiments on intergroup conflict (and how to reduce it) of Sherif (1956; 1972) and the client-centered therapy for conflict resolution of Carl Rogers (1952).

Here, we shall focus on sociology's distinctive contribution to the study of conflict situations—the study of large-scale *social* conflict, including the highly disorganized form found in mobs and riots and the organized variety termed war.

During the past decade, America has been simultaneously involved in international war (Vietnam) and internal conflict (the peace and race riots). Thus the topic of social conflict has assumed central importance. It is now assumed that conflict and violence are integral parts of social history. As Rose (1969) explains, there is always on the one hand the organized violence of social control and, on the other hand the violence of dissent and rebellion, accounting for change. In the extreme, repressive violence leads to totalitarianism and revolutionary violence to anarchy. America, like many other societies, swings somewhat wildly between these two poles.

The sociological study of conflict sometimes leads one to an examination of social movements as well as of the role played by mass media and mass communication in modern society, but most of the subject matter belongs to the subdiscipline called *collective behavior* (cf. Turner and Killian, 1957) or *collective dynamics* (cf. Lang and Lang, 1961; 1962). As the latter authors define this field, it "studies patterns of social action that are spontaneous and unstructured inasmuch as they are not reducible to social structure."

As we saw in Chapter 4, the foundations for this field were laid in the nineteenth century be two French sociologists, Gabriel Tarde and Gustave Le Bon. Tarde believed that human behavior was the result of imitation and suggestion, while Le Bon studied the many crowds, riots, and revolutions that were taking place in France at that time. Tarde's heritage, then, has become the study of how people are influenced, sometimes indeed mesmerized, by television and other mass media, and how susceptible and suggestible they are to such things as advertising and propaganda. Le Bon's heritage is the study of crowds, riots, and other forms of conflict. In both instances, sociology is dealing with the less rational and, one might say, less appealing sides of human nature.

Empirical research on crowds and mobs has been carried out by Allport (1972), Kerckhoff (1973), Lang and Lang (1961), Milgram (1972), and Swanson (1953), among others. Crowd behavior generally increases during periods of restlessness, when integrated groups are breaking down. Crowds are fickle and changeable, and the members of a crowd are less self-conscious and self-controlled than people are otherwise. Therefore crowds may be important instruments of social change. Indeed, crowds must not be seen as being inevitably destructive, since they often signify the rise of important new social movements (cf. Roberts and Kloss, 1974).

There are several different kinds of crowds. One is the *acting crowd*, which is also called a *mob*. The acting crowd is homogeneous, emotional, irrational, and purposive—for example, a lynching mob, or a food riot, or a revolutionary crowd. The formation of an acting crowd occurs through *rumor* (cf. Shibutani, 1966). Rumor is, of course, a form of communication that emerges as an alternative to and when formal communication channels break down. Rumor gradually builds up tension and increasingly distorts what it transmits. Eventually, the role of suggestion becomes central, and as Le Bon already indicated, crowd behavior can at times become hypnotic behavior.

A second type is the *expressive crowd*.

Here, there is no objective, no collective response, merely a collective rhythm and excitement. Examples are religious revivals and the Japanese snake dance.

Finally, there is the *audience crowd,* for example, the crowds listening to the speeches of charismatic leaders such as Adolph Hitler and Fidel Castro.

To control or disperse a crowd, one must attempt one of the following strategies. (1) The common focus of attention (the leader, or the flag, or the cross, or any other rallying symbol) must be displaced or seized, so as to "break the spell." Or, (2) one might use shock effect, as when a minister jolts a rampaging mob into guilt, turning its feelings inward, from rage into shame. (3) A further logical possibility is, of course, armed intervention. (4) Authorities might simply decide to let a mob run its course: once a mob has accomplished its objective, or once it has lasted long enough to dissipate enough energy, it will disintegrate.

As mentioned earlier, a considerable amount of research on crowd behavior has been done since the 1960s, obviously because there has been an increase in the amount of such behavior. Fisher (1972) has studied protest demonstrations, Zimmerman (1969) has described that perennial marcher, Dr. Spock, I. F. Stone (1969) has written about the pilgrimage of Malcolm X, Martin Luther King (1969) wrote about the Montgomery bus boycott, and Learner (1969) described the riots during the 1969 Chicago Democratic Convention. The number of books and articles dealing with student riots, peace demonstrations, and youth dissent can no longer be estimated. It includes Becker (1970), Freedman (1969), Keniston (1971), Lambert and Heston (1971), McPhail (1972), and Pinard and others (1973). This literature includes descriptions of such events as the San Francisco State and Berkeley riots, studies of various sit-ins, and other forms of protest. It is good to remember that draft riots also occurred during previous wars, for example the Civil War (cf. Headley, 1969), and that there was a direct and causal relationship between the Vietnam war and youth unrest in the 1960s.

The peace movement, then, was a social movement, a direct response to a temporary but severe social problem—war. The counterculture showed us one way in which to cope with violence: fleeing from it (cf. Allen and West, 1970).

The relationship between social problems, collective behavior, and social movements has always been a close one (cf. Blumer, 1975; Roberts and Kloss, 1974; Mauss, 1975; Toch, 1965). We have just touched on that relationship with specific reference to the turbulent 1960s. In addition, we must also remember the role played by the mass media in this relationship. As Sherif noted, during critical periods such as wars and depressions, the role of the media becomes one of propaganda. Propaganda, like advertising and hypnosis, exerts control through *suggestion.* That is, it is accepted even in the absence of logically adequate grounds (cf. Lindesmith and Strauss, 1956). The aim of propaganda, unlike that of education, is not to inform but to convert and to facilitate speedy collective action in the face of crisis. This depends, to a large extent, on successful mass persuasion (cf. Cartwright, 1964).

The mass media, then, play a crucial role in determining public opinion (cf. Katz and Lazarsfeld, 1971) and, as Hubbard and associates (1975) recently showed, in determining society's response to social problems. For example, the media play an active role in determining and altering the racial stereotyping (Cox, 1973) and prejudice (Schary, 1969) that go on in society, and they also had some impact on the public's attitude toward the Vietnam war (Wright, 1973).

We have dealt with riots and mobs primarily in the context of social movements. Indeed, this type of conflict must, in the end, be recognized as one form of political behavior, that is, as one form of power negotiation. The other major social problem of the decade—race—was fought along the same lines. The Watts riots (cf. Ransford, 1973; Stark et al., 1974) were, of course, a cry for power and part of the long-term struggle for black power (cf. Cleaver, 1967).

Finally, international war itself (cf. Etzioni and Wenglinsky, 1970) is the ultimate struggle for power. Sociologically, this is the important point, rather than questions about the motives that prompt men to fight (cf. Moskos, 1973). Mead (1956:260) once drew the profound distinction between imperialism and internationalism, noting that the Romans were internationalists rather than imperialists. Since we incessantly criticize America for its foreign involvements, we might want to remember Mead's distinction. The choice may not be between foreign involvement and isolationism but between the constructive and benevolent exertion of power—internationalism—and its destructive application.

SOCIAL CHANGE

This chapter has examined the social-psychological meaning of deviance, social problems, aggression, and conflict. The final and perhaps most fundamental meaning of these processes remains to be discussed—change. Personal change and development were dealt with in the chapter on socialization. Here, our interest is social change.

Although the entire book has followed a dynamic and processual model, we now introduce explicitly the time dimension into the discussion. This book approaches time in the same fashion as it has approached other aspects of society: phenomenologically. Time—or, we should say, temporality—is a subjective reality (cf. Schutz, 1970). It is "an intrinsic property of consciousness" (Berger and Luckmann, 1966:26). Temporality refers to intrasubjective experiences and intersubjective definitions. For example, statements such as

"it takes the waitress a long time to bring the menu" or "our society is changing rapidly" reflect subjective experiences and definitions. A rural Mexican may not become as readily impatient with the waitress as a New York businessman. His time consciousness—culturally acquired—may be different.

Time may be an objective reality—cosmic time (cf. Berger and Luckmann, 1966:27)—but the meaning of time is inevitably a function of context and social definition. Is one hour a long time? It depends whether it is spent sipping cognac and listening to music with one's lover or waiting for the bus in icy weather.

If it is agreed that temporality is the experience of things occurring rapidly or slowly, then how can it be asserted, as is currently fashionable (cf. Toffler, 1970), that contemporary society is changing with unusual speed and that in general modern society is dynamic whereas traditional society has been static? It may be that there is, in human nature, a rock-bottom standard of time and change that we can only transgress at the risk of mental illness and social disorganization, as Toffler and many others seem to be arguing in their critical appraisals of the modern technocracy. However, there is no evidence for this yet. Assertions about the rapidity of change and of the pace of life in contemporary America, for example, may reflect an emerging consciousness rather than objective conditions, a new consciousness that, paradoxically, might signify that Americans are becoming tired of the bustling business ethic, that is, that they are slowing down!

What is culture?

To the social psychologist, social change is *cultural change*. It is change occurring in the minds of people.

Traditionally, the dominant conception of culture found in sociology and anthropology has been one of an all-encompassing complex of knowledge, belief, art, morals, law, custom, and any other capabilities and habits acquired by man as a member of society (Tylor, 1871). Classical social theorists like Hegel, Durkheim, and Wundt tended to view culture as a monolithic *Volksgeist,* a folk mind or group mind that molds the behavior of individuals.

The interactionist emphasis has been a different one. Culture, as W. I. Thomas (1936) for example points out, refers merely to the way individuals collectively, but actively, arrive at certain interpretations; that is, it refers to the definition of the situation. While the social construction of reality does acquire a certain external facticity (Berger and Luckmann, 1966), interactionists are careful not to reify culture (cf. Shibutani, 1961), not to view it as an external and inevitable reality that leads an existence independent from that of the members of society but as something that is always enacted, negotiated, changed, and interpreted *by people.*

If it is recognized that culture is of our making and that we are not enchained by our cultural heritage, then this raises the matter of choice. Jaeger and Selznick (1973), Kando (1975; 1976), and others have argued that the conception of culture found in anthropology may be too broad. Whatever custom, belief, or value happens to exist in society is accepted as a legitimate part of the culture. Perhaps a more *normative* conception of culture is required, at least for some purposes. If it is agreed that culture must not be reified and that the doctrine of cultural determinism has been exaggerated, one may perhaps begin to make some necessary judgments, recognizing that it is within our power to mold our culture, improve it, change it, humanize it. A humanistic conception of culture must find a middle ground between the all-encompassing anthropological definition and the elitist conception of high culture.

Sexual change

Change, then, is viewed here as change in consciousness, change in social definitions. Collective behavior aimed at solving a perceived social problem sometimes takes the form of social movements (cf.

Roberts and Kloss, 1974), one of the major forms of social change today.

First, then, a change in consciousness occurs, a change in the definition of the situation. Then the process may focus itself on some concrete areas. A crystallization occurs, and this may finally lead to concrete and specific political action.

A good example is what has happened in the realm of sex and sex roles in America since World War II. At first, there was a diffused liberalization process in the air, changing attitudes and values with respect to sex behavior (cf. Ellis, 1961; Kinsey et al., 1948; Sorokin, 1956), the so-called new permissive morality responsible for so much of the generation gap (cf. Mead, 1970; Riesman, 1964). This was clearly a case of cultural change, and only cultural change.

With the new sexual morality came, inevitably, a certain equalization of the sexes. In addition, technological and political factors (at least one major war every decade) also made for sex role equalization. Thus a new social problem emerged: women's sex roles. The early 1960s already produced a substantial literature dealing with this problem (cf. Bailyn, 1964; Daedalus, 1964; Henry, 1966; Komarovsky, 1966; Owen, 1962), but later on it assumed truly diluvial proportions (cf. Chafetz, 1974; Seward and Williamson, 1970).

In the meantime, the cultural revolution proceeded at an accelerated pace, producing extreme countercultural manifestations as well as, for those more committed to the system, a more respectable middle-class *Playboy philosophy.* Formerly tabooed sex research was now not only tolerated but welcomed (cf. Masters and Johnson, 1966; Brecher and Brecher, 1966), alternative life-styles, including mate-swapping, key clubs, and communal living, became popular (cf. Delora and Delora, 1972), divorce became the norm rather than the exception, and the monogamous lifelong nuclear family became everybody's whipping boy, at least among liberal social scientists (cf. Cadwallader, 1969; Johnson, 1969). By the mid-1970s, the media were so busy pushing and legitimizing the new morality that it had become an integral part of law and order itself, such as when television's cop Bronk first apprehends a criminal and, at the conclusion of the show, walks off with a policewoman toward a motel.

Interestingly, the new morality is, in some blatant instances, the very antithesis of the movement for sexual equality. *Playboy* magazine has been repeatedly singled out as a target of the women's movement. But whether recent social change in America has been paradoxical or not, the new consciousness eventually led to a genuine social and political movement—women's liberation.

Over three decades ago, Myrdal (1944) had already pointed out the parallels between the fate of blacks and that of women. Thus in the 1960s a neologism was coined, after the word racism: *sexism.* The women's movement has generated an immense flood of publications indicting America's sexist ideology, our sexist socialization procedures, and our discriminatory practices on the job market, in the bedroom, and in all other areas of life (cf. Amundsen, 1971; Andreas, 1971; Bem and Bem, 1975; Boston Women's Health Book Collective, 1973; Davis, 1972; Epstein, 1971; Friedan, 1963; Gornick and Moran, 1971; Horner, 1975; Micossi, 1973; Sullerot, 1971; Tanner, 1970). While much of this literature combines empirical work on sex roles with ideological polemic, we mention it here primarily in the context of the latter: since the mid-1960s, the transition from social problem consciousness to social movement has been made.

Because so few dared to state the dialectical reaction, the sporadic publications that did so deserve mention. Goldberg (1973), as noted earlier, wrote a book about the biological inevitability of patriarchy, and Gilder's (1973) book argues

that women's liberation is directly responsible for sexual suicide, that is, for the ultimate destruction of American civilization. All one can say about such statements is that they are rather bold, given the existing climate. The wave has yet to crest; the Equal Rights Amendment has a good chance of being ratified, more and more states pass stringent new antirape legislations. In sum this social movement is successfully making the transition from cultural change to political action.

The changing American consciousness

The changes in American society go, of course, far deeper than a changing sexual morality and changing sex roles.

Since World War II, countless social observers have documented the changes in the consciousness and in the national character of the "typical American." These include Berger and colleagues (1973), Bronfenbrenner (1971), Dubin (1962), Fromm (1947), Kando (1975), Mills (1951), Reich (1970), Riesman et al. (1950), Wheelis (1958; 1973), Whyte (1956), and Zijderveld (1971).

The common theme found in most of these writings is a general impression that Americans have become less individualistic, less autonomous, less inner-oriented, less innovative, and more other-directed, conforming, sheepish. Perhaps the classical statement on this was Riesman and associates (1950). Others have focused on the ramifications of this trend in specific areas of life. For example, Bronfenbrenner (1971) examines the contribution made to the trend by the emerging socialization and family patterns. Dubin (1962) documents the absence of the work ethic among modern American industrial workers. Kando (1975) discusses the emerging leisure consciousness. Reich (1970) speculates that we shall, as an outcome of these cultural trends, eventually all become hippies.

Most of the authors not only note these trends but also deplore them. Mills (1951) and Whyte (1956) decry the new bureaucratic ethos (the new motto is "to get along, not to get ahead"), the new emphasis on adaptability and role-playing. Fromm (1947) deplores what he terms the new marketing personality: modern man sees himself as a commodity to be marketed. His self-esteem depends on the ability to favorably impress others, not on inner convictions. Wheelis (1958), Zijderveld (1971), and others are similarly critical of these trends, many of which can be subsumed under the concepts of alienation and dehumanization.

The recent (1973) book by Berger and his colleagues, *The Homeless Mind,* picks up the theme once again, attributing dehumanization and alienation to technological modernization. It is, according to these authors, in the modern technocracy that man suffers the most profound loss of meaning and identity. While contemporary Americans long to belong more desperately than ever, they belong nowhere anymore—they are homeless.

The various countercultural and cultist manifestations of the past few years may be viewed as reactions to the technocratic dehumanization. Hippies, Jesus communities, and other groups of people have begun to form their own alternative lifestyles, building self-sufficient and isolated rural communities in Colorado, Illinois, California, Virginia, and elsewhere. Often these communities believe in occult, non-Western types of religions (cf. Simmons, 1964), they are often referred to as communes (cf. Kanter, 1972), and many of them are milleniarian, that is, they await the end of the world, which they know is imminent and inevitable (cf. Lofland and Stark, 1975).

One such community is located in Stelle, Illinois, where a few hundred young adults and their children have built their own little society, with local factory, school, residences, and all. The people of Stelle believe the world will end about the year 2000 but that they will survive the end of the world because of their education. They send their children to school from ages three to twenty-one (Sacramento Union, 1974).

Berger and associates (op. cit.) believe that man's psychological problems are the product of modern society, and that tribal man, for example, was not homeless. To what extent this may be a romantic fallacy (cf. Kunkel, 1974) and to what extent intellectuals such as Peter Berger may be projecting their own existential anxiety onto the average man remain to be seen.

SUMMARY AND CONCLUSION

This final chapter began with a theoretical and empirical discussion of deviance and social problems, explaining the fallacy of the traditional approach to those phenomena. Traditionally, deviance and social problems have been assumed to be objective phenomena and therefore amenable to scientific solution. As we saw, this is not the case. Deviance and social problems are a function of social definitions and they must be approached as such, through human dialogue. Furthermore, deviance and social problems do not refer to the behavior of one party (an individual or a group[3]) but to a process of interaction between two or more parties, for example, between an ingroup and an outgroup or between a self and others. Deviance and social problems are *relational* terms, like conflict. They are not merely behavioral terms. It therefore follows that the important question with respect to these phenomena is not "why?" but "how?". For example, when a marriage suffers from excessive quarrelling, it is generally best to

_____
[3]A common misconception occurs when laymen and students are introduced to sociology; the notion that "psychology studies the behavior of the individual" whereas "sociology studies the behavior of several or many individuals." To simply add up the behavior of a number of individuals does not make it sociology. Such a conception of sociology would imply that most human behavior consists of the type of conduct observed in about two-year-old children and called *parallel play*—behavior occurring in the presence of others but devoid of mutual interaction. It must be understood that sociology studies social *interaction*.

assume that both partners must share the blame and to proceed from there. To ask "why?" and to attempt to pin down the blame—in whatever proportion—is likely to be counterproductive. To understand the flow of interaction—viewing the family as a unit—is the more promising approach, as shown by Waller (1975), among others.

Having discussed deviance and social problems, we then examined conflict, and this finally led to a discussion of social change.

The pervasive feeling in America has been that change is necessarily for the better. Traditionally, change has mostly meant technological change, and it has been in that materialistic sense that change and progress have been equated. Today, there is the following paradox: the dominant radical liberalism now rejects the doctrine of progress through technology, attacking business, industry, and a capitalist growth economy and proposing instead new values, including environmental conservation, collectivism, a leisure ethic, and egalitarianism. As Tom Hayden said, the radicalism of the 1960s has become the common sense of the 1970s. Yet is this new consensus not another declaration of progress and the belief in the necessity of change?

As we saw earlier, Berger and his colleagues (1973) are among those who have recently questioned the benefits of modernization. Elsewhere, Berger (1974) makes the same point, vividly depicting the intolerable human cost of the modernization and economic development of the third world, whether along capitalist or socialist lines. Marris (1975), too, shows how rapid change can do violence to basic human needs. Of course, earlier sociologists like Durkheim, Thomas, and Znaniecki had already noted that social change and social disorganization are two sides of the same coin.

The questions one must ask are: What are the human costs of social change? Do those costs outweigh the benefits? If we are going to have change, change for what? Sociologists (such as Berger et al., op. cit.) and social psychologists (Marris, 1975; Shibutani, 1961) believe that there may be some *immanent* human requirements that can be ignored or transgressed only at the risk of doing serious harm to man himself. These may include a need to feel at home with oneself, society, and the world, a need for values and meaning. Modern technology has radically altered the social structure, creating a mass society and magnifying the potential for human manipulation and exploitation (cf. Shibutani, 1961: 616). However, human nature has not changed (loc. cit.).

The central task of a humanistic social psychology (cf. Smith, 1974) is to determine the facts about human behavior without doing violence to basic humanistic values and human needs. To exclude the moral question under the guise of science is an error, for man is by nature a moral creature.

The reintroduction of morality at this point may seem paradoxical, after having argued throughout this chapter and much of the book that there are no absolutes. Yet it is not: humanism does not mean nihilism. It means behavior guided by humanistic values, values that are in harmony with man's nature and that reflect this by virtue of being of his own free formulation. While this comes perilously close to an appeal to human nature, it means, of course, something entirely different than the biological determinism of the instinctivists or any other form of determinism. Throughout history, various models of man have been proposed. Aristotle's was *political man,* the classical economist's was *Homo economicus,* Huizinga (1949) wrote about *Homo ludens* (man the player), and others have postulated a *Homo faber* (man the worker) as well as various other concepts. Now, humanisitc social psychology proposes to view man essentially as a *social animal* (cf. Aronson, 1976) and, above all, a *moral animal.*

Lyman and Scott (1970) point out that a humanistic paradigm must reject the functionalists' metaphysical assumptions that social order, justice, and virtue are given. It must face the reality of conflict, power, and pluralism and the possibility of chaos and injustice. However, it is an *inner-worldly humanism* that is being proposed: social order and values are possibilities *insofar as they are accomplished by man*. Thus the total rejection of value—under the guise of either science or freedom—is a misconception of both the notion of progressive change and the humanistic ideas presented in this book. As Wheelis (1973:4) recently noted, ". . . some things are not permitted . . . there are immanent standards, of man's making but not of man's design . . . they are, therefore, to be discovered but not created . . . though not absolute they change but slowly . . . to live by them is what is meant by being human."

The question, then, is: change for what? Much change in the twentieth century has reduced man to a means while elevating ideologies and institutions to ends, thereby causing more human death and suffering than all previous centuries combined. As we forge toward the end of the century, the trend does not seem to be abating. On the left and on the right, causes, ideologies, institutions, movements, and systems are more powerful than ever, dwarfing the individual in his alienation and impotence. Perhaps we should pause before we relinquish individualism altogether and take another good look at places where it has been "transcended." It was Hitler, after all, who admonished his followers that "your people are everything; you are nothing."

Do we need change? Perhaps. But inasmuch as contemporary social change is largely unguided by humanistic values, much of it may not be for the better.

REFERENCES

Abramson, H. A. (ed.)
  1966 The Use of LSD in Psychotherapy and Alcoholism. Indianapolis: The Bobbs-Merrill Co., Inc.
Akers, R. L. et al.
  1968 "Opiate use, addiction and relapse." Social Problems 15:459-469.

Allen, James R. and Louis J. West
  1970 "Flight from violence: hippies and the green rebellion." In Youth and Drugs: Perspectives on a Social Problem. John H. McGrath and Frank R. Scarpitti (eds.). Glenview, Ill: Scott, Foresman and Co., pp. 169-177.
Allen, Vernon L. (ed.)
  1970 Psychological Factors in Poverty. Chicago: Markham Publishing Co.
Allport, Floyd H.
  1972 "Social stimulation in the group and the crowd." In Classic Contributions to Social Psychology. Edwin P. Hollander and Raymond G. Hunt (eds.). New York: Oxford University Press, pp. 306-319.
Amundsen, Kirsten
  1971 The Silenced Majority: Women and American Democracy. Englewood Cliffs, N.J.: Prentice-Hall, Inc.
Andreas, Carol
  1971 Sex and Caste in America. Englewood Cliffs, N.J.: Prentice-Hall, Inc.
Anonymous
  1972 "The doctor talks about frigidity." In Social Problems in America: Costs and Causalities in an Acquisitive Society. Harry C. Bredermeier and Jackson Toby (eds.). New York: John Wiley & Sons, Inc., pp. 124-127.
  1974 "Losing: an attempt at stigma neutralization." In Deviance: Field Studies and Self-Disclosures. Jerry Jacobs (ed.). Palo Alto, Calif.: National Press Books.
Ardrey, Robert
  1966 The Territorial Imperative. New York: Dell Publishing Co.
Arnold, David O.
  1969 "The American way of death: the roots of violence in American society." In The Age of Protest. Walt Anderson (ed.). Pacific Palisades, Calif.: Goodyear Publishing Co., Inc., pp. 262-268.
Aronson, Elliot
  1976 The Social Animal (ed. 2). San Francisco: W. H. Freeman & Co.
Bailyn, Lotte
  1964 "Notes on the role of choice in psychology of professional women." Daedalus 93 (Spring): 700-710.
Ball, Donald W.
  1970 "An abortion clinic ethnography." In Social Psychology Through Symbolic Interaction. Gregory P. Stone and Harvey A. Farberman (eds.). Waltham, Mass.: Ginn-Blaisdell, pp. 196-207.
  1975 "Privacy, publicity, deviance and control." Pacific Sociological Review (July):259-279.

Bandura, A. et al.
1963 "Imitation of film-mediated aggressive models." Journal of Abnormal and Social Psychology 66:60-72.

Bardwick, Judith M.
1971 Psychology of Women: A Study of Bio-Cultural Conflicts. New York: Harper & Row, Publishers.

Barron, Frank et al.
1964 "The hallucinogenic drugs." Scientific American (April):29-37.

Barton, Anthony
1974 Three Worlds of Therapy: An Existential-Phenomenological Study of the Therapies of Freud, Jung, and Rogers. Palo Alto, Calif.: National Press Books.

Becker, Howard S.
1953 "Becoming a marihuana user." American Journal of Sociology (November):235-242.
1962 "Marihuana use and social control." In Human Behavior and Social Processes. Arnold M. Rose (ed.). Boston: Houghton Mifflin Co., pp. 589-607.
1963 Outsiders: Studies in the Sociology of Deviance. Glencoe, Ill.: The Free Press.
1964 (ed.) The Other Side: Perspectives on Deviance. London: Collier-Macmillan Limited.
1967 "Whose side are we on?" Social Problems (Winter):239-247.
1969 "Social bases of drug-induced experiences." In Readings in Social Psychology. Alfred R. Lindesmith and Anselm L. Strauss (eds.). New York: Holt, Rinehart and Winston, pp. 156-175.
1970 Campus Power Struggle. Chicago: Aldine Publishing Co.

Bell, Robert R. and Michael Gordon (eds.)
1972 The Social Dimension of Human Sexuality. Boston: Little, Brown and Co.

Bem, Sandra L. and Daryl J. Bem
1975 "Homogenizing the American woman: the power of an unconscious ideology." In Psychology is Social. Edward Krupat (ed.). Glenview, Ill.: Scott, Foresman & Co., pp. 60-73.

Benjamin, H.
1954 "Transsexualism and transvestism as psycho-somatic and somato-psychic syndromes." American Journal of Psychotherapy 8:219-230.
1966 The Transsexual Phenomenon. New York: Julian Press.

Berg, Ronald H.
1969 "Why Americans hide behind a chemical curtain." In Current Perspectives on Social Problems (ed. 2). Judson R. Landis (ed.).

Belmont, Calif.: Wadsworth Publishing Co., Inc., pp. 68-80.

Berger, Peter L.
1974 Pyramids of Sacrifice: Political Ethics and Social Change. New York: Basic Books, Inc.

Berger, Peter et al.
1973 The Homeless Mind: Modernization and Consciousness. New York: Random House, Inc.

Berger, Peter L. and Hansfried Kellner
1970 "Marriage and the construction of reality." In Recent Sociology. Hans Peter Dreitzel (ed.). New York: The Macmillan Co., pp. 49-72.

Berger, Peter L. and Thomas Luckmann
1966 The Social Construction of Reality. Garden City, N.Y.: Doubleday & Co., Inc.

Berkowitz, Leonard
1972 "The study of urban violence: some implications of laboratory studies of frustration and aggression." In Black Psyche: The Modal Personality Patterns of Black Americans. Stanley Guterman (ed.). Berkeley, Calif.: The Glendessary Press.

Bittner, Egon
1972 "Police discretion in emergency apprehension of mentally ill persons." In An Introduction to Deviance: Readings in the Process of Making Deviants. William J. Filstead (ed.). Chicago: Markham Publishing Co., pp. 161-180.

Blauner, Robert
1964 Alienation and Freedom. Chicago: University of Chicago Press.

Bloomberg, Warner, Jr.
1969 "American violence in perspective." In Violence in America: A Historical and Contemporary Reader. Thomas Rose (ed.). New York: Vintage Books, pp. 359-371.

Blum, Richard H.
1970 "Drugs, behavior, and crime." In Youth and Drugs: Perspectives on a Social Problem. John H. McGrath and Frank R. Scarpitti (eds.). Glenville, Ill.: Scott, Foresman & Co., pp. 158-169.

Blum, Sam
1972 "Suicide." Playboy (November):148-150, 268-274.

Blumer, Herbert
1975 "Social problems as collective behavior." In Readings in Social Psychology. Alfred R. Lindesmith et al. (eds.). Hinsdale, Ill.: Dryden Press, pp. 59-66.

Bogardus, E. S.
1928 Immigration and Race Attitudes. Boston: D. C. Heath.

Boston Women's Health Book Collective
1973 Our Bodies, Our Selves. A Book by and for Women. New York: Simon and Schuster.

Bowers, Malcolm B.
1974 Retreat from Sanity: The Structure of

Emerging Psychosis. New York: Human Sciences Press.

Brecher, Ruth and Edward Brecher (eds.)
1966 An Analysis of Human Sexual Response. New York: New American Library.

Breed, Warren
1964 "Suicide and symbolic interaction." Proceedings of Southwestern Sociological Association (March):80-81.

Bronfenbrenner, Urie
1971 "The changing American child—a speculative analysis." In Selected Readings and Projects in Social Psychology. Richard R. MacDonald and James A. Schellenberg (eds.). New York: Random House, Inc.

Brown, D. B.
1961 "Transvestism and sex-role inversion." In The Encyclopedia of Sexual Behavior. A. Ellis and A. Abarbanel (eds.). New York: Hawthorne Books, Inc.

Bruce, Virginia
1967 "The expression of femininity in the male." Journal of Sex Research (May):129-140.

Bryan, James H.
1973 "Apprenticeships in prostitution." In Social Psychology in Everyday Life. Billy J. Franklin and Frank J. Kohout (eds.). New York: David McKay Co., pp. 432-446.

Buckner, H. Taylor
1970 "The transvestic career path." Psychiatry 33:381-389.
1971a "Deviants as clients and as fillers for social control agencies." In Deviance, Reality and Change. H. Taylor Buckner (ed.). New York: Random House, Inc., pp. 245-249.
1971b "Societal reactions to bad." In Deviance, Reality and Change. H. Taylor Buckner (ed.). New York: Random House, Inc., pp. 106-110.

Burgess, Ernest W.
1962 "Social problems and social processes." In Human Behavior and Social Processes. Arnold M. Rose (ed.). Boston: Houghton Mifflin Co., pp. 381-400.

Burgess, R. L. and R. L. Akers
1966 "A differential association-reinforcement theory of criminal behavior." Social Problems 14:128-147.

Burke, Peter
1969 "Scapegoating: an alternative to role differentiation." Sociometry (June):1-10.

Cadwallader, Mervyn
1969 "Marriage as a wretched institution." In Current Perspectives on Social Problems (ed. 2). Judson R. Landis (ed.). Belmont, Calif.: Wadsworth Publishing Co., Inc., pp. 231-239.

Cain, Arthur H.
1969 "Alcoholics Anonymous: cult or cure?" In Current Perspectives on Social Problems (ed. 2). Judson R. Landis (ed.). Belmont, Calif.: Wadsworth Publishing Co., Inc., pp. 80-92.

Caldwell, John M., Jr.
1948 "The present status of neuropsychiatry in the army." Military Surgeon 102:479-482.
1949 "Current developments and problems in military neuropsychiatry." American Journal of Psychiatry 105:561-566.

Cameron, Mary Owen
1973 "Identity and the shoplifter." In Deviance: The Interactionist Perspective. Earl Rubington and Martin S. Weinberg (eds.). New York: The Macmillan Co., pp. 376-380.

Cameron, N.
1943 "The paranoid pseudo-community." Journal of Marriage and the Family 26:32-38.

Cantor, Donald J.
1969 "The right of divorce." In Current Perspectives on Social Problems (ed. 2). Judson R. Landis (ed.). Belmont, Calif.: Wadsworth Publishing Co., Inc., pp. 256-265.

Cartwright, Dorwin
1964 "Some principles of mass persuasion." In Dimensions of Social Psychology. W. Edgar Vinacke and Warner W. Wilson (eds.). Chicago: Scott, Foresman and Co., pp. 297-306.

Cavan, Sherri
1966 Liquor License; An Ethnography of Bar Behavior. Chicago: Aldine Publishing Co.

Chafetz, Janet Saltzman
1974 Masculine, Feminine or Human? Itasca, Ill.: F. E. Peacock Publishers, Inc.

Chappell, Duncan et al.
1971 "Forcible rape: a comparative study of offenses known to the police in Boston and Los Angeles." In Studies in the Sociology of Sex. James H. Henslin (ed.). New York: Appleton-Century-Crofts, pp. 169-193.

Chauncey, Robert L.
1975 "Comment on the labelling theory of mental illness." American Sociological Review (April):248-251.

Chesler, Phyllis
1972 Women and Madness. Garden City, N.Y.: Doubleday & Co., Inc.

Christiansen, Karl C.
1970 "Industrialization and urbanization in relation to crime and juvenile delinquency." In Crime in the City. Daniel Glaser (ed.). New York: Harper & Row, Publishers, pp. 41-47.

Cicourel, Aaron V.
1968 The Social Organization of Juvenile Justice. New York: John Wiley & Sons, Inc.

Clausen, John A.
1971 "Mental disorders." In Contemporary Social Problems. Robert K. Merton and Robert A. Nisbet (eds.). New York: Harcourt, Brace.

Cleaver, Eldridge
1967 Soul on Ice. New York: McGraw-Hill Book Co.

Clinard, Marshall B.
1970 "The role of motivation and self-image in social change in slum areas." In Psychological Factors in Poverty. Vernon L. Allen (ed.). Chicago: Markham Publishing Co., pp. 326-347.

Cloward, Richard A.
1959 "Illegitimate means, anomie and deviant behavior." American Sociological Review (April):164-176.

Cohen, Albert K.
1959 "The study of disorganization and deviant behavior." In Sociology Today. R. K. Merton, L. Broom, and L. S. Cotrell (eds.). New York: Basic Books, Inc., pp. 461-484.

Coles, Robert
1969 "Journey into the mind of the lower depths; violence in ghetto children; stripped bare at the follies; a review; Appalachia: hunger in the hollows." Violence in America: A Historical and Contemporary Reader. In Thomas Rose (ed.). New York: Vintage Books, pp. 296-311.

Cooley, Carol H.
1951 Social Aspects of Illness. Philadelphia: W. B. Saunders Co.

Cory, Donald Webster
1971 "The unrecognized minority." In Deviance, Reality and Change. Taylor Buckner (ed.). New York: Random House, Inc., pp. 289-293.

Coulter, Jeff
1973 Approaches to Insanity: A Philosophical and Sociological Study. New York: John Wiley & Sons, Inc.

Cox, Keith K.
1973 "Changes in stereotyping of Negroes and whites in magazine advertisements." In Social Psychology in Life. Richard I. Evans and Richard M. Rozelle (eds.). Boston: Allyn and Bacon, Inc., pp. 174-180.

Cressey, D. R.
1955 "Changing criminals: the application of the theory of differential association." American Journal of Sociology 61:116-120.
1962 "Role theory, differential association, and compulsive crimes." In Human Behavior and Social Processes. Arnold M. Rose (ed.). Boston: Houghton Mifflin Co., pp. 443-467.

Cumming, John and Elaine Cumming
1968 "On the stigma of mental illness." In The Mental Patient: Studies in the Sociology of Deviance. Stephan P. Spitzer and Norman K. Denzin (eds.). New York: McGraw-Hill Book Co., pp. 409-418.

Daedalus
1964 "The woman in America." Daedalus, Journal of the American Academy of Arts and Sciences 93(2) (Spring).

Daniels, Arlene Kaplan
1970 "Development of the scapegoat in sensitivity training sessions." In Human Nature and Collective Behavior. Papers in Honor of Herbert Blumer. Tamotsu Shibutani (ed.). Englewood Cliffs, N.J.: Prentice-Hall, Inc.
1972 "The social construction of military psychiatric diagnoses." In Symbolic Interaction. Jerome G. Manis and Bernard N. Meltzer (eds.). Boston: Allyn and Bacon, Inc., pp. 554-571.
1973 "The philosophy of combat psychiatry." In Deviance: The Interactionist Perspective. Earl Rubington and Martin S. Weinberg (eds.). New York: The Macmillan Co., pp. 132-141.

Davis, Elizabeth Gould
1972 The First Sex. Baltimore: Penguin Books.

Davis, Fred
1961 "Deviance disavowal: the management of strained interaction by the visibly handicapped." Social Problems (Fall):120-132.
1969 "Definition of time and recovery in paralytic polio convalescence." In Readings in Social Psychology. Alfred R. Lindesmith and Anselm L. Strauss (ed.). New York: Holt, Rinehart and Winston, pp. 148-155.
1972 Illness, Interaction, and the Self. Belmont, Calif.: Wadsworth Publishing Co.

Delora, Joan S. and Jack R. Delora (eds.)
1972 Intimate Life Styles. Marriage and Its Alternatives. Pacific Palisades, Calif.: Goodyear Publishing Co.

Denzin, Norman K.
1968 "The self-fulfilling prophecy and patient-therapist interaction." In The Mental Patient: Studies in the Sociology of Deviance. Stephan P. Spitzer and Norman K. Denzin (eds.). New York: McGraw-Hill Book Co., pp. 349-57.

Denzin, Norman K. and Stephan P. Spitzer
1966 "Paths to the mental hospital and staff predictions of patient role behavior." Journal of Health and Human Behavior 7:265-271.

Deutscher, Irwin
1962 "Some relevant directions for research in juvenile delinquency." In Human Behavior and Social Processes. Arnold M. Rose (ed.). Boston: Houghton Mifflin Co., pp. 468-481.

Dexter, Lewis Anthony
1964 "On the politics and sociology of stupidity in our society." In The Other Side: Perspectives on Deviance. Howard S. Becker (ed.). London: Collier-Macmillan Limited, pp. 37-50.

Dinitz, Simon et al.
1968 "Integration and conflict in self-other conceptions as factors in mental illness." In The Mental Patient: Studies in the Sociology of

Deviance. Stephan P. Spitzer and Norman
K. Denzin (eds.). New York: McGraw-Hill
Book Co., pp. 367-376.

Dollard, John and Neal E. Miller
1950 Personality and Psychotherapy. New York:
McGraw-Hill Book Co.

Douglas, Jack D.
1967 The Social Meanings of Suicide. Princeton,
N.J.: Princeton University Press.
1972 Research on Deviance. New York: Random
House, Inc.

Driscoll, James P.
1971 "Transsexuals." Transaction (March-April):
28-37, 66, 68.

Dubin, Robert
1962 "Industrial workers' worlds: a study of the
'central life interests' of industrial workers."
In Human Behavior and Social Processes.
Arnold M. Rose (ed.). Boston: Houghton
Mifflin Co., pp. 247-266.

Dumont, Matthew P.
1968 The Absurd Healer: Perspectives of a Community Psychiatrist, New York: The Viking
Press.

Durkheim, Emile
1897 Le Suicide. Paris: F. Alcan.
1938 The Rules of Sociological Method. Chicago:
University of Chicago Press.

Durkheim, Emile et al.
1964 Essays on Sociology and Philosophy. Kurt H.
Wolff (ed.). New York: Harper & Row, Publishers.

Duster, Troy
1971 "Conditions for guilt-free massacre." In
Sanctions for Evil. Nevitt Sanford, Craig
Cornstock, and others (ed.). San Francisco:
Jossey-Bass, Inc., pp. 25-37.

Edgerton, Robert B.
1971 The Cloak of Competence: Stigma in the
Lives of the Mentally Retarded. Berkeley,
Calif.: University of California Press.

Edwards, John N. (ed.)
1972 Sex and Society. Chicago: Markham Publishing Co.

Ellis, Albert
1961 The Folklore of Sex. New York: Grove
Press, pp. 235-255.

Emerson, Joan
1970 "Behavior in private places: sustaining definitions of reality in gynecological examinations." In Recent Sociology. Hans Peter
Dreitzel (ed.). New York: The Macmillan
Co., pp. 73-100.

Epstein, Cynthia Fuchs
1971 Woman's Place. Berkeley, Calif.: University
of California Press.

Erikson, Kai T.
1962 "Notes on the sociology of deviance." Social
Problems (Spring):307-314.

Etzioni, Amitai and Martin Wenglinsky (es.)
1970 War and Its Prevention. New York: Harper
& Row, Publishers.

Eysenck, Hans J.
1960 "The effects of psychotherapy." In Handbook of Abnormal Psychology. Hans J. Eysenck (ed.). New York: Pitman Medical Publishing Co.

Farber, Leslie H.
1970 "Ours is the addicted society." In Youth and
Drugs: Perspectives on a Social Problem.
John H. McGrath and Frank R. Scarpitti
(eds.). Glenview, Ill.: Scott, Foresman and
Co., pp. 57-66.

Faris, Robert E. L. and H. Warren Dunham
1939 Mental Disorders in Urban Disorders. Chicago: University of Chicago Press.

Feshbach, Seymore
1961 "The stimulating versus cathartic effects of a
vicarious aggression activity." Journal of Abnormal and Social Psychology 66:381-385.

Filstead, William J. (ed.)
1972 An Introduction to Deviance: Readings in
the Process of Making Deviants. Chicago:
Markham Publishing Co.

Fisher, Charles S.
1972 "Observing a crowd: the structure and description of protest demonstrations." In Research on Deviance. Jack D. Douglas (ed.).
New York: Random House, Inc., pp. 187-
213.

Fisher, Claude S. et al.
1975 "Comments on van den Berghe." American
Sociological Review (October):674-678.

Fortes, Meyer
1962 "Ritual and office." In Essays on the Ritual
of Social Relations. Max Gluckman (ed.).
Manchester: Manchester University Press.

Frankl, Victor
1963 Man's Search for Meaning. New York: Beacon Press.

Freedman, Mervin B.
1969 "Urban campus prototype." In Violence in
America: A Historical and Contemporary
Reader. Thomas Rose (ed.). New York: Vintage Books, pp. 269-279.

Freidson, Eliot
1973 "The production of deviant populations." In
Deviance: The Interactionist Perspective.
Earl Rubington and Martin S. Weinberg
(eds.). New York: The Macmillan Co., pp.
125-128.

Freud, Sigmund
1924 A General Introduction to Psychoanalysis.
New York: Boni & Liveright Publishing
Corp.

Friedan, Betty
1963 The Feminine Mystique. New York: Dell
Publishing Co.

Fromm, Erich
1947 Man for Himself. New York: Rinehart.

1973 The Anatomy of Human Destructiveness. New York: Holt, Rinehart and Winston.

Gaertner, Samuel and Leonard Bickman
1972 "A nonreactive indicator of racial discrimination: the wrong-number technique." In Beyond the Laboratory: Field Research in Social Psychology. Leonard Bickman and Thomas Henchy (eds.). New York: McGraw-Hill Book Co., pp. 162-171.

Gagnon, John H. and William Simon (eds.).
1967 Sexual Deviance. New York: Harper & Row, Publishers.
1970 The Sexual Scene. Chicago: Aldine Publishing Co.

Garfinkel, Harold
1956 "Conditions of successful degradation ceremonies." American Journal of Sociology 61:420-424.
1967 Studies in Ethnomethodology. Englewood Cliffs, N.J.: Prentice-Hall, Inc.

Gaugh, Harrison, G.
1968 "A sociological theory of psychopathy." In The Mental Patient: Studies in the Sociology of Deviance. Stephan P. Spitzer and Norman K. Denzin (eds.). New York: McGraw-Hill Book Co., pp. 60-68.

Gergen, Kenneth J.
1971 The Concept of Self. New York: Holt, Rinehart and Winston, Inc.

Gibbs, Jack P.
1961 "Suicide." In Contemporary Social Problems. Robert K. Merton and Robert A. Nisbet (eds.). New York: Harcourt, Brace & World, Inc., pp. 222-262.
1966 "Conceptions of deviant behavior: the old and the new." Pacific Sociological Review (Spring):9-14.

Gilder, George
1973 Sexual Suicide. New York: Quadrangle.

Glaser, Daniel
1962 "The differential-association theory of crime." In Human Behavior and Social Processes. Arnold M. Rose (ed.). Boston: Houghton Mifflin Co., pp. 425-442.
1970 "Violence and the city." In Crime in the City. Daniel Glaser (ed.). New York: Harper & Row, Publishers, pp. 200-209.

Glaser, Barney G. and Anselm L. Strauss
1965 Awareness of Dying. Chicago: Aldine Publishing Co.

Goffman, Erving
1957 "Alienation from interaction." Human Relations 1:47-59.
1958 "Characteristics of total institutions: the inmate world." In Symposium on Preventive and Social Psychiatry. Washington, D.C.: U.S. Government Printing Office.

1959 "The moral career of the mental patient." Psychiatry (May):123-142.
1961 Asylums. Garden City, N.Y.: Doubleday and Co., Inc.
1963 Stigma: Notes on the Management of Spoiled Identity. Englewood Cliffs. N.J.: Prentice-Hall, Inc.
1969 "The insanity of place." Psychiatry: Journal for the Study of Interpersonal Processes (November):357-388.

Goldberg, Steven
1973 The Inevitability of Patriarchy. New York: William Morrow.

Gornick, Vivian and Barbara K. Moran (eds.)
1971 Woman in Sexist Society. New York: New American Library.

Gottlieb, David
1957 "The neighborhood tavern and the cocktail lounge: a study of class differences." American Journal of Sociology 62:559-562.

Gove, Walter R.
1970 "Societal reaction as an explanation of mental illness: an evaluation." American Sociological Review (October):873-884.
1974 "Individual resources and mental hospitalization: a comparison and evaluation of the societal reaction and psychiatric perspectives." American Sociological Review (February):86-100.

Gove, Walter R. and Jeannette F. Tudor
1973 "Adult sex roles and mental illness." American Journal of Sociology (January):812-836.

Green, Richard and John Money
1969 Transsexualism and Sex Reassignment. Baltimore: Johns Hopkins Press.

Greer, Germaine
1973 "Seduction is a four-letter word." Playboy (January):80-82, 164, 178, 224-28.

Gruenberg, Ernest M.
1954 "The epidemiology of mental disease." Scientific American (March):2-6.

Gusfield, Joseph R.
1972 "Moral passage: the symbolic process in public designations of deviance." In An Introduction to Deviance. William J. Filstead (ed.). Chicago: Markham Publishing Co., pp. 61-77.

Hamburger, Christian, et al.
1953 "Transvestism: hormonal, psychiatric and surgical treatment." Journal of the American Medical Association (May 30):391-396.

Haythorn, William W. and Irwin Altman
1973 "Together in isolation." In Social Psychology: A Transaction—Society Reader. Elliot Aronson and Robert Helmreich (eds.). New York: D. Van Nostrand Co., pp. 151-255.

Headley, Joel Tyler
1969 "Draft riots of 1863." In Violence in America: A Historical and Contemporary Reader. Thomas Rose (ed.). New York: Vintage Books, pp. 112-122.

Heiss, Jerold (ed.)
1968 Family Roles and Interaction: An Anthology. Chicago: Rand McNally.
Henry, Jules
1966 "Forty-year old jitters in married urban women." In Challenge to Women. Farber Seymour (ed.). New York: Basic Books, Inc., pp. 146-152.
1973 On Sham, Vulnerability and Other Forms of Self-Destruction. New York: Vintage Books.
Henslin, James M.
1971a "Criminal abortion: making the decision and neutralizing the act." In Studies in the Sociology of Sex. New York: Appleton-Century-Crofts, pp. 113-137.
1971b (ed.) Studies in the Sociology of Sex. New York: Appleton-Century-Crofts.
Henslin, James M. and Mae A. Biggs
1971 "Dramaturgical desexualization: the sociology of the vaginal examination." In Studies in the Sociology of Sex. James M. Henslin (ed.). New York: Appleton-Century-Crofts, pp. 243-272.
Heron, Woodburn
1957 "The pathology of boredom." In Mass Leisure. Eric Larrabee and Rolf Meyersohn (eds.). Glencoe, Ill.: The Free Press, pp. 136-141.
Hess, Robert D.
1970 "The transmission of cognitive strategies in poor families: the socialization of apathy and underachievement." In Psychological Factors in Poverty. Vernon L. Allen (ed.). Chicago: Markham Publishing Co., pp. 73-92.
Hirschi, T.
1962 "The professional prostitute." Berkeley Journal of Sociology 7:33-49.
Hollingshead, August B. and Frederick C. Redlich
1958 Social Class and Mental Illness: A Community Study. New York: John Wiley & Sons, Inc.
Hooker, Evelyn
1965 "The homosexual community." In Perspectives in Psychopathology. James O. Palmer and Michael J. Goldstein (eds.). New York: Oxford University Press.
Horner, Matina S.
1975 "Femininity and successful achievement: a basic inconsistency." In Psychology Is Social. Edward Krupat (ed.). Glenview, Ill.: Scott, Foresman & Co., pp. 78-85.
Hubbard, Jeffrey C. et al.
1975 "Mass media influences on public conceptions of social problems." Social Problems (October):22-34.
Hughes, Everett C.
1964 "Good people and dirty work." In The Other Side: Perspectives on Deviance. Howard S. Becker (ed.). London: Collier-Macmillan Limited.
Hughes, Langston
1970 "Who's passing for who?" In Social Psychology Through Symbolic Interaction. Gregory P. Stone and Harvey A. Farberman (eds.). Waltham, Mass.: Ginn-Blaisdell, pp. 237-239.
Huizinga, Johan
1949 Homo Ludens: A Study of the Play Elements in Culture. London: Routledge and Kegan Paul Ltd.
Humphreys, Laud
1970 Tearoom Trade: Impersonal Sex in Public Places. Chicago: Aldine Publishing Co.
1972 Out of the Closet. The Sociology of Homosexual Liberation. Englewood Cliffs, N.J.: Prentice-Hall, Inc.
Jackson, Don D.
1962 "Schizophrenia." Scientific American (August): 3-11.
Jacobs, Jerry
1974 "The clinical organization of 'subnormality': a case of mistaken identity." In Deviance: Field Studies and Self-Disclosures. Jerry Jacobs (ed.). Palo Alto, Calif.: National Press Books, pp. 154-163.
Jaeger, Getrude and Philip Selznick
1973 "A normative theory of culture." In Readings in Social Psychology—A Symbolic Interaction Perspective. J. D. Cardwell (ed.). Philadelphia: F. A. Davis Co., pp. 101-126.
Jellinek, E. M.
1952 "Phases of alcohol addiction." Quarterly Journal of Studies on Alcohol 13:673-684.
Jewell, Donald P.
1973 "A case of a 'psychotic' Navaho Indian male." In Deviance: The Interactionist Perspective. Earl Rubington and Martin S. Weinberg (eds.). New York: The Macmillan Co., pp. 69-77.
Johnson, Nora
1969 "A marriage on the rocks." In Current Perspectives on Social Problems (ed. 2). Judson R. Landis (ed.). Belmont, Calif.: Wadsworth Publishing Co., pp. 248-256.
Johnson, Rita Volkman and Donald R. Cressey
1963 "Differential association and the rehabilitation of drug addicts." American Journal of Sociology (September):129-142.
Johnson, Wendell
1973 "Stuttering: how the problem develops." In Social Psychology in Everyday Life. Billy J. Franklin and Frank J. Kohout (eds.). New York: David McKay Co., pp. 202-212.
Jorgensen, Christine
1968 A Personal Autobiography. New York: Bantam Books.
Juhasz, Anne McCreary (ed.)
1973 Sexual Development and Behavior. Homewood, Ill.: Dorsey Press.

Kadushin, Charles
1966 "The friends and supporters of psychotherapy: on social circles in urban life."
American Sociological Review (December):786-802.
Kando, Thomas
1972a "Passing and stigma management: the
case of the transsexual." Sociological Quarterly (Fall): 475-483.
1972b "Role strain: a comparison of males, females and transsexuals." Journal of Marriage and the Family (August):459-464.
1972c "The projection of intolerance: a comparison of males, females and transsexuals." The
Journal of Sex Research 8 (August):
225-236.
1973 Sex Change: The Achievement of Gender
Identity Among Feminized Transsexuals.
Springfield, Ill.: Charles C Thomas, Publisher.
1974 "Males, females and transsexuals." Journal
of Homosexuality (Fall):45-64.
1975 Leisure and Popular Culture in Transition.
St. Louis: The C. V. Mosby Co.
1976 "Any progress on the cultural front? (how to
pass between the scylla of elitism and the
charybdis of know-nothing populism)."
American Sociological Association (August).
Kanter, Rosabeth Moss
1972 Commitment and Community: Communes
and Utopias in Sociological Perspective.
Cambridge, Mass.: Harvard University
Press.
Kaplan, Bert et al.
1968 "A comparison of the incidence of hospital-
ized and non-hospitalized cases of psychosis
in two communities." In The Mental Patient:
Studies in the Sociology of Deviance. Stephan P. Spitzer and Norman K. Denzin
(eds.). New York: McGraw-Hill Book Co.,
pp. 111-121.
Katz, Elihu and Paul F. Lazarsfeld
1971 "Two-step flow of communication." In Selected Readings and Projects in Social Psychology. Richard R. MacDonald and James
A. Schellenberg (eds.). New York: Random
House, Inc., p. 68.
Keniston, Kenneth
1971 Youth and Dissent. The Rise of a New Opposition. New York: Harcourt, Brace, Jovanovich.
Kerckhoff, Alan C.
1973 "Sociometric patterns in hysterical con-
tagion." In Social Psychology in Everyday
Life. Billy J. Franklin and Frank S. Kohout
(eds.). New York: David McKay Co., pp.
495-507.

Kerner, Otto
1968 Report of the National Advisory Commis-
sion on Civil Disorders. New York: Bantam
Books.
Kesey, Ken
1962 One Flew Over the Cuckoo's Next. New
York: Signet.
King, Martin Luther
1969 "The Montgomery bus boycott." In The Age
of Protest. Walt Anderson (ed.). Pacific Palisades, Calif.: Goodyear Publishing Co., Inc.,
pp. 81-92.
Kinsey, A. C. et al.
1948 Sexual Behavior in the Human Male. Philadelphia: W. B. Saunders Co.
Kitsuse, John I.
1972 "Deviance, deviant behavior, and deviants:
some conceptual issues." In An Introduction
to Deviance. William J. Filstead (ed.). Chicago: Markham Publishing Co., pp. 233-244.
1973 "Societal reaction to deviant behavior." In
Deviance: The Interactionist Perspective.
Earl Rubington and Martin S. Weinberg
(eds.). New York: The Macmillan Co., pp.
16-26.
Kitsuse, John I. and Aaron V. Cicourel
1972 "A note on the uses of official statistics." In
An Introduction to Deviance: Readings in
the Process of Making Deviants. William J.
Filstead (ed.). Chicago: Markham Publishing
Co., pp. 244-255.
Klapp, Orrin E.
1962 Heroes, Villains, and Fools: The Changing
American Character. Englewood Cliffs,
N.J.: Prentice-Hall, Inc.
Kohn, Melvin L. et al.
1972 "Situational patterning in intergroup rela-
tions." In Beyond the Laboratory: Field Re-
search in Social Psychology. Leonard Bick-
man and Thomas Henchy (eds.). New York:
McGraw-Hill Book Co., pp. 309-319.
Komarovsky, Mirra
1966 "Women's roles: problems and polemics." In
Challenge to Women. Seymour M. Farber
(ed.). New York: Basic Books, pp. 20-33.
Krim, Seymour
1970 "The insanity bit." In Social Psychology
Through Symbolic Interaction. Gregory P.
Stone and Harvey A. Farberman (eds.).
Waltham, Mass.: Ginn-Blaisdell, pp. 626-
636.
Kunkel, John H.
1974 "Review of the Homeless Mind: Modernization and Consciousness, by Peter Berger."
American Journal of Sociology (September):543-546.
Laing, R. D.
1959 The Divided Self. London: Tavistock Publications.
Lambert, Richard D. and Alan W. Heston (eds.)
1971 "Students protest." The Annals of the Amer-

ican Academy of Political and Social Science
(May).

Lambert, William Wilson
1971 "Cross-cultural backgrounds to personality
development and the socialization of aggression: findings from the six culture study." In
Comparative Perspectives on Social Psychology. William Wilson Lambert and Rita Weisbrod (eds.). Boston: Little, Brown and Co.,
pp. 49-62.

Lang, Kurt and Gladys Engel Lang
1961 Collective Dynamics. New York: Thomas Y.
Crowell Co.
1962 "Collective dynamics: process and form." In
Human Behavior and Social Processes. Arnold M. Rose (ed.). Boston: Houghton Mifflin Co., pp. 340-359.

Learner, Steve
1969 "A visit to Chicago: blood, sweat, and tears."
In Violence in America: A Historical and
Contemporary Reader. Thomas Rose (ed.).
New York: Vintage Books, pp. 317-327.

Lemert, Edwin M.
1951a Social Pathology. New York: McGraw-Hill
Book Co.
1951b "Speech defect and the speech defective."
In Social Pathology. New York: McGraw-
Hill Book Co., pp. 151-153.
1962 "Paranoia and the dynamics of exclusion."
Sociometry (March):2-20.

Lindesmith, Alfred R.
1947 Opiate Addiction. Bloomington, Ind.: Principia.
1968 Addiction and Opiates. Chicago: Aldine
Publishing Co.
1969 "A symbolic interactionist view of addiction."
In Readings in Social Psychology. Alfred R.
Lindesmith and Anselm L. Strauss (eds.).
New York: Holt, Rinehart and Winston, pp.
176-191.
1975 "A Reply to McAuliffe and Gordon's 'A Test
of Lindesmith's Theory of Addiction.'"
American Journal of Sociology (July):147-
153.

Lindesmith, Alfred R. and Anselm L. Strauss
1956 Social Psychology: The Revised Edition.
New York: Holt, Rinehart and Winston.

Lindesmith, Alfred R., Anselm L. Strauss, and Norman K. Denzin
1975 Social Psychology (ed. 4). Hinsdale, Ill.: Dryden Press.

Lippmann, Walter
1922 Public Opinion. New York: Harcourt, Brace.

Loeb, Martin B.
1968 "Some dominant cultural themes in a psychiatric hospital." In the Mental Patient: Studies in the Sociology of Deviance. Stephan P.
Spitzer and Norman K. Denzin (eds.). New
York: McGraw-Hill Book Co., pp. 305-310.

Lofland, John F. and Robert A. Lejeune
1960 "Initial interaction of newcomers in Alcohol-

ics Anonymous." Social Problems 8:102-
111.

Lofland, John with the assistance of Lyn H. Lofland
1969 Deviance and Identity. Englewood Cliffs,
N.J.: Prentice-Hall, Inc.

Lofland, John and Rodney Stark
1975 "Becoming a world-saver: a theory of conversion to a deviant perspective." In Readings in Social Psychology. Alfred R. Lindesmith et al. (eds.). Hinsdale, Ill.: Dryden
Press, pp. 364-382.

Lorber, J.
1967 "Deviance as performance: the case of illness." Social Problems 14:302-310.

Lorenz, Konrad
1966 On Aggression. New York: Harcourt Brace.

Lukacs, John
1969 "America's malady is not violence but sav-
agery." In Violence in America: A Historical
and Contemporary Reader. Thomas Rose
(ed.). New York: Vintage Books, pp. 349-
359.

Lyman, Stanford M. and Marvin B. Scott
1970 "Paranoic, homosexuality, and game
theory." In A Sociology of the Absurd. New
York: Appleton-Century-Crofts, pp. 71-88.
1970 A Sociology of the Absurd. New York:
Meredith Corp.

Mannheim, Karl
1936 Ideology and Utopia. New York: Harcourt,
Brace and World.

Manning, Peter M.
1971 "Fixing what you feared: notes on the
campus abortion search." In Studies in the
Sociology of Sex. James H. Henslin (ed.).
New York: Appleton-Century-Crofts, pp.
137-169.

Marmor, Judd
1969 "Some psychosocial aspects of contemporary
urban violence." In Violence in America: A
Historical and Contemporary Reader.
Thomas Rose (ed.). New York: Vintage
Books, pp. 338-349.

Marris, Peter
1975 Loss and Change. Garden City, N.Y.: Anchor Books.

Martindale, Don and Edith Martindale
1973 Psychiatry and the Law: The Crusade
Against Involuntary Hospitalization. St.
Paul, Minn.: Windflower Publishing Co.

Marx, Karl and Friedrick Engels
1930 The Communist Manifesto. New York: International Publishers.

Maslow, A. H. and Bela Mittelmann
1951 Principles of Abnormal Psychology: The Dynamics of Psychic Illness. New York: Harper
& Row, Publishers.

Masters, William H. and Virginia E. Johnson
1966 "Counseling with sexually incompatible marriage partners." In An Analysis of Human Sexual Response. Ruth and Edward Brecher (eds.). New York: New American Library, pp. 203-219.

Matza, David
1961 "Subterranean traditions of youth." Annals of the American Academy of Political and Social Science (November):102-118.
1969 Becoming Deviant. Englewood Cliffs, N.J.: Prentice-Hall, Inc.

Mauss, Armand L.
1975 Social Problems as Social Movements. Philadelphia: J. B. Lippincott Co.

McAuliffe, William E. and Robert A. Gordon
1974 "A test of Lindesmith's theory of addiction: the frequency of euphoria among long-term addicts." American Journal of Sociology (January):795-840.

McCall, George J. and J. L. Simmons
1966 "Social acts and social objects." In Identities and Interaction. Glencoe, Ill.: The Free Press.

McHugh, Peter
1968 Defining the Situation; The Organization of Meaning in Social Interaction. Indianapolis: The Bobbs-Merrill Co.

McIntosh, Mary
1972 "The homosexual role." In The Social Dimension of Human Sexuality. Robert E. Bell and Michael Gordon (eds.). Boston: Little, Brown & Co., pp. 176-189.

McPartland, Thomas S. et al.
1967 Self-conception and ward behavior in two psychiatric hospitals." In Symbolic Interaction: A Reader in Social Psychology. Jerome G. Manis and Bernard N. Heltzer (eds.). Boston: Allyn and Bacon, pp. 445-459.

McPhail, Clark
1972 "Student walkout: a fortuitous examination of elementary collective behavior." In Symbolic Interaction. Jerome G. Manis and Bernard N. Meltzer (eds.). Boston: Allyn and Bacon, pp. 208-225.

Mead, George Herbert
1956 On Social Psychology. Anselm Strauss (ed.). Chicago: University of Chicago Press.

Mead, Margaret
1970 "The generation gap." In Sex Roles in Changing Society. Georgene H. Seward and Robert C. Williamson (eds.). New York: Random House, Inc., pp. 404-406.

Mechanic, David
1968 "Some factors in identifying and defining mental illness." In The Mental Patient: Studies in the Sociology of Deviance. Stephan P. Spitzer and Norman K. Denzin (eds.). New York: McGraw-Hill Book Co., pp. 195-202.
1969 Mental Health and Social Policy. Howard E. Freeman (ed.). Englewood Cliffs, N.J.: Prentice-Hall, Inc.

Mercer, Jane R.
1973 "Labeling the mentally retarded." In Deviance: The Interactionist Perspective. Earl Rubington and Martin S. Weinberg (eds.). New York: The Macmillan Co., pp. 77-88.

Merton, Robert
1948 "The self-fulfilling prophecy." Antioch Review (Summer).

Merton, Robert K. and Robert Nisbet
1971 Contemporary Social Problems (ed. 3). New York: Harcourt, Brace.

Micossi, Anita Lynn
1973 "Conversion to women's lib." In Social Psychology: A Transaction-Society Reader. Elliot Aronson and Robert Helmreich (eds.). New York: D. Van Nostrand Co., pp. 74-83.

Milgram, Stanley
1965 "Some conditions of obedience and disobedience to authority." Human Relations 18:57-76.

Milgram, Stanley et al.
1972 "Note on the power of crowds of different size." In Beyond the Laboratory: Field Research in Social Psychology. Leonard Bickman and Thomas Henchy (eds.). New York: McGraw-Hill Book Co., pp. 196-199.

Miller, Arthur
1969 "The bored and the violent." In Current Perspectives on Social Problems (ed. 2). Judson R. Landis (ed.). Belmont, Calif.: Wadsworth Publishing Co., pp. 49-59.

Miller, Merle
1972 "What it means to be homosexual." In Social Problems in America: Costs and Causalities in a Requisitive Society. Harry C. Bredermeier and Jackson Toby (eds.). New York: John Wiley & Sons, Inc., pp. 128-133.

Miller, Walter B.
1973 "White gangs." In Social Psychology: A Transaction-Society Reader. Elliot Aronson and Robert Helmreich (eds.). New York: D. Van Nostrand Co., pp. 102-116.

Miller, Walter B. et al.
1961 "Aggression in a boy's street-corner group." Psychiatry 24:283-293.

Mills, C. Wright
1951 White Collar: The American Middle Classes. New York: Oxford University Press.

Morris, Desmond
1967 The Naked Ape. New York: McGraw-Hill Book Co.

Moskos, Charles C.
1973 "Why men fight: American combat soldiers in Vietnam." In Readings in Social Psychology—A Symbolic Interaction Perspective. J. D. Cardwell (ed.). Philadelphia: F. A. Davis Co., pp. 153-168.

Mulford, Harold A.
1968 "Drinking and deviant drinking, U.S.A., 1963." In The Mental Patient: Studies in the Sociology of Deviance. Stephan P. Spitzer and Norman K. Denzin (eds.). New York: McGraw-Hill Book Co., pp. 155-163.

Murphy, H. B. M., E. D. Wittkower, J. Fried, and H. Ellenberger
1968 "A cross-cultural survey of schizophrenic symptomatology." In The Mental Patient: Studies in the Sociology of Deviance. Stephan P. Spitzer and Norman K. Denzin (eds.). New York: McGraw-Hill Book Co., pp. 164-177.

Myrdal, Gunnar, with the assistance of Richard Sterner and Arnold Rose
1944 An American Dilemma. New York: Harper & Row, Publishers.

Natanson, Maurice
1970 The Journeying Self: A Study in Philosophy and Social Role. Menlo Park, Calif.: Addison-Wesley Publishing Co.

Nichols, John R.
1965 "How opiates change behavior." Scientific American (February):80-88.

Nisbet, Richard E. and David E. Kanouse
1972 "Obesity, food deprivation, and supermarket shopping behavior." In Beyond the Laboratory: Field Research in Social Psychology. Leonard Bickman and Thomas Henchy (eds.). New York: McGraw-Hill Book Co., pp. 275-280.

Opler, Marvin K.
1957 "Schizophrenia and culture." Scientific American (August): 3-7.

Opton, Edward M., Jr.
1971 "It never happened and besides they deserved it." In Sanctions for Evil. Nevitt Sanford, Craig Comstock, and others (eds.). San Francisco: Jossey-Bass, Inc., pp. 49-71.

Owen, C.
1962 "Feminine roles and social mobility in weekly magazines." Social Research 10 (November): 283-296.

Palmer, Mary B.
1968 "Social rehabilitation for mental patients." In The Mental Patient: Studies in the Sociology of Deviance. Stephan P. Spitzer and Norman K. Denzin (eds.). New York: McGraw-Hill Book Co., pp. 445-448.

Pauly, Ira B.
1973 "Female transsexualism." In Proceedings of the Second Interdisciplinary Symposium on Gender Dysphoria Syndrome. Stanford, Calif.: Stanford University, Division of Reconstructive and Rehabilitation Surgery.

Payne, William D.
1973 "Negative labels: passageways and prisons." In Readings in Social Psychology—A Symbolic Interaction Perspective. J. D. Cardwell (ed.). Philadelphia: F. A. Davis Co., pp. 49-62.

Perls, Fritz
1969 Gestalt Therapy Verbatim. Lafayette, Calif.: Real People Press.

Pinard, Maurice et al.
1973 "Process of recruitment in the sit-in movement." In Social Psychology in Everyday Life. Billy J. Franklin and Frank J. Kohout (eds.). New York: David McKay Co., pp. 481-494.

Plath, David W. and Yoshie Sugihara
1973 "A case of ostracism and its unusual aftermath." In Social Psychology: A Transaction-Society Reader. Elliot Aronson and Robert Helmreich (eds.). New York: D. Van Nostrand Co., pp. 145-150.

Powell, Elwin H.
1962 "Beyond utopia: the 'beat generation' as a challenge for the sociology of knowledge." In Human Behavior and Social Processes. Arnold M. Rose (ed.). Boston: Houghton Mifflin Co., pp. 360-380.

Rainwater, Lee
1970 "Neutralizing the disinherited: some psychological aspects of understanding the poor." In Psychological Factors in Poverty. Vernon L. Allen (ed.). Chicago: Markham Publishing Co., pp. 9-28.

Ransford, H. Edward
1973 "Isolation, powerlessness, and violence: a study of attitudes and participation in the Watts riot." In Social Psychology in Everyday Life. Billy J. Franklin and Frank J. Kohout (eds.). New York: David McKay Co., pp. 380-395.

Ray, Marsh B.
1961 "Abstinence cycles and heroin addicts." Social Problems (Fall):132-140.

Ray, Oakley S.
1972 Drugs, Society and Human Behavior. St. Louis: The C. V. Mosby Co.

Reckless, Walter C.
1967 "Pioneering with self-concept as a vulnerability factor in delinquency." Journal of Criminal Law, Criminology and Police Science 58:515-523.

Reckless, Walter C. et al.
1957 "The self-concept in potential delinquency and potential nondelinquency." American Sociological Review 25:566-570.

Reckless, Walter C. and Ellen Murray
1956 "Self-concept as an insulator against delinquency." American Sociological Review 21:744-746.

Reich, Charles A.
1970 The Greening of America. New York: Random House, Inc.

Reiss, Albert J., Jr.
1973 "The social integration of queers and peers."

In Deviance: The Interactionist Perspectives. Earl Rubington and Martin S. Weinberg (eds.). New York: The Macmillan Co., pp. 395-406.

Riesman, David
1964 "Two generations." Daedulus 93 (Spring): 711-735.

Riesman, David with Nathan Glazer and Reul Denney
1950 The Lonely Crowd. New Haven, Conn.: Yale University Press.

Roberts, Bertram H. and Jerome K. Myers
1968 "Religion, national origin, immigration and mental illness." In The Mental Patient: Studies in the Sociology of Deviance. Stephan P. Spitzer and Norman K. Denzin (eds.). New York: McGraw-Hill Book Co., pp. 139-147.

Roberts, Ron E. and Robert Marsh Kloss
1974 Social Movements: Between the Balcony and the Barricade. St. Louis: The C. V. Mosby Co.

Rodriguez, Octavio
1974 "Getting straight: reflections of a former addict." In Deviance: Field Studies and Self-Disclosures. Jerry Jacobs (ed.). Palo Alto, Calif.: National Press Books.

Rogers, Carl R.
1952 "Dealing with interpersonal conflict." Pastoral Psychology 3:14-20.
1961 On Becoming a Person. Boston: Houghton Mifflin Co.

Rogler, Lloyd H. and August B. Hollingshead
1971 "Escape into schizophrenia." In Selected Readings and Projects in Social Psychology. Richard R. MacDonald and James A. Schellenberg (eds.). New York: Random House, Inc.

Rose, Arnold M. (ed.)
1962a Human Behavior and Social Processes: An Interactionist Approach. Boston: Houghton Mifflin Co.
1962b "A social-psychological theory of neurosis." In Human Behavior and Social Processes. Arnold M. Rose (ed.). Boston: Houghton Mifflin Co., pp. 537-549.

Rose, Thomas
1969 "How violence occurs: a theory and review of the literature." In Violence in America: A Historical and Contemporary Reader. Thomas Rose (ed.). New York: Vintage Books, pp. 26-57.

Rosen, George
1969 Madness in Society: Chapters in the Historical Sociology of Mental Illness. New York: Harper & Row, Publishers.

Rosengren, William P.
1972 "The self in the emotionally disturbed." In Symbolic Interaction. Jerome G. Manis and Bernard N. Meltzer (eds.). Boston: Allyn and Bacon, pp. 509-520.

Rubington, Earl and Martin S. Weinberg
1973 Deviance: The Interactionist Perspective. New York: The Macmillan Co.

Sacramento Union
1974 "Working for survival." (December 7).

Sagarin, Edward and Donald E. J. MacNamara
1968 Problems of Sex Behavior. New York: Thomas Y. Crowell Co.

Sampson, Harold et al.
1973 "Family processes and becoming a mental patient." In Deviance: The Interactionist Perspective. Earl Rubington and Martin Weinberg (eds.). New York: The Macmillan Co., pp. 42-52.

Sanford, Nevitt and Craig Comstock
1971 "Social destructiveness as disposition and as act." In Sanctions for Evil. San Francisco: Jossey-Bass, pp. 323-337.

Sarbin, Theodore R.
1970 "The culture of poverty, social identity, and cognitive outcomes." In Psychological Factors in Poverty. Vernon L. Allen (ed.). Chicago: Markham Publishing Co., pp. 29-46.

Sartre, Jean-Paul
1956 Being and Nothingness: An Essay on Phenomenological Ontology. New York: Philosophical Library.

Schary, Dore
1969 "The mass media and prejudice." In Prejudice U.S.A. Charles Y. Glock and Ellen Siegelman. New York: Praeger Publishers, Inc., pp. 96-112.

Scheff, Thomas J.
1964 "The societal reaction to deviance: ascriptive elements in the psychiatric screening of mental patients in a midwestern state." Social Problems 11:401-413.
1966 Being Mentally Ill. Chicago: Aldine Publishing Co.
1968 "The role of the mentally ill and the dynamics of mental disorder: a research framework." In The Mental Patient: Studies in the Sociology of Deviance. Stephan P. Spitzer and Norman K. Denzin (eds.). New York: McGraw-Hill Book Co., pp. 8-21.
1970 "Mental illness as residual deviance." In Social Psychology Through Symbolic Interaction. Gregory P. Stone and Harvey A. Farberman (eds.). Waltham, Mass.: Ginn-Blaisdell, pp. 645-652.
1973 "Typification in rehabilitation agencies." In Deviance: The Interactionist Perspective. Earl Rubington and Martin S. Weinberg (eds.). New York: The Macmillan Co., pp. 128-132.
1974 "The labeling theory of mental illness." American Sociological Review (June):444-543.

1975 "Reply to Chauncey and Gove." American Sociological Review (April):252-257.

Scher, Jordan
1970 "Patterns and profiles of addiction and drug abuse." In Youth and Drugs: Perspectives on a Social Problem. John H. McGrath and Frank R. Scarpitti (eds.). Glenview, Ill.: Scott, Foresman and Co., pp. 25-40.

Scherer, Klaus R. et al.
1975 Human Aggression and Conflict. Englewood Cliffs, N.J.: Prentice-Hall, Inc.

Schur, Edwin M.
1971 Labeling Deviant Behavior: Its Sociological Implications. New York: Harper & Row, Publishers.

Schutz, Alfred
1970 On Phenomenology and Social Relations. Helmut R. Wagner (ed.). Chicago: University of Chicago Press.

Schwartz, Richard D. and Jerome H. Skolnick
1964 "Two studies in legal stigma." In The Other Side: Perspectives on Deviance. Howard S. Becker (ed.). London: Collier-Macmillan Ltd., p. 117.

Scott, Robert A.
1972 "The selection of clients by social welfare agencies: The case of the blind." In An Introduction to Deviance: Readings in the Process of Making Deviants. William J. Filstead (ed.). Chicago: Markham Publishing Co., pp. 181-194.

Seward, Georgene H. and Robert C. Williamson
1970 Sex Roles in Changing Society. New York: Random House, Inc.

Shearing, C. D. and M. G. Petrunik
1972 "Normative and phenomenological approaches to the study of deviance." American Sociological Association (August).

Sherif, Muzafer
1956 "Experiments in group conflict." Scientific American (November):2-6.
1972 "Superordinate goals in the reduction of intergroup conflict." In Classic Contributions to Social Psychology. Edwin P. Hollander and Raymond G. Hunt (eds.). New York: Oxford University Press, pp. 384-392.

Shibutani, Tamotsu
1961 Society and Personality: An Interactionist Approach to Social Psychology. Englewood Cliffs, N.J.: Prentice-Hall, Inc.
1966 Improvised News: A Sociological Study of Rumor. Indianapolis: Bobbs-Merrill Co.

Short, J. F. and F. L. Strodtbeck
1965 Group Process and Gang Delinquency. Chicago: University of Chicago Press.

Shostrom, Everett L.
1968 Man, the Manipulator: the Inner Journey from Manipulation to Actualization. New York: Bantam Books.

Simmel, Georg
1971 On Individuality and Social Forms. Donald N. Levine (ed.). Chicago: The University of Chicago Press.

Simmons, J. L.
1964 "On maintaining deviant belief systems." Social Problems 11:250-256.

Smith, Harvey L. and Jean Thrasher
1968 "Roles, cliques, and sanctions: dimensions of patient society." In The Mental Patient: Studies in the Sociology of Deviance. Stephan P. Spitzer and Norman K. Denzin (eds.). New York: McGraw-Hill Book Co., pp. 316-324.

Smith, M. Brewster
1974 Humanizing Social Psychology. San Francisco: Jossey-Bass.

Sobel, Raymond and Ardis Ingalls
1968 "Resistance to treatment: explorations of the patient's sick role." In The Mental Patient: Studies in the Sociology of Deviance. Stephan P. Spitzer and Norman K. Denzin (eds.). New York: McGraw-Hill Book Co., pp. 324-334.

Sorokin, Pitirim
1956 The American Sex Revolution. Boston: Porter Sargent Publications.

Spitzer, Stephan P. and Norman K. Denzin (eds.)
1968 The Mental Patient: Studies in the Sociology of Deviance. New York: McGraw-Hill Book Co.

Stark, Margaret J. Abudu et al.
1974 "Some empirical patterns in a riot process." American Sociological Review (December):865-876.

Stebbins, Robert A.
1972 "Studying the definition of the situation: theory and field research strategies." In Symbolic Interaction. Jerome G. Manis and Bernard N. Meltzer (eds.). Boston: Allyn and Bacon, pp. 337-355.

Stoller, Robert J.
1968 Sex and Gender: On the Development of Masculinity and Femininity. Naw York: Science House.

Stone, I. F.
1969 "The pilgrimage of Malcolm X." In The Age of Protest. Walt Anderson (ed.). Pacific Palisades, Calif.: Goodyear Publishing Co., pp. 121-131.

Storr, Anthony
1972 Human Destructiveness. New York: Basic Books, Inc.

Sullerot, Evelyne
1971 Woman, Society and Change. New York: McGraw-Hill Book Co.

Sullivan, H. S.
1953 The Interpersonal Theory of Psychiatry. New York: W. W. Norton & Co.

Sutherland, Edwin H.
1947 Principles of Criminology. New York: J. B. Lippincott Co.

Swanson, G. E.
1953 "A preliminary laboratory study of the acting crowd." American Sociological Review (October):522-533.

Sykes, Gresham M. and David Matza
1957 "Techniques of neutralization: a theory of delinquency." American Sociological Review (December):667-670.

Szasz, Thomas S.
1956 "Malingering: diagnosis or social condemnation? Analysis of the meaning of diagnosis in the light of some interrelations of social structure, value judgment, and the physician's role." A.M.A. Archives of Neurology and Psychiatry 76:432-443.

1961 The Myth of Mental Illness: Foundations of a Theory of Personal Conduct. New York: Dell Publishing Co.

1963 Law, Liberty and Psychiatry: An Inquiry into the Social Uses of Mental Health Practices. New York: The Macmillan Co.

1970a "Blackness and madness." The Yale Review (Spring):333-341.

1970b The Manufacture of Madness: A Comparative Study of the Inquisition and the Mental Health Movement. New York: Harper & Row, Publishers.

1971 "In the Church of America, psychiatrists are priests." Hospital Physician (October):2-4.

1972a "Scapegoating 'military addicts': the helping hand strikes again." Transaction (January):4-6.

1972b "The ethics of addiction." Harper's Magazine (April):74-79.

Tannebaum, Frank
1938 Crime and the Community. New York: Columbia University Press.

Tanner, Leslie B. (ed.)
1970 Voices from Women's Liberation. New York: New American Library.

Thomas, W. I.
1923 The Unadjusted Girl. Boston: Little, Brown & Co.

1936 "The comparative study of cultures." American Journal of Sociology 42:177-185.

Thomas, W. I. and D. S. Thomas
1928 The Child in America. New York: Alfred A. Knopf, Inc.

Thomas, W. I. and F. Znaniecki
1918- The Polish Peasant in Europe and
1920 America (5 vols.). Chicago: University of Chicago Press.

Toby, Jackson
1972 "Competition for prestige." In Social Problems in America: Costs and Causalties in an Acquisitive Society. Harry C. Bredemeier and Jackson Toby (eds.) New York: John Wiley & Sons, Inc., pp. 60-67.

Toch, Hans
1965 The Social Psychology of Social Movements. New York: Bobbs-Merrill Co.

Toffler, Alvin
1970 Future Shock. New York: Bantam Books.

Townsend, J. Marshall
1975 "Cultural conceptions, mental disorders and social roles: a comparison of Germany and America." American Sociological Review (December):734-752.

Turner, Ralph H. and Lewis M. Killian
1957 Collective Behavior. Englewood Cliffs, N.J.: Prentice-Hall, Inc.

Tylor, E. B.
1871 Primitive Culture, vol. 1. London: John Murray.

van den Berghe, Pierre L.
1974 "Bringing beasts back in: toward a biosocial theory of aggression." American Sociological Review (December):777-788.

1975 Man in Society. A Biosocial View. New York: Elsevier Publishing Co.

Vincent, Clark E.
1968 "Illegitimacy." In Problems of Sex Behavior. Edward Sagarin and Donald E. J. MacNamara (eds.). New York: Thomas Y. Crowell Co., pp. 31-68.

Waller, Willard
1961 The Sociology of Teaching. New York: John Wiley & Sons, Inc.

1975 "The process of alienation." In Readings in Social Psychology. Alfred R. Lindesmith et al. (eds.). Hinsdale, Ill.: Dryden Press, pp. 326-334.

Walters, R.
1966 "Implications of laboratory studies of aggression for the control and regulation of violence." Annals of American Psychology (March):60-72.

Ward, D. A. and G. Kassebaum
1964 "Homosexuality: a mode of adaptation in a prison for women." Social Problems 12:159-177.

Warren, Carol A. B.
1972 "Observing the gay community." In Research on Deviance. Jack D. Douglas (ed.). New York: Random House, Inc., pp. 139-165.

Watts, W. David, Jr.
1971 The Psychedelic Experience: A Sociological Study. Beverly Hills, Calif.: Sage.

Weinberg, S. Kirson
1972 "Incest behavior." In Sex and Society. John N. Edwards. Chicago: Markham Publishing Co., pp. 172-179.

Weiss, Robert S.
1973 Loneliness: The Experience of Emotional

and Social Isolation. Cambridge, Mass.: The M.I.T. Press.

Wender, Paul H.
1968 "Vicious and virtuous circles—the role of deviation amplifying feedback in the origin and perpetuation of behavior." Psychiatry (November):309-324.

Werthman, Carl
1970 "The function of social definitions in the development of delinquent careers." In Crime in the City. Daniel Glaser (ed.). New York: Harper & Row, Publishers, pp. 137-154.

Whatley, Charles D.
1968 "Social attitudes toward discharged mental patients." In The Mental Patient: Studies in the Sociology of Deviance. Stephan P. Spitzer and Norman K. Denzin (eds.). New York: McGraw-Hill Book Co., pp. 401-409.

Wheelis, Allen
1958 The Quest for Identity. W. W. Norton & Co., Inc.
1973 The Moralist. Baltimore: Penguin Books.

Whitehurst, Carol
1974 "The quack as healer: a study in doctor-patient interaction." In Deviance: Field Studies and Self-Disclosures. Jerry Jacobs (ed.). Palo Alto, Calif.: National Press Books.

Whorf, Benjamin Lee
1956 Language, Thought and Reality. Cambridge, Mass.: The M.I.T. Press, pp. 40-42.

Whyte, William H., Jr.
1956 The Organization Man. Garden City, N.Y.: Doubleday & Co., Inc.

Wilkins, Leslie T.
1969 "Deviance and deviance amplification." In Readings in Social Psychology. Alfred R. Lindesmith and Anselm L., Strauss (eds.). New York: Holt, Rinehart and Winston, pp. 343-349.

Williams, Robin
1972 "The reduction of inter-group tensions." In Social Problems in America: Costs and Causalities in an Acquisitive Society. Harry C. Bredemeier and Jackson Toby (eds.). New York: John Wiley & Sons, Inc., pp. 47-49.

Wilson, Thomas P.
1970 "Normative and interpretive paradigms in sociology." In Understanding Everyday Life. Jack D. Douglas (ed.). Chicago: Aldine Publishing Co., pp. 57-59.

Winick, Charles
1964 "Physician narcotic addicts." In The Other Side—Perspectives on Deviance. Howard S. Becker (ed.). New York: The Free Press, pp. 261-281.

Wiseman, Jacqueline P.
1973 "The alcoholic's return to society." In Deviance: The Interactionist Perspective. Earl Rubington and Martin S. Weinberg (eds.). New York: The Macmillan Co., p. 414.

Wright, James
1973 "Life, times, and the fortunes of war." In Social Psychology: A Transaction—Society Reader. Elliot Aronson and Robert Helmreich (eds.). New York: D. Van Nostrand Co., pp. 291-300.

Yarrow, Marian Radke et al.
1973 "The psychological meaning of mental illness in the family." In Deviance: The Interactionist Perspective. Earl Rubington and Martin S. Weinberg (eds.). New York: The Macmillan Co., pp. 32-42.

Yinger, J. M.
1960 "Contraculture and subculture." American Sociological Review (October):625-635.

Zborowski, Mark
1952 "Cultural components in responses to pain." Journal of Social Issues 4:16-30.

Zijderveld, Anton C.
1971 A Cultural Analysis of Our Time. New York: Anchor Books.

Zimbardo, Philip G.
1973 "The psychological power and pathology of imprisonment." In Social Psychology: A Transaction-Society Reader. Elliot Aronson and Robert Helmreich (eds.). New York: D. Van Nostrand Co., pp. 162-165.

Zimmerman, Gereon
1969 "What makes Dr. Spock march?" In The Age of Protest. Walt Anderson (ed.). Pacific Palisades, Calif.: Goodyear Publishing Co., pp. 167-174.

Zinn, Howard
1969 "Violence and social change in American history." In Violence in America: A Historical and Contemporary Reader. Thomas Rose (ed.). New York: Vintage Books, p. 70.

Index